Economic Analysis and Canadian Policy

Second Edition

Economic Analysis and Canadian Policy

Second Edition

David Stager
Associate Professor of Economics
University of Toronto

Butterworth and Co. (Canada) Ltd.
Toronto, Canada

iv

CANADA: BUTTERWORTH & CO. (CANADA) LTD.
                     TORONTO: 2265 MIDLAND AVENUE,
                              SCARBOROUGH, M1P 4S1

UNITED KINGDOM: BUTTERWORTH & CO. (PUBLISHERS) LTD.
                     LONDON: 88 KINGSWAY, WC 2B 6AB

AUSTRALIA: BUTTERWORTH PTY. LTD.
                     SYDNEY: 586 PACIFIC HIGHWAY, CHATSWOOD, NSW 2067
                     MELBOURNE: 343 LITTLE COLLINS STREET, 3000
                     BRISBANE: 240 QUEEN STREET, 4000

NEW ZEALAND: BUTTERWORTHS OF NEW ZEALAND LTD.
                     WELLINGTON: 26/28 WARING TAYLOR STREET, 1

SOUTH AFRICA: BUTTERWORTH & CO. (SOUTH AFRICA) PTY. LTD.
                     DURBAN: 152/154 GALES STREET

ISBN 0-409-86951-1

1 2 3 4 5   80 79 78 77 76

Printed in Canada by the Alger Press Limited

Preface

This second edition has few changes in topics and organization from the first edition, but hardly a page has escaped without some updating of data, legislation, and events, or efforts to clarify the exposition. The objective remains as it was in the first edition — to present a concise introduction to economic analysis and to Canadian economic policy for a wide range of Canadian readers. That the first edition has been used, in roughly equal proportions, by university and community colleges or institutes of technology suggests that instructors have found this text useful in a variety of courses.

Since the majority of students in introductory economics courses do not go further in economics, the primary goal of most introductory courses is to guide students in using economic concepts and reasoning in everyday decision-making, in reading newspaper accounts of economic issues with a critical sense, and in recognizing the economic components of social and economic problems. Many of the problems which students encounter in economics courses arise in the presentation rather than in the nature of economic analysis. The lengthy exposition and complex organization of many elementary economics texts can obscure the basic simplicity of economic reasoning and its application to common economic problems. A concise approach to each topic should therefore help students to see the logical development and the use of economic concepts in various problem areas. Each general topic in this text therefore follows the same pattern in presentation: an explanation of the objectives or goals, followed by the theoretical framework for analyzing the economic activity concerned, and finally the related policy in terms of historical experience, current legislation, or alternative actions.

This book is intended to serve primarily as a core text for a two-semester course, but it is organized so that it can also be used for a sequence of two complete one-semester courses. Each major topic is contained within one chapter such that each chapter can be used as a complete unit of instruction. The length of the second edition has again been deliberately constrained to avoid overwhelming students by sheer size, and so that each instructor can add the most appropriate supplementary material for specific courses or programs.

The major innovation in this second edition is the use of colour — to clarify the interpretation of diagrams and to emphasize important assumptions, observations, and conclusions. The use of a high quality paper and a change of type-faces and layout are all intended to complement the use of colour for easier reading.

Students have found two features particularly helpful in reviewing the main topics of each chapter. The captions accompanying the diagrams explain the main points illustrated by the diagram, often rephrasing the explanation offered in the text. The review of the main points at the end of each chapter is somewhat longer than the summaries included in most texts; it is intended to be a short, precise review without omitting important details. In fact, students have also found the summary to be a useful introduction to the main ideas of the chapter.

I am happy to record a substantial debt to the many instructors who have taken the time to write with comments on the previous edition and to offer useful suggestions. While some of these have been incorporated in this edition, I regret that a number of creative proposals could not be included without expanding the book much beyond what is thought to be its optimum length. Students in my sections of the introductory economics course have contributed more than they realized by spotting typographical errors and questioning difficult or ambiguous passages. My gratitude to those who helped with the manuscript of the first edition remains as great as ever: D.J. Daly and J.W. White read the complete manuscript and offered numerous suggestions; comments on one or more chapters were also provided by D.R. Campbell, Gail C.A. Cook, D.A. Dodge, H.C. Eastman, Sheila B. Eastman, J.A.G. Grant, Arthur Kruger, N.M. Meltz, S.A. Rea, A.E. Safarian, J. Siegel, and L. Waverman. They should, as always, be spared the embarrassment of association with any errors or omissions.

Once more my final debt is to my family — Bev, Andrea, and Martha; that this book is dedicated to them is small compensation for the usual external costs associated with author's activities.

David Stager

Toronto, Ontario
February, 1976

Contents

     A   INDUSTRIAL ORGANIZATION IN CANADA   357
     Industrial Concentration   357
     Size of Firms   358
     Type of Firm   359

     B   PUBLIC POLICY FOR INDUSTRIAL ORGANIZATION   366
     Public Policy for Monopoly and Oligopoly   367
     Public Control of Natural Monopolies   370
     Public Support for Restricted Competition   375
     Public Support for Existing Competition: Agriculture   377
     Public Assistance for Agriculture   381
     Public Policy for Consumer Protection   387
     Foreign Ownership and Control in Canadian Industry   388

Part Four   Distribution of Incomes

13. Rent, Interest, and Profit   398

     A   DEMAND FOR PRODUCTIVE FACTORS   398
     What are Factors and Factor Services?   398
     Demand for Factor Services: The Marginal
     Productivity Theory   399

     B   RENT   406
     Economic Rent and Transfer Earnings   406
     Rent and The Use of Land   408

     C   INTEREST   410
     Valuation of Assets   411
     Interest and The Marginal Efficiency of Capital   412
     The Structure of Interest Rates   414

     D   PROFIT   415
     What Is Profit?   415
     Risk, Uncertainty, and Profit   416
     Competition, Monopoly, and Profits   417

1 Economics: The Analysis of Alternatives

A. Economic Problems: Individual and Social Decisions

What Is Economics?

The question, "What is Economics?" cannot be answered in a few words. This chapter provides at least a partial answer by examining basic economic problems, the way societies organize their institutions to deal with these problems, and methods used for analyzing and solving economic problems. Only after economics is considered in these several ways can simple definitions of economics be interpreted with some understanding. Nonetheless, it is useful to have such definitions as guideposts to what is to come.

Definitions of economics offered by prominent economists have included:

> Economics is a study of mankind in the ordinary business of life; it examines that part of individual and social action which is closely connected with the attainment and with the use of the material requisites of well being.
> — Alfred Marshall

> Economics is the science which studies human behaviour as a relationship between ends and scarce means which have alternative uses.
> — Lionel Robbins

> Economics comes in whenever more of one thing means less of another.
> — Fritz Machlup

> The theory of economics . . . is a method rather than a doctrine, an apparatus of the mind, a technique of thinking, which helps its possessor to draw correct conclusions.
> — John Maynard Keynes

> Economics is whatever economists do.
> — Jacob Viner

These definitions emphasize that economics involves both individual and social decisions and actions; that the means for satisfying

1

human wants are limited and can be used in alternative ways;
that this scarcity requires giving up something to gain something
else; and that the study or economics provides a method, a technique
for thinking about economic problems, rather than settled conclusions. The last of the above definitions may seem facetious; in fact, it
emphasizes that economists are applying basic economic analysis —
or the technique for economic thinking — to an increasing number
of problem areas. Studies of the economics of crime, education,
health, discrimination, housing, poverty, disarmament, and pollution, have all been added to economic literature in recent years.

Economic problems arise from the need to make decisions or
choices about an endless number of alternatives: alternative uses for
the output of economic activity, alternative methods for producing
this output, and alternative ways of distributing this output among
individuals.

The Vocabulary of Economics

Economic problems can be discussed with more clarity by using
terms in a consistent way. These terms will be recognized as common words in our everyday language, but with more specific meanings given to them. New terms are defined as they are introduced in
successive chapters, often in italics to draw attention to them.

A society or country has a variety of resources or *factors of
production* including the *natural resources* of land, water, minerals,
forests, game, and fish; *human resources*, consisting of various
mental and physical abilities and skills; and *man-made or capital
resources* such as roads, dams, machinery, and buildings. These
productive factors can be combined in numerous ways to produce
commodities. All commodities can be described as either *goods* or
services. Each of these may also be described as either *intermediate*
(semi-finished) or *final*; and final goods and services are
categorized, according to their use, as either *consumer goods* or
producer goods.

Goods are tangible commodities such as bread, automobiles,
and sweaters; services are intangible commodities like the repairing
of a flat tire, legal advice, and bus transportation. Intermediate goods
are those which are partly finished, such as bread flour, and require
further processing before they are useful. When they have passed
through all stages of production, they are final goods. Consumer
goods and services are those which individuals value because they
provide direct satisfaction of various kinds: physiological, intellec-
tual, psychological, spiritual, and so on. Such satisfaction usually
derives not from possessing these goods but from using them; this
use of commodities to provide satisfaction is *consumption*. The
satisfaction which consumers realize from commodities is also
called *utility*.

Producer goods and services are those which do not provide satisfaction directly, but are used in the production of other goods and services. *Production* is the creation of utility. Because utility can have different characteristics, so can production. This may be a matter of *form*: making a milk-shake or producing a concert; it may be a matter of *time*: providing storage so that consumers may enjoy a properly aged wine, or fresh apples in February; or it may be a matter of *place*: transporting goods such as new automobiles or fresh lobsters to consumers who are some distance from the origin of these goods.

Scarcity and Choice

Goods can also be described as either *economic goods* or *free goods*. Economic goods are those which are *scarce* — there is not enough of the particular good to provide as much as all consumers would like if the good were free. A free good is one which exists in sufficient abundance to satisfy everyone's wants, even when no price is charged. Drinking water is often regarded as a free good, apart from the municipal service charge for pumping and piping, but in areas of some countries even drinking water is not a free good since it can be bought only in bottled form. One could add other free goods, such as pure air and sunshine, but the list would be extremely short.

The fact that goods are scarce is a reflection of the *scarcity of productive resources to meet unlimited human wants*. The emphasis here is not on *needs* (items necessary to maintain life) but on *wants*. It is clear that the basic needs of people in many parts of the world have not yet been met, but there may be at least some hope of doing so. Indeed, calculations have shown that a redistribution of the world's current output would solve this problem, provided that the redistribution would not lead to an increase in the population. But the wants of individuals, whether rich or poor, seem endless. Without making any judgment on the merits of these wants, it is assumed that not all of these wants can be satisfied.

The scarcity of resources to meet these unlimited wants forces individuals and societies to make *choices*. Choices have to be made among alternative commodities that could be produced, alternative means for producing them, and alternative distributions of the commodities produced among individuals.

These basic choices are common to every society or economy regardless of its political organization or ideology. What distinguishes different economies is the institutions or mechanisms established to make these decisions.

A discussion of different ways in which economies have been or are organized is presented later in this chapter.

Making choices entails giving up or forgoing something if something else is to be enjoyed. This is the common experience of most consumers: purchasing a new house may mean that a family must put off purchasing a new car for a few years. Self-employed professionals face a similar problem: taking an extended holiday requires giving up the income that would have been earned during that period. Students, too, forgo potential earnings to continue their education, as well as forgoing the satisfaction derived from other things which would have been bought with money spent for books and tuition fees.

Opportunity Cost

The satisfaction or output that would have been derived from the best alternative use of resources is termed the opportunity cost of the choice actually made.

Opportunity cost is an important concept in economics because it describes the total cost entailed in choosing one alternative rather than another. Without looking at a potential choice in terms of all that must be given up, one might, for example, measure the cost of a vacation only in terms of actual expenditures and omit either forgone earnings or other enjoyment that might be gained from the given amount of time.

Societies face the same kind of choices involving the consideration of opportunity costs, especially in decisions about dividing resources between the production of privately consumed goods and services and of public goods and services such as defence, education, health, transportation, and so on. The problem is illustrated in Figure 1.1.

If all the economy's productive resources are fully utilized in producing only private goods, the maximum output per year would be OC_3 units; allocating all resources to public goods would yield OP_3 units. Thus there are limits to what the economy can produce, namely OC_3 or OP_3 units, even if all resources are concentrated on one type of good. The economy, however, will probably want some combination of these. The *production-possibilities curve* represented by the curved line between C_3 and P_3 shows the full range of possible maximum combinations of public and private goods which can be produced with the given resources. Suppose an economy is at point A, enjoying OC_2 units of private goods and OP_1 units of public goods. If it wants to increase its output of public goods to OP_2 units, the production-possibilities curve shows that individuals must then forgo the difference between OC_2 and OC_1 units of private goods. This reduction in private goods is the opportunity cost of the increase in public goods. The new combination would be OC_1 and OP_2 units, represented by point B.

The economy would be able to increase its output of public goods without reducing private goods only if the economy were not at its *production-possibilities frontier* or *boundary*. If productive resources are not being fully utilized, the economy will be inside

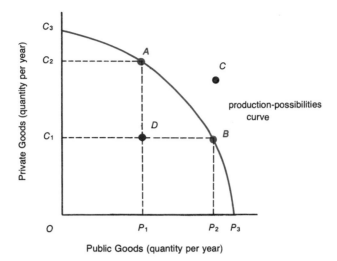

Figure 1.1   A Production-Possibilities Curve

Any point on the production-possibilities curve indicates one of numerous combinations of maximum output which can be obtained by the use of available resources and current technology. Moving from *A* to *B* requires giving up some private goods to obtain more public goods. *C* represents an unattainable combination and *D* represents a combination which does not make full or efficient use of resources. Any other two commodity categories could be portrayed on a similar curve.

this boundary, perhaps at point *D*. In this case, output of public goods could be increased from *OP₁* to *OP₂* units by improving the use of resources, without reducing private consumption, and thus without incurring an opportunity cost. All combinations within the production-possibilities curve are possible combinations, but only combinations on the curve represent maximum combinations of output. Point *C* lies beyond the curve, representing a combination of public and private goods unattainable with the given quantity of productive resources and the existing state of technology.

Basic Economic Decisions

The basic economic decisions facing all economies have been mentioned briefly above; they are described further here as an outline of the topics to be examined in the rest of the book.

1.   Allocation of Resources: What is to be produced?

An economy can produce thousands of different commodities and in numberless combinations of quantities of each. Thus decisions must be made not only on the kinds of commodities but also on the quantity of each that should be produced. The combination of commodities produced will reflect the different goals held by various societies; that is, even economies with similar resources and technology may produce a different collection of commodities. In most cases, this total collection will include some producer goods both to maintain existing productive capacity and to incorporate advancing technology in new equipment. This requires a further decision about the opportunity cost, in terms of forgone satisfaction from current consumption, that should be incurred to gain increased future output. In other words, what resources should be released from the production of consumer goods to increase the production of producer goods?

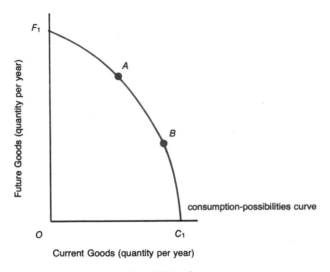

Figure 1.2   A Consumption-Possibilities Curve
Productive resources can be used to produce alternative combinations of consumer goods and producer goods. A higher proportion of the latter, represented by *A*, increases the quantity of consumer goods available in the future. Choice of combination *A* rather than *B* implies a higher rate of economic growth.

This decision is illustrated in Figure 1.2 using a *consumption-possibilities curve.* Note the similarity of this curve with the production-possibilities curve of Figure 1.1. If all existing productive resources are allocated to current consumption, OC_1 units can be enjoyed now. But if the same resources, except those required to sustain life, are used for producer goods to increase the output of consumer goods in the future, OF_1 units of consumer goods can be enjoyed in the future. Note that OF_1 is greater than OC_1. Of course, some resources must be used to produce commodities for current consumption and some for at least maintaining current productive capacity. The actual combination chosen will lie somewhere along the consumption-possibilities curve, perhaps at either point *A* or point B. An economy which chooses combination B over A is said to have a higher *rate of time preference* because its preference for current goods over future goods is stronger than that exhibited by an economy which chooses combination A.

2. Production Methods: How will the commodities be produced?

Virtually all commodities can be produced using different techniques. Roads can be built by using people working with shovels and picks, or by using fewer workers and some light machinery, or by using very few workers and huge earth-moving and paving machines designed specifically for road-building. Similarly, most consumer goods can be produced using mainly manual labour, or with little labour and much machinery.

The production methods chosen will depend on the state of technology in the economy and the relative availability of capital, or producer goods, and labour of various skill levels. Technology — the knowledge of alternative processes, raw materials, and sources of raw materials for producing specific commodities — is generally available to any economy although some resources are required to train researchers to adapt technology developed in other countries to the needs of a particular economy. Thus the major condition influencing the choice of production methods is the amount of labour and capital available and the willingness to forgo current consumption to develop capital goods and to improve the level of education and skill in the labour force.

3. Commodity Distribution: Who will get how much of the commodities produced?

An economy must also decide who will receive how much of each of the commodities produced. Although production problems received much of the attention for many years, distribution problems have received an increasing proportion of economists' attention with the recent emphasis on poverty. Some have even suggested that production problems have been solved, in the sense that the world's existing resources and technology are capable of producing at least a minimum standard of living for the world's population, and that only the distribution problem remains. It is in this area that political and social considerations enter most strongly, and therefore where the type of decision-making mechanism or organization is most important.

4. Other Economic Decisions

The preceding three sets of questions are the basic ones facing any economy. They are often stated succinctly as *How? What? For Whom?* Other decisions can be extracted from these for special attention. They include questions about the rate of economic growth, the level of resources used in the economy, and how to provide flexibility in response to economic and other changes.

The desired rate of economic growth is one aspect of the resource allocation decision. Economic growth can be illustrated, as in Figure 1.3, as an outward shift of the production-possibilities curve. In Figure 1.1, combination C was unattainable because sufficient resources were not available to produce this combination of commodities. However, if the economy decides to allocate some of its resources to producer goods to expand its productive capacity, the curve may shift outwards over time, as shown by the outer curve in Figure 1.3. Combination C becomes attainable, indicating that more of both public goods and private goods can be made available.

The level of resources used in the economy has been taken as fixed at any given time. While this is so, the quantity of resources actively used, and particularly labour services, can be changed fairly quickly. This involves decisions both about the quantity of labour service to be made available and the quantity of labour service actually used. The former decision concerns the number of hours per week and weeks per year that persons will work in paid employment, and who will be available for employment. The decision about the quantity of labour actually used determines whether everyone who wants to work will be able to find employment; that is, whether

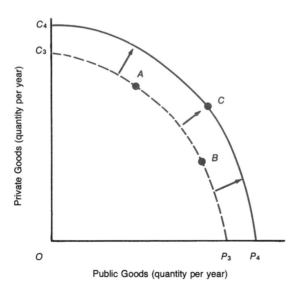

Figure 1.3 Outward Shift of Production-Possibilities Curve
Choosing a higher proportion of producer goods, (reflecting a higher preference for future consumer goods), leads to greater economic growth, with an outward shift of the production-possibilities curve. Full use of available resources produces a larger total output of both public and private goods than the maximum combinations shown in Figure 1-1

the economy will decide that full employment has a high priority, or must be governed by other considerations.

How to provide for flexibility in response to changing conditions is a question which arises when the three basic questions are considered over time rather than at any point in time. Each of the What? How? and For Whom? questions may be answered differently as available resources, technology, consumer preferences, and political values are changed. Part of the answer to each of the basic questions must therefore include a means for responding to such changes.

Economic Systems

Every economy faces the same basic economic questions but each has a different way of determining the answers. An economy can therefore be classified in terms of the method used to make its basic economic decisions. Each of the wide variety of *economic systems* in existence uses a combination of decision-making arrangements. To understand their operation more fully, it is useful to consider the pure forms of economic systems that can be defined according to different types of decision-making. Although these pure forms do not exist in any economy, some of their characteristics occur in varying degrees in each of the world's economies. The three basic types of economic system are: traditional economy, planned economy, and market economy.

Traditional Economy

The traditional economy is usually based on small units, such as families or villages, each producing everything it consumes with little need for specialization of labour and exchange of goods. Everyone joins in to help with harvesting crops and building new homes and a few persons become skilled craftsmen to produce clothing and equipment.

Decisions about the allocation of resources, mainly labour and land, are rather simple in a traditional economy. Food, clothing, buildings, and tools are those which have been produced as long as the members of the economic unit can remember. Tradition not only dictates what commodities are to be produced, and how much is required to maintain the unit, but also how these commodities are produced. Tradition also determines who — often the oldest male — will make any remaining decisions. A few centuries ago, this was the dominant form of economic organization, but colonization, political independence, and worldwide emphasis on economic development have transformed almost all of the earlier examples of traditional economies.

Planned Economy

The essential feature of a planned economy is that a central authority makes all of the important decisions concerning the basic economic problems. In practice, this method is often used by a totalitarian form of government and thus is sometimes called a *command economy*. Furthermore, the central authority usually, but not necessarily, owns the productive resources of land and physical capital.

The economy is operated on the basis of a series of plans, each usually covering a period of five years, and consisting of further annual plans for each year in the period. These specify the total output of each commodity, how much each production unit will produce, and how much of the economy's productive resources will be made available to each unit. Within this framework, labourers and consumers are free to realize the greatest satisfaction possible. They are constrained to the extent that only certain jobs will be available in specific areas, and only certain consumer goods and services will be available and at specified prices.

The central authorities thus decide what will be produced and in what quantity, what production methods will be used and, by setting wages and prices, determine how the output will be distributed. The major problems of a planned economy are to provide sufficient consumer goods and services to maintain the confidence and support of the population, to utilize resources efficiently, and to take account of all the detailed decisions required to make the plan operational. Authorities must also maintain the structure of the plan while remaining sufficiently flexible to deal with unforeseen events such as droughts, wars, and new technology.

Pure planned economies do not exist, but the major characteristics of a planned economy dominate the economies of the U.S.S.R., most eastern European countries, and China. Each of these, however, has some elements of the traditional economy, and to a 'greater extent, the market economy.

Market Economy

The main feature of the market economy is that prices are determined in a separate market for each commodity and factor of production, with these prices in turn determining the answers to each of the basic economic questions. Various terms have been associated with this form of economic organization: the terms *price system* and *pricing mechanism* stress that prices are central to the decision-making in a market economy; *free-enterprise economy* appropriately describes only one aspect of the pure form whereby any individual is free to produce any commodity in any quantity and by any method; and *capitalist economy* emphasizes that individuals may own physical capital, thereby realizing larger incomes than if they offered only their labour services. These latter two terms, however, have ideological connotations which can detract from an understanding of the essential elements of the market economy.

Prices are determined in the markets for specific goods and services in the manner described in the next chapter. A *market is the organized collection of potential buyers and sellers for a specific commodity*. Markets, and therefore prices, for different commodities and productive factors are interdependent because buyers have alternative commodities available to them and suppliers can use resources to provide other commodities.

Prices, and particularly differences between prices, determine what will be produced and in what quantity, because producers will supply those commodities which can be sold for at least the cost of producing them. The prices of productive resources determine what production methods will be used: as the price of labour increases relative to the cost of machinery, more of the latter will be substituted for labour. The distribution of consumer goods and services is determined by the price that an individual receives for his labour services and for the use of his physical capital and land.

Not only does the pure market economy not exist, but economies which have come closest to this system are now tending to place less reliance on the market or price system to determine the answers to their basic economic questions. All economies are more appropriately described as *mixed economies*. This term is not very informative; rather, its value lies in emphasizing that elements of each of the pure forms can be found in any existing economy. In the Canadian economy, for example, the market system is dominant but there are also features of the planned and traditional economies. Formal education, for example, is provided mainly through a planning mechanism with authorities at different levels of government deciding who shall go to school (under the compulsory attendance legislation), where schools shall be built and what shall be taught. Elements of the traditional economy are found in Eskimo settlements, some Indian reservations, and some remote rural districts.

There are at least two criteria for choosing which of these systems should be followed, or how dominant each system should be in a mixed economy. One is economic performance — achieving maximum output per person or per person employed — and the other is the freedom of choice available to producers and consumers.

The conflicts between these two criteria are found in any economy, but they are particularly evident in countries such as India and France, which have substantial elements of central economic planning but also try to maintain the freedoms of a market system.

B. Economic Analysis:
Towards Rational Decisions

Economic Analysis and Economic Policy

This part of the chapter describes methods used in analyzing economic behaviour and the application of the results obtained to solve economic problems. Economists often disagree on the results of economic analysis, the conclusions to be drawn from these results, or the appropriate prescriptions for individual decisions or for social policies. Some of the disagreement stems from problems with analytical techniques and inadequate statistics; but more often the disagreement stems from differences in political or social judgments about what should be done in response to economic problems.

These two types of disagreement reflect different aspects of economics: economic analysis and economic policy.

Policy refers to a course of action that is expected to bring about some specific objective or goal.

Policy thus includes a statement of what the goals should be as well as the means for attaining such goals. It is at this point that the role of the economist is sharply questioned; that is, should his or her studies be confined to *positive economics*, or should these deal in *normative economics* as well? *Positive economics is concerned with describing and analyzing the way things are. Normative economics emphasizes the way things should or ought to be.* Positive economics would, for example, be interested in the price of milk as a matter of fact, perhaps as an indication of the effects of a particular policy, without being concerned about whether this price was "good" or "bad". Normative economics, however, would make a judgment about the price of milk, perhaps that it was so high that some children received too little milk, or so low that dairy farmers received an inadequate income.

Disputes in positive economics can be settled by appealing to the relevant facts and the analytical techniques. If there is agreement on what the facts are and how they should be analyzed, there is no reason for further dispute; the conclusions should be the same. Because economists have been concerned with developing analytical techniques, they are equipped to handle problems in positive economics. However, they have no similar tools for dealing with disagreements about the *value judgments* made in normative economics. When people hold different basic political views, these cannot be reconciled by other than persuasion or the voting process. For this reason many economists and other social scientists have traditionally declared that they should restrict their work to positive studies, leaving value judgments to politicians and their electorates.

Although this distinction can be made clearly in abstract

discussions, it cannot be drawn so clearly in specific economic studies. The categories established for collecting and analyzing data, assumptions made to simplify the analysis, and the particular type of analysis used can reflect the values or personal concerns of the researcher. Moreover, what is left out of the analysis can be as important in determining the results as what is included. Thus conclusions drawn from similar economic studies can vary, depending somewhat on the views of persons doing the studies. The reasons for such differences can usually be determined, however, by examining the data and techniques used. Articles in economic journals often appear to be quite technical because it is as important to know how an economist arrived at the conclusion as it is to know what conclusions were reached.

The problem areas selected for economic analysis also reflect value judgments, to the extent that some problems are considered more important than others. Several factors influence an economist's choice of topics for analysis: availability of data, previous work done in the field, interest of other economists in the same topic, and adequate financial assistance. But an important consideration is whether the economist perceives the problem as a serious social issue. Until recently, for example, there have been relatively few studies of the economics of advertising, and the economics of urban problems such as housing and transportation. Economists and financial sponsors such as governments have been increasingly criticized for these oversights.

The distinction between normative and positive economics is made more difficult because intelligent normative statements involve an element of positive analysis. The statement that the legal minimum wage should be raised, as one means for dealing with poverty, requires an accurate knowledge of the consequences. A higher minimum wage may result in more unemployment but also result in higher total wage payments to the low-income groups that remain employed. It is also possible that both employment and total wage payments would be reduced.[1] A judgment about minimum wage legislation therefore requires both an understanding of its various effects, and a further judgment about whether the number of persons employed is more important or less important than the total wages paid to the lowest income group.

Despite these various difficulties in distinguishing normative and positive economics, it is usually possible to determine at least which statements can be settled by agreeing on the analysis used and which statements can be settled only by agreeing on value judgments. Provided that this is done, an increasing number of economists share the view that they should not restrict themselves to positive economics.

---

[1] The possible consequences of minimum wage legislation are discussed in Chapter 2.

Scientific Method In Economics

The social sciences, including economics, have been called the "soft sciences" because they usually have not been able to employ the scientific method as rigorously as have the "hard sciences" of physics, chemistry, and biology. This is not because the social sciences are less careful in the use of scientific enquiry, but rather because experimentation is more difficult than in the physical or natural sciences.

The scientific method requires examining questions by referring to actual evidence rather than to intuition, judgment, or personal experience.

Evidence or facts must be gathered and analyzed to arrive at conclusions. Suitable evidence, however, usually must be drawn from controlled experiments. This involves controlling or manipulating the relevant variables so that the effects of particular actions can be isolated from the effects of all other actions. Physical scientists are able to do this by controlling temperature, light, moisture, or whatever other variables might affect the results. Biological scientists can control their experiments by, for example, adding a particular nutrient to one group of plants or animals but not to another group which is similar in all other respects. The results obtained in each case are then compared and conclusions are drawn.

The scientific method also involves the development of laws or principles through repetition of such experiments until it can be concluded that there is a very high probability that the matter under examination will behave in a certain way when specific conditions exist. The bodies of knowledge represented by different sciences are based, for example, on laws concerning heat, sound, gravity, or genetics. Frequently the question is raised whether a social science is even possible; that is, whether laws can be determined for human behaviour since humans have free will to decide how they will behave under various circumstances.

Long and continued observation of human behaviour has shown, however, that while the actions of a particular individual may be unpredictable, the behaviour of groups of individuals in response to specific situations can be predicted. The more precisely the situations can be defined or described the more accurate the predictions can be. Many studies have found, for example, that a lesser quantity of a good will be sold when the price of the good increases. There may be some situations, however, in which this does not occur. The prediction about what will happen when the price increases can be made more accurately if information is also available about other important factors such as whether incomes are also rising, whether the good is being advertised, and whether the prices of similar goods are also increasing. When large groups of individuals are seen to behave similarly in well-defined situations after repeated observations, economic laws can be stated which have at least considerable predictive power in economic analysis, if not the universal validity of the laws of physical sciences.

Theories, Models, and the Real World

Behavioural laws provide the basis for predictions of what will happen in certain circumstances. They do not, however, explain why these things happen. If one knows the reason why certain events occur, then it may be possible to alter the circumstances so that they will not happen, or alternatively, so that they will happen more frequently. A theory about why such things happen will provide the basis for a policy or a set of actions to be taken to achieve the desired ends. *A theory is an explanation of the relationships between situations and events:* it is more powerful than a law in that it provides both an explanation and a basis for predictions.

A theory also provides the framework for observation. Observation of "facts" is meaningful only when what is observed has some relationship to other items of interest. One could, for example, collect information on the prices of sugar in every grocery store and supermarket in the country. The information would be meaningless unless one had some theory about why such prices should be the same or different in different types of stores, different regions of the country, or in cities and towns of various sizes. A theory therefore assists in defining the data to be collected for economic analysis.

A theory has three component parts: a set of *definitions of terms* used in the theory; a set of *assumptions defining the conditions* in which the theory is applicable; and *hypotheses concerning the relationships* among the situations and events the theory is intended to explain. Each of these components will limit the applicability of the theory. The definitions may be so restrictive as to exclude significant aspects of the situation. A definition of labour services, for example, may define labour as undifferentiated with respect to skills whereas everyone knows that there is a wide variation in skills among members of the labour force. Whether this kind of definition imposes a serious limitation on the theory's validity depends on what the theory is intended to explain. Thus the definitions used in a theory must be examined to see how they influence the conclusions reached.

Similarly, assumptions may be made which initially seem inappropriate or contrary to what one knows to be true. In a theory explaining the effects of price changes, for example, it may be assumed that consumers' incomes are constant, even though it is known that incomes have been rising. Assumptions of this kind are made as substitutes for the regulation of variables in controlled experiments. By assuming first that incomes are constant and then that incomes are rising, a theory can be used to explain the specific effect that increasing incomes have on prices.

Such limitations only point out the respects in which a theory is inadequately specified, rather than requiring it to be discarded. Too often, one hears such expressions as, "That's too theoretical", or, "That's all right in theory but not in practice". Sometimes these expressions reflect a person's dislike for a complex explanation of events, but more often they stem from the view that a theory is too simple to take account of specific cases or complicated situations. In this case, one can reply that a simple theory can at least explain the general relationships and, furthermore, form the basis for more complex theories that take into account greater variation in the circumstances or observed outcomes.

The validity of a theory is tested by comparing its predictions with evidence drawn from actual experience; such evidence must of course be classified according to the definitions used in the theory. If actual experience coincides with the predictions, a valid theory has been devised and only needs to be tested from time to time to recertify its validity. If experience differs from the predictions, two alternatives are available: either to determine that another existing theory would have predicted the actual outcome more accurately, implying that the theory in question should be abandoned; or to improve the theory by examining the evidence closely for modifications that should be made. Note that in the latter case, the initial theory, although imperfect, provides a framework for interpreting the new evidence.

Economic Models. Economists have taken the scientific method as applied to economics one step further than the development of theories, by combining theories to construct models of the operation of segments or the whole of the economy. Such models provide a kind of laboratory in which controlled experiments can be conducted to provide detailed predictions of the economic performance, under alternative conditions, of firms, industries, or the entire economy. Models of an economy require much time and effort to construct and maintain, and thus reflect the cooperative effort of many economists. Such models of the Canadian economy have been developed at the Bank of Canada, the Economic Council of Canada, and the University of Toronto, and are used to ascertain both what would happen if certain policies were introduced and what can be expected to happen because of policy actions already taken.[2]

The terms "model" and "theory" are sometimes used interchangeably: one may talk about either a model or a theory of national income determination, but generally a model represents a more complex set of relationships than does a theory. Moreover, a model often includes a quantitative specification of the relationships indi-

---

[2] For example, see the Economic Council of Canada, *Ninth Annual Review: The Years to 1980*, for a description of the Council's model (called CANDIDE) and the economic predictions based on that model.

cating, for example, not only that an increase in the labour force would increase output but how large an increase in output would be associated with a specific increase in the labour force.

Economic models are constructed by *abstracting* from real-world situations. Abstraction involves, as it did in developing theories, identifying the important features or variables such as income levels, unemployment and inflation rates, and tax rate structures, and stating the expected relationships among these. The model is next tested against the evidence by using data from previous years to determine whether the model would have predicted the actual outcome. When the model is correctly specified in this sense, it can then be used for experimentation. Tariff rates on imported goods could be varied, for example, to determine the effects of these changes on other variables such as employment and prices of domestic commodities. This information can then provide guidance for designing the federal government's tariff policy. If policies based on experimental results are actually implemented, the real-world results can be compared with the model's predictions. Any important discrepancies will indicate how the model should be modified for future experimentation and policy development.

Microeconomics and Macroeconomics

The study of economics can be divided into two major areas: microeconomics and macroeconomics. "Micro" is derived from a Greek word meaning "small": *microeconomics is concerned with small or specific segments of the economy* such as the behaviour of individual consumers and firms, of labour groups, and of groups of firms in industries. The branches of economic analysis falling within microeconomics include the theory of consumer behaviour, the theory of the firm, the theory of price and wage determination, the theory of income distribution, and most aspects of international trade theory. "Macro" is derived from the Greek word for "large": *macroeconomics deals with large segments, or with the whole economy.* Emphasis is on the broad aggregates of total employment, total output and incomes, total money supply, and so on. Part Two of this book examines macroeconomics; it will be seen from these chapters that the major objectives of macroeconomic studies are an understanding of and solution for the problems of unemployment, inflation, stability in national and international economic relations, and economic growth. Some topics are difficult to classify as either microeconomics or macroeconomics because they involve elements of theory drawn from both areas. An analysis of the government or public sector, for example, involves microeconomic studies of specific programs but macroeconomic studies of the overall effects of government taxation and expenditures.

Some Basic Concepts

Some basic concepts are introduced here because they are frequently used in economic analysis and thus appear at many points throughout this book.

Rationality. One of the basic assumptions in economic analysis is that individuals will behave rationally. At one time, this assumption was incorporated in the concept of *economic man.* Individuals were assumed to be primarily interested in increasing their material well-being. If someone were offered a higher wage for his service or a higher price for his output, it was expected that he would take it. The emphasis then shifted from the assumption that *all* individuals are *always* seeking to improve their material well-being to the assumption that most individuals will *usually* behave in this way. This meaning of rationality is still specific to the extent that a particular objective is assumed — improvement of material well-being — as well as behaviour leading to that objective. The more general meaning of rationality is that individuals will behave or take such actions as are necessary to achieve their objectives, whatever these may be.

"Other Things Being Equal". The phrase "other things being equal" — or its Latin equivalent, *ceteris paribus* — is used to compensate for the inability to control particular variables in the real world. Economists *assume* that other things are equal or unchanged, that is, they reason *as if* this is the case. A common example is the statement that "as the price of a good increases, fewer units of the good will be purchased, *other things being equal".* Because factors influencing the purchase of goods, other than the price, do not remain unchanged, the specific effect of a price change can be isolated only by making this assumption. Moreover, the assumption can be changed gradually — economists usually say an assumption is "relaxed" — to allow each of the other factors to change separately so that their specific effects can also be determined.

Stock and Flows. Much of economics is concerned with total quantities involved at a point in time and with changes in quantities over a period of time. This distinction can be made by reference to stocks and flows. *A stock is the quantity which exists at any particular point in time.* To describe a stock properly requires both a statement of the quantity and the time at which it is measured. Thus the Canadian labour force can be stated as a stock: there were 9.9 million persons in the labour force in April, 1975.

A flow is the change in the quantity occurring during a period of time. To describe a flow properly requires both a statement of the quantity and the length of time involved. Thus the net change in the

Canadian labour force is stated as flow: 336,000 persons were added to the labour force during the twelve months prior to April, 1975.

Difficulties With Measurement

The discussion in this part of the chapter has tended to emphasize the necessity for measurement of economic activity. Development of economics as a science requires that observations be expressed in quantitative terms if theories and models are to be tested and ultimately judged valid. Some of the concepts used in economics, however, cannot be measured easily, if at all. This does not mean that such concepts must be discarded. In fact, some economic relationships can be explained only by drawing on concepts which can be described qualitatively, but which cannot be measured.

The *satisfaction* or enjoyment provided by clothing, food, or entertainment, cannot be measured precisely because individuals can only say, for example, that they like beef better than fish. Yet the concept of satisfaction or utility is used extensively in economics.

Another measurement problem follows from the *need to rely on samples* when it is not possible to examine the entire population of the group in question, usually due to the extreme expense of collecting information on the complete group. A chemist can work with any sample of pure sulphur dioxide, knowing that every other sample would have the same properties. An economist, however, must be certain that the sample accurately represents the population, at least with respect to the characteristics under study. Furthermore, conclusions drawn from one sample may be valid only for a limited time, requiring that subsequent studies be undertaken whenever it is suspected that the circumstances affecting the sample have changed.

Economics and the Use of Graphs

Much of economics, but not all of it, as the preceding section indicates, is concerned with the quantitative relationships among different events or actions. The relationships can be described verbally; indeed, many economics books consisted almost entirely of verbal description and reasoning until three or four decades ago. Verbal presentations have the advantage of making an economist's work available to a wide audience and in forcing an author to be quite precise in arguments. However, verbal presentations have a disadvantage: they usually require a lengthy discussion of a topic which might be stated more concisely in mathematical terms.

Geometry has been used in economics because its pictorial aspect often makes an explanation clearer with one diagram than could be achieved with several pages of prose. Although geometry limits the analysis to two or three variables or dimensions, geometrical presentations are satisfactory for an exposition of basic economic principles and their applications. Graphs are therefore used at many points in this text to illustrate economic relationships. However, students who have no training in geometry, or who have forgotten the fundamentals of geometry, should have little difficulty in working with graphs following this brief review.

A graph consists of 2 coordinates, or straight lines, intersecting each other at an angle of 90 degrees at a point called the origin. Figure 1.4 shows a coordinate graph dividing space into 4 quadrants. The vertical coordinate is labelled y and the horizontal one, x. Positive values of y are measured above the origin and negative values below. Positive values of x are measured to the right of the origin and negative values to the left. The upper right-hand quadrant thus contains positive values of both x and y. Frequently only this quadrant is used because the values of variables concerned are often both positive.

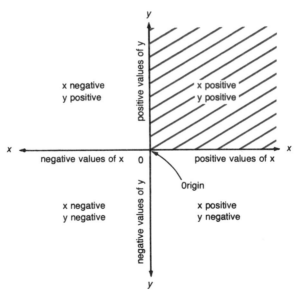

Figure 1.4 A Coordinate Graph

A coordinate graph divides space into four quadrants. Relationships between two variables are specified by plotting the value of one variable on the horizontal, x axis and the value of a second variable on the vertical, y axis. Since economics is usually concerned with variables having positive values, often the only quadrant used is the one where both x and y are positive.

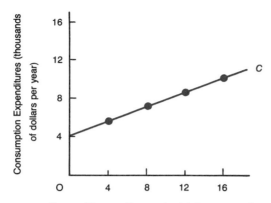

Figure 1.5   *Hypothetical Consumption Curve*
Consumer expenditures are a function of, or are dependent on, the level of personal income. Consumption expenditures observed at each level of income are plotted on a coordinate graph to illustrate the relationship between consumption and personal income as consumption curve *C*.

In specific cases, the coordinates or axes are labelled according to the variables involved. Figure 1.5 is an example of a graph depicting the relationship between annual personal income and consumption expenditures: consumption is on the vertical or y axis; annual personal income is on the horizontal or x axis. (Consumption expenditures are positive even when income is zero since some expenditures are necessary for survival; the individual is assumed to borrow or draw on savings to provide this amount.) Consumption expenditures are assumed to be a function of income; that is, the amount of these expenditures will *depend* on the level of income.

The dependent variable (consumption) is conventionally shown on the vertical axis and the independent variable (income) is shown on the horizontal axis. An important exception to this convention occurs in supply and demand analysis: there the independent variable, price, is on the vertical axis and the dependent variable, quantity demanded or supplied, is on the horizontal axis.

The line representing the consumption function in Figure 1.5 happens to be a straight line but functions more often are non-linear or curved. In fact, the functions plotted on a graph are generally referred to as curves even when they are straight lines. Curves are described as being upward-sloping, or downward-sloping, to the right. A curve which is upward-sloping to the right has a positive slope; a negative slope is represented by a curve sloping downward to the right.

Review of the Main Points

1. Because human wants are unlimited, resources used in producing goods and services to satisfy these wants are scarce. This scarcity requires that choices be made about the use of available resources and the distribution of the commodities produced. Such choices involve opportunity costs: the forgone satisfaction or output that would have been derived from the next best alternative.

2. A production-possibilities curve shows the maximum possible combinations of two commodities (or two types of commodities) which can be produced with the resources available, and illustrates the choice that must be made among alternative combinations.

3. The basic economic decisions are (a) what commodities should be produced in what quantities, including decisions about private and public goods, and current and future goods, such that the total combination of commodities provides the maximum satisfaction possible with the given resources; (b) how these commodities will be produced, given the state of technology and the relative availability of labour and physical capital, to make the most efficient use of productive resources; and (c) how the commodities will be distributed among the population to reflect generally held views about social justice.

4. Three types of economic systems can be defined according to the way the basic economic decisions are made; these are the traditional economy, the planned economy, and the market economy.

5. The traditional economy consists of small self-sufficient units of families or villages, with decisions made according to traditional practices. The planned economy is directed by planning authorities who decide how these basic questions will be answered. The market economy is directed by the set of prices determined in markets for each commodity and factor of production.

6. Pure forms of these economic systems do not exist; each economy combines features from each pure system and thus should be described as a "mixed economy". Nevertheless, economies are often classified according to the most dominant features; thus the U.S.S.R. is predominantly a planned economy and Japan, a market economy.

7. Positive economics deals with an analysis of the way things are; normative economics is concerned with the way things should be. The latter involves making value judgments about economic goals or objectives and thus is not properly included in a science of economics. But assumptions and classifications used in economic analysis reflect value judgments which can cause disagreements about the results of economic analysis.

8. The scientific method consists of gathering information or facts, and analyzing these to arrive at conclusions. Economists usually cannot perform controlled experiments and thus must make numerous observations to identify the laws or principles of economic behaviour.

9. Laws state what will happen in particular situations but do not explain why. Theories provide this explanation, as well as predictions, and a framework for collecting information. A theory includes definitions of terms, assumptions defining conditions for its applicability, and hypotheses about the relationships among the events or conditions the theory is intended to explain. The validity of a theory is tested by comparing its predictions with evidence drawn from actual experience. Any discrepancy requires that the theory be modified to provide more accurate predictions.

10. A model of economic behaviour is usually a combination of theories representing large segments or the whole of the economy, but its construction involves the same process used for theories. Models are used to experiment with policy alternatives or to predict the effects of actual policies.

11. Economics is often divided into microeconomics and macroeconomics; the former deals with specific segments of the economy while the latter deals with the whole economy.

12. Some basic concepts used in economic analysis include rationality, the assumption that individuals will act to achieve their objectives; "other things being equal", the assumption that all other factors influencing a particular condition remain constant; and stocks and flows, a distinction made between the quantity existing at one time and the change in quantity occurring during a period of time.

13. In some cases economics is imprecise, or involves only qualitative statements, because some concepts such as consumer satisfaction are immeasurable or because only samples of a total population can be analyzed.

14. Economic principles can be presented verbally but mathematical exposition often is more precise. Geometric graphs are widely used to illustrate verbal explanations.

Review and Discussion Questions

1. Do you think it is valid to assume that not all wants can ever be satisfied? Why?

2. Canada is sometimes described as an affluent society, yet economists continue to base their analyses on the fact of scarcity. Can these two situations be reconciled? Explain carefully what "scarcity" means in this context.

3. Why is the opportunity cost concept so important in economic analysis and economic decisions?

4. Assume you are the chief planner in a planned economy. How will you decide what to produce and how much to produce of each commodity?

5. Could there ever be a pure market economy? Explain.

6. Many of the House of Commons debates focus on economic issues. Should there therefore be a large proportion of economists among the MPs elected to Parliament? Why?

Sources and Selected Readings

Boulding, Kenneth E. *Economics as a Science*. New York: McGraw-Hill, 1970.

Brewis, T. N. "Economic Analysis and Policy" in T. N. Brewis, et al, *Canadian Economic Policy*. Toronto: Macmillan, 1965.

Friedman, Milton. *Capitalism and Freedom*. Chicago: University of Chicago Press, 1962.

Grossman, Gregory. *Economic Systems*. Englewood Cliffs, N.J.: Prentice-Hall, 1967.

Heilbroner, Robert L. *The Making of Economic Society*, 4th ed. Englewood Cliffs, N.J.: Prentice-Hall, 1972.

Hitch, Chas. L. "Uses of Economics" reprinted in M.H. Watkins and D.F. Forster (eds.) *Economics: Canada*. Toronto: McGraw-Hill, 1963, pp. 2-13.

Hutchison, T.W. *'Positive' Economics and Policy Objectives*. London: Allen & Unwin, 1964.

Kuhlman, John M. *Studying Economics*. Pacific Palisades, California: Goodyear, 1972.

Nove, Alex. *The Soviet Economy*, rev. ed. London: Allan and Unwin, 1965.

2 Private Markets and Public Decisions

A. Demand, Supply, and Market Prices

The previous chapter showed that the scarcity of productive resources requires choices to be made in the use of resources; in virtually all contemporary economies these choices are based on prices. Prices are determined either by the forces of supply and demand or by government decree. In either case it is important to understand how consumers and producers react to changes in prices; and conversely, how consumers and producers can influence the level of prices. These relationships are examined by *supply and demand analysis*. Forces influencing the market for each commodity could be grouped or categorized in several ways. The most obvious groupings, however, consist of all the forces affecting buyers and all those affecting sellers. Separating the demand and supply sides of markets emphasizes that these two sets of forces act *independently* of each other. This independence of buyers and sellers cannot be stressed too often. The common factor to which each group responds is the price of the commodity, while at the same time, the price is determined by the independent actions of buyers and sellers.[1]

Demand for Consumer Goods and Services

Although "demand" is used in several ways in everyday language, it has only one specific meaning in economics. Economists avoid using the term "demand" to describe the unlimited wants or desires of individuals and societies discussed in the last chapter. A person might *want* to travel around the world, live in a palace with many servants, own several cars and a huge wardrobe, and so on. But economics is not concerned with such extreme desires, except as they offer evidence for the fundamental assumption that not all human wants can be met.

The demand for a commodity is the quantity that would be purchased at each of various alternative prices, at a particular time, given (or holding constant) all the other conditions that influence purchases of a commodity.

---

[1] The analysis developed in this chapter is based on the assumption that there are many buyers and sellers for each commodity. Chapters 9 and 10 extend this analysis; alternative market conditions are examined in Chapter 11.

There will be only one price-quantity combination observed for any commodity in a given market at a particular point in time; the quantities which would be purchased at other prices are hypothetical. How then can one establish a schedule of demand, or how much would be purchased at prices other than the prevailing price? One could ask individuals how much they would be willing to buy at a variety of possible prices or, in some cases, it is possible to determine the demand for a commodity by examining the amounts purchased at different times in the past as the price of the commodity changed. But this *historical approach* is unreliable if other factors affecting purchases have changed along with the price of the commodity. Because these factors do change quite frequently, an alternative, *survey approach* is sometimes considered more dependable. The limitations of this approach may also be obvious since people are simply asked what they *would* do. Most people find it difficult to answer with certainty what quantity they would purchase at each of various alternative prices. Nevertheless, the concept of demand as defined above provides a useful tool for analyzing the effects of a wide variety of forces influencing the market for any commodity.

Demand Schedules

The relationship between prices and the quantity purchased at each price can be shown as a *demand schedule* as in Table 2.1. Suppose that an individual has been asked about his demand for cups of coffee to be provided by an office "coffee-pool". His answers as presented in Table 2.1 indicate that if the price were $.50 per cup he would buy no coffee — and perhaps bring his own thermos from home. At $.40, however, he would buy one cup each day; he needs this to overcome his mid-morning drowsiness and the lower price would cause him to forgo the nuisance of carrying a thermos. As the price dropped further, he would buy more coffee throughout the day. At $.05 per cup, for example, he would buy five cups. Note that even if the coffee were provided at zero price (free), he would take a total of only seven cups.

Table 2.1
Individual's Demand Schedule for Coffee

Price ($ per cup)	Quantity demanded (cups per day)
.50	0
.40	1
.30	2
.20	3
.10	4
.05	5
.00	7

Demand Curves and the Law of Demand

The information provided in a demand schedule can be plotted on a graph as a *demand curve*. The conventional practice is to show prices per unit on the vertical axis and quantities purchased in a given period of time on the horizontal axis. The individual's demand schedule for coffee is shown as a demand curve in Figure 2.1. The separate combinations of quantity and price (zero cups at $.50, one cup at $.40, etc.) have been plotted at the appropriate point on the graph. These points are then joined by a smooth line to determine the continuous demand curve, *DD*.

The demand curve illustrates the effect of a basic economic principle:

The law of demand states that as the price of a commodity falls, the quantity purchased will increase, all other things being equal, or alternatively, that the quantity purchased will decrease as the price rises.

Within limited price ranges there occasionally can occur exceptions to the law of demand. One such case is related to the difficulty in determining quality differences among similar commodities.

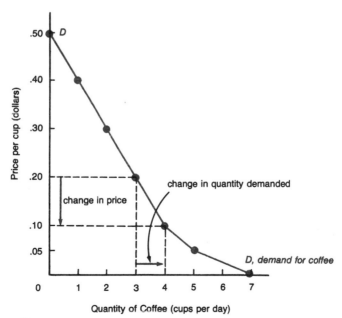

Figure 2.1 *Individual's Demand Curve for Coffee*
The individual's demand schedule for coffee is plotted as demand curve *DD*. The downward-sloping curve shows that price and quantity are inversely related: the quantity demanded increases as the price decreases. This is true for almost all goods, and hence provides a basic economic principle, the law of demand.

Some people tend to judge the quality of a good by its price: a manufacturer of plastic garbage bags, for example, may find that he sells less of his product at a low price than he would if he introduced the bags at a higher price. Another apparent exception occurs when the satisfaction derived from some good is directly dependent on its price. To the extent that diamonds are a source of satisfaction for some people mainly *because* they are expensive, fewer diamonds would be purchased at lower prices. If a good can be stored for future use, an increase in price may lead to a greater quantity purchased if consumers expect that the price will rise again in the near future.

Change in Quantity Demanded vs. Shift in Demand

Demand has been defined as a schedule or listing of the quantities of a commodity which would be purchased at various prices, when other factors are held constant. The quantity which will be bought at a specific price is referred to as the *quantity demanded*. It is difficult to talk about, for example, the "demand for coffee" because this involves a description of the entire demand schedule or curve. Rather, when people talk about the "demand" for a commodity, they are usually referring instead to the *quantity demanded*, or purchased, at the prevailing market price. When this price increases, people may also tend to say that the "demand has fallen", when in fact they are referring to a *change in the quantity demanded*. Refer again to Figure 2.1. The change in quantity demanded as the price of a cup of coffee drops from $.20 to $.10 is the increase from three to four cups. If all other factors are unchanged, a change in price must result in a change in the quantity demanded or purchased.[2]

The law of demand included the words "all other things being equal", and in the last sentence above the words "if all other factors are unchanged". What are these other factors which determine an individual's demand for a commodity, and which explain, for example, why the coffee consumer would buy four cups at a price of $.10 instead of either three or five cups? Clearly, there are a host of factors that could be listed to explain this result. A closer look at such a list would suggest that there are three major groupings for these items:

- the prices of related commodities;
- the consumer's income level;
- the consumer's taste or preference for
  the commodity relative to other commodities.

Relative Prices of Related Commodities. Consider each of these factors in relation to the coffee consumers' demand for coffee. If the prices of tea, milk, and soft drinks should fall, the quantity of coffee

---

[2] One exception to this occurs in the rare case when demand is perfectly inelastic, as explained on p. 32.

purchased at each of the various prices would probably be less than that shown in Table 2.1. But if the price of each of these substitute beverages should rise, the quantity of coffee purchased might be more than was shown in Table 2.1. This indicates that if the price of a commodity (tea) which is a close substitute for the good in question (coffee) should increase, there would be an *increase in demand* for the good in question (coffee). This would be represented by a *shift in demand*, or a shift of the demand curve to the right and upward. This is illustrated in Figure 2.2 where the original demand for coffee is shown as *DD*. The new demand curve resulting from the shift in demand is D_1D_1. The shift is described as being both upward and to the right because more of the commodity is bought at the *same price* (a rightward shift), or alternatively, the *same quality* would be purchased at a higher price (an upward shift).

There is a shift or change in demand with a change in the price of *complementary goods*, as well as with the price of *substitutes*. It may be obvious that the demand for coffee depends on the relative prices of substitutes such as tea and milk. Perhaps it is less obvious that the demand for a commodity also depends on the prices of

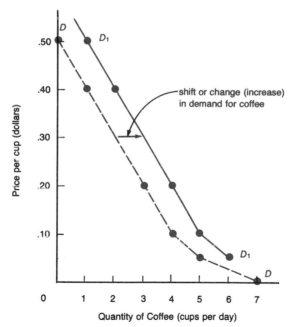

Figure 2.2 A Shift in Demand
A change in price leads to a change in the quantity demanded, but a change in other factors produces a shift in demand: the entire demand curve shifts to a new position on the graph. An outward shift, or an increase in demand to D_1D_1, means that a greater quantity is purchased at any given price. This would follow from an increase in the consumer's income, an increase in the price of close substitutes for the product, or the consumer's increased preference for the product.

complements, or commodities which are usually used along with the particular commodity. If the coffee-drinker could not possibly take his coffee without cream and sugar, and if the supplier charged $.25 for each of these, the demand curve for coffee probably would have been to the left of and lower than the *DD* curve shown in Figure 2.1. Notice that an increase in the price of complements will decrease the demand for the good in question, while an increase in the price of substitutes will have the opposite effect.

Consumer Income. The second major determinant of demand is the *consumer's income level.* Assume now that the coffee-drinker's income is much greater than it was when the demand schedule in Table 2.1 was determined. Since he now has a higher level of income, with more to spend on all items, he probably will also spend more to satisfy his desire for coffee. At a price of $.40 he might now be willing to buy two cups instead of one. A similar increase in the quantity purchased could be anticipated for each price level. Thus an increase in income usually leads to an upward and rightward shift in demand or to an increase in demand; a decrease in income would lead to a downward and leftward shift in demand.

Preferences. Thirdly, the *consumer's set of preferences or tastes* for all commodities will also influence his demand for any given commodity. Such tastes usually change slowly, being altered by increasing age or changing life-style, or experience with different commodities. Rather abrupt changes in tastes may occur, however, with specific circumstances. The information that cigarette-smoking causes cancer has immediately changed at least some individuals' preference for cigarettes relative to, for example, their preference for cigars or pipe tobacco. Preferences among brands of cigarettes may be modified by advertising campaigns. In fact, the primary purpose of advertising can be described as an attempt to shift outward the demand curve for the advertised product.

Elasticity: Sensitivity to Price Changes

That the quantity demanded of a good will increase as its price falls, all other things being equal, usually comes as no surprise to anyone. Further, the law of demand is not particularly useful by itself. It is more important to know how sensitive consumers are, or how strongly they react, to a price change. The concept of *elasticity* is used to measure this relationship between the price change and the resulting change in quantity demanded.

The general concept of elasticity is defined as the percentage change in one variable resulting from a given percentage change in another variable.

Elasticity can therefore be used to measure several economic relationships: the change in demand for a product with a change in income; the change in investment with a change in interest rates; and so on.

The measure of the relationship of price and quantity demanded is termed *price elasticity of demand*, or more specifically, the *elasticity of demand for x with respect to the price of x*. Using the general definition given above in this specific context yields the following definition of the price elasticity of demand:

$$E_D = -\frac{\text{percentage change in } Q_X}{\text{percentage change in } P_X}$$

where E_D is the coefficient or measure of elasticity, Q_X is the quantity demanded of product x, and P_X is the price of x.

Note that there is a minus sign in the above formula. Since there is normally an inverse relationship between changes in price and in quantity demanded, a decrease or negative change in price will result in a positive change in quantity and vice versa. The elasticity coefficient would therefore be negative; including the additional minus sign ensures that the measure will be positive — a simple convenience now generally adopted.

Elasticity, or the degree of responsiveness of consumers to price changes, usually is different for each price level. Elasticity is therefore ideally measured at a particular price, or at a particular point on the demand curve. This is described as *point elasticity*. But changes in price and quantity of such small dimensions that they can be referred to as points are not measurable except with calculus.

An alternative measure, *arc elasticity*, can be used to approximate the value of the point elasticity. This measures the responsiveness of consumers over a short segment or arc of a demand curve rather than at a particular point. This can be illustrated using the coffee-drinker's demand schedule in Table 2.1. If the price of coffee falls from $.20 to $.10, he would increase his quantity demanded by one cup, going from three to four cups per day. The percentage price decrease is calculated by dividing the change in price by the *average* of the old and new prices and multiplying by 100. It is this averaging of prices which permits the approximation of elasticity at a point. Thus the percentage *price* change is

$$\frac{\Delta P}{\frac{P_1 + P_2}{2}} \times 100 = \frac{-10}{\frac{10 + 20}{2}} \times 100 = -67\%$$

The Δ sign is the Greek letter *delta* and means *change in*. The value of ΔP is negative because the price fell.

Similarly, the percentage change in *quantity demanded* would be calculated by the formula:

$$\frac{\Delta Q}{\dfrac{Q_1 + Q_2}{2}} \times 100 = \frac{1}{\dfrac{3 + 4}{2}} \times 100 = 29\%$$

The price elasticity of demand for coffee, *over the price range from $.10 to $.20* is therefore:

$$E_D = -\frac{-29}{-67} = .43$$

The complete formula by which this was obtained is:

$$E_D = -\frac{\Delta Q}{\dfrac{Q_1 + Q_2}{2}} \times 100 \div \frac{\Delta P}{\dfrac{P_1 + P_2}{2}} \times 100$$

This can be simplified to:

$$E_D = -\frac{\Delta Q}{\Delta P} \times \frac{P_1 + P_2}{Q_1 + Q_2}$$

Although there are many instances when it is necessary to know the precise value of the elasticity measure, more often it is sufficient to discuss the elasticity of demand in general terms. *Five elasticity categories* can be used for this purpose. In the above example the quantity demanded changed proportionately less than the change in price: a 67 per cent change in price led to a 29 per cent change in quantity demanded. The elasticity measure, E_D, was therefore less than one; in this case the demand is said to be *inelastic*. If quantity demanded had changed proportionately more than price, E_D would have been greater than one, and the demand would be described as *elastic*. If E_D had been exactly equal to one — the percentage change in quantity demanded the same as the percentage change in price — the condition would be one of *unitary elasticity*. Summarizing briefly:

> when $E_D < 1$, demand is inelastic;
> when $E_D = 1$, demand is of unitary elasticity;
> when $E_D > 1$, demand is elastic.

The other two cases are the extreme limits of elasticity. When there is no change in the quantity demanded as price changes, demand is *perfectly inelastic* and $E_D = 0$. But if there is an infinitely large change in quantity demanded with the most minute change in price, the demand is *perfectly elastic* and $E_D = \infty$ (infinity).

Price Effects on Total Revenue

Elasticity can also be defined in terms of the effect of price changes on the total revenue received from the sale of a commodity, or on the total amount paid by the consumer. If the coffee-drinker found the price to be $.20, he would buy three cups of coffee for a total expenditure of $.60. At a price of $.10 per cup, his purchase of four cups would entail a total expenditure of $.40. The decrease in price would result in decreased total revenue or total expenditure for coffee. Over this price range, the elasticity was found previously to be inelastic. Thus one can conclude that *if a price decrease results in a decreased total revenue, the demand is inelastic. Alternatively, if a price decrease increases the total revenue, the demand is elastic. When the total revenue remains unchanged with changes in price, there is unitary elasticity of demand.*

This second definition suggests why the elasticity of demand for any product is of considerable interest to producers and governments. Although an industry will usually increase the number of units sold if the price of its product falls, it may also find that its total revenue *falls*, if the demand is inelastic. Similarly, a government seeking more revenue will want to increase sales taxes on products for which the demand is *inelastic* so that there is relatively little reduction in the quantities purchased after the tax is imposed, and so that total revenues, including the tax revenues, are increased.

Calculating the precise elasticity of demand for a product can be difficult because it involves either undertaking expensive market surveys, or examining data on quantities sold as prices changed over the past, adjusting for the effects of price changes in related products and changes in consumers' incomes and, if possible, their changing tastes. But the approximate degree of elasticity sometimes can be estimated from the nature of the product in question.

The demand for goods and services will tend to be more elastic or less inelastic:

1. If there are a number of close substitutes for the product. As the price of one good rises, consumers will switch to other goods if these are close substitutes.
2. If the good is a luxury item. When consumers can easily do without a particular good, they will be readier to forgo its purchase as its price increases.
3. If the good represents a significant item in the consumer's budget. If a consumer usually buys a large quantity of beef each year, he will be more likely to reduce his beef consumption as its price increases relative to the price of other meats, than if beef is a minor item in his budget.

Conversely, *the demand for goods and services will tend to be more inelastic or less elastic:*

1. If there are few close substitutes. Since there are apparently no close substitutes for milk in the diet of small children, there will be little change in quantity demanded as the price of milk rises.
2. If the good is a necessity. A specific good, such as salt, which is considered a necessity will be purchased in the necessary quantity regardless of its price.
3. If the good represents an insignificant part of the consumer's budget. A person who buys one package of tulip bulbs each year probably will not be very responsive to increasing tulip bulb prices, but a city parks department which has spent large amounts for tulip bulbs in the past will likely switch to other bulbs or plants.

Total Market Demand

So far the discussion of demand curves has been concerned with the individual's demand curve. Specifically, the coffee-drinker's demand for coffee has provided a simple example to develop a number of concepts relating to consumers' demand for goods and services. Practical interest in demand, however, usually is directed to the *total market demand* for a particular product. Since this total demand consists of the demand expressed by all individuals in the market, *the market demand curve is derived by adding the demand curves or schedules of all these individuals.*

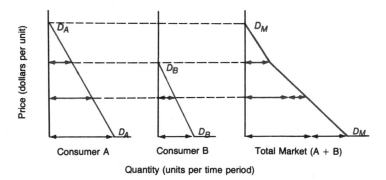

Figure 2.3 *Adding Individuals' Demand Provides Market Demand*
The market demand curve, D_M D_M, is derived by adding horizontally the individual demand curves for all consumers in the market.

Adding the demand schedules requires that the quantities that all persons would buy *at a given price* and at a given time be totalled. The relevant market in the coffee example might be the total group of employees in the office building. If each employee were asked about his demand for coffee it might be found that a total of 30 cups would be sold at $.60, 75 cups at $.40, 150 cups at $.20, and so on. The adding of demand curves requires that the curves for each individual be added *horizontally*, as shown in Figure 2.3.

Since the market demand curve is simply a summation of individuals' demand curves, the special features of these demand curves are also applicable to the market demand. Shifts in market demand, changes in the quantity demanded by the market, and the price elasticity of market demand, are all defined in the same manner as presented for individuals.

Consumer demand is further examined in Chapter 9. This introduction is sufficient, however, when combined with the following section on supply, to see how the market process determines prices.

Supply of Consumer Goods and Services

It is now time to turn to the sellers' side of the market. This discussion of supply can be briefer than the section on demand because there are several similarities in the way each side of the market is analyzed. Care must be taken of course to note the important differences.

Just as "demand" was given a specific definition to distinguish it from the everyday usage of the word, so "supply" is given a special meaning.

The supply of a commodity is the quantity that would be offered for sale at each of various alternative prices, at a particular time, given (or holding constant) all the other conditions that influence a producer's willingness to supply that commodity.

As in the case of demand, there can be only one price-quantity combination observed for any commodity in a given market at a particular time. Any other prices and related quantities are hypothetical. Again, the complete supply schedule or curve would be determined by interviewing potential suppliers, or possibly by examining data on previous prices and quantities offered at these prices. The *market* supply schedule would be derived by adding the supply schedules for each of the several suppliers in a market.

The supply curve, as illustrated in Figure 2.4, usually slopes upwards to the right: the quantity that would be supplied increases with higher prices. Although the downward slope of the demand curve is so common that it has been treated as a fundamental law, there is *not* a similar "law of supply". The reasons for this are outlined in Chapter 10; for the present discussion, the assumption —

which is generally valid — of an upward-sloping supply curve is sufficient. As prices rise, existing producers are tempted to produce more, and more producers will be attracted into the market, so that a larger quantity will be offered at each increase in price. But as more producers enter the market, and more units of the good are produced, the prices of the inputs used in producing the good will be bid up. As production costs per unit rise with increasing output, suppliers will be willing to offer a greater quantity only if the price increases still further.

Change in Quantity Supplied vs. Shift in Supply

Provided that "all other things are equal", or that there is no change in the factors influencing the suppliers' decisions, the actual quantity supplied can change only with a change in prices. Or alternatively, *whenever there is a change in price, there must be a change in the quantity supplied.* Figure 2.4 shows that a change in price, from OP_1 to OP_2, results in a change in the quantity supplied from OQ_1 to OQ_2.

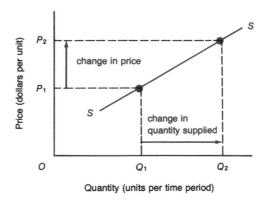

Figure 2.4   Individual Producer's Supply Curve
The producer's supply curve, *SS*, shows the quantity that would be offered at each price. An increase in price would result in an increase in quantity supplied because producers could then cover the higher costs per unit associated with a larger output. Note that the supply curve would not intersect the quantity (*Q*) axis, and likely would intersect the price (*P*) axis, because the supplier must receive at least a price greater than zero before any quantity would be offered to the market.

A change in supply or a shift of the supply curve will occur when any of the factors change which were previously assumed to be held constant. These are quite different factors from the ones which caused the consumer's demand curve to shift to the left or right.

It is because different factors influence supply than influence demand that supply and demand are said to be independent.

The factors causing a shift in the supply curve are related to the suppliers' production costs. Such factors can be placed in three categories:

1. the cost of the inputs or factors of production;
2. changes in the technique or technology related to the production of the specific good;
3. time available to adjust to price changes.[3]

If the costs of labour, raw materials, electrical power, or manufacturing equipment should increase, manufacturers would find that the production cost per unit would also increase and they would be willing to offer fewer units at any given price. This is represented by a leftward shift of the supply curve as illustrated in Figure 2.5. It is unlikely that the costs of inputs would decrease, assuming that there is no change in the technology relating to the production of the good. Thus there is unlikely to be an outward shift of the supply curve when technology is not improving.

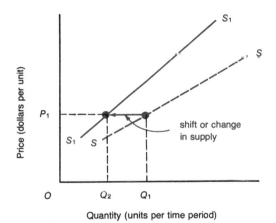

Quantity (units per time period)

Figure 2.5   A Shift in Supply

An increase in the price of productive factors, such as labour, increases the producer's cost per unit. Thus, a lower quantity, OQ_2, will be offered at the same price, OP_1. Since the cost per unit is higher at any output quantity, the entire supply curve shifts to S_1S_1. Technological changes which reduce the producer's cost per unit would shift the supply curve to the right of SS.

Technological changes, however, may lead to quite substantial outward shifts of the supply curve. Economists give "technology" a very broad definition. A change in technology with respect to the production of any good would include a new source of raw materials or other inputs, new kinds of inputs, new transportation methods for

---

[3] Time periods are given detailed examination in Chapter 10, in the discussion of the short run and the long run.

either the inputs or the products, as well as new combinations of inputs or a new technique for combining the inputs used previously. Given this wide interpretation of technology, there are obviously many potential ways for reducing the production cost per unit for any particular good, and thus for shifting its supply curve outward.

Supply Elasticity

Just as demand elasticity measures responsiveness of consumers to changes in product prices, the elasticity of supply measures the responsiveness of producers to changes in product prices. *The elasticity of supply with respect to price is the percentage change in the quantity supplied divided by the percentage change in the price.* This can be represented by the formula:

$$E_s = \frac{\Delta Q}{\Delta P} \times \frac{P_1 + P_2}{Q_1 + Q_2}$$

Note that a minus sign is not added to the right-hand side of the formula as it was for demand elasticity. This is because a positive change in price is assumed to result in a positive change in quantity supplied. In such cases the coefficient or measure of supply elasticity will be positive.

The general categories of supply elasticity are the same as those used for demand elasticity:

when $E_s = 0$, supply is perfectly inelastic;
when $E_s < 1$, supply is inelastic;
when $E_s = 1$, supply is of unitary elasticity;
when $E_s > 1$, supply is elastic;
when $E_s = \infty$, supply is perfectly elastic.

The alternative definition used for demand elasticity, based on the effect of a price change on total revenue, is *not* applicable to supply elasticity since any increase in price will increase total revenue.

Supply elasticity varies for different products for two main reasons:

- the *availability of inputs* to produce the commodity in question;
- the *time* required to adjust production to the new price level.

The *availability of inputs* can be illustrated by the case of residential housing. As the price of housing increases, for example, there will be little increase in the number of new houses offered for sale in a specific area if the land zoned for residential housing has been exhausted. Supply would be almost perfectly inelastic when such an important input is unavailable. In the case of a commodity like bread, however, the supply would be much more elastic if there is no difficulty in obtaining more bread flour and semi-skilled labourers, and in operating the bakery for longer hours.

Time is an important determinant of supply elasticity because most inputs which are not immediately available can be produced over longer periods of time; more land can be annexed and zoned for housing, or more flour can be milled, in the examples cited above. Furthermore, a significant price increase may induce producers to change production techniques or their productive capacity over a longer period of time. But these changes would also depend on the producers' *expectations*. If they expect that the price rise is a temporary one, no such change in productive capacity or techniques is likely.

Price Determined by Supply and Demand

Treating demand and supply separately emphasizes their independence and shows the separate responses of consumers and producers to price changes. The preceding sections took different prices as given; now it is time to see how demand and supply interact to determine the price of any commodity. Figure 2.6 shows the market demand and supply curves for coffee on the same graph. The demand curve indicates that *if* the price is $.60 per cup, 50 cups will be

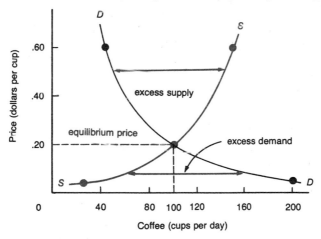

Figure 2.6 Equilibrium Price Determined By Market Demand and Supply
The equilibrium price of $.20 per cup is determined by the intersection of the market demand curve, *DD*, and the market supply curve, *SS*. At a price above $.20 per cup, suppliers would offer more than consumers are willing to purchase: there would be an excess supply. Similarly, at a price below $.20, there would be an excess demand. At $.20, however, the quantity supplied, 100 cups per day, exactly equals the quantity demanded.

purchased each day, but producers will supply 150 cups per day. There will be a *surplus* or *excess supply* of 100 cups per day. This condition causes producers to lower the price of coffee to dispose of the surplus, or to assure that they will not be left with a surplus on future days. As the price falls, consumers will be willing to buy more, but producers will supply less. The process of adjusting to the surplus, and the resulting downward pressure on prices, thus involves the consumers as well as the producers.

Suppose producers become impatient with this adjustment process and decide that they will be able to dispose of all their coffee only when the price is as low as $.05. (Producers are assumed to have done no market research and do not have the advantage of examining Figure 2.6.) At $.05 per cup, producers are willing to provide only 25 cups per day, but customers want to buy 200 cups per day. Producers find that their coffee is sold quickly, and many disappointed customers are still in the lineup to buy coffee for $.05. In fact, they would like to buy another 175 cups, the amount of the shortage or excess demand.

Through this trial-and-error procedure, the price might just happen to be set at $.20. At this price, 100 cups per day are offered by suppliers and exactly the same number is purchased by the customers.

This price, which will just clear the market while leaving no disappointed consumers, is the equilibrium price, or the price at which the quantity demanded is equal to the quantity supplied.

When the price was $.60, the excess supply or surplus was a pressure on the downward movement of the price. At $.05, the excess demand exerted an upward pressure. Since at $.20 there is neither excess demand nor excess supply, there are no such pressures and the market is in equilibrium. The quantity that is offered and purchased at the equilibrium price is the *equilibrium quantity*.

Change in the Equilibrium Price

"Equilibrium" is used to describe a price-quantity combination at which the forces acting on demand and supply are in balance, or exactly offset each other. There is no suggestion that these are necessarily ideal or desirable prices and quantities, or that they will remain at these levels for any length of time. In fact, since the given demand and supply curves are not necessarily true for more than one point in time, an excess of demand or supply may easily arise at what had previously been the equilibrium price; the equilibrium price of the product may change as the forces influencing either supply or demand change.

Supply and demand analysis can be used both to explain why the price of a product might have changed in the past, and what will happen to the price if demand and/or supply are changed in the

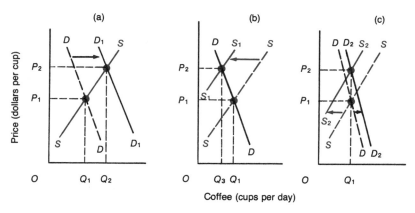

Figure 2.7 Shifts in Supply or Demand Affect Equilibrium Price and Quantity
A higher equilibrium price, OP_2, can result from either an outward shift in demand
(to D_1D_1) or an inward shift in supply (to S_1S_1), or some combination of these shifts
in both demand and supply. In the latter case, the equilibrium quantity may be
unchanged despite an increase in price.

future. Consider the coffee market again. Suppose that the equilibrium price of a cup of coffee had been $.20 in the past. A coffee-drinker returns to this particular office after an absence of some months to find that the price is now $.25. Why has the price increased? Can he make some informed guesses using his knowledge of supply and demand in the coffee market?

One possible set of reasons for the price increase is suggested by Figure 2.7a. If the quantity sold has increased along with the price, there has been an increase in demand, or an outward shift of the demand curve. This may have been due to a recent pay increase received by the office personnel, or to substantial rise in the price of tea and milk, or even to the (improbable) medical discovery that coffee was the key to longevity. Note there has been an increase in the *quantity supplied*, as the demand curve shifted upward along the existing supply curve.

Alternatively, the curious coffee-drinker may find that the increased coffee price has been accompanied by a decrease in the quantity sold. This implies that there has been a decrease in supply, or an upward shift of the supply curve, as illustrated in Figure 2.7b. The shift of the supply curve upwards along the existing demand curve may have been due to an increase in the price of coffee beans or in the wages paid to the producers' employees. In this case there has been a shift in supply and a decrease in the quantity demanded, but no change in the demand for coffee.

Finally, the coffee-drinker may find that there has been no change in the quantity sold, even though the price has increased. As Figure 2.7c suggests, this would occur only if there was a shift in both supply and demand. The demand curve has shifted outward, and the supply curve inward, just enough to leave the quantity sold unchanged.

The coffee-drinker, who did not have the benefit of Figure 2.7, could deduce only that if the quantity sold has increased, demand has increased by more than supply has decreased. Conversely, if the quantity sold has decreased, supply has decreased by more than the increase in demand.

Interdependence of Markets and General Equilibrium

The equilibrium price and quantity in each market is dependent on changes occurring in other markets. The example of coffee drinkers and suppliers examined only one market. It was suggested, however, that one possible reason for the outward shift of the coffee demand curve with the resulting price increase, was an increase in the price of milk. That is, what happens in the coffee market is partly dependent on what happens in the milk market. But why would the price of milk increase? Perhaps this was due to a leftward shift of the milk supply curve caused by an increase in the price of feed for dairy cattle, which in turn was due to an increased demand for feed for beef cattle, due to an increase in demand for steaks, due to an increase in wages of automobile workers, due to an increase in demand for automobiles, and so on and on.

Although this example of related markets gives the impression of a chain of effects, the interdependence of markets is more appropriately seen as a network. Increased wages for automobile workers, for example, might increase not only the demand for steaks but for many other consumer goods and services as well. The market for each of these would in turn directly influence several other markets.

For some purposes, it may be sufficient to know the effect of increased wages on only one market, but for other purposes it may be necessary to know the effect on what is termed the *general equilibrium* of the economy. A market is in equilibrium at the price where the quantity demanded exactly equals the quantity supplied. The economy is in equilibrium when *each* market has reached this equilibrium state, or when the forces operating to change the market prices and quantity of each product or productive factor exactly offset each other so that there is no change. When such a condition exists, all products are being produced as efficiently as possible and each person is realizing as much satisfaction as possible, given the state of technology and the level and distribution of incomes.

Such a condition is not likely to occur. It may be that a product can be produced more efficiently by using more equipment and less labour. This shift would have effects on both the equipment market and the labour market, with further consequences working their way through all other markets. Similarly, a consumer may decide he would be happier if he attended more movies and bought fewer clothes. Again the consequences would ripple through a succession of markets. Thus, the concept of general equilibrium is of more practical significance in its explanation of the *adjustment process* of interdependent markets and for its prediction of the *direction* in which the economy will move than for the determination of prices and quantities which will actually exist at any time.

B.   Market Failure and Social Decisions

Why Markets Fail

An economy's use of the market system, with its price mechanism for allocating resources and distributing finished products, is based on the argument that this provides the most efficient use of resources and the greatest possible satisfaction for the total group of consumers. The case made for the market system two centuries ago by Adam Smith, in his book *The Wealth of Nations*, has often been cited to demonstrate the merits of a market economy:

> Every individual endeavours to employ his capital so that its produce may be of greatest value. He generally neither intends to promote the public interest, nor knows how much he is promoting it. He intends only his own security, only his own gain. And he is in this led by an *invisible hand* to promote an end which was no part of his intention. By pursuing his own interest he frequently promotes that of society more effectually than when he really intends to promote it.

The "Invisible hand" described by Adam Smith was the price mechanism at work: allocating or guiding resources to the most efficient production of commodities most desired by consumers. All of this was done without restricting individuals' freedom to determine their own role in the economy. But Smith was writing at a time (1776) when the prevailing concept of individual freedom included freedom from a collective will as well as from authoritarian command. Furthermore, the economic organization Smith observed in England and Scotland, and particularly in his home city of Glasgow, was quite different from what he would see today in Canada, or in the United States, Japan, and Western Europe. Although the many small shopkeepers such as butchers and bakers that formed the core of Smith's economy are still evident, they are overshadowed by giant, multinational corporations and international labour unions.

Nevertheless, Adam Smith recognized that the "invisible hand" would not provide a satisfactory answer in every case. He argued, for example, that parents would not always recognize the advantages of providing an education for their children. Even if they did recognize the advantages they either would not or could not pay for the education, and at best would not provide as much education as would be in the public interest.

Many other inadequacies in market solutions to economic problems have since been recognized. These are commonly described as instances of *market failure; the failure of the market to produce an outcome that agrees with the currently prevailing notion of social justice.* There are two basic reasons for market failure: *imperfect competition* and *the existence of non-market problems.*

Imperfect Competition

Economies such as Canada's are not organized to meet all the criteria required for the price mechanism to achieve the most efficient use of productive resources. Instead of perfectly competitive markets, where there are many producers of each commodity and new firms can easily be established to produce these commodities, there are frequently only a few large firms, each powerful enough for various reasons to keep out any potential competition.

Unemployment. One of the market system's most serious failures has been its inability to maintain the full employment of the labour services offered by individuals in the economy. Part of this is due to instability or unsteady economic growth (examined in Chapters 4 and 6). But unemployment is also due to the lack of labour market information, the existence of large firms and labour unions, and other imperfections in the operation of the economy which prevent the expansion of firms or the reduction of wages to the point where employers will want to hire all those who want to work.

Adjustment Lags. A partial explanation for unemployment and several other market failures is that the market system may be slow to adjust to changes in consumer tastes and technology. Labour mobility is far from perfect; workers often are slow in making occupational, industrial, and geographical shifts to take advantage of wage differences because retraining is costly in human effort and time, and moving to another locality imposes many social costs. Increased mechanization and scale of production has "locked-in" producers to particular commodities, techniques, and plant size, for longer periods of time. Financial resources are often unavailable for new projects because lenders take a "wait-and-see" attitude.

Tendency to Monopolistic Power. A basic difficulty with the market system is that it has tended to encourage the development of monopolistic power in many markets. The rapid adjustment implied in the price mechanism requires competition among many producers. Producers, however, would prefer to avoid such adjustments and hence strive to gain more control of their markets. Chapters 11 and 12 explain the consequences of monopolistic control: potential competitors are excluded, output is restricted, and prices are higher than when no producer has such control.

Although competition may spur technological change, this in turn can foster monopolistic control. Modern technology generally can be implemented most successfully when firms are assured of large markets and have access to large-scale financing, specialized management, and dependable sources of raw materials. Thus producers will strive to control the factor markets from which they obtain their productive resources as well as their product markets.

One response to the monopolistic power of producers has been the emergence of large unions. This development of "countervailing power" improves the position of workers but may lead the market system further from its most efficient allocation of resources.

Barriers to Markets. Monopolistic power of producers and unions bars other firms from entering some product markets and other workers from some labour markets. Other factors, especially personal and social prejudices, also bar individuals from product markets (refusing to rent to black people or barring Jews from country clubs), and from factor markets (refusing to hire women or denying a business loan to an ex-convict).

Non-Market Problems

There are an increasing number of questions requiring a collective or social decision: questions, for example, of equitable income distribution, conservation of resources, and abatement of pollution. The market is not designed to provide a satisfactory solution to such questions, even if the economy were organized for the ideal operation of the market system. Rather, social questions require social intervention in private markets.

Equitable Income Distribution. The price mechanism allocates consumer products according to individuals' ability to pay for them, which in turn is determined by prices established for the productive resources individuals offer to factor markets. The market system, it is argued, is an inadequate means for determining how commodities should be distributed because some individuals are able to accumulate more physical capital and land relative to others than is considered just or fair, especially if these are accumulated through successive inheritances. As a result the market system allocates more resources to producing luxury goods for the wealthy and fewer necessities for the poor.

Even if incomes were not realized from inheritances or simple good luck, a normative or ethical question would remain. Should an individual's enjoyment of goods and services be related directly to his *economic* role in society, or should some other standard be used for distributing income or goods and services? Although there appears to be wide agreement that the market system fails to distribute income equitably, there is much disagreement on alternatives.

Controversial Consumer Wants. One aspect of the individual freedom associated with the market system is *consumer sovereignty:* the power the consumer has to determine what shall be produced by directing his expenditures to the products he wants most. Although consumer sovereignty has been diminished by monopolistic producers (only to emerge again recently in the political form of "consumerism"), the market system still responds by offering whatever consumers will buy. The market makes no value judgment about what should be produced. Thus some goods and services become the focus of social controversy: alcohol, tobacco, marijuana, heroin, prostitution, pornography, betting shops, lotteries, and guns. The political system is used to correct what are regarded as failures or undesirable consequences of the market system: alcohol is sold by government agencies, tobacco advertising is banned, prostitution is made illegal, lotteries are licensed, books and films are censored, safety standards are imposed for automobiles, and so on.

A wider range of consumer wants are also often questioned. The fact, for example, that more homes in Canada have television sets (96.6 per cent) than have flush toilets (95.5 per cent) is cited as an example of misguided consumer sovereignty.[4] The current rejection of materialism by some young people has been a forceful statement about what they judge to be the inappropriate outcome of consumer sovereignty and monopoly power in the marketplace.

Unmet Public Needs. Even if society judged all consumer wants to be merited, the market would still fail to provide public needs or *public goods. These are items which, if not purchased collectively, will not be purchased at all.* This is because they would be equally available to everyone due to the difficulty in excluding those who would not pay. Strictly speaking, many public goods and services could be purchased individually but their effectiveness is far greater when purchased collectively: imagine, for example, an economy in which individuals made their own arrangements for police and fire protection, and even for weather forecasts. Everyone's health is improved if chest X-rays and vaccinations are provided to all persons in the community, rather than to the few who choose to purchase them individually. Public action through governments is required to make collective purchases that would not occur if the market system were left to make these decisions.

Externalities Ignored. Externalities are economic effects or consequences of actions by producers or consumers for which no compensation is paid; that is they are external to market transactions. An individual who improves the appearance of his home usually provides his neighbours with an external economy or benefit, if only because they can realize a higher price for their own homes due to

---

[4] Statistics Canada, *Household Facilities and Equipment, May 1971.*

the improved appearance of the neighbourhood. Conversely, a factory which pollutes a river, making it unsuitable for swimming, imposes an external diseconomy or cost on a downstream resort owner who no longer can provide a swimming area as one of his attractions.

Externalities are quite common in everyday experience, but the market system ignores them. If individuals who improved the appearance of their homes could collect the value of the benefits realized by their neighbours, homeowners would allocate more resources to this activity because there would be a greater monetary return from the costs they incur. If resort owners who were harmed by a factory's pollutants could collect full compensation for the harm caused, factories probably would change their techniques or disposal systems in response to the higher cost of using the existing systems. In each case, resource allocation would come closer to maximizing society's satisfaction than occurs under an unregulated or free market system.

J. Kenneth Galbraith, in writing about the failure of the market system to take externalities into account, portrays one small instance of the consequences as follows:

> The family which takes its mauve and cerise, air-conditioned, power-steered, and power-braked automobile out for a tour passes through cities that are badly paved, made hideous by litter, blighted buildings, billboards, and posts for wires that long since should have been put underground. They pass into a countryside that has been rendered largely invisible by commercial art. . . . They picnic on exquisitely packaged food from a portable icebox by a polluted stream and go on to spend the night at a park which is a menace to public health and morals. Just before dozing off on an air mattress, beneath a nylon tent, amid the stench of decaying refuse, they may reflect vaguely on the curious unevenness of their blessings.[5]

Government in the Market Economy

Examining the implications of the market system makes it easier to understand the role of government in a market economy. More public action is required than the traditional views of writers on liberal democracy would suggest. Not only must governments provide the legal foundation for a market economy, including laws of property, contracts, and incorporation, and police protection and national defence; they must also give the market economy some social direction or objectives. The major failures of the market system stem from the fact that in its pure form it has no aim other than to provide efficiently the commodities demanded by individuals controlling the

---

[5] J. Kenneth Galbraith, *The Affluent Society*, Boston: Houghton Mifflin, 1958, p. 253.

productive resources. Social activity, however, consists of individuals acting interdependently; thus not all of their economic wants can be met by individual, independent decisions.

This does not mean that the market system must be rejected if social objectives or wants are to be satisfied. Rather, the market system can be adapted as an instrument for effecting social or public policy. Society can make normative decisions about desirable outcomes of the market and alter the market forces to achieve them. It may be necessary, for example, to transfer income to some groups by taxing it from others, but the recipients of income transfers can then spend these as they wish. Governments can direct producers to take external costs into account by taxing pollution or specifying installation of non-polluting equipment. Producers of external benefits can be subsidized by taxing persons who enjoy the benefits.

If the market system is to provide the results assumed for its purely competitive form, government intervention is also required to bring some stability to the fluctuations of individual decisions, hasten adjustments to changing conditions, and restrain monopolistic tendencies and private control of unique resources.

These several roles for governments in a market system can be grouped into three categories: allocation, distribution and stabilization.

Allocation activities include purchasing or providing public goods; making externalities explicit in individuals' decisions by taxation, subsidy, or regulation; and regulating the structure of markets to obtain more competitive conditions. This category probably accounts for the largest portion of governments' involvement in economies. Government direction of resource allocation is considered in several chapters, but especially in Chapter 8.

The *distribution function* is largely a matter of arranging direct income transfers by taxing higher-income persons and making grants to lower-income persons in the form of welfare payments, unemployment compensation, pensions, and other financial assistance. However, almost all government spending has some redistributive effect because the income-class composition of persons receiving government goods or services usually differs from the income-class composition of taxpayers supporting the expenditures. Government regulations can also have a redistributive impact: anti-pollution legislation reduces the profit of the polluting factory, reduces the real income of its customers by increasing the price of the product, but increases the profit of the downstream resort owner. Government redirection of income distribution is treated primarily in Chapter 15.

Stabilization is pursued mainly by varying the government's expenditure and taxation program, although monetary and foreign trade policies also are designed to stablize economic activity. Since these policies may also embrace government actions to improve resource allocation or income distribution, the latter activities can also have stabilizing or destabilizing effects; for example, under certain conditions, increasing income transfers to low-income groups can send the economy off on an inflationary spiral. Governments therefore not only need to determine the appropriate extent of their involvement in each aspect of economic activity, they must also decide the priorities for such involvement due to potential conflicts in the goals they pursue through the market system. This latter problem is raised again in Chapters 4 and 6.

Cautionary Note. Descriptions of market failures and government intervention to set things right again can leave the impression that the only problem is for the public to determine the appropriate nature and priority for government involvement in any given area. As the proportion of government activity in the economy increases, however, it is increasingly important that society be alert to government decisions which have the same faults that were noted for markets. Public highway projects, for example, may be planned with little regard for the external costs these impose through environmental damage. The political goal of "citizen participation" can become a matter of "citizen protest" unless governments avoid elements of monopolistic control, external costs, adjustment lags, and so on, in their own economic actions.

Using the Price Mechanism for Public Policies

Governments can attempt to correct the perceived failures of the market system in several ways: commonly, they take actions which will directly influence the results obtained through the price mechanism. Two types of actions of this kind are the setting of maximum or minimum prices and the taxing or subsidizing of particular commodities. Some existing or proposed public policies are examined here to illustrate the effects of government intervention and the significance of supply and demand elasticities in designing a policy which will have the desired results.

Maximum or Ceiling Prices: Rent Controls

A common proposal for increasing the real incomes of persons living in rented apartments is to set maximum rental rates, thus leaving these persons a larger portion of their incomes to spend on other goods and services. The general consequences of such a policy are illustrated by Figure 2.8 on page 50. Suppose that only highrise apartments are covered by the policy, thus omitting housing alternatives such as flats and rooms in other houses, duplexes and townhouses.

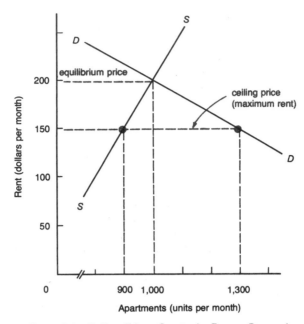

Figure 2.8   Ceiling Prices Create An Excess Demand
Setting the maximum apartment rent at $150 per month, below the equilibrium
price of $200 per month, increases the quantity demanded to 1,300 units but
reduces the quantity supplied to 900 units. The difference, 400 units, is an excess
demand which results in illegal, black-market transactions and possibly in government allocation or rationing of the 900 units supplied.

Over the relevant price range, demand is neither very inelastic,
because housing alternatives are available; nor very elastic, because
some form of housing is necessary and for some people the alternatives to highrise apartments may not be very good substitutes. Supply is fairly inelastic on the assumption that costs of labour, land,
and materials all increase sharply as more apartment buildings are
constructed and because other buildings cannot be readily converted to apartments. The equilibrium price before the rent control
policy is $200 per month; the equilibrium quantity in this local
market is 1,000 units.

If the maximum rent is set at $200 per month or more, (at or
above the equilibrium price), this policy will have no effect on the
market unless supply decreases (the supply curve shifts leftward), or
demand increases (the demand curve shifts rightward). Assume,
however, that the maximum rent is set at $150 per month. The quan-
tity demanded will increase, as a result of the price decrease, to
1,300 units per month. People who have been living in other types of
accommodation or who have been sharing other accommodation
will want to rent units at this lower price. But the quantity supplied
will decrease to 900 units per month, perhaps because apartment

owners can convert housing units to offices for doctors, dentists, or other professionals. *The result is an excess demand or shortage of 400 units.* Note however that there is no change in the *equilibrium price,* because there is no change in demand or supply. That is, there is no shifting of these curves. The rent control policy has created *disequilibrium* in the housing market.

When the price mechanism is working freely, it is this mechanism that allocates or rations the available goods or services among potential buyers. The constraint placed on the price mechanism in the form of a ceiling price requires that some other means be found for allocating the 900 units among the 1,300 customers willing to pay the price of $150. In this particular case, the 900 units will probably be made available to the tenants who were fortunate enough not to be in apartments withdrawn from that market. Some of the 900 units will be vacated by persons moving from the area or to other accommodation; their apartments will be eagerly sought. Apartment superintendents may lease these apartments to the first-comers, but more likely will practise some discrimination, such as selecting persons who are likely to give the superintendents the least trouble, or persons who are highly recommended by current tenants. Alternatively, the superintendent may accept or insist on payments or gifts and, in effect, auction the apartments to the highest bidder. *When price controls are in effect, suppliers are able to do what they cannot do in a free market: exercise some preference among potential buyers.* This often results in political pressure to allocate the available units through a method which is acknowledged to be fairer or more just than allowing individual suppliers to decide. The responsible government department or agency might, for example, establish a means test or other standards for considering applications.

Despite the appearance of a "fair" allocation system for the 900 units, there remain 400 unsatisfied prospective tenants. The pressure for more apartments created by their frequent enquiries about vacancies is likely to stimulate the development of a *black market: the buying and selling of a commodity at prices above the maximum legal price.* Apartment owners may offer to rent a "business office", for example, which is actually a housing unit, at a higher price than $150 per month. Apartment superintendents may insist on an additional payment of up to $50 per month with the threat of harassment if the bribe is not paid. Or there may be a number of additional charges, for keys, use of kitchen appliances and other furniture, or parking, to raise the full price of the apartment substantially above the legal price. As this occurs, more apartments will be provided, and the number demanded will decrease, until the market equilibrium is re-established at $200 per month for 1,000 units.

Other policies which have been proposed as alternatives to rent controls include subsidies for housing construction and additional income supplements or housing grants for low-income families and individuals. The former policy would shift the supply curve outward, lower the equilibrium price and increase quantity, as is explained in the last section of this chapter. If the costs of subsidies were met from additional income tax revenues, everyone would benefit from the lower rents but the middle- and higher-income groups would bear most of the cost.

Housing grants for persons with lower incomes would help them pay their rents. Although the additional income would also be expected to increase demand for housing and increase the equilibrium price slightly, this increase would be less than the amount of the housing grant.

Price controls are frequently used in wartime to restrain the rapid inflation that would occur in consumer goods as resources are shifted to defence production. Rationing of the inadequate quantity supplied is usually done by issuing *ration coupons*. A potential consumer needs both money and ration coupons to buy one unit of a good. Only enough coupons are issued to buy the quantity available at the legal price. Since a demand curve for rationed commodities is influenced by individuals' levels of "coupon income" as well as money income, a limited distribution of coupons is intended to shift the demand curve leftward to the point where it intersects the supply curve at the maximum price. When price controls are used in peacetime, governments attempt to offset the excess demand by trying to stimulate an increase in the supply of commodities covered by the controls.

Minimum or Floor Prices: Minimum Wages

Minimum wage laws and guaranteed floor prices for selected agricultural products are two common examples of minimum price setting by governments. (The latter case is examined in Chapter 12.) All provincial governments and the federal government have enacted minimum wage legislation enabling them to issue regulations specifying the minimum hourly wage that can be paid in certain areas, occupations, or industries. When such legislation is introduced or new minimum levels are announced, most employees are at a wage rate above that level. Usually only some categories of unskilled labour are affected.

Suppose the market for unskilled labour in a particular area is represented by the supply and demand curves shown in Figure 2.9. The equilibrium hourly wage is $2.00 at a quantity of 20,000 man-hours per week. A legal minimum wage of $2.00 or less per hour will have no effect on the market. Assume, however, that the minimum wage is set at $2.25 per hour. The result is that employers want only 16,000 man-hours per week but 24,000 man-hours are offered. Those who remain employed receive a higher wage, but (assuming a 40-hour week) 100 persons lose their jobs. The unemployed include not only the 100 persons who were employed previously, but also a

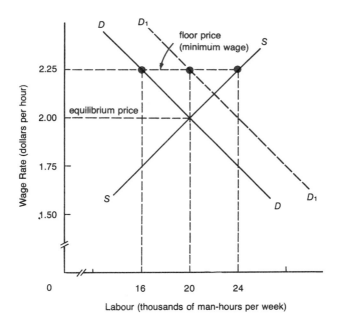

Figure 2.9   Floor Prices Create An Excess Supply
Setting the minimum wage rate at $2.25 per hour, above the equilibrium rate of
$2.00 per hour, increases the quantity of labour supplied and reduces the quantity
demanded. The excess supply, or unemployment of labour, would be 8,000 man-
hours per week. Even if employers can shift their demand curve to D_1D_1 by making
more efficient use of their existing employees, new entrants to the labour market,
at the higher wage, will not be employed.

further 100 persons who would like to work at the higher wage and
who were not in the labour market at the previous wage of $2.00 per
hour.

This unemployment might be reduced if the higher wage for
those remaining in employment leads to increased consumer expenditures and hence to an outward shift in the demand for labour
and more persons employed at the minimum wage or above. If the
demand for unskilled labour is elastic, a wage increase will reduce
the total wages paid, reduce the level of consumer spending, shift
the demand for labour leftward, and increase unemployment.

It is often argued, however, that one result of minimum wage
legislation is that employers are stimulated to make better use of
their unskilled labour so that their existing employees will be worth
more to them, hence justifying a higher wage. This is in effect an
outward shift of labour demand curve to D_1D_1. Should this occur,
none of the existing employees would lose his job, but the additional 4,000 man-hours per week offered to this market would find
no takers. There would still be unemployment resulting from the
new wage legislation.

The actual effects of minimum wages remain the subject of much controversy. Empirical studies are hampered by the problem of isolating other changes occurring in the economy at the same time. Minimum wage legislation frequently has been introduced in different provinces or states, or the minimum wage has been increased, in a period of economic prosperity when the labour demand curve is shifting outward faster than the supply curve, with the result that actual unemployment has been slight or negligible. It is extremely difficult to estimate how much greater employment would have been in the absence of such legislation.

A black market will not emerge as it does when price ceilings are imposed. However, employers may find prospective workers pressing them for employment at a wage below the legal minimum, or workers may offer to work more hours than they would be paid for. The government therefore appoints employment inspectors to guard against such violations when minimum wage legislation is implemented.

Effects of Sales Taxes

All taxes have an effect on commodity or factor markets — income taxes, for example, influence the quantity of labour offered in the labour market — but the effect of a government's intervention in the working of the price mechanism can be seen most clearly in the case of sales taxes. A general sales tax, one which requires that a tax of 5 per cent, for example, be paid on the value of all purchases except necessities like food, is levied primarily as a source of government revenue. Taxes on specific commodities, however, are sometimes intended to curtail the consumption of those items. One common proposal, for example, is that governments should impose a much higher sales tax on cigarettes, if they wish to reduce smoking, rather than requiring a health warning to be printed on the package or banning cigarette advertising. Similarly, it has been proposed that marijuana be legalized but taxed heavily. Opponents of automobile exhaust pollution who are skeptical about emission control devices argue that increasing the gasoline tax is the most effective means for reducing such pollution. Controversy on such proposals concerns not only whether the quantity purchased would be substantially reduced but also whether the producer or consumer would bear the cost of the tax.

Consider the case of automobile gasoline. Assume the existing supply and demand are as shown in Figure 2.10a. At a current equilibrium price of $.55 per gallon, 500 gallons are sold each day. Assume further that the provincial government increases the gasoline tax by $.20 per gallon. If gas stations are to continue supplying 500 gallons, they must now receive $.75 per gallon if they are to meet their own costs and pay the higher taxes. In fact, to provide any given quantity after the new tax is in effect, the supplier will require

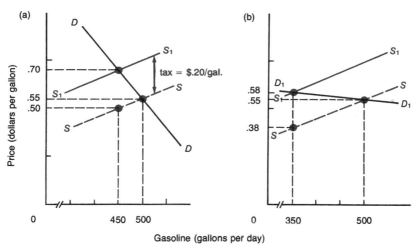

Figure 2.10 Incidence of A Sales Tax Depends on Elasticities of Supply and Demand
Imposing a gasoline sales tax of $.20 per gallon shifts the market supply curve upward, to S_1S_1, by the amount of the tax. The increase in the equilibrium price, however, is less than the tax: the more elastic the demand (compare D_1D_1 and DD), the less the price increase, and the lower the incidence of the tax on the consumer.

$.20 per gallon more than he did before the tax. This is reflected in an upward shift of the supply curve to S_1S_1 by a vertical distance equal to $.20. A specific tax, one which states an absolute amount to be paid on each unit, results in a uniform vertical shift of the supply curve. If the new tax had been an ad valorem tax, stated as a percentage of the selling price, the new supply curve would have had a steeper slope because the absolute amount of the tax would be higher for each selling price.

Tax Incidence. Figure 2.10a shows that the effect of the increased tax is to raise the price to $.70 per gallon, but gasoline consumption is reduced by only 50 gallons per day since this portion of the demand curve is inelastic. (Calculate the elasticity over the range of the price change.) Since the tax increase of $.20 must be deducted from the new price of $.70, producers receive only $.50 per gallon for each of the 450 gallons sold. (Part of this will also be deducted to pay the original tax.) Thus consumers pay $.15 more per gallon and producers receive $.05 less per gallon than before the new tax was imposed. Although the producer will make the actual tax payment to the government, consumers bear three-quarters of the tax while producers bear one-quarter. That is, the *incidence* or ultimate burden of the tax falls mainly on the consumers. The government may decide that consumer protest about higher gasoline prices would be too great compared with the minor effect of the tax on reducing gasoline consumption and therefore forgo imposing such a tax.

But what would the effect be if the demand for gasoline were quite elastic, as in Figure 2.10b? This implies that there are close substitutes for gasoline, or automobile transportation, such as public transit. The price will increase only slightly, from $.55 to $.58, but the quantity sold will fall to 350 gallons per day. (Calculate the elasticity of demand in this case.) The incidence of the tax falls almost entirely on the producers who receive a much lower price per gallon for fewer gallons. In this case, consumers may not react very strongly to the small price increase but the producers probably will lobby the government vigorously to withdraw the tax. Nevertheless, the government may decide that the significant reduction in gasoline consumption outweighs the protests from the gasoline industry.

This comparison of two cases of demand elasticity illustrates some conclusions that can be drawn about the effects of a sales tax:

- Provided that the demand is not perfectly elastic, a sales tax will increase the price paid by consumers and lower the amount received by suppliers, by less than the full amount of the tax in each case.
- The more *inelastic* is the *demand* for a commodity, the *higher* is the new market price and the portion of tax borne by consumers.
- The more *inelastic* is the *supply* of a commodity, the *lower* is the new market price and the portion of the tax borne by consumers.
- Except when either demand or supply are perfectly inelastic, a sales tax will reduce the quantity bought and sold. The more elastic are both demand and supply, the greater is this reduction in quantity.

The example considered above assumed that the purpose of the tax was to reduce consumption. A government is also interested in the revenue realized from a sales tax; this will also differ depending on the elasticity of demand and supply. The more inelastic is demand or supply, the less the quantity bought and sold is reduced by the tax and hence the higher is the tax revenue. Governments therefore will find sales taxes more effective in reducing consumption the more elastic is demand or supply for the commodity concerned, but more effective in raising revenue the more inelastic is demand or supply for the commodities to be taxed.

Effects of Subsidies

A subsidy is a payment to a producer to offset part of his production costs; the payment may be either a flat or fixed sum or a sum which varies directly with the quantity produced. Subsidies are paid when a government wants to increase the production of a particular item, without involving the government directly in its production and distribution. It has often been proposed, for example, that the federal government increase its financial assistance to Canadian publishing firms so that Canadians will be encouraged to read more works by Canadian authors.

To determine the effects of implementing this proposal consider an example which makes some simplifying assumptions. Suppose the demand for Canadian paperback books can be represented by a single demand curve as shown in Figure 2.11. Since for the general reader there are many close substitutes, ranging from foreign books to Canadian magazines, the demand is assumed to be quite elastic. Supply is also assumed to be elastic because the costs of labour and materials probably do not rise very quickly with increased output. The current equilibrium price is $2.95 per book; 10,000 books are sold at this price each month.

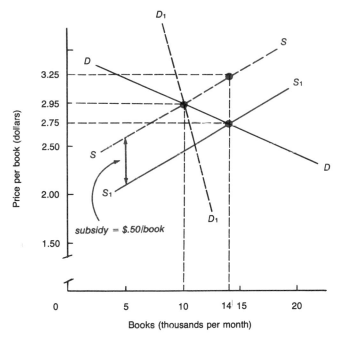

Figure 2.11 Effect of a Subsidy Depends on Supply and Demand Elasticities
A government subsidy of $.50 per book shifts the market supply curve downward to $S_1 S_1$ by the amount of the subsidy. However, the equilibrium price falls by less than the full subsidy: the more elastic the demand curve, the less the price falls but the more quantity is increased. The broken-line demand curve can be used to visualize the subsidy's effect on price and quantity when demand is more inelastic.

Next assume the government offers Canadian publishers a subsidy of $.50 per paperback book.[6] Since publishers are currently willing to supply 10,000 books per month at a market price of $2.95, they should be willing to supply the same 10,000 books at a market price of $2.45 when the government pays a $.50 subsidy. *Thus the effect of the subsidy will be to shift the supply curve downward by the amount of the subsidy.* The new supply curve, S_1S_1, intersects the demand curve at a lower price and higher quantity. The new market price is $2.75 and 14,000 books are sold each month.

The subsidy in this case does substantially increase the consumption of Canadian books. The incidence or economic benefit of the subsidy lies mainly with the producers. They now receive $.30 more per book while consumers pay $.20 less: three-fifths of the subsidy accrues to producers, two-fifths of the subsidy is realized by consumers.

As in the case of a sales tax, however, the elasticity of demand and of supply have a significant effect on the incidence of a subsidy. An alternative, inelastic demand curve is also shown in Figure 2.11 to make it easier to compare the influence of different demand elasticities on the price and quantity effects of a subsidy. In the alternative case, the subsidy would lead to a greater reduction in price but a lower increase in quantity. The incidence of the subsidy would have fallen mainly on the consumers. Some general conclusions can be drawn from this comparison:

- Provided that the demand is not perfectly elastic, a subsidy will decrease the price paid by consumers and increase the amount received by suppliers, by less than the full amount of the subsidy in each case.
- The more *inelastic* is the *demand* for a commodity, the *lower* is the new market price and the greater is the benefit of the subsidy to consumers in terms of a price reduction.
- The more *inelastic* is the *supply* of a commodity, the *higher* is the new market price and the greater is the benefit of the subsidy to producers in terms of additional amount received.
- Except when either demand or supply are perfectly inelastic, a subsidy will increase the quantity bought and sold. The more elastic are both demand and supply, the greater is this increase in quantity.

Review of the Main Points

1. Many factors influence the price of a commodity. These act either on the demand side or on the supply side of the market, and are independent of each other.

---

[6] This is the case of a *per unit* subsidy. The effect of a *flat sum* subsidy can be determined using the theory of the firm, as developed in Chapters 10 and 11.

2. Demand is the quantity of a commodity that would be purchased at each of various alternative prices, at a particular time, holding constant all other conditions that influence purchases of a commodity. The list of these price-quantity combinations is a demand schedule; plotting this schedule on a graph yields a demand curve.

3. The law of demand states that as the price of a commodity falls, the quantity demanded will increase, all other things being equal, or alternatively, that the quantity demanded decreases as the price rises. A change in quantity demanded is the result of a change in price with all other factors held constant; a change in demand is the result of a change in one or more other factors which influence consumers' purchases. "Other factors" are the prices of related commodities, the consumer's income level, and the consumer's set of tastes or preferences.

4. The elasticity of demand for a good with respect to price is defined as the percentage change in quantity demanded divided by the percentage change in price. When $E_D < 1$, demand is inelastic; when $E_D > 1$, demand is elastic; and when $E_D = 1$, demand is of unitary elasticity. When total revenue increases as price increases, the demand is inelastic; but if total revenue falls, the demand is elastic. When total revenue is unchanged as price changes, demand is of unitary elasticity.

5. The total market demand for a commodity is found by adding the quantity demanded at each price by each consumer in the market.

6. The supply of a commodity is the quantity that would be offered for sale at each of various alternative prices, at a particular time, holding constant all other conditions that influence a producer's willingness to supply the commodity. The supply curve usually slopes upward to the right.

7. A change in the quantity supplied results from a change in price, but a shift in supply is the result of changes in other factors. These are the cost of inputs used to produce the good and the technology related to the production of this good.

8. The elasticity of supply with respect to price measures the responsiveness of suppliers to changes in produce prices, and is defined as the percentage change in the quantity supplied divided by the percentage change in price. When $E_S < 1$, supply is inelastic; when $E_S > 1$, supply is elastic; and when $E_S = 1$, supply is of unitary elasticity.

9. The price elasticity of supply depends on the availability of inputs within a given production period, the time required to adjust production to the new price level, and whether the supplier expects the price change to be only temporary.

10. A product market is in equilibrium at the price where the quantity supplied is equal to the quantity demanded. At a price above the equilibrium price, the pressure of excess supply leads to a lower price; at a price below the equilibrium price, the pressure of excess demand leads to a higher price. The equilibrium of a product market will be disturbed, leading to a new equilibrium price and quantity, when there is either a shift in demand or in supply. It is possible that a shift of both demand and supply will leave *either* price *or* quantity unchanged, but not both.

11. The equilibrium price and quantity in each market is dependent on changes occurring in other markets. When all markets are in equilibrium, the economy is in general equilibrium; all products are being produced as efficiently as possible and all individuals are realizing as much satisfaction as possible, given the state of technology and the level and distribution of incomes. The concept of general equilibrium is most useful in explaining the process whereby markets adjust to changes and in predicting the direction of changes in each market.

12. Markets provide some answers which do not accord with the prevailing notion of social justice. Evidence of market failure due to imperfect competition is found in the existence of unemployment, adjustment lags, a tendency to monopoly power, and barriers preventing some persons from having access to all markets. Furthermore, a market system makes no judgments about income distribution and consumer wants; does not provide public goods and services such as national defence; may not provide enough quasi-public goods such as education and health; and ignores external benefits and costs.

13. The rationale for government involvement in a market system is to correct the results of market failure, through legislation and direct participation in specific markets. Governments can use the price mechanism to achieve certain results, for example, by imposing price ceilings or price floors and by levying sales taxes or offering subsidies; but governments need to be aware of the consequences of these actions.

14. A price ceiling such as rent control creates an excess demand or shortage; rationing may therefore be used to reduce effective demand. A black market is also likely to arise. A price floor such as a legal minimum wage creates a surplus or excess supply (unemployment). Employers may effectively increase the demand for labour by improving the utilization of labour. There is also an incentive for potential employees to offer their labour services, illegally, below the minimum wage.

15. A sales tax shifts the supply curve upward by the amount of the tax per unit and hence increases the equilibrium price and reduces the quantity sold. The more inelastic the demand and the

more elastic the supply, the higher is the new price and the greater the incidence of the tax on the consumer. A subsidy shifts the supply curve downward by the amount per unit of the subsidy, reduces the equilibrium price and increases the quantity sold. The more inelastic the demand and the more elastic the supply, the lower is the new price and the greater the benefit realized by the consumer.

Review and Discussion Questions

1. Why are price differences more important than absolute price levels in the operation of the market system?

2. Why is price elasticity defined in terms of percentage changes in price and quantity rather than changes in the absolute values of these?

3. (a) List five commodities for which you think the demand is inelastic, and five for which the demand is elastic, over the range of prices usually observed for these commodities. Explain why demand would be inelastic or elastic in each case.

   (b) List five pairs of commodities which are very close substitutes. Can you think of any *perfect* substitutes, that is, commodities which are perfectly interchangeable from a consumer's point of view? List five pairs of commodities which are complementary goods. Are there any *perfect* complements?

4. What forces are at work to move the price of a commodity toward its equilibrium price? Can you think of any markets which appear to be in equilibrium? What use can you make of the market equilibrium concept?

5. Use a supply and demand diagram to explain the probable changes in price and quantity purchased if the sale of marijuana were to be legalized and conducted without government controls.

6. List as many instances as you can of external costs you have experienced today and external benefits you have enjoyed. What legislative or other changes might be made to bring these effects within the decision-making of persons who produced these effects?

7. "The market system assures the best possible allocation of resources and distribution of incomes." Do you agree? Why?

Sources and Selected Readings

Boulding, Kenneth E. *Economic Analysis, Volume 1: Microeconomics*, 4th ed. New York: Harper & Row, 1966.

Dorfman, R. *Prices and Markets*, 2nd ed. Englewood Cliffs, N.J.: Prentice-Hall, 1972.

Galbraith, J. Kenneth. *The Affluent Society*. Boston: Houghton Mifflin, 1958.

Leftwich, R.H. *The Price System and Resource Allocation*, 5th ed. Hinsdale, Ill.: Dryden Press, 1973.

Radford, R.A. "The Economic Organization of a P.O.W. Camp", *Economica*, Vol. XII (November 1945), pp. 189-201.

Stigler, George L. *The Theory of Price*, 3rd ed. New York: Macmillan, 1966.

3 Measuring Canada's Economic Performance

Canada's Economic Goals

Canada's economic goals have emerged gradually through political consensus. They were stated explicitly by the Economic Council of Canada in its *First Annual Review* and, with some variation, were repeated in its subsequent *Reviews*. The Council has recognized five basic economic goals: *reasonable price stability, full employment, a high rate of economic growth, a viable balance of payments*, and *an equitable distribution of rising income*. However, the Council has also emphasized that the various goals are not always compatible with each other:

> Policies designed to accomplish a particular aim such as full employment or a rapid rate of growth may be in conflict with the policies needed to avoid inflation or to maintain a viable balance of payments. There is always the overriding requirement to reconcile conflicting tendencies and to achieve consistency.[1]

The following chapters in Part Two examine the structure and operation of the economy and consider the policies that might be pursued to achieve the first four of these goals. The problem of income distribution is reserved for Part Four.

In order to determine whether progress is being made toward achieving Canada's economic goals, some method is required for measuring the economy's performance as it affects these objectives.

The measures currently used to assess this performance are described in this chapter. They are examined to determine whether they should be modified to provide a more accurate indication of how the economy is performing. The combination of these various measures forms the framework for the overall assessment of the government's economic policies. In the past, critics of these policies were generally willing to accept this framework as a common ground for discussion, but even the measures are now being challenged. It is therefore essential in the following sections to pay close attention to the detailed definitions being used.

---

[1] Economic Council of Canada, *First Annual Review: Economic Goals for Canada to 1970*. Ottawa: Queen's Printer, 1964, p. 2.

Inflation and Price Stability

Inflation is often defined as an increase in the general level of prices. Preferably, inflation should be defined as *an increase in the general level of prices of consumer goods and services.* Prices of intermediate goods or producer goods may rise, but if producers are able to take some offsetting action, such as accelerated productivity increases or narrower profit margins, so that prices of consumer goods and services are unchanged, most of the undesirable effects of inflation will not be realized. Governments do watch the prices of intermediate goods, especially of important products like steel, because they know an increase in prices of raw or semi-finished products or in wholesale prices often leads to an increase in the price of consumer goods.

The Economic Council of Canada defined "reasonable price stability" as the average annual rates of change in prices and costs in Canada from 1953 to 1963, (the decade prior to the Council's appointment), or about 2 per cent annually. Strictly speaking, price stability should be defined as *no change* in prices. However, the Council was reflecting the common view that, since some inflation seems inevitable, price stability can be defined as a low, steady increase in the price index. In 1972, the Council set the target inflation rate at 3 per cent; but in 1973, an absolute target was abandoned in preference to the objective that Canada's inflation rate should not exceed that of other major countries.

In addition to the most commonly used measure of price change, the *Consumer Price Index (CPI)*, the Council selected a number of other indices to be used in monitoring prices and costs. These included an index for each of the following: wholesale prices, prices of industrial materials, farm product prices, average hourly earnings in manufacturing, corporate profits and labour cost per unit in manufacturing, and the Gross National Expenditure price deflator. This last item is discussed later in this chapter. The choice of these indices reflects the fact noted above, that governments are also concerned about prices outside the consumer sector.

Consumer Price Index

Each month the federal government's statistics bureau, Statistics Canada, announces changes in the Consumer Price Index (the CPI) from the previous month and from the same month one year ago. The CPI is intended to measure changes in the purchasing power of consumers' incomes. If a person's income is unchanged from the previous year, but prices of consumer goods and services have increased by 5 per cent, the individual's purchasing power has fallen accordingly. If his income has increased by 5 per cent, while prices have risen by the same amount, then he is able to buy exactly the same physical quantity of goods and services that he purchased the previous year.

The CPI is calculated by comparing current prices of commodities generally purchased by consumers with the prices of the same commodities in an earlier, *base year*. The set of prices are compared for the next several years. The base year is usually the most recent one in which there was little price change.

The current prices of goods and services are expressed as a percentage of the base year prices. Thus, if the base year price of a light-bulb was $.50 and the current price is $.65, the price index for light-bulbs would be 130, since $65 \div 50 \times 100 = 130$. The relative importance of each commodity included in the CPI is indicated by a weight which reflects the share of the consumer's total expenditures directed to this item. Housing and food, for example, have large weights in the CPI; recreational items have a much lower weight. The CPI therefore reflects both the average prices paid and the relative quantities purchased by the average Canadian consumer.[2] Persons who divide their personal budgets differently from the weights used in the CPI, perhaps spending unusually large amounts on fashionable clothing or recreation, will find that the CPI is not a satisfactory measure of changes in the purchasing power of their own incomes if the prices of these items move differently from prices of most other goods.

Because the base year quantity weights remain constant while the actual distribution of the consumer's budget may change over time, the CPI may not be an accurate reflection of changes in purchasing power. The base year is therefore revised occasionally to keep abreast of these changes. It may be assumed that the CPI will slightly overstate the inflationary effect actually experienced by consumers since they will tend to reduce their expenditures on those items whose prices are increasing most quickly.

Revision of the base year also overcomes another problem associated with price indices, the changing quality of the commodity concerned. For example, changes in automobile styles and features, along with unequivocal improvements, make price comparisons difficult over a range of more than a few years.

Figure 3.1 on page 66 illustrates Canada's experience with inflation since 1951. Prices soared upward rapidly in that year, but for the next fifteen years, prices rose at an average of about 2 per cent annually. Inflation has received increasing attention because recent annual increases in the CPI have greatly exceeded this long-term average annual rate which the Economic Council described as "reasonable". Consequently, the federal government implemented a price and income control program in late 1975. This is discussed at the end of Chapter 6.

---

[2] Specifically, the CPI is based on the relative quantities of about 300 items purchased by families of 2 to 6 persons, with an annual income in 1967 of $4,000 to $12,000, and living in cities of at least 30,000 population. The base year has been changed from 1961 to 1971 for price comparisons, but the broad category weights are based on 1967 expenditures, while the detailed weights within the food category are for 1969.

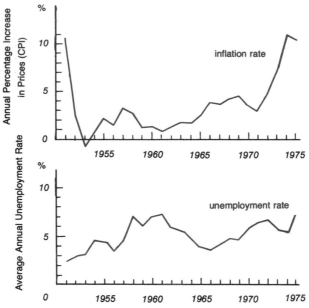

Figure 3.1 *Inflation and Unemployment in Canada, 1951-75*
From 1952 to 1962 the inflation rate was less than 2 percent annually but inflation
was above 3 percent annually during 1965-70. The unemployment rate has tended
to be high when the inflation rate is low, but in the late 1960s both rates were
increasing. Inflation exceeded 10 percent in both 1974 and 1975.
Source: Statistics Canada, *Canada Year Book* and *The Labour Force*.

Problems of Inflation

Inflation is of public concern because it has different effects on
the purchasing power of different groups of people, and can adversely affect Canada's competitive position in world markets. If
everyone could anticipate precisely the annual price increases and
could adjust his income and financial assets or debts accordingly,
the disadvantages of inflation would be sharply reduced. Although
there has been some improvement in this direction, for example,
through the introduction of cost-of-living adjustments in some wage
contracts and pension plans, the effects of inflation remain severe for
some groups.[3] Persons on unadjusted pensions and other fixed in-

---

[3] The Economic Council notes in its *Annual Review* for 1974 that the use of
  cost-of-living adjustments or "indexation" varies widely among different
  levels of government and between government and private sectors:
  "About 90 percent of all federal transfer payments to individuals are explicitly indexed, whereas the majority of provincial and municipal transfers
  outside Quebec are not. In the private sector, the occurrence of indexation
  is increasing but remains infrequent".

comes experience a reduction in real income as prices rise. Creditors may also lose since $500 repaid after ten years will buy fewer goods and services than would $500 when the loan was made. Creditors try to estimate the extent of inflation and include an allowance for this in the interest rate on loans. But forecasting the rate of inflation for several years hence is a difficult art. Creditors may overestimate the extent of inflation; to this extent they impose an unnecessary burden on borrowers and contribute to further inflation, for example, through higher rents and higher mortgage costs for home-owners. In general, inflation has the effect of shifting real income from the older to the younger generations because older generations tend to include a larger number of creditors and persons living on fixed incomes.

If the rate of inflation is higher in Canada than in other countries, Canada's foreign trade position may be adversely affected. As the prices of Canadian products rise relative to the prices in the other countries, Canadians increase their purchases of imported goods and sell fewer goods abroad. Hence, the Economic Council proposed a new indicator that would establish a relative standard rather than an absolute one. That is, there should be zero difference between the movement of the CPI in Canada and the weighted index of consumer prices in the United States, United Kingdom, West Germany, Japan, France, and Italy. (These are Canada's major trading partners, as is shown in Chapter 7, Table 7.2).

A discussion of the causes of inflation and policies for dealing with it is included in Chapter 6.

How Much Unemployment Represents Full Employment?

When the Economic Council first attempted to define "what would be a reasonable employment target for the Canadian economy", it stated candidly:

> The concept of full employment varies considerably from country to country. Nowhere does it mean 100 per cent of the labour force. In any free society — even in countries experiencing an intense labour shortage — there will always be a certain minimum amount of voluntary or unavoidable unemployment as workers move from one job to another.[4]

In 1964, the Council concluded that a 3 per cent rate of unemployment represented a reasonable employment target for Canada. However, the Council recognized in 1972 that this was a very ambitious target, when taken together with its inflation target of less than 2 per cent, and noted that "Not once during the last fifteen

[4]Economic Council of Canada, *op. cit.*, pp. 37-38.

years has the Canadian economy even approached both goals simultaneously". The Council therefore suggested that for the immediate future the temporary objective should be an average annual unemployment rate of 4.5 per cent and an inflation rate of 3 per cent. In 1973 and 1974, the Council continued to propose 4.5 per cent as the target unemployment rate, but raised this in 1975 to a target of 5.6 per cent averaged over 1975 to 1980.

Full Employment

The concept of full employment is usually limited to the labour resources of an economy, but a broader interpretation of full employment includes the full utilization of all productive resources: the productive plant and equipment and land, as well as the labour force. This broader definition is seldom used in measuring economic activity because arbitrary decisions are required to determine when a plant is working at full capacity. Is it 10 hours per day for 5 days per week? or for two 8-hour shifts? or for three 8-hour shifts? "Full capacity" however, can be applied to such plants as steel mills, which are normally in continuous operation.

"Full employment" therefore usually refers only to the labour force, for the reasons noted above, and because unemployment of labour represents a serious social problem as well as an underutilization of economic resources. The common definition of full employment, however, is concerned with whether a person has an income-earning job, and not with the number of working hours per week that is either possible or desirable. Thus, *full employment is defined as the situation in which everyone aged 14 or over who is willing and able to work for pay has an income-earning job.*

Unemployment

The unemployment rate is calculated once each month by Statistics Canada. This is based on a monthly survey of about 30,000 Canadian households. *Employed persons* include those who during the survey week worked for one hour or more as paid employees, or were self-employed, or worked without pay for a family farm or business, or who did not actually work but were only temporarily absent from their jobs due to weather, illness, industrial disputes, or vacations. *Unemployed persons* include those who were not at work during the survey week but who were able to work and had actively looked for work. The *labour force* is defined as the total of employed and unemployed persons. The *unemployment rate* can then be calculated simply: the number of persons unemployed as a percentage of the total labour force.

These definitions raise a number of problems concerning the measurement of unemployment. First, it should be clear that "the unemployed" do not include all those who are not earning income.

Large groups of people are considered to be outside the labour force: housewives who are not at work outside the home, full-time students who do not have part-time jobs, all persons under 14 years of age, most retired people, persons in correctional institutions, and Indians on reservations. Another important group not in the labour force are those who have been employed, moved into the unemployed group, became discouraged by the lack of employment opportunities, and are no longer actively seeking work.

One may wonder why there can be so many unemployed persons at the same time as so many job vacancies exist. Part of the explanation is that some people are not able to find work for which they are trained and at the wage level they expect. They may have decided that it pays them to spend some time looking for the proper job rather than to accept the first one available. Secondly, job vacancies may occur in one area of the country but the unemployed persons are living in a different area. Again, it may be more rational for an unemployed person to seek work near his home rather than bear the cost of moving.

Another problem is that the current definition of unemployment does not include *disguised unemployment* or *underemployment*. This occurs when people have jobs, but are not working at jobs which would fully utilize their specific skills. An unemployed chemical engineer may decide to drive a taxi or work on a construction site until he can find work in his field. He would not be counted as unemployed in the labour force survey; nevertheless, he may be actively seeking some other employment.

Persons working fewer hours per week than they prefer, for example, a waitress restricted to working in the peak hours, are also underemployed. Some people are able to "moonlight" — take a second job — but it is often difficult to find two jobs which can be held conveniently at the same time. A survey conducted by Statistics Canada in January, 1973 found that only 3 per cent of the employed labour force held more than one job.

The unemployment rate reflects only the number of persons unemployed; it does not measure directly the average *duration* of unemployment. Unemployment is obviously more serious if persons have been out of work for three or four months rather than for a week or so.

Finally, a problem may arise in understanding monthly reports on unemployment rates because the monthly rates are said to be *seasonally adjusted*. This means that the rate calculated from the monthly labour force survey is adjusted to take account of the fact that the unemployment rate is usually higher in the winter and lower in the summer. If a review of recent years shows the unemployment rate as usually 1.5 times greater in January than it is for the twelve-month average, the actual rate for January will be divided by 1.5 to obtain the *seasonally adjusted rate*. If the unemployment rate is worse in January this year than it was in January last year, this difference will be reflected in the adjusted rate. However, the difference in the actual unemployment rates for January and for July is substantially reduced by the adjustment.

Figure 3.1 shows the upward trend of the unemployment rate in recent years. The most troublesome feature of this development is that it has occurred along with an increase in the rate of inflation. Much more will be said about this compounded problem in Chapter 6.

The differences in unemployment rates among different groups and in different regions of Canada are shown in Table 3.1. Note that the unemployment rate is generally higher for males than for females. This is not necessarily because women are better able to find a job or to hold one, but because women who are the secondary earner in households tend to spend less time looking for a job before giving up if jobs are scarce. Younger people have a higher unemployment rate for a number of reasons: the survey may have found them when they were just entering the labour force for the first time and had not yet found a job; they are often the first to be laid off due to lack of seniority; or they may lack the experience many employers are seeking. Reasons for the higher unemployment rates in the Atlantic provinces and Quebec are examined in Chapter 15.

Table 3.1

**Average Annual Unemployment Rates
by Age, Sex, and Region, Canada, 1974**

Age	Unemployment Rate	Region	Unemployment Rate
14-19	11.7	Atlantic Provinces	9.7
20-24	8.3	Quebec	7.3
25-44	3.9	Ontario	4.1
45-64*	3.5	Prairie Provinces	2.8
		British Columbia	6.0
Males	5.7		
Females	4.9	Canada	5.4

* Number over 64 years in Labour Force Survey too small to provide reliable estimate.

Source: Statistics Canada, *The Labour Force*.

Economic Growth and the National Accounts

Economic growth can be defined and measured in a number of ways, but there are basically two approaches to defining economic growth: one focuses on the increase in *actual output* of goods and services while the other refers to an increase in the economy's productive capacity or its increased *ability* to produce goods and services. A common definition based on the former concept is the *rate of increase in real Gross National Product per capita.*[5] This simple definition requires more complex measurements than were used for either price stability or full employment. Before turning to the meaning of "real" or "per capita", it will be necessary to focus on Gross National Product (GNP) and other related measures of national income.

Why Measure Growth?

Economic growth is one of the basic economic goals because an annual increase in goods and services available to each consumer is a major step toward improving an individual's well-being, although it is also recognized that this depends on several other, non-economic conditions. Moreover, people increasingly recognize that the methods used to achieve economic growth have serious consequences for their total well-being. Smelters and pulp mills, automobiles and pop-cans may contribute to one's enjoyment but these may also contribute to an unpleasant environment. Technological improvements can increase the incomes of many persons, but put others out of work, perhaps permanently. Alternatively, these improvements may lead to a shorter work week, leaving employees with both higher pay and more leisure time. Ideally, these and many similar effects should be included in any measure of collective and individual well-being. But until better measures are developed, it is useful to use the total output of the economy as an indicator of consumer satisfaction.[6]

Another reason for measuring this output is to determine how well the Canadian economy is being managed. On the basis of experience with this and other economies, economists can estimate what would be produced if all available physical and human resources were fully employed, albeit according to some arbitrary definition of full employment. If the actual output falls below the estimated potential level, the economy is not performing at full capacity. Changes should then be made in the organization of the economy and the economic policies of governments.

Comparisons of economic performance from year to year provide a measure of how successful economic policies have been, and whether other policies or programs will be required. Past rates of economic growth provide a basis for forecasting future growth rates, and thus for determining what the level of output will be several

---

[5] The Economic Council, however, has tended to emphasize the growth in labour productivity — the increase in output relative to the manpower resources used — as its measure of economic performance for policy purposes.

[6] Some attempts to develop better measures of well-being are discussed following the description of national income accounts.

years hence. These estimates can aid governments, for example, in determining whether existing tax structures will yield sufficient revenues to finance planned expenditure programs. Firms can estimate whether consumer incomes will increase enough to merit expansion of productive capacity.

What Is Measured?

Measurement requires a basic unit such as inches, litres, or degrees. The most obvious unit for measuring output and incomes is the currency unit of the economy. Although the thousands of different goods and services produced each year can be aggregated only by using the Canadian dollar as a common unit, there is a disadvantage in using a money measure: only goods and services which are bought and sold will have an explicit price. Although an artist may be able to estimate the market value of his painting, for example, no one can determine its price precisely until it is sold. Thus, *only the goods and services which are exchanged for money can be included in the measure of economic growth.* Work around the house such as cleaning, cooking, caring for children, carpentry, and painting, is not included unless someone has been paid for this work. Illegal activities such as drug-trafficking, prostitution, and bootlegging are also economic activities but are omitted from the measured output of the economy because it is difficult to estimate the total economic value of these activities.

The Circular Flow

Each of the many goods and services produced every year must be classified in such a way that none is omitted or counted twice. A classification system established by tracing the flows of payments through the economy must separate two basic flows of economic activity: the flow of goods and services, and the flow of payments made for these goods and services. Only the latter is used since this provides the required monetary measure.

In a simple economy payments flow in only two directions. Producers or firms pay individuals, or households, for the use of their labour, land, and capital in the form of wages, rent, and interest. Households pay the firms for the goods or services produced.

The flow of payments in a more complex economy is illustrated in Figure 3.2. This economy has four parts or sectors: households, firms, governments, and trade with foreign countries. *Households* pay firms for consumer goods and services and receive payments from *firms* in the form of wages, interest, rent, and dividends. Some firms buy the products of other firms but these goods and services are used up in producing the final products for consumers or households.

Governments add another dimension to the flow of payments

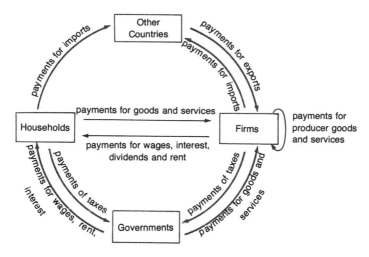

Figure 3.2 The Economy's Circular Flow of Payments
The simplified basic flow of payments in the economy consists of payments made by firms (producers) to households (of one or more individuals) for the use of productive factors — labour, land, and capital — and payments from households to firms for final goods and services. Firms also make payments to other firms for producer goods and services. Governments receive payments as taxes, and make payments to buy final products from firms and productive services from households. Trade with other countries requires payments for imports and returns payments for exports.

since they receive tax payments from both households and firms. Government payments are made to households for labour and other productive services, and to firms for the goods and services purchased by governments. Payments also flow out of the economy to purchase the products and the productive services of *other countries*, which also purchase products and productive services from this economy.

This description of the circular flow of payments illustrates two approaches to measuring an economy's productive activity. *Payments for productive services* — wages, interest, rent, and dividends — can be aggregated to determine total incomes, while *payments for goods and services* purchased by consumers, governments, firms, and foreign countries can be added to determine the total output. Payments to foreign countries must be subtracted from payments received from foreign countries to obtain the net increase (or decrease) in incomes or products of the Canadian economy.

Value Added

These two approaches to measuring economic activity are reflected in two sets of accounts: the *national income* accounts and the *national expenditure* accounts. It is relatively easy to keep track of all income payments but expenditures for firms' goods and services present a serious problem. Which expenditures are for products used by consumers and which are for products to be used by other firms? If all sales by all firms were totalled, the economy's total output could be greatly increased simply by having a larger number of more specialized firms. Totalling all sales made by all firms involves counting the value of iron ore and steel several times, whereas the additional value added to the economy by these products is reflected in the value of a final product such as an automobile.

The solution to this problem of double-counting is to measure only the value added to the final product by each specific process. The method for calculating the value added is illustrated in Table 3.2. A rancher sells a steer to a cattle-buyer for $500. The buyer transports the steer to a central yard and feeds it for a short time until it is sold to a meat packer for $700. The packer takes the steer to his plant where it is killed, cleaned, quartered, and sold to a supermarket for $1,000. Finally, the supermarket's butcher divides the quarters into the desired cuts, trims the fat, and packages the meat, for a final price of $1,400.

Table 3.2

Value Added: Three Calculation Methods

		Payments to Productive Factors			
	Purchases from Other Firms	Wages	Interest and Rent	Profits	Value of Sales
Rancher	$ 0	$420	$ 30	$ 50	$ 500
Cattle Buyer	500	100	40	60	700
Meat Packer	700	140	60	100	1,000
Supermarket	1,000	200	100	100	1,400
Totals	$2,200	$860	$230	$310	$3,600

Value Added =
1. Payments to Productive Factors = $860 + 230 + 310 = $1,400
   or
2. Value of Finished Product (Supermarket sales) = $1,400
   or
3. Total Sales minus Purchases from Other Firms = $3,600 − 2,200 = $1,400

The value added at each stage of the process is calculated by subtracting the purchases from other firms or suppliers from the selling price of the item at that stage. The value added by the meat packer, for example, is his selling price of $1,000 minus the $700 he paid the cattle buyer. The total value added by the complete process is the total value of all sales, $3,600, minus the $2,200 paid in purchases from other firms, or $1,400. This is equal to the selling price of the final consumer goods at the supermarket. By subtracting the value of purchases from other firms, one can isolate the intermediate goods from the final goods. (Recall from Chapter 1 that intermediate goods are those which will be processed further while final goods are used either as producer goods or consumer goods.)

It is not a coincidence that the total payments made through the entire process for wages, interest, rent, and profits, equal the value added as calculated above. The price paid by the household or firm is the total payment for all the productive services required to provide the final product.

Thus the value of all incomes received in the economy must equal the value of all final goods and services produced.

Economic growth can be measured therefore either in terms of total income or total expenditure for final products.

The National Income and Expenditure Accounts

Gross National Product

The Gross National Product includes all payments made to factors of production, plus some additional adjustments, in one year. These items and their amounts are shown in Figure 3.3. *Compensation of employees* comprises wages and salaries (including military pay and allowances), plus any supplementary income or bonuses paid to employees. These items are calculated as gross pay before taxes, union dues, pension contributions, and similar payments, are deducted by employers.

Incomes of self-employed persons appear as *entrepreneurial income*. This includes the incomes of the thousands of farms and small businesses, after deducting the expenses incurred in operating the business. *Rent and interest income* also includes the estimated rental value of owner-occupied homes. This provides a more accurate total value of the use of housing and avoids the misleading increase in GNP that would occur if an unusually large number of people decided to rent rather than buy homes.

Corporation profits before taxes are adjusted in two ways before they are entered in the national accounts: dividends paid to non-residents are subtracted since these are not income for Canadians; and corporations' inventory values are adjusted for price changes occurring during the year.

Indirect taxes (sales and excise taxes) paid by businesses are not a cost of production; they are added to GNP since these taxes are included in the selling price of finished products and thus are included in Gross National Expenditure. *Subsidies* to producers must

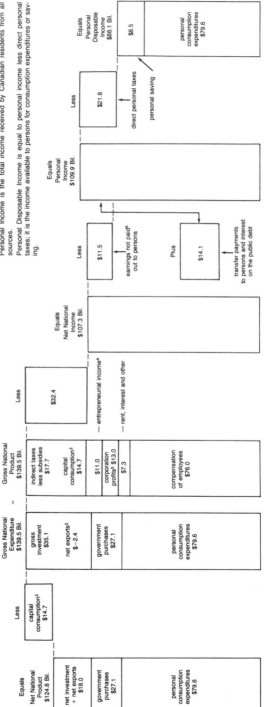

Figure 3.3 NATIONAL INCOME AND EXPENDITURE ACCOUNTS, CANADA, 1974

Gross National Product, Net National Income[1] at Factor Cost, Personal Income, Personal Disposable Income, and Personal Net Saving, Canada 1974.

Gross National Expenditure = Gross National Product is the market value of the total of goods and services produced by Canadian residents during the year.

Net National Income at Factor Cost is the total earnings of labour and property from the production of goods and services.

Personal Income is the total income received by Canadian residents from all sources.

Personal Disposable Income is equal to personal income less direct personal taxes; it is the income available to persons for consumption expenditures or saving.

[1] at factor cost, i.e. at the cost of the labour and capital used
[2] exports valued at $38.3 minus imports of $40.7 and miscellaneous valuation adjustments
[3] and miscellaneous valuation adjustments
[4] includes accrued net income of farm operators from farm production and net income of non-farm unincorporated business
[5] including inventory valuation adjustment and minus dividends paid to non-residents
[6] such earnings are mostly undistributed corporation profits, corporation profit taxes, government investment income, and employer and employee contributions to social insurance and government pension funds.

Note: Some columns do not add because of rounding
Source: Canadian Statistical Review.

be subtracted. Although these form part of the payments to productive factors, selling prices of the goods do not need to cover all costs since part of these is met by the subsidy.

Depreciation, or *capital consumption allowance*, is not a direct payment to productive factors but does represent a cost through the need to replace worn-out or obsolete plant and machinery. The last item in the GNP account, the *residual error of estimate*, is the statistical correction required to equate total income with total expenditure for final products. Since some entries in both sets of accounts are estimated, the totals may differ slightly. Half the difference is subtracted from the higher amount and added to the lower amount so that income will equal expenditure.

Net National Income

The term "national income" is often used to describe the general level of economic activity without specifying one of the several concepts or accounts outlined in this section. The most precise meaning of national income is *Net National Income: the total of all incomes received by the economy's productive factors*. NNI is the sum of wages and salaries, interest and rent, corporate profits before taxes, and the income of unincorporated enterprises. Since these are all included in GNP, Net National Income or NNI can be computed by subtracting indirect taxes and depreciation from GNP, and adding subsidies.

Personal Income

Some of the income included in Net National Income does not go directly, or even eventually, to individuals. Corporations pay part of their profits to governments as corporate income tax, another part takes the form of shareholders' dividends, with the balance — retained earnings or undistributed corporate profits — held by the corporations. This may be held in the form of securities, or used to expand the business, or loaned to other firms.

Personal incomes are increased by the transfer payments made by governments to individuals. *Transfer payments* are those for which no goods or services are provided in exchange, such as family allowances, pensions, and welfare assistance. *Personal income is equal to Net National Income minus undistributed corporate profits and corporate income taxes plus government transfer payments.* Private transfer payments — another term for gifts — are not included in these calculations since they redistribute, rather than increase, total personal income.

Personal Disposable Income

Individuals are free to decide how to dispose of only a part of their incomes. Personal income taxes must be subtracted from Personal Income to determine Personal Disposable Income which people can use however they wish. Although there are thousands of such decisions open to each individual, the basic decision concerns the portion of one's income to be spent on goods and services now, and the portion to be saved for the enjoyment of goods and services in the future. Disposable Income can be used only for *current consumption*, or for the postponed consumption represented by *savings*.

Gross National Expenditure

Gross National Expenditure (GNE) is the sum of expenditures for all final goods and services in the economy during the year. The components of GNP were categorized in terms of the factors of production; components of GNE are grouped according to the users of the final products. These are consumers, governments, businesses, and other countries. Purchases by governments and by other countries, are itemized separately so that changes in the importance of the public sector and the foreign trade sector can be measured easily in the national accounts.

Gross National Expenditure includes personal expenditures on consumer goods and services, government expenditures for goods and services, gross investment, net exports of goods and services, and the residual error of estimate as defined above for GNP. Gross investment includes "business gross fixed capital formation", which is new residential and non-residential construction and new machinery and equipment, and the value of physical change in inventories. The latter is included because semi-finished goods, and finished goods which have not been sold, have required income payments to productive factors which were included in GNP.

Net exports of goods and services; that is, exports minus imports, are also termed *net foreign investment*. A country which exports more than it imports is postponing consumption; future enjoyment of goods and services can be bought with the net payments it receives from other countries.

Net National Product

Net National Product is GNE minus estimated depreciation or capital cost allowance. Gross National Expenditure is the market value of the total output of final goods and services of an economy. It is not the most suitable measure of the year-to-year increase in goods and services, however, because some goods are used just to maintain the economy at its previous productive capacity. Some producer goods, such as cement and paint, are used to repair roads, schools, houses, and other buildings; other producer goods replace worn-out machinery. It is virtually impossible to determine how much of the gross investment, or total output of producer goods, is used to maintain the existing capital stock and how much represents net additions to housing or productive capacity. Instead, depreciation occurring each year is estimated and subtracted from gross investment. The difference is net investment.

Thus far, six concepts of national income or output have been described; each has a particular significance or use. Gross National Product is the total annual income of the economy; Net National Income is the total payments to factors of production; Personal Income is the income of individuals; Disposable Income is the amount that individuals have available for personal use; Gross National Expenditure is the market value of the total output of the economy; and Net National Product is the net output after allowing for depreciation.

Gross Domestic Product

Gross National Product includes the incomes of Canadian citizens working abroad as well as of residents of Canada. Another account, *Gross Domestic Product*, includes only the payments to factors of production located in Canada. GDP is equal to GNP minus indirect taxes less subsidies, minus income received from non-residents, plus income paid to non-residents.

Real Income and Output Per Capita

A major use of the national income accounts is to measure the change in output and incomes from year to year, but such comparisons require further adjustments of GNP or GNE. The GNE for a given year may be greater than the GNE in the previous year, but if all of the increase in measured output was due to price increases physical output would be no greater than the previous year. Values calculated in the national accounts must therefore be adjusted in such a way that comparisons of GNE over time show changes in real or tangible output rather than in the monetary value of the output.

This adjustment requires an index of the change in prices during the year. The Consumer Price Index is unsuitable for this purpose, since GNE includes other goods and services as well as consumer items. Thus, a GNE Price Index has been developed to take account of price changes and the relative weights in the major expenditure categories included in Gross National Expenditure. Real GNE is obtained by dividing the GNE, measured in current prices, by the GNE Price Index. The latter is sometimes referred to as the "GNE deflator" because the continuous rise in prices means that current GNE is being deflated rather than inflated.

Conversion of GNE in current dollars to real GNE in constant (1971) dollars is shown in Table 3.3. GNE as measured by the current prices for each year increased 135 per cent from 1961 to 1971, but the increase in real GNE during the same period was only 70 per cent. The difference is explained by the 38 per cent increase in prices.

Table 3.3

Gross National Expenditure, Canada

Year	GNE in Current Dollars (millions)	GNE Implicit Price Index (1971 = 100)	Real GNE in 1971 Dollars (millions)	Canada's Population on June 1 (millions)	Real GNE per Capita
1961	39,646	72.4	54,741	18,238	3,001
1971	93,462	100.0	93,462	21,569	4,333
1974	140,880	129.4	108,862	22,446	4,850

Source: Statistics Canada, *Canadian Statistical Review*.

Real GNE may rise, for example, 5 per cent each year, but this does not necessarily mean that individuals' real incomes will also rise by 5 per cent. Increases in the real output per person will depend on the relative rates of increase in population and in real output. Table 3.3 shows that although real GNE grew by 70 per cent between 1961 and 1971, the real GNE per capita rose by only 44 per cent between 1961 and 1971 because Canada's population increased by 18 per cent during this period. Note that GNE is the measure of final goods and services produced over the period of one year and that the population by which it is to be divided changes daily during the year; the mid-year population estimate is therefore used to represent the population when GNE per capita is calculated.

National Income at Full Employment

National income accounts not only measure how an economy has performed in the past year; they can also indicate by how much the economy fell short of its potential output. Full employment is one of the basic economic goals, but apart from counting the number of persons who are looking for work at any given time, there are few measures of the extent to which an economy is utilizing its productive resources. It was noted previously that persons may be employed in part-time jobs or in jobs which do not make full use of their skills. Plant and equipment may also be operating at less than full capacity. By subtracting the total output achieved under these conditions from the estimated potential output, the extent of underutili-

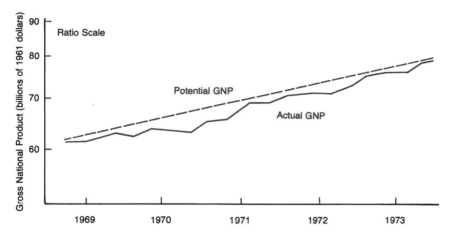

Figure 3.4   Potential and Actual GNP
Canada's actual GNP has been less than the potential GNP because productive resources, especially labour, have not been fully utilized. The Economic Council of Canada estimates the GNP potential growth rate to be about 5.3 percent for 1966-77.
Source: Economic Council of Canada, *Economic Targets and Social Indicators*, 1974.

zation of productive resources can be obtained. This estimate is at the same time a clear statement of the cost of underutilization in terms of the additional goods and services which could have been produced and the additional incomes which could have been earned.

The Economic Council's estimates of potential output are compared with actual output in Figure 3.4. In its discussion of "the GNP Gap", the Council states that:

> For the third consecutive year [1973], the economy expanded faster than the potential growth rate, reducing to only a fraction the large GNP "gap" that emerged during the slowdown in 1970. The level of real output over the year averaged about 1.5 per cent below the potential ceiling, comparing favourably with gaps of 3.7 per cent in 1970, 3.5 per cent in 1971, and 3.0 per cent in 1972.[7]

Innovations in Measures of Economic Performance

The national income accounts have served as the main measure of economic progress in Canada since they were introduced in 1926. Definitions have been improved, data collection techniques have been revised almost continuously, and historical data have been modified to reflect revised definitions. But at their best, the national

---

[7] Economic Council of Canada, *Eleventh Annual Review: Economic Targets and Social Indicators*, Ottawa: Information Canada, 1974, p. 18.

income accounts measure only the level of marketed output and monetary incomes.

Considerable work is now underway to improve national income accounting so that it will provide more accurate measures of output and income, and the distribution of these. Some economists are attempting to estimate, for example, the value of items not in the accounts — such as students' time spent in educational institutions and housewives' work at home — as well as expenditures that are required simply to avoid a decline in social progress. As an example of the latter case, it can be argued that:

> Programs designed to reduce environmental deterioration — investment in pollution control, for example — are quite apt to show up as increased real output, as indeed they should if the benefits from the program exceed the costs. However, the level of output would still be overstated relative to the level in past years when there was no need for pollution control because there was less pollution.[8]

A second major proposal for improving measurement of progress toward social and economic goals is a set of *social indicators*. The national accounts, even if revised to take account of expenditures required to maintain the social and physical environment and unmarketed labour services, cannot indicate how well output has been utilized to achieve other national goals. Social scientists have therefore begun to develop a system of social accounts or social indicators to monitor progress in such areas as health, education, crime prevention, and housing. Progress toward methods of measuring social progress, however, is bound to be exceedingly slow. The Economic Council of Canada has stated quite plainly that "the search for a unique all-inclusive measure or index of human well-being does not seem very promising except in the longest of long runs."[9] Such a measure depends on the almost impossible task of measuring individual satisfaction, and then of aggregating such measures for the whole population. Nevertheless, in its 1974 *Annual Review*, the council presented specific indicators to monitor progress in housing, health, and environmental quality.

The Balance of International Payments

The fourth major economic goal is maintenance of "a viable balance of payments". This refers to the Balance of International Payments, another important set of accounts used to measure Canada's

---

[8] National Bureau of Economic Research, *Economics — A Half Century of Research, 1920-1970*. New York: National Bureau of Economic Research, 1970, p. 10 fn.

[9] Economic Council of Canada, *Eighth Annual Review: Design for Decision-Making*. Ottawa: Information Canada, 1971, p. 24.

economic performance. *The Balance of International Payments is a record of all economic transactions between residents of Canada and the residents of all foreign countries during one year.*

The goal of a viable balance of payments has been defined by the Economic Council as being not merely the maintenance of an inflow of payments from other countries equal to the outflow of payments from Canada to all other countries, but also as a strengthening of Canada's international economic position. This would be reflected particularly in the reduction of "the current account deficit" relative to Canada's Gross National Product, and in a reduction of "net capital inflow" relative to domestic investment. The terms used in expressing this goal are drawn from the following description of the Balance of International Payments.

The separate factors influencing the overall balance of payments can be seen by examining the detailed structure of the international accounts. There are three major sections in the Balance of International Payments: the *Current Account*, the *Capital Account*, and the *Changes in Holdings of Foreign Exchange and Gold*. Each account is divided into a number of other sections related to the specific form or nature of the transaction. Entries in each account are categorized as either credits or debits. Items which increase the flow of foreign currencies into Canada are credits; items which increase the flow of foreign currencies out of Canada are debits. Credit items, from Canada's point of view, also include reductions in Canadian dollars held by foreigners, in addition to increases in the flow of foreign currencies into Canada. Alternatively, a debit item could reduce Canadian residents' holdings of foreign currencies, for example, in foreign bank accounts. These distinctions can be illustrated by examining the items in each account.

Current Account. Items included in the current account can be seen in Table 3.4. The current account is divided into the merchandise (or goods) account and the services account. The balance on merchandise account, or the *balance of trade*, shows the net position for the year with respect to trade in goods. Countries traditionally attempted to develop a "favourable balance of trade" by exporting more than they imported in order to accumulate gold or foreign currencies. A glance at the current account in Table 3.4, however, shows that Canada's positive balance on the merchandise account was more than offset in 1974 by the negative balance in the non-merchandise or services account.

The major non-merchandise items include travel, interest and dividends, and freight and shipping. When Canadians travel abroad or use foreign transportation services, they are "importing" services provided by other countries. Similarly, there are large outflows of interest and dividend payments for the use of foreign-owned capital. Inheritances and migrants' funds are not payments for foreign goods

Table 3.4

Canadian Balance of International Payments, 1974
(millions of dollars)

	Current Receipts		Current Payments		Balance*
Current Account					
Merchandise (exports or imports)	32,493		31,473		+1,020
Services	5,759		9,264		−3,505
Travel	1,684		1,986	−302	
Interest and dividends	784		2,276	−1,492	
Freight and shipping	1,602		1,783	−181	
Other services	1,689		2,786	−1,097	
Transfers		1,363	755		+608
Inheritances and					
migrants' funds	718		155	+563	
Other transfers	645		600	+45	
Total		39,615	41,492		−1,877
Capital Account					
Long-term capital					944
Direct investment				−210	
Stocks and Bonds				1,905	
Other long-term capital				−751	
Short-term capital					957
Bank deposits, other financial assets				1,097	
Other short-term capital				−140	
Total net capital movements*					+1,901
Changes in Holdings of Foreign Exchange and Gold					
Net Change in official international reserves					+24

*A minus sign, except for official monetary movements, indicates net outflow of funds from Canada.

Source: Statistics Canada, *Canadian Statistical Review*, May 1975.

or services; rather, they represent international *transfer payments* through bequests or funds accompanying immigrants or emigrants.

These components of the current account can thus be used to monitor the effects of policies to stimulate exports, reduce imports, encourage foreign tourists to visit Canada, and so on. The balance on current account reflects the net effect of these policies and is one key indicator of progress toward a viable balance of payments.

Capital Account. The capital account is divided to show the flows of long-term capital and short-term capital. An inflow of foreign capital has the same effect on currency movements as does an outflow of export goods: there is an inflow of foreign currencies to Canada. Inflows of foreign capital are therefore treated as credits in the balance of payments. This should not be confused with the fact that borrowings of foreign capital add to Canada's foreign indebtedness; the inflow of currency is accompanied by an outflow of certificates (stocks and bonds) indicating foreign ownership or foreign indebtedness.

Movements of long-term capital can take the form of direct investment in Canada by foreigners (a credit) or Canadian residents' direct investment in other countries (a debit). Such investment would include the purchase of an existing Canadian firm, for example, or the construction of a new branch plant to be operated by the foreign owners. International purchases of stocks and bonds include both new and existing issues of these securities. Short-term capital movements include changes in bank deposits and short-term bills foreigners hold in Canada or Canadian residents and governments hold abroad.

The item which brings the balance of payments into balance is the "other short-term capital". This is a residual item which is calculated after all other entries in the international accounts have been estimated.

Changes in Holdings of Foreign Exchange and Gold. The third main section of the balance of payments shows the changes in official or government holdings of foreign exchange and gold. These changes reflect the net deficits or surpluses on the other two accounts, apart from the balancing or residual item discussed above. A surplus on either the current or the capital account would add to Canada's holdings of foreign currencies, but this could be offset by a deficit in the opposite account.

Basic Balance

The balance on current account is often cited as a measure of health of the balance of payments since a chronic deficit balance represents a growing debt to other countries. But a surplus on capital account can offset part or all of this deficit. The concept of a *basic balance* has been developed to show the net effect of movements in both the current and capital accounts in order to calculate the net result in holdings of foreign currencies.

A *basic balance exists when the Current Account balance is equal to the long-term capital balance.* Movements of gold and foreign currencies and the short-term capital balance are removed from this equation since a balance which depended on either of them would be precarious, particularly under a fixed foreign exchange rate. Countries could not sustain an outflow of foreign exchange and gold over a long period since stocks of each of these are limited. Nor can short-term capital movements be depended upon since the movement of these funds changes quickly with changes in short-run conditions. A more complete examination of the international balance of payments and factors affecting it is presented in Chapter 7.

Review of the Main Points

1. Canada's basic economic goals are: reasonable price stability, full employment, a high rate of economic growth, a viable balance of payments, and an equitable distribution of rising incomes.

2. Inflation is an increase in the general price level of consumer goods and services. Price changes in consumer goods and services are measured by the Consumer Price Index (CPI); price changes for all final goods and services are measured by the GNE Price Index. The CPI is calculated by comparing current prices of consumer commodities with the prices of the same collection of commodities in the base year. Changes in the quality of commodities and in the combination of commodities produced or consumed make it necessary to change the base year every five to ten years.

3. Inflation reduces the purchasing power or the real income of persons living on fixed incomes such as pensions, reduces the real value of repayments of debts to creditors, and may increase the prices of a country's exports relative to those of other countries.

4. Full employment of all productive resources is difficult to measure because it is almost impossible to define the full utilization of all factors. "Full employment" is therefore usually related only to the labour force and is defined as the situation in which everyone aged 14 or over who wants to work for pay, and is able to do so, has paid employment. The full employment goal however, is often expressed in terms of an acceptable or target rate of unemployment.

5. The labour force consists of everyone who is at work and persons who are unemployed but who are looking for work. However, the current measure of unemployment does not take account of underemployment or underutilization of the labour force due to persons working at jobs not making full use of their skills or time.

6. Economic growth is usually measured by the rate of increase in real Gross National Product per capita. In fact, there are two measures which produce equivalent results. The circular flow of payments for productive factors and payments for finished goods and services means that the economy's performance can be measured either in terms of incomes received by productive factors or by the market values of the finished products.

7. In order to avoid double-counting of commodities, the values added at each stage of a productive process are summed to determine the total value added throughout the process. The value added at each stage is calculated by subtracting the purchases

from other firms from the total receipts from the sale of the product of any given firm.

8. The GNP and GNE accounts are supplemented by other accounts which provide measures of income or output for more specific purposes. Net National Income includes only the payments to factors of production; Personal Income includes income and transfer payments received by individuals; Disposable Personal Income is the balance of Personal Income remaining after deducting personal income taxes; Net National Product is Gross National Expenditure minus depreciation and thus measures the net addition to goods and services after allowing for replacement of obsolete or worn-out plant, equipment, and housing.

9. Real increases in income and output are distinguished from the monetary value of income and output by adjusting the current value of GNP and GNE for the price changes (usually increases) occurring during the year. Such price changes are reflected in the GNE Price Index, commonly called the "GNE deflator". A similar adjustment must be made for the annual increase in population if current per capita output is being compared with that for previous years.

10. The national accounts of income and expenditures provide a measure of the economic activity of a country, but are only a proxy measure of the well-being of its population. An attempt is therefore being made to develop other social accounts or indicators to measure progress toward the achievement of national goals.

11. The goal of a viable balance of payments is concerned with maintaining an acceptable balance between the inflow and outflow of international payments for goods and services, and of long-term capital. The Balance of International Payments includes the Current Account of payments for goods and services and international transfer payments, the Capital Account of international long- and short-term capital flows, and the account showing Changes in the Holdings of Foreign Exchange and Gold.

Review and Discussion Questions

1. Are there other economic goals that you would add to, or substitute for, the five goals stated by the Economic Council of Canada? How would you rank the Council's five goals in order of priority? Explain why.

2. "Inflation is a much more serious problem than unemployment because inflation affects everyone while unemployment is a problem only for those out of work." Explain carefully what is meant by inflation and unemployment and why you agree or disagree with this statement.

3. Why are real estate assets said to be a "hedge against inflation"?

4. Explain why GNE must logically be equal to GNP.

5. If you have been given the current value of GNP, what further information is required to calculate Personal Disposable Income? Can this be calculated if GNE is used as a starting point? Explain.

6. Why is it necessary to remove government transfer payments from total government expenditures before estimating GNE? Why do private transfer payments (or gifts) not appear in any of the national income accounts?

7. Why are intermediate goods not included in the estimates of GNE? How would you decide whether a good is an intermediate good? Should all automobiles sold each year be included in GNE? Why?

8. Suppose the government paid living allowances to all full-time students. Trace the effects of this policy on the components of GNP and of GNE.

9. Why would GNP not provide an adequate comparison of the standard of living in different countries? Explain how you would interpret "standard of living". How would you modify the national income accounts to provide better international comparisons of standards of living?

10. Describe how you would estimate the potential GNE or GNP at full employment. What are the main determinants of the potential output of an economy Why is the full employment of the labour force, rather than full employment of all productive factors, emphasized as a policy objective?

Sources and Selected Readings

Dernberg, Thomas F., and Duncan M. McDougall, *Macroeconomics*, 4th ed. New York: McGraw-Hill, 1972.

Economic Council of Canada. *First Annual Review: Economic Goals for Canada to 1970*. Ottawa: Queen's Printer, 1964. Also, *Annual Review* for subsequent years.

Mishan, E.J. *The Costs of Economic Growth*. Harmondsworth, Middlesex: Penguin, 1969.

Raynauld, André. *The Canadian Economic System*. Toronto: Macmillan, 1967.

Sirkin, Gerald. *Introduction to Macroeconomic Theory*, 3rd ed. Homewood, Ill.: Irwin, 1970.

Statistics Canada. *Canada Year Book*. Ottawa: Information Canada, annual.

_____. *National Income and Expenditure Accounts*. Ottawa: Information Canada, quarterly.

_____. *Prices and Price Indexes*. Ottawa: Information Canada, annual.

_____. *Quarterly Estimates of the Canadian Balance of Payments*. Ottawa: Information Canada, quarterly.

_____. *The Labour Force*. Ottawa: Information Canada, monthly.

Urquhart, M.C., and K.A.H. Buckley. *Historical Statistics of Canada*. Toronto: Macmillan, 1965.

4   Changing Levels of National Income and Output

A. Aggregate Demand and Equilibrium National Income

The national income accounts measure changes in the level of national income but the accounts cannot by themselves explain why there are unemployed resources, nor what action is required to achieve full employment. The general causes of changing levels of national income and employment are found in the *theory of national income determination*. The main elements of this theory, which presents a model of the operation of the economy were developed during the Depression of the 1930s. In 1936, John Maynard Keynes published a book in which he showed how it was possible for the economy to become stuck at high levels of unemployment. Prior to that time, any unemployment was expected to last only a short time; the natural tendency in any economy was thought to be toward full employment of all productive resources. Widespread and persistent unemployment during the Depression, however, was evidence that some assumptions of earlier economic theory were inappropriate.

National Income Determination in Classical Economics

Many economists preceding Keynes believed that the economy would function effectively if market forces were allowed to follow a natural course. This *laissez-faire* view that there was no need for government intervention at the aggregative or national levels of economic activity was based on the assumption that wages, prices, and interest rates were perfectly flexible, and thus would move up and down freely with changing economic conditions. It also assumed that there would be an effective domestic and international financial system.

The classical or traditional view of aggregate economic activity was stated most simply by a French economist, Jean Baptiste Say (1767-1832). According to Say's Law — the *Law of Conservation of Purchasing Power* — "supply creates its own demand". This has become a simplified statement of Say's more elaborate explanation of the automatic forces keeping an economy at, or close to, the full employment level. Employees would be paid according to the value of the goods they produced. They would, in turn, spend their earnings on commodities produced by other workers. If all incomes were spent, the total purchases would be just equal to the total output of the economy, since the total purchasing power was exactly equal to the value of all goods produced.

Although economic growth received only minor attention until early in the nineteenth century, growth could be taken into account in Say's model. As technological change enabled the factors of production to increase their outputs, the wages and interest paid would be increased proportionately. Additional income would thus be available to purchase the increased output.

Some temporary unemployment was possible, but when this arose, the basic economic forces would return the economy to full employment. If, for example, demand for a certain good had fallen and workers were unemployed, the general level of wages would fall as some workers offered to work for less while others left the labour force. Lower wages would encourage other employers to hire more labour, bringing the economy back to full employment. The mobility of labour and other productive factors was thus an additional basic assumption in the classical analysis.

The simplest version of the classical model assumed that workers would spend all of their earnings, and without delay. What would happen if this were not the case? If individuals decided to save some of their incomes, there would be more funds available as loans to investors. The rate of interest would fall, investors would increase their purchases of investment goods, demand would be maintained, and with it, the validity of Say's Law.

An important assumption in classical economics was that employees' wages would be equal to the value of their output. Karl Marx later argued that unemployment arose partly because this was an invalid assumption. Employees were "exploited" by being paid less than the value they contributed to output. The total demand for output would be inadequate since employers were not likely to spend enough to compensate for the employees' declining purchasing power. Marx also argued that unemployment would increase as more machinery was substituted for labour in productive processes. But both Say's Law and the Marxian analysis of unemployment were effectively challenged by John Maynard Keynes.

Keynesian Model of National Income Determination

An important landmark in the development of our understanding of the economic environment was John Maynard Keynes' book, *The General Theory of Employment, Interest and Money*.[1] The

---

[1] In a letter written to George Bernard Shaw on January 1, 1935, Keynes stated: "I believe myself to be writing a book on economic theory which will largely revolutionize — not, I suppose, at once but in the course of the next ten years — the way the world thinks about economic problems."

"Keynesian revolution" consisted of a detailed attack on the classical economists' explanation for the level of employment and output, and Keynes' conclusion that government intervention rather than *laissez-faire* was required to move the economy to the full-employment level. Forty years later, the Keynesian view of the government as manager of the economy is still referred to as "the new economics" because the full implications of his argument were recognized and accepted only after a number of years of discussion.

The foundation stone of the Keynesian model or explanation of the operation of the economy is *aggregate demand*.

This is the total demand of all consumers, business, governments, and foreign buyers, for all types of final goods and services produced within the economy concerned. Say's Law had stated that this aggregate demand would be just equal to the aggregate supply or output, especially if foreign trade in exports and imports is omitted from the simple classical case. Keynes disputed this. He argued that individuals would choose to save some part of their incomes, and that there was no logical reason for foreigners or businesses to buy precisely the same amount that would offset this short-fall in aggregate demand. Governments were thus required either to encourage more consumer and investor spending by reducing taxes or to increase government spending directly.

The balance of this chapter is concerned with a more detailed examination of this model for the operation and management of the economy. A first step in developing this model is to examine the factors influencing the separate components of aggregate demand: consumption, investment, government spending, and exports.

Consumption and the Propensity to Consume

The largest component of aggregate demand is consumption.

Consumption, in the model presented here, includes all current spending for consumer goods and services produced domestically, that is, within the national economy.

The consumption category in national income accounting, as presented in Chapter 3, included spending for imported consumer goods and services because these could not easily be separated from consumption spending for domestically produced goods and services. Imports were excluded by subtracting them from exports. In the theoretical model, consumer spending for domestically produced commodities can be separated conceptually from imports; these can then be treated as a distinct category.

The total income of an economy, represented in the simple model outlined here by the Gross National Product (GNP), can be used in only four ways: for consumption of domestically produced commodities, for savings, for purchases of imports (goods and services produced in other economies), and for tax payments. That is,

$$Y = C + S + M + T$$

where Y is national income (GNP), C is consumption, S is savings, M is imports, and T is taxes. To simplify the model, it is assumed that saving is done only by households and not by business firms.

Savings are defined as postponed consumption because they represent future purchasing power, or the ability to buy goods and services in the future. Some initial difficulty in understanding this definition may result from the usual narrow use of the word "savings", for example, in reference to bank savings deposits. But this is only one form in which savings can be held. These can also be held through the purchase of bonds, stocks, real estate, or other similar forms. Since savings represent the postponement of consumption, people try to hold their savings in a form which will preserve the real value of this postponed enjoyment of goods and services, and which may even increase this value. Such financial assets are widely described as "investments", but economists reserve this latter term for real output which takes the form of buildings and equipment used to produce consumer goods, housing, and inventories which will be consumed in the future.

One must also distinguish between the term "savings" when it is used to refer to a *stock*: the total value of savings at a point in time, and when it is used to refer to a *flow*: the total amount of saving that is done over a period of time. The latter is the concept used in the national income model.

The major influence on the level of consumption is the level of current disposable income. Individuals are obviously strongly governed in their spending decisions by the income available to them after income taxes are deducted. From the perspective of the overall economy, however, and to simplify further the development of the national income model, the level of consumption can be said to be determined by the level of the Gross National Product. In more complex models, individuals' consumption decisions would also be related to their long-run average annual incomes (generally termed "permanent income") to take account of the year-to-year fluctuations in incomes of, for example, salespersons, entertainers, farmers, and small retailers. The size of one's wealth also has some influence on consumption, since one can draw on wealth (or accumulated assets) to finance major purchases such as automobiles and furniture. Financial assets, however, have their major effect on consumption through the annual income they yield in the form of interest, dividends, and rents.

Individuals must decide how much of their annual incomes will be spent immediately and how much will be saved. Families with lower incomes may find it necessary to spend all of their incomes; some may even spend more than their current incomes by borrowing against anticipated increases in future incomes. A few may be able to consume more than their current incomes by drawing on the savings from incomes in previous years. Families with higher incomes may decide that some of their income should be saved for future uses such as travel, furnishing a home, financing children's education, or for a "rainy day".

Propensity to Consume. Families at any given income level have a propensity or tendency to allocate a certain proportion of their incomes to consumption. High-income families consume more than low-income families, but they also save more. Usually, the higher the family income, the lower is the proportion of income consumed and the higher the proportion saved. *The proportion of income going to consumption is described as the propensity to consume.* As noted previously, "income" for the purpose of the model presented here is being defined as the GNP. However, the simple concept of the propensity to consume can be more readily illustrated by reference to hypothetical families and their annual disposable, or after-tax, incomes. This is done in Table 4.1. As family incomes rise, the share or proportion of the income going to consumption falls, that is, the propensity to consume declines. The remaining portion of the income goes to saving and imports.

Table 4.1

**Marginal Propensities to Consume, Save, and Import:
Some Hypothetical Examples**

Dis-posable Family Income	Consump-tion	Saving	Imports	Additional Consump-tion	Additional Saving	Additional Imports	Marginal Propensities To Con-sume	To Save	To Import
$5,000	$5,100	$-100	$ 0						
				900	100	0	0.9	0.10	0.00
6,000	6,000	0	0						
				800	150	50	0.8	0.15	0.05
7,000	6,800	150	50						
				700	200	100	0.7	0.20	0.10
8,000	7,500	350	150						
				600	250	150	0.6	0.25	0.15
9,000	8,100	600	300						

The information in Table 4.1 is shown in graphic form in Figure 4.1. Since the scale on each axis is the same, any point along the line drawn at a 45° angle to each axis represents equal values for consumption and disposable income. That is, if a family's entire disposable income were spent for consumption at each income level, the consumption curve or function would appear as the 45° line marked $C=DI$ in Figure 4.1. This "equality line", together with the consumption curve marked C, makes it easier to see that the percentage of income consumed declines with increasing income levels. One

can also identify the income level at which all the annual income —
but only that amount — goes to consumption, namely at $6,000. At
lower incomes, families are dissaving: they are borrowing or drawing on previous savings to finance current consumption.

Since disposable income can only be spent for domestic consumption or imports, or be saved, the vertical distance between the
equality line and the consumption curve shows the amount used for

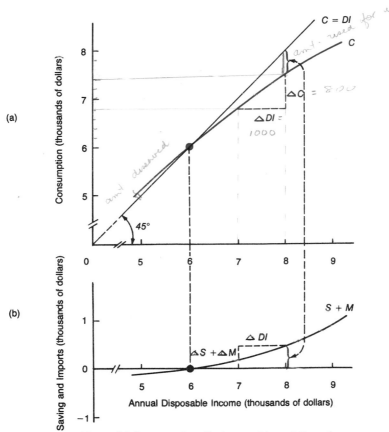

Figure 4.1 Consumption, Saving, and Import Spending
Depend on Disposable Income

As a family's disposable income rises, it tends to spend a lower percentage on
consumption of domestic goods and services, and to increase the percentages
saved and spent for imported goods. Data provided in Table 4.1 are plotted to
obtain the family's consumption curve, C, and its saving and imports curve, S + M.
At income levels below $6,000, the family spends more than its current income on
domestic consumer goods and services. The marginal propensity to consume,
MPC, is the increase in consumption, $\triangle C$, associated with a given increase in
income, $\triangle DI$; the combined marginal propensities to save and to import, MPS +
MPM, are calculated from the increase in saving and imports, $\triangle S + \triangle M$, associated with an increase in income, $\triangle DI$.

imports and saved (or dissaved) at each income level. Import spending and savings can be plotted against income levels in Figure
4.1(b) to obtain the savings and imports curve marked $S + M$.

These diagrams also illustrate both the average and marginal
propensities to consume. The *average propensity to consume*, *APC*,
is the proportion of total disposable income, *DI*, used for current
consumption of goods and services, *C*, and is calculated by the simple formula:

$$APC = \frac{C}{DI}$$

For the data in Table 4.1, the *APC* at the $7,000 level is 6,800 ÷
7,000 or 0.97; at the $9,000 level the *APC* is 0.90.

Similarly, the *average propensity to save*, *APS*, is the proportion
of disposable income which is saved and is calculated as

$$APS = \frac{S}{DI}$$

The *average propensity to import* is

$$APM = \frac{M}{DI}$$

Even more important than knowing the proportion of total income households allocate to consumption, is knowing how consumption changes with any change in income.

The marginal propensity to consume, *MPC*, is the change in
consumption associated with a change in income.

Economists usually use the term marginal, but this has the same
meaning as additional, extra, or incremental. Table 4.1 shows that
when the family which has had an income of $6,000 receives an
additional or extra income of $1,000, the additional consumption is
$800. The *MPC* is 800 ÷ 1,000, or 0.8. For the family which was
previously at the $8,000 level, the *MPC* is 0.6. The *MPC* formula
therefore is:

$$MPC = \frac{\Delta C}{\Delta DI}$$

where Δ is interpreted as "marginal" or "incremental".

The values for ΔC and ΔDI are shown on Figure 4.1(a) between
the $7,000 and $8,000 income level. Note that these amounts also
represent the "rise" and the "run" for this section of the consump-

tion curve. Since the definition of the slope of a line is rise divided by run,

$$\frac{\Delta C}{\Delta DI} = \text{the slope of the curve.}$$

Thus the MPC is equal to the slope of the consumption curve. The gradual flattening of the consumption curve, or its decreasing slope, reflects the decrease in MPC as income rises as shown in Table 4.1. Similarly, the marginal propensity to save, MPS, is equal to the slope of the savings curve, and *increases* with income. A straight line for the consumption or saving curve would indicate a *constant* MPC or MPS.

Note that the total of the values for MPC, MPS and MPM at each income level in Table 4.1 equals 1. This follows from the condition that families can only consume, save, or import with their disposable incomes. Thus it will always be the case that:

$$APC + APS + APM = 1$$

and

$$MPC + MPS + MPM = 1$$

Alternatively,

$$APC = 1 - (APS + APM)$$

and

$$MPC = 1 - (MPS + MPM)$$

Although savings can be calculated by subtracting consumption and imports from disposable income, one should not assume that the amount saved is simply the residual effect of a decision to spend a certain amount for consumption. There must be extremely few families who would have difficulty in spending all of their disposable incomes, leaving nothing to be saved. Usually saving and spending decisions are made together: a family may want a new sofa now but it wants even more an extensive trip during the summer vacation next year. Families and individuals vary greatly in their saving goals and habits. Some may have specific reasons for their savings while others simply try to save an increasing amount as their incomes rise.

A family or individual at a given level of income may have a different MPS or MPC under different conditions. The $7,000 family, for example, may have a higher MPS in wartime than in peacetime, both because prices of some goods are so high that purchases are postponed and because the government is urging citizens to buy more government savings bonds. These changing conditions and decisions would be reflected in *shifts* of the consumption curve upward in peaceful, prosperous times and downward in wartime — accompanied by shifts in the savings curve in the opposite direction. Under wartime conditions, the imports curve is also likely to shift downwards, reinforcing the upward shift of the savings curve.

A Warning! Be careful to distinguish between a *movement along* the consumption curve and a *shift* of the whole curve. As noted earlier, consumption tends to increase with increased income, although less than proportionately. This declining proportion is due to increased saving and/or increased spending on imports. These changes occur as individuals and economies move along the consumption curve. An upward *shift* in the consumption curve results from a decision to save and/or to import less *at a given level of income.*

Since most economies have experienced continuously rising levels of income, it may be difficult to imagine changed spending patterns at a given level of income. One might more readily understand these shifts occurring at the same time national income is increasing. To cite an extreme example, the removal of all tariffs next year would lead to a sharp increase in imports, far greater than the slight increase that might have been expected with no change in tariffs and a small increase in consumers' incomes. This is illustrated in Figure 4.2. The M_t curve indicates that when disposable income is $60 billion in year t, the value of imports is $6 billion. If DI rose to $65 billion in year $t + 1$, imports would rise to $7 billion. The removal of tariffs in year $t + 1$, however, results in imports of $10 billion: one-quarter of the $4 billion increase is due to the increased DI but the balance is due to the upward shift of the import curve, from M_t to M_{t+1}. The consumption curve would shift downward by the same amount, unless the savings curve also shifted downward.

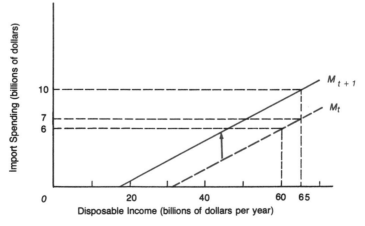

Figure 4.2   A Shift in the Propensity to Import
A distinction must be made between a movement along a planned spending curve and a shift of the entire curve. The propensity to import curve, M_t, indicates that an increase in Disposable Income from $60 to $65 billion increases import spending to $7 billion. An upward shift in the propensity to import, to M_{t+1}, increases import spending by a further $3 billion, at the same level of Disposable Income.

Propensity to Consume and the GNP. As noted previously, the propensity to consume concept is introduced in terms of families and their disposable incomes because this is more readily visualized and understood. However, these concepts must now be redefined in terms of the spending decisions of the total economy and the national income or GNP. The average propensity to consume becomes the proportion of GNP going to consumption; hence,

$$APC = \frac{C}{Y}$$

where Y is the GNP or national income. The marginal propensity to consume becomes the change in consumption associated with a change in GNP; and hence

$$MPC = \frac{\Delta C}{\Delta Y}$$

Similarly,

$$APS = \frac{S}{Y} \text{ and } APM = \frac{M}{Y}; \text{ also, } MPS = \frac{\Delta S}{\Delta Y} \text{ and } MPM = \frac{\Delta M}{\Delta Y}$$

The shift from disposable income to GNP requires that income taxes be returned to the discussion. This introduces two further concepts, the average and marginal propensities to make tax payments. Clearly, these terms stretch the notion of "propensity" as a voluntary inclination or tendency. For the sake of consistency, however, the terminology is retained. The average propensity to pay taxes is the proportion of GNP directed to income tax payments and the marginal propensity to pay taxes is the change in income tax payments associated with a change in GNP. Hence,

$$APT = \frac{T}{Y} \text{ and } MPT = \frac{\Delta T}{\Delta Y}$$

Note that MPT resembles in concept, but is not the same as, the marginal tax rate that is used in calculating personal income taxes.

Investment

The second major component of aggregate demand is gross investment.

Investment is defined as purchases of new productive capacity (plant and equipment), new residential housing, and real additions to inventories.

Gross investment rather than net investment is the proper category since some investment spending is for replacement of depreciated and obsolete items. Gross investment includes, for example, all new equipment purchased; net investment is the net addition to equipment after allowing for the replacement of obsolete and worn-out equipment.

The reason for investment spending is to realize a monetary return on the investment. The firm or individual who decides to invest in new plant and equipment is influenced not so much by the current level of income as by the *expected rate of return on the planned investment* and the *rate of interest charged on funds to be borrowed* for the investment. If the expected yield rate is greater than the interest rate, the project is expected to realize a net profit and thus is undertaken. As an increasing amount is invested in the economy, the expected yield on each *additional* investment project is assumed to fall. This follows from the assumption that rational investors will undertake the highest yielding projects first. The yield or rate of return on additional or marginal investment is termed the *marginal efficiency of investment, or MEI.*

The expected yield rate on plant and equipment is calculated by comparing the expected after-tax profits with the total cost of the plant and equipment. The rate of return on housing owned by apartment developers is obviously the net profit compared with the cost of the housing project. For owner-occupants, the yield is the implicit rental value of housing. Inventories are considered a necessary component of production since inventories (or the available stock of any given good) must be large enough to fill customers' orders or, in the case of raw and semi-finished materials, to assure continued production. The larger the inventories, the greater are the potential sales and profits, but it is the additional profit associated with additional inventories that represents the marginal yield on that form of investment. This must be weighed against the cost of holding inventories. Firms must finance the wages and other costs entailed in unsold products, either from their own funds or with short-term loans.

There is some doubt about the effect of the interest rate on investment decisions; this is explored in more detail in a later section of this Chapter. However, this does not diminish the importance of *profit expectations* in determining the level of investment. Such expectations depend partly on the current level of technology, and partly on the level of national income, since higher consumer spending means a potentially larger market for the firm's products. Thus, the level of investment usually is expected to rise with higher levels of national income. But in this initial description of the national income model, investment is unrelated to income levels.

Finally, it should be noted that for the purpose of examining aggregate demand, investment is defined here as including only the investment goods produced domestically, just as consumption was restricted to consumer goods and services produced domestically.

Government Spending

The third component of aggregate demand is government spending for domestically produced goods and services. Each level of government — federal, provincial, and municipal — is included. This category excludes *government transfer payments* which are made to transfer income from one group (taxpayers) to another group (recipients of payments such as family allowances, government pensions, unemployment insurance). Transfer payments are excluded from government spending because they become part of consumers' disposable income, and thus are included in consumption, saving, or imports.

Governments' purchases of goods and services may be used directly in administration, or for provision of public services and facilities such as defense forces, highways, and parks. Generally, total government expenditures rise with income levels, often faster than the increase in income, but government spending may also rise abruptly in wartime and fall slightly thereafter. Government spending is both for consumer (final) goods and services and for investment goods, and might therefore have been included under the preceding consumption and investment categories. It is isolated for separate treatment because these expenditures will be seen to play a major, independent role in determining the level of national income.

Exports

The final component of aggregate demand is exports. Since demand for exports is expressed from outside the country concerned, there are many factors influencing the level of receipts from export sales which do not directly affect the other components of aggregate demand, from weather conditions in other countries to their changes in government. It should be noted that in the national accounts, one of the Gross National Expenditure components was net exports. In the present case, however, gross exports is the proper category. In the national accounts, the spending of consumers, governments, businesses, and even exports, included spending for imports. These were then subtracted from gross exports to avoid double-counting. But in this chapter, consumption, investment, government spending, and exports include domestic goods and services only, that is, goods and services produced within the national economy.

Toward Equilibrium National Income

The separate components of aggregate demand can now be combined as shown in Figure 4.3. At this initial stage of the development of the national income model, the simple assumption is made that the level of investment, government spending, and exports, are all independent of the level of national income; that is, spending for these three components is not influenced by the level of national income. This independence from the effects of national income is reflected in the horizontal curves for *I*, *G*, and *E* in Figure 4.3. A later, more realistic case will show each of these curves rising toward the right, indicating increasing *I*, *G*, and *E* spending with increases in national income. This simple case, however, is satisfactory for an examination of the basic behaviour of the income determination model.

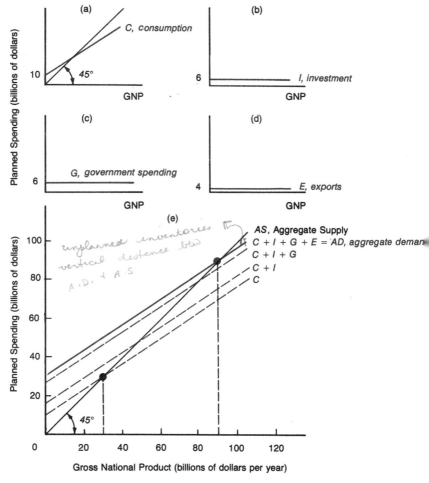

Figure 4.3   Aggregate Demand and Aggregate Supply
Determine Equilibrium National Income or GNP
Planned aggregate demand consists of planned spending for domestic consumption, investment, government goods and services, and exports. Initially, the latter three components are assumed to be unaffected by the level of GNP. Thus, *I, G,* and *E,* are constant, while *C* rises with increasing income. The aggregate demand, *AD*, is plotted in Figure 4.3e by adding vertically the values for *C, I, G,* and *E* at each income level. When planned aggregate demand equals aggregate supply, *AS*, the economy is at its equilibrium level of GNP, namely, $90 billion.

Note that the horizontal (income) axis is now labelled *GNP* rather than *DI* as in Figure 4.1 because governments, businesses, and foreign buyers are now included in the analysis. The $C + I + G + E$ curve in Figure 4.3e is also labelled *AD*, for aggregate demand. The consumption curve is plotted first (from Figure 4.3a), then the $6 billion for *I*, $10 billion for *G*, and $4 billion for *E* are added successively. Since these amounts are fixed regardless of income level, the addition of each item produces a parallel upward shift of the total spending curve.

Aggregate supply, AS, can be represented by the 45° angle or equality line shown in Figure 4.3e. This line relates the total amount of spending required to purchase all of the output to each level of national income. The aggregate supply curve appears as an "equality" line, when the scales on each axis are the same, because the value of the output at any level of national income is *necessarily* equal to the national income. This is because the national income was earned precisely by producing the total output — or the aggregate supply — that is shown for each income level. For example, at an income or GNP of $60 billion, the aggregate supply is $60 billion because the GNP represents the total factor payments included in producing a total output valued at $60 billion.

Equilibrium Level Defined

Economists use the concept of *equilibrium* in explaining why specific features of an economy either change or remain static over time. *The equilibrium level of national income is the level at which national income will remain unless some forces are operating to move it to a higher or lower level.* If all of the factors influencing national income remain unchanged, or if forces acting in opposite directions exactly offset each other, national income will be unchanged.

The equilibrium level of national income is not necessarily the desirable level. In fact, Keynes recognized that the major economies during the Depression of the 1930s were more or less in equilibrium — or were stuck — at undesirably low levels of national income. By examining the forces which could move the economies away from this low equilibrium level, Keynes was able to suggest remedies for moving to higher equilibrium levels.

An important distinction must be made between *planned* expenditures and *actual* expenditures. Planned expenditures may also be described as intended, desired, or *ex ante* (before), and actual expenditures may be described as *ex post* (after). This distinction emphasizes that at a given level of national income, the separate sectors representing investment, government spending, and exports have independent plans to spend certain amounts for the existing output of goods and services. The total of these planned purchases together with consumption may be more, less, or equal to the actual level of output.[2]

An economy is said to be at its equilibrium level of national income when the planned level of aggregate demand is equal to the aggregate supply at that level of income.

In other words, the total amount that consumers, investors, governments, and foreign purchasers of exports, plan to spend for domestic goods and services is just equal to the amount produced.

If at any given level of GNP, the aggregate demand is less than the value of actual output, or aggregate supply, there will be unpurchased goods left in the stores and warehouses of the economy. These unpurchased goods represent an *undesired or unplanned inventory* of goods from the producers' point of view. Businessmen want to hold some goods as inventories but the *desired or planned level of inventories* was included in the investment component of aggregate demand.

Excess inventories are undesirable because businesses do not have the cash income from those potential sales to pay for the labour and other inputs used to produce the excess goods and services. It may be necessary to borrow this extra money. The interest payments then add to the producers' costs and reduce their expected profits. Producers respond to this situation by deciding to produce less the following year, both to get rid of the undesired inventories and to prevent the same thing from happening again. In Figure 4.3e the unplanned inventories are shown as the vertical difference between the aggregate demand and aggregate supply curve at, for example, a GNP of $100 billion. The economy is *not* at equilibrium national income at this level because there are forces (the undesired inventory level and producers' revised decisions) preventing the economy from remaining at this level.

Suppose that producers react by cutting their output back to a level represented by a GNP of $80 billion. Employees are laid off, purchases of other input services and raw materials fall, and incomes fall to the $80 billion level. The economy is again out of equilibrium, but this time the planned level of aggregate demand exceeds aggregate supply. Although aggregate demand has been reduced somewhat due to the effect of declining incomes 'on consumers' demand, there is still such a demand for goods and services that inventories fall below the level planned or desired by businessmen. Shelves are emptied and warehouse stocks are depleted. The next response is to increase output. Employees are rehired, more raw materials are purchased, and incomes rise. If producers have estimated correctly, the level of GNP might rise to $90 billion where

---

[2] This use of "planned" does *not* refer to the decisions of a planned economy such as is described in Chapter 1; rather, the reference is to the plans or intentions of individual businesses, governments, and foreign buyers.

aggregate demand will be just sufficient to purchase the aggregate supply. The equilibrium level of national income has been reached. It is unlikely, however, that it will remain there for very long, for reasons to be discussed in the next section.

Moving the Equilibrium Level

Imagine the planned aggregate demand curve shifting up or down from the position it takes in Figure 4.3e. Wherever it shifted, it would still intersect the aggregate supply curve at some point. Any point along the 45° line represents a potential equilibrium level of GNP. By examining the separate components of aggregate demand, to determine why each of these may change, it is possible to see why aggregate demand shifts, and how the equilibrium level of national income can be changed.

Consumption. A shift in the consumption curve may result either directly from decisions about spending on domestic goods and services, or indirectly from decisions about saving and importing or changes in the level of disposable income.

One major reason for a downward shift in the consumption curve is an increase in personal income taxes. This would reduce disposable income, although national income is unchanged. Similarly, a reduction in income taxes would increase disposable income and would likely shift the consumption curve upward.

An upward shift may also occur if consumers expect their incomes to rise fairly quickly. Anticipation of rising income may lead them to spend more now, saving less for a "rainy day", or for extended holidays which they believe can be financed directly from their higher future incomes. The consumption curve may continue to shift upward over time as consumers' choice widens and as they experience more ways to spend their incomes. Easier and faster air travel for vacations and growing concern about health care, are only two of many such possibilities.

The consumption curve may shift downward if the yield on savings improves sharply. A substantial increase in interest paid on bank savings deposits and savings bonds is comparable to an increase in the price of current goods relative to the price of future goods.

Investment. The investment curve will shift with changes in profits, expectations, interest rates, and availability of borrowed funds. Profit expectations depend on many factors, from advances in technology to political conditions in Canada and abroad. If businessmen become pessimistic about the effects of foreign trade barriers on their ability to export their products, for example, the investment curve may shift downward. A reduction in corporate income tax rates or interest rates would shift investment upward.

Government Expenditures.   The shifts in government expenditures play an especially important role in aggregate demand because governments can attempt to offset any undesirable shifts in the other components of aggregate demand. Government budgets may be designed to provide substantial increases in spending if, for example, it appears that the investment curve is shifting downward. In severe wartime situations, the government may have less freedom to decide whether spending will be increased or not. Even in these conditions, spending on government programs other than military activities, can be reduced if necessary to achieve the desired level of national income.

Exports.   Shifts in the foreign demand for exports also occur for a wide range of reasons. In the Canadian case, these wide shifts are usually the outcome of special agreements or arrangements such as the Automotive Agreement or the sale of unusually large quantities of wheat to foreign countries. An unusually sharp increase in prices of Canadian goods will reduce export sales if similar price increases have not occurred elsewhere. A devaluation of some foreign currencies, relative to the Canadian dollar, will have the same downward effect on the exports curve.

Alternative Definition of Equilibrium

It is possible — although rather unlikely — that the various shifts in the components of aggregate demand may offset each other, with the net result that planned aggregate demand will remain equal to aggregate supply at the given level of national income. If the forces which tend to push the economy out of equilibrium do not counterbalance each other exactly, the economy will move to a new equilibrium level of national income. These forces or factors can be categorized as *planned injections* and *planned withdrawals. Injections are additions to planned aggregate demand, or additional planned spending on domestic goods and services at a given national income level. Withdrawals are reductions in planned aggregate demand, or decreases in planned spending on domestic goods and services.*

Withdrawals include savings, taxes, and imports. Increases in each of these components reduce the amount of spending available for purchases of domestic goods and services. Injections include additions to investment spending, to exports, and to government spending. Consumption is *not* included in this latter list because changes in domestic consumption from a given level of disposable income are necessarily reflected in changes in savings and imports. Changes in disposable income reflect changes in personal income taxes. It should now be apparent that the economy will remain at its equilibrium level of national income if the injections equal the withdrawals, or if

$$I + E + G = S + M + T$$

where I = Investment   and S = Savings
          E = Exports M = Imports
          G = Government spending T = Taxes

Thus there are two definitions of the equilibrium level of national income: (1) that income at which planned aggregate demand equals aggregate supply, and (2) that income at which planned injections, $I + E + G$, equal planned withdrawals, $S + M + T$.

Note that some of the withdrawals may be used to provide some

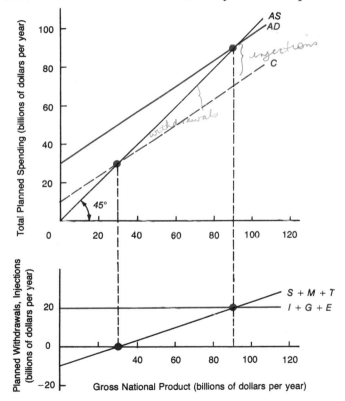

Figure 4.4   Equilibrium GNP Occurs When AD = AS or S + M + T = I + G + E
The economy is at its equilibrium level of GNP, $90 billion, when planned aggregate demand, *AD*, is equal to the aggregate supply of final goods and services, *AS*. This condition occurs when planned injections of spending for investment, government goods and services, and exports (*I* + *G* + *E*) are equal to withdrawals for saving, imports, and taxes *(S* + *M* + *T)*. Injections equal the vertical distances between *C* and *AD*, while withdrawals equal the vertical distance between *C* and *AS*.

of the spending for the injections, but that there is no reason to expect that planned withdrawals will necessarily equal planned injections. Savings will be used to finance some of the investment spending, but some savings may be held in the form of foreign bank deposits or foreign real estate holdings. Similarly, investment may be financed partly by foreign creditors or shareholders. In some years, government spending may exceed taxes, with the difference financed partly by foreign borrowing; in other years tax revenues may exceed government expenditures with the surplus used to retire government bonds held by foreigners. Similarly, the value of exports is seldom exactly equal to the value of imports.

The two definitions of equilibrium national income are illustrated in Figure 4.4. The aggregate supply and aggregate demand curves are the same curves shown in Figure 4.3e. The injections curve $I + G + E$ is equal to the difference between C and AD and appears as a horizontal line because injections are assumed at this stage to be independent of the level of income. The withdrawals curve $S + M + T$ is obtained from the difference between the consumption and aggregate supply curves. Since the gross income paid to the factors for the production of the aggregate supply can be used only for consumption, taxes, savings, or imports, the difference between aggregate supply and consumption must equal withdrawals. Thus, at the income level where $C = AS$, the withdrawals are zero and the $S + M + T$ curve intersects the horizontal axis. The upward slope of the $S + M + T$ curve indicates that savings, imports, and taxes increase with higher levels of income.

B.   Multiplier, Accelerator, and A Dilemma

The preceding sections have been concerned with explaining why national income is at a particular level, and what forces may move it away from this level. The next part of this chapter describes why small changes in aggregate demand may result in much larger or multiplied changes in the level of national income.

The Multiplier Effect

Small changes in aggregate demand can produce large changes in national income due to the existence of the *multiplier*. Like the wind, the multiplier cannot be observed directly; one can only examine its effects. Careful readers may have noted in Figure 4.3 and 4.4 that when planned injections were added vertically to the consumption curve to obtain the aggregate demand curve, equilibrium national income increased by more than the addition to spending. Assume that in Figure 4.5, aggregate demand initially consists only of consumption spending. The equilibrium national income would then be $30 billion. By a net addition of $20 billion to aggregate planned demand, equilibrium income is increased by $60 billion to the $90 billion level. The final increase in national income is *three times* the initial increase in spending.

This multiple by which initial changes in spending change the national income is called the multiplier.

Further inspection of Figure 4.5 will suggest that if the consumption curve rose less steeply, the addition of the same total amount for $I + G + E$ would produce an aggregate demand curve with a flatter slope, and that AD_1 and AS would intersect at a lower income level. One might conclude from this that the multiplier effect is related to the slope of the consumption curve. Moreover, it should be recalled that the slope of the consumption curve is equal to the marginal propensity to consume. A high marginal propensity to consume is represented by a steeply sloped consumption curve and leads to a high multiplier effect on national income of the initial changes in aggregate demand.

In order to find an explanation for this effect, it is necessary to recall some of the initial discussion of consumption and saving in this chapter. When families or individuals received an addition to their incomes, part of this was spent on domestic consumer goods,

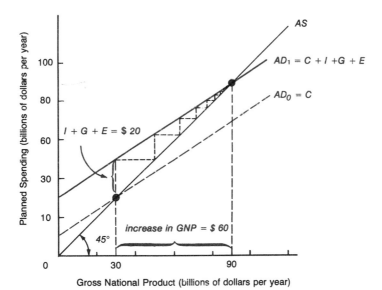

Figure 4.5 Multiplier Effect of Increased Spending
Injections of spending *(I + G + E)*, additions to these components, or increases in planned consumption have a final effect on GNP which is greater than the initial change. With *MPC* = ²/₃, the addition of $20 billion for *I + G + E*, increases equilibrium GNP by $60 billion. The larger the value of the multiplier, the larger the final change in GNP.

some was spent on imports and some was saved. The fraction consumed was termed the marginal propensity to consume, MPC. Now suppose for the sake of simplicity that $MPC = \frac{2}{3}$ for every family and individual in the economy. If a firm decided to build a new plant it might first employ an architect, paying him a fee of $10,000. He would spend two-thirds of this amount; one-third would go to savings and imports. The $6,666.67 for consumption would go to many other persons and firms in the economy, each of which would also consume two-thirds of their additional incomes, for a further increase in consumption spending of $4,444.44. The next round of consumption spending would amount to $2,962.96. This process would continue until the successive amounts of consumption spending become infinitely small. By that time, the total *additional* spending, including the original $10,000 would amount to $30,000.

The final effect on national income of the initial increase in spending can be determined from the formula for the sum of a geometric progression. The values for the successive rounds of spending were calculated by multiplying the previous spending times the MPC, or $\frac{2}{3} \Delta I + (\frac{2}{3})^2 \Delta I + (\frac{2}{3})^3 \Delta I + \ldots + (\frac{2}{3})^{n+1} \Delta I$, where ΔI is the initial increase in investment spending.

The formula for the sum of a geometric progression is

$$\Sigma \infty = a \frac{1}{1 - r}$$

where a is the initial change (ΔI in this case) and r is the value by which it is multiplied in the series. Thus

$$\frac{1}{1 - r} = \frac{1}{1 - \frac{2}{3}} = 3.$$

When the MPC is two-thirds, the effect of the original spending will be a threefold increase in spending, and in the level of national income. If the MPC had been three-quarters, each round of spending would have been larger and the final effect would have been greater. Check this by letting $r = \frac{3}{4}$. Then $1/(1 - \frac{3}{4}) = 4$. With an MPC of three-quarters, there will be a fourfold increase in national income for any given increase in spending.

The formula for the multiplier thus is $\dfrac{1}{1 - MPC}$.

Since $1 - MPC = MPS + MPM + MPT$, this can also be written as

$$\frac{1}{MPS + MPM + MPT}$$

The multiplier therefore can be defined as the reciprocal of the sum of the marginal propensities to save, import, and pay taxes. This is an extremely useful conclusion, indicating that the higher the marginal propensity to save, to import, and to pay taxes, the lower will be the effect of increased spending on the equilibrium national income. The importance of this effect can be recognized by letting $MPC = 1$. The value of the multiplier would be infinitely large; an increase in spending of only one dollar (or even less) would be sufficient to keep the national income increasing indefinitely!

The multiplier has the same effect on withdrawals as on injections, but in the opposite direction. If someone decides to increase his savings by $1,000, this reduces spending by the same amount. That spending *would have* generated more spending, but now incomes are reduced for each of the potential recipients in what would have been successive spending rounds. The total decline in spending and national income is equal to the original decrease times the multiplier of 3 (when $MPC = \frac{2}{3}$), or $3,000.

Special Cases of the Multiplier

There are two special applications of the general multiplier, one related to foreign trade, and the other to government spending and taxes. The *foreign trade multiplier* has the same formula as the general multiplier described above but emphasizes that an economy which attempts to expand its exports in order to bolster aggregate demand must be prepared to take one step back for each few steps forward. An increase in exports of $1,000 represents an increase in spending and in incomes, but part of this increased income will be saved and part will be spent on imports. When $MPC = \frac{2}{3}$, $MPS = \frac{1}{6}$, $MPM = \frac{1}{6}$ (and $MPT = 0$ for simplicity), an increase in export sales of $1,000 results in increased income of $3,000, but one-sixth or $500 of this is spent on imports. The *net* increase in foreign trade is equal to the increase in exports less the increase in imports of $500.

The *balanced budget multiplier* also has the same formula as the general multiplier but refers to the particular case of a balanced change in a government's budget. One might expect that when tax revenues and government spending are each increased by the same amount there will be no change in national income. To determine what *does* happen, consider the following example.

Assume again that $MPC = \frac{2}{3}$ and that $(MPS + MPM + MPT) = \frac{1}{3}$. If government spending increases by $3 million, the multiplier effect results in an increase in national income of $9 million. An increase in personal income taxes of $3 million reduces potential spending by $3 million, but only two-thirds or $2 million of this would have been spent on domestic consumption. The other third would have been saved or spent on imports. Therefore the (downward) multiplier effect is based on only the initial $2 million decrease in consumption spending. The effect of a $3 million increase in taxes is a $6 million decline in national income. The *net* effect of the balanced or equal increase in taxes and in government spending is a $3 million increase in national income.

Try a similar case using a balanced increase, of say $15 million. One should find that the net effect is a $15 million increase in national income. In fact, *the balanced budget multiplier will always have a net effect on national income equal to the initial change in taxes and in government spending, provided that these amounts are equal.* Because a change in government spending has a greater effect on national income than an equal change in taxes, government spending is said to be a more powerful weapon in influencing national income than is a change in taxes.

Note that the value of the multiplier used in these examples is derived from hypothetical assumptions about marginal propensities. Empirical studies of the Canadian economy have found that the value of the multiplier for government budgetary changes is less than 2; one study estimated the multiplier effect of a change in government expenditure on non-farm output as 1.7, and 1.42 for a personal income tax reduction.[3] The low multiplier values reflect the influence of import spending, time lags, and built-in stabilizers. The latter two items are described in Chapter 6.

The Paradox of Thrift

The practice of saving some part of one's income has generally been regarded as a prudent habit. Not only would one be in a better position to meet financial emergencies, but well-managed savings could be expected to increase future income through interest and dividends on financial assets. It may seem paradoxical therefore that an increase in the desire to save can have a deterrent effect on national income, and will likely even lead to a lower level of actual savings.

Up to this point, the components of aggregate demand other than consumption have been assumed to be unaffected by the level of national income. It is more likely of course that planned investment and planned government spending will rise with increasing national income. Exports are less likely to be related to national income levels, although some increase in exports may be expected with higher levels of output if this leads to more competitive prices for exports due to specialization and economies of scale.

An increase in $I + G + E$ with increases in the level of national income is shown by the upward slope of the $I + G + E$ curve in Figure 4.6. The $S + M + T$ curve reflects the initial relationship between planned savings, imports, and taxes, at the given level of

---

[3] Sydney May, "Dynamic Multipliers and their Use for Fiscal Decision-Making," in Economic Council of Canada, *Conference on Stabilization Policies*, Ottawa: Queen's Printer, 1966. See also D.J. Daly, *Fiscal Policy — An Assessment*, Toronto: Collier-Macmillan, 1972, for a discussion of the multiplier estimates.

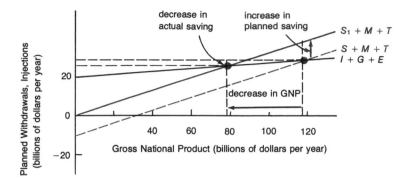

Figure 4.6 The Paradox of Thrift
With planned withdrawals at $S + M + T$, the economy is in equilibrium at a GNP of
$117 billion. If at this GNP level, households and firms decide to increase saving,
the equilibrium level of GNP falls to about $78 billion because increased saving
reduces consumption which then increases inventories beyond the desired level.
Employment and output is reduced until the economy returns to equilibrium at the
lower GNP. Actual saving when GNP is $78 billion is less than the actual saving
when GNP was $117 billion: the attempt to save more finally led households and
firms to save less.

GNP. If persons should decide that at this level of national income
they would like to save more, with no change in planned imports or
taxes, the change in desired savings would shift the $S + M + T$ curve
up to $S_1 + M + T$ as in Figure 4.6.

The increase in planned savings has two important effects. The
increase in planned withdrawals from spending is not matched by a
change in planned injections of $I + G + E$. The economy therefore is
being forced away from the initial equilibrium level of national income. The multiplier increases the effect of the initial increase in
saving (and decrease in spending) such that total decline in spending is somewhat greater than the initial increase in saving. National
income reaches an equilibrium level at a much lower level than the
initial equilibrium point.

As the level of national income falls, the average income of
families and individuals also falls. The absolute level of saving will
also fall. The *Paradox of Thrift is that the intended increase in
saving has led to a decrease in actual saving.*

The Acceleration Principle and the Multiplier

Apart from government policies, the acceleration principle is one of
the most important factors influencing the level of aggregate demand and national income. This principle, often referred to simply

as the *accelerator*, defines the relationship between a change in consumption, through the effect on investment, and a change in national income. A simple arithmetic example may illustrate this relationship and the assumptions underlying the acceleration principle.

Table 4.2 presents hypothetical data for a firm producing Canadian flags. Assume that for every 10,000 flags produced annually the firm requires one sewing machine, and that the firm replaces one worn-out machine each year. In the years prior to 1966, the firm was selling a constant 50,000 flags annually; thus there was no change from year to year in the level of flag consumption or of sewing machine purchases. But in 1966, with the approach of Expo and Centennial Year, flag sales rose by 20 per cent. In addition to purchasing the usual replacement machine, the firm added another machine to its capital stock; this represented an increase of 100 per cent in its annual level of gross investment. Centennial Year brought a boom in flag sales: flag consumption rose by 67 per cent while machine purchases rose by 150 per cent. Although the 1968 sales held steady at the 1967 level, the firm was able to reduce its purchases of sewing machines to the one machine required annually as a replacement for old equipment. The annual level of gross investment fell by 80 per cent. In 1969, the level of investment again increased sharply, but then fell back just as quickly. There was no *fixed* relationship between the percentage changes in consumption and in investment; the 20 per cent increase in consumption in 1966 *accelerated* investment to a 100 per cent increase but to maintain the doubling of investment realized in 1969, consumption would have had to increase in 1970 by 27 per cent.

Table 4.2

Accelerator Effects on Investment:
Example of A Hypothetical Flag Firm

Year	Consumption (flags per year in thousands)	Machines Required	Investment			Investment Change %	Consumption Change %
			Additional	Replacement (number of machines)	Total		
1965	50	5	0	1	1	0	0
1966	60	6	1	1	2	100	20
1967	100	10	4	1	5	150	67
1968	100	10	0	1	1	−80	0
1969	110	11	1	1	2	100	10
1970	120	12	1	1	2	0	9
1971	120	12	0	1	1	−50	0

Important assumptions underlie the acceleration principle. Although it is not illustrated in the example, it is assumed that when consumption falls, firms do not dispose of unused machinery. However, if flag sales had dropped to 50,000 units in 1968, the firm *might* have sold its unused machines to firms using such machines for another product, *if* the flag firm expected sales to remain at the new low level for some time. If firms could and would dispose of unneeded machinery when sales fell in one area, an increase in sales in another area would not have so strong an effect on investment because productive capacity would be transferred to where it was required.

It is also assumed that firms are operating at full capacity. If the flag firm had been operating at only five-sixths of its capacity when flag sales were at 50,000 units, the increased sales of 1966 could have been produced without adding to productive capacity and without any change in the usual level of annual investment.

The acceleration principle also assumes that firms expect annual sales to remain at the new higher level; otherwise it would be unprofitable to purchase a new machine for short-term use.

Finally, it is assumed that firms supplying the investment goods (sewing machines) can respond immediately to meet the accelerated demand for this equipment. Although none of these assumptions is universally valid, the effects of the acceleration principle are nevertheless evident and have been shown to account for some of the wide swings in economic activity.

Since the multiplier plays an important role in amplifying the effects on national income of a change in planned investment, the multiplier also interacts with the accelerator to reinforce the effects on national income of a change in consumption and investment. The increased investment means higher output and incomes in the machine industry. This higher income is then multiplied through successive rounds of spending to result in higher national income. Similarly, sharp declines in investment due to the accelerator effect can be multiplied, leading to even sharper drops in national income.

Equilibrium National Income At Full Employment

The components of aggregate demand have been examined to this point for the effects they have on the equilibrium level of national income. Nothing has been said about what constitutes a *desirable* level of national income, or how aggregate demand can be influenced to bring the economy into equilibrium at some specified level of national income.

Two of the basic economic goals outlined in the last chapter were full employment and price stability. A desirable level of national income would be the level at which these two goals could be achieved. The economy's objective therefore is to realize an equilibrium level of national income at full employment and without inflation.

The estimated potential output at full employment, as defined

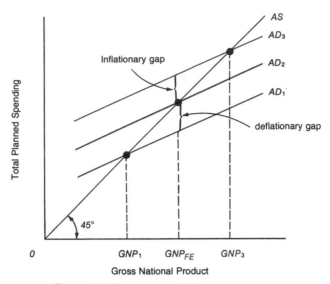

Figure 4.7 Inflationary and Deflationary Gaps
AD_2 shows the level of aggregate demand required at various levels of *GNP* to move the economy to the full-employment level of *GNPFE*. The deflationary gap is the difference in planned spending between AD_1 and AD_2 at *GNPFE*. Similarly, the inflationary gap is the vertical distance between AD_2 and AD_3 at *GNPFE*.

in the last chapter, is shown in Figure 4.7. When planned aggregate demand $C + I + G + E$ is at AD_2, the economy will be in equilibrium exactly at the full employment level of national income because planned spending is just sufficient for the full employment of the economy's resources. But because the total of planned spending is dependent on many diverse factors there is no reason to expect that aggregate demand will necessarily be at AD_2, or that it will remain at this level for any length of time.

If planned aggregate demand is at AD_1, spending will not be sufficient to maintain full employment. The *additional* spending required to bring the economy to the full employment level of national income is referred to as the *deflationary gap* because the inadequacy of spending has a deflating or depressing effect on the economy. Note that the size of the deflationary gap shown in Figure 4.7 is less than the difference between national income at full employment and the national income resulting from the lower aggregate demand. This illustrates the potential effect of the multiplier. If an initial injection of spending equal to the deflationary gap can be realized, the multiplier will act on this spending to raise the national income by some multiple of the initial expenditure. Since the deflationary gap is measured at the full employment level of national income, an estimate of this level and an estimate of the value of the multiplier are required before the size of the required increase in spending can be determined.

What happens if aggregate demand is at AD_3? In this case the economy can be in equilibrium only if the total value of output *exceeds* the full employment level. The amount by which planned spending exceeds the spending required for full employment is termed the *inflationary gap*. This term emphasizes the fact that an equilibrium level of national income above the full employment level can be achieved only through inflation, or an increase in prices. There would be no increase in *real* output but the increase in prices would increase the *monetary value* of the full employment level of output. It is only in this sense that there can be an equilibrium level of national income above full employment. This is the condition which has led to the popular definition of inflation as "too much money chasing too few goods".

The Inflation and Unemployment Dilemma

The concept of an inflationary and deflationary gap will be useful in Chapter 6 in exploring the kinds of action which might be taken in trying to push the economy to full employment or to reduce inflation. But the circumstances implied in the description of equilibrium levels of national income above and below full employment are seldom found in actual experience. It is now widely recognized that both inflation and unemployment can occur at the same time, and more specifically, that in recent years there have been high levels of inflation even though the economy is also experiencing high average annual unemployment rates.

This effect is illustrated in Figure 4.8. At low levels of real output, corresponding to the equilibrium national income when aggregate demand is at AD_1 in Figure 4.7, the unemployment rate is very high but there is no inflation. In fact, if the unemployment rate is high *and rising* there may even be some deflation, or declining prices, as indicated by the dotted path. As real output reaches level Q_1, unemployment may still be quite substantial but inflation begins. With the economy closely approaching the full employment level of output, Q_{FE}, inflation proceeds more quickly until, at Q_{FE}, full employment has been reached and inflation could potentially increase at a rapid rate.

At levels of real output between Q_1 and Q_{FE}, any attempt to reduce inflation also has a depressing effect on employment, while efforts to increase employment would also stimulate a general rise in prices. This dilemma of having to choose between unemployment and inflation as the priority problem, and the policies that might be pursued to deal with this dilemma, will be discussed in Chapter 6.

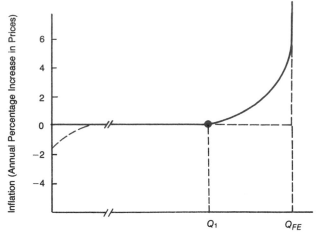

Figure 4.8 Inflation and Unemployment Can Occur Simultaneously
The basic national income determination model assumes that increased aggregate demand will increase real output until the economy reaches the full-
employment level of real output, Q_{FE}. Further increases in aggregate demand
would result in inflation as additional spending bid up prices of the maximum fixed
output. Experience shows, however, that inflation may begin at lower output levels,
such as Q_1, and become worse as output increases, even though there is some
unemployment. Similarly, at very low output levels, some deflation may occur.

C. Money and National Income

Up to this point, aggregate demand and aggregate supply of goods
and services have been the major factors determining the equilibrium level of national income. Now it is necessary to examine the
interaction of the *real sector*, (the markets for goods and services),
and the *monetary sector*, (the money market), to see the direct effect
of changes in the demand for and supply of money on the level of
national income. This combination of the real and monetary sectors
is often referred to as a post-Keynesian or neoclassical model of the
economy because Keynes had attached greater importance to the
effects of government spending and taxes on the general performance of the economy. More recently, however, some economists
have revived the earlier significance which the classical economists
placed on the role of money.

Money in the Classical Model

The classical economists placed primary emphasis on the stock or
quantity of money existing in the economy at any given time. The
stock of money is determined by adding the coins and paper currency in circulation (outside the banks) and bank deposits. The definition of money, and changes in the quantity of money are consi-

dered in more detail in the next chapter, but a simple definition of money as the total stock of purchasing power immediately available to individuals, businesses, and governments, is satisfactory for this section. Bank deposits, apart from some special savings deposits, are included because cheques can be written on them to pay for goods and services. Bonds and other financial assets are not counted as money because these must be converted to cash or bank deposits, possibly at a loss, before they can be used to pay for goods and services.

The *Quantity Theory of Money* of the classical economists took two forms: the crude theory and the sophisticated theory. The *Crude Quantity Theory* stated simply that the general price level in the economy would vary directly and proportionately with the level of money. This could be expressed as

$$P = kM$$

where k is the value of the constant relationship between the general price level, P, and the stock of money, M. If the quantity of money were doubled, the crude quantity theory would predict that prices would be doubled. This result was based on two of the classical assumptions outlined earlier: that individuals would spend all of their incomes, and that the economy was normally at the full employment level. Thus, if the quantity of money were increased, people would spend the increased quantity also. But since it was assumed that the economy was normally at full employment, the increased spending could only result in a bidding up of prices for the fixed levels of goods and services. Money in the crude classical model had the effect of increasing national income, but only by increasing the *monetary value* of the output, not by increasing the *real* output.

The *Sophisticated Quantity Theory*, or what is more properly called the *equation of exchange*, modified the crude theory to take into account that it is not only the *quantity* of money available which affects the economy, but also the *velocity* of money, or how quickly money circulates in the economy. Two different measures of the velocity of money have been used: the transactions velocity and the income velocity.

The *transactions velocity of money* is calculated by dividing the total value of all transactions or sales made during the period of a year by the average stock of money available during the same period. The formula for the transactions velocity is therefore:

$$V_T = \frac{P \times T}{M}$$

where V_T is the transactions velocity, P is the weighted average price of transactions, T is the total number of transactions, and M is the quantity of money. If one knew that the total value of transactions, $P \times T$, in one year was \$300 billion and the stock of money was \$30 billion, the velocity calculation would show that, on average, each dollar was exchanged ten times during the year.

Income velocity is the proper concept, however, for examining transactions of final goods and services. Income velocity is calculated by dividing the GNP or GNE, in current dollars, for a given year by the stock of money. The formula is the same as for the transactions velocity except that Y (output of final goods and services) is substituted for T and P is the weighted average price of final goods and services. Hence:

$$V_Y = \frac{P \times Y}{M}$$

The income velocity will be considerably smaller than the transactions velocity since national income measures only the final goods and services, and not the many transactions that occur as each good moves toward the final production stage. Nevertheless, since it is *changes* in the velocity of money that are important, the income velocity can serve as an indicator of the changes in the speed at which money is circulating in the economy.

The *quantity equation of exchange* is so called because it is an equation which relates the quantity of money to the value of goods and services exchanged. By definition, the total value of these commodities must be equal to the total spending. That is, $M \times V_Y = P \times Y$ because V_Y was defined as $P \times Y$ divided by M. This equation is also often written as

$$M \times V = P \times Q$$

This equation is described as a *truism* or *identity* because it states what is necessarily true, rather than expressing a causal relationship. Nevertheless, the quantity equation of exchange emphasized a point made by the later classical economists, namely that the crude theory omitted the possibility of a change in the velocity of circulation of money. It was assumed, however, that the velocity was reasonably stable in the long run, and that changes in the quantity of money would lead directly to proportionate changes in the price level. The introduction of real goods into the equation, in the form of T or Y, also opened the possibility of an economy which was at less-than-full employment responding to an increase in M by increasing real output. Finally, the equation also showed that even when the money supply remained constant, an increase in velocity could result in an increase in national income.

Although the quantity equation did try to show how money could affect the levels of real output and prices, it was not very useful for explaining the mechanisms underlying these changes. Keynes argued that an analysis of the role of money needed to examine the *demand for money*, or why people would hold different amounts of money under different conditions.

The Demand for Money

It is easy to understand why there is a demand for real goods and services, and why the quantity demanded should vary inversely with the price of a good. It may not be quite so obvious why people should want to *hold* money, apart from using it immediately to purchase commodities. The *motives for holding money* can be described under three categories: (1) transactions; (2) precautionary; (3) speculative.

The *transactions demand* for money arises because one needs money to make routine purchases over a short period of time. It would be possible — but foolish — to buy bonds or other financial assets with one's weekly or monthly pay as it was received and then "cash" these each time money was needed to buy the groceries or pay the rent. In addition to the inconvenience, there are costs in buying and selling some financial assets. Instead, most people keep some cash in their wallets or purses and a reasonable balance in chequing accounts to meet regular expenses.

The *precautionary demand* for money is closely related to the transactions demand. One can estimate weekly or monthly requirements for regular expenditures on food, housing, clothing, and transportation, but other expenditures are less predictable. A sudden illness, the opportunity to join someone else on a trip, or a clearance sale of "real bargains" may suddenly require cash. One usually maintains a bank balance somewhat above the bare minimum for these and similar "rainy day" reasons.

The *speculative demand* for money is related to a small percentage of the population who hold some assets in bank accounts in order to take advantage of opportune times to buy other financial assets. When investors, for example, believe that common stock prices are about to fall for a short time, they may sell stocks and hold their funds as bank deposits until it seems time to buy stocks again.

These are reasons for holding money, but they do not suggest how much money people will hold.

The quantity of money demanded at any time, given one's level of income and "taste" or preference for holding money, depends on the rate of interest.

This is illustrated in Figure 4.9. The demand for money curve, D_M, resembles a typical demand curve: a larger quantity is demanded as the price falls. Since the demand for money reflects the preference which people have for liquidity or liquid assets, as compared to purchasing power in other forms, *the demand for money is referred to as liquidity preference.*

The price or cost of holding money is the rate of interest. When the interest rate is high, holding large cash balances is very expensive in terms of the interest that could be earned by holding assets in other forms. This is reflected in the fact that one can usually observe

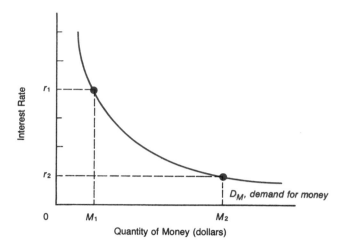

Figure 4.9   Liquidity Preference: Demand For Money
At any given level of income the quantity of money, held as coins, currency, or
bank deposits, is greater the lower the interest rate. As the interest rate falls from r_1
to r_2, the quantity demanded increases from OM_1 to OM_2 because the cost of
holding money — the forgone return on other financial assets — is lower at lower
interest rates.

a shift of deposits from chequing accounts to (non-chequing) savings
accounts, bonds, and stocks, when interest rates rise sharply. When
interest rates are low, the cost of retaining these balances in a chequing account is much less; many people find it "more trouble than it's
worth" to estimate more precisely the amounts they must hold in a
chequing account.

Nevertheless, some money must be held for transactions and
precautionary reasons whatever the level of interest. This is reflected
in Figure 4.9. M_1 is the amount of money being held for these
reasons even at high interest rates. At these high rates virtually no
money will be held for speculative reasons because there will be
more rewarding opportunities in holding other assets. But as interest
rates fall, from r_1 to r_2, more money will be held for transactions and
some will be held for speculative reasons. When the rate drops to r_2
— which may be the counterpart of 2 to 3 per cent interest rate on
savings deposits — large amounts of money will be held for speculation.

The liquidity preference curve is shown to flatten out at an
interest rate of about r_2. This long "tail" on the right-hand end of the
liquidity preference curve was described by Keynes as the *liquidity
trap*. He argued that at very low interest rates, such as are experienced in severe recessions, investors will hold exceptionally large
quantities of money instead of other assets. The cost of holding
assets in liquid form at r_2 is not sufficient to offset the risk of holding
assets in other forms. However, such low interest rates have not been

experienced for so long that the liquidity trap is now considered to be of historical interest only.

Determination of the Rate of Interest

The liquidity preference curve will vary with different individuals. Just as some individuals will buy several bottles of a fine wine at a given price while others buy few or none, some people will hold large amounts of money at a given interest rate while others hold little. Although people vary significantly in their preferences for holding money rather than other assets, depending on their willingness to take some risk, the major factor determining the amount of money held is the level of individuals' incomes. At any given interest rate, the higher one's income, the larger the amount of money required for transactions, and the higher the cost one is willing to afford for the convenience of holding money for precautionary and speculative purposes.

Suppose the liquidity preference curve for the entire economy is the demand curve shown as D_1D_1 in Figure 4.10. In addition, suppose the quantity of money available at this time is M_1. The supply curves for money are shown as vertical lines — that is, as perfectly inelastic with respect to the interest rate — because the quantity of money

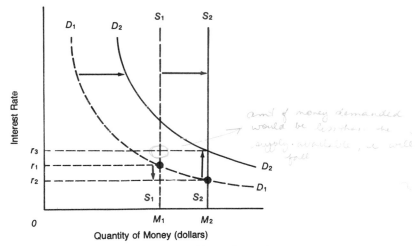

Figure 4.10 Supply Of And Demand For Money Determine The Equilibrium Interest Rate

The quantity of money supplied is assumed to be independent of the interest rate, or perfectly inelastic with respect to the interest rate, because the money supply is decided by the Bank of Canada. The intersection of the demand curve, D_1D_1, and the supply curve, S_1S_1, determines the equilibrium interest rate, r_1. An increase in the money supply to S_2S_2 (or to quantity OM_2), would lower the interest rate to r_2. An increase in the demand for money shifts the demand curve to D_2D_2 and raises the interest rate to r_3.

available at a particular time is dependent on decisions of the monetary authorities, and not on the interest rate. In the next chapter, the methods used by the monetary authorities for varying the supply of money over time are discussed, but these are not necessary for the present section.

In Figure 4.10 it can be seen that the money market will be in equilibrium only when the interest rate is r_1, given the demand curve, D_1D_1, and the supply curve, S_1S_1. If the interest rate was higher than r_1, the amount of money demanded would be less than the amount available and the interest rate would fall, for example, as banks offered loans at lower interest rates. The interest rate would drop still further, to r_2, if the money supply was increased to M_2, as shown by the supply curve, S_2S_2. But if during the period that the supply of money was being increased, the demand for money should also increase, to D_2D_2, the interest rate would rise to r_3.

The equilibrium rate of interest is determined by the supply of and demand for money.

In the short run, the liquidity preference or demand curve tends to shift very little. The more important infleunce is a short-run change in the supply of money. In the longer run, however, the demand for money tends to rise with increases in national income, so that both supply and demand affect the interest rate.

Money, Interest Rate, and Aggregate Demand

The money market and the market for real goods and services are linked through the effect of the interest rate on the level of investment. When interest rates are high, investors will borrow less to undertake new investments because there will be fewer investment possibilities for which the expected rate of return exceeds the rate of interest. This effect is illustrated in Figure 4.11. In the initial equilibrium condition of the money market, the interest rate is r_1. At this interest rate, businesses find it profitable to continue investing up to a level of investment, I_1, since at this level of investment the marginal efficiency of investment, or rate of return, is just equal to the cost of borrowing money. If they invested more, the returns would fall below their interest costs with a net loss as the result. When businesses plan a level of investment of I_1, planned aggregate demand will be AD_1, given the other components of aggregate demand, and the equilibrium level of national income will be GNP_1.

Now suppose the money supply is increased to M_2. Provided that the demand for money is unchanged, the interest rate falls to r_2. With this decline in the interest rate, investors will increase the level of their planned investments to I_2. The increase in planned invest-

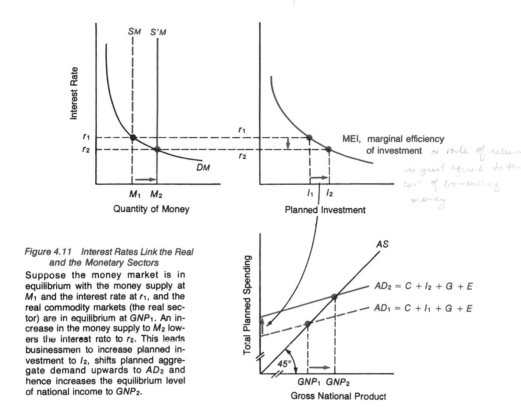

Figure 4.11   Interest Rates Link the Real and the Monetary Sectors

Suppose the money market is in equilibrium with the money supply at M_1 and the interest rate at r_1, and the real commodity markets (the real sector) are in equilibrium at GNP_1. An increase in the money supply to M_2 lowers the interest rate to r_2. This leads businessmen to increase planned investment to I_2, shifts planned aggregate demand upwards to AD_2 and hence increases the equilibrium level of national income to GNP_2.

ment increases the level of aggregate demand to AD_2, with a resulting increase in the equilibrium level of national income to GNP_2. Conversely, if the amount of money available drops below M_1 (the S_M curve shifts to the left), the interest rate would rise, planned investment would fall, aggregate demand would fall, and thus the equilibrium level of national income would fall.

This important effect of the interest rate on national income, through the effect on planned investment, is based on the assumption that investors' plans are quite sensitive to changes in the rate of interest.

While it is true that for large investment projects, of say $10 million, an increase of one percentage point in the interest rate represents a substantial cost increase — in this example it would be $100,000 — several other factors must also be considered in a project of this magnitude. For example, this may represent a new plant being opened in an area where there is still some uncertainty about consumer response to the proposed product, or it may be the first plant ever to use a new technique. The risk of technical failures and the uncertainty of consumer response are frequently the major considerations. Furthermore, the usual financial sources for projects of this kind may have their funds "tied up" in loans on other projects. Some firms prefer to finance new projects from their retained earnings: whether or not a project is undertaken could depend more on whether funds were available than on the current interest rate.

These several factors have led some economists to emphasize the *availability* of money, rather than the interest rate, in explaining the effect money has on the level of national income. Although this is an important distinction, it does not significantly alter the basic explanation since both factors operate in the same direction. That is, an increase in the money supply has the effect of both increasing the availability of money and decreasing the interest rate; in either case, an increase in planned investment can be expected. However, firms with a large fund of retained earnings may use this to finance new projects even when interest rates are high. To this extent, the link between money supply and business investment is somewhat weakened. However, empirical evidence indicates that there is a much stronger effect of the availability of money and the interest rate on investment in residential housing.[4]

General Equilibrium
in the Real and Monetary Sectors

When the real sector of the economy was examined in the first part of this chapter, it was found that national income would be at an equilibrium level when planned aggregate demand was equal to aggregate supply, or when planned injections were equal to planned withdrawals. These conditions would determine a specific equilibrium level. The introduction of a variation in the interest rate, however, introduces a corresponding variation in equilibrium levels of national income. Figure 4.12a shows five possible levels of aggregate demand, and thus five possible equilibrium levels of national income, associated with five different interest rates: the higher the interest rate, the lower the level of investment and aggregate demand. The five combinations of interest rates and corresponding levels of national income are plotted in Figure 4.12b. The resulting curve, IS, represents the many possible equilibrium levels of national income. The IS curve, (or Investment = Savings curve), indicates that given a particular interest rate, r_2, planned investment (or total injections) is equal to planned savings (or total withdrawals) at the corresponding level of national income, GNP_4. But the IS curve

---

[4] See, for example, a survey by D.J. Daly, "The Scope for Monetary Policy — A Synthesis" in Economic Council of Canada, *Conference on Stabilization Policies*, Ottawa: Queen's Printer, 1966.

also raises the question of whether the economy *can* ever actually be in equilibrium if each point on the curve represents a potential equilibrium level of national income.

The answer to this question is found by turning to the money market or monetary sector as depicted by Figure 4.12c. With a given amount of money available, M_1, the interest rate will rise with each increase in the demand for money. As explained earlier, this demand will increase as national income rises in order to meet the transactions needs and because more people will hold money for speculative reasons. The five demand curves shown in Figure 4.12c represent the demand for money at five levels of national income; the D_5 curve is associated with the highest level of income. Thus the increasing interest rates, r_1 to r_5, are associated with increasing

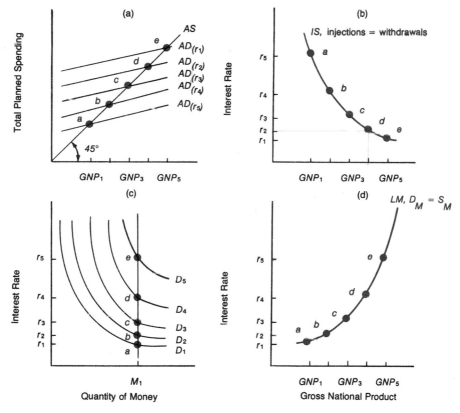

Figure 4.12 *Alternative Equilibrium Conditions in Real and Monetary Sectors*
The real sector can be in equilibrium at a wide range of GNP levels, depending on the interest rate: a high interest rate, r_5, is associated with a low level of planned investment and planned aggregate demand, AD_5, and hence a low level of national income, GNP_5. The *IS* curve shows the interest rate associated with each equilibrium level of GNP. Similarly, the *LM* curve shows the equilibrium interest rate associated with each level of GNP. When the money supply is fixed at M_1, increases in GNP shift the money demand curve upward, resulting in higher equilibrium interest rates.

levels of national income. These combinations of interest rate and national income are plotted in Figure 4.12d as the *LM* curve, so called because it shows many combinations of interest rates and national income at which the amount of money demanded and supplied are equal. (*L* stands for liquidity preference or demand for money; *M* stands for the supply of money.) This time, the question raised is whether there can be any single equilibrium level of the interest rate in the monetary sector.

As one might have guessed by this point, the answer to each of the questions concerning single equilibrium points in the real and the monetary sectors lies in combining the *IS* and *LM* curves on one graph, as in Figure 4.13b.

With the given supply of money M_1, the real sector *can* be at an equilibrium level of national income, GNP_3, when the interest rate is r_3. The monetary sector, however, can be in equilibrium at a national income of GNP_3 *only* if the interest rate is r_3. Thus the combination of GNP_3 and r_3 represents the *only* conditions under which both sectors can be in equilibrium at the same time, and therefore, the only conditions under which the total economy can be in general equilibrium.

Recall what it means for an economy to be in equilibrium. The level of national income will remain at GNP_3 so long as there are *no changes* in any one or more of the several components of the national income model. But if there is a change in any of the components of aggregate demand, or in the demand for or supply of money, the economy will likely be moved away from the current level of national income. It is *likely* that this will happen, although the changes in the components may just happen to be exactly offsetting or counter-balancing so that equilibrium is maintained.

An example of one possible shift, and its consequences, is shown in Figure 4.13. If, as in Figure 4.13a, the supply of money is increased from M_1 to M_2, there will be a lower interest rate for any given level of national income than if the supply had remained at M_1. This effect is reflected in the downward (or outward) shift of the *LM* curve in Figure 4.13b. The *LM* curve "slides down" the *IS* curve, from LM_1 to LM_2, to a higher equilibrium level of national income at a lower interest rate. A decrease in the supply of money would have shifted the *LM* curve upward to the left with a resulting higher interest rate and lower national income.

From Figure 4.12a, one should be able to predict that if planned aggregate demand should increase — with the supply of money and interest rates initially unchanged — that the *IS* curve in Figures 4.12b and 4.13b would shift upward to the right. An increase in planned government spending, for example, would lead to a higher equilibrium level of national income which in turn would increase the demand for money. But with no increase in the supply of money, the increased demand for money would force up the interest rate.

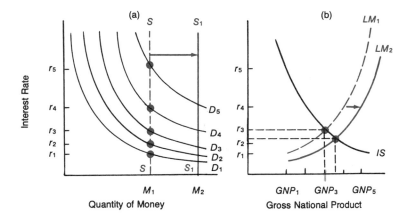

Figure 4.13   General Equilibrium: LM and IS Determine Equilibrium
The real sector can be in equilibrium at any combination of *r* and *GNP* on the *IS*
curve, and the monetary sector, at any combination on the *LM* curve. The two
sectors together, or the total economy, can be in equilibrium only at the interest
rate, r_3, and the national income, GNP_3, where *IS* and LM_1 intersect. An increase in
the money supply to M_2 will shift the money supply curve to S_1S_1 and hence will
shift the *LM* curve to LM_2. The economy will be in equilibrium at a lower interest
rate and higher GNP.

The final result would be higher national income at a higher interest
rate.

The model or explanation of the operation of the economy at the
aggregate level is now complete — at least in its simple form! This is
the model or the *analytical framework* which will be used in Chapter 6 to examine the actions which governments can take in an attempt to achieve the economic goals of full employment and price
stability. But before turning to such an analysis of economic
policies, it is necessary to look at the banking system and how it can
alter the money supply.

Review of the Main Points

1. Classical economists argued that "Supply creates its own demand", or that all output would be purchased. Flexible prices,
   wages, and interest rates would assure that there would always
   be full employment. However, Keynes observed during the Depression of the 1930s that an economy could become stuck at
   high levels of unemployment.

2. In the Keynesian model of national income determination, the
   major components of aggregate demand are consumption, investment, government expenditures, and exports. Consumption
   is spending for domestic goods and services; saving represents
   the postponement of consumption. The fraction of total income
   used for consumption is the average propensity to consume; the

fraction of additional income going to consumption is the marginal propensity to consume. Similar calculations are made for the average and marginal propensities to import and to save. $APC + APM + APS = 1$ and $MPC + MPM + MPS = 1$.

3. Investment is new plant and equipment, new residential housing, and real additions to inventories. As long as the marginal efficiency of investment, or the expected rate of return on each additional investment project, exceeds the interest rate on borrowed funds, there will be investment spending. In the simple case, investment is autonomous — or unaffected by changes in the level of national income. In the complex model, some investment is induced by increasing incomes.

4. Government spending in the national income model excludes transfer payments since most or all of these increase aggregate demand through consumption spending out of individuals' incomes. Again, in the simple case, government spending may be assumed to be autonomous, but in a more complex model, government spending rises with national income. Export spending consists of foreign purchases and therefore is the component of aggregate demand least dependent on the level of national income.

5. Each major sector — consumers, investors, governments, and foreign buyers — determine their planned expenditures independently and for each level of income. The economy is at its equilibrium level of national income when the total planned expenditure, or aggregate demand is equal to aggregate supply or output. Thus, if any of the sectors changes its planned expenditures, the economy will likely return to equilibrium only at some other level of national income.

7. The multiplier effect of successive rounds of spending increases national income by more than the initial increase in spending. The size of the multiplier is the reciprocal of the sum of the marginal propensities to save and to import. Two special cases of the general multiplier — the foreign trade multiplier and the balanced budget multiplier — emphasize that an increase in exports will usually induce an increase in imports, and that an equal increase in government expenditures and tax revenues will increase national income by the same amount.

8. If individuals collectively try to increase saving at any given level of income, they will actually save less because the withdrawal of spending will lead to a lower level of national income: this is called the Paradox of Thrift.

9. The accelerator is the effect that a change in consumption has on the level of investment. Accelerated investment, when combined with the multiplier effect, can produce wide swings in the level of economic activity.

10. A deflationary gap is the additional spending required to raise the level of aggregate planned demand sufficiently to lead the economy to the full employment level of national income. An inflationary gap is the reduction in planned aggregate demand required to return the economy to the full employment level of output.

11. The Keynesian model of national income determination implies that inflation will not occur until the economy is at the full employment level of output, but it is now widely observed that inflation and unemployment occur at the same time.

12. Because the classical economists assumed full employment would prevail, they assumed that an increase in the money supply could only increase the level of prices. Later, in the quantity equation of exchange, they recognized that an increase in the velocity of money could also increase prices, and that both increased money supply and velocity could increase real output if there was some unemployment.

13. Keynes linked the real sector with the monetary sector through the effect of interest rates on investment. Interest rates are determined by the supply and demand for money. Money is demanded (or held) for transactions, precautionary reasons, and speculation. The higher the level of income, the more money will be held at any given interest rate. Thus the money market can be in equilibrium at different interest rates. The economy will be in general equilibrium at the interest rate and level of national income which produces equilibrium in both the real and monetary sectors.

Review and Discussion Questions

1. Can the MPC be equal to 1? Can the MPC be equal to the APC? Explain. Why is it important to know the MPC for specific groups and for the whole economy?

2. Distinguish between a shift in the propensity to consume and a movement along the consumption curve. What explanations could be offered for each type of change?

3. Why is the value of the multiplier calculated from the marginal propensity to consume, rather than from the average propensity to consume?

4. "Since actual saving must equal actual investment (when there are no government or foreign trade sectors), there is no reason to worry about the relationship between planned saving and planned investment." Do you agree? Why?

5. Why are $AS = AD$ and $I + G + E = S + T + M$ both suitable as definitions for the equilibrium level of national income? Is one preferable to the other for any reason?

6. Which is generally the more important factor in its effect on national income, the multiplier or the accelerator? Why?

7. Explain why the aggregate supply curve is shown as a 45° line in Figure 4.3.

8. Why do economists not include an individual's purchases of stocks or bonds in the definition of investment?

9. Why is the quantity equation of exchange necessarily true?

10. Trace carefully the process by which an increase in the supply of money could lead to an increase in the level of employment. In what circumstances would such an increase in the money supply have no effect on employment?

11. "The federal government should try to maintain a stable interest rate to maintain the economy at its general equilibrium level of GNP." Do you agree? Why?

Sources and Selected Readings

Ackley, Gardner. *Macroeconomic Theory*. New York: Macmillan, 1961.

Branson, W.H. *Macroeconomic Theory and Policy*. New York: Harper and Row, 1972.

Dillard, Dudley. *The Economics of John Maynard Keynes*. New York: Prentice-Hall, 1948.

Hansen, Alvin. *A Guide to Keynes*. New York: McGraw-Hill, 1953.

Heilbroner, Robert L. *Understanding Macroeconomics*, 4th ed. Englewood Cliffs. N.J.: Prentice-Hall, 1972.

Keynes, John Maynard. *The General Theory of Employment, Interest and Money*. London: Macmillan, 1936.

Sawyer, John A. *Macroeconomics: Theory and Policy in the Canadian Economy*. Toronto: Macmillan, 1975.

Schultze, Chas. L. *National Income Analysis*, 3rd ed. Englewood Cliffs, N.J.: Prentice-Hall, 1972.

Sirkin, Gerald. *Introduction to Macroeconomic Theory*, 3rd ed. Homewood, Ill.: Irwin, 1970.

Stewart, Michael. *Keynes and After*. Baltimore: Penguin Books, 1967.

5   Money and Banking in Canada

What Is Money?

Since changes in the money supply can have a substantial effect on the performance of the economy, it is important to know precisely what is meant by "money" and how it is possible to change the total quantity of money available to the economy. Consider first something that is equally as interesting to most people, namely food. Two different answers might be given to the question "What is food?" One answer would list the *functions* of food: it nourishes the body; it provides epicurean delight; it may even act as a pacifier for neurotics. A different type of answer would list the numerous *items which serve as food*, from raw fish to baked Alaska. Similarly, the question "What is money?" is answered in terms of its functions and the items serving these functions.

Functions of Money

The most obvious use for money is in the innumerable transactions occurring every day in the Canadian economy. No longer does anyone purchase goods or services by offering goats, beads or beaver skins. Occasionally a guitar may be swapped or traded for part-ownership of a motorcycle but this can be treated as a unique case: the person who gave up the guitar does not make a continuous practice of purchasing items by trading guitars. Instead, it is money that is normally used to buy goods and services and it is money that is readily accepted by the sellers of these commodities.

Money is therefore defined as something readily and widely accepted as a medium for the exchange of goods and services.

An equally common but less obvious function of money is as a *unit of account*; prices of all goods and services can be expressed in terms of money. The selling price of an automobile is stated as 4,295 dollars, not 7 cows or 65 days of manual labour. Anyone who has travelled in another country can appreciate how important it is that prices be expressed in terms of the medium of exchange (or currency) with which he is familiar. Canadian tourists have been heard to mutter in front of store windows around the world, "How much is that in our money?" Although they may be carrying foreign currency, the unit of account they are using to determine the relative prices of the goods is the Canadian dollar.

The third function of money is as a *store of value*. Since the value of the goods and services which can be purchased in the present can be expressed in terms of money, it follows that the total claim on future goods and services can also be expressed in terms of money. To say that one's assets are worth $10,000 is to say that one has a claim on goods and services valued or priced at a total of $10,000. Money is an extremely convenient way to postpone consumption of goods and services since money can be stored more easily than any other commodity. One disadvantage, however, is that prices may rise, resulting in a lower future consumption in real terms. Some people who expect price increases may prefer to buy and store goods, while others hold assets, such as real estate, which tend to rise in price as the prices of consumer goods rise.

Alternatively, if prices fall, the person who holds money rather than stocks will find that he can buy more goods in the future. But even if inflation seems inevitable, most persons will use money as some of their store of value because it is so convenient to have these funds available as they are required in the near future.

Since money serves so well as a store of value or as a measure of one's assets, it also serves well as a standard of deferred payments, or debts. One's debts can be recorded in terms of money, and can be repaid with money.

Characteristics of Money

The purposes money must serve determine its major characteristics. There are many transactions to be made every day and in several locations: at the bus stop, the cafeteria, the newsstand, the drycleaner, and so on. Money not only must be readily acceptable; it must also be easy to carry, but not so small that it is easily lost. A five-dollar coin the size of a Canadian nickel could be lost or misplaced easily. Alternatively, the use of paper currency for denominations of less than one dollar would be a nuisance.

Money must also be divisible, so that very small transactions (such as the purchase of postage stamps and matches) can be accommodated. Thus most monetary units, whether dollars, pounds, francs, or liras, are divided into 100 parts, called cents, centimes, and so on. Money should be durable enough to be exchanged in many transactions and to be carried or held by many persons.

Development of Money

Money is one of the major inventions of mankind, making it possible to abandon the barter system and to develop the division and specialization of labour. Barter required what has been called a coincidence of wants. Someone who wanted a cow and was willing to offer fifty bushels of grain in exchange needed to find a person who not only wanted to trade a cow, but also was willing to take fifty bushels of grain (or less) in return. The barter system acted as a deterrent to the specialization of labour and trade since it was more convenient to be self-sufficient, producing only the amount of each commodity that one's family required.

Early Problems. Items such as spices, salt, and finely made clothing or shoes could not be produced by each family, however, and early forms of money appeared to facilitate trade in these items. Gold, silver, and other rare metals were used because the demand for them for ornamental uses had established their high value. Thus the physical amount required for most transactions was quite small. The convenience of gold to facilitate trade was partly offset by other problems. Since every transaction required a different amount of gold, it was necessary to measure precisely the right number of ounces or grams in each case. This was not only a nuisance, it also provoked numberless disputes about the reliability of the weigh-scales in question. This problem was met by striking coins containing a specific amount of gold or other metal. This amount was then stamped on the face of the coin. Coins of various values were produced so that the proper combination of coins could be presented to meet almost any asking price.

Goldsmith Receipts. Money also had to be kept safe from theft. Persons who had considerable quantities of gold and gold coins began to deposit these with the local goldsmith or jeweller for safe-keeping. The goldsmith issued a receipt for the deposit, perhaps adding that he promised that the required amount of gold would be available whenever the depositor required it. People soon realized that it was a nuisance to collect gold from the goldsmith each time a large purchase was made, and to take gold back to his shop following each major sale. The goldsmith's receipt could be exchanged instead. This process could continue as long as the recipients of the goldsmith's receipt were confident that there actually was gold "backing" the receipt or certificate. Only occasionally would someone demand gold from the goldsmith in exchange for the receipt, perhaps to make a purchase in another town, or because a prospective seller would not accept the receipt, or simply to confirm that the gold was available.

The goldsmith found that on any given day he would be asked for only a very small proportion of the gold he held for his depositors. Some of the gold could be loaned to borrowers, provided that the goldsmith did not loan too much and that the repayments were arranged to assure that the goldsmith would always have enough to meet his depositors' demands. The borrowers likely would not take loans in the form of gold, but rather as goldsmith's receipts, since they too were able to use his receipts to make purchases. Thus gold held by the goldsmith represented only a fraction of the claims on gold represented by his outstanding receipts. The smaller this fraction, the larger were the profits to be made on loans. But the risk of being unable to meet the demand for gold on any given day also became greater as the ratio of claims to actual gold holdings increased.

From Goldsmith to Banker. Gradually, the goldsmiths found it more profitable to spend their time as bankers than as craftsmen. As banks developed, the goldsmith's receipt was replaced by paper currency printed by the banks. This paper currency needed to be backed by gold or silver, at least to some reasonable fraction of the face value of the currency, if it was to be readily accepted. A "run" on a bank would occur when it was discovered that a bank could not meet demands to convert the bank currency into gold or silver. Even the suspicion that a bank was not holding sufficient gold could lead to its collapse if enough depositors demanded their funds at one time. Many such "runs" occurred and many banks failed during the nineteenth and early twentieth century, until banks came under closer government regulation and supervision.

Fiat Money. It is only recently, by comparison with the long history of banking, that the paper currency of the private banks has been replaced by the *legal tender* or *fiat money* issued by central banks under government direction. Most countries now have a central bank operating under varying degrees of government control. The Bank of Canada, described more fully later in this chapter, is the only bank in Canada which can issue legal tender: the only currency which, by law, *must be accepted for payments of debts.*

The Bank of Canada issues both coins and paper currency. Although the metal contained in the coin has some value, this is much less than the face value of the coins. There is no gold, other metal, or any other commodity backing Canada's paper currency. The value of the Bank of Canada currency depends entirely on the willingness of Canadians to accept the currency. What now matters more than whether paper currency is convertible into gold, is whether the currency can be easily counterfeited, whether too much or too little money is put into circulation, and whether the government is pursuing other appropriate policies for price stability.

Cheques. The practice of depositing gold or gold coins with the goldsmith gave rise to another form of money in addition to the goldsmith's receipt or gold certificate. A depositor might not wish to transfer *all* of his gold holdings to someone else; he could not therefore simply pass on the goldsmith's receipt for the full amount. Instead, the depositor could write a note requesting the goldsmith to give a stated amount of gold to the person specified in the note. The recipient of the note might decide to "cash" the note, that is, actually withdraw the gold, or he might simply have the goldsmith issue a receipt acknowledging this transfer of a claim to a specified amount of gold. This process has continued almost unchanged to the modern use of bank deposits, with cheques written against these deposits or accounts to make payments as required. Note that it is the deposit account, and not the cheque, which is counted as money. The cheque simply provides a convenient method for transferring this money.

Alternative Definitions of the Money Supply

The quantity of money available in the economy at any given time is often defined simply as the total value of coins and paper currency in circulation outside the banks and the total value of bank deposits.

Coins and paper currency held by the banks cannot be included since this money is not immediately available for spending. It becomes available only when a deposit is withdrawn in the form of currency, or a cheque is "cashed" rather than deposited. Table 5.1 shows that at the end of 1974 the value of coins and currency in circulation was $5,791 million.

Table 5.1
Money Supply in Canada
December*, 1974
(millions of dollars)

Currency outside banks:		5,791
Notes	5,145	
Coins	646	
Chequable deposits (Can. $ only):		
Chartered banks: Government of Canada	4,834	
Personal savings	6,052	
Demand	9,515	
Trust companies	492	
Mortgage loan companies	166	
Total		21,059
Non-chequable, term, or notice deposits:		
Chartered banks: Personal	23,394	
Non-personal	11,770	
Credit unions and caisses		
populaires	7,507	
Trust companies	10,890	
Mortgage loan companies	4,627	
Quebec savings banks	850	
Provincial governments banks	693	
Total		59,731
Money Supply		
Narrow definition: currency and chartered bank demand deposits		15,306
Conventional definition: currency and chartered bank deposits, excluding Government of Canada deposits		56,522
Broad definition: currency and all deposits in all financial institutions		86,581

* Data for currency and chartered bank deposits are December averages. Other data are as of December 31.
Source: *Bank of Canada Review.*

The growth of non-bank financial institutions which hold deposits for the general public has led to some dissatisfaction with the simple definition of money: not all bank deposits can be spent immediately, and cheques can be written on some deposits at the other institutions.

Consequently, the quantity of money is said to be "narrowly defined" or "broadly defined" depending on the type of deposits included in the definition. The *narrow definition* (frequently termed "M-1") includes coins and paper currency in circulation and demand deposits at the chartered banks. A common or *conventional definition* of money (frequently termed "M-2") includes narrowly defined money plus all other deposits at chartered banks, with the exception of Government of Canada deposits. The *broad definition* (some would say "broadest", and describe M-2 money as broadly defined) includes currency in circulation plus all deposits at chartered banks and other financial institutions such as credit unions, mortgage and trust companies, and provincial savings banks.

Deposits at non-bank financial institutions are sometimes omitted from definitions of money because they are not subject to the same regulations that cover deposits at chartered banks but they nevertheless function as money. Government of Canada deposits at chartered banks are usually omitted when the emphasis is on changes in the money supply because these deposits can be changed as part of the program to implement a specific monetary policy, as will be explained near the end of this chapter. Federal government deposits are nonetheless available for spending and constitute a substantial part of the money supply.

A related category, *near-money*, should be considered when the money supply is measured because some types of assets can easily be converted into bank deposits, and thus represent a potential sharp increase in the money supply. Near-money includes the general public's holdings of federal government bills, bonds, and savings bonds because these can be readily sold or redeemed and converted to chequable deposits. They are not money because they cannot be used directly as a medium of exchange.

The Canadian Banking System

The Canadian *banking system* consists of the chartered banks and a central bank, the Bank of Canada. These form an important part of the larger *financial system* which includes institutions performing only some of the functions of chartered banks: trust companies, insurance companies, mortgage companies, savings banks, credit unions, mutual and pension funds, consumer finance and other financial acceptance companies, and stock and bond brokers. These other financial institutions are closely related to the chartered banks through the similarity of the services provided by each type of institution: provision of loans and mortgages, administration of trusts and funds, as well as the acceptance of deposit accounts. The banks, however, have unique privileges and responsibilities which distinguish them from the other institutions and which are discussed at length in the next section.

The number of chartered banks varies as existing banks merge or close and new banks are established. As of January, 1976, there were ten active Canadian chartered banks. In order of their total assets in 1975, they were the Royal Bank, Canadian Imperial Bank of Commerce, Bank of Montreal, Bank of Nova Scotia, Toronto Dominion Bank, Banque Canadienne Nationale, Banque Provinciale, Mercantile Bank, Bank of British Columbia, and Unity Bank. In addition, there was the Canadian Commercial and Industrial Bank which had just been chartered in July, 1975. Some of these banks have branches in every province and in several other countries while other banks operate primarily in a single province. Each bank — but not each branch — is chartered, or licensed, by Parliament under the Bank Act and is regulated by the provisions of this Act.

The Bank of Canada

The Bank of Canada Act of 1934 provided for the creation of a central bank, the Bank of Canada. The responsibilities of the Bank were summarized in the preamble to the Bank of Canada Act in the following terms:

> to regulate credit and currency in the best interests of the economic life of the nation, to control and protect the external value of the national monetary unit [the dollar], and to mitigate by its influence fluctuations in the general level of production, trade, prices and employment, so far as may be possible within the scope of monetary action, and generally to promote the economic and financial welfare of the Dominion.

In other words, the Bank of Canada was charged with regulating the supply of money in an effort to achieve full employment, price stability, economic growth, and a viable balance of payments. The federal government appoints the Bank's directors who in turn appoint the Governor of the Bank for a term of 7 years. It must be emphasized, however, that the Bank of Canada is not a direct part of the government as is, for example, the Department of Finance. The Governor of the Bank is responsible to Parliament rather than to a particular cabinet minister: nevertheless, the federal cabinet can veto the decisions of the Bank's executive council.

The Bank's monetary policy was therefore expected to be interdependent with the federal government's actions designed to meet these goals. Nevertheless, the Bank of Canada was intended to be *independent* of the direct control of the federal government in order to exercise separate judgment on the policies most suitable for particular circumstances, and on the techniques for implementing these policies.

The principles governing the relationship of the Bank of Canada and the federal government were made more explicit by Mr. Louis Rasminsky when he became Governor of the Bank of Canada in 1961:

> I believe that it is essential that the responsibilities in relation to monetary policy should be clarified in the public mind and in the legislation. I do not suggest a precise formula but I have in mind two main principles to be established: (1) in the ordinary course of events, the Bank has the responsibility for monetary policy, and (2) if the Government disapproves of the monetary policy being carried out by the Bank, it has the right and responsibility to direct the Bank as to the policy which the Bank is to carry out.[1]

In practice, however, the Minister of Finance and the Governor of the Bank have tended to coordinate directly their economic policies in pursuit of their common goals.[2]

The regulation of the money supply to stabilize employment, prices, and the foreign exchange rate of the dollar is the main responsibility of the Bank of Canada. The Bank does, however, have a number of other important functions. These can be described simply as acting as "the government's bank" and as "the bankers' bank".

In its role as the federal government's bank, the Bank of Canada provides *economic advice* to the government, through meetings of Bank officials with people from the federal Department of Finance, and more formally through the annual report of the Governor and his occasional speeches. The balance sheet of the Bank of Canada as presented in Table 5.2 illustrates some of the other ways in which the Bank serves the federal government. Some of the government's bank deposits are held at the Bank of Canada, although a comparison of Tables 5.2 and 5.3 shows that at the end of 1974, the government held only $17 million at the Bank of Canada, while it held almost $4.7 billion at the chartered banks. Although this ratio varies somewhat, the largest part of government funds are held at the chartered banks.

The Bank of Canada manages the government's *bond issues*: the sale to the public of new federal government bonds, the retirement of maturing government bonds, and the conversion of existing bonds to new bonds. The Bank can also make *advances* or loans to the

---

[1] *Submission by the Bank of Canada to the Royal Commission on Banking and Finance, May 31, 1962*, p. 23.

[2] One major exception to this practice was the growing conflict between the views of Mr. James Coyne when he was Governor, and the Minister of Finance, Mr. Donald Fleming, which ended with the resignation of Mr. Coyne in 1961.

Table 5.2

**Bank of Canada
Assets and Liabilities, December 31, 1974
(millions of dollars)**

Assets		Liabilities		
Government of Canada securities 6,979		Notes in circulation		6,291
Treasury bills	1,590	✓Held by chartered banks	1,078	
Other securities	5,389	Held by others	5,213	
Advances		Deposits (in Canadian dollars)		2,479
to Government of Canada	0	Government of Canada	17	
to chartered banks and		✓ Chartered banks	2,361	
savings banks	8	Foreign chartered banks		
Foreign currency	578	and others	101	
Investments in I.D.B.	965	Foreign currency liabilities		2
Other assets	654	Other liabilities		412
Total Assets	9,184	Total liabilities		9,184

Source: *Bank of Canada Review.*

federal government, but this is not a significant function because the Bank can provide funds to the federal government in other forms.

Much more important is the Bank's role in handling the government's weekly sale of *treasury bills*. These are short-term (3 or 6 months) bonds which provide the major day-to-day cash needs of the government. Treasury bills have a high face value, of $100,000 or more, and are purchased by the chartered banks and other large financial institutions. The face value of the treasury bill is the amount for which the bill will be redeemed on maturity. In order to realize a return on these short-term assets, potential purchasers tender an offer to purchase at some amount below the face value. The difference represents the net return which is expressed as the treasury bill yield.

The bills are sold, in quantities determined by the government's current financial needs, to the highest bidder, who is thus the one willing to accept the lowest yield. If, however, the tendered prices are not high enough — that is, if the yield demanded is thought to be too high relative to other prevailing interest rates — the Bank of Canada buys as many of the bills as are necessary to meet the government's needs. This mechanism enables the Bank of Canada to provide funds for the government but only after funds have been sought from the private financial sector at competitive interest rates. It also enables the federal government to obtain the required funds without causing interest rates to be bid up, should the Bank decide that it is inappropriate for rates to rise in the existing circumstances. In a similar manner, the Bank of Canada may buy new federal government bonds if an insufficient number of these is sold in the private sector.

The Bank of Canada acts as a *bankers' bank* mainly by accepting deposits of the chartered banks, foreign central banks, and other official foreign institutions. The deposits of the chartered banks are the portions of the chartered banks' cash reserves which these banks choose to hold at the Bank of Canada rather than in the form of paper currency and coins in their own tills or vaults. The liability items in Table 5.2, "notes held by the chartered banks" and "Canadian dollar deposits of chartered banks" show the proportion of each held in the central bank and at the chartered banks. The value for these two items equal the assets entry in Table 5.3, "Bank of Canada deposits and notes".

The Bank of Canada may also make *advances, or loans, to the chartered banks,* but only as "a lender of last resort". The Bank prefers not to make loans to the chartered banks and thus usually sets the interest rate it charges on these advances, the *Bank Rate,* just high enough so that the chartered banks will look to other banks and financial institutions for the funds required. During the 1970s, the Bank Rate has been in the range of 5¼ to 9¼ per cent. In practice, advances from the Bank of Canada are for 7 days only; this together with a Bank Rate set at the appropriate level keeps Bank of Canada advances at low levels, usually less than $10 million.

Finally, the Bank of Canada acts as a *clearing house* for the chartered banks by transferring deposits from the account of one chartered bank at the Bank of Canada to the deposit account of another chartered bank. When cheques are cleared at the clearing houses of the Canadian Bankers' Association, by totalling the amounts drawn against one bank to be deposited in any of the others, the clearing houses advise the Bank of Canada of the net credits or debits so that the Bank can make these adjustments. Since only chartered banks can hold accounts at the Bank of Canada, other financial institutions must hold accounts at the chartered banks in order to participate in this clearing process.

Banking as a Business

The federal government and the Bank of Canada determine how much money should be available in Canada at any given time, but the operations of the chartered banks are essential in determining whether this decision will be realized.

It is because banks operate as private, profit-seeking businesses that the monetary authorities can predict fairly accurately the effects of their initial decisions on the chartered banks. The specific effects on prices and real output are much more difficult to determine. Some of the reasons for this are discussed in terms of the limitations on monetary policy in Chapter 6.

Banks have several sources of income. Although they pay interest on the savings accounts of their depositors, they also receive income from the services provided for depositors. A fee is charged for processing cheques on chequing accounts, for the use of safe deposit boxes, for cashing foreign cheques, and for exchanging foreign currencies. The major portion of bank income, however, is earned through the use of depositors' funds to purchase securities such as government bonds and to make loans for consumer purchases, business activities, and mortgages.

The consolidated balance sheet for all chartered banks is shown in Table 5.3 as a summary of the principal business activities of banks. Almost 90 per cent of the chartered banks' liabilities are in the form of deposit accounts. The banks hold some deposits of the federal and provincial governments, and of other banks but the largest part of the deposits are public savings and other notice or non-chequing deposits. Since these are the funds the banks will use to earn income, the banks compete actively to attract depositors.

Table 5.3

Canadian Chartered Banks
Assets and Liabilities, December 31, 1974
(millions of dollars)

Assets		Liabilities		
Bank of Canada deposits and notes	3,439	Deposits (in Canadian dollars)		58,798
Canadian day-to-day loans	343	Government of Canada		4,682
Treasury bills	3,703	Provincial governments		622
Government of Canada bonds	4,358	Personal savings	29,789	
Call and short loans	1,029	Other notice	11,210	
Net foreign currency	−803	Other banks	925	
		Other demand	11,570	
Loans	38,255	Advances from Bank of Canada		8
Mortgages	6,023	Acceptances, guarantees, credit		4,288
Other Canadian securities	2,957	Other liabilities		2,144
Net Canadian dollar items in transit	2,542	Shareholders' equity		2,465
Other assets	5,859	Total Liabilities		$67,703
Total Assets	$67,703			

Source: *Bank of Canada Review.*

More than one-half of the banks' assets take the form of loans; another major item is Government of Canada bonds. The amounts shown for these items would be even larger, since these are important income-earning assets, but for the fact that the chartered banks are required by the Bank Act to hold some assets in liquid or very short-term forms. The banks must hold *primary or cash reserves* (as deposits at the Bank of Canada or currency notes at the banks) equal to 12 per cent of the demand or current deposits and 4 per cent of the savings and notice deposits. Since the dollar value of savings and notice deposits is larger than the value of demand deposits, the total cash reserves of chartered banks have been about 6 per cent of total deposits.

The chartered banks are also required to hold *secondary reserves* of near-money in the form of day-to-day loans and treasury bills. Day-to-day loans are very short-term loans made mainly to securities dealers; treasury bills are short-term federal government bonds. Although most treasury bills have a 3-month maturity date, they can easily be bought or sold and therefore are highly liquid assets: they are readily converted into money at only a slight discount from face value.

The secondary reserve requirement may be varied by the Bank of Canada, as a percentage of the chartered banks' total deposits, between 0 and 12 per cent. It has ranged from a high of 9 per cent in 1970-71 to a low of 5.5 per cent in 1975. Altering the secondary reserve requirement instead of the primary reserves enables the Bank of Canada to alter the supply of funds available for longer-term loans while still allowing the banks to earn some return on these reserve assets. Increasing the secondary reserve requirement also has the effect of forcing the chartered banks to increase their purchases of treasury bills at a time when the federal government needs to use this method to increase its funds.

Expansion and Contraction
of Chartered Bank Deposits

The main purpose of this chapter is to show how it is possible to change the money supply. This occurs primarily through the actions of the chartered banks as the economy's principal source of loans.

One of the most fascinating aspects of the banking system is its ability to expand substantially the total bank deposits on the basis of small initial changes in these deposits. This process can be illustrated by following a particular case through the banking system. Suppose that a college student receives a money order from England for $1,000 as an inheritance from the estate of his wealthy aunt. He takes the money order to the bank and asks to have it credited to his deposit accounts, one part to his savings account and the rest to his chequing account. This action increases the deposit liability of his bank by $1,000 but it also increases the bank's assets by $1,000 when the bank clears the money order with the English bank that originally issued the money order. *Assume* the division between the student's savings and chequing account was such that the bank is required to hold an average primary reserve of 10 per cent ($100) against the combined deposits.

The bank now has *excess reserves* of $900 since its cash reserves increased by $1,000 but it must hold only an additional $100 in reserves against the new deposit of $1,000. In order to increase its income, the bank will want to put the $900 into income-earning assets such as loans. (Some income-earning assets must be in very short-term form to meet the secondary reserve requirements but this can be ignored in this simplified explanation.) These changes can be shown in an abbreviated form of the chartered banks' balance sheet. Instead of showing the several items appearing in Table 5.3, the balance sheet below simply indicates the *changes* which take place. Increases are shown by a plus sign and decreases by a minus sign.

Chartered Banks' Balance Sheet

Assets		*Liabilities*	
Reserves	+1,000	Deposits	+1,000
[*required* +100 / *excess* +900]			

Fortunately for the bank, another student appears to obtain a loan, and by convenient coincidence he would like $900. The bank makes the loan by crediting his chequing account with the $900; he can now write cheques to meet his outstanding account at the college for tuition and residence fees. For the sake of convenience, assume that the bank is required to hold 10 per cent or $90 reserves against this new chequing deposit, rather than the statutory requirement of 12 per cent. These further changes are shown as the second stage changes in the banks' balance sheet.

Chartered Banks' Balance Sheet

Assets		*Liabilities*	
Reserves	+1,000	Deposits	+1,000 [*1st stage*]
[*required* +100 / *excess* +900]			
Loans	+ 900	Deposits	+ 900 [*2nd stage*]

Since the borrowing student has immediate debts to meet, he writes cheques on his new account for $900 and gives these to the college fees office, which in turn deposits this amount in the college's chequing account at another bank. This transaction reduces the deposits at the first bank by $900, reduces the reserves it is required to hold by $90, but leaves the increased assets in the form of a $900 loan unchanged. Meanwhile the second bank has increased its deposit liabilities by $900 and its reserve requirements by $90. But the new deposit liability also enables it to increase its loans by 90 per cent of $900, or $810. Note that the new $900 deposit at the second bank resulted in a transfer of $900 reserves from the first bank to the second bank. This transfer takes place between the accounts each chartered bank holds at the Bank of Canada.

Again assume someone appears seeking a loan of $810, opens an account and has this amount credited to his account. The banks' balance sheet would now show the following changes:

Chartered Banks' Balance Sheet

Assets			*Liabilities*		
First Bank					
Reserves		+1,000	Deposits	+1,000	[*1st stage*]
required	+100				
excess	+900				
Loans		+ 900	Deposits	+ 900	[*2nd stage*]
Reserves		− 900	Deposits	− 900	
					[*3rd stage*]
Second Bank					
Reserves		+ 900	Deposits	+ 900	
required	+ 90				
excess	+810				
Loans		+ 810	Deposits	+ 810	[*4th stage*]

This process would continue as long as borrowers wrote cheques for the full amount of their new deposits and recipients of these cheques deposited the receipts instead of "cashing" the cheques by requesting currency. Continuation of the process also depends on the banks' making loans for the full amount of their excess reserves. Since the banks may not always be "fully loaned up" and since some of the cheques may be "cashed", the process is unlikely to continue to the point where new loans and deposits are infinitely small. If the processs continued through several stages, however, one can see that the sum of all the deposits resulting from the initial deposit of $1,000 would be substantial. By the end of the fourth stage shown in the balance sheet, net deposits have increased by $1,710 in addition to the initial deposit. The next stage would show the cancellation of the $810 deposit credited to the second borrower but remaining for the recipient of these funds, then there would be a deposit of $729, and so on.

The final or total increase, including the initial deposit can be calculated using a formula similar to the one used in Chapter 4 to compute the value of the national income multiplier.

The final change will be equal to 1/*R* multiplied by the value of the initial deposit, where *R* is the ratio of required reserves to the total deposits.

$$\frac{1}{R} \times 1,000$$
$$\frac{1}{\frac{1}{10}} \times 1,000$$

Thus, the final increase in this case will be $1,000 × 10, or $10,000. If the required cash reserve ratio had been 5 percent or 1/20, the final change would have been $1,000 × 20, or $20,000. Since the actual cash reserve requirement in the Canadian banking system has averaged about 6 per cent, the potential expansion is about 16 times any initial change in deposits. The actual expansion, however, is limited by the secondary reserve requirement. That is, some of the banks' reserves in excess of the primary reserve requirement must be held as secondary reserves — mainly treasury bills — rather than being available for loans.

Although there is an apparent similarity between the national income multiplier and the expansion of bank deposits, particularly in the formulae for calculating the final results, these two processes should not be confused in any way. They deal with quite different features of the economy. The term "multiplier" is reserved for the particular process of an expansion or contraction in national income resulting from an initial change in spending. This term *cannot* be used for the expansion and contraction of the money supply. In fact, there is no similar generally accepted term in the latter case; one simply refers to the deposit adjustment process. The process by which the money supply is contracted will be described in the next section on the operations of the Bank of Canada.

Techniques for Regulating the Money Supply

The most important activity of the Bank of Canada is regulating the total amount of money available in the economy. The Bank is able to do this through a number of techniques, some of which involve *the unique power of the Bank of Canada to create chartered bank reserves*. There is no longer any "backing" for money created by the Bank of Canada. Prior to World War II, the Bank was limited to creating money equal to four times the value of its holdings of gold. This ceiling was removed in 1940 to allow the Bank to meet the increased monetary requirements of the wartime economy.

The only factor now governing the expansion of the money supply is the confidence of the Canadian public, and other countries, that the Bank of Canada is maintaining the proper monetary level for the best performance of the economy. This explains why the Bank can create money, but not how it does so. Perhaps an even greater puzzle is how the Bank can *reduce* the money supply, since regulating the money supply entails being able to reduce the amount as well as to increase it. The methods the Bank can use to change the money supply are described in this section, but a discussion of when the money supply should be changed is reserved for the next chapter, which deals with the joint actions of the Bank and the government in pursuing full employment and price stability, and in Chapter 7 where international finance is discussed.

Open Market Operations

The Bank of Canada's buying and selling of securities such as federal government bonds and treasury bills is termed the Bank's *open market operations*. The market in which these securities are traded is the bond market; it is "open" because there is essentially no restriction on who can buy or sell bonds. The bond market is not as well defined as the stock market — with the Vancouver, Toronto, and Montreal Stock Exchanges to bring buyers and sellers together — but nevertheless bond trading occurs daily on a large scale through a communications network of telephones and telex machines linking bond brokers' offices. The Bank of Canada, like the chartered banks and many other financial institutions, holds government securities as part of its assets. Of the federal government's outstanding marketable bonds and treasury bills, representing a debt of approximately $21 billion on June 30, 1975, the Bank of Canada held $7.4 billion and the chartered banks held $7.6 billion.[3] Since the Bank of Canada's holdings form such a substantial part of the outstanding government securities, the Bank can exercise considerable influence on the prices of these securities.

What happens when the Bank of Canada deals in government securities in the open market? The bonds which are traded carry a stated maturity value and interest rate. A one-year bond may state, for example, that one year after the bond was issued, the government will redeem the bond for the face value of, say, $1,000 and will pay interest of 6 per cent. If the Bank of Canada wishes to *sell* bonds it can offer to sell this $1,000 bond for $980. The actual yield to the bearer will therefore be the $60 interest payment plus the additional gain of $20 when the bond is redeemed. The yield is $80 on an asset of $980, or 8.2 per cent. If the Bank wishes to *buy* bonds, it would offer to pay a price above the face value, of say $1,020. Thus the Bank of Canada can alter the price at which it is willing to buy or sell bonds until other institutions dealing in the bond market, mainly chartered banks, are willing to buy or sell bonds to the total value desired by the Bank.

Deposit Expansion. The effect on the money supply of the Bank's open market operations can be traced in the following steps. If the

---

[3] In addition to the $20 billion in marketable securities, the federal government had a further debt of $13 billion in non-marketable Canada Savings Bonds and $750 million in securities held by federal government accounts and funds.

Bank buys a bond for $1,000 from an insurance company, the company sends the bond to the Bank and in return receives a cheque for $1,000. The insurance company presents this cheque to its chartered bank to be credited to the deposit account of the company. The chartered bank thus increases its liability to the company by $1,000. When the chartered bank presents the cheque to the Bank of Canada, the Bank creates assets for the chartered bank in the form of $1,000 bank reserves. The Bank of Canada has increased its liabilities by $1,000, in the form of chartered bank reserves, but it has also added the $1,000 bond to its assets. These *changes* are shown below in the balance sheets of the three institutions involved.

Insurance Company Balance Sheet

Assets		Liabilities
Securities	−$1,000	[*no change*]
Deposits	+$1,000	

Chartered Bank Balance Sheet

Assets		Liabilities	
Bank reserves	+$1,000	Deposits	+$1,000

Bank of Canada Balance Sheet

Assets		Liabilities	
Securities	+$1,000	Bank reserves	+$1,000

The process does not stop at this point. The initial increase in bank deposits leads to an expansion of deposits in the same manner as did the $1,000 inheritance discussed in the section on expansion of bank deposits. Assume a cash reserve requirement of 10 per cent: the chartered bank is required to hold only $100 in reserves against the new deposit of $1,000. It is therefore anxious to loan the excess reserves of $900 in order to obtain additional income. The process can be traced through to the point where the initial $1,000 deposit has led to an additional $9,000 in deposits, for an overall increase in the money supply of $10,000. Thus the Bank of Canada can be said to have *created* money to the extent that its cheque, which was written against no deposit account, became a $1,000 deposit in the banking system. Of greater quantitative significance, however, is the subsequent *expansion* of the money supply which occurred through the banking system.

Deposit Contraction. If the Bank of Canada wishes to contract the money supply, it can do so by reversing the process that is initiated through its open market operations. Suppose the Bank of Canada sells a $1,000 bond to the insurance company. The company writes a cheque for $1,000 on its deposit account and sends this to the Bank of Canada in exchange for the bond. The Bank reduces its liability to the chartered bank in question by reducing the bank reserves in an amount of $1,000. The chartered bank in turn reduces its liability to the insurance company by deducting $1,000 from the company's account. But again this is not the end of the process. The chartered bank's reserves have fallen by $1,000, only $100 of which was being held against the $1,000 deposit of the insurance company. The bank must therefore reduce other loans, and hence deposits, until it is back to the required level of cash reserves. Chartered banks do this either by calling in some of their demand loans, or more likely, by simply not re-lending funds received in repayment of loans. Thus, the initial sale of a $1,000 bond by the Bank of Canada leads to a $10,000 reduction in deposits and a $9,000 reduction in loans outstanding.

Features of Open Market Operations. There is one important difference between the expansion and the contraction of the money supply. The extent of the expansion depends on whether banks are able to loan all of their excess reserves, and whether all payments from deposit accounts are redeposited. The full extent of the contraction *must* occur, however, unless the banking system has been holding substantial amounts of excess reserves.

Open market operations influence the rate of interest, as well as the money supply, both directly and indirectly. If the Bank of Canada must make significant changes in the price of government bonds in order to obtain the desired changes in the money supply, these price changes will be reflected in the actual yield on bonds. An increase in the price of bonds lowers the bond yield; this has a downward influence on other interest rates since government bonds are one of several alternative assets for financial institutions. An increase in the money supply, given the demand for money, will also lower the interest rate, since banks will have to lower the rates charged on loans in order to find borrowers for the increase in available loan funds.

The advantage of open market operations is that they effect frequent small changes in the money supply without making it appear that the Bank of Canada is exerting authority in the financial system. Changes occur quickly and can be as widespread as the holding of government bonds. But the effects are not always predictable since the Bank does not have direct control of the consequences; it can only make the sale or purchase of bonds as attractive as possible. Moreover, to obtain a specific change in the money supply, the Bank may need to alter bond prices, and thus interest rates, by more than the Bank regards as reasonable. This would be particularly undesirable from the Bank's point of view if, for example, it forced interest rates upward just when it was also necessary to introduce a new issue of government bonds. Since the Bank acts on behalf of the government, it would be expected to minimize the interest rate the government needed to pay for its borrowed funds.

Transfer of Government of Canada Deposits

Since the Bank of Canada acts as banker for the federal government, the Bank has available a second technique for changing the level of bank reserves, and hence, deposits. If the Bank transfers federal government deposits from a chartered bank to the Bank of Canada (termed a "draw-down"), this has the same effect as the sale of bonds in the open market. If the Bank switches $10,000 from a chartered bank's reserves at the Bank of Canada to the Government of Canada account at the Bank of Canada, the chartered bank finds that it must make up cash reserves of $9,000. This leads to a contraction of deposits and loans as described previously.

Conversely, if the Bank switches $10,000 from the Government of Canada account at the Bank to the federal government's account at a chartered bank, by increasing the bank's cash reserves by $10,000 (termed a "redeposit"), there can be a further expansion of deposits and loans. Again, the potential total contraction must occur, but the expansion does not necessarily run to its full limit. The transfer of government deposits provides a useful method for reinforcing the effect the Bank is trying to achieve through open market operations. Although the transfer of deposit is used primarily when there are large seasonal withdrawals of currency, for example just prior to the Christmas vacation period, this technique is increasingly used as a day-to-day tool of monetary policy.

Changes in the Bank Rate

The Bank of Canada may also influence bank reserves and the money supply by changing the Bank Rate, the interest rate the Bank charges for advances or loans it makes to the chartered banks. If the Bank of Canada lowers the Bank Rate, financial institutions must also lower the rate they charge on loans to the chartered banks; otherwise, the chartered banks would borrow from the Bank of Canada. If a chartered bank borrows from the Bank of Canada, the Bank increases the chartered bank's cash reserves by the amount borrowed. The expansion of money then proceeds as in the previous cases of monetary expansion. But the effect will be short-lived, unless further advances are made, since these loans must be repaid within 7 days.

In practice, the Bank of Canada maintains the Bank Rate just high enough to encourage chartered banks to borrow elsewhere. The Bank Rate is a useful technique, however, for the Bank of Canada to influence interest rates directly. The Bank changes the Bank Rate fairly frequently (five times in 1973, four times in 1974, and twice in 1975), both as a *signal* of the monetary policy it is pursuing and in response to changing demands for funds in the private sector. A low Bank Rate indicates that banks will be able to obtain less expensive loans from the Bank of Canada if necessary, and that they should therefore lend to their customers more freely and at lower rates. A high Bank Rate would indicate that the Bank of Canada wants a reduction in the availability of loans and a higher interest rate. A change in the Bank Rate is used to bring about prompter changes in the monetary situation than would be possible if the Bank relied only on its open market operations and transfers of federal government deposits.

Changes in the Secondary Reserve Ratio

The three preceding techniques represent the methods commonly employed by the Bank of Canada in controlling the money supply. Another of the Bank's powers, that of specifying the percentage of chartered bank deposits to be held as secondary reserves (day-to-day loans and treasury bills), is used to reinforce the effects the Bank is trying to achieve through its other methods. When the Bank of Canada was established in 1934, there was no mention of secondary reserves in the Bank Act. The chartered banks were required to hold primary or cash reserves equal to 5 per cent of their deposits. In 1954, this requirement was amended to allow the Bank of Canada to vary the cash reserve ratio from 8 to 12 per cent of deposits in order to give the Bank another method of regulating the money supply.

An increase in the cash reserve ratio would have the same kind of contractive effect as a sale of bonds in the open market or a transfer of government deposits to the Bank of Canada. If the chartered banks had been "fully loaned up", that is if they had no excess reserves, the need to increase their cash reserves would lead them to reduce their loans and hence their deposits. Such a change in the cash reserve ratio, even if as small as a fraction of a percentage point, would require quite large and immediate changes in cash reserves on the part of all banks. Since this was such a powerful, blunt technique, it was never used by the Bank of Canada. The cash reserve requirement remained at 8 per cent from 1954 to 1967. A revision of the Bank Act in 1967 fixed the cash reserve requirement at 4 per cent of time or notice deposits and 12 per cent of demand deposits.

At the same time, the Act introduced a requirement of secondary reserves. The Bank of Canada was given the authority to vary this ratio between 0 and 12 per cent. Changes in the secondary reserve ratio have approximately the same effect on the money supply as would changes in the primary reserve ratio. In either case, an increase in the required ratio compels the banks to reduce their loans and deposits. But an increase in the secondary reserve requirement still allows the banks to earn some income on their reserves.

Moral Suasion

No discussion of techniques used by the Bank of Canada to control the money supply would be complete without a reference to "moral suasion". Because there are so few chartered banks in Canada, it is often suggested that the Governor of the Bank of Canada should be able to call together the bank presidents and persuade them to follow the monetary policies desired by the Bank. For example, the Bank might wish to avoid overall increases in the money supply while making more funds available for small businesses or residential mortgages. A selective policy of this kind could not be achieved with other techniques such as open market operations because their effects on the money supply are so widespread.

Selective controls of this kind, however, are difficult to implement because the banks are in competition with the other near-bank financial institutions like the trust companies and savings banks. If the chartered banks did try to comply with the wishes of the Bank of Canada, the near-banks probably would provide the funds to potential borrowers who had been turned away from the chartered banks. At a time when the chartered banks controlled a larger proportion of the economy's loanable funds, moral suasion was more feasible than it now is with the increasing significance of the near-banks. The use of moral suasion also depends very much on the attitude of the Governor toward the freedom of the chartered banks to operate within the conditions established by the Bank's other activities.

Another difficulty in implementing selective controls is the possibility that loans obtained for one purpose may be transferred to other uses. For example, if mortgage funds are to be made available but loans for consumer durables such as automobiles and household appliances are to be restricted, a family may take a larger mortgage on its new house and use some of the funds to purchase new appliances.

Money Supply and the Foreign Exchange Rate

Another important function of the Bank of Canada, as stated in the Bank of Canada Act, is "to control and protect the external value of the national monetary unit". The "external value of the national monetary unit" is the rate at which the Canadian dollar can be exchanged for other national currencies such as the American dollar, British pound, French franc, and so on. In other words, the Bank of Canada is responsible for the *foreign exchange rate* of the Canadian dollar. Much more will be said about foreign exchange rates in Chapter 7. A short note is required here, however, on the relationship of the money supply, foreign exchange reserves, and the foreign exchange rate of the Canadian dollar in preparation for the discussion of fiscal and monetary policy in the next chapter.

Foreign Exchange Rates. Foreign exchange rates can be determined either by government decree or by the unregulated market forces of supply and demand. In the first case, the rate is said to be *pegged* or *fixed*; in the second case, the rate is *floating* or *fluctuating*. When the foreign exchange rate is free to fluctuate, the rate is determined by the supply and demand for Canadian dollars. When foreign consumers want to buy more Canadian exports, payment must ultimately be made in Canadian dollars. Foreign currencies offered in exchange for Canadian exports are sold in foreign exchange markets operated by the central banks in exchange for Canadian dollars. This increase in the demand for Canadian dollars raises the price of the Canadian dollar in terms of other currencies. In other words, the foreign exchange rate of the Canadian dollar rises. Similarly, if foreign countries buy fewer Canadian exports, or Canadians increase their import expenditures, the foreign exchange rate of the Canadian dollar falls. The supply and demand for Canadian dollars depends not only on exports and imports, but also on the other items in the Balance of International Payments Accounts presented in Chapter 3.

Pegged Exchange Rate. From 1962 until 1970, the foreign exchange rate of the Canadian dollar was pegged by the Canadian government at the rate of $1.00 (Can.) = $0.925 (U.S.). The Canadian dollar was therefore worth about 8 per cent less than the American dollar in terms of foreign purchases or payments. In fixing the foreign exchange rate at this level, the Canadian government agreed that it would take the appropriate action necessary to offset supply or demand for Canadian dollars, in order to keep the rate within a narrow range around the agreed rate.

The major role of the Bank of Canada in maintaining the pegged rate was its administration of the Exchange Fund Account. When the foreign demand for Canadian dollars increased, the Bank of Canada used Canadian dollars from the Exchange Fund Account to buy foreign currencies. In this way, more Canadian dollars were made available and some foreign currencies were removed from the foreign exchange market, thus curtailing the upward pressure on the Canadian foreign exchange rate.

The Canadian dollars in the Exchange Fund Account were drawn either from the federal government's deposits at the chartered banks or by borrowing from the Bank of Canada. The effect of the latter action was to increase the money supply, since the money created by borrowing from the Bank of Canada was transferred to the chartered bank that sold the foreign exchange to the Exchange Fund Account. The operation of the Exchange Fund Account could therefore lead to an increase in the money supply which was not otherwise intended or desired.

Conversely, the Bank's actions in changing the money supply could have an impact on the Exchange Fund Account. Increasing the money supply would lower the interest rate which in turn would cause short-term deposits to be moved to other countries in search of higher interest rates. This would result in a downward pressure on the Canadian foreign exchange rate. To offset this, the Bank of Canada would need to sell foreign currencies and buy Canadian dollars. This could be difficult when the Account's supply of foreign currencies was low. In such circumstances, the Bank of Canada was constrained from increasing the money supply by as much as it might have if only domestic conditions had been considered.

Floating Exchange Rates. From 1950 until 1962, and again since May of 1970, the foreign exchange rate of the Canadian dollar has been free to fluctuate with the supply and demand conditions in foreign exchange markets. The Bank of Canada therefore is no longer concerned with maintaining an official exchange rate for the Canadian dollar, although it appears to have a view on the appropriate range for the exchange rate and frequently buys or sells Canadian dollars in the foreign exchange market to influence the rate. This arrangment is often described as a "managed float" — or even a "dirty float", as in 1970 and 1971 when the Bank intervened frequently to keep the exchange rate within a narrow (but unannounced) range.

Review of the Main Points

1. Money is something that is readily and widely accepted as a medium for the exchange of goods and services. Money also serves as a unit of account, a store of value, and a standard of deferred payments or debts.

2. Whatever is used as money must be easily carried or transferred, divisible into small units, durable, and not easily reproduced. Precious metals, particularly gold, served as money for a long time; gold certificates, and later bank deposits evolved from the practice of depositing gold for safekeeping. Coins and paper currency are fiat money or legal tender: money the government decrees must be accepted for payment of debts or for exchange.

3. An economy's money supply includes all coins and paper currency circulating outside the banks and the total value of chequable deposits. A broader definition of money includes time or notice deposits. The money supply can be expanded or contracted through the banking system since the chartered banks can make loans equal to a large percentage of their deposits. The potential total expansion, equal to the reciprocal of the cash reserve ratio multiplied by the amount of the initial deposit, is realized only if the banks maintain no excess cash reserves and if

all payments from deposit accounts are redeposited. The potential total contraction, calculated in the same way, must take place since chartered banks must maintain the required reserves.

4. The Bank of Canada acts as the federal government's bank by providing economic advice, holding some of the government's deposits, making loans to the government, and managing its issues of bonds and treasury bills. The Bank also acts as a final clearing house for the chartered banks and as a lender of last resort by making loans available at the Bank Rate.

5. The Bank of Canada regulates the money supply by creating or removing chartered bank reserves through open market transactions in government securities and by transferring federal government deposits between the Bank and the chartered banks. Varying the Bank Rate and the secondary reserve requirement directly influences the chartered banks' lending activities, and hence, the money supply. The Bank may use "moral suasion" to gain the cooperation of the chartered banks in pursuing particular monetary policies.

6. The foreign exchange rate of the Canadian dollar — the rate at which it is traded for foreign currencies — may be pegged, or fixed, by the government or it may be free to fluctuate according to the supply and demand for Canadian dollars. When the rate is pegged, the Bank of Canada is responsible for holding the rate within the agreed range by selling or buying Canadian dollars through the Exchange Fund Account.

7. When there is a low stock of foreign currencies in the Exchange Fund Account, the Bank of Canada is restrained from increasing the money supply. An increase would lower the interest rates, some deposits would leave the country, and there would be a downward pressure on the exchange rate, requiring the Bank to buy Canadian dollars with its diminishing stock of foreign currencies.

8. When the exchange rate is unpegged, the Bank will be required to modify the supply or demand for Canadian dollars if there is a danger of a continuing deficit in the balance of payments. This would also restrain the Bank from increasing the money supply when the exchange rate is unduly low, or from decreasing the money supply when the rate is unduly high.

Review and Discussion Questions

1. It is often said that Canada will soon be a "cashless" society. What does this mean? Describe some of the changes that would be required to achieve a completely cashless society. What advantages and disadvantages would there be? Could Canada also become a "moneyless" society?

2. Could the "gift certificates" of a large retail department store ever function as money? Explain.

3. Give as many reasons as you can for not holding more currency than you usually do. What would cause you to hold more?

4. What happens to the level of the money supply when someone withdraws $500 in currency from his bank account for a vacation trip? Does it ultimately matter whether the trip is within Canada or to another country? Why?

5. Why do changes in the Bank Rate have so much significance if the chartered banks borrow relatively small amounts from the Bank of Canada?

6. Trace the effects through the balance sheets of the Bank of Canada and the chartered banks of (a) a transfer of $2 million in Government of Canada deposits from the Bank of Canada to one of the chartered banks; and (b) the sale of a $100,000 bond by the Bank of Canada to a chartered bank. By how much will each of these actions change the money supply? (Assume that the cash reserve requirement is 10 per cent and that there is no secondary reserve requirement.)

7. Why can one say that the banking system creates money if a bank is permitted to lend only part of its deposits?

8. Since chartered bank's depositors are protected by deposit insurance, what purpose is served by chartered banks' cash reserves and secondary reserves?

9. Suppose that chartered banks were required to hold cash and secondary reserves equal to 100 per cent of their deposits. Would this mean that the Bank of Canada could no longer change the money supply?

10. Bank of Canada actions to increase the money supply have been described as "trying to push on a string". Is there any validity to this analogy?

Sources and Selected Readings

Bank of Canada. *Report of the Governor of the Bank of Canada*. Ottawa: Bank of Canada, annual.

Bank of Canada Review. Ottawa: Bank of Canada, monthly.

Binhammer, H.H. *Money, Banking and the Canadian Financial System*, 2nd ed. Toronto: Methuen, 1972.

Bond, D.E., and R.A. Shearer. *The Economics of the Canadian Financial System*. Scarborough, Ont.: Prentice-Hall, 1972.

Boreham, G.F. et al. *Money and Banking: Analysis and Policy in a Canadian Context*. Toronto: Holt, Rinehart and Winston, 1968.

Cairns, James P., and H.H. Binhammer (eds.) *Canadian Banking and Monetary Policy*. Toronto: McGraw-Hill, 1965.

Galbraith, J.A. *Canadian Banking*. Toronto: Ryerson Press, 1970.

Neufeld, E.P. *Bank of Canada Operations and Policy*. Toronto: University of Toronto Press, 1958.

———. (ed.) *Money and Banking in Canada*. Toronto: McClelland and Stewart, 1964.

———. *The Financial System of Canada*. Toronto: Macmillan, 1972.

Report of the Royal Commission on Banking and Finance. Ottawa: Queen's Printer, 1964.

6 Fiscal and Monetary Policies for Economic Stability

A. Stabilization Policies and Problems

Instability in the general equilibrium level of national income was shown in Chapter 4 to follow from changes in components of aggregate demand. Changes in these items could cause the level of national income to swing through a wide range from serious unemployment to rapid inflation. Major responsibility for moderating such unemployment and inflation while encouraging a high rate of economic growth rests with the federal government, with the assistance of the Bank of Canada. Some provincial governments also try to design their expenditure programs to counteract unemployment and inflation but there frequently are significant differences among the priorities of the various governments, with resulting conflicts among their policies for dealing with inflation and unemployment.

The federal government's responsibility for influencing aggregate demand to maintain economic stability has been widely accepted only in the past two or three decades. Keynes' analysis of high unemployment levels experienced during the Depression led him to argue that governments must use their taxation and spending powers to offset swings in economic activity. This view was advocated in Canada in 1940 by the Royal Commission on Dominion-Provincial Relations, and stated as government policy in 1945 in a White Paper on employment and income.

Actions taken by the federal government and the Bank of Canada to reduce unemployment and inflation are collectively described as stabilization policies.

These have also been called counter-cyclical policies, but the former term is now more commonly used. These actions consist of *fiscal policy*: the government's expenditure and taxation programs, and *monetary policy*: the Bank of Canada's actions to regulate the money supply and influence interest rates. A third group of policies is concerned with international economic relations and includes *policies on tariffs, foreign exchange rates, and foreign investment*. These are treated in some detail in the next chapter. International economic policies are determined to a certain extent in cooperation with other countries, and for the moment can be considered constraints within which domestic economic policies must be designed.

The Inflation-Unemployment Trade-Off

The numerous combinations of actions available to the federal government and the Bank of Canada to influence aggregate demand and the money supply make it difficult to determine the most suitable stabilization policy for Canada at any particular time. Further complicating this, however, is the need to choose between inflation and unemployment as the primary problem to be attacked. Toward the end of Chapter 4, the inflation-unemployment dilemma was outlined briefly as a variation from the basic Keynesian model of national income determination.

The simple Keynesian model portrayed inflation as occurring only when the economy was at full employment. This conclusion was based on the premise that, if aggregate demand increased during periods of unemployment, the result would be increasing employment and real output rather than increasing prices. In actual experience, however, prices tend to rise even when there is substantial unemployment, and to rise more quickly as the economy approaches the full-employment level. Some reasons for this are discussed in the next section on the causes of inflation and unemployment.

This varying combination of rates of unemployment and inflation can be shown by a curve relating the average unemployment rate and inflation rate for particular periods. Such a curve is often called a *Phillips curve*, after one of the first economists to analyze the relationship of these and similar indicators of economic activity. Figure 6.1 presents a hypothetical Phillips curve to show the nature of the basic decision facing a government before it can proceed with outlining a stabilization policy. Suppose the economy is currently experiencing a combination of inflation and unemployment represented by point *A*: inflation at the rate of 3 per cent annually and an average annual unemployment rate of 4 per cent. Assume further that the target level of economic "stability" is actually defined as 2 per cent inflation and 3 per cent unemployment, represented by point *B*.

The government may choose to fight inflation, trying to reduce it from 3 to 2 per cent, but must then accept 6 per cent unemployment (point *D*). Alternatively, the government may try to reduce unemployment to 3 per cent, meanwhile allowing inflation to rise to 4 per cent (point *C*). Of course, it may also opt for any combination along the Phillips curve, perhaps even at a point lying outside the range between *C* and *D*. Since the government must trade off some inflation to reduce unemployment, and vice versa, the Phillips curve is also termed a *trade-off curve*.

Ideally, the government would like to move the economy toward point *B*, and certainly to keep it away from *E*, a combination of high unemployment and high inflation. The Phillips curve shown in Figure 6.1 illustrates only the nature of the trade-off decision facing the government; it does not present actual data for the Canadian economy.

Historical Phillips curves are useful in understanding how the economy has performed in the past, but they do not provide an adequate basis for designing future stabilization policy.

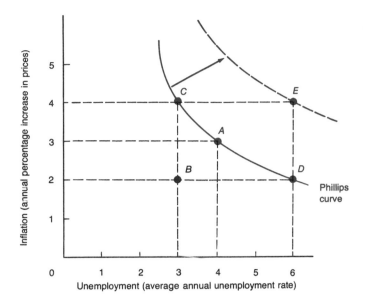

Figure 6.1   The Phillips Curve: Inflation and Unemployment Trade-Off
A Phillips curve shows the various combinations of unemployment and inflation
rates which have occurred in an economy's recent past. Usually, high unemployment rates have been associated with low inflation rates, and vice versa. However,
the historical Phillips curve cannot be used to determine by how much inflation will
increase for a given decrease in the unemployment rate, for example in moving
from *D* to *A*, because the curve tends to shift with other economic changes.

That is, the government cannot determine how much inflation it
should expect for each percentage point it seeks in the reduction of
the unemployment rate, because this relationship appears to change.
Recent evidence suggests that the Phillips curve for Canada is shifting outward.[1]

This outward shift is due partly to inflation expectations or an
"inflation psychology" in the population. If, for example, the government is fighting unemployment and thus lets inflation proceed at
a higher rate than in the previous year, workers and lenders anticipate continuing inflation and demand higher wages and interest
rates. They thus create the inflation they expected. The prevailing
unemployment rate is associated with a higher rate of inflation than
in the past; that is, the Phillips curve shifts outward.

Other reasons suggested for the changing relationship between
inflation and unemployment include the possibility that the structure or nature of unemployment is different now than it was five to

---

[1] S.F. Kaliski, *The Trade-Off Between Inflation and Unemployment: Some
Explorations of the Recent Evidence for Canada,* Economic Council of
Canada, Special Study, (Ottawa: Information Canada, 1972).

ten years ago. The greater number of "secondary" workers — persons who work part-time or who are in the labour force intermittently — may increase the measured unemployment rate at any given level of inflation, while there is a relatively low unemployment rate among "primary" workers, the full-time members of the labour force. The geographical immobility of workers may also affect the trade-off: if there is a strong demand for workers in one part of the country while unemployment is high in a particular region, the national relationship of inflation and unemployment is different from a condition in which there is substantial unemployment in all regions.

There have been suggestions that the Phillips curve is not a necessary feature of the Canadian economy; rather, that the continuing coexistence of inflation and unemployment is the result of uncoordinated economic policies. There is no apparent evidence, however, that zero inflation and full employment can be achieved simultaneously, mainly due to the "structural" causes of inflation and unemployment outlined in the next section. Instead, the serious question is whether fiscal and monetary policies can only move the economy back and forth along an outward-shifting Phillips curve, or whether they can also shift the curve toward lower levels of both inflation and unemployment. These alternative possibilities are the basis for the argument between those who believe that actions such as an incomes policy and manpower policies are required to shift the Phillips curve inward, and those who believe that an incomes policy is unnecessary and that manpower policies should be designed for long-term economic growth rather than for short-term economic stabilization. An assessment of this debate requires some examination of the causes of inflation and unemployment.

Some Causes of Inflation and Unemployment

Inflation

Several explanations for inflation have emerged from intensive theoretical analysis and empirical research in the past two decades. These can be grouped within three major categories: *demand-pull*, *cost-push*, and *structural change*.

Demand-Pull Inflation. The traditional explanation for inflation has been the one presented in Chapter 4 as part of the theory of national income determination: planned spending at the prevailing price level exceeds the value of goods and services available at the full-employment level. The excess demand can arise because the four general groups of buyers — consumers, businesses, governments, and foreign buyers — make their plans independently and the spending of the latter three was seen to have only a partial relationship to the level of national income. The demand-pull explanation assumes that prices of factors and products are flexible enough to move upwards under the pressure of increased demand. In fact, as was suggested in Chapter 4, this pressure may result in some price increases before the economy reaches the full-employment level. Nevertheless, the essential point is that inflation is explained in terms of excess demand. Consequently, the traditional policy prescription is to reduce aggregate demand through fiscal and monetary policies.

Cost-Push Inflation. Cost-push inflation, or "sellers' inflation" is so named to emphasize that the inflationary pressure arises on the supply side of product markets or factor markets. In the case of labour markets, this has been described as a "wage-price spiral". However, the wage-push aspect of cost-push inflation depends on a number of critical assumptions: that workers can obtain wage increases proportionately greater than any increase in labour productivity; that the wage increase leads to an increase in the labour cost per unit; that this necessarily increases the total production cost per unit; and that producers increase selling prices whenever production costs rise.

For this process to occur labour must have strong bargaining power — usually in the form of strong unions — and producers need some monopolistic power in product markets to pass on the price increases. Thus, cost-push inflation is more likely to occur in industries where there are strong unions and only a few producers, and can occur at high levels of unemployment, especially when this is concentrated in other industries or regions. Although the cost-push explanation has tended to emphasize the role of labour unions, suppliers of any materials or productive factors who can exercise some market power — or some direct control over their selling prices — can contribute to cost-push inflation.

Fiscal and monetary policies are less effective in dealing with cost-push inflation because substantial reductions in planned spending will have their effects primarily through increasing unemployment to serious levels. A strong union, for example, may be able to maintain its bargaining power until higher levels of unemployment reach the industry concerned.

Structural Inflation. The structural-change explanation for inflation is based on changes in the *composition* of aggregate demand, and suggests that inflation may arise even when there is no overall excess demand nor cases of substantial market power. For example, as consumer demand shifts to products such as automobiles and recreational equipment, there may be less spending on commodities such as railway transportation, cotton textiles, and domestically produced furniture.

The increased demand for automobiles can lead to price increases in that industry, especially when it is operating at full capacity; but because wages and prices are apparently inflexible downward, the reduced demand for the other products does not lead to a corresponding fall in their prices. Thus, the overall level of prices rises while there may be increasing unemployment in the industries where demand has fallen. Again, fiscal and monetary policies designed to restrain aggregate demand are only partly effective because they will probably increase unemployment while having only a modest impact on rising prices in the expanding industries.

Unemployment

The various causes of unemployment can be grouped in four major categories: *inadequate demand, frictional, seasonal*, and *structural*.

Inadequate-Demand Unemployment. The converse of demand-pull inflation is inadequate-demand unemployment; this is the result of insufficient aggregate demand to produce employment for all labour offered at the prevailing wage level. Some years ago, this would have been termed *cyclical* unemployment, corresponding with the fluctuations in demand for labour over the course of the business cycle. However the fact that the demand for labour does not always correspond closely to the business cycle has caused this term to be abandoned.

Inadequate aggregate demand tends to be more variable in its effect on different industries than is the effect of excess demand on product prices. When labour is employed under two- or three-year contracts, for example, a decrease in demand can have less effect than when contracts cover shorter periods, or unions have less influence on temporary laying-off of workers. It will also have less effect on skilled and technical employees who are retained during slack periods so that employers will not have to compete in tight labour markets for special skills when demand begins to rise again.

Frictional Unemployment. At any point in time, there will be some people looking for work who have just left a job or who are just entering or re-entering the labour force; this is frictional unemployment. and is generally regarded as the least serious form of unemployment. In fact, frictional unemployment is likely to be highest when aggregate demand and output is rising quickly and workers therefore believe there is a good possibility of finding a better job. Conversely, frictional unemployment usually declines during slack periods because workers are less venturesome in leaving their current jobs to look for others and relatively fewer people are attracted into the labour market.

Frictional unemployment could become more serious, however,

if the *duration* of this unemployment increased due to increased difficulty in locating suitable work.

Seasonal Unemployment. The seasonality of some work, especially in temperate countries like Canada, leads to substantial seasonal unemployment. Construction, agriculture, forestry, fishing, and some parts of the retail and recreation industries have a fluctuating demand for labour due to climatic restrictions on their work or climatic influences on the demand for goods and services. A broader definition of seasonality includes fluctuations in the demand for labour over the course of one year due, for example, to layoffs during retooling for new models in the automobile industry.

Seasonal unemployment, especially due to climatic conditions, is becoming quantitatively less important as a smaller percentage of the labour force is engaged in agriculture and other primary industries; as construction technology changes to make outdoor work possible year-round; and as winter sports stabilize the demand for recreational equipment and facilities.

Structural Unemployment. The unusually high unemployment rates of the early 1960s provoked much debate about whether the unemployment was due to inadequate demand or to structural changes in the demand for labour, following from changes in the composition of demand for goods and services and improvements in technology. The latter factors were expected to produce *structural unemployment* among persons in some goods-producing industries, since services constituted a larger share of final demand, and among unskilled workers displaced by technological changes. Structural unemployment is also described as long-duration unemployment because workers displaced by structural changes may not be able to find work again in the same occupation, industry, or locality. A change in occupations or a move to another area may be postponed for some time until all other prospects have been exhausted.

Although an outline of different types of unemployment is useful in explaining variation in unemployment rates and the average duration of unemployment at different times, the simple categories of causes do not directly suggest the most appropriate corrective policies. Someone may have lost his job due to declining consumer demand for the product of a particular industry, but the reason he cannot find another job may be that the demand for his type of labour skills has declined only temporarily — for seasonal or aggregate demand reasons — or it may have declined permanently, due to technological change. A different policy would be required in each case. Consequently, a variety of employment and manpower policies were used in combination in an attempt to restrain the rising unemployment rates of the late 1960s and early 1970s.

The rest of this chapter deals mainly with fiscal and monetary policies for regulating aggregate demand because these continue to be the major tools available to the government for curtailing both inflation and unemployment. More specific policies are required to supplement these general tools when either inflation or unemployment are particularly serious; these are examined briefly at the end of the chapter in the sections on *incomes policies* and *manpower policies*.

B. Fiscal Policy

Although fiscal policy can be defined simply as the government's expenditure and taxation programs, any discussion of a specific fiscal policy should consider the effects particular taxation and spending measures are intended to achieve. Different types of taxes can have different effects on consumption, investment, and export goods and services, depending on which items and whose incomes are taxed. Government expenditures can have widely varying effects depending, for example, on whether they are transfer payments or payments for goods and services.

Fiscal policy can be further defined as either *automatic* or *discretionary*. Automatic fiscal policy consists of what are commonly called *automatic or built-in stabilizers*: government programs designed to vary the amount of tax revenues or government expenditures automatically as the levels of employment and prices change. *Discretionary fiscal policy* requires a specific decision by the government; that is, the government must use its discretion in determining the level and type of taxation and expenditures needed to combat current economic problems.

Automatic Stabilizers

Two types of automatic stabilizers are at work in the economy: private economic behaviour in response to changing incomes, and government programs. The private "built-in" stabilizers are the marginal propensities to save and to import described in Chapter 4. As individuals' and corporations' after-tax incomes rise, the marginal propensity to save tends to rise also. The proportionately greater saving has a dampening effect on aggregate demand, thereby constraining the inflationary effect of rising incomes. Conversely, as incomes fall, the marginal propensity to save decreases and proportionately more income is directed to consumption or investment goods, with the effect of maintaining aggregate demand and employment at a higher level than would occur if the marginal propensity to save was constant for all levels of income. The marginal propensity to import tends to act in the same way, increasing with rising incomes and thus reducing their potential inflationary effect.

Built-in stabilizers in the form of government programs include *transfer payments* for income and price maintenance schemes and *tax revenues* from the progressive personal income tax structure. Transfer payment programs include unemployment insurance, welfare assistance, and farm price supports.

Unemployment Compensation. As the level of unemployment rises, accompanied by a fall in employment earnings, government expenditures for unemployment compensation are increased. Although these payments do not fully offset the decline in incomes, they keep consumer demand closer to its previous level than it would be without the payments. Similarly, when the economy is moving closer to full employment, unemployment compensation payments decline so that aggregate demand does not push up prices quite so quickly.

Welfare Assistance Payments. Welfare assistance payments tend to act in the same way as unemployment compensation in stabilizing consumer demand. However, welfare schemes are generally provided for persons experiencing long-term unemployment or persons who are not in the labour force, and so do not perform quite so effectively as automatic stabilizers in short-run changes in aggregate demand.

Agricultural Price Supports. Agricultural price support schemes (described more fully in Chapter 12) provide payments to producers whenever the price of the commodity concerned falls below the guaranteed price. Depending on the scheme in effect, the government either pays the difference between the price received in the market and the guaranteed price, or buys the quantity which is not sold at the guaranteed price. These payments have the same effect as the unemployment and welfare payments in keeping agricultural producers' incomes closer to the previous level. As agricultural prices rise, the payments to producers decline.

Progressive Personal Income Tax Structure. The progressive tax structure on personal income acts as one of the strongest and most immediate stabilizers. When incomes rise, a larger percentage of the additional income is taken for taxes. Consumers' disposable incomes thus rise less quickly than their gross incomes. When personal incomes fall during a recession, a lower proportion of incomes is deducted for taxes and disposable incomes fall more slowly than total incomes. One study has estimated, for example, that the ratio of the percentage change in tax yields to the percentage change in GNP, for Canada, over the short run, is about 2.2. That is, a 1 per cent increase in GNP will produce a 2.2 per cent increase in tax revenue.[2]

---

[2] D.J. Daly, *Fiscal Policy — An Assessment*, Toronto: Collier-Macmillan, 1972.

The automatic stabilizers built into government programs are always at work and respond relatively quickly to income changes. Depending on the level of economic activity, they are slowing down either the decline or the increase in disposable incomes. Although government action was needed to initiate the programs, and may be taken again to alter the payments or tax rates, no specific decision is needed as the economy moves through changing levels of inflation and unemployment.

The advantage of built-in stabilizers is that they operate automatically, but they also have a disadvantage: they reduce the effectiveness of discretionary policies to deal with inflation and unemployment. The progressive income tax structure, in particular, causes what has been termed *fiscal drag*: as government actions to reduce unemployment begin to take effect and national income rises, the higher marginal tax rates increase tax revenues and reduce aggregate demand. The opposite effect also occurs. As anti-inflation policies begin to work and national income falls, lower marginal tax rates leave consumers with a higher proportion of gross incomes available for spending. These effects are reinforced by the other automatic stabilizers. The government must therefore consider the action of automatic stabilizers when discretionary fiscal policy is being determined.

Discretionary Fiscal Policy

Discretionary fiscal policy can be defined as a *deliberate effort by the government to achieve not only stable prices and full employment but also economic growth, favourable income distribution, and equilibrium in the balance of payments, through the appropriate composition and size of its expenditures and tax revenues.*

Numerous alternatives on each side of the budget are open to the government, each with different effects. Indeed, the government is constantly encountering pressure from various groups to favour them by reducing taxes or increasing government spending in each new budget. The consequences of alternative budgetary positions available to the government can be analyzed using the theory of national income determination presented in Chapter 4.

Basic Effects of Fiscal Policy

Consider a situation in which the economy is experiencing high unemployment and only minor inflation. The government is formulating an *anti-unemployment* or *expansionary fiscal policy*. It has three basic choices:

- to increase government expenditures, leaving tax revenues unchanged;

- to decrease tax revenues, leaving government expenditures unchanged;
- to increase both government expenditures and tax revenues.

Assume further that government economists have determined that to reduce unemployment to the desired level (presumably to create full employment), the required increase in national income is $6 billion and that the economy's marginal propensity to consume is 2/3. How large would the changes need to be in each of the three choices open to the government? From the information on marginal propensities, the government knows the value of the multiplier to be 3. (Recall that the multiplier = $1/(1 - MPC)$).

Increased Government Expenditures. Government expenditures for goods and services directly increase aggregate demand. Since any increase in government expenditures has a multiplied effect on aggregate demand and thus on national income, an increase of $2 billion in government expenditures will, with a multiplier of 3, increase national income by $6 billion. This is illustrated in Figure 6.2. The result is an initial increase in government spending to G', with the multiplier effect resulting in a $6 billion increase in GNP.

Decreased Tax Revenues. A decrease in personal or corporate income taxes does not have the same effect as an equal increase in

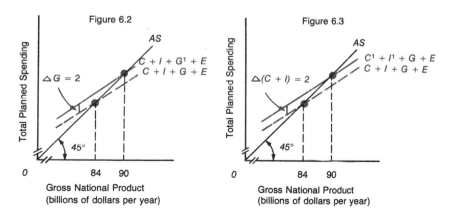

Figure 6.2 Increased Government Expenditures
A $2 billion increase in government expenditure will have a multiplied effect on national income. When $MPC = 2/3$, the value of the multiplier is 3, and GNP is increased by $6 billion.

Figure 6.3 Decreased Personal and Corporate Income Taxes
A $3 billion decrease in personal and corporate income taxes increases disposable income by $3 billion, but if the $MPS + MPM + MPT$ for consumers and firms is 1/2, C and I increase by only $2 billion. With a multiplier of 3, this increase leads to an increase in GNP of $6 billion.

government expenditures. Although a decrease in taxes increases personal or corporate after-tax income, one-third of the increased income goes to savings, imports, and even *some* taxes. The multiplier effect will occur only on the additional spending for domestically produced goods and services; this is equal to two-thirds of the increase in disposable income. Tax revenues must therefore be reduced by more than an increase in government expenditures if this second approach is to have the same effect on national income as the first.

A $3 billion decrease in tax revenues produces an initial increase of $2 billion in domestic spending, and a final increase in national income of $6 billion. Thus the tax reduction needs to be 50 per cent greater than the increase in government expenditures to have the same effect on national income. (Note that when $MPC = \frac{1}{2}$, tax reductions must be double the expenditure increase; and when $MPC = \frac{3}{4}$, tax reductions must be 33 1/3 per cent larger than expenditure increases.) The effect of a tax reduction of $3 billion is illustrated in Figure 6.3. Government expenditures and exports are unchanged but consumer spending and investment initially increase by a total of $2 billion, from C to C' and I to I'.

Equal Increases in Taxes and Expenditures. The fact that tax reductions must be greater than increases in government expenditures to obtain the same increase in national income hints at the changes required if the government chooses to follow the third alternative: an equal increase in taxes and expenditures. If taxes are increased by $2 billion, domestic spending will decrease initially by two-thirds of this amount, or $1 1/3 billion, and the final decrease in national income will be $4 billion. An increase of $2 billion in government expenditures, however, leads to an increase in national income of $6 billion. The combined effect of a $2 billion increase in both government spending and taxes will therefore be a *net* increase in national income of $2 billion. Thus, to achieve the objective of a $6 billion increase in national income, both taxes and government expenditures must be raised by $6 billion.

This third alternative is a specific case of the *balanced budget multiplier* which was introduced in Chapter 4. The particular result obtained here can be expressed in general terms:

A balanced or equal change in taxes and government spending will change national income by the same amount, given that the value of the multiplier is uniform throughout the economy.

The government may also choose to combine two of the basic alternatives. To combat high unemployment, for example, it may combine tax reductions with increased government expenditures. In this case, a $6 billion increase in national income can be achieved through decreasing tax revenues by $1 billion and increasing government expenditures by $1 1/3 billion. Alternatively, especially perhaps just prior to an election, tax revenues might be decreased by $1½ billion and government expenditures increased by $1 billion, with the same effect on national income.

Limitations of Fiscal Policy

Although only the basic elements of a fiscal policy have been outlined, it should be clear that the government is faced with difficult decisions each time it designs new fiscal policy. When unemployment is high, should taxes be cut? government expenditures increased? some of each action taken? or a budget balance be maintained with much larger increases in both taxes and spending? Some considerations in making these choices fall into three general categories: 1. the timing of specific changes in taxation and spending; 2. the immediate effects of the policy, apart from the longer-run desired effects on employment, prices, and national income; and 3. the problem of managing budgetary deficits that result when expenditures exceed revenues, and budgetary surpluses when revenues exceed expenditures.

Timing of Fiscal Policy. Several factors compound the problem of timing in implementing fiscal policies. It is so difficult to predict the future, even for a few months hence, that too much emphasis is often placed on present conditions in designing fiscal policy. This difficulty is illustrated hypothetically in Figure 6.4. For example, after a slow but steady growth in GNP through time periods, t_1 to t_2, with unemployment probably at a higher-than-normal level, the economy

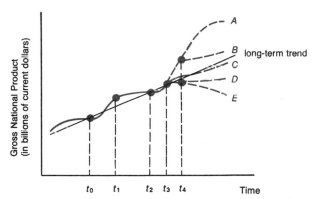

Figure 6.4 Predicting Future Economic Activity For Policy Decisions
At time period t_2, the economy may seem to be moving toward its long-term trend line (path C). There may therefore be a recognition lag between t_2 and t_3 before the actual path A is recognized. A further decision lag may delay action beyond t_2, with the implementation of a policy not occurring until t_4 or later. Contractionary policy implemented at t_4 may put the economy onto path B. But if the strength of the original expansion was wrongly judged, and the economy was moving onto path D, a contractionary policy will reinforce the recession, indicated by path E.

begins to "heat up", GNP rises more quickly from t_2 to t_3, the unemployment rate drops slightly, and economic advisors warn that increased inflation is ahead. Should the government assume there will be a prolonged expansionary period, with the economy moving along path A? Or is the current burst likely to be as short-lived as it was during t_0 to t_1, moving the economy along path D? Or is the economy moving onto its long-term steady growth path shown as C?

If the future path is actually A, this illustrates the first type of timing problem: there may be a *recognition lag* such that the economy is well into an inflationary period (or a recession) before corrective action is even considered. This lag is represented in Figure 6.4 as the period from t_2 to t_3.

Secondly, there is a *decision lag* while government economists and advisors agree that the economy is indeed on path A, that a contractionary fiscal policy is required, and that this should, for example, take the form of both reduced government expenditures and tax increases. The decision period may be prolonged because tax changes, in this case possibly an income surtax, are normally announced only when the finance minister presents his budget or his "mini-budget". However, even if this decision is announced by the government shortly after t_3, a further, *implementation lag* is also experienced: changes, in income taxes particularly, usually are not effective until some time after the announcement.

Expenditure changes generally can be effected more quickly than tax changes, but most major programs or projects cannot be terminated abruptly. A decision, for example, to cut back on defence expenditures would result in the signing of fewer new production contracts, rather than the breaking of existing contracts. Fewer personnel would be recruited, and military commitments abroad would gradually be reduced.

The same type of lags would occur if an expansionary policy was required: time to recognize the need, to determine a new policy, and to put it into action. The first Opportunities For Youth Program, for example, required time to make the program known, for applications to be received, processed, and approved, for the first grants to be awarded, for the funds to be spent by the recipients, and for the multiplier to begin to take effect.

The combined decision lag and implementation lag is represented by the period from t_3 to t_4 in Figure 6.4. During this period, the rate of inflation has been high. Although the policy begins to have an effect at t_4, the economy moves along path B, representing a higher level of inflation than if it had been on path C without these lags.

There is an even more serious problem associated with these lags. Suppose that the economy were actually on path D, rather than on path A as determined by the government. A contractionary policy having its effect at t_4 would initiate a recession represented by path E.

Regional Versus National Effects. The second set of problems associated with fiscal policies concerns the location of their effects. If unemployment is high in some regions but not in others, a tax cut may reduce the high unemployment but add to inflationary pressures in the other regions. Such cases require government expenditure programs specifically designed to put purchasing power into the hands of low-income persons in the high unemployment regions. A program such as Opportunities For Youth was popular with some government economists because it met these requirements ideally: applications could be approved for areas experiencing high unemployment and grants paid to persons who would spend all of this income.

Conversely, if there is a widespread recession with unemployment at an unusually high level across the country, a tax cut usually is the preferable strategy. The implementation period can be short and the consequences immediate and widespread.

Budget Deficits and Surpluses

A potential political limitation on discretionary fiscal policy results from the diversity of views on the maximum budgetary deficit government should incur. Three general views can be identified as:

- balance the budget for each year;
- balance the budget over the cyclical fluctuations in economic activity, or over a five to ten year period;
- balancing the budget is unimportant: use whatever combination of expenditures and taxes will bring about non-inflationary full employment.

Annually Balanced Budget. Prior to the Keynesian analysis of national income determination, and especially during the Depression, it was generally accepted that a government should balance its budget each year; after all, that was what prudent individuals would do. When the economy was in a slump, it would be irresponsible for the government to push the country further into debt by allowing expenditures to exceed tax revenues. Advocates of this policy failed to recognize that when incomes declined during the Depression, tax revenues also fell. If a balanced budget was to be maintained, the government would need to increase tax rates in order to keep tax revenues constant, or decrease government expenditures, or do both. Each of these policies would reduce aggregate demand and produce further unemployment.

During an inflationary period, tax revenues would rise, and if expenditures remained constant, a surplus would result. Maintenance of a balanced budget would require the government to lower the tax rates, or increase government expenditures, or do some of each. These actions would add to aggregate demand and thus increase the rate of inflation. It is evident then, that an annually balanced budget would worsen whichever problem, unemployment or inflation, was present.

Budgets Balanced Over the Cycle. Some persons who recognized that an annually balanced budget could be an irresponsible fiscal policy argued that governments should pursue a counter-cyclical policy but that the budget should be balanced over the cycle. As incomes rose, taxes should be increased faster than expenditures so that a budget surplus would be accumulated. But as this contractionary action slowed down the rate of inflation and unemployment began to increase, expenditures should be increased faster than tax revenues, wiping out the surplus and even producing a budgetary deficit. This approach seemed plausible when fairly regular cycles were experienced, but failed to answer the problem that arose when a recession continued for some time or when government expenditures were unusually large for some time, as occurred during World War II.

Deficit or Surplus As Required. Recognition of the limitations in balancing the budget annually or cyclically led to acceptance of the government's budget as a tool for combating inflation or unemployment, with only secondary importance attached to the resulting surplus or deficit. This position is sometimes referred to as *functional finance*: a budgetary deficit or surplus has a particular function and should be judged by how well this function is served rather than by the size of the deficit or surplus. In fact, a recent version of this view suggests that what is relevant is not the actual deficit or surplus shown in the government's budget, but what the budgetary balance would be if the economy were at the full-employment level.

Full-Employment Deficit or Surplus. Most economists now emphasize the full-employment deficit or surplus, or the *full-employment balance.* It is recognized that a deficit budget introduced when unemployment is high may so effectively stimulate the economy that the increased incomes associated with full employment will produce a balanced budget, possibly a surplus, or at least a lower deficit. This concept can be illustrated as in Figure 6.5 Government expenditures, G, are assumed to rise slightly with increasing national income. Tax revenues, T, rise more rapidly due to the progressive tax rates and constant basic tax exemptions. The given tax and expenditure programs produce a deficit when the economy is at a less-than-full-employment level of national income, GNP_1, and a surplus when national income is beyond the full-employment level at GNP_2. The particular deficit incurred at GNP_1 produces a balanced budget at the full-employment level represented by GNP_{FE}.

The government's role is to make sure that the tax structure and

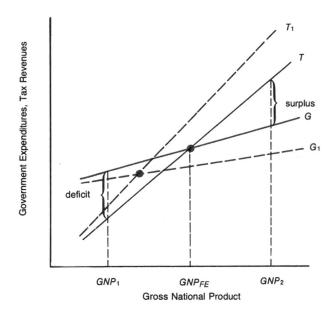

*Figure 6.5   A Budgetary Deficit May Produce
a Balanced Budget at Full Employment*

Given the government's planned spending for various levels of national income, G, and the tax revenues realized as national income increases, T, a budget deficit $(G - T)$ at GNP_1 may stimulate economic activity enough to produce a balanced budget $(G = T)$ when the economy is at full-employment national income, GNP_{FE}. The given planned G and T would also produce the necessary surplus budget to restrain the inflation which could be expected at even higher levels of national income, such as GNP_2. A more contractionary budget, represented by G_1 and T_1, provides stronger restraint against inflationary pressure.

the level of government expenditures are such that a budgetary balance is achieved at the full-employment level. Suppose that tax rates had been set higher in Figure 6.5, for example at T_1, and government expenditures were lower, at G_1. This may have produced the deficit budget required to deal with high unemployment at GNP_1, but this pattern of revenues and expenditures would also have produced a surplus before the economy reached full employment. Such a policy may be satisfactory, however, if the government anticipates that inflation will proceed more rapidly as the economy approaches full employment and if the objective would therefore be changed from reducing unemployment to restraining inflation.

Managing Deficits and Surpluses

The government may need to incur a deficit over an extended period to reduce a stubborn, high level of unemployment. Since a deficit represents expenditures in excess of tax revenues, where does the additional revenue come from to make these expenditures possible? One might think that the government should be able to draw on accumulations of past surpluses, but many governments have acquired such large debts in the past, primarily through war expenditures, that any previous surplus has generally been used to reduce this debt. A deficit therefore requires governments to borrow.

Borrowing for Deficits. There are two sources for such borrowing: the general public (including the chartered banks) and the Bank of Canada. If the government borrows from the public by issuing government bonds — such as the Canada Savings Bonds issued each fall — private spending is reduced. Individuals may reduce their consumption spending slightly to purchase government bonds; more likely, they hold their savings in the form of government bonds instead of other forms which would have made their savings available for private investment spending.

Government bonds purchased with savings which otherwise would be held in cookie jars, or used to purchase foreign securities, do not reduce aggregate private demand. Borrowing from the public can also increase aggregate demand if government expenditures are directed to individuals whose marginal propensity to consume is higher than that of persons who otherwise would have received these funds through private spending.

Since borrowing from the public can diminish the stimulating effect of a deficit budget, the government is more inclined to borrow from the Bank of Canada. When the government sells bonds to the Bank, the bonds are added to the Bank's assets; the Bank's liabilities are increased in the form of Government of Canada deposits at the Bank. The government can then issue cheques directly against this account or transfer its deposit to the chartered banks. In either case, the effect is to create new money.

When a cheque drawn against the government's account at the Bank of Canada is deposited by a recipient at his chartered bank, monetary expansion begins, following the process outlined in Chapter 5. Financing a budgetary deficit by borrowing from the Bank of Canada has a doubly stimulating effect. It adds new government spending to aggregate demand and encourages investment through the lower interest rates and availability of loans which result from an increased money supply. Note, however, that the effect on interest rates may be slight, since the increased national income due to new government spending will also increase the demand for money.

Disposing of Surpluses. Budget surpluses may be handled in either of two ways: the surplus revenues may be used to repay some of the government's debt, or they may be held in the government's bank accounts. A surplus budget, however, is intended to reduce inflation by reducing aggregate demand. If the surplus is used to reduce the debt, bond-holders will receive some of the surplus, probably use these funds for consumption and investment spending, and thus diminish the anti-inflationary effect of the surplus.

Alternatively, the government can retire some of the debt held by the Bank of Canada. The procedure is the reverse of that followed when the government borrows from the Bank of Canada. Cheques are drawn on the government's deposits at the chartered banks to pay the Bank of Canada for the government bonds it surrenders. The Bank of Canada "cashes" them by reducing the chartered banks' reserves at the Bank. Not only is aggregate demand reduced by the amount of the budget surplus; the money supply is being reduced, initially by the reduction of bank reserves, and later by the contractive process as the chartered banks seek to restore the minimum cash reserve requirement. Thus, using a surplus to retire publicly held debt *may* offset part of the deflationary effect of the budget, but retiring debt held by the Bank of Canada will augment the deflationary effect.

If the government holds the surplus as idle bank balances at the chartered banks, aggregate demand is reduced but there is no change in the money supply, since the deposits are simply transferred from individuals' and corporations' accounts to those of the government.

The Public Debt

A distinction is seldom made between the terms *public debt* and *national debt*. Strictly speaking, the public debt includes the outstanding debt (or liabilities) of all governments: municipal and provincial, as well as federal. The national debt, which more correctly would be called the *federal debt*, refers only to the debt of the federal government. Perhaps because the latter debt forms such a large part of the total public debt (see Table 6.1), the two terms are often used interchangeably.

Table 6.1

Public Debt*, by Government Level, Canada
(millions of dollars)

Year	Federal	Provincial	Municipal	Total
1973	55,500	17,000	11,500	84,000
1967	32,567	8,384	8,083	49,034
1960	21,372	3,666	4,770	29,808
1950	16,690	2,005	1,301	19,996
1941	6,630	1,798	1,114	9,542
1933	3,029	1,354	1,371	5,754

*Direct debt less sinking funds. Totals include intergovernmental debt. Data are estimated for 1973.
Source: Statistics Canada, *Canada Year Book*; and M.C. Urquhart and K.A.H. Buckley, *Historical Statistics of Canada*.

Some people advocated an annually balanced budget because they feared that continuing deficits could lead the country to accumulate very large debts which never could be repaid. Whether the public debt *should* ever be completely paid off is a question to be considered shortly. Even supporters of budgetary deficits to control unemployment are concerned about the public debt, but less about the absolute size of the debt than about the effects of its existence and its management. It must also be noted that the gross debt is largely offset by public assets. The *net* public debt in 1973, for example, was about $27 billion — just under one-third of the gross debt.

Size of the Public Debt

The public debt is the current total amount owed by all levels of government, principally municipal debentures, provincial bonds, and federal bonds and treasury bills. Table 6.1 shows the composition of the public debt over the past several years. The public debt increased rapidly during World War II, when the federal government borrowed heavily to finance defence expenditures. Although the public debt has also grown considerably since 1945, the ability of the country to carry this debt has grown even more quickly. This is reflected in the declining ratio of public debt to GNP. In 1950 the gross debt was greater than the total output of goods and services, but now the gross debt represents only about 70 per cent of GNP, and the net debt represents about 22 per cent of GNP.

Another comparison can be made, between interest payments required to carry the debt and the annual GNP. Table 6.2 shows that although the ratio of total debt to GNP has declined steadily since 1933, the percentage of GNP required to meet the interest charges has increased slightly in recent years due to higher interest rates. This second comparison represents the actual cost of the public debt and is thus the comparison to be considered when budgetary deficits are evaluated.

Table 6.2

Public Debt, Interest Payments, and GNP, Canada
(millions of dollars)

Year	Gross Public Debt	Interest Payments on Debt	GNP	Public Debt as % of GNP	Interest as % of GNP
1973	84,000	4,709	118,678	71	4.0
1967	49,034	2,081	66,409	75	3.1
1960	29,808	1,093	38,359	78	2.8
1950	19,996	544	18,491	108	2.9
1941	9,542	291	8,282	115	3.5
1933	5,754	283	3,492	165	8.1

Source: Statistics Canada, *Canada Yearbook*.

Burden and Benefits of the Public Debt

An evaluation of the costs and advantages of the public debt requires that some unique features of the debt be recognized.

Income Redistribution. It is often said that "we all owe the public debt to ourselves". More correctly, the debt is owed by everyone in the country, but only to some persons. Repayment of outstanding debt can be made only by borrowing more money from ourselves or by raising our own taxes. This means that the total consumption of goods and services is not reduced, as it would be when a private debt is repaid, but there may be a transfer of income to the extent that the persons to whom the debt is repaid are different from those who provide the new borrowed funds or who pay the taxes.

Most bondholders are corporations or individuals in the higher-income groups, but some of the tax revenues raised to pay the interest charges or to repay part of the debt comes from the lower-income groups. The resulting income redistribution toward the higher-income groups can be considered a burden of the public debt, especially if one objective of the government's fiscal policy is to redistribute income toward the lower-income groups.

Tax Disincentives. If marginal tax rates are increased to raise tax revenues for interest payments or debt repayments, this may act as a disincentive, or discourage individuals from earning higher incomes and corporations from investing in new and riskier projects. However, even if higher marginal tax rates have such a disincentive effect, it would represent only a minor burden of the debt, since such a small part of tax revenues are used for payments of interest and principal on the public debt that the rate increase would be similarly small.

Inflationary Effects. The public debt represents the accumulation of budget deficits intended to have an expansionary effect. This effect may continue, however, even when the need for it has passed. Holdings of highly liquid assets like Canada Savings Bonds create what has been termed a "wealth effect". Individuals feel wealthier than if their assets were in less liquid forms, like real estate, and consequently have a higher consumption level at any given income level. This can add to the rate of inflation when the economy is close to full employment.

Externally Held Debt. Provincial governments do not have the advantage of being able to sell their bonds to the Bank of Canada to finance a budget deficit. Consequently, a small but significant portion of the provincial debt — and some of the federal debt — is held by residents of other countries. This externally held debt represents a burden to the extent that residents of Canada must forgo some consumption to pay the interest charges and eventually to repay the debt. In this sense, the public debt does resemble a private debt.

Possible Burden on Future Generations. It is sometimes argued that the public debt places a burden on future generations by requiring them to pay interest and principal on a debt they did not incur. However, to the extent that government expenditures have been used productively, future generations will enjoy a higher level of goods and services than would have been possible otherwise. Current government expenditures for items such as education, health care, and transportation facilities are expected to produce substantial future economic benefits from which the costs of the debt can be met. Wasteful government expenditures which did not produce such benefits would, however, represent a future burden. Furthermore, *failure* to increase the public debt can also become a burden if the current generation allows what is called "social overhead capital" to degenerate. If roads, schools, hospitals, airports, and other public facilities are not properly maintained, large future deficits with sharp increases in public debt will be required to bring these structures back to the original operating standard.

Limitations on Monetary Policy. Several times each year it is necessary to refinance part of the public debt as matured bonds are presented for payment. The government would like to arrange this refinancing — issuing new bonds to raise funds for repayment of mature bonds — during recessions, when interest rates tend to be low, in order to minimize future interest payments. But if the sale of government bonds is concentrated in such periods, this will increase the general level of interest rates, discourage private investment, and prolong the recession, just at the time when the Bank of Canada would be attempting to lower interest rates to stimulate the economy. Conversely, the government will be reluctant to see interest rates increased during inflationary periods if it must refinance part of the debt, while the Bank will be trying to raise interest rates to restrain aggregate demand.

Basis for Open Market Operations. The principal advantage of the public debt is the stimulating effect of the budget deficit financed by the debt. A second advantage is the existence of a large quantity of widely held government bonds which are the basis for the Bank of Canada's open market operation. Recall that the Bank can effect subtle, daily changes in the money supply by buying and selling government bonds. In the absence of such a monetary tool, the Bank would be forced to rely on more disruptive devices: changing reserve requirements or the Bank Rate or both.

C. Monetary Policy

Monetary policy is the deliberate effort by the government, acting through the monetary authorities (the Bank of Canada), to vary the money supply in order to move the economy toward non-inflationary full employment, and to maintain a viable balance of payments and the proper foreign exchange rate when this is pegged. This latter concern of monetary policy was introduced in Chapter 5 and is examined again in Chapter 7.

The classical view of money's role emphasized its direct influence on the price level, but the neo-Keynesian view stresses the effect of the money supply on interest rates. (This relationship was explained in the latter part of Chapter 4.) Because the interest rate has some effect on the level of investment, particularly in residential construction, and hence on employment and national income, there is continuing controversy about whether the monetary authorities should pay more attention to interest rates or to the money supply.

It has been argued, for example, that monetary authorities should strive to maintain stable interest rates as one means of achieving a stable economy. But the explanation of general equilibrium in the economy, based on the interaction of the real and the monetary sectors, showed that full-employment national income could be achieved at various interest rates. Thus monetary policy cannot simply attempt to maintain a stable rate or to assume that a specific low rate is required for an expansionary policy and a specific high rate is required for a contractionary policy. Instead, monetary policy requires an appropriate *change* in interest rates, regardless of whether these are currently high or low. Recognition of this fact has shifted the emphasis in monetary policy toward its earlier concern with the level of the money supply rather than of interest rates.

Effect of Monetary Policy

To trace the sequence of effects of monetary policy on national income, (and thus on unemployment and inflation), assume that the Bank of Canada is pursuing an expansionary policy by buying bonds in the open market. The purchase of bonds increases national income directly by increasing chartered bank reserves, making more loans available, and thus stimulating investment and consumption spending.

Bond purchases also affect national income less directly through changes in the interest rates. The Bank can usually acquire enough bonds to realize its policy objectives only if it offers a higher price for bonds than would otherwise prevail in the bond market. A higher bond price results in a lower yield or interest rate than the face-value interest rate stated on the bonds. The lower interest rate can have two general effects. A lower interest rate is expected to encourage firms to increase their investment in plant and equipment, to increase their inventories of semi-finished and finished goods, and to increase residential construction.

Briefly, the Bank's action has these consequences. The purchase of bonds:

- increases bank reserves, making more loans available and at lower interest rates;
- increases the price of bonds and lowers interest rates, inducing more residential construction, expenditures on consumer durables, and possibly more business investment.

Limitations of Monetary Policy

The use of fiscal policy was seen to have a number of limitations or qualifications. Monetary policy is similarly constrained, but for different reasons.

Asymmetry of Monetary Policy. The major limitation is the asymmetry of monetary policy: the Bank of Canada can force a contraction in bank deposits but it can only encourage an expansion by increasing chartered banks' excess reserves. Monetary expansion is curtailed if the banks are not "fully loaned up"; that is, if banks are not able to find borrowers for all of their excess reserves. Fewer new deposits are created than is indicated by the reciprocal of the required reserve ratio. Such a situation might occur when interest rates are quite high. In this case, stronger expansionary monetary policy would be required to force interest rates down far enough to attract a substantial number of borrowers. The banks might use some of their excess reserves to buy bonds from the general public, thus adding to bank deposits; but if the Bank's open market operations have pushed up bond prices very far, the yield rate on bonds will be too low to attract the banks.

Liquidity Trap. At very low interest rates, the liquidity preference or demand for money curve is assumed to flatten out to form a *liquidity trap*. This was illustrated in Figure 4.9. At such low interest rates, people are quite prepared to increase their bank deposits in exchange for bonds. At this point, the Bank's purchase of bonds has little effect on the rate of interest because only a small increase, if any, in bond prices is necessary to provide the Bank with whatever quantity of bonds it seeks. In these circumstances, the money supply can be increased, but not interest rates. But when interest rates have reached such a low level, the economy probably is experiencing such high unemployment that little investment or consumption spending can be induced simply by increasing the money supply to make loans available.

The concept of a liquidity trap was important to Keynes' analysis of Depression conditions, but it has little relevance in current economic conditions, with higher interest rates than have prevailed in previous decades.

Investment Inelasticity. Investment spending may in some cases be inelastic with respect to changes in the interest rate. If for example firms are skeptical that the government's expansionary policies will be effective in increasing aggregate demand, they will not increase investment spending even at much lower interest rates. This also illustrates, incidently, another limitation on monetary policy: that business expectations contrary to the desired direction of government policy can severely weaken its effect.

Investment spending may also be interest-inelastic for high-yield, high-risk projects. Whether the project is undertaken will depend on the firm's assessment of many factors influencing the potential success of the venture, rather than on the interest rate.

Finally, larger firms may have sufficient funds among their highly liquid assets to undertake whatever investment projects they may be considering. The increased scarcity of loans would have little effect on their investment decisions; only a very high interest rate would cause them to question whether such funds should be held in higher yielding assets rather than in the firms' own investment project. Smaller firms, however, are not so likely to have internal funds, and therefore are more affected by changes in monetary policy.

Effect of Near-Money. Asset holdings in the form of near-money or highly liquid assets can offset much of the potential effect of a contractionary monetary policy. Chartered banks can sell their government bonds to provide loan funds; firms and individuals can sell their more liquid assets to maintain their investment and consumption spending.

Changed Velocity of Circulation. A problem similar to that posed by near-money is presented by changes in the velocity of money. Recall from the quantity equation of exchange, $MV = PQ$, that an increase in V will have the same effect on national income as an increase in M. Velocity tends to increase during an expansionary period, when monetary policy usually is attempting to restrain increases in the money supply, because individuals want to hold less money as interest rates rise. Higher interest rates encourage savings and trust companies to be more active in attracting and loaning funds during an expansionary period. This further increases the velocity of money, partly offsetting the effect of contractionary monetary policy.

Fixed Foreign Exchange Rates. Under a fixed foreign exchange rate, monetary policy designed to achieve domestic stability can cause difficulties for monetary authorities. If the money supply is increased and interest rates fall, short-term foreign capital tends to leave the country in pursuit of higher interest rates elsewhere. This puts a downward pressure on the foreign exchange rate; more foreign currency must be sold from the Exchange Fund Account in exchange for Canadian dollars to maintain the pegged rate within the agreed range. When holdings of foreign currencies are low, the Bank of Canada will be reluctant to pursue an expansionary policy which would further drain the Exchange Fund Account by lowering interest rates.

The Bank will also be reluctant to pursue a vigorous expansionary policy if there is a serious deficit on the current account in the balance of payments. Such a policy would tend to increase product prices, reduce exports, and increase imports, thereby worsening the current account deficit. One of the major advantages of a freely floating exchange rate is that monetary and fiscal policies are free to deal with domestic problems without such concern for the balance of payments and foreign exchange rates. However, a "managed float" requires that monetary policy still be constrained by these external considerations. (This is discussed further in Chapter 7.)

Conflict with Debt Management. The discussion of the public debt raised the problems that debt management poses for monetary policy. The government would like to refinance its maturing bonds during recessionary periods when interest rates are low. But substantial sales of government bonds would increase interest rates and discourage investment expenditures. At the same time, the Bank should be buying bonds in the open market to lower interest rates in order to induce more investment spending. Thus the Bank faces a dilemma posed by its two roles as manager of the public debt and as agent of monetary policy.

Timing and Location of Effects. Monetary policy appears to have about the same overall time lag that is encountered with fiscal policy. The recognition or identification lag may be equally long, but the decision lag can be much shorter than for fiscal policy since the Bank's senior officers alone usually decide day-to-day policy. (The Finance Minister and his advisors are consulted on longer-range monetary policy.) The implementation lag can also be somewhat shorter because the Bank's techniques for changing the money supply act immediately to alter chartered banks' reserves, but the subsequent expansion stage may take longer if the banks have difficulty in finding borrowers for their excess reserves. The contraction process, however, must proceed quickly, particularly when the banks have been holding no excess reserves.

Conversely, the *location* of the effects of monetary policy cannot be controlled as can some aspects of fiscal policy, particularly on the expenditure side. Effects of monetary policy are seen first in the larger financial centres of the country, but the branch banking system assures that these effects are quickly dispersed. An excess or deficit of bank reserves is reported only for each chartered bank; the head office of these banks can therefore manage its reserves within its branches as it chooses. In an expansionary situation, for example, all branches of a bank will be advertising for potential borrowers in order to loan out the total excess reserves held by that bank. This universality of effects can be an advantage when the entire country faces similar inflation or unemployment, but a disadvantage when conditions vary significantly among different regions.

D.   Monetary, Fiscal, or Other Policies?

Monetary or Fiscal Policy?

Monetary and fiscal policy represent two distinct sets of actions the government can take in its efforts to control inflation and unemployment. Each has limitations and advantages. Which should be emphasized, and when? Economists have debated this question extensively, especially in recent years with the revival of an active monetary policy at the Bank of Canada. The argument is even more vigorous in the United States where the Federal Reserve System has much more independence in designing a monetary policy than does the Bank of Canada.

Supporters of fiscal policy maintain that, although both fiscal and monetary policy should be used, the former is more effective in bringing about economic stability because it can be designed to act more directly on particular problems. Monetary policy, they argue, has its main effect, through changes in interest rates, on the level of residential construction and consumer durables; this can be slow and unpredictable. Monetary policy should therefore be used only to reinforce fiscal policy, and specifically to offset the effects of higher interest rates generated by deficit financing in an expansionary fiscal policy.

The advocates of monetary policy — the "monetarists" — argue that fiscal policy acts too slowly, and indeed has worsened economic problems when, for example, an expansionary policy has its major effect after the recession is past and inflation is a serious threat. Fiscal policy therefore should be restricted to the minimum government expenditures required to provide necessary public services, with sufficient tax revenues to finance these. Moreover, money is said to have a stronger, more direct, impact on aggregate demand than simply by affecting interest rates.

The key to this argument is the stability in the demand for money. There is said to be a normal relationship between the quantity of money individuals and firms wish to hold and the level of national income. This implies that the velocity of money tends to return to a normal rate following any fluctuations in velocity. If the money supply increases beyond the quantity individuals want to hold at a particular level of national income, this excess money will be spent, increasing national income to the point where the normal relationship between the demand for money and national income has been reestablished. Similarly, a reduction in the money supply will lead to a reduction in spending until national income has fallen to the level appropriate to the quantity of money held. This can be recognized as a restatement of the quantity equation of exchange: $MV = PQ$. If V is assumed to be constant, an increase in M will increase P or Q or both; that is, the level of national income will rise.

In this context, fiscal policy can be viewed as a special case of monetary policy. When a deficit budget is financed by borrowing from the public, the expansionary effects are not nearly so strong as when the government borrows from the Bank of Canada. In the latter case, money is created and deposit expansion occurs. The monetary advocates point out that it is actually the increase in the money supply which increases aggregate demand rather than the deficit budget *per se*.

Rules Versus Discretionary Policy

Professor Milton Friedman has argued[3] that analyses of money's impact on national income leads not only to the conclusion that monetary policy is more effective than fiscal policy for economic stability but that a monetary *rule* should replace discretionary monetary policy: *that the money supply should be increased each year at the same annual rate projected for real growth in Gross National Product.* This follows from his view that not only is monetary policy important, but that changes in the money supply have too strong an effect on the economy to leave decisions about these changes to monetary authorities. In fact, he suggests that monetary policy has had a *destabilizing* effect because changes have been too large or too small in given situations, and have been made too late to have their intended effect. If the economy is basically stable, as Friedman claims, his rule would allow economic growth to proceed steadily.

Normative Aspects of the Debate

Economists recently have given more attention to the use of monetary policy but most are not prepared to abandon discretionary

---

[3] Milton Friedman. *Dollars and Deficits.* Englewood Cliffs, N.J.: Prentice-Hall, 1968.

policies, fiscal or monetary, in favour of rules because the economy is not basically stable: each period requires judgment and knowledge about economic conditions and policies to design an appropriate policy for the following period. Thus, more emphasis has been placed on selecting appropriate combinations of fiscal actions, proper financing of deficits, timing of policies, and especially coordinating monetary and fiscal policies.

The debate as outlined above is concerned with positive economic analysis. Despite extensive research on the efficacy of monetary and fiscal policies, much disagreement remains on basic relationships in the economy (such as between income and the demand for money) and on the data and techniques used in analyzing policy impact on economic activity. In time, such disagreements may be resolved through further theoretical and empirical research.

An overriding aspect of the debate, however, concerns normative judgments about the role of government in the economy.

Some advocates of more emphasis on monetary policy would like to see the Bank of Canada become more independent of the federal government so that it is free of what such advocates regard as short-run, political considerations. However, even with the close relationship between the Bank and the federal government, they argue that more reliance on monetary policy would slow down the expansion of the government sector in the economy. (As Chapter 8 shows, total government spending, including transfer payments, now accounts for almost 40 per cent of the Gross National Product.) Fiscal policy, in practice, is seen as gradually increasing the government share of GNP because politically it is difficult to eliminate or to reduce spending on specific programs after they have been in effect for a few years. Thus, contractionary fiscal policy can be implemented only by increasing taxes: the alternative action, of reducing expenditures, is said to be unavailable to the government. This effect is sometimes described as "creeping socialism".

To a certain extent, this second level of the debate could be resolved by examining government budgets to discover whether significant expenditure reductions had occurred when restrictive fiscal policies were required, but the disagreement is largely a matter of political ideology. Nevertheless, economists have an obligation to show how economic policies affect the political organization of the country, as well as how they affect specific economic objectives. From this perspective, normative disagreements can be a stimulating, enlightening contribution to policy-making, provided that they are based on sound evidence and reasoning.

Canadian Experience with Monetary Policy

A number of influential economists emerged from the closely controlled economy of World War II, anxious to use the new

Keynesian prescriptions for fiscal policy. These seemed ideally designed, particularly those concerning budgetary deficits, to deal
with the anticipated recession following the war. Monetary policy
was largely ignored. This was partly due to the Bank of Canada's
views on the nature of the economic problems and their inexperi-
ence in using monetary policy. From the beginning of its operations
in 1935 and 1939, the economy had been recovering from the Depression; since an expansionary policy was required throughout this
period, there was little opportunity for learning to use the tools of
monetary policy under various economic conditions.

The monetary situation during World War II also offered little
opportunity to experiment with monetary policy. Large-scale government borrowing to finance war expenditures required a continuation of the expansionary policy to maintain low interest rates. This
was accomplished through the Bank of Canada, which purchased
large quantities of government bonds. This action both increased the
money supply and directly maintained low interest rates by not
allowing bond prices to fall.

The wartime monetary policy was continued into the immediate
postwar years because a recession was expected to follow from the
sharp reduction in the government's war expenditures. The strong
inflationary pressure which emerged instead, as individuals spent
their savings on the limited output of consumer goods, was not
recognized for a few years. The Bank took little action except, in
1948, to suggest that chartered banks restrain their granting of loans.
There was a mild recession in 1949, but serious inflationary conditions returned in 1950.

The Bank of Canada's first significant use of monetary policy
took the form of increasing the Bank Rate from 1½ to 2 per cent in
late 1950. In early 1951, moral suasion was used to gain the chartered banks' agreement to restrict less essential loans and to accept
an overall ceiling on deposit expansion. Setting a ceiling rather than
attempting to restrain monetary expansion by using open-market
operations indicated the Bank's initial reluctance to develop day-
to-day use of monetary policy.

The ceiling was removed in 1952 but loans continued to be
restricted. The recession which emerged in late 1953 brought no
monetary action until late 1954, when the money supply was increased by reducing the cash reserve ratio from 10 to 8 per cent. The
return of inflation in 1955 evoked a stronger monetary policy consisting of open-market operations, an increase in the Bank Rate, and
moral suasion. The latter included an agreement to restrain loans
and to maintain an additional 7 per cent reserve in highly liquid
assets. This became an informal secondary reserve requirement, but
in 1967 it was made mandatory by the revision of the Bank Act.

A restrictive monetary policy was maintained throughout the
late 1950s until early 1961, despite the serious recession that developed in 1958 through 1961 when unemployment rose to over 7

per cent. This perverse monetary policy reduced the effectiveness of the government's expansionary fiscal policy, resulting in a sharp dispute between the Governor of the Bank and the Minister of Finance. Following Senate hearings on this disagreement about appropriate monetary policy, the government accepted the resignation of the Governor, Mr. James Coyne.

The new Governor, Mr. Louis Rasminsky, immediately introduced an expansionary monetary policy based on open-market bond purchases. Except for monetary restraint in 1962 when the Canadian foreign exchange rate was pegged at 92½ cents in terms of the American dollar, the expansionary policy continued to 1965, using open-market purchases and reductions in the Bank Rate. Some restraint on the money supply was exercised in 1965 as the sustained economic growth of 1961 to 1965 threatened to bring faster price increases, but expansionary conditions generally prevailed until 1967.

Early in 1968, Canada's foreign exchange reserves fell sharply as monetary authorities bought Canadian dollars to maintain the pegged exchange rate. The Bank introduced severe monetary restraint to increase rates and attract foreign deposits. By June 1968, the immediate crisis had passed and monetary restraint was eased. But the restrictive monetary policy had not been as effective in restraining inflation as had been thought, and unemployment became a more serious problem. Monetary restraint was again exercised by open-market bond sales, and a number of increases in the Bank Rate and the secondary reserve requirements. This restrictive policy was maintained until mid-1970. From then until late 1972 the Bank Rate was reduced frequently, from a high of 8 per cent to 4¾ per cent. The secondary reserve requirement was maintained at its high of 9 per cent until the end of 1971 but then was reduced twice within a month to 8 per cent to allow the banks to divert funds from treasury bills into loans and hence encourage expansion of consumer and investment spending.

The rapid increase in the money supply that occurred through 1971-72 was tempered during 1973 in a belated effort to restrain inflation. The Bank Rate was raised five times in the five months from mid-April to mid-September, from 4¾ to 7¼ per cent. Inflation continued at a high rate in early 1974; the Bank Rate was raised again three times, in April, May, and June, to 9¼ per cent and credit conditions tightened. The high interest rates attracted deposits to savings and term accounts with a resulting rapid increase in the broadly defined money supply.

Meanwhile, the foreign exchange value of the Canadian dollar rose to a premium of over 4 per cent on the American dollar and the balance of payments on current account was showing an increasing deficit. These latter considerations apparently influenced monetary policy most strongly in late 1974 as the Bank Rate was dropped back to 8¾ per cent in November and to 8¼ per cent in January, 1975. But by the latter half of 1975, however, domestic inflation was of primary concern; the Bank Rate was raised to 9 per cent in September, 1975.

The secondary reserve requirement had been held at 8 per cent from January, 1972, to the end of 1974 when it was reduced to 7 per cent; this was the first step in a further reduction to 6 per cent in January, 1975, and to 5½ per cent in March, 1975. Since the federal government had met its revenue requirements through record sales of Canada savings bonds in the fall of 1974, it did not need to rely on the chartered banks to take up its offerings of treasury bills and hence the Bank of Canada could reduce their secondary reserve requirements. The massive flow of funds that would have been available for loans, with resulting inflationary pressures, were substantially offset by the Bank of Canada's contractionary open-market operations. Meanwhile, the foreign exchange rate of the Canadian dollar fell from $1.02 in October, 1974, to $.96 in August, 1975, and then began to ease upwards again.

Manpower Policies

In the early 1960s, when there was increasing support for the structural-change explanation of unemployment, there were frequent proposals for manpower policies designed to reduce such unemployment and hence to shift the Phillips curve to lower levels of both inflation and unemployment. At the same time there was considerable support for manpower policies to deal with the poverty problem and to encourage economic growth. These were longer-range objectives, however, and any success in meeting these through manpower programs would not be available immediately. Manpower programs were sometimes used primarily as stabilization programs, but not in a way that would necessarily improve the trade-off relationship. In the case of retraining programs, for example, putting unemployed persons into classrooms would temporarily reduce the unemployment rate and their maintenance allowances would stimulate aggregate demand, but if they were put back into the labour force without adequate training in appropriate occupational skills the process would be repeated during the next recession. However, if manpower policies are properly designed — and applied — to meet the objective of economic growth by improving labour productivity, they can at the same time contribute to economic stabilization. The major components of Canada's manpower policy include programs for retraining, counselling and job placement, and labour mobility.

Retraining. Although some provinces have retraining programs, the major program in Canada is conducted under the federal government's Adult Occupational Training Act (1967). Training is provided to persons who are expected to benefit through increased earnings, who are above the school-leaving age, and who have been out of school for at least one year. The training generally consists of classroom instruction in educational institutions established by provincial governments. There is increasing evidence, however, that on-the-job training is more effective in improving a worker's skills and future employment opportunities, and hence the federal government has tended to shift the program in this direction.

Counselling and Job Placement. Canada Manpower Centres have been established in more than 300 municipalities across Canada to collect and provide information on job vacancies, to counsel workers on employment prospects and training opportunities, and to refer workers to specific training programs. Employers are encouraged to list job openings with the Centres; other job information is collected through a job vacancy survey conducted by Statistics Canada.

Labour Mobility. A federal Manpower Mobility Program was introduced in 1965 to assist workers in finding employment in other geographical areas. Grants are available for workers who need to travel to other areas to take training programs not available in their home areas, to assist workers in exploring job possibilities in nearby areas, and to cover moving and travel expenses for workers and their families who have secured employment elsewhere. Eligibility for such grants is restricted to persons who are unemployed or underemployed and who cannot find suitable work in their home areas.

Other programs, both federal and provincial, are concerned with improving the operation of the labour market. One important policy is legislation forbidding discrimination in employment practices, particularly regarding race, religion, national origin — and in some provinces — sex and age.

Prices and Incomes Policy

The dilemma of simultaneous inflation and unemployment described earlier in this chapter is a serious enough problem for government policy-makers, but two additional factors have led them to look more widely for stabilization policies. First, the Phillips curve apparently is shifting outward: that is, higher inflation is associated with any given unemployment rate; and second, monetary and fiscal policies have not worked as well as desired, requiring massive and often disruptive changes to obtain significant reductions in inflation or unemployment. Attention has turned to prices and incomes policy as an additional tool for dealing with these problems, particularly following introduction of such a policy in Britain and the United States.

A prices and incomes policy has three components: a set of general targets or objectives concerning incomes which are expected to lead to economic stability, such as a statement that the average level of wages should rise by not more than 8 per cent; a set of principles for translating the general targets into specific wage and price decisions in each sector, industry, and firm; and a method for either inducing voluntary acceptance of these objectives and principles, or for enforcing them if a voluntary program is not successful.

Canadian Experience. Faced with accelerated inflation in 1966, the Canadian government suggested that wage increases should be voluntarily restrained to not more than 6 per cent annually. Workers responded by pressing more vigorously for wage increases, to keep ahead of both the rising cost of living and possible government attempts to introduce a more formal wage policy.

In 1969, the federal government appointed a Prices and Incomes Commission to examine the major causes of the rapid inflation and to suggest means for dealing with it. The Commission attempted to obtain voluntary support for restraint of wage and price increases but the labour unions refused to cooperate. The Commission's final report before it was abolished in June, 1972, took note of experience with wage and price controls elsewhere and suggested that something similar might be necessary in Canada, at least for a temporary period. Any temporary controls, however, may be expected to have only temporary effects, with the result that such controls would need to be reintroduced from time to time. This seems to have been the experience in the United States, and particularly in Britain, as described in the section below.

Temporary wage and price controls, as proposed by the Conservative party in the July 1974 election, were rejected by the Canadian electorate. In October 1975, a "restraint" program was introduced which proposed limiting most wage, salary, and professional fee increases to 10 per cent annually, and allowing prices to rise only by the amount of increased production costs. An Anti-Inflation Board was appointed to monitor wage and price increases, to seek public support for the program, and to coordinate the federal program with the provincial legislation that was required to give legal power to some parts of the program.

Soon after the program began, the prime minister stirred national controversy by suggesting that "the market system was not working" and thus that more government intervention was required. This was a direct reference to the problems described in Chapter 2 in the section on market failure. That is, where markets have become monopolistic, cost-push inflation becomes stronger, and governments must encourage greater competition. An incomes policy is useful, however, only if it provides a period within which other legislation can be introduced to improve the market system over the long run.

American Experience. The American experience with an incomes and prices policy began in 1962. The U.S. President's Council of Economic Advisors advocated wage and price "guideposts"; these recommended average wage increase in each industry equal to the annual increase in productivity (or output per man-hour). Prices were to be reduced if an industry's productivity increase was greater than the national average, and vice versa. The guideposts had no legal status, but they did have the strong support of Presidents Kennedy and Johnson. Generally it is agreed that this approach had some restraining effect on prices and wages, largely because the presidents were prepared to cite specific cases as being contrary to the public interest.

As inflation became a more serious problem in the late 1960s, presidential influence was much less effective, partly because this inflation stemmed from the government's Vietnam War expenditures. President Nixon finally turned, in 1971, to direct controls by forbidding any increases in wages and prices for 90 days. Following this period, a Cost of Living Council was created to direct two agencies, a Pay Board which would review and judge proposed wage increases, and a Price Commission to do the same for prices. Controls of this type might have been instituted in any case, but they seemed to be particularly necessary in 1971 because President Nixon was also proposing several tax reductions in order to reduce unemployment. The wage and price freeze was intended to curtail inflation so that increased disposable income would generate more real output and employment. This was followed in January, 1973, by a voluntary system of price restraints, then in mid-1973 by a short return to a price freeze, and then by wage and price review boards again.

British Experience. The British experience with incomes policies has been long and rather unsuccessful. The postwar Labour government introduced a "wage freeze" and "dividend restraint" policy in 1948, but wages nevertheless increased by an average of 6 per cent during the following year. Although wages for a particular occupation and grade classification remained fixed, employees were simply promoted to higher classifications. That is, employers competed for labour by offering higher job classifications instead of higher wages. During the early 1950s, the Conservative government relied on exhortations to management and unions to restrain wage increases. In 1961, a "pay pause" was introduced to give the government's new National Economic Development Council time to discover means for increasing productivity which would justify subsequent wage increases.

In 1962, about the same time the Americans were being urged to follow wage and price "guideposts", the British government issued a White Paper proposing a "guiding light": that wage increases should average 2.5 per cent annually. A National Incomes Commission which was to assist the government in implementing this policy received little support from the unions with the result that the guiding light was ignored in many industries.

The election of a Labour government in 1964 led to an agreement among government, employers, and unions, to plan jointly for increasing productivity and income restraints. Two further White Papers in 1965 set a norm of 3 to 3.5 per cent as the average annual increase in money incomes, but earnings rose by three times this amount during the following year. The result was a tougher policy: from October 1966 until August 1967 an "incomes freeze" was in effect. This was more successful than the earlier recommendations and exhortations. Nonetheless, Britain found it necessary to devalue the pound in November 1967 to maintain competitive prices in international markets, and then to allow the foreign exchange rate of the pound to float in June of 1972. In early 1973, a 90-day wage and price freeze — this time a "standstill" — was introduced. For the rest of 1973, wage increases could not exceed 6.5 per cent. Nevertheless, Britain experienced rampant inflation and in July 1975, introduced new guidelines which limited wage increases in the following year to £6 (about $13.80) per week, with no increases for those earning over £8,500 (about $18,000) per year.

Review of the Main Points

1. The federal government's fiscal and monetary policies are part of its overall stabilization policy to reduce inflation and unemployment. Because these generally occur together, the government must choose to reduce inflation while accepting higher levels of unemployment, or vice versa. At the same time, the government attempts to shift the Phillips curve downward so that a lower rate of inflation occurs with any given unemployment rate; but in fact, the curve appears to be shifting outward despite government efforts.

2. For policy and analysis purposes, three types of inflation are identified; demand-pull, cost-push, and structural change. The first is caused by excess aggregate demand, the second by increases in production costs per unit of output, and the third by changes in the composition of demand such that increased prices in some sectors are transmitted to other sectors. Similarly, four types of unemployment are identified: inadequate demand, frictional, seasonal, and structural. The first is caused by inadequate aggregate demand, the second by persons leaving one job to look for another, the third by seasonal fluctuations in the demand for labour, and the fourth by changes in the composition of demand for final goods and by changes in production technology.

3. Fiscal policy includes both automatic and discretionary elements. Automatic stabilizers include the higher marginal propensities to save and to import at higher income levels, government programs which automatically vary transfer payments as

incomes change, and the progressive income tax structure which reduces the proportion of disposable income as gross incomes rise.

4. Discretionary fiscal policy includes the actions taken by the government to achieve not only stable prices and full employment but also economic growth, favourable income distribution, and balance of payments equilibrium, through the appropriate composition and size of its expenditures and tax revenues. Alternative fiscal policies are available, for example, to reduce unemployment. The three basic approaches are: an increase in government expenditures, a decrease in tax revenues, or an equal increase in both tax revenues and expenditures.

5. The size of the change required varies for each of these alternatives. Because the multiplier affects the full amount of government expenditures, these need to be increased the least. Since the multiplier acts only on the consumption component of increased disposable income, tax revenues must be decreased by more than the increase in government expenditures to have a given effect on national income. Finally, if the value of the multiplier is uniform throughout the economy, an equal change in tax revenues and government expenditures will change national income by the same amount.

6. A major problem in designing discretionary fiscal policy is to determine how long current increases in inflation or unemployment are likely to last if current fiscal policy is not revised. A strong deflationary policy, for example, could produce a recession if the strength of a current inflationary trend is overestimated.

7. Other problems include the time lags in recognizing an emerging problem, deciding on the proper action, and implementing this policy; and the problem of determining how this public action will indirectly affect private spending and how particular areas and individuals will be affected by a general policy.

8. An annually balanced government budget would reinforce any delfationary or inflationary trend in the economy. Balancing the budget over the cycle is generally impossible because the size and duration of recessions and expansionary periods are seldom equal. Instead, governments should have budget deficits or surpluses as required to guide the economy to non-inflationary full employment. The relevant consideration is not the actual deficit or surplus but the potential budgetary position that would be realized if the economy were at full employment.

9. Deficits may be financed by borrowing from the general public or from the Bank of Canada. Borrowing from the public transfers private consumption and investment to government spending. A net increase in spending results if private funds would have been

dormant or used to purchase foreign securities, or if the multiplier is greater for government expenditures than for private spending. Borrowing from the Bank of Canada creates new money and thus has a much stronger expansionary effect.

10. Surpluses generally are used to reduce the outstanding public debt. Repayment of publicly held debt transfers aggregate demand from taxpayers to bondholders but repayment of a debt held by the Bank of Canada reduces the money supply and then the level of aggregate demand.

11. Monetary policy is the deliberate use of variations in the money supply to move the economy toward non-inflationary full employment. When the foreign exchange rate is pegged, effects of monetary policy on the balance of payments and on the exchange rate must also be taken into account.

12. Monetary policy effected through open market operations influences aggregate demand by changing bank reserves available for loans and thus the interest rate on loans, and by directly changing interest rates through changing bond prices.

13. The limitations on monetary policy include: the asymmetry of its effects — contraction of the money supply must occur but expansion depends on the ability of banks to increase their loans; the liquidity trap, or the inability of the Bank to reduce interest rates further once they have reached a low level; the interest-inelasticity of investment under certain conditions; the possibility of near-money, or highly liquid assets, being converted to money and thus offsetting a restrictive monetary policy; changes in the velocity of circulation which tend to vary inversely with the money supply; the need to maintain high interest rates when there is downward pressure on a pegged exchange rate; the difficulty of keeping interest rates low during a recession while the sale of government bonds exerts an upward pressure on interest rates; the time lag in implementing an appropriate policy; and the universality of effects which may be inappropriate to specific regional needs.

14. Controversy exists among government and academic economists on the appropriate roles for fiscal and monetary policy. Fiscal policy is preferred by some because it can be designed to deal directly with specific problems, while others argue that fiscal policy can act so slowly that an expansionary policy may spur the economy at the wrong time. Still others argue that even discretionary monetary policy is too destabilizing and propose that the money supply be increased at the same rate as the potential growth rate of GNP.

15. Canadian experience with active monetary policy was negligible during the Depression and World War II. A restrictive policy was generally maintained through the 1950s regardless of economic

conditions. A more active, expansionary policy following 1960 included regular open market operations, but the pegging of the exchange rate from 1962 to 1970 limited its effectiveness on domestic conditions. An anti-inflation policy was pursued from 1968 to 1970. An expansionary policy followed from 1970 to 1972; and then from 1973 to 1976, monetary policy was mildly contractionary. Monetary policy since 1960 has included greater use of changes in the Bank Rate and, since 1967, changes in secondary reserve requirements.

16. Manpower programs have been introduced, partly in an effort to shift the Phillips curve downward by reducing cost-push inflation and structural unemployment. Retraining, job counselling and placement, and mobility programs are designed to increase the supply of specific labour skills in areas where there appear to be an excess demand for these skills.

17. A prices and incomes policy has often been proposed as an additional stabilization policy. The United States and Britain have both resorted to direct control of wage and price increases, with limited success. Canada introduced a mandatory restraint program in late 1975.

Review and Discussion Questions

1. Why is the problem of time lags so important in setting monetary and fiscal policy?

2. If a given increase in government expenditures has a greater impact on GNP than an equal decrease in tax revenues, why would the government ever decrease taxes as part of a fiscal policy to reduce unemployment?

3. Suppose someone suggested to you that the federal government should pay off the national debt completely. Outline your response in terms of how this might be accomplished and what the consequences would be.

4. Why is monetary policy likely to be more effective in curtailing inflation than in reducing unemployment?

5. Write a letter to your Member of Parliament explaining your views on the federal government's prices and incomes policy.

Sources and Selected Readings

Buchanan, James M., and Richard E. Wagner, *Public Debt in a Democratic Society*. Washington, D.C.: American Enterprise Institute, 1967.

Economic Council of Canada, *Third Annual Review: Prices, Productivity and Employment*. Ottawa: Queen's Printer, 1966.

Johnson, H.G. "The Keynesian Revolution and the Monetarist Counter-Revolution," *American Economic Review*, May 1971.

Officer, L.H., and L.B. Smith (eds.) *Issues in Canadian Economics*. Toronto: McGraw-Hill Ryerson, 1974, Part I.

Prices and Incomes Commission. *Inflation, Unemployment and Incomes Policy*. Ottawa: Information Canada, 1972.

Safarian, A.E. *The Canadian Economy in the Great Depression*. Toronto: University of Toronto Press, 1949.

Sawyer, J.A. *Macroeconomics: Theory and Policy in the Canadian Economy*. Toronto: Macmillan, 1975.

Sirkin, Gerald. *Introduction to Macroeconomic Theory*, 3rd ed. Homewood: Ill.: Irwin, 1970.

Smith, David C. *Incomes Policies: Some Foreign Experiences and Their Relevance for Canada*. Ottawa: Queen's Printer, 1966.

Tobin, J. "Inflation and Unemployment," *American Economic Review*, March 1972.

7   International Trade and Finance

Anyone who reads a Canadian newspaper regularly knows how important are the international aspects of Canada's economy. In fact, it sometimes seems that there are more articles on these concerns than on domestic economic problems. Large export sales of wheat, another trade mission to Asia, the foreign exchange value of the Canadian dollar, amendments to the Canada-United States Automotive Agreement, arguments over the sale of Canadian water, petroleum, gas, or uranium, and international monetary crises: all are treated as major news items. This chapter deals with Canada's international trade and finance; then in Chapter 8 attention is focused on the government sector and its relationship to the rest of the economy. Since the foreign trade and government sectors were featured prominently in the theory of national income determination, as presented in Chapter 4, it is important to understand how each of these sectors functions and how each influence the other two major components: domestic consumption and investment.

A.   International Trade

Canada's Pattern of Foreign Trade

One major feature of Canada's international economic relations is foreign trade, and particularly trade in goods. Recall from the discussion of the Balance of International Payments in Chapter 3 that international payments include capital flows, income transfers and payments for goods and services. This section, however, is concerned only with trade in physical or tangible commodities. Canada's pattern of foreign trade is examined by asking the following questions: how large is Canada's foreign trade relative to its GNP? Who are the major trading partners? What is exported and to whom? What is imported and from whom?

Table 7.1 shows that in 1972 Canada ranked sixth in the world in the total value of its exports. More significantly, Canada's exports equalled 23 per cent — almost one-quarter — of its total production of goods and services. Although the United States is the world's largest exporter, its exports represent only 4 per cent of its GNP. Only West Germany and the United Kingdom are more significant exporting countries than Canada when both the value of exports and exports as a share of GNP are taken into account.

Table 7.1

Major Exporting Countries, 1972

	Value of Exports ($ U.S. millions)	Percentage of World Exports	Percentage of own GNP
United States	48,979	12	4
West Germany	46,208	11	22
Japan	28,591	7	11
France	25,848	6	18
United Kingdom	24,344	6	22
Canada	20,178	5	23
Italy	18,548	4	20
Total, 7 countries	212,696	51	
Total, world	414,400	100	

Source: United Nations, *Statistical Yearbook*, 1973.

Canada's major trading partners are shown in Table 7.2. Note that in most cases the main purchasers of exports are also the main suppliers of imports. In 1974, Canada had a positive balance of trade with most of these trading partners. Although only one-quarter of American exports (1 per cent of the American GNP) came to Canada in 1974, Canada's trade with the United States far exceeds that with any other country, accounting for two-thirds of Canada's exports and imports. For this reason, Canada is very much concerned about the domestic economic policies of the United States. When unemployment is high in the United States, Canada's export sales may fall; when inflation is a problem in the United States, Canada may "import" some of this inflation through purchases of American goods.

Table 7.2

Canada's Major Trading Partners, 1974

Country	Merchandise Exports		Merchandise Imports		Trade
	Value ($ millions)	Percentage of Total	Value ($ millions)	Percentage of Total	Balance ($ millions)
United States	21,325	66.3	21,306	67.3	+ 19
Japan	2,229	6.9	1,427	4.5	+ 802
United Kingdom	1,904	5.9	1,126	3.6	+ 778
West Germany	545	1.7	767	2.4	− 222
Italy	464	1.4	316	1.0	+ 148
China	439	1.4	61	.2	+ 378
France	318	1.0	394	1.2	− 76
Venezuela	205	0.6	1,288	4.1	−1,083
Iran	62	0.2	618	2.0	− 556
Rest of World	4,686	14.6	4,336	13.7	− 350
Total	32,177	100.0	31,639	100.0	+ 538

Source: Statistics Canada, *Exports* and *Imports*.

Table 7.3

Canada's Major Merchandise Exports, 1974

Item	Value ($ millions)	Percentage of Total
Motor vehicles and parts	5,578	17.8
Crude petroleum	3,408	10.9
Wheat	2,401	6.5
Wood pulp	1,861	5.9
Newsprint	1,722	5.5
Lumber	1,289	4.1
Copper ore and concentrates	647	2.1
Copper	644	2.1
Iron ore and concentrates	574	1.8
Total Exports (excluding re-exports)	31,292	

Source: Statistics Canada, *Canadian Statistical Review*.

The major commodities exported by Canada are displayed in Table 7.3. Motor vehicles and parts head the list of exports, a result of the Canada-United States Automotive Agreement by which tariffs were removed from motor vehicles and parts imported by automobile manufacturers to increase specialization in automobile production and expand Canada's sale of these to the United States. Most of the other items in this list reflect the importance of products from primary industries: newsprint, wood pulp, and lumber from forestry; wheat from agriculture; crude petroleum, iron ore, copper and copper ore from mining and smelting. The value of the least-processed products on this short list alone — wood pulp, wheat, lumber, crude petroleum, and iron and copper ore — accounts for about 30 per cent of Canada's exports.

Conversely, Table 7.4 shows that a large share of Canada's imports are fully manufactured or finished products. The imports of motor vehicles and parts also reflect the effects of the Automotive

Table 7.4

Canada's Major Merchandise Imports, 1974

Item	Value ($ millions)	Percentage of Total
Motor vehicles and parts	6,995	22.2
Crude petroleum	2,645	8.4
Communications equipment	956	3.0
Farm machinery and parts	800	2.5
Iron and steel	787	2.5
Aircraft and parts	667	2.1
General purpose machinery	617	2.0
Office machines	608	1.9
Total Imports	31,578	

Source: Statistics Canada, *Canadian Statistical Review*.

Agreement. The net trade effect of this agreement can be seen by subtracting the value of vehicles and parts imported from those exported. The apparent paradox of both exporting and importing crude petroleum is explained by the concentration of petroleum production in Western Canada, its consumption in Eastern Canada, and the high cost of transporting or moving petroleum between these two areas. Thus Quebec imports petroleum from Venezuela by means of ocean tankers to Maine and pipeline from Maine to Quebec while Alberta exports petroleum to the United States.

These patterns of foreign trade vary somewhat from year to year as new sources of raw materials are discovered and developed, as new agreements are made with other countries, as wheat harvests change with weather conditions in Canada and abroad, as technology and consumer demands change, and as international monetary arrangements are revised. Nevertheless, some of the main features have dominated Canada's foreign trade pattern throughout its history: the export of raw or semi-finished materials and the import of manufactured goods; the increasing prominence of trade with the United States; and the large export component in Canada's total production of goods and services.

Rationale for International Trade

Why do countries trade with other countries? Why not attempt to become a self-sufficient economy? One might suggest that one way to increase a country's employment and income is to increase exports. But this policy necessitates buying the exports of other countries if other countries are to have the funds to buy one's own exports. This brings us back to the question, why import and export goods rather than produce domestically all that a country needs? This is the question to be examined in this section. The next part of the chapter deals with the financial arrangements for international trade. Unfortunately, more popular attention, and perhaps professional attention, is given to financial or monetary problems than to the trade problems. Basic issues in the trading of real goods and services need to be understood before there can be a proper examination of what are often political questions concerning international financial arrangements.

The rationale for the exchange of goods and services among countries, or for foreign trade, is basically the same as the rationale for trade among regions within a country, or for the specialization of labour. In the latter case, individuals specialize in providing the type of labour service which will earn them the highest monetary return, and then sell their goods or labour services so that they can purchase other goods and services. A dentist, for example, may also be skilled as a do-it-yourself carpenter. He may be even more skilled in carpentry than are the carpenters available locally. Nevertheless the dentist will probably hire a carpenter to put a den in his basement rather than do the job himself. When the dentist calculates the income he can earn during the three days it would take him to build the den (after subtracting income tax from such earnings), he finds that he can earn more as a dentist than he must pay the carpenter. Thus, by hiring a carpenter he can have his den and extra income as well. The carpenter gains through having a higher income than he would have had otherwise.

Similarly, some areas of Canada are especially suited to the production of apples: the Annapolis Valley of Nova Scotia, the Niagara Peninsula in Ontario, and the Okanagan Valley of British Columbia. Each of these areas could also support beef production, but if this were done the value of the potential beef output would be less than the value of apple production on these lands. Other areas can produce beef cattle, sometimes not so efficiently as in the areas mentioned above, but more efficiently than they can produce apples. Again, specialization in the commodity produced relatively more efficiently, with subsequent exchange of goods between the areas, leaves each area better off than if each produced both beef and apples.

The gains realized through specialization in each of the above cases — the dentist and the carpenter, the apple and beef producers — were possible only because there was an exchange of services or goods.

International trade is an extension of this local and regional specialization and exchange which further increases the economic gains from specialization.

The explanation for the benefits to be realized through such trade is termed the *theory of comparative advantage*. The argument that individuals and areas can be better off through specialization and exchange is widely applied in economics; economists frequently refer to the "comparative advantage" of certain individuals or regions. But the theory of comparative advantage needs to be advocated frequently with respect to different countries because there are so many barriers or limitations to the free exchange of goods and services among countries.

The Theory of Comparative Advantage

The theory of comparative advantage states that the commodities (goods and services) which a country should produce and trade with other countries are the commodities that it produces relatively more efficiently than do other countries.

The concept of comparative advantage and its role in the argument for unimpeded specialization and free exchange among countries can be illustrated by a simple example. Suppose that there are

only two countries to be considered: Canada and England. Assume
further that each country produces and consumes only two goods,
cheese and beef. Each country has only land and labour resources;
labour is fully employed but there is no limit on available land. All
labour is of uniform quality within each country. Productive resource requirements can thus be expressed simply in terms of labour
units, such as one day of labour. The production conditions in each
country are such that, as shown in Table 7.5, Canada can produce
both cheese and beef more efficiently than can England. The production of 100 pounds of beef requires 3 units of labour in Canada and 6
units in England; the production of 100 pounds of cheese requires 2
labour units in Canada and 3 in England.

Canada has an *absolute advantage* in the production of both
beef and cheese because fewer labour units are required to produce a
given quantity of each good in Canada than in England. One might
suggest that Canada should produce both beef and cheese for its own
consumption, ignoring any possibility of trade with England, since
Canada can produce both goods more efficiently. The theory of
comparative advantage, however, states that it is not absolute advantage or absolute efficiency that matters, but rather comparative advantage or comparative efficiency. Table 7.5 shows that Canada is
twice as efficient as England in producing beef: 3 labour units compared with 6; but only 1.5 times more efficient in producing cheese:
2 labour units compared with 3. Canada is *relatively* more efficient
in producing beef than cheese: Canada's *comparative advantage* is
in beef production and England's comparative advantage is in
cheese production.

Table 7.5

Relative Efficiency and Costs Before Trade

	Resource Requirements in labour units		Opportunity Costs	
	Beef (100 lb.)	Cheese (100 lb.)	Beef (1 lb.)	Cheese (1 lb.)
Canada	3	2	1½ lb. cheese	²/₃ lb. beef
England	6	3	2 lb. cheese	½ lb. beef

Now the example must be pursued in more detail to see how
both Canada and England can gain by specialization and trade. The
information in Table 7.5 indicates the cost of each product in each
country in terms of productive resources. But the cost of each good
can also be expressed in terms of its opportunity cost, or how much
of the other good must be given up to increase the output of the first
good. At this point, the comparison is not *between* countries but
simply of the two goods *within* each country.

For every 100 pounds of beef produced in Canada, 150 pounds of cheese must be given up or forgone because the 3 labour units required to produce beef are not available for cheese production. This is another illustration of the *opportunity cost* concept introduced in Chapter 1. The cost of 100 pounds of beef is the opportunity that is forgone to enjoy 150 pounds of cheese. Thus one can say that one pound of beef "costs" 1½ pounds of cheese. The price of one pound of cheese is 2/3 pounds of beef. Similarly, the price of one pound of beef in England is two pounds of cheese; and the price of one pound of cheese is ½ pound of beef. This is another way of determining comparative advantage: beef is relatively cheaper in Canada (one pound costs 1½ pounds of cheese compared with two pounds in England) and cheese is relatively cheaper in England (one pound costs ½ pound of beef compared with 2/3 pound in Canada).

It is because these cost ratios are different in each country that trade can be an advantage to both.

If the cost ratios were the same, this would be comparable to saying that neither country was *relatively* more efficient in the production of one good than the other and that therefore neither country had a comparative advantage in the production of either good. If in Table 7.5, for example, England's production cost of cheese had been 4 labour units, Canada would have been *equally more efficient* in producing both goods and England would have been *equally less efficient*. In this case there would be no benefit to either country in specialization and trade. Canada would, of course, have a higher consumption level than England because its resources were more productive, but it could not become even better off through trade. Canada and England each could only attempt to produce the particular combination of beef and cheese which gave the greatest satisfaction to the consumers in each country.

The possibility that the production cost ratios will be exactly the same for each country is quite remote. The many conditions affecting the production of any good vary so much among countries that a country can be expected to have a comparative advantage in at least a few goods, and therefore have a reason for foreign trade. The question of costs implied in the Table 7.5 data does, however, emphasize an important assumption underlying the discussion of equal cost ratios. This is that the price of one good expressed in terms of the other is constant regardless of the level of production. Even if the production cost of cheese in England had been 4 labour units *at a given level of production*, for example when labour resources were equally divided between beef and cheese production, the cost of cheese might have dropped to 3 labour units at a higher level of cheese production. This would imply that there were *economies of scale* (cost per unit decreased with increases in output) in England's cheese production. If this were the case, then specialization would be an advantage. In this simple example illustrated by Table 7.5 it is assumed that the production costs per unit are constant for all levels of production; economies of scale are at least temporarily ruled out.

The increased output made possible when countries produce according to their comparative advantages can be seen by extending this simple example of two countries and two commodities. Assume that Canada's labour resources are 1,200 labour units per week and England's are 1,800 labour units per week. How these labour resources are actually divided between the production of beef and cheese in each country depends on relative supply and demand conditions for each product. Assume the labour distribution is as follows: Canada allocates 450 labour units for beef and 750 for cheese; England allocates 1,200 for beef and 600 for cheese.

Table 7.6

Gains in Real Output Through Specialization and Trade

	Beef		Cheese		
	Production (100 lb.)	Labour Used (units)	Production (100 lb.)	Labour Used (units)	Total Labour Used (units)
Before Specialization					
Canada	150	450	375	750	1,200
England	200	1,200	200	600	1,800
World	350		575		
After Specialization					
Canada	400	1,200	0	0	1,200
England	0	0	600	1,800	1,800
World	400		600		

Since in Canada 3 labour units are required to produce 100 pounds of beef, 450 labour units will yield 150 units of beef, each unit weighing 100 pounds. The production level for each of the other cases are shown in Table 7.6. Total world production is 350 units of beef and 575 units of cheese. But if Canada produces only beef and England produces only cheese, world output increases to 400 units of beef and 600 units of cheese.

Terms of Trade

The sharing of increased production between the two countries will depend on the *terms of trade* which are established, or the quantity of one good which will be traded for a given quantity of another good. The precise terms of trade, or the prices for each good when trade takes place, depend on the supply and demand conditions in each country. But the *limits* of these terms of trade or exchange prices can be determined from the relative production costs assumed earlier. Prior to specialization, one unit of beef cost or was exchanged within Canada for 1.5 units of cheese. Consumers in Canada will therefore not be willing to pay more for 1.5 units of cheese imported from England than the one unit of beef they paid previously for Canadian cheese. Similarly, prior to specialization in England, one unit of beef was exchanged for two of cheese. If trade is to take place, the consumers in England will not pay more than this price for imported beef. The terms of trade must lie between 1:1.5 and 1:2. If the ratio is 1:1.8 both countries will be willing to trade because Canada will receive 1.8 units of cheese, instead of 1.5 units, for each unit of beef it gives up, while England needs to give up only 1.8 units of cheese, instead of two units, for each unit of beef.

International specialization and trade has one major benefit: prices of goods and services are reduced, or alternatively, real wages are increased. Since labour and other resources are directed to their most productive use, a given number of labour units will yield a greater output and thus a higher real wage. This, rather than lower prices, is generally the specific objective of international trade policies.

Conditions Fostering International Trade

An almost endless list of specific conditions contribute to the development of international trade, through enhancing the comparative advantage each country has in the production of particular commodities. Nevertheless, the following general factors encompass most of the reasons that enable a country to produce some goods at relatively lower costs.

Physical or Geographical Differences. Unique combinations of climatic and geographical features account for a large proportion of the cases of specialization in agricultural products. Wheat could be grown in almost every temperate-zone country of the world, but the special combination of terrain, precipitation, and temperature gives only a few countries like Canada, the United States, Australia, and Argentina, a strong comparative advantage in wheat production because the production costs per bushel are much lower than they are in other areas.

The combination of a large water supply and a sharp drop in land elevation at Niagara Falls gave Ontario a comparative advantage in producing low-cost hydroelectric power for a long time. Development of other sources of energy, however, have diminished much of this cost advantage. The combination of natural resources close to ocean ports has also been a spur to foreign trade. British Columbia's forest industries depend on shipping from Vancouver and other ports; Venezuelan oil can be shipped to many countries due to its proximity to the sea. In these cases, the transportation costs per unit are much lower than they would be for countries with similar natural resources located further from water transportation.

Differences in Technology and Labour Resources. Some countries such as Japan, Great Britain, and Germany, do not have major cases of comparative advantage based on geographical conditions, but they have become major exporters through technological innovations and development of skilled labour. Other countries have enhanced their natural advantages by adding massive amounts of physical capital to the productive process. The United States, for example, has been able to maintain a comparative advantage in producing some agricultural commodities despite increasing land and labour costs by mechanizing and automating much of its agricultural industry.

Economies of Scale. The realization of economies of scale is a case of developing a comparative advantage that did not exist at lower output levels. One reason that Britain joined the European Common Market was to maintain a large enough European market for some of its products so that it could continue to enjoy economies of scale. Similarly, the Canada-U.S. Automotive Agreement was designed to encourage such economies in Canadian automobile production by increasing the length of production run: the number of automobiles of a specific model that are produced on a given assembly line without change-overs.

Tastes or Preferences. There are a few cases where countries produce such a unique product that it may seem to be an exaggeration of the principle of comparative advantage to explain trade in these terms. French wines, for example, cannot be reproduced in other countries. Given the worldwide demand for these, it is quite rational for France to specialize as much as possible in wine production and import other products. But if Italian or Portuguese wines were a perfect substitute for French wines, this comparative advantage would disappear.

Apart from governments' policies on foreign trade, which are discussed later, a general factor *discouraging* international trade should also be noted. This is the *cost of transporting goods* between countries. Some countries may have a comparative advantage in certain products when only the domestic production costs are considered, but the cost of moving the goods to foreign markets may wipe out this advantage. Tropical countries clearly have a comparative advantage in the production of cut flowers, but these are so perishable that expensive air transportation is necessary to deliver them to snow-bound Canadian consumers. The result is domestic greenhouse production of such flowers with little foreign competition. However, the importance of transportation costs varies with the mode of transportation required and the size of the item relative to its selling price.

Restrictions on International Trade

Although the general validity of the principle of comparative advantage has been widely recognized, and many economists have long advocated free or unimpeded international trade, several types of barriers remain. Restrictions are found on both sides of international trade; some directly or indirectly discourage exports while others impede imports. Most of the attention in this section is directed to imports because restrictions on these are generally quite specific. But there are some issues on the export side which must at least be raised because they have increasing importance in Canadian economic policies.

Discouraging Exports

What is often described as "an abundance of natural resources" has been a major source of Canada's exports throughout its history. But doubts are being raised about whether Canada should export natural resources such as water and petroleum. The economic problem, however, is not whether to export but how to determine the proper price. By exporting large quantities of water at a price which currently seems reasonable, even attractive, Canada may find in future years that the price of domestic water is much higher than it would have been otherwise. Given some uncertainty about the size and location of industry and population in the future, projecting the future domestic demand for water is difficult. The problem is one of weighing increased current income and consumption against the possibility of lower real income and consumption in the future if the cost of bringing water to Canada's domestic users should increase. This question becomes more complex when income distribution is taken into account: only some people would benefit directly from the sale of water but all consumers would pay the higher future prices.

For the same reason, there is increasing opposition to export sales of crude petroleum and other non-reproducible resources such as copper and iron ore. Again, it is a question of whether the price should be higher or an export tax levied. *Export duties*, or taxes on exports, are more common in less-developed countries which rely on income from export sales. When such incomes are unusually high they are taxed to provide income for the periods when receipts from exports are low, and to redistribute the benefits of export sales.

Indirect restrictions on exports operate through policies for *diversification*, rather than specialization, of industrial production, and through various factors *reducing the geographical, occupational, and industrial mobility of labour.* Diversification of industrial production may be advocated for several reasons; one is to reduce dependence on income from exports if there tend to be fluctuations in export sales of commodities such as wheat. When export sales drop, governments are pressed to provide income supplements to the producers. Another reason is to maintain a basic self-sufficiency in essential commodities to avoid dependence on other countries in case of war, adverse economic policies, or simply changes in the terms of trade.

Specialization usually requires the mobility of labour within a country. In most cases this would be carried out at high economic and social cost to the individuals concerned. Plants in some parts of the country would have to be closed, families would need to move to other centres to find work, and workers would need to be trained for new jobs. Although monetary costs would be more than offset if the area for specialization were properly identified, some persons would place a high value on remaining in a familiar community and region. The result is pressure for industry to be subsidized in various ways so that geographical relocation is not necessitated by economic pressures.

These considerations do not invalidate the principle of comparative advantage. Rather, they emphasize the broader range of costs and the distribution of potential benefits and costs that need to be taken into account when potential areas of specialization are examined.

Restrictions on Imports

Although there are several kinds of restrictions on imports, these can be divided into two basic categories: taxes and regulations on quantities. Taxes on imports are termed tariffs or import duties. An ad valorem tariff states the tax as a percentage of the price of a good; a specific tariff specifies the amount to be paid on each unit regardless of its price. Another minor type of import tax is a licence fee which may be required to import specific goods. The cost of the licence usually is fixed, whatever the quantity imported, and thus the effective tax rate is reduced with an increasing quantity of imports.

Quotas are limitations on the quantity of a good which can be imported. Such quotas may be expressed in terms of the quantity which can be imported each month or each year, or from particular countries. Quotas may also be combined with an import licence so that the importer is paying a fee to import a specific amount. The most stringent form of quota is an embargo, or sanction. Examples of these are an embargo or prohibition against the importation of cattle when there is an outbreak of a cattle disease in another country; and the sanction Great Britain placed against the importation of Rhodesian goods such as tobacco when Rhodesia unilaterally declared its independence.

The general economic effects of tariffs and quotas are so similar that the balance of this section deals with import restrictions in terms of tariffs only. These effects can be explained using the supply and demand analysis presented in Chapter 2. Figure 7.1a shows the

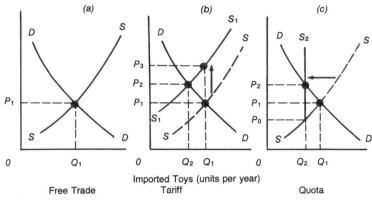

Figure 7.1   *Tariffs and Quotas Reduce the Quantity of Imports and Increase Prices*
When there are no restrictions on international trade, OQ_1 units of toys are imported each year and the price is OP_1 per unit. Imposing a tariff shifts the supply
curve upward, to S_1S_1, by the amount of the tariff, P_1P_3. The price increases by
less than the tariff amount, to OP_2, and the quantity imported falls to OQ_2. (Compare this with the case of a sales tax on domestic goods, as shown in Figure 2.10).
A quota which restricts the quantity imported to OQ_2 effectively shifts the supply
curve to SS_2 and increases the price to OP_2.

supply and demand for imported children's toys in Canada prior to
any restriction on such imports; the equilibrium price is OP_1 per
unit, and quantity is OQ_1 per year. If a specific tariff is imposed, the
importer is willing to supply OQ_1 of the toys only if the price is high
enough to cover his previous costs plus the new tax. The result
shown in Figure 7.1b is an upward shift of his supply curve to S_1S_1.
The amount of the tariff is the difference between OP_1 and OP_3. A
new equilibrium price is established at OP_2, with the quantity demanded reduced from OQ_1 to OQ_2. The same effect would follow, as
indicated by Figure 7.1c, if a quota on imported toys were set at a
quantity of OQ_2. This represents a shift of the supply curve from SS
to SS_2, with SS_2 being perfectly inelastic above a price of OP_0. The
new price is again OP_2. Since the price and quantity effect of tariffs
and quotas can be the same from the perspective of the consumer,
governments favour the tariff form of restriction which produces tax
revenues as well as the quantitative limitation on imported goods.

Reasons for Tariffs and Other Trade Restrictions

If tariffs raise the prices of imported goods and reduce the quantity consumers can enjoy, why do governments continue to impose
tariffs? There are many reasons; some are based on political objectives while others are related to economic objectives. Only in some
cases, however, do tariffs contribute effectively to achieving these
objectives.

Political Independence. Any country wants to be as independent as possible in determining its foreign relations. Unless it is willing to be closely allied with some other countries in mutual defence agreements, it must develop its own defence industries and encourage other industries which can be converted to defence production in wartime.

Countries also want to be independent of foreign decisions about the domestic services they will have. Most countries, for example, have established national airlines so that they can determine how their cities and regions will be served, rather than depend on foreign airlines, which might be less expensive, to provide this service. By limiting the access of foreign airlines, countries are in effect imposing a quota on foreign air service.

Countries also tend to protect their agricultural producers by high tariffs, when food products could be obtained more cheaply abroad, because it would be so disruptive socially and politically to re-establish the numerous small farmers in other occupations and because countries fear the uncertain consequences of losing part of their agricultural industry.

The cost of pursuing political goals by restricting imports and encouraging higher-cost domestic production is not easily determined. Such political objectives could be accomplished more precisely, with a full appreciation of the cost of doing so, if selected domestic industries or commodities were *subsidized* directly and foreign suppliers were discouraged by the lower domestic prices made possible by the subsidy. Governments and their electors could then determine whether the cost of these objectives was too great or whether more should be spent to pursue them more effectively. Although people might object to paying more taxes for such subsidies, they would need to weigh this against the higher prices they pay for domestically produced commodities when foreign goods and services are excluded.

Maintenance of Full Employment and Protection of Industry.

The most common economic reason given for tariffs is that they protect established industries and their employees. If tariffs on certain commodities were reduced or removed, prices of the imported commodities would fall and domestic firms would be forced either to close, putting employees out of work, or to become more efficient in the use of resources. This, of course, is exactly the process implied in the principle of comparative advantage. It is also the main reason why free trade is not more widely practised in spite of the economic advantages. Although consumers pay a higher price for some domestic goods because foreign competition is excluded by tariffs, governments find it politically more desirable to maintain tariffs than to admit cheaper imports. Alternatively, tariffs could be removed with a tax placed on consumers who enjoy cheaper goods to subsidize the establishment of more competitive firms and retrain or relocate the workers for the new firms. Governments are seldom willing to consider this alternative, however, because consumers seem more willing to pay higher prices than to be taxed to assist the readjustment of production. Similarly, firms and employees appear to be more concerned about short-run relocation costs than the longer-run benefits from the more productive use of resources.

A related argument states that tariffs "help keep money in the country". When consumers buy domestic goods instead of imports, employment and incomes are maintained. But this is only another form of the argument considered above. Specialization based on comparative advantage would raise real incomes and increase real purchasing power such that employment would increase with the removal of tariffs.

Increased Government Revenues. If the demand for the imported good is elastic with respect to price, a tariff decreases the quantity demanded proportionately more than the price increase. (Recall the explanation of price elasticity in Chapter 2.) Government revenue from a tariff on such a good may not be very substantial but at least it is greater than zero. However, an attempt to increase this by raising the tariff will reduce the tariff revenue. Tariffs are more effective in producing government revenue in cases where the demand is inelastic. But inelastic demand implies that there are no close substitutes: domestic commodities are not directly in competition with that particular import. Thus, a tariff which raises substantial government revenue usually provides little protection for domestic industry. Furthermore, tariffs yielded only an estimated $1.8 billion for 1975 while the cost of tariffs in terms of inefficient production has been estimated as well over $10 billion. At existing federal rates, this additional output would yield an additional estimated $3 billion in tax revenues.

Improved Balance of Payments. When a country is experiencing a continuing deficit in its balance of trade, or on its current account in the balance of payments, there may be much support for raising tariffs to curtail imports. This action will reduce the physical volume of imports. If the demand for imports is inelastic, total expenditures on imports will increase but payments abroad will decrease since the import duty goes to the home government. This temporarily improves the balance of payments situation. If demand for imports is elastic, total expenditures on imports as well as payments abroad, will fall, again temporarily improving the balance of payments. The decrease in foreign payments, however, provides other countries with less foreign currency to spend on their imports. The result may be a reduction in exports and, therefore, possibly a return to an adverse balance of payments condition.

Retaliation. Even if any of the preceding reasons were valid arguments for imposing tariffs, there would be the danger that other countries would retaliate by imposing tariffs on their imports, possibly reducing export sales and at least partly offsetting any advantage conveyed by the tariff. This should also emphasize that the least acceptable argument for tariffs is simple retaliation in reaction to tariffs being imposed elsewhere. When another country takes the initiative in raising tariffs, this presents one barrier to the economic gains of free trade, but retaliation by a second country further diminishes the possibility of gains realized through specialization and trade.

Protection of Infant Industries. The single economic argument for tariffs which does not conflict with the principle of comparative advantage is that a tariff should be imposed to protect an industry or firm that appears to be *developing* a comparative advantage. If a tariff is not imposed it may be difficult to get past the initial stage of high costs associated with low levels of production. However, the danger in governments' acceptance of this argument is that once the low-cost production level has been reached, it will be politically difficult to remove the tariff.

The argument can also be appealing to governments anxious to justify support for a certain industry. In such circumstances, protective tariffs may be imposed without satisfactory evidence that the industry is likely to develop a comparative advantage. Even in this case, the objective might be achieved more effectively by subsidizing the developing industry rather than through a protective tariff. The subsidy can be identified clearly as a cost of obtaining future gains from trade; judgments can therefore be made about the amount of present consumption that should be given up for potential increased future consumption from more productive use of resources. The subsidy also provides a reason for the government to scrutinize the operations of the new industry more closely, whereas the tariff offers the industry little incentive to reduce costs unless there is an explicit timetable for the gradual reduction of the tariff. However, the subsidy could also be reduced gradually to provide the same incentive.

There is only one answer to each of the several reasons given for tariffs: raising the price of imports maintains domestic industries at a less efficient level of production than would occur under free trade and encourages tariff retaliation from other countries, thus compounding the loss of real income and output that would be realized by specializing in areas of comparative advantage. The non-economic arguments for tariffs which are related to other political or social objectives cannot be sustained either, since subsidies provide a more efficient means for pursuing these objectives. Canada's tariff policies and the economic effects of these policies are examined in more detail following the next section.

Opening the Way for Trade

Both the international and domestic conditions facing an economy change substantially from time to time and, with these changes, attitudes towards free trade or protective tariffs also vary. The result has been a variety of arrangements for obtaining some of the advantages of foreign trade while retaining some features of a protected economy. These have ranged from special trade agreements on particular commodities to the economic integration of geographical areas.

Agreements

International agreements on reducing tariff barriers may be either *multilateral agreements* or *bilateral agreements*, that is, among several countries or between two specific countries. The most important multilateral agreement is GATT, *the General Agreement on Tariffs and Trade*. Immediately after World War II, a number of countries tried to establish an international trade organization to act as an agency of the United Nations and as a counterpart to similar United Nations organizations concerned with labour, agriculture, and education. Opposition to the proposed international trade organization led to the substitution of the somewhat weaker arrangement, GATT.

The General Agreement on Tariffs and Trade, now signed by about 80 countries, sets out regulations governing the conduct of international trade, including the frequently cited "most-favoured nation" clause. This states that a country may not discriminate among trading partners by imposing a higher tariff against the imports of one country than against another. (Some of the discriminating tariff schedules which existed at the signing of GATT, such as the Imperial Preference tariffs levied by British Commonwealth countries on each other's imports, were allowed to continue.) The other major effect of GATT arrangements has been a succession of multilateral trade negotiations designed to reduce tariff schedules by stages. The last round of negotiations (the Kennedy Round) lasted from 1964 to 1967, but resulted in an agreement that, during a 5-year transition period from 1967 to 1972, the average tariff level in most of the major exporting countries would drop to 7 or 8 per cent. The current round of negotiations were to begin in late 1973 but were postponed until the United States passed a Trade Act to give its officials authority to participate. GATT meetings are expected to continue until mid-1977, with resulting tariff reductions and removal of non-tariff trade barriers being phased in over a 5- to 10-year period.

Non-tariff barriers will receive particular attention in negotiations because they have been used more frequently in the early 1970s, partly in response to the Kennedy Round tariff reductions and partly to the recession. Such barriers include: quotas on quantity or total value of specific imports; export subsidies, tax concessions, and other government aid to exporters; customs procedures which delay shipments and product standards which are more stringent for imports than for domestic goods; some anti-dumping regulations; legislation and campaigns to give preference to domestically produced goods.

A number of *multilateral trade agreements* have each been concerned with only a single commodity: wheat, tin, cotton, and others. These agreements sought primarily to establish a price range within which the commodity would be traded internationally in an effort to stabilize prices. Such stability would encourage continued specialization by the exporting countries in the particular commodity and thus continue the gains to be realized from that trade.

Bilateral agreements are, strictly speaking, in contravention of the GATT "most-favoured nation" clause but have won acceptance where other countries are not seriously harmed, or where the protests of injured nations have been successfully ignored. The Canada-U.S. Automotive Agreement is a prominent example of a bilateral agreement, requiring that each country remove tariffs against imports of motor vehicles and parts from the other country. However, the Agreement is discriminatory only on the American side: the United States has removed tariffs from Canadian automotive products but not from those of other countries, whereas Canada's side of the agreement permits Canada to remove tariffs on automotive products from other countries.

Integration of Trade Policies

Agreements of the type just discussed are either concerned with partial reduction of tariffs on all commodities or complete removal of the tariff against specific commodities. The next step toward free trade is the integration of trade policies, but this can take different forms.

Free Trade Areas or Associations. A *free trade area* or *free trade association* is a group of countries who have agreed to reduce the tariffs imposed against imports from each of the other countries, usually with the objective of complete removal of these tariffs. However, each country can maintain its own trade policy with respect to other countries outside the free trade area. A major example of this kind was the *European Free Trade Association* (EFTA) formed in 1960 by seven Euopean countries: Austria, Denmark, Great Britain, Norway, Portugal, Sweden, and Switzerland. This group was formed in an effort to replace the trade they feared would be lost when other European countries established the European Economic Community, discussed next.

Customs Unions and Common Markets. A customs union goes one step further than the free trade area in integrating members' trade policies. In addition to removing the tariffs against imports from each other, the member countries agree to a common tariff schedule each will charge against imports from outside the group. A *common market* takes integration another important step by permitting the free flow of productive resources, namely labour and capital, among the member countries. At the final stage of development of the common market, common fiscal and monetary policies are required, as well as a common trade policy. By this point, the countries will also have provided for substantial political integration as well.

The *European Economic Community* (EEC) is commonly called the European Common Market, but it has not yet reached the final stages of the pure common market described above. Nevertheless, the EEC has since its formation in 1957 succeeded in establishing free trade in the products of each country and in permitting the free flow of labour and capital among its members. When Britain joined the EEC in 1971, EFTA was so seriously weakened that Denmark and Ireland decided to seek membership in the EEC, and the remaining EFTA countries signed free trade agreements for non-agricultural products with the EEC.

Canada's Tariff Policies

Protective tariffs have had a substantial, long-term effect on the character of the Canadian economy. Long periods of high tariffs on manufactured goods have stimulated a larger manufacturing sector than would have emorged otherwise and, with it, a higher proportion of foreign capital and labour. Tariffs have also led to more inefficiency in manufacturing than would have occurred otherwise and, consequently, lower real incomes, higher relative prices, and fewer exports of manufactured products.

Until 1879, tariffs served mainly as a major source of government revenues. Sir John A. Macdonald's National Policy shifted the emphasis to protection: tariff rates were raised to 25 to 30 per cent, from a previous average of about 10 per cent. Tariff rates continued upward for another decade to reach an average of over 30 per cent. British preference tariffs were introduced in 1899; these provided for lower duties on British goods than on goods imported from other countries. In 1911, the Laurier government negotiated a trade reciprocity agreement with the United States: each country would remove all tariffs on imports of lumber, fish, agricultural produce, and mineral ores from the other country; and lower tariffs would be applied on some manufactured goods. But the government was defeated in the 1911 election, partly on its Reciprocity policy, and the trade agreement was never implemented.

Tariff rates fell gradually from the introduction of British Preference until 1930. Tariffs were then raised quickly to the former high levels, partly in an effort to protect domestic employment during the Depression and partly as retaliation against sharp increases in American tariffs. In 1932, the Ottawa Agreements established Imperial Preference tariffs among British Commonwealth countries, thus extending the preferential tariffs Canada and Britain has established earlier. A trade agreement with the United States in 1935 reduced the tariffs that had been pushed so high 5 years before.

Table 7.7

Canadian Nominal Tariff Rates, for Selected Commodities

Commodity	Pre-Kennedy Round	Post-Kennedy Round
High Tariff Items	%	%
Distilled beverages	20.0	20.0
Tobacco products	30.0	25.0
Shoes	25.6	23.3
Woolen cloth	23.8	21.6
Fur goods	24.5	22.0
Knitted goods	27.6	24.1
Office furniture	22.0	17.0
Pens and pencils	21.1	17.4
Low Tariff Items		
Process cheese	5.9	5.9
Fish products	7.1	3.6
Publishing and printing	1.4	1.4
Aluminum: rolled, cast, extruded	3.0	2.2
Clay products	9.5	7.8

Source: J.R. Melvin and B.W. Wilkinson, *Effective Protection in the Canadian Economy*, Ottawa: Queen's Printer, 1968, Table 3.

The General Agreement on Tariffs and Trade (GATT), initiated in 1948, has been the major element in Canada's postwar tariff policy. Through periodic meetings of GATT members, a series of multilateral tariff reductions have been achieved. Most recently, the Kennedy Round of tariff negotiations led Canada to reduce tariffs on many items, some of which are shown in Table 7.7. A bilateral agreement, the Canada-United States Agreement on Automotive Products, was signed in 1965, as noted previously. In 1973 Canada introduced a general preferential tariff for developing countries to provide for reductions in the tariffs on imports from these areas.

The Economic Council of Canada proposed in a recent report[1] that Canada should pursue a free trade policy, preferably with all nations but particularly with the United States, the European Economic Community, and Japan. Even if bilateral free trade could

[1]Economic Council of Canada, *Looking Outward: A New Trade Strategy for Canada*. Ottawa: Information Canada, 1975.

not be realized, Canada should undertake unilateral abolition of its tariffs. The Council recognized, however, that while the economic advantages were unequivocal, Canada would need to examine the social and political implications of such a policy. The major reason for the Council's recommendation was that Canada's rate of increase in productivity, under tariff protection, was one of the lowest among the industrialized countries.

B.   Financing International Trade and Capital Flows

International trade in goods and services and securities requires that payments be made in the currency of the country supplying these items. This in turn requires that a rate of exchange between foreign currencies be determined; the system used to determine these rates will have implications for the balance of payments equilibrium. Should there be a continuing disequilibrium in the balance of payments, and especially on the deficit side, corrective action will need to be taken by the country concerned. But the close trading relationships of some countries requires that enduring solutions for such deficits be arranged by international agreement, and even reforms of the international monetary system. These are the problems to be treated in the rest of this chapter.

Foreign Exchange Markets

Foreign exchange markets include all the buyers and sellers of particular currencies in every country. There is not a separate market for each currency, as there is for each of all other commodities such as bread or milk, because a currency can be bought only with another currency — and any other currency which can be exchanged internationally will do: a Canadian dollar can be bought with Swiss francs, Italian liras, Greek drachmas, and so on. Exchange of currencies usually occurs in chartered or commercial banks, which in turn deal with the central banks of each country or with the major commercial banks of other countries. Foreign currencies are also exchanged at airport booths, on the street-corners of some countries, and in firms which make foreign currency exchange their principal business. The major commercial banks and large foreign exchange dealers account for most of the world's trade in foreign currencies.

These dealers and banks issue quotations on foreign exchange rates, or prices of foreign currencies, several times weekly. These are *ratios* at which one currency can be traded for another. The foreign exchange rate or price of the Canadian dollar can be expressed in terms of numerous other currencies, although it is most often stated in terms of the American dollar. But if Canadian dollars can be traded in many different places at the same time, how can there be only one price for the Canadian dollar?

There may, in fact, be slight differences in this price at any given time but such differences are quickly reduced by *arbitrage*. Persons who watch for these differences and make a profit by buying and selling foreign currencies simultaneously are called arbitragers. If the Canadian dollar is selling for 66.1 Spanish pesetas in Toronto but for 66.2 pesetas in Madrid, an arbitrager in Toronto will call a broker in Madrid, buy 100,000 pesetas, and sell them immediately in Toronto. The 100,000 pesetas will cost him $15,106 in Madrid but he can exchange them for $15,129 in Toronto, with a profit of $23. Since this may not cover the costs of telephone calls and broker's fees, he will deal in larger quantities or look for other currencies and centres where the price difference is greater. As arbitragers rush to make their gains on these differences, their own actions alter the supply and demand for currencies and move the prices for a particular currency toward a common level around the world.

Determination of Foreign Exchange Rates

Although arbitrage does have a slight but important influence on the supply and demand for currencies, other factors determine the general level of prices for foreign currencies. Toward the end of Chapter 5, foreign exchange rates were described as being either "pegged" or "floating". Exchange rates which are floating will fluctuate with changing market conditions for foreign currencies. When rates are pegged they will also be influenced by marked conditions but only within the permitted range; market pressures tending to move the rate outside this range will be offset through direct intervention in the currency market by a government or its monetary authorities.

The supply and demand for currencies derives from five types of international transactions:

1. capital flows;
2. trade in goods and services and transfer payments;
3. speculation;
4. government intervention to maintain pegged rates; and
5. arbitrage.

Capital flows arising, for example, when a Canadian firm borrows funds in New York, require that Canadian dollars be bought with the American dollars being loaned so that the borrowing firm will have Canadian currency to spend in Canada. This transaction adds to the demand for Canadian dollars in the American foreign exchange market or to the supply of American dollars in Canada. When the Canadian firm pays interest on the loan, its Canadian dollars must be converted to American dollars, with the opposite effects on the American or Canadian foreign exchange markets.

Trade in goods and services has the same type of effects. A Canadian firm importing automobiles from Japan must pay the producer in Japanese yen. The result is an increase in the demand for Japanese yen in Canada or in the supply of Canadian dollars in Japan.

Speculation in foreign currencies is essentially the same as speculation in other markets, from common shares to real estate to agricultural commodities; if speculators expect the price of the item to rise they will buy more, selling it later at (they hope) a higher price. Note that speculation differs from *arbitrage*; the speculator holds the item for resale later, while the arbitrager buys and sells simultaneously in two markets. If speculators expect the price of a currency to rise, they buy and hold the currency until the expected price is reached, or it becomes unprofitable to wait longer. When speculators are especially active in buying or selling a particular currency, their own actions may bring about the results they anticipated.

Government intervention, through a central bank, to maintain pegged rates is described later in this chapter.

The foreign exchange rate, or the price of one currency in terms of another, is determined by supply and demand forces just as the equilibrium prices of goods and services were seen to be determined in Chapter 2. Hypothetical supply and demand curves for Canadian dollars in terms of Swiss francs are shown in Figure 7.2. Assume for the moment that the exchange rate for neither currency is pegged. The demand curve indicates that when more Swiss francs must be paid for a Canadian dollar, fewer Canadian dollars would be demanded by persons wishing to buy them with Swiss francs. This reflects the fact that as the price of the Canadian dollar rises in terms of Swiss francs, Canadian goods become more expensive for Swiss importers. Although the price of a woollen blanket in Canada, for example, may remain at $8, an increase in the price of a Canadian dollar from 2 francs to 3 francs means that Swiss importers must pay 50 per cent more for the blanket — fewer Canadian goods would be bought and fewer Canadian dollars would be required. The demand curve for Canadian dollars therefore has the conventional downward slope to the right.

Why is the supply curve shown to slope upward to the right? An increase in the price of the Canadian dollar implies a decrease in the price of Swiss francs. Swiss watches, for example, would be less expensive in Canadian dollar terms and more of these would be purchased by Canadian importers. Although a greater quantity of *watches* would be purchased, it is not certain that a greater quantity of dollars would be offered for exchange with francs. This depends on the elasticity of demand for Swiss watches.[2] If this is *inelastic*,

---

[2] Recall from Chapter 2 that a price increase results in a greater total expenditure if demand is inelastic, but a lower total expenditure if demand is elastic.

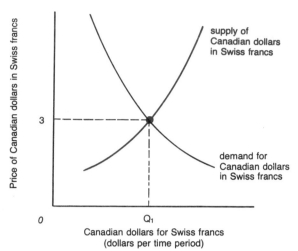

**Figure 7.2 Unpegged Foreign Exchange Rates Are Determined
By the Supply Of and Demand For Currencies**

When the foreign exchange rate of the Canadian dollar is free to fluctuate, the
exchange rate between the Canadian dollar and, for example, the Swiss franc is
determined by supply of Canadian dollars exchanged for Swiss francs and the
demand for Canadian dollars purchased with Swiss francs. At a price of 3 Swiss
francs for one Canadian dollar, the quantity of Canadian dollars purchased in the
given time period is OQ_1. At a higher price, there would be an excess supply of
Canadian dollars and at a lower price, there would be an excess demand for
Canadian dollars.

the total expenditure of Canadian dollars will be less, and fewer
Canadian dollars will need to be exchanged for Swiss francs to
purchase the greater number of watches. The supply curve will be
downward sloping to the right. If there is unitary demand elasticity
the supply curve will be vertical because there is no change in the
total expenditure of Canadian dollars or in the number of dollars to
be exchanged for francs; and if the demand for watches is elastic, the
quantity of Canadian dollars offered will rise. For simplicity, it is
this last case which is assumed in the upward slope of the supply
curve shown in Figure 7.2.

Balance of Payments Equilibrium

When the Balance of International Payments was discussed in Chapter 3, the concept of a "basic balance" was used to explain why the
balance of payments always balanced. The balance of payments was
seen to include three sets of accounts: the current account recorded
international transactions in goods and services; the capital account
recorded international short-term and long-term capital flows; and

the third account recorded changes in official holdings of foreign exchange and gold. The inflows of payments balanced the outflows because movement of gold, foreign currencies, and short-term capital offset any net surplus or deficit on the other accounts. The balance of payments was therefore said to have a "basic balance" only when these latter movements were not required as the balancing items; that is, when the current account balance was equal to the long-term capital balance. *When the balance of payments does not have this basic balance, there is either a surplus or deficit in the balance of payments and thus it is in disequilibrium.*

One of Canada's economic goals listed in Chapter 3 is "a viable balance of payments"; that is, avoiding the kind of disequilibrium described above. A country attempts to overcome a balance of payments disequilibrium, particularly a continuing deficit disequilibrium, because this requires a continuing payment of gold and foreign exchange to other countries, and a rising indebtedness to them, neither of which can be sustained indefinitely. A continuing surplus disequilibrium entails a continuing accumulation of foreign exchange and debts of other countries. Although this may seem desirable, a continuing surplus is a source of inflation because the net inflow of foreign currency increases the money supply as the chartered banks sell this currency to the central bank in exchange for the domestic monetary unit. The central bank is thus required to offset this increase by contractionary operations. A continuing surplus on current account also represents a giving up of current consumption (in the export of goods and services to other countries) in exchange for a claim on goods and services in some indefinite future. Like a large personal savings account, a surplus yields satisfaction only when it is being spent. Hence a country will wish to correct a balance of payments disequilibrium — whether a deficit or a surplus — but its actions in doing so will depend on whether it has a floating or pegged exchange rate.

Floating Exchange Rates and the Balance of Payments

When a currency's price or exchange rate is free of government control, it fluctuates with changes in the supply and demand for the currency. Consider again the case of Swiss watches. If there is an increase in the price of Canadian-made watches, there will likely be an increase in Canada's demand for Swiss watches. The supply curve of Canadian dollars in Swiss francs shifts outward; that is, there will be more Canadian dollars offered in exchange for Swiss francs at any price level (that is, at any exchange rate). Figure 7.3a shows this outward shift of the supply curve with the resulting decrease in price of the Canadian dollar as more are offered in exchange for Swiss francs.

When the price of a currency falls, it is said to *depreciate*; if it rises, it is said to *appreciate*. Figure 7.3b shows that depreciation of

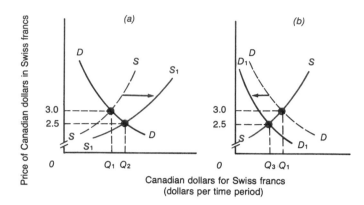

*Figure 7.3   Shifts in Supply or Demand for Currencies Cause
Foreign Exchange Rates to Change*
An increase in the supply of Canadian dollars that can be exchanged for Swiss
francs shifts the supply curve outward to S_1S_1, hence lowering the exchange rate
of the Canadian dollar in terms of Swiss francs and increasing the quantity of
Canadian dollars demanded. Alternatively, a decrease in the demand for Cana-
dian dollars, to D_1D_1, also lowers the exchange rate but reduces the quantity of
Canadian dollars demanded.

a currency can occur not only with an increase in its supply, but also
with a decrease in demand for the currency. The downward shift of
the demand curve reflects a decrease in the Swiss demand for Canadian dollars, perhaps because Canadian blankets have become relatively more expensive than English blankets, or because Swiss investors are buying fewer shares on the Vancouver Stock Exchange.

What will be the effect on Canada's balance of payments of a
depreciation in the Canadian dollar's exchange rate? (Although the
analysis is presented for Canadian-Swiss trade only, the conclusion
can be generalized to include trade with all other countries.) Assume
that both the long-term capital account and the current account are
in balance before depreciation occurs. The net effect will depend on
the price elasticity of demand by the Swiss for Canadian imports and
by Canadians for Swiss imports. *If both demands are elastic,* a depreciated Canadian dollar, and the lower price of Canadian goods for
the Swiss, will lead initially to a surplus on Canada's current account. But the increased quantity of Canadian dollars demanded by
the Swiss, and the decreased quantity of Swiss francs demanded by
Canadians, results in an appreciation of the Canadian dollar. The
balance of trade shifts in the other direction and Canada's surplus on
current account disappears. Thus when both demands are elastic,
the balance of payments will tend toward long-run equilibrium.

When both demands are inelastic, depreciation of the Canadian
dollar leads Canada to buy fewer Swiss goods but to pay more Canadian dollars in total for them; the Swiss buy more Canadian goods
and pay more dollars in total because the Swiss pay the same dollar
price per unit even though the price of Canadian goods has fallen in

terms of Swiss francs. Hence, there may be a net deficit for Canada. In this case the Canadian dollar depreciates further still and, if the elasticity of the Swiss demand plus the elasticity of the Canadian demand, for each other's goods, is less than one, the balance of payments tends toward a long-run disequilibrium.

The disequilibrium that results when the combined elasticities of demand is less than one can persist only if there is a surplus on the long-term capital account. If the Swiss (or all other countries generally) are willing to continue buying Canadian stocks and bonds, the deficit on current account may be offset. But in some countries, and notably in Canada, concern has been expressed about the level of foreign indebtedness or foreign investment. This may be deemed an unacceptable price to pay for a continuing current account deficit.

A country faced with a balance of payments disequilibrium due to inelastic demand for its exports and imports would find a solution difficult. Apart from direct controls, which are discussed later, the main attack on the disequilibrium must come through domestic policies designed to lower the price of domestic goods in order to reduce imports. This would include anti-inflation policies as well as longer-run programs for improving labour productivity. In most cases, however, this problem would not arise. The demand for another country's goods tends to be elastic because there are a number of close substitutes, either produced domestically or available from a number of other countries.

Fixed Exchange Rates and the Balance of Payments

The origin of fixed exchange rates lies in the gold standard which governed the financing for foreign trade until the Depression of the 1930s. Countries that were "on the gold standard" agreed to buy and sell gold at a fixed price expressed in terms of their own currencies. Since the prices of currencies were fixed in terms of a common commodity, gold, they were also fixed in terms of each other. This was brought about by the arbitrage process described earlier, although some small variation in exchange rates could remain, due to the cost of shipping gold.

The rate of exchange among currencies remained fixed despite changing supply and demand for imports and exports because gold formed part of the money supply of the countries concerned. When a country's international payments exceeded its receipts, the deficit resulted in a net outflow of gold. Since this reduced the country's money supply, prices of its goods and services would fall — or so it was assumed under the crude quantity theory of money described in Chapter 4. The inflow of gold to foreign countries would raise their prices, exports to those countries would increase and imports from them would decrease, until there was a balance in foreign trade. The gold flow would then cease. To the extent that prices were flexible and responded quickly to changes in the money supply, a country would not incur a deficit or surplus on its balance of payments for very long. Note that under the gold standard, domestic prices change to maintain an equilibrium in the balance of payments; under floating exchange rates, domestic prices are constant and exchange rates change to maintain an equilibrium in the balance of payments.

A *gold exchange standard* evolved early in this century as smaller countries began to hold the currencies of larger countries like the United States and Great Britain in place of gold and as the gold standard countries made more of their international payments in foreign currencies instead of gold. The prices of currencies continued to be expressed in terms of gold but a world shortage of gold diminished its actual use in foreign trade.

Toward the end of World War II, most of the major nations met to establish the *International Monetary Fund* (IMF) in an effort to stabilize foreign exchange rates and to help countries that would have balance of payments difficulties in the postwar period. In joining the IMF, countries agreed to fix their exchange rates in terms of gold or the American dollar. Canada attempted to fix an appropriate pegged rate but the fluctuating foreign demand for Canadian dollars in the postwar period caused Canada to free the dollar in 1951 to find an appropriate level. A pegged rate was established from 1962 to 1970 at $1.08 Canadian for $1.00 American, but the Canadian dollar was unpegged again in 1970.

Under a fixed exchange rate system, a government agrees to maintain the price of its currency within a very narrow range around the *par value* or pegged rate.

It does this, as explained in Chapter 5, by buying or selling foreign currencies from its Exchange Fund Account, or a similar account, to offset the effects of supply and demand for its currency arising from other international transactions. Because the foreign exchange rate cannot fluctuate significantly, there are no effects on the balance of payments equilibrium of the kind described in the preceding section.

This does not mean, however, that a fixed exchange rate has no implications for the balance of payments. Indeed, a serious problem arises if there is a persistent or chronic deficit because a country must continue paying out foreign currencies to meet this deficit. A chronic balance of payments deficit usually is an indication of an *overvalued currency*: that is, that the exchange rate has been set too high. At the fixed exchange rate of an overvalued currency, the price of a country's own goods will be expensive compared with the same goods in other countries. The result is a strong incentive to import and a difficulty in promoting exports.

An *undervalued currency* leads to chronic surpluses on the balance of payments. Although this may be considered a less serious situation, an undervalued currency requires a country to pay more for its imports and to earn less from its exports.

Correcting Balance of Payments Deficits

A country experiencing a chronic deficit due to an overvalued currency can take a number of different actions to reduce its deficit. It can:

1. pursue contractionary monetary and fiscal policies;
2. impose tariffs;
3. subsidize exports;
4. devalue its currency;
5. impose exchange controls; or
6. allow the exchange rate to float.

Contractionary monetary and fiscal policies should have the effect of restraining inflation, thus improving the competitive position of exports and discouraging imports. Such policies also curtail imports by slowing the growth of incomes. At the same time, high interest rates implied in the restrictive monetary policy should encourage a larger inflow of short-term capital. Such actions may impose a high cost in terms of unemployment. Nevertheless, the IMF generally insists that a member country experiencing a chronic deficit should implement more restrictive domestic policies.

Imposing tariffs will reduce imports by making them expensive but at best will have no effect on exports. More likely, imposing or increasing tariffs will cause other countries to retaliate; there likely will be no improvement in the balance of payments and any previous advantages of foreign trade will be lost.

Export subsidies probably will encourage increased receipts from exports and reduce the balance of payments deficit. There may also be retaliation by other countries. In any case, taxes must be raised to pay the subsidies; this entails a gift to other countries who enjoy the cheaper exports at the expense of the taxpayers.

Devaluation is a reduction in the pegged value of the foreign exchange rate. This represents an abrupt change in the rate compared with the gradual *depreciation* that might occur with a floating exchange rate. The effect of the devaluation will be the same as in the case of depreciation: the quantity or volume of imports will decline, the value of exports will rise, but the net effect on the balance of payments depends on the price elasticities of demand for imports and exports.

Exchange controls are used by some countries which have experienced chronic deficits for some time. Persons receiving foreign currency, whether through export sales, gifts, or otherwise, are required to present it to the government in exchange for the domestic currency at a specified rate. Persons who require foreign currencies to pay for imports, travel abroad, and so on, must apply to the government; currency can thereby be rationed for purposes receiving government approval.

Allowing the exchange rate to float is perhaps the final alternative that a country would consider since it could expect strong criticism from the IMF. Britain, for example, had devalued the pound twice in the postwar period, from $4.03 to $2.80 (U.S.) in 1949 and to $2.40 in 1967, before it allowed the pound to float in June, 1972.

By mid-1973, most of the major currencies were floating and the sense of "international disgrace" that once accompanied unilateral decisions to float a country's currency had largely disappeared. Some of the other remedies described above were still relevant, however, as countries tried to manage the range within which they thought their currencies should float. Hence, monetary policy was usually designed with domestic and international considerations in mind.

Fixed or Floating Exchange Rates?

The unsettled international monetary situation in the early 1970s raised again the debate on the merits and disadvantages of fixed and floating exchange rates. The latter allows the balance of payments to adjust to equilibrium automatically, except in the unusual case of inelastic demand for the countries' exports and imports. Currency prices are determined in the market rather than by arbitrary government decision. There is no need to maintain foreign reserves simply to maintain a fixed rate. Domestic fiscal and monetary policies do not need to be tempered by considerations of the balance of payments situation. Moreover, inflationary pressures are reduced under a floating exchange rate system. If the exchange rate is fixed, the domestic price level rises with price increases in other countries. This occurs because higher foreign prices attract domestic production into exports and hence there is a fall in the supply of goods and services to the domestic market. Under floating rates, export sales would cause the foreign exchange rate to rise and hence higher foreign prices would be less attractive to exporters.

Fixed exchange rates are usually defended on the grounds that they stabilize the prices of goods and services entering into international trade, and thus encourage such trade. This can be important in a recession when declining imports, under floating rates, would improve the trade balance, push up the foreign exchange rate, and thus reduce exports. Under pegged rates, the exchange rate would not rise and exports would be maintained.

Floating exchange rates are said to encourage speculation which in turn will reinforce any fluctuation in an exchange rate. A fixed exchange rate, however, can also encourage speculation. When a country has a serious deficit on its balance of payments, is running low on foreign reserves to maintain the agreed rate, and has too much unemployment to implement a restrictive stabilization policy, there is a high probability that it will devalue its currency. Speculation that this will occur involves large-scale selling of the country's currency on foreign exchange markets, creating extreme pressures on the lower limits of the agreed range for the currency's exchange rate. Such speculation is frequently the reason for the final decision to devalue. Proper evaluation of both systems of exchange rate determination can be made, however, only in the light of recent problems and changes in the international monetary system.

Reforming the International Monetary System

The problem of dealing with chronic balance of payments deficits in several major trading countries, and especially with the United States' frequent deficit and its decling gold stock, led to numerous proposals and some actions for reforming the system of international payments. The problem arose primarily from the pegging of foreign exchange rates and the use of gold as the ultimate medium of international exchange. Consequently, the major changes have been in these two areas.

Gold in International Payments

During the late 1930s and World War II, much of the world's stock of gold was accumulated in the United States. This was partly due to the movement of gold out of Europe with the rise of Nazi Germany, and partly to the United States' commitment to buy gold from world producers at a fixed price of $35 per ounce. This price, established in 1934, was inadequate to stimulate substantial gold production in the face of rising mining and smelting costs. However, as long as the United States was running large balance of payments deficits, gold and American dollars were being made available to other countries to finance their international payments.

In the early 1960s, however, the American gold stock was sharply reduced. A shortage of *world liquidity* — gold and key currencies such as the American dollar — was foreseen since world trade was expanding much more rapidly than the output of gold and the movement of key currencies into international finance. Moreover, industrial and other private demand for gold was increasing. The international monetary system clearly was dependent on continuing balance of payments deficits in the United States to increase holdings of gold and foreign exchange in other countries. A common proposal was to increase the price of gold: this would both stimulate increased gold production and increase the value of the existing gold stock. But it would also entail a devaluation of the American dollar, a consequence the American government was not prepared to accept.

By early 1968, there was mounting speculation that the price of gold would be raised. Speculators bought gold at an increasing pace. This upward pressure on the price of gold was offset by the American Federal Reserve which sold gold to foreign central banks. Some of these in turn sold the gold to speculators, thus continuing the upward pressure on gold, draining the American gold reserves, and pushing the American dollar closer to devaluation.

In March of 1968, the ten major trading nations, the Group of Ten, agreed to suspend payments of gold to private purchasers and thus separated the official gold market from the private gold market. Gold would continue to be exchanged at $35 per ounce in the "official tier" but would be free to find its own price in the "free market tier". The existing gold reserves in the central banks of the Group of Ten would be used for international payments, when gold was required, at the official price.

The separation of the official and private gold markets became less distinct in November, 1973, when it was agreed that central banks would be able to sell gold in the free market. The "two-tier" system was completely abandoned in 1975 when the IMF members agreed to abolish the official price of gold and to end the requirement that gold be used in transactions with the IMF. One-sixth of the Fund's gold would be sold at market prices and the resulting profits used to provide financial assistance for developing countries experiencing chronic balance of payments problems. Another one-sixth of the Fund's gold would be resold to member countries at the previous official price in proportion to their original quotas. The Group of Ten also agreed not to peg the price of gold (that is, not to fix the rate of exchange of their currencies in terms of gold) and not to increase their official holdings of gold for at least 2 years.

By these actions, official holdings of gold became more valuable: central banks could use gold to settle transactions at the market price ($140 per ounce when the IMF decision was made) rather than at the previous official price. Even though the market price of gold fell sharply with the announcement that the IMF would be willing to sell some of its gold, the value of the total official holdings of gold increased by more than 200 per cent. Consequently, countries with large gold holdings will be able to finance balance of payments deficits longer than they could at the previous official price, with the further result of continuing inflationary pressures in world trade.

SDRs: Special Drawing Rights

The 1968 agreement on a two-tier system for gold prices temporarily solved the problem of speculation against an increase in the price of gold but it did not solve the problem of an inadequate stock of gold for international payments. This was partly resolved when members of the International Monetary Fund agreed in 1967 and again in 1969 to create *Special Drawing Rights* or SDRs; these have been termed "paper gold" since they serve the same function as gold in international payments.

SDRs are an international fiduciary currency: they are created and accepted by agreement of IMF members. The annual stock of SDRs is determined by an 85 per cent vote of IMF members and are distributed in proportion to the quota of reserves members are required to hold at the IMF. SDRs came into effect in 1970 with the decision to create $9.5 billion of SDRs for the 1970-1972 period.

SDRs will not replace gold as the major medium for international payments — at least not for some time. Nevertheless, the international agreement to create a world currency represents a major step toward replacing the unpredictable output of gold by the regulated creation of a currency which can match the world's needs for international payments.

Although SDRs are viewed as currency, they are treated as a loan to the extent that countries using SDRs to make payments to other countries are encouraged to redeem (or buy back) these SDRs; countries using SDRs are to pay 5 per cent interest to the recipients of their SDRs.

An SDR was originally valued at US $1.00 but in 1974 the IMF decided to let the value of the SDR fluctuate with the rate of exchange between 15 major world currencies and the American dollar. Each currency used in computing this average would be weighted in proportion to its country's share of world trade.

Floating the American Dollar

The third major change in the international monetary system occurred in 1971 when the United States announced that it would increase the price of gold to $38 per ounce, but that the American dollar would not be convertible into gold. This effectively unpegged or floated the foreign exchange rate of the American dollar and, with it, the foreign exchange rates of all other countries. During the four months from President Nixon's August announcement until the December meeting of IMF members, the value of currencies in terms of each other were determined by the same interaction of supply and demand that was described earlier for floating exchange rates.

When the IMF members met in December, 1971, they established a new structure of pegged foreign exchange rates but with wider margins within which the rate was to be maintained, namely, plus or minus 2¼ per cent instead of the original 1 per cent. (A few countries did not establish new pegged rates due to continuing uncertainty about what the rate should be. Canada's foreign exchange rate had been unpegged since May, 1970.) This was the first major realignment of foreign exchange rates to occur since the original structure was set in 1944, although some countries had individually changed their foreign exchange rates during this long period.

The new agreement did not remain intact for long. In June of

1972, Britain announced that it was floating the pound; the Swiss franc was floated in January, 1973. Then, following several months of trying to maintain the American dollar at the agreed exchange rate, the United States devalued its dollar by 10 per cent in February, 1973. The counterpart of this action was an increase in the price of gold from $38 to $42.22 per ounce. At the same time, Japan and Italy decided to allow their currencies to float.

Shortly thereafter, however, continued downward pressure on the American dollar led the EEC countries (except Britain, Ireland, and Italy) to agree on a "joint float": the exchange rates of the EEC members' currencies would be fixed in relation to each other but would float with respect to all other currencies. This final attempt at pegging exchange rates was substantially weakened when France and Germany temporarily left the joint float in 1974. The floating exchange rate system which had evolved through the 1971 to 1974 period was officially acknowledged by the IMF in January, 1976.

Managed Float or Sliding Pegs?

Some countries were reluctant to shift to an international monetary system based on floating exchange rates completely free of any government intervention. There was general agreement, however, that the previous rigid structure of fixed exchange rates made it increasingly difficult to effect the large rate revisions necessary to overcome long-run disequilibria in balances of payments. The emerging compromise on floating exchange rates was based on assurances — particularly from the United States — that governments would intervene in foreign exchange markets to prevent erratic currency movements. There remained some doubt, however, that a "managed float" could survive.

An exchange rate system based on "sliding pegs" is therefore often proposed as a means for retaining the stability of pegged rates, while providing for the gradual and continuing correction of imbalances through flexible rates. The sliding peg system would also widen the range within which exchange rates would be allowed to fluctuate.

Under a sliding peg system, a par value or official rate would be established. A country would be permitted, however, to change the par value according to an agreed formula by, say, 1 or 1½ per cent a year. Such changes could continue on a monthly or annual basis until the balance of payments disequilibrium was corrected. Moreover, the range of permitted fluctuations around the par level would be widened to a proposed 10 per cent above and below the parity rate. Thus, exchange rates could move over a relatively broad range in reaction to short-term influences, but would be changed gradually in response to longer-term conditions. Such a system could be expected to avoid the international monetary crises experienced in the recent past due to speculation that a currency would be devalued.

Review of the Main Points

1. Canada's annual exports of goods are equal to more than one-fifth of its GNP, and ranks sixth in the world in total value of exports. Trade with the United States accounts for two-thirds of Canada's exports and imports. Apart from trade in motor vehicles and petroleum, Canada's major exports come from primary industries while imports are mainly manufactured goods.

2. The theory of comparative advantage is an extension of the principle of specialization and exchange to trade among countries. This states that a country should produce and trade those commodities in which it has a comparative advantage, namely, commodities it can produce relatively more efficiently than can any other country. Even if a country has an absolute advantage in all commodities, that is, if it is more efficient in the production of all commodities than other countries, it will be still better off by producing commodities in which it has a comparative advantage.

3. The terms of trade between countries or within a country is the ratio of the quantity of one good which will be exchanged for a given quantity of another good. No trade will occur between countries unless this ratio is within the limits established by the terms of trade within each country.

4. International trade, when based on the principle of comparative advantage, reduces commodity prices or alternatively, increases real wages.

5. Import restrictions include tariffs and quotas. The reasons generally advanced for tariffs are: to maintain political independence; to protect domestic industries and employees; to raise government revenues; to reduce a balance of payments deficit; to retaliate against tariffs imposed by other countries; and to foster new industries which are expected to develop a comparative advantage. Tariffs reduce the gains from trade and implicitly impose a tax on consumers, by requiring them to pay a higher price for commodities, or a tax on workers, by reducing real wages.

6. International trade has been encouraged by international agreements, such as GATT, which have led to reduced tariffs, and by integration of trade policies through free trade associations, customs unions, and common markets.

7. Foreign exchange markets operating in each country are closely linked by arbitrage, the simultaneous buying and selling of two currencies in two countries.

8. Foreign exchange rates, whether floating or pegged, reflect the supply and demand for foreign currencies, and indirectly, the

supply and demand for exports and imports. Speculation in currency also affects foreign exchange rates.

9. A country's balance of payments is in disequilibrium when there is a deficit or surplus in the combined balances of the current account and the long-term capital account. The effect on the balance of payments of fluctuating exchange rates depends on the elasticity of demand for exports of the two countries involved. If both demands are elastic, there will be a tendency to long-run equilibrium; if inelastic with a combined value less than one, there will be long-run disequilibrium. A chronic deficit on current account can be sustained by a surplus on the capital account but this implies an increasing level of foreign indebtedness.

10. Under fixed exchange rates, a balance of payments disequilibrium is not corrected automatically. A continuing deficit (or surplus) reflects an overvalued (or undervalued) currency. A country can try to correct a deficit by restrictive monetary and fiscal policies, imposing tariffs, subsidizing exports, devaluing the currency, imposing exchange controls, or allowing the exchange rate to float.

11. Fluctuating exchange rates allow the balance of payments to adjust automatically but entail more variation in prices of internally traded goods. Fixed exchange rates can stabilize such prices but fixed rates require an arbitrary decision on the appropriate rate and a foreign exchange account to maintain the agreed rate. Fixed exchange rates also curtail the use of monetary and fixed policy in pursuing domestic objectives and attract speculation when a country is having difficulty maintaining a fixed rate.

12. Numerous proposals have been made for reforming the international monetary system. Recent changes include: the implementation in 1968 of a two-tier system to separate the official and the market prices of gold and then in 1975 abolition of an official price for gold; the introduction in 1970 of Special Drawing Rights to finance a small part of international trade; and in 1971 the floating and depreciation of the American dollar, with consequent changes in the relative exchange rates of several other national currencies. A frequently proposed compromise between fixed and floating exchange rates is an exchange rate system based on "sliding pegs", whereby a country's foreign exchange rate could be changed frequently and could fluctuate within a wider range.

Review and Discussion Questions

1. What is the difference between absolute advantage and comparative advantage? Why is comparative advantage the relevant concept for explaining international trade?

2. Suppose that the United States were more efficient than any other country in producing all commodities purchased by American consumers. Would there be any reason for the United States to import some goods from other countries?

3. "International trade is indirect production. It is more efficient production." Explain.

4. "A tariff cannot be effective in providing government revenues if it provides effective protection for domestic producers." Explain why you agree or disagree.

5. "Tariffs are necessary to protect Canadian workers from the competition of lower-wage countries such as Hong Kong." Do you agree? Why?

6. What does it mean to say that there is an imbalance in the balance of payments? How can an imbalance be corrected? Why should it be corrected?

7. Should Canada have a fixed or a fluctuating foreign exchange rate? Give a detailed explanation for your position.

Sources and Selected Readings

Dales, John H. *The Protective Tariff in Canada's Development*. Toronto: University of Toronto Press, 1966.

Eastman, H.C. "On Pegging Us to a Cross of Gold" *Canadian Forum*, June, 1962.

Eastman, H.C., and S. Stykolt. *The Tariff and Competition in Canada*. Toronto: Macmillan, 1967.

Economic Council of Canada. *Looking Outward: A New Trade Strategy for Canada*. Ottawa: Information Canada, 1975.

English, H. Edward, B.W. Wilkinson, and H.C. Eastman. *Canada in a Wider Economic Community*. Toronto: University of Toronto Press, 1972.

Johnson, Harry G. "Inflation, Unemployment and the Floating Rate," *Canadian Public Policy*, Spring 1975.

Kenen, Peter B. *International Economics*, 2nd ed. Englewood Cliffs, N.J.: Prentice-Hall, 1967.

Kindleberger, Chas. P. *International Economics*, 5th ed. Homewood, Ill.: Irwin, 1973.

Wonnacott, Paul, and Ronald J. Wonnacott. *U.S.-Canadian Free Trade: The Potential Impact on the Canadian Economy*. Montreal: Private Planning Association of Canada, 1968.

8   Economics of the Public Sector

Government policies determine the framework for all economic activity in Canada. It might therefore seem unnecessary to devote a separate chapter to the economics of governments, or the public sector, when public policies are examined in most of the other chapters. This chapter, however, emphasizes governments' direct involvement in allocating resources and distributing final products through their expenditures and taxation programs. It is precisely here that the "mixed" aspect of a mixed economy is most pronounced. When transfer payments are included, governments determine the spending of almost 40 per cent of Canada's GNP; these are spending decisions made by a political process rather than through the market system. The second part of the chapter examines the principles and structure of the taxation system used to collect the revenues for financing these expenditures.

A. Government Expenditures

The Growth in Government Spending

Total expenditures by all levels of government in Canada have increased dramatically in the past several decades; for example, the federal government's expenditure in 1867 was about $14 million, by 1926 it was $306 million, and in 1974 it was $25 billion — or about 1800 times what it was in 1867. Such growth is due to a number of factors: *inflation* is an obvious one. The price level has risen by over 200 per cent since 1926, implying that the real increase in government expenditures is much less than a comparison expressed in current dollars would indicate. Second, the *population* of Canada has increased by over 125 per cent since 1926. One would therefore expect an increase in government expenditures that approximately matched the population growth. Third, Canada was involved in two *major wars* during this century, and in other defence commitments, which resulted in continuing expenditures for veterans'pensions and other benefits, and for interest payments on the debt incurred during the war periods.

If these were the only factors influencing government expenditures, the increase would be much less than the above comparison indicates. Governments would still be spending approximately the same low share of the Gross National Product that they controlled several decades ago. Figure 8.1 indicates, however, that each level of government — federal, provincial, and municipal — continues to claim an increasing share of the Gross National Product.

Public sector expenditures represented about 45 per cent of the GNP during World War II but fell sharply to 23 per cent by 1950. The public sector share rose slowly during the 1950s and early 1960s,

Figure 8.1   Government's Spending, Including Transfer Payments,
as a Percentage of Canada's GNP, 1926-1973

Federal government spending increased sharply, to over 45 per cent of GNP, during World War II, but provincial and municipal governments reduced their spending. The federal share of GNP rose slightly in the 1953-54 and 1960-62 recessions. Municipal and provincial governments' share of GNP has increased fairly steadily in the postwar period, with provincial governments showing the sharpest increase since the mid-1960s. Intergovernmental payments are excluded.

Source: Canadian Tax Foundation, *The National Finances, 1974-75*, Table 2-12.

reaching temporary peaks as government expenditures were increased to deal with the recessions of 1953-54 and 1960-62. Since 1965, however, the government share has risen to over 35 per cent, its highest peacetime level.

The relative sizes of federal, provincial, and municipal expenditures have also changed during the same period. Prior to the 1930s, municipal expenditures were about double those of the provincial governments. Since 1945, the total expenditures of these two levels of government have been roughly equal, but most recent trends suggest provincial expenditures will rise more quickly than those of the municipalities. Meanwhile, federal expenditures have followed the same general pattern shown for the total of all governments, but as a percentage of GNP they remain below the levels reached during the 1950s and early 1960s.

Expenditures by Government Function

The primary reason for the absolute growth in government expenditures in Canada — in addition to the effects of inflation, population growth, and war — has been an increasing emphasis on governments' role in providing education, health, and welfare assistance. Figure 8.2 shows the percentage of the total government expenditures allocated to each major function, for 1959 and 1972.

A comparison of the percentages of total government spending allocated to specific functions in 1959 and 1972 shows that the traditional functions of government — defence, transportation, protection, and general administration — have received a lower or constant share of the total spending. The major increases in the share of government spending have been in health, education, and social welfare. This reflects increases in the relative costs of providing such services, increases in the proportion of transfer payments, and a shift of expenditures for some of these services, especially in the health field, from the private to the public sector.

Public expenditures for health services rose sharply with the introduction of the Medical Care Act, under which the federal and provincial governments share the cost of health programs arranged by the provinces. Welfare assistance expenditures include old age pensions and family allowances, which are paid to all eligible persons regardless of income level, in addition to income-support payments under the Unemployment Insurance programs and the Canada Assistance Plan. Education expenditures, as a percentage of total government spending, rose quickly for three reasons: the proportion of the population in the school-age group increased in the 1950s and 1960s; the percentage of the school-age group remaining in the educational system beyond the compulsory age has continued to rise, as have the real educational costs per student. However, the declining birth rate of the past decade may lead to a levelling off in the share of government spending going to education.

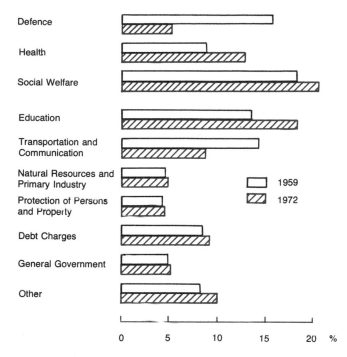

Figure 8.2   Major Government Expenditures as a Percentage of Total Government Spending, 1959 and 1972

About 50 per cent of the combined spending by all levels of government in 1972 went to education, health, and social welfare. The share of governments' budgets directed to these three categories increased substantially from 1959 to 1972, while the share going to defence, and transportation and communication declined.

Source: Statistics Canada, *Consolidated Government Finance*.

The Economic Functions of Government

The expenditure patterns presented in the previous section showed how the relative importance of spending by different levels of government, and of their specific expenditure programs, has changed substantially in the past several decades. This summary did not explain, however, why the roles of governments are changing or even why there should be direct government involvement in the economy. These questions are answered in a general way by recalling the economic role of governments as described in Chapter 2. Government functions in the economy are:

- to stabilize the level of economic activity over a long-term upward trend in GNP;
- to assure that income is distributed in a manner that is considered equitable or fair; and

- to encourage more efficient use of productive resources and to provide commodities which would not be produced in sufficient quantity, if at all, in the absence of government action.

Governments also have political and social functions such as curtailing crime, setting and enforcing safety standards; and regulating social practices concerning marriages, divorce, and property ownership. Some of these functions have economic consequences, but this section discusses only the direct economic responsibilities of governments listed above, and particularly the allocation function.

The stabilization role of government has been examined previously; in Chapter 4 it was seen that government expenditures and taxation affect the level of aggregate demand, and thus the level of employment, output, and income. In Chapter 6 more detailed attention was given to the discretionary and automatic fiscal policies that governments could pursue in an attempt to stabilize prices and employment. The stabilization role of government has been much more widely accepted since the Depression and the adoption of Keynesian and post-Keynesian macroeconomic theories.

To agree on what constitutes an acceptable combination of inflation and unemployment — or what constitutes a stable economy — is difficult enough, but is is even more difficult to agree on what represents an equitable distribution of income. Governments must therefore constantly seek and guide a national consensus on this question, and then determine what means can be used to achieve the appropriate redistribution of income. The pattern of income distributions, and especially the incidence of poverty, is discussed in Chapter 15, as are the causes of poverty and the approaches governments can take to alleviate it.

Stabilization of the economy and redistribution of income involve governments primarily in decisions about the *transfer* of purchasing power both over time (in the case of deficit and surplus budgets) and among individuals. The resource allocation role of government is more directly concerned with determing how resources should be used. The many factors influencing these latter decisions, and the several methods for guiding resource allocation will be considered next.

Government's Responsibility for Resource Allocation

Governments have taken greater responsibility in the past several years, not only for economic stabilization and income distribution, but also for assuring that the economy's productive resources are used efficiently and are used to provide the goods and services desired by the public.

Regulation. Although direct government control over the use of resources, through its expenditures on goods and services, has been shown to be substantial and growing steadily, governmental influence on resource allocation is even more significant through its regulation of the private sector. The maintenance of competition involves legal restraints on monopoly practices such as mergers, price fixing, and market sharing. Chapter 12 explains why competition usually leads to more efficient resource use, and describes the many types of regulations governments can impose on the private sector in an effort to achieve this efficiency.

Public Goods. The second major rationale for government control of resource allocation concerns what are called public goods or collective consumption goods. Since some confusion can arise about the use of terms in this area of economics, it is necessary to specify further that this section deals with pure public goods, while the next section examines quasi-public goods. One of the earliest economic functions of government was to provide pure public goods: goods — or more often, services — which one person can use or enjoy without interfering with the use of that good or service by anyone else.

For something to qualify as a public good, it must be impossible to exclude anyone from using it or otherwise benefitting directly from it.

It is this exclusion principle which dictates that some services, if they are to be available at all, must be made available through collective action since they would be equally available to everyone once they were produced.

National defence is the most obvious public good. No one living within the country concerned can be excluded from the general effects of a defence program. If a few individuals were to establish an effective defence program, everyone else would benefit as much as the persons who paid for the program. In such cases, it is likely that each person would refrain from providing defence — or other similar services — for himself, knowing that he could derive the benefits at no cost to himself, if only someone else would take action. Consequently, everyone waits for "someone else" to do it, and nothing happens. Hence the only way that such services can be provided is for individuals to agree that governments should tax each of them and provide the services collectively.

Quasi-Public Goods. Pure public goods account for only a minor part of governments' expenditures. Why then, do governments undertake the rest of their expenditure programs? Prices could be charged for items such as highways, education, health care, and parks. Individuals unwilling to pay the price could be excluded. These services could therefore be provided by the private sector — and indeed, each of these examples has been or is available from private producers. In some cases, *the cost of collecting the price charged* would be too great for the private entrepreneur to realize a profit on his activity. It was possible to collect tolls, for example, when there were only a few roads: early photographs of some Canadian cities show toll booths at the main intersections. But the proliferation of roads, with the spread of residential areas and increased numbers of vehicles, led to the collective action of paying property taxes and gasoline taxes to provide a system of public streets and highways.

Another, more important, reason for the collective provision of some services is that there are *economies of scale* in the production of these services. Several producers could provide postal, transportation, or communications services — and they have. But it was realized, for example, that the transportation services provided by several private companies in Toronto's suburbs could be produced more efficiently by combining these operations, and hence the Toronto Transportation Commission was formed. Similarly, many of the early telephone companies and a number of the railroads were combined to form the Bell Telephone System and the Canadian National Railway. These latter two examples illustrate alternative methods of government control: Bell Canada remains a private firm with its rates set by a government board, whereas the CNR is government-owned.

Externalities constitute the third and most important reason for governments to provide services such as education, health, and science research. Externalities were defined in Chapter 2 as the economic effects of actions of producers and consumers for which no compensation is paid, or economic effects which are not considered in decisions about market transactions. Environmental pollution is a common form of externality. Factories emitting sulphur dioxide, noisy trucks passing through residential communities, boats discharging sewage into lakes, all impose a "cost" on people adversely affected by these actions. If no compensation is charged against the offender, the effects are *external diseconomies* or external costs.

Alternatively, there can be positive effects or benefits for which the person affected is not required to compensate the producer of the effects. Examples of such *external economies* or external benefits range from the enjoyment of shade from a neighbour's tree to the improvement in one's own health when everyone has had inoculations against contagious diseases.

If these external effects are not taken into account by collective action, resources will not be allocated in what, from the whole economy's point of view, is the most efficient manner.

When the producer of external diseconomies is not required to pay the cost of preventing pollution or to compensate those adversely affected, more of his goods will be produced than should be because the full cost is not considered in his production decisions. The result is an inefficient use of resources. Similarly, external benefits enjoyed by other individuals are not taken into account in private decisions, for example, about health and education expenditures. Unless activities like education or disease prevention are subsidized, individuals underestimate the full benefits associated with the costs of particular activities and thus there will be too few resources allocated to these activities. Governments are therefore expected to try to assess externalities and to regulate or tax those who cause external diseconomies while subsidizing the producers of external economies.

Alternatives in Providing Public Goods

Direct Production. Governments can provide public goods and services, and can represent the public interest in the private sector, through a number of alternative techniques. The most obvious one is *direct production by government-owned firms or through various government departments.* Governments can become direct producers by employing labour and purchasing other supplies to provide many types of public services. The Department of National Defence, for example, hires and trains personnel and purchases equipment to provide defence services. Similarly, land is purchased and persons hired to provide the services of national parks. Police protection is "produced" directly by provincial and municipal governments.

There is considerable disagreement on how many and what types of goods and services should be produced directly by governments. One part of this debate focuses on the question of "nationalizing" some industries such as petroleum, steel, and banking, to produce more efficiently the goods and services supplied by these industries. Another part of the debate is concerned with the extent to which governments should control publishing and broadcasting, for example, and whether these industries would have any independence under government ownership. Somewhat less attention is paid to whether governments should be direct producers of all the many services already under their control.

A major argument favouring government production is that where the economies of scale are such that one producer could provide the output required more efficiently than could several firms, the government should be that single producer in order to provide any specific quantity at the lowest possible price. This condition is termed a natural monopoly and is examined in detail in Chapter 12.

Another argument is that governments need to have direct control over vital services such as defence, and police and fire protection. These have been government functions for so long that it is impossible for some people to imagine them being arranged privately. Yet fire protection was provided privately in some parts of Canada during the last century by the fire insurance companies, and some aspects of police service are available privately through firms providing security guards and private detectives. There are, in fact, a number of alternative arrangements open to governments for the provision of most services now appearing in public budgets.

Purchases. Another alternative is to purchase the goods or services from the private sector or from other governments instead of producing them directly. Governments are increasingly considering this "make or buy" decision. The federal government, for example, currently buys student-places in educational institutions to provide further training for people who qualify under the Adult Occupational Training Act. Under a previous technical training Act, the federal government participated jointly with the provinces to "make" technical training.

Regulations. The simplest, and often least expensive, alternative is the use of legislation and regulations to control the private sector. Monopolies such as Bell Canada are allowed to exist in the private sector because governments can regulate the prices they charge for their services.[1]

Subsidies. Yet another alternative is to increase the production of some goods and services, notably those with associated external economies, by direct subsidies to private producers. For example, some universities in Canada are legally private institutions but they receive substantial grants from governments so that they can offer services (instruction) at prices (tuition fees) lower than their full cost.

Taxes. Although taxation is discussed in the second part of this chapter, it must be noted here that taxes can be used to achieve the opposite effect of a subsidy. Taxes can be imposed on private firms so that fewer goods are produced and at higher prices. It has been argued, for example, that pollution could be controlled more effectively by taxing pollution rather than by using legislation to forbid it. A sufficiently high tax on pollution might reduce pollution further and at less direct cost to the government by comparison with the difficult and costly process of prosecuting every apprehended case of pollution.

Preparing the Public Budget

Even if it can be assumed, at least for the moment, that the redistribution and stabilization functions of the government budget have

---

[1] See Chapter 12 for a discussion of government regulation of natural monopolies.

been taken into account, the allocation function raises a number of problems. Not only do governments need to decide which of the several methods should be used for providing or encouraging public services, they must also decide how much of each good or service should be available. How much *should* be allocated to each of the many government activities?

The traditional answer to this question has been that the elected representatives of the people vote on each issue and thereby determine how much will be allocated to each activity. The debate on governments' spending estimates is an important feature of the parliamentary process and, especially where there are strong opposition parties, gives rise to close scrutiny of a government's proposed expenditure program.

Do the elected members always know what their constituents want, and do they always vote according to these wants? Some economists have developed models to explain how the political process is used to determine the output of public goods and services.[2] Such models, for example, suggest that individual members and political parties arrange their voting to maximize the probability of their being reelected, and especially reelected as the government. Governments will therefore provide the minimum services required to gain the votes of each interest group, and try to realize the maximum number of votes with a minimum of tax revenues. The voting process can partly take account of externalities, but since each voter has only one vote, the size or importance of external effects cannot be reflected in voting. Someone who will be severely harmed by a new expressway or airport has no more effect on the political decision than someone who will realize almost negligible benefits. Consequently, political pressure groups or lobbies are formed to offset this inadequacy in the voting system.

Benefit-Cost Analysis

A technique now widely used by governments to evolve rational expenditure programs, and to persuade the electorate that their programs *are* rational, is program budgeting. Its full name is the *Planning-Programming-Budgeting System*, or PPBS. The essential feature of this approach is that government expenditures are allocated to programs or functions of governments, rather than, as in the past, to government departments. However, departments have been retained for administrative purposes. Under PPBS, a government decides how much to allocate to its total health program, and then assigns the administration of various parts of the program to different departments. Developing the total expenditure program through

---

[2] See, for example, Albert Breton, *The Economic Theory of Representative Government*, Chicago: Aldine, 1974; and Anthony Downs, *An Economic Theory of Democracy*, New York: Harper, 1957.

PPBS has three steps: a government outlines its objectives and priorities in the form of a *plan*; this plan is then translated into the several *programs* required to meet the various objectives; and the total *budget* is the sum of expenditures allocated to each program.

How could a government determine how much to spend on each program? The approach usually used in PPBS is *benefit-cost analysis*. Although benefit-cost analysis is regarded by some people as a complicated approach to government spending decisions, the basic concept is familiar to everyone. This is simply a comparison of the benefits of a project with its cost — a comparison that everyone makes, although perhaps sometimes unconsciously, when deciding how to spend his time or money.

Benefit-cost analysis was used initially in public allocation decisions to evaluate proposed water resource developments. Since there were many potential benefits of a proposed dam, some way had to be found to include all of them — flood control, irrigation, electric power production, and recreational use — within a single measure to be compared with the costs of land acquisition and dam construction. More recently, benefit-cost analysis has been used to evaluate expenditure proposals in education, vocational training, health, transportation, parks, research and development, housing, and crime prevention. In fact, the list could include almost all government programs.

An Example. With the increasing use of this technique, there has been increasing criticism of the interpretation of its results. Benefit-cost analysis, and difficulties associated with its application, can best be understood through an example. Consider the case of a government which must decide whether a community college should be added to the post-secondary educational system. Since governments are responsible for encouraging the most productive use of an economy's resources, this project should be evaluated from the point of view of the whole economy; this requires that *all* benefits and *all* costs be included in the analysis.

The costs include the direct costs of constructing, or renting, the college buildings as calculated on an annual basis; the salaries of instructors, and other staff; the books, supplies, and transportation costs of students; and other miscellaneous expenses. Indirect costs include the earnings which students forgo because they are not in the labour force; and the cost of municipal services supplied to the colleges, such as snow and garbage removal, and police and fire protection. There may also be some nonmonetary costs, such as the noise of students' motorcycles disturbing the neighbourhood.

The direct benefits include the additional output of the graduates, beyond what they would have produced had they not attended the college. The indirect benefits vary from local prestige due to the presence of a college, to the community involvement of its staff, to the availability of more meeting and conference spaces if these facilities are open to the community.

A conceptual outline of the costs and benefits can be prepared without much difficulty, but problems arise with the attempt to put dollar values on each item in the list. How should the buildings be depreciated in estimating the annual cost of their use? Are high school graduates' wages a satisfactory measure of the forgone earnings of college students? Does it cost the municipality anything more to include the college within its fire protection program? How can the neighbourhood's costs, such as motorcycle noise, be measured?

Even more difficult questions arise in evaluating the benefits. Are the earnings of the other college graduates a suitable measure of the potential output of college graduates in question? How will these estimated earnings change over the years with changing conditions in the supply and demand for such graduates? What is the possibility that the graduates will emigrate, or that they will not be in the labour force, or that they will not live to retirement — whatever that age might be? How should one estimate the value to the community of locating a college there?

These are the kind of questions which the critics of benefit-cost analysis have raised, and indeed the questions which analysts must answer. Nevertheless, assumptions can be made to deal with each question. By using alternative sets of assumptions, one can determine whether varying the value assigned to any one cost or benefit component has a significant effect on the final calculations.

The actual calculations of the costs and benefits include an estimate of the total cost of producing one "average" college graduate and the total benefits associated with the graduate for his lifetime.[3] If the benefits exceed the costs, the college represents a reasonable use of productive resources. Whether the project will actually be undertaken depends on whether the net benefit is greater in this project or in some other public projects under consideration. That is, priorities will be established on the basis of the benefit-cost calculations and other political considerations.

It remains for the government to decide what share of the costs should be borne by the individual student and what share should be met by public funds. Again leaving aside other considerations of income redistribution (or equality of opportunity) and stabilization of employment, the public contribution should be just large enough to attract enough students so that the bidding up of instructors' salaries and the declining average benefits associated with an increasing number of graduates will reduce the net benefits to zero; at this point the total benefits are just equal to the total costs.

In practice, governments do not determine their policies quite so precisely. This type of calculation, however, affords some guidance on whether public policies are even moving in the appropriate direction. A project, for example, which cannot be justified on the basis of benefit-cost analysis, requires the politicians to justify or reject it by looking more closely at the nonmonetary and indirect effects.

---

[3] The benefits and costs must be *discounted* to a common base year before the net benefit, or *net present value*, is calculated. This procedure is explained in Chapter 13.

Which Level of Government?

The history of the public sector in Canada includes many disputes about which level of government should be responsible for which public service. Generally the issues have focused on an interpretation of the responsibilities allocated to the federal and provincial governments by the British North America Act of 1867, or on the financial resources available to different governments to meet their responsibilities. These questions are considered more closely when intergovernmental tax agreements and revenue transfers are discussed later in this chapter.

The *economic* rationale for determining the appropriate level of government to be responsible for different public services is essentially the same as the justification for the public provision of services other than pure public goods, namely the existence of *economies of scale* and *externalities*. The existence of economies of scale, for example, led some provinces to amalgamate local school boards into county or district units. Specialized programs could be provided by small, local boards only at very high per-student costs, but county boards can provide a wider variety of programs at lower average costs — or so it was assumed. There is some conern, however, that these economies of amalgamation may be partly offset by higher costs for administering the larger units.

Education also provides an example of how external benefits, or *spillover benefits*, lead to a change in the level of government responsible for a given function. Although the increasing share of education costs assumed by some provincial governments is explained in part by problems associated with using property taxes to finance education, this shift in responsibility is also based on the argument that graduates of the local schools are more likely to leave the local community than was the case in earlier years. Local residents are less willing to bear the education costs of children who will not be productive members of the local labour force.

In contrast, residents of larger metropolitan areas often object to paying for the welfare services of persons moving into the area from other centres. The provincial governments, and in some cases the federal government, are pressed to assume larger shares of the cost of what have traditionally been municipal functions as the population becomes more mobile.

The external effects argument is, however, not inconsistent with *decentralization* of the provision of public services. Local residents, and their elected municipal representatives, may be in a better position to determine, for example, whether the benefits of a neighbourhood park justify the cost of providing it. Governments may not make the proper decisions about public services if they are too far removed from persons who will enjoy the benefits or who will bear the nonmonetary costs of some types of projects. For this reason a number of provinces, and particularly the higher-income provinces, are arguing that they can determine the value or priority of some public services better than the federal government. At the municipal level, local ratepayers associations are beginning to discuss the establishment of ward councils, as municipal councils enlarge their geographical areas and become further removed from specific neighbourhood problems.

B. Taxation

Principles of Taxation:
Who and What Should Be Taxed?

There is much truth in the old adage about the inevitability of death and taxes. Almost anything can be — and has been — taxed. Taxes have been levied on every type of luxury, from windowpanes to wives, on necessities such as salt, and on the incomes of the poor as well as the wealth of the rich. Economic analysis can indicate how governments should allocate their expenditures to achieve specific objectives, but it is more difficult to say how governments should collect revenues to finance these expenditures. There is not, for example, an analytical technique like benefit-cost analysis which can be applied to the taxation side of government budgets. Instead, a set of principles or standards must be used to judge the merits of a proposed tax. Although normative judgments underlie taxation decisions, objective analysis is important in assessing the effects of different types of taxes. In discussing these principles, it is again assumed that the government's stabilization function has been taken into account. But the question of redistribution must be given at least as much attention as the allocation function in examining a proposed tax, as will be evident from the following principles of taxation.

The principles or standards for assessing the effects of taxation have evolved through a long history of financing public expenditures. Although there is widespread agreement on the principles, the relative emphasis to be placed on each one will vary among different groups in the population and at different points in time. There can also be considerable disagreement about the extent to which any particular tax is in accord with the accepted principles.

The three basic principles of taxation are: *equity*, *neutrality*, and *efficiency*.

Principles of Tax Equity

The equity principle states simply that the tax system should be fair. But what constitutes a fair, just, or equitable tax system? Three conditions have been proposed as a test of equity. Each of these yields a different answer on whether a particular tax can be said to be "fair". As a result, the major disagreement about taxes centres on which of these tests is most appropriate. The three alternatives for judging tax equity are based on the *benefits received*, the *ability to pay*, and the *equal treatment of equals*.

Benefits Received. The principle of benefits received states that *individuals (and corporations) should pay taxes equal to the benefits they receive from government programs.* As governments increasingly move into areas of quasi-public goods, and especially those areas which have come under public control for reasons of efficiency, there is growing support for the principle of benefits received. This is often expressed in terms of a proposal that public services be financed by "user charges", or that the user of the service be charged directly. Thus subway-riders would be charged the full cost of providing subway transportation. But this proposal can err in focusing only on those who benefit directly from a service. The major beneficiaries of a city's subway system include not only the subway riders but also the inter-city residents who are freed from automobile noise and congestion, the merchants who no longer need to provide customer parking, and so on. Obviously, it would be difficult to assess a benefits tax against this more diffused group.

It is at least as difficult to determine who benefits, and especially to what extent, from most other public services. Does everyone benefit equally from national defence or police protection? If some persons benefit more than others, how are the relative amounts to be measured? This is not to suggest that the benefits principle is inappropriate, but rather that its application is not as easy as some advocates would argue. There are, however, cases in which the benefit principle has been applied using some rough approximations. For example, the gasoline tax was initially "ear-marked", or reserved, for use in highway construction and maintenance, on the assumption that the amount of gasoline purchased would be in direct proportion to the benefits derived from highway use. But "ear-marked" taxes have become less popular because the revenues from such taxes were sometimes insufficient to meet the demand for the services they were to provide, or alternatively, because governments wanted to use those revenues for other programs.

Ability to Pay. The principle of ability to pay, sometimes termed the principle of equal sacrifice, states that *individuals should be taxed according to their ability to pay.* The underlying reasoning is that individuals should make an equal sacrifice in paying taxes, in terms of the private goods and services they forgo in order to enjoy the public services. Since a tax of $100 represents a larger sacrifice for the poor than for the rich, the rich are expected to pay more in order to make a comparable sacrifice. What constitutes an equal sacrifice, however, is also an almost impossible question to answer. The debate on how the ability-to-pay principle should be applied has therefore produced a third equity principle, which is in fact, a refinement of preceding principles.

Equal Treatment of Equals. The third equity principle states that *equals should be treated equally: persons with equal ability to pay, or enjoying equal benefits, should pay equal taxes.* Since this suggests looking at persons who, by some standard, are considered to be at the same level, this condition is termed *horizontal equity.* It follows from this principle that "unequals should be treated unequally" and that such a condition can be termed *vertical equity.* While it is difficult to be certain that apparent "equals" are indeed equal in every important respect, it is an even greater problem to determine how unequally the unequals should be taxed.

The application of the ability-to-pay principle, together with the conditions of vertical and horizontal equity, raise the same types of questions about what constitutes ability as were raised in determining who benefits and by how much. In this case, there are two basic questions: how should ability to pay be defined, and how much should be paid by persons at any specific level of ability? Several measures of ability to pay have been used or proposed. Annual incomes are an obvious indication of individuals' ability to pay, but difficulties arise in determining what constitutes income. In addition to employment earnings, incomes are received in the form of interest, rent, dividends, profits on unincorporated businesses, sale of assets, gifts, inheritances, as well as in tangible goods and services. Some incomes are easier to identify than others and the recipients of these are less likely to be able to evade or avoid taxes. Partly in an attempt to get around the evasion and measurement problems, other measures of ability to pay have included real estate or property holdings, wealth or assets in other forms, and purchases of consumer goods, especially luxuries.

The second question is one of determining what represents an equitable sacrifice for each ability level: how much tax should be paid by each group? The tax burden, when compared with an individual's income, can be described as *regressive, proportional,* or *progressive.* At first glance, it might appear that a proportional tax, with everyone paying the *same percentage* of his income, would be most equitable. It is generally agreed, however, that even the same percentage, let alone the same dollar amount, would represent a greater sacrifice for low-income groups. A tax of 10 per cent of an income of $5,000 would require a greater sacrifice, it is argued, than

10 per cent of a $50,000 income. Progressive taxes, with the higher-income person paying a *higher percentage* of his income in taxes than the low-income person have therefore become more acceptable. The opposite case, a regressive tax, is one which claims a *lower percentage* from the high-income persons. Note that the emphasis is on the *percentage* of income which is paid in taxes. High-income persons may pay a higher absolute amount in the case of a regressive tax, even though the percentage is lower than for low-income persons.

Other Taxation Principles

Prior to the discussion of the equity principle, two other desirable features of a tax system were also mentioned. These were neutrality and efficiency. *The neutrality principle states that taxes should have a neutral effect on private decisions and on the operation of private markets*, unless a tax is explicitly intended to alter private sector activities in some way. A tax on pollution or on liquor, are examples of taxes intended to be *non-neutral* in their effects. Alternatively, there are many taxes which are not primarily intended to alter private decisions but which do have that effect. It is unlikely that any tax is perfectly neutral; rather, taxes must be compared on the basis of their relative neutrality — or the comparative strength of their effects on private decisions.

The principal of efficiency includes several features in the administration of a tax system. It should be viewed by the taxpayers as *reasonable and fair*, so that tax evasion does not become widespread. It should be *simple to administer* so that the costs of collecting the tax do not represent a high percentage of the tax revenue. It should be *enforceable*; when evasion of a tax is fairly common, it is no longer regarded as fair and tax revenues decline. Finally, the tax should provide a *predictable revenue* for the government so that it is not necessary to change the tax rates or the tax base too frequently.

These several taxation principles do not, unfortunately, point to what can be regarded as the ideal tax. Instead, the *existing tax system reflects a compromise of these principles*; the continuing analysis and debate on the tax system is an attempt to discover what is at any particular time the most widely accepted compromise.

Taxation In Canada

The British North America Act specifies the types of items which can be taxed by each level of government. Under this Act, the federal government has the right to collect revenues by "any mode or system of taxation", but provincial governments are restricted to direct taxation within their own province. Since municipalities are governed by provincial legislation, they are also confined to direct taxation.

Direct taxes are those levied on the persons intended to pay the tax: these include income taxes, estates taxes or succession duties, and real estate taxes. *Indirect taxes* are those levied on goods and services, and therefore indirectly on persons who are not identified until they purchase the commodities taxed; these include excise or sales taxes, and tariff duties on imports. By explicit agreements with the federal government, however, provinces have been permitted to levy sales taxes.

Table 8.1

Tax Revenue Sources by Government Level, Canada, 1974

Tax Source	Percentage of Total Tax Collected			
	Federal	Provincial	Municipal	Total
Incomes				
Corporations	21	10	—	15
Individuals	44	36	—	37
Interest, dividends going abroad	2	—	—	1
General and other sales	12	25	—	16
Gasoline, fuel oil sales	—	10	—	3
Customs and excise duties and				
excise taxes	8	—	—	4
Real and personal property	—	—	86	9
Gift tax, succession duties	—	1	—	1
Health insurance premiums	—	5	—	2
Other	13	13	14	12
Total tax revenue ($ millions)	22,650	14,201	4,517	41,368
(%)	100	100	100	100

Source: Canadian Tax Foundation, *The National Finances*, 1974-75, and *Provincial and Municipal Finances, 1975*.

Federal Taxes

Personal Income Tax. The federal government's major source of revenue is the tax on personal incomes. Table 8.1 shows that 44 per cent of federal tax revenue was raised by this means in 1974. This percentage has increased sharply in the postwar period and may continue to do so as personal incomes rise. This follows from the progressive rate structure for personal income taxes, shown in Table 8.2; a higher percentage of one's income is paid in taxes with increasing income levels.

The personal income tax meets most of the criteria of a good tax: it is simple to collect, provides a predictable level of revenue, and is difficult to evade. Although it bears no direct relationship to benefits received, it is based on one of the best measures of ability to pay.

A major criticism of the personal income tax is that it is hard to determine how unequally the unequals should be treated. That is, how progressive should the progressive rate structure be? The rate levied on the highest bracket of a person's income, the *marginal tax rate*, is the one a person considers when deciding whether to take a higher-paying job, or to earn additional income through overtime work or moonlighting. Because a high marginal rate, of say 50 per cent, may discourage a person from earning additional income, a highly progressive rate structure — where the marginal tax rates increase sharply — is said to restrain economic activity. How serious this effect actually is, however, is still strongly debated among economists. Nonetheless, the 1972 tax reform legislation removed the progressivity of the personal income tax structure at the higher income levels by setting 47 per cent as the marginal rate of federal tax on taxable income over $60,000. Previously, the marginal rate continued to rise to a maximum of 60 per cent at $400,000 and above.

Table 8.2

Personal Income Taxes and Tax Rates, 1975
For Married Taxpayer with Two Dependent Children under age 16

Assessed Income	Taxable Income*	Marginal Tax rate** %	Taxes Paid	Average Tax Rate %	After-tax Income
$ 2,500	0	2.75	0	0	$ 2,500
5,000	136	2.75	34	25.0	4,966
7,500	2,813	26.10	554	19.7	6,946
10,000	5,294	27.41	1,234	23.3	8,766
12,500	7,794	30.02	1,987	25.5	10,513
15,000	10,294	32.63	2,809	27.3	12,191
20,000	15,294	40.46	4,620	30.2	15,380
30,000	25,294	43.93	8,879	35.1	21,121
50,000	45,294	48.95	18,766	41.4	31,234

* Deductions from assessed income include personal exemptions for a married taxpayer (who supported a spouse and 2 dependent children) of $4,226, standard deduction of $100, employment expense deduction of $150, and actual unemployment insurance and Canada Pension Plan contributions.

** Federal tax rate plus provincial tax at 30.5 percent of federal tax.

Another important feature of the 1972 tax reform was the addition of capital gains to personal and corporate incomes for tax purposes. A capital gain (or loss) is the difference between the purchase and selling prices of assets such as real estate, common shares, and works of art. One-half of such gains is to be taxed at the appropriate personal or corporate rate, but one-half of any capital loss may be deducted from taxable gains. Capital gains realized on the sale of one's home, and on non-financial assets sold for less than $1,000 are exempt.

A further reform, introduced in 1973, provided for adjustment of tax deductions, exemptions, and "tax brackets" — the taxable income levels at which higher marginal rates were applicable —

according to changes in the Consumer Price Index. Without such "tax indexing", especially in years of high inflation rates, taxpayers would be paying a higher percentage of their incomes in taxes even though their increased incomes might represent no increase in their real standard of living.

Corporation Income Tax. The corporation income tax also provides a large part, about 21 per cent, of the federal government's tax revenues. This tax is levied on the net income of corporations, after eligible business expenses have been deducted from the firm's gross receipts. The tax reforms introduced an incentive for small businesses with a rate of 25 per cent on the first $100,000 of business income of Canadian-controlled private corporations, provided the total taxable income is less than $500,000. The general tax rate for all other corporations is 46 per cent.

The corporate income tax has been criticized because it is said to represent double taxation of income — the earnings of firms are taxed as corporate income and again as personal income in the form of shareholders' dividends. This problem is met in part by providing a tax credit equal to one-third of the dividend income of individuals: that is, this amount can be deducted from the total tax that would otherwise be paid if dividends are included in income. Another criticism of the corporate income tax is that it is *shifted forward*, or passed on, to individuals through higher prices of goods and services. But, as with the case of the marginal tax rate on personal income, the results of several empirical studies can be interpreted in ways which leave economists debating the actual incidence of this tax.

Another controversial feature of the corporate income tax is that mining and petroleum firms are allowed to deduct a "depletion allowance" from gross receipts; this is somewhat comparable to the depreciation allowance related to physical assets. Previously the depletion allowance was computed as a percentage of profits and continued as long as the mine or well was in operation. This provided a large deductible item which did not represent an actual expense to the firm. Depletion allowances will now be related to actual expenditures: $1 in depletion allowance being "earned" for each $3 of expenses. One significant result of depletion and similar specific allowances has been a wider variation in the effective tax rates for corporations. The non-neutral effect of this has led to greater growth of the mining industry than would have occurred otherwise.

Excise and Sales Taxes and Customs Duties. Excise taxes are taxes levied on specific goods, while sales taxes are levied on broad categories of goods. The federal government levies a *general sales tax* at the manufacturer's level of goods produced and used in Canada, and on goods imported into Canada, with the exception of some goods such as most foodstuffs and equipment used in manufacturing, transportation, and primary industries.

There are also *special excise taxes* levied, in addition to the general sales tax, on items such as tobacco products, wines, cosmetics, and jewelry. Excise taxes are levied on what may be regarded as luxury items, or what one provincial treasurer called "avoidable tastes". Such taxes produce high levels of revenue relative to the price of the goods because the demand for these tends to be price-inelastic. That is, an increase in the price results in a less-than-proportionate decrease in the quantity of the goods purchased.

Taxes in the form of tariffs or customs duties are levied on many goods imported into Canada. Such taxes are intended both to produce revenues for the federal government and to protect domestic producers from the competition of lower foreign prices. To the extent that the tariff succeeds in reducing the purchase of imports, however, it reduces government revenues from such duties. Sales and excise taxes and customs duties account for just under 30 per cent of federal tax revenues.

Provincial Taxes

Personal and Corporate Income Taxes. Each province levies a personal income tax, in addition to that levied by the federal government, equal to 30 to 43 per cent of the total federal tax. (The Quebec personal income tax is levied directly on taxable income reported to the province.) The federal government collects this tax for the provinces, with the exception of Quebec, and "abates" or refunds the appropriate amounts to the provinces. Similarly, the corporation income tax imposed by each province is collected and refunded by the federal government, with the exception of Ontario and Quebec where the corporation tax is collected directly.

Sales and Excise Taxes. All provinces except Alberta impose a sales tax, of from 5 to 8 per cent. Sales taxes are an increasingly important source of revenue for these provinces, both because total sales revenues are increasing and because sales tax rates have been increased as provinces require more tax revenues. Some of the provinces have designated the sales tax according to the purpose for which the revenue is raised, such as a "social security tax"; nevertheless these are sales taxes since they are levied on the sale of goods and expressed as a percentage of the retail price.

Provinces also levy excise taxes on specific goods, often the same goods which bear a federal excise tax, such as tobacco products and alcoholic beverages. Other commodities such as gasoline or motor fuel are taxed by what is essentially a sales tax, but this tax was originally justified as a user charge on vehicles using the highways constructed by the provinces. Taxes are also levied on the transfer of land and securities as these are bought and sold.

Estate and Gift Taxes. The federal estate and gift taxes were eliminated under the 1972 tax reform. Only Ontario, Quebec and British Columbia had levied estate taxes prior to this time, but the withdrawal of the federal government from this field opened the way for the other provinces to impose such a tax. Manitoba and Saskatchewan joined the other three provinces in imposing an estate tax, and all five also levy a gift tax.

Property Taxes. Some provinces also levy a property or real estate tax, usually because a province has assumed responsibility for most or all of the costs of local services such as education, and thus uses the property tax which would have been levied by the municipalities to finance these costs.

Municipal Taxes

Property or Real Estate Taxes. A property tax may be levied on *personal property* such as jewelry and antiques or on *real property* including land and buildings. Personal property taxes are now so rare that the terms property tax, real property tax, and real estate tax, are used interchangeably. Almost all of the municipalities' tax revenues are raised through the real estate tax. Historically, this was considered to be related to benefits received when municipal expenditures were mainly for police and fire protection, roads and garbage disposal. Reliance on this tax has been criticised recently, however, because property owners have borne the rapid increases in education costs without necessarily having a proportionate increase in the means to pay this tax.

Other Revenue Sources

Each level of government has other sources of revenue in addition to the taxes outlined above. The federal government receives income from some of its crown corporations, and realizes interest on its loans, deposits and special funds. Other non-tax revenue includes licences and fees charged on a variety of activities controlled by the federal government.

Provincial governments derive substantial revenue from motor vehicle registrations and operators' licences, profits on the sales of alcoholic beverages and other provincial enterprises, and several other fees and licences, as well as fines and penalties.

Municipal governments realize some additional revenue through licence fees on the operation of businesses such as retail stores, barber shops, and taxis, and from traffic and parking fines.

Fiscal Federalism and Intergovernmental Transfers

In addition to tax revenues, provincial and municipal governments derive substantial revenue from grants made by the higher level of government. Such grants may be either *conditional*, paid for definite purposes and under specific conditions, or *unconditional*, leaving the recipient government free to spend the funds in any way.

Federal Grants

Unconditional Grants. Historical circumstances account for the unconditional grants paid by the federal government to the provinces. The British North America Act required the provinces to withdraw the sales and excise taxes that had provided such a large part of their revenues. In compensation, the federal government provided *statutory subsidies*, based on provincial populations, with additional allowances for costs of government administration, debt charges, and special grants. In 1974-75, these amounted to only $34 million.

The BNA Act permitted the provinces to levy personal and corporation income taxes, but when the federal government required a sharp increase in its revenues to finance expenditures for World War II, it entered into Wartime Tax Agreements with the provinces whereby they withdrew from the income tax field. In return, the federal government made a cash grant to the provinces equal to the previous year's revenue from these taxes. The wartime agreements were replaced in 1947 with agreements that were renewed every five years, currently termed the Federal-Provincial Fiscal Arrangements Act.

Under this Act, the federal government makes three types of payments to the provinces: abatements, equalization grants, and stabilization grants. Throughout the postwar period, the federal government has gradually transferred or abated to the provinces a larger share of the revenue collected from personal and corporate income taxes. The payments made to the provinces are referred to as *tax abatements*. Some provinces receive lower tax abatements per capita than other provinces because, for example, one percentage point of the federal personal income tax produces lower revenues per capita where the taxable income base is lower.

The federal government therefore makes an *equalization payment* to the lower-income provinces so that an abatement of one percentage point in the personal or corporate income tax is of equal value per capita to each province. *Stabilization payments* are made when necessary, to maintain a province's tax revenue at not less than 100 per cent of the previous year's revenues, on the basis of the previous year's tax rates.

Conditional Grants. Conditional grants, or grants-in-aid, are usually made as the federal government's portion of cost-sharing programs. There are now fewer such programs both because it was difficult for the federal government to control the expenditures under these arrangements, and because some provinces chose to "opt out" of the program, receiving instead increased tax abatements. Recent examples of shared-cost programs are the Hospital Insurance Plan, Medicare, and the Canada Assistance Plan. Under the latter plan, for example, the federal government pays 50 per cent of provincial expenditures for a variety of welfare assistance programs. A special form of *adjustment payment* is also made to the provinces under an arrangement whereby the federal government pays 50 per cent of post-secondary education costs. If the tax abatements specified for this purpose are less than 50 per cent of the costs, an adjustment payment is made for the difference.

Federal Grants to Municipalities. Federal grants are also made to municipalities to compensate them for the federal properties which are exempt from real property taxes.

Provincial Grants

Provincial governments make both unconditional and conditional grants to municipalities; these account for almost 50 per cent of municipal governments' total revenues from taxes and other sources. Unconditional grants, including payments in lieu of property taxes on provincial government properties, are designed to reduce the municipal tax burden on residential and farm properties. About three-quarters of the conditional grants represent contributions to primary and secondary education; other shared-cost programs include roads and highways, unemployment assistance and winter works projects, police services, recreation, and housing.

Review of the Main Points

1. Total government expenditures in Canada represent about one-third of the Gross National Product. These expenditures have increased sharply due to inflation, population growth, wars, and increasing emphasis on public provision of education and health services.

2. Economic functions of government include stabilization of aggregate economic activity, redistribution of income in an equitable manner, and reallocation of productive resources to more efficient uses.

3. Reallocation of resources involves both regulation of private sector production and direct production of goods and services within the public sector. Public goods and services such as defence are those which would not be produced except through

collective action. Quasi-public goods like highways, education, and health care are produced collectively due to high costs of excluding non-contributors, economies of scale, or external benefits.

4. Public and quasi-public goods and services may be provided through direct production by government departments or agencies, by purchasing the goods or services from the private sector, by regulating private monopolies, by subsidizing producers, or by imposing taxes on activities which are contrary to the public interest.

5. Benefit-cost analysis is the principal technique in the Planning-Programming-Budgeting System (PPBS) most governments have introduced for determining their expenditure programs; benefit-cost analysis consists of comparing all benefits with all costs of a project and selecting the projects with the highest net benefits.

6. The appropriate level of government to provide particular services depends on economies of scale and externalities associated with each program. The greater the economies of scale, and external benefits for other areas, the stronger is the case for passing responsibility to a higher level of government. However, lower levels of government may be better able to determine the local benefits of a program.

7. The three basic principles of taxation are: equity, neutrality, and efficiency. Three alternatives for judging tax equity are based on the benefits received, the ability to pay, and the equal treatment of equals. The first alternative states that taxes should be equal to the benefits received; however, some direct benefits, and most indirect benefits, are hard to measure, and such taxes usually are difficult to collect. Ability to pay is defined as requiring an equal sacrifice from all individuals, but this too is difficult to determine. Equal treatment of equals applies to each of the other two alternatives; the major difficulty is deciding how unequally the unequals should be treated.

8. A progressive tax is one which collects a higher percentage of the tax base, such as income, the larger the tax base; while a proportional tax collects the same percentage and a regressive tax, a lower percentage, from larger tax bases.

9. The neutrality principle states that taxes should have a neutral effect on private decisions and on the operation of private markets unless a tax is explicitly intended to alter these. The efficiency principle requires that a tax be reasonable and fair, simple to administer, enforceable, and provide predictable revenue.

10. The federal government relies on personal and corporation income taxes, excise and sales taxes, and customs duties for its tax

revenue; roughly two-thirds of federal revenue comes from income taxes. Provincial governments raise almost one-half of their tax revenue through income taxes, about one-quarter through sales taxes, and the balance through taxes on gasoline and other sources. Municipal governments raise more than four-fifths of their tax revenues through real property taxes. Each level of government also has non-tax revenues from crown corporations and other public agencies, interest on financial assets, and various licences, fees, and fines.

11. Unconditional grants are made by the federal government to provincial governments, mainly as equalization payments to compensate lower-income provinces that would otherwise have to impose higher taxes on their populations to provide public services comparable to those provided in higher-income provinces. Conditional grants represent the federal contributions to shared-cost programs.

Review and Discussion Questions

1. What conflicts are there among the three basic economic functions of government: allocation, distribution, and stabilization? Which of these functions should receive highest priority? Why?

2. Why has the total government share of GNE increased so much over the past decade? How high should this percentage go? Why?

3. Should governments provide any goods or services they do not now provide? Specify and explain why. Are there any goods or services currently provided by governments that should be provided instead by the private sector? Specify and explain why.

4. List as many external benefits as you can that are associated with a graduate of the program in which you are currently enrolled. How would you measure the value of each type of benefit?

5. Do you favour the ability-to-pay or the benefits-received principle of taxation? Why? Which principle is the easier one to apply? Which of the existing taxes collected by any level of government do you favour and which do you oppose most strongly? Why?

5. Do you think a tax on gasoline is progressive, proportional, or regressive? Why?

Sources and Selected Readings

Bird, Richard M. *The Growth of Government Spending in Canada*. Toronto: Canadian Tax Foundation, 1970.

Breton, Albert. *The Economic Theory of Representative Government*. Chicago: Aldine, 1974.

Canadian Tax Foundation. *The National Finances.* Published annually by the Foundation.

_____. *Provincial and Municipal Finances.* Published biennially by the Foundation.

Dupré, J. Stefan. "Tax Powers Versus Spending Powers: A Historical Analysis of Federal-Provincial Finance" in A. Rotstein (ed.) *The Prospect of Change.* Toronto: McGraw-Hill, 1965, pp. 83-101.

Economic Council of Canada. *Sixth Annual Review: Perspective 1975.* Ottawa: Queen's Printer, 1969.

_____. *Eighth Annual Review: Design for Decision-Making.* Ottawa: Information Canada, 1971.

Haveman, R. H. *The Economics of the Public Sector.* New York: Wiley, 1970.

McKean, R.N. *Public Spending.* New York: McGraw-Hill, 1968.

Musgrave, R.A. *The Theory of Public Finance.* New York: McGraw-Hill, 1959.

Phelps, Edmund S. (ed.) *Private Wants and Public Needs,* rev. ed. New York: Norton, 1965.

Report of the Royal Commission on Taxation. Ottawa: Queen's Printer, 1966.

9 Consumer Demand and Consumer Decisions

The many factors influencing demand were discussed in Chapter 2 to show how prices are determined in individual commodity markets. Such an analysis of supply and demand factors provides an explanation for the behaviour of prices, and the response to prices in terms of quantities demanded, but it does not offer a more general explanation of the overall economic behaviour of consumers. The law of demand predicts that a consumer will buy more of a good when its price falls, but provides no answers on how a consumer will spend his income among the thousands of goods and services available to him.

Why does a consumer buy some goods and not others? Why does he buy a great deal of one product but only a little of another? If his income increases by 10 per cent, will he spend 10 per cent more on each good he has bought in the past, or will some of the increase be allocated to new goods? How will his collective purchases change if the prices of some goods rise while the rest remain constant? Answers to these questions require a *theory of consumer behaviour*. The rest of this chapter is concerned with such a theory, which otherwise might be called "On getting more for one's money".

Price Versus Value

An old proverb states that "He who knows the price of everything knows the value of nothing". Although this expression exaggerates the case, it nevertheless makes the basic point that troubled early economists: the value, or usefulness, of a commodity often seemed to be quite different from the price of the item. Water was valued highly because it was so important to life, yet water was either free, or available at a low price. Conversely, some luxury items such as spices and silks commanded high prices.

Marginal Utility and Consumer Decisions

Utility is Satisfaction

Toward the end of the last century, economists gave increasing attention to the usefulness or satisfaction that consumers derived from their purchases. Not only was the satisfaction or enjoyment derived from each commodity seen to be important to a consumer, but also the total enjoyment derived from the combination of all his purchases. This satisfaction or usefulness was termed *utility*. Commodities would be purchased only because they provided some utility for the consumer. The utility of a particular commodity would vary among consumers depending on each consumer's set of preferences or tastes. Moreover, the utility derived from each particular unit of a commodity would depend on how much of that commodity an individual had previously consumed or used during a given time period.

Marginal Utility

At the same time, economists recognized that a consumer did not decide how to spend the whole of his income at any given moment. Rather, he was constantly faced with specific decisions such as whether to buy another shirt or another roast of beef. These items were described as being at the *margin* of his consumption of such goods. The *marginal unit* of beef would be the specific roast of beef he is considering buying. Although marginal is the term usually used in economics for this concept, other terms such as *additional*, or *incremental*, also appear occasionally.

Table 9.1

Individual's Utility Schedule for Milk-Shakes

Milk-shakes per day	Total Utility	Marginal Utility
0	0	
1	12	12
2	19	7
3	23	4
4	25	2
5	25	0
6	24	−1

The concepts of utility and marginal units are combined in the term *marginal utility*. While granting that utility cannot be measured objectively, economists assume that individuals can and do make subjective comparisons of marginal utility, both among marginal units of various commodities and among various quantities of the same commodity.

Marginal utility can be illustrated by the example presented in Table 9.1 and Figure 9.1. Someone who has not had a milk-shake for a long time probably derives a great deal of enjoyment or utility from a milk-shake, especially on a hot day. In fact, he may decide to have a second. But the second milk-shake probably is less satisfying than the first. A third milk-shake may also be enjoyed, but with even less satisfaction than the second. And a fourth milk-shake is only barely satisfying. Part-way through the fifth milk-shake he is beginning to feel sorry that he ordered it. Irrationally, he goes on to order a sixth and soon regrets it! In this case, the *total utility* or enjoyment of the milk-shakes increased during the consumption of the first four, but the fifth and sixth milk-shakes reduced his overall enjoyment. The *marginal utility*, however, declined for each additional milk-shake following the first one; this decline continued until there was even some disutility associated with the last two.

This declining satisfaction from each additional unit of a commodity is described as *diminishing marginal utility*.

Law of Diminishing Marginal Utility

The declining satisfaction obtained from each additional unit of a commodity was observed so widely that economists chose to regard it as a law, or one of the basic principles, of economics. More recently, economists have questioned whether something which

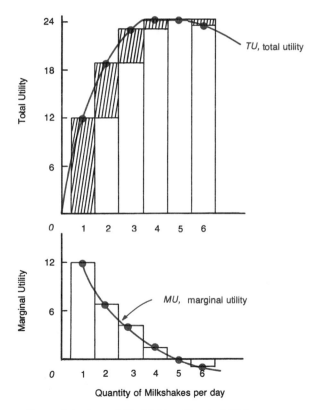

Figure 9.1   Law of Diminishing Marginal Utility
Marginal utility is the change in total utility associated with each additional unit consumed. The total utility curve, *TU*, shows the cumulative total utility at each level of consumption. Shaded areas represent the additional utility or satisfaction associated with each particular milkshake. Marginal utilities plotted in the lower graph illustrate the law of diminishing marginal utility: each additional unit provides less utility. When marginal utility becomes negative, total utility begins to decline.

cannot be measured — utility — should be the basis of an economic law. Nevertheless, they are satisfied that consumers behave *as if* the law of diminishing marginal utility is valid. As the marginal utility or satisfaction derived from each additional unit diminishes, it is apparent that consumers will buy *additional* units only at a lower price. The law of diminishing marginal utility thus provides a logical basis for the law of demand: if consumers will buy additional units only at a lower price, they will buy a larger total quantity only at a lower *average* price per unit.

Rational Consumer Decisions

Diminishing marginal utility provides the key to an explanation for consumers' purchases of particular combinations of commodities, given their income levels. At the same time, this explanation provides a rule for determining a consumer's optimal combination of purchases. The rule for consumer decision-making assumes that consumers will act rationally, that is, that they will make decisions conducive to achieving their objective. It is also assumed that their objective is to derive the greatest possible utility or satisfaction from their individual monetary incomes, or in other words, that consumers wish to maximize their total utility. The concept of an equilibrium position can be applied to consumers, as it has been to commodity markets in Chapter 2 and to national income in Chapter 4.

The combinations of consumers' purchases are in equilibrium when consumers have obtained the maximum total utility with their given individual incomes.

When this point is reached, there are no pressures forcing consumers to change their combination of purchases in striving for greater satisfaction.

A rule for consumer decision-making becomes more apparent if one focuses on the consumer's *marginal expenditure* rather than on his total expenditure. Although a consumer may agree that his marginal dollar should be spent where it will realize the highest marginal utility, he may wonder what to do when a good will afford more utility but also costs more than another potential purchase. In this case *he must choose the good which yields the highest marginal utility per dollar*. If a $15 sweater will give exactly twice as much satisfaction as a $6 shirt, the shirt should be purchased since this provides more utility per dollar than does the sweater.

This suggests the rule for rational behaviour in allocating one's income:

The total income should be spent on various commodities such that the marginal utility per dollar spent on one commodity is equal to the marginal utility per dollar spent on each and every other commodity.

This rule can be expressed in general terms as follows:

$$\frac{MU_a}{P_a} = \frac{MU_b}{P_b} = \frac{MU_c}{P_c} = \ldots = \frac{MU_n}{P_n}$$

where MU_a is the marginal utility of good a, and P_a is the price of good a, and so on to the last or nth good.

The rule for rational allocation of incomes has a wider application to the use of all resources. Most people who are concerned about making good use of their *time* follow this rule, perhaps without recognizing how "economical" they are. In the interval remaining before leaving for a trip, writing an examination, or moving to a new job, they will spend their time on those things which are most important or where the results will be most effective in achieving their objectives. Consider a student, for example, who wishes to obtain a high average mark on his examinations. He may be able to improve the mark in his best subject by five points if the entire remaining week is spent on that subject. But his *average* mark, or the total mark for all examinations, may be improved still further by allocating study time so that the anticipated improvement (or marginal gain) per hour of study is the same for each subject.

Changing Equilibrium Conditions

No one is likely to be able to estimate the marginal utility derived from each unit of a commodity so accurately that he can achieve precisely his optimum allocation of expenditures. But the decision rule that commodities should be purchased until their marginal utilities are proportional to their prices can guide consumers *toward* more rational decisions. Moreover, even if one could achieve the equilibrium condition, forces would be acting in such a way that a new combination of expenditures probably would be indicated. Changes in tastes leading to changes in marginal utilities of different goods, changes in the relative prices of commodities, and the availability of new commodities, all would require a reallocation of expenditures.

Consumer Surplus

The concept of marginal utility provides some insight into the suggestion raised earlier, namely that the value of a good may seem unrelated to its price. Consider the case of someone who is very fond of corned-beef sandwiches. Figure 9.2 shows this person's demand curve for his particular gastronomical delight. At the prevailing price of corned-beef sandwiches, $.40, he purchases four of these per week. The *economic or market value* of these four sandwiches is $1.60. But the demand curve indicates that he would have been

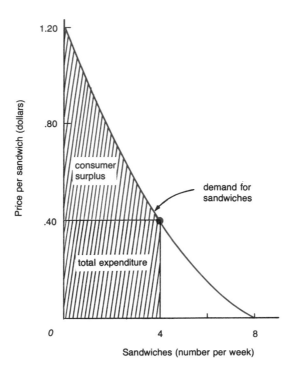

Figure 9.2   *Consumer Surplus*
The consumer's demand curve indicates that he would be willing to pay more than
$.40 for 1, 2, or 3 sandwiches, but since the market's equilibrium price is $.40, he
can buy each of his 4 sandwiches for that price. The difference between what he
would be willing to pay in total for the 4 sandwiches if purchased separately, and
what he does pay, is called consumer surplus.

willing to pay about $1.00 for the first sandwich, about $.75 for the
second, about $.50 for the third, as well as $.40 for the fourth. The
total value to the individual of the four sandwiches is much greater
than the market value calculated by multiplying the price by the
number of sandwiches purchased. This total value to the individual
is a reflection of his total utility, although the actual total utility
cannot be calculated in dollar terms. What is clear, however, is that
the sandwich-lover would be willing to pay more in total for his four
sandwiches than he has been required to pay. The difference between these two amounts is termed the *consumer surplus*.

   Suppliers would, of course, like to be able to collect this consumer surplus as well as the total revenue they realize from their
market sales. One technique for realizing at least a large part of this
surplus is to sell goods by *auction*. At an antique auction, for example, there may be four Early Canadian crocks to be sold. Instead of

offering the four crocks at one time, the auctioneer will usually sell them individually. The person who offers the highest price for the first one will get it. That buyer may be willing to pay even more than anyone else for the second. And for the third. If he buys the four crocks separately, he will have paid a higher total price than if he had bought the four at once. Note, however, that he might have been willing to pay still more for the crocks, even though they are sold separately. He has only been required to offer a higher price than anyone else. Even this difference — between what the buyer thinks each is worth and the price he pays — can be collected from the buyer by using the "Dutch auction" technique. In this case the auctioneer starts with an unreasonably high price, dropping the price until the most anxious buyer makes an offer.

Indifference Curves and Consumer Decisions

The consumer's decision rule, that the ratio of marginal utility to price should be equal for all commodities, is useful for a general or qualitative explanation of consumer behaviour, but it does not provide an operational method for quantitative analysis of consumer behaviour. Economists have therefore modified this approach so that it is not necessary to measure utility directly. The more modern method for examining consumer behaviour is *indifference curve analysis*.[1]

Indifference Schedules, Curves, and Maps

Indifference Schedule. Even though someone cannot say by how much more or less he would enjoy a slice of pizza compared with a piece of barbecued chicken, he should be able to say how much pizza would give him approximately the same satisfaction as one piece of chicken. If the answer is three slices, then he is said to be *indifferent* between having one piece of chicken and three slices of pizza. Furthermore, he will be indifferent between various *combinations* of pizza and chicken. By listing these combinations in an *indifference schedule* and then plotting this schedule on a graph, one can obtain the individual's indifference curve for these two goods.

---

[1] A still more recent approach examines the consumer's "revealed preference". This is presented in more advanced textbooks such as the one by Wm. J. Baumol included in the selected readings list at the end of this chapter.

Table 9.2

Combinations Yielding Equal Total Satisfaction

Combination	Pizza (pcs. per wk.)	Chicken (pcs. per wk.)
A	25	5
B	20	6.5
C	15	10
D	10	15

Table 9.2 presents one person's indifference schedule for combinations of pizza and barbecued chicken. The information provided indicates that he is equally satisfied with, or is indifferent among, four different combinations of pizza and barbecued chicken. Any one of these combinations might be consumed each week: 25 slices of pizza and 5 pieces of chicken provide the same satisfaction or utility as 10 slices of pizza and 15 pieces of chicken. Different persons could have quite different combinations of pizza and chicken depending on their relative tastes for these two foods.

Indifference Curve. The four combinations shown in Table 9.2 are plotted as points A to D in Figure 9.3. A smooth curve is drawn through these points to show the other combinations which presumably would be equally acceptable. This becomes indifference curve, I_1. Note that the individual is indifferent between combination A and combination B; it is *not* a matter of being indifferent, for example, between 25 pizza slices and 5 pieces of chicken.

The process can be repeated to develop other indifference curves for the same individual and the same goods. By beginning with a less desirable combination of, say, 15 pieces of pizza and 5 of chicken, (point E) and obtaining other equally satisfactory combinations, a lower indifference curve, I_0 is obtained. Alternatively, asking for other combinations which would yield the same satisfaction as 15 pieces each of pizza and chicken (point F) provides the higher indifference curve, I_2. That is, 15 pieces of each item, and all other equally satisfactory combinations, would yield a higher level of satisfaction or utility than the combinations represented by I_1.

Each indifference curve represents a distinct level of utility provided by various combinations of the two goods.

Indifference Map. Since there can be many different levels of utility or satisfaction derived by consuming various amounts of one good while the quantity of the second is unchanged, there can similarly be many indifference curves relating to these two goods. For example, points E and F in Figure 9.3 were derived by holding the quantity of

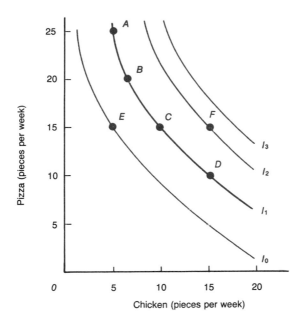

Figure 9.3 An Individual's Map of Indifference Curves
Each indifference curve represents a specific level of satisfaction that can be enjoyed by consuming various combinations of pizza and chicken. Examples of equally satisfying combinations are shown as points A, B, C, and D, on indifference curve I_1. Total satisfaction increases as one shifts to combinations represented by points on indifference curves, such as F on I_2, which are further from the origin.

pizza constant at 15 pieces and varying the quantity of chicken combined with the pizza to yield lower and higher levels of satisfaction than are represented by combination C. Then alternative combinations are determined which yield the same satisfaction provided by combination E, and similarly for combination F, to derive the two additional indifference curves I_0 and I_2. One can imagine the other indifference curves that would result as the quantity of chicken combined with the fixed quantity of pizza varied from 1 to 20 pieces, and the alternative "equal satisfaction" combinations were determined. The end result would be a whole *family of indifference curves* or an *indifference map*.

The indifference map presents a complete picture of an individual's preferences for various combinations of two goods.

It is also a map of the total utility he enjoys with different combinations of the goods. The indifference curve I_3 represents a higher level of total utility than does I_1, although one cannot measure the difference between these two utility levels.

Indifference curves can never intersect. If I_2 intersected I_1 at B, this would imply that the consumer was indifferent between combinations B and F. But since he is also indifferent between B and C, this would also imply that he was indifferent between C and F. Such a result would be foolish because combination F provides him with more chicken than does combination C, while the quantity of pizza remains the same. Since he cannot be indifferent between F and C, curves I_1 and I_2 cannot intersect.

Marginal Rate of Substitution

Note that the indifference curves in Figures 9.3 have a particular shape: they bow inward, or are *convex to the origin*. This reflects the fact that as one moves downward along the indifference curve, or as more chicken is combined with less pizza, more chicken is required to compensate for the loss of each unit of pizza if total utility is to remain unchanged. Figure 9.4 shows that as one moves from A to B on indifference curve I_1, 1.5 pieces of chicken can be substituted for 5 of pizza. But in moving from C to D, 5 pieces of chicken must be substituted for 5 of pizza. As the individual consumes more chicken, each additional piece of chicken provides less satisfaction and thus more must be added to compensate for the reduction in pizza.

The law of diminishing marginal utility discussed earlier reappears in indifference curve analysis as the *law of diminishing marginal rate of substitution*.

The marginal rate of substitution is the quantity of one good that an individual will give up in exchange for one unit of another good without changing the total satisfaction obtained from the two or more goods he consumes.

In Figure 9.4 the marginal rate of substitution between points A and B is 5 pieces of pizza for 1.5 of chicken, or 3.3 to 1. But when more chicken and less pizza is included in the combination, the marginal rate of substitution is 1 to 1, that is, 1 piece of chicken for 1 of pizza.

The law of diminishing marginal rate of substitution therefore states that as more of a good is consumed, the marginal rate at which it can be substituted for another good will diminish.

Consumer Decisions with Given Incomes

Budget Line. If a consumer is indifferent among a large number of alternative combinations of pizza and chicken, how does he decide which specific combination of purchases to make? The answer lies in relating his income and the relative prices of these goods to his indifference map.

To present a simple example, suppose that a consumer allocates $15 each week for lunches or snacks; that these consist of only pizza

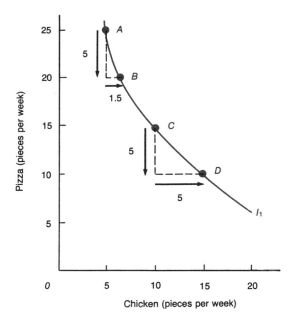

Figure 9.4   Law of Diminishing Rate of Substitution
A movement downward along indifference curve I_1, implies that equal satisfaction combinations include more chicken and less pizza. More chicken must be added in moving from C to D, than in moving from A to B, to compensate for the loss of a given quantity (5 pieces) of pizza, because each additional piece of chicken provides less satisfaction. That is, as more of a good is consumed, the marginal rate at which it can be substituted for another good will diminish.

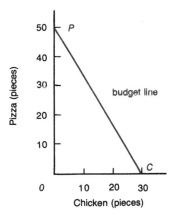

Figure 9.5   Consumer's Budget Line
The budget line PC shows the various combinations of pizza and chicken which can be purchased with a given money income ($15) and at given prices ($.30 per slice of pizza and $.50 per piece of chicken). Higher incomes would shift the budget line outward since more of each good could be purchased, provided prices remained constant.

or chicken; that pizza is $.30 per slice while chicken is $.50 per piece. This information provides a *budget line* or *consumption-possibilities curve*. If he spends all of the $15 on chicken, he can buy 30 pieces; alternatively, the $15 would buy 50 slices of pizza. These alternatives are illustrated in Figure 9.5. The budget line, *PC*, shows the various combinations of pizza and chicken which can be purchased with $15 — from 50 pizza slices and no chicken to 30 chicken pieces and no pizza.

The budget line is a straight line because *the slope of the line is the ratio of the prices of the two goods.* Since the prices do not change with different quantities purchased of each good, the ratio, and thus the slope of the line, is constant for all combinations of the two goods.

Consumer Equilibrium. By plotting the budget line on the indifference map, it is possible to determine the combination of pizza and chicken which will yield the highest total utility, given the level of income and prices of each good. This combination can be described in terms of Figures 9.6 as point K: 30 pieces of pizza and 12 pieces of chicken. Since the budget line is just touching the indifference curve I₂, or is *tangential* to I₂, this is the highest level of utility that can be obtained with an expenditure of $15. Other combinations, such as those represented by L and M, would just exhaust the $15 budget,

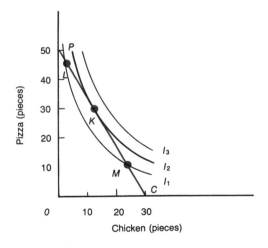

Figure 9.6   Consumer Equilibrium
The consumer will reach his maximum satisfaction level, given his budget line *PC*, by consuming combination *K*: 30 pieces of pizza and 12 pieces of chicken. Although his income would also buy combinations *L* and *M*, these are on a lower indifference curve, *I₁*, and thus provide less satisfaction. The greatest satisfaction he can afford is therefore represented by the highest indifference curve he can reach; this occurs at *K*, where *PC* is tangent to *I₂*. Unless the consumer's tastes or income change, or there is a change in prices of these goods, the consumer will continue to purchase combination *K*.

and the consumer is indifferent between them, but these would provide a lower level of satisfaction because they are on a lower indifference curve. Point K thus becomes the consumer's equilibrium position, given the information assumed at the beginning of this example. The combined purchase of 30 pieces of pizza and 12 pieces of chicken per week is the most rational expenditure he can make.

The consumer's equilibrium condition is defined as the purchase of two goods such that their marginal rate of substitution is equal to the ratio of their prices.

This condition is derived from the fact that at the point where the budget line is tangential to the indifference curve, the slopes of the two lines are equal. Since the slope of the budget line is the ratio of prices and the slope of the indifference curve is the marginal rate of substitution or the substitution ratio of the two goods, these two ratios must be equal at point K, the consumer's equilibrium position.

Notice the similarity of this equilibrium condition with the rule for consumer expenditures under marginal utility analysis. This latter rule required expenditures on two goods such that

$$\frac{MU_1}{P_1} = \frac{MU_2}{P_2} \text{ or } \frac{MU_1}{MU_2} = \frac{P_1}{P_2}$$

That is, the ratio of marginal utility is equal to the ratio of prices for two goods. In indifference curve analysis, the rule is

$$\frac{P_1}{P_2} = MRS_{\text{(1 for 2)}}$$

where MRS is the marginal rate of substitution between good 1 and good 2.

Thus, MU_1/MU_2 has been replaced by $MRS_{\text{(1 for 2)}}$. This provides an objective measure of utility but in terms of quantities of goods that substitute for one another. To obtain such a measure, it is necessary only that a consumer be able to say which combinations of goods provide equal satisfaction; and not how much more satisfaction he derives from one good than from another.

Derivation of the Consumer's Demand Curve

Indifference curve analysis makes it possible to derive the consumer's demand curve from his indifference map. For each of the two goods involved, the quantity that would be demanded at each price can be found by varying the price of the good and determining the quantity of that good which would be included in the various

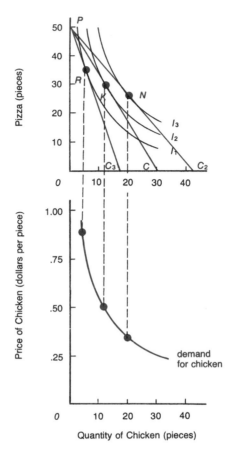

Figure 9.7   Effects of Changes in Relative Prices
A decrease in the price of chicken enables the consumer to buy more chicken with
a given income: the budget line shifts to PC_2, and the highest-satisfaction combination is N. Similarly, an increase in the price of chicken shifts the budget line to PC_3
and combination R is purchased.

Figure 9.8   Deriving the Demand Curve
The consumer's demand curve for chicken can be derived from information in
Figure 9.7. The quantity of chicken which would be purchased is shown by combi-
nations R, K, and N, for each of the prices represented by the three budget lines.

equilibrium combinations of purchases. This is illustrated in Figure
9.7. When the price of chicken is $.50, the consumer will buy 12
pieces. If the price drops to $.35, with the price of pizza unchanged,
the budget line becomes PC_2 since an expenditure of $15 would buy
43 pieces. The new equilbrium is on a higher indifference curve, at
point N, and 20 pieces of chicken would be purchased. Similarly, if
the price of chicken increases to $.88, the budget line shifts to PC_3,

the new equilibrium point is R and only 7 pieces of chicken are purchased.

The combinations of chicken prices and quantities demanded are plotted in Figure 9.8. These provide three points on the consumer's demand curve for chicken. By assuming alternative prices for chicken, other equilibrium points could be found in Figure 9.7 and plotted in Figure 9.8. These points are then joined to derive the complete demand curve, given a specific level of the consumer's income, constant prices of other products, and no changes in the consumer's tastes.

Income and Substitution Effects

The law of diminishing marginal utility provided one explanation for the downward slope of the consumer's demand curve. This explanation was not entirely satisfactory, however, because marginal utility could not be measured and one needed to rely on intuitive or subjective judgments about the validity of this explanation. Indifference curve analysis affords a more precise and objective explanation in terms of the *income effect* and the *substitution effect*.

The income effect is the effect of a price change on the total purchasing power of a given monetary income.

If the price of chicken falls, more chicken can be purchased, just as if there had been an increase in income. Similarly, an increase in the price of chicken has the same effect as a decrease in income: less chicken can be purchased.

The substitution effect is the effect of a change in the relative prices of two goods, leading to a substitution of some of the good which has become relatively cheaper, for some of the good which has become relatively more expensive.

This effect can be explained by reference to Figure 9.9. A fall in the price of chicken shifts the budget line from PC_1 to PC_2. In moving to the new equilibrium combination, the consumption of pizza decreases and the consumption of chicken increases. But only part of the increased chicken consumption is due to the substitution effect. The income effect is measured by drawing another line, P_3C_3, parallel to the original budget line and tangent to the same indifference curve reached by the new budget line, PC_2. Budget line P_3C_3 shows the extent to which the consumer is better off, or enjoys a higher level of real income, as a result of the decreased price of chicken. That is, the consumer can buy more pizza, as well as more chicken, when the price of chicken falls. This analysis shows that the income effect of the price change has increased consumption of chicken from 12 to 18 pieces. The substitution effect has increased consumption further still, from 18 to 30 pieces. The income effect is measured by moving from one indifference curve to the other; the substitution effect is measured by moving along the new indifference curve. It is these two effects taken together which explain the downward slope of the consumer's demand curve: as the price of a good falls he buys more, both because the relatively lower price leads him to substitute this good for other goods and because the lower price makes it possible for him to buy more goods, including the good in question, with his given monetary income.

Consumer Expenditure Patterns

Indifference curves are used in the previous section to analyze a consumer's response to price changes, but indifference curve analysis can also be used to determine how consumers will respond to income changes. In Figure 9.9, for example, the budget line P_3C_3

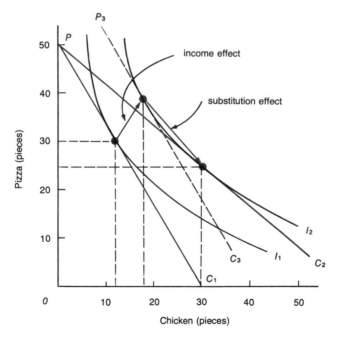

Figure 9.9 A Price Change Has Two Effects
When the price of chicken falls, the budget line shifts from PC_1 to PC_2. Chicken consumption increases from 12 pieces to 30 pieces. Part of the increase is an income effect: since a price decrease enables one to purchase more real goods with a given money income, there is an increase in real income. This is represented by a parallel shift of PC_1 to P_3C_3, and an increase in chicken consumption to 18 pieces. The further increase in chicken consumption from 18 to 30 pieces is a substitution or price effect: the decreased chicken price relative to the pizza price leads one to substitute chicken for pizza.

shows the real income effect of a price change. However, P_3C_3 also shows how consumption would change if prices remained constant and the consumer's income increased. The income increase is shown by a shift of the budget line from PC_1 to P_3C_3. Similarly, if several budget lines, representing different income levels, were drawn parallel to P_3C_3, a line connecting the points of tangency of the budget lines and the various indifference curves would show the quantities of chicken and of pizza that would be consumed at various income levels. From this information one could plot a curve, termed an *income-consumption curve*, which shows the quantity of each good which will be purchased at various levels of income. These are also termed *Engel curves*, after a nineteenth-century German statistician, Ernst Engel. By using data for expenditures on broad categories of consumer goods at different income levels, Engel observed that the percentage of consumer incomes spent on food usually declined as incomes increased. This commonly observed fact became known as Engel's Law. Other similar observations led to a set of Engel's Laws, namely, that as consumers' incomes increased, the percentage spent on housing remained almost constant, the percentage spent on clothing remained the same or increased slightly, and the percentage spent on most other items increased. With the exception of minor variations, these laws have remained valid for different countries and over long periods of time.

Table 9.3

Consumption Expenditure Patterns of Families and Unattached Individuals, by Selected Income Classes, Canada,* 1972

| | *Annual Income* | | | | |
| | All Classes | 4,000 to 5,000 | 8,000 to 9,000 | 12,000 to 15,000 | Over 25,000 |
	percentage of total consumption expenditure				
Food	23	25	23	22	20
Shelter	21	26	22	20	19
Household operation	5	5	5	5	7
Furniture, equipment	6	3	5	6	7
Clothing	10	7	9	10	11
Health, personal care	6	6	6	5	6
Tobacco, alcoholic beverages	5	6	6	5	5
Travel, transportation	16	11	16	17	15
Recreation	5	5	5	5	6
Reading, education	2	3	1	2	3
Miscellaneous	2	1	3	3	2
Total**	100	100	100	100	100
Total Consumption Expenditures	$ 8,191	4,369	7,226	9,794	17,357
Net Income before Taxes	$11,118	4,481	8,488	13,358	33,794

* Eight major cities representing 92 per cent of the Canadian population.
** Components may not add to totals due to rounding.
Source: Statistics Canada, *Urban Family Expenditure, 1972.*

An annual survey of families and unattached individuals, conducted by Statistics Canada, provided information which can be used to plot similar curves for broad categories of consumer items. Table 9.3 shows, for example, how consumer expenditures vary by income level for food, shelter and household operation, transportation, clothing, and recreation. The consumption expenditure patterns for selected levels of income, as shown in Table 9.3, generally are in accord with the Engel's Laws outlined previously. As income increases, the percentage spent for food decreases, the combined percentages for shelter and household operation remains almost constant, except at the lowest income level, and the proportion of income that goes for clothing increases slightly.

Note also that consumption expenditures as a percentage of total income decline substantially as income rises. The difference consists of both savings and personal income taxes. As real incomes rise over a period of time, and a larger percentage of families move into the higher income classes, the share of national income going to consumption expenditures tends to fall. From 1961 to 1974, for example, consumer expenditure as a percentage of GNP fell from 65 per cent to 57 per cent.

Income Elasticity of Demand

The effect of a change in income on the quantity demanded of a specific commodity can be described in terms of the general elasticity concept that was introduced in Chapter 2:

Income elasticity of demand is the percentage change in quantity demanded divided by the percentage change in income.

The formula for calculating income elasticity can be derived from this definition in the same way that the price elasticity was derived in Chapter 2. Hence, income elasticity is calculated as follows:

$$E_y = \frac{\Delta Q}{\Delta Y} \times \frac{Y_1 + Y_2}{Q_1 + Q_2}$$

where E_y is the coefficient of income elasticity, ΔY is the difference between the two income levels, Y_1 and Y_2, and ΔQ is the difference between the two quantity levels, Q_1 and Q_2.

For most commodities, the quantity demanded — or the expenditure on the commodity when prices are constant — increases as income increases. The income-elasticity coefficient will therefore be positive, since the direction of change is the same for both the quantity demanded and income. Table 9.4 presents the income elasticities of demand for food, tobacco and alcoholic beverages, and travel and transportation at each of various income levels. Each income-elasticity coefficient is positive, indicating that, at all levels of income, an increase in income produces an increase in expenditures on the three commodity categories concerned. Commodities for which the income-elasticity coefficient is positive are termed *normal goods* because consumers purchase a greater quantity of these, or spend more for these goods, as their incomes rise. Common examples of goods with a high income elasticity include filet mignon, theatre box-seats, and rare wines.

Note in Table 9.4 that the income-elasticity coefficients for food and for tobacco and alcoholic beverages decline as income increases. If this continued to the point at which the coefficient became negative, these goods would be described as *inferior goods* for persons at the income level associated with the negative coefficients. Inferior goods, or goods for which the quantity purchased declines as income increases, include the cheaper meat cuts and tobacco brands, and lower quality wines.

Table 9.4

Income Elasticity of Demand for Selected Commodities and Income Levels, Canada,* 1972

Annual Family Income	Food	Tobacco and Alcoholic Beverages	Travel and Transportation
$ 6,000	1.05	1.93	1.25
8,000	.89	.72	1.83
10,000	.48	.71	2.18
15,000	.54	.68	1.06

* For families of two or more persons, in eight major cities representing 92 per cent of the Canadian population.
Source: Calculations are based on data from Statistics Canada, *Urban Family Expenditure, 1972.*

Review of the Main Points

1. The theory of consumer behaviour attempts to explain why consumers allocate their expenditures as they do, and how consumers will change their purchases as relative prices change.

2. Utility is the satisfaction, enjoyment, or usefulness individuals derive from a commodity. Marginal utility is the utility derived from the marginal or additional unit purchased. Total utility is the utility derived from the total quantity of the good consumed in a given period.

3. The law of diminishing marginal utility states that as more of a particular good is consumed, the marginal utility of each additional unit will diminish.

4. Consumers can maximize the total utility derived from a given level of income by arranging their purchases so that the marginal

utility per dollar spent on one commodity is equal to the marginal utility per dollar spent on every other commodity. This is the equilibrium combination of purchases, given the consumer's tastes and the relative prices of consumer goods. The equilibrium combination will change whenever there is a change in his tastes, relative prices, or an introduction of new commodities — unless the influence of these changes exactly offset each other.

5. Consumer surplus is the difference between the total revenue suppliers receive for the total quantity exchanged in the market for a good and what consumers would be willing to pay as an expression of the total utility they derive from the good.

6. Indifference schedules are lists of combinations of goods such that each combination provides the same satisfaction to the consumer. Indifference schedules can be plotted on a graph as indifference curves. An individual's indifference map is a set of indifference curves, with each curve representing a specific level of satisfaction or utility. Since each indifference curve represents a different level of utility, indifference curves cannot intersect.

7. The shape of indifference curves — downward sloping and convex to the origin — is due to the diminishing marginal rate of substitution. That is, as the quantity consumed increases, more of a good must be substituted for a given reduction in the consumption of another good.

8. A budget line shows the combinations of two goods which can be purchased, given their prices, with a given total expenditure. The slope of this line is the ratio of the prices of the two goods. Since the ratio is constant for all combinations of the two goods, the budget line is a straight line.

9. The consumer equilibrium condition, or the condition for maximizing total utility with a given income, is reached by purchasing the combination of goods represented by the point of tangency of the budget line and an indifference curve. The slopes of each of these are equal at the tangency point, indicating that the ratio of prices is equal to the marginal rate of substitution of the two goods, or that $P_1/P_2 = MRS$ (1 for 2).

10. As the price of a good changes relative to the price of another good, the position of the budget line changes and thus the equilibrium combination of goods also changes. By plotting the quantities of a good which will be purchased as its price changes, the consumer's demand curve can be derived from an indifference map.

11. The combined income and substitution effects of a change in the price of a commodity provide an explanation for the downward slope of a consumer's demand curve. That is, a price decrease results both in an increase in a consumer's real income and in a

change in the relative prices of two goods, leading to the substitution of some of the cheaper good for some of the more expensive good.

12. An income-consumption curve, showing the quantities of a good which will be purchased at different income levels, can be derived by shifting the budget line outwards across a consumer's set of indifference curves. Such curves, also called Engel curves, provide information for calculating the income elasticity of demand for a commodity: the percentage change in quantity demanded divided by the percentage change in income. If the quantity demanded increases, or if the income elasticity is positive, as income increases, the commodity is a normal good; a decrease in quantity demanded or a negative income elasticity would indicate that the commodity is an inferior good.

13. Data from surveys of family expenditures tend to confirm the Engel's Laws: that as income increases, a lower percentage is spent for food, a constant percentage is spent for housing, a slightly increasing percentage is spent for clothing, and an increasing percentage is spent for most other items, particularly luxuries.

Review and Discussion Questions

1. "Consumer sovereignty is a fiction. Producers develop new products and then use advertising to persuade consumers that they should buy these products." Do you agree? Why?

2. Can total utility be positive when marginal utility is negative? Can total utility be increasing when marginal utility is positive but decreasing? Explain.

3. Why does the optimum allocation of a consumer's income require the same ratio of marginal utility to price for all commodities purchased? What basic objective is assumed in stating this rule?

4. Draw an indifference curve which shows various combinations of ice-cream cones and apples which would give you equal satisfaction. Add other indifference curves showing higher and lower levels of total satisfaction. Add a budget line representing a total expenditure of $2 per week, if cones cost 20¢ and apples cost 10¢. Next, add budget lines as the price of apples varies from 2¢ to 40¢. Derive your demand curve for apples. Does it agree with what you believe your demand for apples actually is? If not, examine your indifference map and explain the discrepancy. As the price of apples increases from 10¢ to 20¢, is the income effect greater or less than the substitution effect?

5. Draw an indifference curve for two commodities that are perfect substitutes, and one for two commodities that are perfect complements.

6. What use could producers make of information about the income-elasticity, and price-elasticity, of demand for their products?

7. What explanations can you offer for the Engel's Laws, and the related evidence shown in Table 9.3?

Sources and Selected Readings

Baumol, Wm. J. *Economic Theory and Operations Analysis*, 2nd ed. Englewood Cliffs, N.J.: Prentice-Hall, 1965.

Due, John F., and Robert W. Clower, *Intermediate Economic Analysis*, 5th ed. Homewood, Ill.: Irwin, 1966.

Duesenberry, J.S. *Income, Saving and the Theory of Consumer Behavior.* Cambridge: Harvard University Press, 1949.

Ferber, Robert. "Consumer Economics: A Survey," *Journal of Economic Literature*, December 1973.

Green, H.A.J. *Consumer Theory.* Harmondsworth, Middlesex: Penguin, 1971.

Katona, George. *The Powerful Consumer.* New York: McGraw-Hill, 1960.

Stonier, Alfred W., and Douglas C. Hague. *A Textbook of Economic Theory*, 4th ed. London: Longmans, Green, 1973.

Watson, Donald S. *Price Theory and Its Uses*, 3rd ed. Boston: Houghton Mifflin, 1972.

10   Production Costs and Competitive Supply

A. *Production Costs*

When the supply curve was introduced in Chapter 2, it was stated simply that this curve was determined by the costs of production. This chapter examines how production costs vary under different conditions, how producers make their supply decisions, and thus how the market supply of certain products is determined.

What are Costs?

The basic cost concept, *opportunity cost*, was defined in Chapter 1 as the satisfaction or output forgone by choosing one alternative instead of the next best alternative. The opportunity cost of a productive factor is the output forgone by using that factor for the given purpose rather than in its best alternative use. The cost of labour hired by a firm, for example, will be the wage the firm must pay to attract that labour away from its best alternative employment.

Explicit and Implicit Costs. A firm's costs are both *explicit* and *implicit*. Explicit costs are a firm's direct expenditures for productive factors such as labour services, materials, electricity, transportation, rental of space, and so on. Implicit costs are related to the use of productive factors owned by the firm. Most firms recognize, for example, that if part of their plant stands idle, a cost is involved even if the firm makes no mortgage payments or maintenance expenditures for the idle space. This is the opportunity cost represented by what could be earned through the productive use of the space. Since implicit costs can only be estimated, implicit costs are also referred to as imputed costs.

Using the opportunity cost concept to estimate implicit costs often leads to the erroneous impression that only implicit costs are opportunity costs. Rather, *all costs are opportunity costs*. The firm could use the productive resources purchased with direct expenditures, as well as the factors it owns, to produce other commodities, just as an individual's opportunity cost of attending a movie is related to both the admission price and the time spent at the theatre. Each could have been used to realize satisfaction or enjoyment in alternative ways.

Normal Profits are Costs. One of the opportunity costs of producing a particular commodity is the profit forgone by not producing some other commodity.

Implicit costs therefore include normal profit: the minimum profit required to retain the firm in the production of the specified commodity.

Any profit made in excess of the normal profit is termed an *economic profit* or *pure profit.* (Normal profits are also termed zero profits because they include no pure profit; conversely, pure profits are also termed excess, supernormal, or extranormal profits because they are in excess of normal profits.) Although a businessman may be inclined to calculate his firm's profit by subtracting explicit costs from total revenues, an economist would calculate pure profit by subtracting both explicit and implicit costs, including normal profits, from the total receipts.

The Short Run and the Long Run. Production costs are also classified according to the period within which the firm can vary the quantity of specific factors used in producing a given quantity of output. Some factors such as casual labour can be varied on a daily basis; others such as skilled labour and some materials may be varied according to a contractual period of perhaps three months to two years, while changes in machinery or plant size may require an even longer time.

The *short run* is the period within which it is possible to change the quantity produced by altering the quantity of some factors, such as labour and raw materials, but within which it is not possible to alter the quantities of all factors. During the short run, for example, the firm may employ more labour to utilize idle machinery or to work an additional shift.

The *long run* is the period long enough to enable a firm to alter the quantity produced by altering the quantity of all resources used to produce the good, including changes in the type of resources used.

The short run and long run do not refer to specific time periods in terms of weeks or months; they can be defined only by reference to the production of particular commodities and prevailing practices concerning, for example, contractual employment of managerial personnel and the length of collective agreements with labour unions. Thus the short and long runs are more appropriately viewed as *planning periods* than as calendar time periods.

Short-Run Production and Costs

Production costs per unit of output usually vary with the length of the planning period because different combinations of productive resources can be used in the different planning periods. The resources required and the cost per unit produced in the short run can be examined using a simple *production function.* Such a function is illustrated by the *production schedule*, shown in Table 10.1, and plotted as a *total product curve* in Figure 10.1a. These show how a firm's total output changes as additional units of a factor are added to the firm's existing productive factors. Suppose that a firm is producing a standard ceramic mug for sale in craft and gift shops. Assume for simplicity that the only productive resources required are physical capital in the form of pottery wheels, and skilled labour, or potters. (The raw material, clay, is assumed to be a free good in a huge mound outside the pottery shop.) Assume also that the firm has five pottery wheels and is determining how its output would vary with different amounts of labour.

Table 10.1

Production Schedules for a Pottery Firm

Variable Factor* (man-days of labour) Q_L	Total Product per day TP	Average Product per day AP	Marginal Product per day MP
0	0	0	
1	20	20	20
2	76	38	56
3	183	61	107
4	304	76	121
5	410	82	106
6	486	81	76
7	518	74	32
8	520	65	2
9	513	57	−7

*Fixed factor consists of 5 pottery wheels.

Table 10.1 shows the total product, average product, and marginal product associated with various quantities of labour. *Total product*, TP, is the total quantity produced per time period (one day) by the total productive factors of the firm. *Average product*, AP, is the quantity produced per unit of a variable productive factor, or by each man-day of labour service in this particular example. *Marginal product*, MP, is the change in the total product associated with each additional or marginal unit of a productive factor, in this case with an additional man-day of labour. Thus:

$$AP = \frac{TP}{Q_L} \text{ and } MP = \frac{\Delta TP}{\Delta Q_L}$$

where Q_L is the quantity of labour in man-days. (Recall from Chapter 4 that Δ is a Greek letter used to represent "change in".)

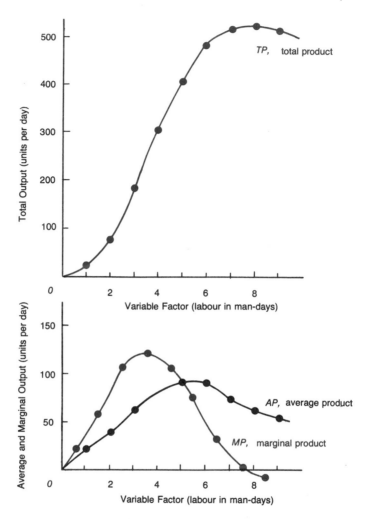

Figure 10.1   The Law of Diminishing Returns
When the quantity of one productive factor is fixed, the addition of increasing
quantities of a variable factor eventually leads to a decline in the total product. In
this example, adding a ninth man-day of labour to the pottery firm's five wheels,
results in lower total product. The shape of the total product curve, *TP*, is determined by the marginal product, *MP*, associated with each additional man-day of
labour. When *MP* becomes negative, *TP* begins to decline. Average product, *AP*,
is the total product divided by the quantity of labour. Marginal product is equal to
average product where average product is at a maximum.

The total product curve is plotted in Figure 10.1a; the average
and marginal product curves are plotted in Figure 10.1b. The quantity of the variable factor, labour, at which the total product curve
reaches its maximum output level is the point of *diminishing
productivity*. Similarly, the quantity of labour at which the average

product curve reaches its maximum output level is the point of *diminishing average productivity*; for the marginal product curve it is the point of *diminishing marginal productivity*.

Law of Diminishing Returns

Reference is made in everyday language to the "law of diminishing returns", often with some vagueness about its meaning. The example just presented shows that there are three possible meanings, depending on whether one refers to total, average, or marginal productivity. Different explanations for variation in output with changes in the quantity of a productive factor could be given for each productive process. Generally, this effect is due to a normal relationship betwoen labour and machinery, and the possibility for division of labour. Presumably the machinery/labour relationship in the pottery firm is that one person operates one wheel. If fewer than five persons are employed, at least one wheel is idle. If more than five persons are employed, the additional workers can add to total output only by performing other specialized tasks such as preparing and rough-shaping the clay, fitting handles to the mugs, glazing, packing, and handling orders. But the number of persons required for these additional tasks is also related to the fixed capital, the total number of pottery wheels. When all wheels are in use, the data provided in Table 10.1 indicates that the ninth person cannot be fully occupied, distracts the other workers, and the firm's total output is reduced.

Note that the marginal product is not necessarily the actual product of a particular additional person, but reflects the effect of an additional worker on the total productive process, usually by making further division of labour possible.

The law of diminishing returns thus states that, given a fixed quantity of one productive factor, the economies realized by division of labour eventually diminish as increasing quantities of this variable factor are added, or more generally, that the continued addition of the variable factor eventually leads to a decrease in the total product.

Because the proportions of the two factors vary as more of one is added, the law is also termed the *law of variable proportions*.

Total, Average, and Marginal Costs

The production costs of the firm can be determined from its production schedule and the prices it pays for productive resources. In this simple case, it is assumed that the firm's purchases of productive resources are too small to influence their prices, so that the price of any factor of production to this firm is constant regardless of the amount the firm buys.

Fixed and Variable Costs. The total cost of producing any given quantity of output can be divided into fixed costs and variable costs.

Fixed costs are those costs which do not vary with changes in quantity of output.

They are also termed *overhead costs*; they must be incurred even if the firm produces no output. These would include payments for insurance, licences, property taxes, interest on loans and bonds, and imputed costs of plant and equipment. In the pottery firm example, the estimated or imputed cost of the pottery wheels is treated as a fixed cost.

Variable costs are costs which vary directly (but not necessarily in proportion) with changes in the quantity of output.

These usually include items such as wages, materials, fuel, and transportation. The variable costs of the pottery firm are its wage payments. The fixed, variable, and total costs are shown in Table 10.2, and are plotted as curves in Figure 10.2. The total fixed cost is set at $50, the imputed cost of the five wheels, for all levels of output. The total variable cost rises slowly at first because the marginal product of additional labour is rising. When the point of diminishing marginal productivity is reached, the total variable cost begins to rise more quickly because additional units of labour produce fewer additional units of output. Note that the total fixed cost is added vertically to the total variable cost at each level of output to determine the total cost.

Table 10.2

Production Costs for a Pottery Farm

Variable Factor (man-days of labour) Q_L	Total Product (mugs per day) TP	Total Cost			Average Cost			Marginal Cost (per unit)
		Fixed TFC	Variable TVC	Total TC	Fixed AFC	Variable AVC	Total ATC	MC
1	20	$50	$100	$150	$2.50	$5.00	$7.50	
2	76	50	200	250	.66	2.64	3.30	$1.79
3	183	50	300	350	.27	1.64	1.91	.94
4	304	50	400	450	.16	1.32	1.48	.83
5	410	50	500	550	.12	1.22	1.34	.94
6	486	50	600	650	.10	1.23	1.33	1.32
7	518	50	700	750	.10	1.35	1.45	3.11
8	520	50	800	850	.10	1.54	1.64	50.00

Average Costs. *Average total cost, ATC, or the total cost per unit, is the total production cost for a given quantity of output divided by that quantity or number of units produced. The average fixed cost and average variable cost are defined and calculated similarly. These cost schedules are also shown in Table 10.2, and are plotted as cost* curves in Figure 10.3. The average fixed cost curve falls continuously as output increases because the fixed cost is being divided by an increasingly larger quantity. This is the effect commonly described as "spreading overhead costs".

The average variable cost curve, AVC, is U-shaped; it declines initially, reaches a minimum cost, and rises again. The output level at which the *AVC* curve is at its minimum is the same point at which the average product curve reaches its maximum in Figure 10.1. When the average product per unit of labour is at a maximum, the cost of such labour in each unit of output, the *AVC*, is at a minimum. Similarly, when the average product is rising, the *AVC* is falling and

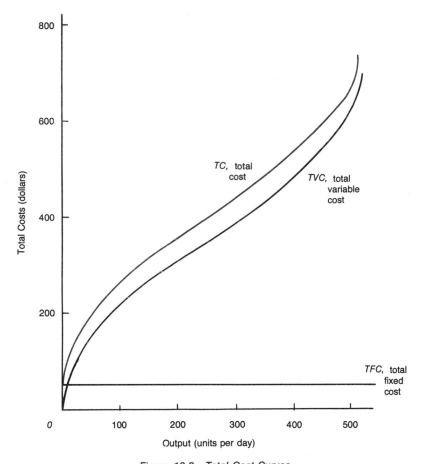

Figure 10.2   Total Cost Curves
The total cost curve, *TC*, is obtained by adding vertically the total variable cost, *TVC*, and total fixed cost, *TFC*, at each level of output. Fixed cost does not vary with output. Variable costs usually increase at a decreasing rate, and then at an increasing rate, with higher levels of output because of diminishing marginal productivity of variable factors such as labour.

vice versa. Thus the law of diminishing average productivity implies that the average cost, or cost per unit, will eventually rise. The actual point at which this occurs, as noted before, depends on the particular conditions for producing each commodity. If the firm is a sufficiently large employer of labour, the average cost will rise sooner since the firm will be bidding up the cost of labour services as it employs increasing numbers of workers, unless the large number of employees also makes substantial specialization of labour possible.

The *average total cost curve, ATC,* is again determined by adding vertically the average variable and average fixed costs at each level of output, or by dividing the total cost by the quantity produced. At the lowest output levels, the shape of the *ATC* curve is influenced mainly by the *AFC curve,* but as *AFC* diminishes, the *ATC* curve approaches the *AVC* curve. The output level at which the *ATC* curve is at a minimum is defined as the firm's *capacity* or *optimum rate of output.* Although the firm can produce more than this quantity, operating above capacity increases average costs; operating with excess capacity, or at a lower output level, also results in higher average costs than could be realized by increasing output.

Marginal Cost. Apart from the basic concept of opportunity cost, the most important single cost concept in economic analysis is marginal cost:

Marginal cost is the change in total cost associated with the production of each additional unit.

Marginal cost can also be calculated from changes in the total variable cost since fixed cost does not vary with the quantity produced. Note, however, that it *is* possible to have a change in the fixed cost within the short-run period, such as an increase in property taxes or in the price of a business licence. But this increase must be paid regardless of the level of output and thus does not affect the marginal cost of additional units.

The marginal cost curve, as shown in Figure 10.3, is also U-shaped and for the same general reasons that the average variable cost curve takes this shape. Marginal cost is at its minimum at the output level where the marginal product curve begins to fall, the point of diminishing marginal productivity. Note that as the marginal cost curve rises it intersects the average variable cost curve from below and at its minimum level. The output level at which this equality of marginal cost and average variable cost occurs is the same output level at which marginal product and average product are equal.

Marginal cost schedules and curves are important because they show the increase in total cost for each additional unit, or the amount by which total cost can be reduced with each unit decrease in the level of production. The average cost schedules do not provide this information: although average costs vary with level of output, the change in average cost is *not* the cost of producing one more or one less unit. The significance of marginal cost in the firm's decision about the quantity to produce is explained later in this chapter.

Although the marginal cost and average variable cost curves shown in Figure 10.3 have a pronounced U-shape for expository purposes, marginal cost remains constant in many actual cases, over a wide output range, because diminishing returns are not experienced until higher output levels are reached. But although constant marginal costs may be observed in studies of the actual costs of firms or industries, this constancy cannot continue at much higher levels of output. Eventually, the law of diminishing returns has its effects, and marginal cost begins to rise. It will be seen later that this rising

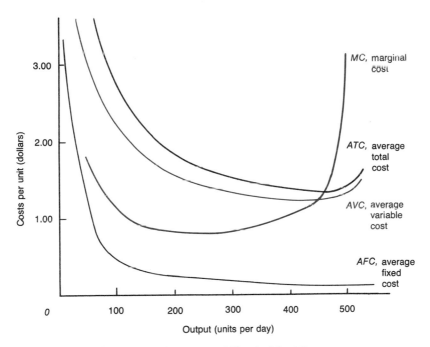

Figure 10.3 Average and Marginal Cost Curves
The average fixed cost, *AFC*, average variable cost, *AVC*, and average total cost, *ATC*, are calculated by dividing the total cost by the quantity produced. The marginal cost, *MC*, is the change in total cost associated with each additional unit produced. *AFC* declines with increasing output, but *AVC* and *ATC* fall and then rise as *MC* rises more sharply. *MC* always intersects the *AVC* and *ATC* curves at their lowest points.

portion of the marginal cost curve is critical to the firm's output decisions; it is this section of the curve therefore that is commonly used in analyzing such decisions.

Long-Run Production and Costs

The long run was defined as the time required to change or vary all factors of production, particularly plant and equipment. In the long run, a firm can change its plant size or the amount and type of machinery it uses, as well as alter the amount and proportions of such factors as labour, raw materials, and so on. Moreover, the number of firms in the industry producing a specific commodity may also change as some firms leave or others enter the industry.

Since all factors are variable in the long run, the distinction between fixed and variable costs is not relevant in the long run: reference can therefore be made simply to total costs. The alternatives open to a firm in the long run are examined in terms of average total costs and alternative plant sizes.

Suppose the pottery firm were trying to determine the plant size at which it could produce 500 mugs at the lowest possible average cost. Figure 10.4 shows that a plant size of 5 pottery wheels, represented by the ATC_1 curve, would result in an average total cost of $1.40. The 500 mugs could be produced in the smaller plant represented by ATC_0 or in the larger plant represented by ATC_2 but at a higher average cost in each case. (Note that it is not a question of

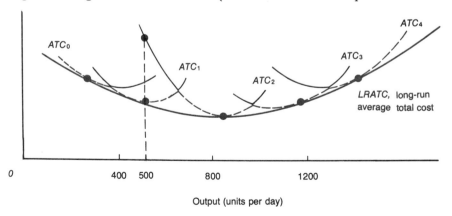

Figure 10.4 Long-Run Average Total Cost Curve
When all possible short-run average total cost curves are plotted on a graph (only 5 are illustrated here), the minimum *ATC* for producing any given level of output can be determined. Joining the minimum *ATC* for each level of output provides the long-run average total cost curve, *LRATC*. Note that only at the minimum point of the *LRATC* (at about 850 units) does the *LRATC* curve coincide with the minimum point of any short-run *ATC* curve; in this case, it is ATC_3. The broken curve shows the *LRATC* if only five plant sizes are possible; the smooth curve shows the *LRATC* when there are an unlimited number of plant sizes.

finding the output which can be produced at the minimum average cost in a plant of given size, but rather, finding the plant size at which a given output can be produced at the lowest average cost.)

Similarly, the firm could determine the plant size that would result in the lowest average cost for producing 1,000 mugs. Figure 10.4 indicates that a plant size with either ATC_2 or ATC_3 would lead to approximately the same average cost for 1,000 mugs, but the larger plant would enable the firm to expand production at lower average costs per unit than would the smaller plant. This would be true until output reached 1,300 mugs when the firm would want to increase to the plant size implied in the ATC_4 curve.

If the ATC curves of all possible plant sizes were plotted in Figure 10.4, it would be possible to determine the plant size with the lowest average total cost for producing each level of output.

The curve showing the lowest average total cost for each output level is the long-run average total cost curve, LRATC.

Returns to Scale

The shape of the long-run average total cost curve is determined by variations in the returns to scale. These are *not* due to the law of diminishing returns; that law described the effect on output of continuing to add more of one productive factor while the quantity of all other factors was held constant. *Returns to scale result from varying the quantities of all factors.*

There are three different cases of returns to scale: *increasing returns, constant returns,* and *decreasing returns.* The decreasing portion of a long-run average total cost curve, such as the *LRATC* curve in Figure 10.4, reflects increasing returns. The minimum, flatter portion reflects constant returns, and the increasing portion represents decreasing returns.

Increasing Returns. Increasing returns to scale are also referred to by a number of other terms: economies of scale, of large scale, of mass production. Firms or industries experiencing increasing returns are sometimes called decreasing-cost firms or industries. The increase in returns refers to the decrease in average total cost that can be realized as output increases faster than inputs with increasing plant size.

Increasing returns occur for various reasons: technical, managerial, marketing, and financial. *Technical economies* can be realized in several ways: large batches or mass production makes increased specialization of labour possible; some machinery may be quite expensive and therefore lead to low unit costs only with large scale production; a large firm may be able to enlarge the number of commodities it produces and thus make use of by-products from the production of its major item. A common technical economy in the chemical and petroleum industries, for example, is realized by increasing the diameter of pipelines. The volume carried per hour can be increased without any, or comparable, increase in labour.

Managerial economies can be realized by large plants which use special managers for each type of activity and who in turn can afford to purchase more information and advice on their part of the plant's operations. Also, some managerial personnel may be underutilized in a small plant because they are capable of dealing with more responsibility in terms of production, sales, or employees than would be found in a small plant.

Marketing economies are possible because some sales activities such as market research, advertising, and establishment of distribution outlets usually require large expenditures to be effective.

Financial economies are related, for example, to a large firm's ability to borrow funds at a lower interest rate, or even to issue public shares to raise investment funds, and to finance a broader research and development program which leads to further economies.

Constant Returns. Constant returns or constant costs mean that output and the use of productive factors are increasing at the same rate. This is the case of a firm which has become large enough to take advantage of the economies of scale just described, but which has not expanded to the point where diseconomies begin to take effect. Since constant returns often are realized over a wide range of output quantities, many of Canada's larger firms are in a constant returns situation.

Decreasing Returns. Decreasing returns to scale, or increasing average total costs, would occur for reasons opposite to those explaining increasing returns. For example, management of very large firms may become less effective in controlling and coordinating the firm's diverse activities. Beyond a certain size, there may be no further economies to be realized through specialization of the managerial function. Also, one important assumption made thus far, that the quantity of labour and materials purchased by the firm is such a small part of the market quantity that their prices are unaffected, usually does not hold for very large firms. If the automobile producers, for example, substantially expanded their scale of production, their purchases of more steel and certain skilled workers would increase the prices of these factors, and thus raise their average total costs, unless there is a perfectly elastic supply of these factors in the long run.

While any one of these situations may be found in large firms, it is doubtful that the net effect of many factors would be to increase the average total costs with large-scale production. That is, the production level at which decreasing returns begin for one factor may also be the level at which increasing returns begin for other reasons.

There has been much debate, with relatively little evidence, on whether the long-run average total cost curve normally rises at high levels of output.

B. Supply Determination in Competitive Markets

Market Structure

The quantity of output a firm will supply to a market depends on both its production costs and the structure of the market. Market structure is defined in terms of the nature and number of buyers and sellers and the characteristics of products. Each supplier or seller is treated as a single firm; all firms supplying a particular product are collectively described as the industry for that product.

Although many types of market structure have been identified, four basic types are sufficient to illustrate the principles governing a firm's output decisions under alternative market conditions. Two market structure models represent the extreme limits of possible conditions: *pure competition* and *pure monopoly*. Two other models represent the actual conditions faced by a large number of firms: *monopolistic competition* and *oligopoly*. Only pure competition is discussed in this section; the other three models are considered in Chapter 12.

Pure Competition

The distinguishing feature of pure competition, or perfect competition as it is sometimes called, is that *individual firms cannot influence the price of the product in any way*. Regardless of the quantity supplied, a firm faces the price prevailing in the market at any given time. Firms in pure competition are therefore described as *price-takers*.

A second basic feature of pure competition is that *there are no barriers or obstacles preventing new firms from entering the industry, or preventing existing firms from leaving it*. Any firm which wishes to produce and sell a product in a perfectly competitive market is free to do so.

A number of conditions give rise to these two essential characteristics of pure competition.

- There are many sellers of the product, such that no individual seller produces a significant share of the quantity available to the market. The actions of any one firm, for example, in offering the product at a different price, are not taken into account by other firms.

- All firms produce exactly the same product. Because "product" is defined broadly enough to include associated services such as free delivery, advice, and maintenance service, buyers have no reason to purchase the product from one firm rather than another. The products of all firms are therefore said to be homogeneous.
- All buyers have full information about the market, in terms of the product, prices, and suppliers. For example, if one firm offered the product at a lower price than its competitors, all potential buyers would be aware of this.
- Productive resources are perfectly mobile; any firm or potential firm can acquire whatever resources it requires for producing the commodity in question.

Such conditions rarely exist in any market; pure competition is therefore almost unknown in actual practice. Nevertheless, an analysis of firms' behaviour under pure competition is a useful approach to studying the diversity of existing market conditions. As successive features contrary to the conditions of pure competition are introduced into market structure models, the separate effects of such conditions can be identified. By associating these effects with market conditions, firms can decide which changes would be favourable to their objectives. It will be shown later that pure competition generally leads to the most efficient use of resources, and therefore provides a standard for evaluating the efficiency of resource use under other market conditions.

There are, however, some markets which are more closely approximated by the pure competition model than by other models. The markets for farm products have traditionally provided examples of pure competition. The classic case portrays, for example, the egg industry, with many producers and numerous buyers, standard products (determined by egg-grading standards), resources readily moved into or out of egg production, and buyers aware of at least many if not all producers and their prices. Any single egg producer supplies such a small share of the market quantity that he cannot affect the market price. Firms can easily enter or leave the industry because resources such as grain, labour, land, and buildings can be readily transferred between egg production and other agricultural uses.

In many countries, *agricultural products* are still marketed under conditions very similar to pure competition. In other countries, including Canada, producer cooperatives or marketing boards have been established for several agricultural commodities. These have often been formed in response to the existence of only a few buyers, such as large supermarkets or food processors. The result is a market with only one seller, the cooperative or board, and a few buyers. A substantial element of pure competition remains in such a market, however, in that individual producers receive the same price for their products and each producer can supply any quantity at that price unless there are quotas assigned to each producer. The creation of the Canadian Egg Marketing Agency thus ended most of the conditions necessary for perfect competition in the egg industry: production is regulated by quotas and most eggs are marketed through a provincial board.

The *fishing industry* has also provided examples of pure competition, but here also cooperatives have been formed to market the fish from local areas. Both fishing and agricultural production have also been modified by contractual arrangements whereby a large buyer agrees to buy all, or a specified quantity, of the product from individual suppliers, and at predetermined prices. Furthermore, the supplier may sell his product only to the buyer holding the contract.

Examples which closely resemble pure competition can be found in local markets, for example, for *handicraft products* such as leather-goods, pottery, wood-carvings and hooked rugs, where any of these is a specialized handicraft of the area. Tourists travelling across the country frequently encounter a series of roadside stands with each producer offering essentially the same product at very similar prices.

Output and Price under Pure Competition

The effect of *time* on production conditions has previously been described in examining short-run and long-run production costs. In the short run, the quantity produced can be changed only by altering the use of variable resources, but in the long run, the quantity produced can vary more widely because all resources are variable. The elasticity of supply therefore varies with the time period; the longer the period considered, the more elastic is the supply.

Yet another time or planning period can be introduced: this is the *market period* or *momentary period* which is *the period within which the quantity to be supplied has already been produced.*

The *market period* is appropriate only to perishable products which, once produced, must be supplied to the market. In cases where storage may be part of the production process, products are not considered perishable until they have been removed from storage for delivery to buyers. Since the quantity of perishable products is fixed, supply is perfectly inelastic. This is illustrated in Figure 10.5, using lettuce as an example. The quantity of lettuce offered in a particular market area on any given day is represented by the vertical or perfectly inelastic supply curve, SS, at quantity OQ_m. The market price, OP_1, is determined by the intersection of the supply and demand curves. If the quantity of lettuce supplied each day remains at OQ_m, the price of lettuce will vary with shifts in the demand curve.

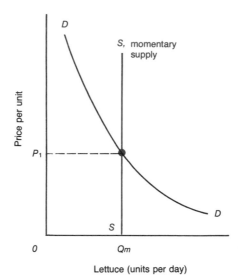

Lettuce (units per day)

Figure 10.5   Momentary or Market Period

In the momentary or market period the quantity supplied, Q_m, has been deter-mined previously, and thus the supply curve, SS, is perfectly inelastic. The equilib-rium price can vary only with changes in demand.

Short-Run Output under Pure Competition

Firms' Objectives. In the market or momentary period, a firm has no choice about the quantity to be supplied; this has already been de-termined. In the short-run, however, a firm must decide what quan-tity will be produced. This will depend on the firm's objectives or reasons for being in business.

The long-standing assumption has been that firms want to realize the highest possible profit; firms are described as "profit-maximizers".

Not only does this assumption seem to fit with general observa-tions of firms in the real world; there are also some advantages in making this assumption. It is easier to analyze firms' behaviour if only one objective, rather than several, is considered; the output level at which maximum profit is realized can be determined pre-cisely when cost and revenue information is given; and the profit-maximization assumption can be used to determine output under alternative market conditions.

Some controversy has arisen, however, on the validity of the profit-maximization assumption. Critics have argued that firms, especially the larger ones, may have objectives other than profit maximization. Two alternative hypotheses about firms' objectives are actually variations of the profit-maximization assumption. One suggests that firms are more concerned with realizing a *satisfactory profit* than the maximum profit. Firms are seen as attempting to achieve or maintain a certain level or rate of profit; once this is assured, firms make little effort to improve profits further. Another hypothesis is that firms are concerned only with *long-run profit maximization*, and will take whatever short-run decisions are necessary to achieve this goal. Maximizing the short-run sales revenue, for example, is said to be a short-run means toward this long-run end. Increasing sales will enable the firm to expand in the longer run, thus realizing economies of scale and higher profits.

The latter variation has been further modified as a distinct alternative to the profit-maximizing assumption; *firms are said to hold sales maximization as their major objective, even in the long run.* Firms want to achieve the highest possible sales revenue, even if this means sacrificing some profits. The basis for this argument is that the objectives of large firms (especially the giant corporations) are determined by managers rather than shareholders. Such firms will make sufficient profits to satisfy the shareholders, but will be primarily concerned with the salary and prestige of the higher levels of management. A large firm generally pays higher managerial salaries and confers more prestige and political power, even though its profit rate may be smaller than for some smaller firms.

Hypotheses about objectives of firms are difficult to test and validate. Because each hypothesis advanced here has contained at least some element of profit maximization, and for other reasons given above, the profit maximization assumption remains a basic element in economic analysis of firms' behaviour.

Short-Run Profit Maximization. The fact that a purely competitive firm is a "price-taker" was defined to mean that it could not affect the product price regardless of the quantity it supplied, because its output would represent only a very small share of the market quantity. The result is that a purely competitive firm faces a perfectly elastic demand curve for its product, as shown in Figure 10.7, because there can be wide variation in the quantity purchased from the firm even though there is no change in the price received by the firm.

Given the firm's cost conditions and the perfectly elastic demand for its product, the firm has two decisions to make: What quantity should it produce? and Should it produce at all?

Two approaches or rules can be used for answering these questions. The firm can compare its total revenues with its total costs, or it can compare marginal revenues and marginal costs. Both approaches will be seen to provide the same answers. These are illustrated by returning to the example of the pottery firm producing ceramic coffee mugs.

Total Revenue Minus Total Cost Rule. The total revenue received from the sale of the firm's mugs is calculated by multiplying the quantity sold times the price per mug. This is expressed as $TR = Q \times P$. Table 10.3 presents the firm's total revenue and repeats the total cost data shown in Table 10.2. The product price is assumed to be $2 per unit. The profit (or loss) for each level of production is calculated by subtracting the total costs from the total revenue. A loss is incurred at low levels of production because the fixed costs are paid regardless of quantity produced, and because, as Table 10.1 shows, the marginal product of the first few workers is low. A profit can be made as output approaches 183 mugs but the maximum profit can be obtained by producing 486 mugs.

Table 10.3

Total Revenues and Costs for a Pottery Firm

Variable Factor (man-days of labour) Q_L	Total Product (mugs per day) TP	Total Revenue (p = $2.00) TR	Total Costs TFC	TVC	TC	Profit (+) or Loss (−)
0	0	$ 0	$50	$ 0	$ 50	$− 50
1	20	40	50	100	150	−110
2	76	152	50	200	250	− 98
3	183	366	50	300	350	+ 16
4	304	608	50	400	450	+158
5	410	820	50	500	550	+270
6	486	972	50	600	650	+322
7	518	1,036	50	700	750	+286
8	520	1,040	50	800	850	+190

The total revenue and total cost data are plotted in Figure 10.6. Note that the total revenue curve is a straight line; this is because the perfectly elastic demand curve faced by a purely competitive firm means that the firm receives the same price for each unit it sells. The total cost curve increases throughout its length, but rises more quickly at high levels of output due to the diminishing marginal productivity of additional units of labour. The profit or loss is the vertical distance between the total revenue and total cost curves, measured at each quantity level. The level of output at which the total cost curve lies furthest below the total revenue curve is therefore the quantity at which maximum profits are realized. In Figure 10.6, this is again found to be at 486 mugs.

Suppose the price had been $1.25 per mug instead of $2.00. The total revenue received by the pottery firm when the price is $1.25 is shown as TR' in Figure 10.6. The new total revenue curve is also a straight line because the price received for each mug is constant for all levels of output, but the curve has shifted downward as a result of the lower price. The new total revenue curve lies below the total cost curve for all output levels, indicating that the firm cannot make a profit. It can, however, *minimize losses* when the price is $1.25, by producing 410 mugs. At this point, the loss is $38.

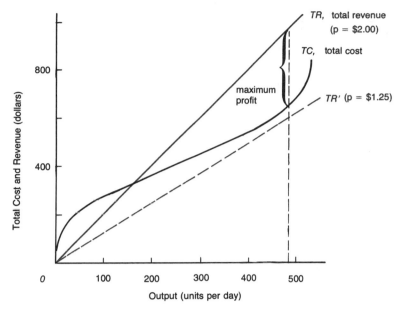

Figure 10.6 Pure Profit = TR − TC
Pure profit (or loss) at each level of output is represented by the vertical distance
between the total revenue curve, *TR*, and the total cost curve, *TC*. When the price
per unit is $2.00, profit is maximized at 486 units. When the price falls to $1.25, *TR*
is below *TC* at all output levels: no profit is possible and the loss is minimized at
410 units. The *TR* curves are straight lines because the price received by the firm
does not vary with output in the case of pure competition.

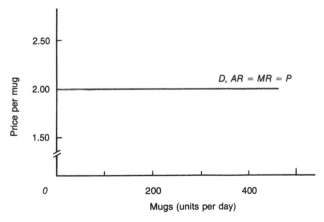

Figure 10.7 Purely Competitive Firm's Demand Curve
The demand curve facing a purely competitive firm is perfectly elastic, or a horizontal line at the prevailing market price ($2.00 per unit). The price received by the firm
at each level of output is the average revenue, *AR*. Since this is constant for a
purely competitive firm, the average revenue is also the marginal revenue, *MR*.

Marginal Revenue Equals Marginal Cost Rule. The second approach
to calculating the firm's profit-maximizing quantity of output is to
compare the marginal revenue and marginal cost.

Marginal revenue, MR, is the change in total revenue due to the
sale of an additional unit of output.

That is,

$$MR = \frac{\Delta TR}{\Delta Q}$$

Since the price or revenue received by the firm remains the same for
each additional unit sold, marginal revenue is equal to the price.
Thus, for the purely competitive firm, $P = AR = MR$. Furthermore.
since the demand curve is a horizontal straight line at the market
price, the marginal revenue and average revenue curves are the demand curve for the firm. These curves are shown for the pottery firm
in Figure 10.7.

The second rule for determining the profit-maximizing quantity
is:

The firm should produce the quantity at which marginal revenue is equal to marginal cost, or at which $MR = MC$.

Since marginal revenue equals price, but only in the case of a
purely competitive firm, this can also be stated as *the quantity at
which P = MC*. This rule follows from the fact that a profit is realized
on each unit of output which can be produced at a cost less than the
revenue received for that unit. Each unit of output which returns a
profit adds to the total profit of the firm. Thus the firm should increase the quantity produced to the point where the cost of an additional unit is just equal to the additional revenue. At this point there
is no further increase in total profits; the *maximum profit* point has
been reached. This is illustrated in Figure 10.8, again using the case
of the pottery firm and the relevant data drawn from Table 10.2.

First, note that the marginal cost curve, MC, intersects the marginal revenue curve, MR, at two points, indicating that MC equals
MR at quantities of 40 units and 486 units. The first point, where the
MC curve intersects the MR curve *from above or where the MC curve
is falling*, is *not* relevant to the profit-maximization rule. On all
quantities of less than 40 units the firm realizes a loss. Since marginal cost refers only to variable costs, this is a loss in addition to the
fixed costs. Only at quantities greater than 40 units does the firm
begin to make a profit. But this profit is not realized on each of the
units; it is realized on only those units produced in excess of 40.

The total profit on 125 units, for example, is found by calculating the total loss on the first 40 units (including the fixed costs) and
subtracting this from the total gain on the next 85 units. The shaded

area above the MR curve in Figure 10.8 represents a loss; the shaded area below the MR curve represents a profit. Comparison of these areas (recalling that the MC curve extends much further up the vertical axis than is shown in Figure 10.8), suggests that a small profit is realized on 125 units.

On each additional unit between 40 units and 486 units, the firm realizes a profit; the total profit therefore continues to increase up to an output of 486 units. Above this quantity level, marginal cost exceeds marginal revenue and each unit produced in excess of 486 reduces total profit. The profit-maximizing level of output is therefore 486 units. This concurs with the result obtained by subtracting total cost from total revenue shown in Table 10.3, namely that the firm should produce 486 units. This quantity was associated with the employment of six workers. Adding a seventh worker would bring output to 518 units, at a marginal cost per unit of $3.11, and to a point where the firm begins to incur losses which would reduce its

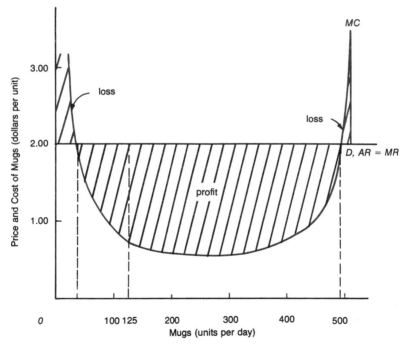

Figure 10.8 Maximum Profit is Realized When MC Equals MR
Profit is realized on any unit of output which the marginal revenue exceeds the marginal cost. Thus output should be increased to the point at which MC equals MR, or 486 units. Beyond this level, MC exceeds MR and the loss reduces the total profit realized on previous units. Although MC also equals MR at 40 units, this is not a profit-maximizing output because MC intersects MR from above and thus represents the level at which the firm only begins to realize a profit on each unit.

profit. Ideally, the firm would employ six full-time workers and use a seventh worker on a part-time basis just to the point where 486 units were being produced. *It is therefore at the quantity level where MC = MR, when marginal costs are increasing, that the firm reaches its profit-maximizing output.* At this point the firm is in equilibrium; given the market price and its production costs, the firm will not alter this profit-maximizing level of output.

Shutdown Price. Should the firm produce at all if it cannot make a profit? At a price per mug of $1.25, the answer is yes. In fact, as long as the market price per mug is greater than $1.20, the firm should produce. Although the firm loses $38 by producing 410 mugs when the price is $1.25, it would lose the full amount of its fixed costs, $50, if it did not produce at all. By producing 410 mugs, it receives a total revenue of $512. This provides $500 to meet its total variable costs, with an additional $12 to meet part of its fixed costs.

When the price drops below $1.20, however, the firm should shut down. At $1.20, total revenue for the 410 mugs is $492, just about enough to cover total variable costs but with nothing left over to meet fixed costs. At a lower price, the total revenue will be less than total variable costs; there is clearly nothing to be gained by continuing production. These alternative situations have been illustrated by allowing the price to vary while costs are unchanged. Both price and costs could of course change simultaneously. The firm's shutdown price, therefore, is defined as *the price at which total revenue is equal to or less than total variable costs at all except zero output.* This can also be expressed as *the price at which the average revenue is equal to or less than the average variable cost at all possible levels of output.* Since the total revenue is the price multiplied by the quantity sold, the average revenue (total revenue divided by the quantity) is equal to the price. Thus, a third definition of the shutdown price is the *price which is equal to or less than average variable cost at all possible levels of output.*

The shutdown condition can be stated simply as:

$$TR \leq TVC$$
$$\text{or:} \quad AR \leq AVC$$
$$\text{or:} \quad P \leq AVC$$

Shutdown Price: A Second Approach. The profit-maximizing rule, — produce the quantity at which MC equals MR, — can also be used to determine whether or not the firm should shut down. For the sake of brevity, the pottery firm is momentarily set aside to consider the two general cases illustrated in Figure 10.9.

In Figure 10.9a, the firm realizes its minimum loss at quantity OQ_1 where MC equals MR. Total revenue is price, OP_1, times quantity, OQ_1. Total cost is average total cost, OP_2, times quantity, OQ_1.

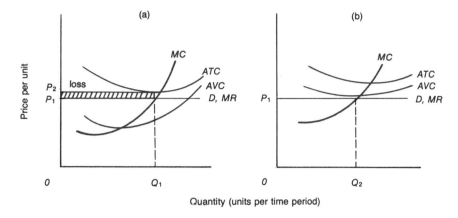

Figure 10.9 Alternative Short-Run Loss Conditions
The firm represented by Figure 10.9a minimizes its loss by producing OQ_1. At this point its average revenue, OP_1, exceeds its average variable cost, AVC, so it is earning some revenue to meet its fixed costs. It will therefore continue to produce OQ in the short run. The firm in Figure 10.9b, although it would minimize its loss at OQ_2 will not produce at all. There is no output level at which its average revenue, OP_1, would exceed its average variable cost, AVC, and hence it will shut down in the short run.

Total cost exceeds total revenue at OQ_1 by the amount of loss shown as a shaded area. However, at OQ_1 the average variable cost, AVC, is less than the price or marginal revenue. The firm therefore receives more than the cost of variable factors used to produce OQ_1, and has some revenue to offset part of its fixed costs. The firm pictured in Figure 10.9a should continue to operate, producing quantity OQ_1.

In Figure 10.9b, the firm minimizes its losses at OQ_2, where $MC = MR$. But at OQ_2 the average variable cost is greater than the price. The firm therefore does not receive a high enough price to cover the variable cost of producing OQ_2. The firm illustrated by Figure 10.9b should shut down because its average variable cost exceeds the price received. Only if the AVC curve falls, or the price rises, is it rational for the firm to remain in operation.

Competitive Firm's Short-Run Supply Curve

The purely competitive firm has been shown in the preceding section to adjust its output, given the market price and its cost conditions, in order to maximize profits. Purely competitive firms can therefore be described as "quantity-adjusters" as well as "price-takers". If a firm's cost conditions remain unchanged, the firm simply adjusts the quantity it supplies as the market price changes. But the supply of a commodity was defined in Chapter 2 as the quantity that would be supplied at each price. Thus, in adjusting quantity to different market prices, the firm is actually determining its supply curve.

Since the quantity which will be provided at each market price is determined by the marginal cost curve, the firm's supply curve is its marginal cost curve above the shut down point.

The fact that the supply curve coincides with the marginal cost curve is illustrated in Figure 10.10 by returning to the pottery firm example. It was determined previously that the firm would shut down if the price were $1.20 or less; that is, at these prices the quantity supplied would be zero. The firm's marginal cost curve is shown as a broken line at prices below $1.20 in Figure 10.10 to emphasize that this lower part of the marginal cost curve is *not* part of the supply curve. Instead, a horizontal straight line is drawn at $1.20 to indicate that zero quantity would be supplied at any lower price.

The supply curve above the $1.20 price is derived by drawing a series of demand or marginal revenue curves — horizontal straight lines — at alternative prices. The quantities at which the MR curves

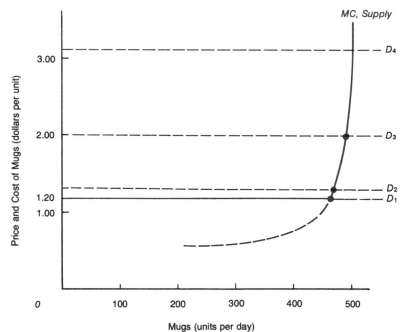

Figure 10.10 *Marginal Cost Curve Is Competitive Firm's Supply Curve*
Since maximum-profit output is realized when *MC* equals *MR*, any point on the firm's *MC* curve represents a potential output level. But since *P* equals *MR* for a purely competitive firm, any point on the *MC* curve also indicates the quantity that would be supplied at the related price level. Hence, the purely competitive firm's *MC* curve, above the price at which the firm would shut down ($1.20), is also the firm's supply curve.

intersect the *MC* curve are the quantities which would be supplied at each of the alternative prices. Thus, 442 units would be supplied at a price of $1.21, 460 at $1.32, 486 at $2.00, and 518 at $3.11. The supply curve is found by joining these points. Since all of these points are on the marginal cost curve, the supply curve *is* the marginal cost curve — *but only above the price which the firm would shut down.*

Short-Run Equilibrium of Competitive Industries

All of the firms producing a particular commodity constitute an industry.

An industry's supply curve is therefore the summation of supply curves for individual firms in the industry.

These are summed or aggregated in the same way that consumers' demand curves were added to find the market demand curve in Chapter 2: the total of quantities supplied by each firm at a particular price is the total quantity supplied by the industry at that price.

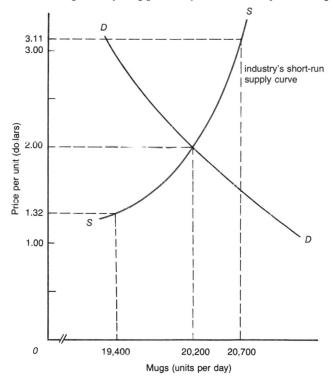

Figure 10.11 Industry's Supply, Demand, and Equilibrium Price
Supply curves for individual firms are added horizontally to obtain the industry's supply curve, *SS*. Intersection of the supply curve with the market demand curve, *DD*, determines the equilibrium price, $2.00 per unit, which is the price faced by individual firms.

Suppose that there are forty pottery firms supplying ceramic mugs. If one firm supplies 486 mugs at a price of $1.32, each of the other firms probably will supply about the same number. This is not an essential condition of a purely competitive industry, but is likely to be the outcome of other specified conditions such as the mobility of resources and full knowledge of production and marketing in the industry. The total quantity supplied to the market at $1.32 would be about 19,400 mugs. Similarly, assume that the forty firms supply a total of 20,200 at $2.00 and 20,700 at $3.11. These points are plotted in Figure 10.11 to show the industry's supply curve.

Although a firm in pure competition faces a perfectly elastic demand curve, the industry faces the downward-sloping market demand curve. Such a market demand for ceramic mugs is also shown in Figure 10.11. The equilibrium price and quantity is $2.00 and 20,200 mugs per week; this market equilibrium price is thus the given price, shown in Figures 10.7 and 10.8, to which individual firms adjust their output in the short run.

Long-Run Equilibrium: Industry and Firm

Firms and industries can be in short-run equilibrium without being in long-run equilibrium.

Adjustments to achieve long-run equilibrium are likely to involve changes in both the number of firms in the industry and the average size of firms.

Changes in the number of firms will depend on whether any existing firms are making pure profits or realizing losses in the short run. Firms will continue to enter or leave the industry until the total revenue of each firm is sufficient to cover its total costs, including a normal profit, but no firm is realizing a pure profit. This will occur when each firm is at the output level where its average total cost is at a minimum.

To see how this adjustment occurs, suppose that existing firms in a particular industry are making economic or pure profits. A typical firm in this industry is illustrated in Figure 10.12. The firm is in short-run equilibrium, producing OQ_1, units per week, the quantity at which $MC = MR_1 = OP_1$. Pure profit is shown as the shaded area between price and average total cost for OQ_1 units.

When it is known that pure profits are being made in this industry, new firms will be established to produce the same commodity. More firms result in a greater quantity being supplied at each price: there is an outward shift of the short-run supply curve. If demand remains constant (no shift in the demand curve), the outward shift in the supply curve leads to a lower equilibrium price. Both the new and old firms had, however, based their output decisions on the assumption that the price would remain at OP_1 and hence produced OQ_1. The fall in price to OP_2 therefore causes firms to incur a loss, the difference between OP_2 and the average total cost at OQ_1. Firms will continue producing in this second short-run period because the price more than covers their average variable cost at OQ_1. In the next short-run period, however, some firms will leave the industry. They are not covering their fixed costs; they are not making the normal profit required to keep them in the industry.

The departure of firms reduces the quantity supplied in the next short-run period, shifts the industry supply curve to the left, and leads to a higher equilibrium price. If the new price happens to be OP_3, firms will make a sufficient profit to keep them in the industry, but there will be no pure profit to attract new firms. The firms will have reached the output level, OQ_3 where their average total cost is at a minimum. But since at this output quantity, marginal cost equals marginal revenue, and this is equal to price, the minimum average total cost is also equal to the price.

This is one of the conditions for long-run equilibrium of a purely competitive industry, namely that the firms' average total cost is equal to the market price. The second equilibrium condition is that firms adjust their size so that they are producing the quantity at which the long-run average total cost is at a minimum.

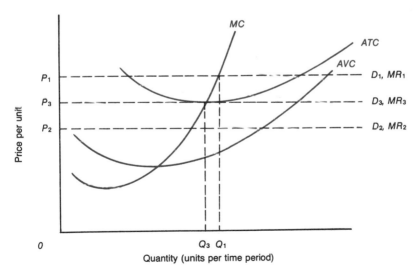

Figure 10.12   Entry of Firms Reduces Existing Firms' Profits
In the first short-run period, a purely competitive firm is realizing its maximum profit at OQ_1. New firms enter the industry in the next short-run period, shifting the industry's supply curve outward and reducing the equilibrium price to OP_2. But since firms had expected the price to remain at OP_1, they continue to produce OQ_1, realizing a loss per unit equal to the difference between OP_1, and ATC at OQ_1. In the next period, some firms will leave the industry, the industry's supply curve shifts leftward, and the equilibrium price increases to OP_3. The remaining firms adjust their output to OQ_3, at which they realize only a normal profit.

This means that in terms of Figure 10.13, (note the similarity with Figure 10.4), firms will adjust their fixed factors until their average total cost curve is represented by ATC_2. If, for example, firms are producing OQ_1 at an average total cost of OP_1 (and price equals MC_1), the industry will be in equilibrium but only to the extent that firms are neither leaving nor entering.

The long-run average total cost curve, $LRATC$, of Figure 10.13 indicates that there are returns to scale to be realized if firms adjust their fixed factors to increase their plant size. In pure competition, this opportunity is available to all firms since there are no restrictions on the use of resources. The same process leading firms to produce where price equals minimum average total cost will lead them to expand their output to OQ_2 with a resulting market price of OP_2. *This fulfills the second condition for long-run equilibrium of a purely competitive industry: that firms produce the quantity where price equals the minimum long-run average total cost.*

Changes in Long-Run Costs. In this account, it has been implicitly assumed that the entry or exit of firms did not change production costs by raising or lowering the prices of productive factors. This would be the case of a *constant-cost industry, one in which changes in the number of firms does not affect the prices of production factors.* The long-run supply curve of such an industry will be perfectly elastic — a horizontal straight line P_1 — shown in Figure 10.14 as S_{LR}. An increase in demand, or a shift of the demand curve from DD to D_1D_1 will initially raise the market price, leading to pure profit,

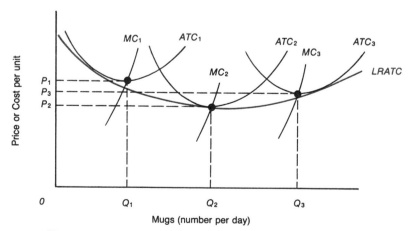

Figure 10.13   *Long-Run Equilibrium in Purely Competitive Industry*
In the long run, the number of firms in a purely competitive industry is adjusted, such that each firm is producing the output, OQ_2, at which the market price, OP_2 is equal to the average total cost. Each firm adjusts to the plant size, represented by ATC_2 at which it can produce OQ_2 at the minimum long-run average total cost, OP_2.

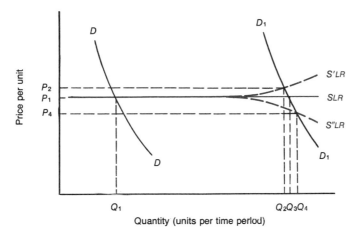

Figure 10.14 Alternative Long-Run Industry Supply Curves
The long-run supply curve of a purely competitive industry may either be upward-sloping (S'_{LR}), perfectly horizontal (S_{LR}), or downward-sloping (S''_{LR}). The shape of the long-run supply curve depends on the effect new firms have on the costs of productive factors. If these rise with increased output, the supply curve is upward-sloping and a long-run increase in demand, to $D_1 D_1$, results in a higher product price, OP_2. A downward-sloping supply curve usually is due to external economies. In the latter case, a long-run increase in demand can result in a lower product price, OP_4.

and attract new firms. As explained previously, this will shift the short-run supply curve outward and reduce the market price. Hence the perfectly elastic long-run supply curve.

However, if prices of productive factors are raised by the entry of new firms, production costs are increased: cost curves are shifted upwards. The short-run supply curve will not be shifted outward quite as far as in the constant-cost case and a higher equilibrium price and a lower quantity will be established. *This is the case of an increasing-cost industry, in which the entry of new firms raises the prices of productive factors, and the industry's long-run supply curve slopes upward to the right.*

A third possibility may exist: *the decreasing-cost industry in which the entry of new firms reduces the prices of productive factors.* Such a case is unlikely because an increased demand for productive factors would normally lead to higher production costs. However, it may happen, for example, that an increase in the number of firms employing welders in a certain area would stimulate the training of welders, resulting in so many with this skill that the price of welding services would fall. The general explanation for decreasing-cost industries is the existence of external economies: additional firms in an area, for example, may attract services such as improved transportation which will reduce the costs of all firms.

Review of the Main Points

1. All costs are opportunity costs: these include explicit or direct costs and implicit or indirect costs. Normal profit, the minimum profit required to retain a firm in a particular industry, is also a cost of production.

2. The short run is the period within which quantity produced can be varied even though some factors, such as plant size, remain constant. The long run is the period within which all factors of production can be changed. Variable factors are factors which can be varied in the short run; fixed factors are those that can be varied only in the long run.

3. Total product is the total quantity produced in a given time period; average product is the quantity produced by one unit of a variable factor; marginal product is the change in total product associated with an additional unit of the variable factor. The quantity of the variable factor employed when the total product reaches a maximum is the point of diminishing total productivity. Diminishing average and marginal productivity are defined similarly for the average product and the marginal product.

4. The law of diminishing returns states that as increasing quantities of a variable factor are combined with a fixed factor, the total product will eventually decline.

5. Fixed costs are those which must be incurred regardless of the level of output; variable costs vary directly with changes in the level of output. Total costs include both fixed and variable costs.

6. The average fixed cost decreases as long as output is increasing; the average variable cost usually declines initially, then increases at the output level where average product begins to decline. The average total cost curve is also U-shaped; a firm's capacity is defined as the output level at which average total cost is at a minimum. Marginal cost, the change in total cost associated with producing an additional unit, begins to increase at the output level where marginal product reaches a maximum. When AVC and ATC are at a minimum, they are also equal to the marginal cost. The long run average total cost curve shows the lowest average total cost at which each quantity can be produced.

7. Returns to scale may be increasing, constant, or decreasing. These refer to variations in the average total cost for a given quantity of output which are associated with different quantities of fixed factors. Increasing returns arise for technical, managerial, marketing, and financial reasons, including, for example, fuller utilization of managerial skills at higher output levels.

8. "Pure competition" describes a commodity market in which in-

dividual firms face a perfectly elastic demand curve and thus adjust their output quantities to a given price, and a market in which any firm is free to enter or leave. Conditions for this situation are: there are many sellers, none of which produces a significant share of the quantity supplied to the market; all firms produce the same product; all buyers and sellers have full information about product prices and production costs; productive resources are available without restrictions to any firm.

9. Equilibrium quantity and price for a commodity market will vary for different planning periods. The momentary or market period is the period within which the quantity to be supplied has already been produced. In the short run and the long run, however, firms can adjust output in accordance with their objective. This is generally assumed to be profit maximization, although other objectives have been hypothesized.

10. The profit-maximizing output can be found by determining the output level at which the difference between total revenue and total cost is greatest. A firm may produce even though total revenue is less than total cost, but it should shut down unless total revenue exceeds total variable cost.

11. The maximum profit is also realized at the output level where marginal revenue equals marginal cost. For a purely competitive firm, marginal revenue is constant and is equal to average revenue or price. Thus the profit-maximizing output is that at which marginal cost equals price, when marginal cost is rising.

12. A firm's short-run supply curve is the portion of its marginal cost curve beyond the price at which it would shut down.

13. All firms producing a specific commodity constitute the industry for that commodity. Hence, the industry's supply curve is the summation of the supply curves of all firms in the industry. The intersection of the industry's short-run supply curve, which is also the market supply curve, with the market demand curve determines the equilibrium output and price.

14. If existing firms are making economic profits or incurring losses, the number of firms will be altered in the long run such that each firm is producing the quantity at which its average total cost is equal to the market price. The size of a firm will be adjusted until firms are producing at the long-run minimum average total cost.

15. The shape of the industry's long-run supply curve depends on the effect new firms have on production costs. An increasing-cost industry has an upward-sloping long-run supply curve; a constant-cost industry, a perfectly elastic supply curve; and a decreasing-cost industry, a downward-sloping supply curve.

Review and Discussion Questions

1. Why are normal profits, but not pure profits, considered to be a cost of production?

2. Explain the relationship between marginal cost per unit of output and the law of diminishing marginal productivity.

3. Explain why the MC curve always intersects the ATC and AVC curves at the lowest points on these curves. Why does the ATC curve usually fall at low levels of output and then rise as output is increased further?

4. "The existence of economies of large scale contradicts the law of diminishing returns." Do you agree? Why? Which concept is relevant in the short run? Which is relevant in the long run? Explain.

5. An individual dairy farmer does not advertise his product but the Dairy Farmers of Canada (representing all dairy farmers) may decide to advertise the advantages of milk. Is each acting rationally? Why? Use a supply and demand diagram to show the possible effects of advertising for the dairy industry and for the individual dairy farmer.

Sources and Selected Readings

Baumol, Wm. J. Economic Theory and Operations Analysis, 2nd ed. Englewood Cliffs, N.J.: Prentice-Hall, 1965.

Due, John F., and Robert W. Clower. Intermediate Economic Analysis, 5th ed. Homewood, Ill.: Irwin, 1966.

Lancaster, Kelvin. Introduction to Modern Microeconomics, 2nd ed. Chicago: Rand McNally, 1974.

Leftwich, Richard H. The Price System and Resource Allocation, 5th ed. Hinsdale, Ill.: Dryden Press, 1973.

Stigler, G. The Theory of Price, 3rd ed. New York: Macmillan, 1966.

Stonier, A. W., and D. C. Hague. At Textbook of Economic Theory, 4th ed. London: Longmans, Green, 1973.

11 Imperfect Competition: Private Power in the Market Place

Pure or perfect competition is the form of market structure with which all other market conditions can be compared. Other market structures are generally described collectively as *imperfect competition*. Pure monopoly properly should be excluded from this category because it is the case of only one seller and hence a condition of *no* competition. For convenience in discussion, however, imperfect competition is frequently considered to include pure monopoly as well as other principal forms of market structure: oligopoly and monopolistic competition. Each of these two terms, in turn, describes a wide variety of market conditions.

A. Pure Monopoly

A pure monopoly is a market in which only one firm produces a commodity for which there are no close substitutes.

The monopolist therefore faces no competition from other producers. Such a condition is rare because there are substitutes for almost all commodities. The products of firms commonly regarded as monopolies have some substitutes: a telegram substitutes for a telephone call; natural gas and fuel oil can substitute for electricity used in heating; aircraft and buses provide transportation alternatives to trains. The definition and identification of monopoly therefore depends on *the closeness or similarity of such substitutes, and thus on the extent of the firm's power to affect the price of the product by controlling the quantity supplied to the market.* A monopolist thus is described as a *price maker*.

Barriers to Entry

Other firms are prevented from producing the same commodity by various barriers to entering the industry. Some monopolistic conditions are created by *government actions*, including the granting of patents, creation of public utilities, sale of franchises, and the placing of quotas or embargos on specific imports.

Patents granted to inventors give them exclusive rights to produce their products for a period of 17 years. Alternatively, patent holders may sell their rights to other firms or licence firms to produce the patented products. A patent may also create a monopoly in

317

the production of a product and it may also allow a firm to extend a monopoly position if the firm requires licencees to purchase other products from it as well.

Public utilities are often created when there appears to be a *natural monopoly* condition. The economies of large scale associated with natural monopolies generally are due to large fixed costs; a very large output can be provided before declining fixed costs are offset by rising variable costs. There may also be situations in which competition may reduce the quality of service or increase its price. Urban bus transportation, for example, is generally provided by a single firm — a public utility — due to economies of large scale and the inconvenience to passengers of a variety of bus tokens and incompatible timetables if a number of firms provided this service. In such cases, governments retain the right to regulate the prices and types of service offered.[1]

Franchises are granted, often with some payment made to a government, for the exclusive right to provide a service even though a natural monopoly condition does not exist. In some cities, for example, a taxi company has the exclusive right to transport people from the airport to the city, although other taxis may take them to the airport. Fares might be lower if several firms could transport people from the airport, but in granting the franchise the government is able to insist that sufficient taxis be available at all times to meet travellers' needs.

Quotas limit the quantity, and *embargoes* forbid the importation of specific imports, to the advantage of a domestic producer. To maintain a monopoly position against potential domestic producers, however, other types of barriers must exist.

In addition to such government actions, a second general type of barrier is a monopolist's *ownership or control of unique resources* used in producing the commodity concerned. Such control is particularly evident in cases of rare deposits of mineral ores. For example, the International Nickel Company controls about 90 per cent of the world's nickel deposits, and the Aluminum Company of America, prior to World War II, controlled virtually all sources of the bauxite ore used in producing aluminum.

A third general type of barrier can arise with *large-scale production relative to the size of the market, especially when the firm has been established for some time*. The costs of entry are thus extremely high and discourage potential firms from entering the industry. When the quantity which could be sold, even at a very low price, is relatively small and there are significant economies of scale, it may not be possible for more than one firm to make a profit. Potential competitors may recognize that if other firms enter the industry, all firms will incur losses. An existing monopolist will, of course, try to

---

[1] A more elaborate discussion of natural monopolies is presented in Chapter 12.

encourage this impression. Furthermore, a large, well-established firm will have a well-known product and dependable sources of financing which place a new entrant at a distinct disadvantage.

Short-Run Price and Output in Pure Monopoly

A pure monopolist has been described as a *price maker* or *price searcher*. In the monopoly case, the firm *is* the industry because a monopoly is defined as an industry in which there is only one seller.

The demand curve faced by the monopolist is the market demand curve for the product in question.

Since the demand curve indicates what quantity will be purchased at each price, the price set by the monopolist must be the price associated with the quantity he wishes to sell.

As in the case of purely competitive firms, a monopolist's objective is assumed to be profit maximization. A monopolist thus is concerned with determining the quantity of output required to meet this objective. The basic decision rules for maximizing the monopolist's profit are the same as those for the purely competitive firm: produce the quantity at which total revenue exceeds total cost by the greatest amount, or at which marginal cost is equal to marginal revenue. For a purely competitive firm, this rule could be expressed in terms of marginal cost equalling price, because the demand curve facing the firm was perfectly elastic. It is highly improbable, however, that a monopolist would face a perfectly elastic demand curve because it faces the total demand curve for the market. This difference in the demand curves facing the two types of firm is one of the two major features distinguishing pure competition from pure monopoly, the other feature being the difference in ease of entry to the industry.

A monopolist's price and output decision can be illustrated by the following example. Suppose someone holding a commercial pilot's licence decides to provide a scheduled air service in a small, remote community. The service offered is measured as miles of air travel. To avoid the complication of unfilled seats, it is assumed that the plane carries only one passenger and that only chartered service is offered. Fixed costs are high relative to the small market to be served, and the pilot has an outstanding reputation for long, accident-free experience with local flying conditions. It is improbable therefore that other firms will be in competition with him.

Monopolist's Revenue

A market research firm engaged by the monopolist has found that the demand for local air service is as shown in Table 11.1. This market demand schedule indicates the number of miles of air travel that will be purchased each month at each of several prices, and thus the number of travel-miles the monopolist can expect to sell at each price.

Table 11.1

Revenues and Costs for a Monopoly Airline Service

Quantity (thousands of miles) per month	Price, Average Revenue	Total Revenue	Marginal Revenue	Total Cost	Average Total Cost	Marginal Cost	Profit (+) or Loss (−)
0	1.00	0		1,000			−1,000
1	.91	910	.91	1,250	1.25	.25	− 340
2	.81	1,620	.71	1,490	.75	.24	+ 130
3	.72	2,160	.54	1,740	.58	.25	+ 420
4	.63	2,520	.36	2,000	.50	.26	+ 520
5	.54	2,700	.18	2,300	.46	.30	+ 400
6	.45	2,700	.00	2,640	.44	.34	+ 60
7	.36	2,520	−.18	3,030	.43	.39	− 510
8	.27	2,160	−.36	3,490	.44	.46	−1,330
9	.18	1,620	−.54	4,020	.45	.53	−2,400
10	.10	1,000	−.62	4,670	.47	.65	−3,670
11	.00	0	−1.00	5,410	.49	.74	−5,410

The total revenue that can be realized at each quantity is calculated by multiplying the price by the quantity that would be sold at that price. From the total revenue schedule the marginal revenue schedule can be calculated, since *marginal revenue is the change in total revenue associated with each additional unit sold.* The demand schedule is also the average revenue schedule because average revenue is the total revenue, at each price, divided by the quantity.

Each of these schedules is plotted in Figure 11.1 as the demand or average revenue curve, marginal revenue curve and, below them, the total revenue curve. These show important differences from the revenue curves of the purely competitive firm. The monopolist's average revenue curve slopes downward because he faces the total demand curve of the market for his product. His marginal revenue curve is *not* identical with his average revenue curve because the monopolist can increase the quantity he sells only by reducing the price. The lower price relates not just to the additional unit sold, but also to all other units sold. For example, the pilot can sell 4,000 miles at $.63 per mile but to sell 5,000 miles he must lower the price to $.54 per mile. Thus the *average* revenue per mile drops only from $.63 to $.54, but the *marginal* revenue per mile for the additional 1,000 miles is only $.18 because he has had to accept a lower price for the first 4,000 miles in order to sell the additional 1,000 miles. *At any level of output the marginal revenue will be less than the average revenue if the average revenue or price is declining.*

Although the average revenue is always positive, *marginal revenue becomes negative* when the quantity produced increases from 5,000 to 6,000 miles, and is increasingly negative for higher levels of

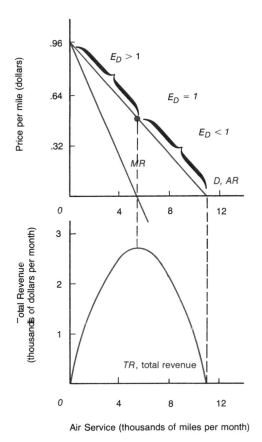

Figure 11.1
Monopolist's Revenue
Curves

The demand curve faced by a monopolist is the market demand curve since he is the only firm producing the product. The demand curve is also his average revenue curve, *AR*, because the demand curve indicates the price he can charge to sell any given level of output. His marginal revenue curve, *MR*, lies below the *AR* curve because additional output can be sold only if a lower price is charged on all units. At high prices, demand is elastic; total revenue, *TR*, increases with increasing sales; and *MR* is positive. When demand is of unitary elasticity, *MR* is zero, and *TR* reaches a maximum. At lower prices, demand is inelastic, *MR* is negative, and *TR* declines.

Air Service (thousands of miles per month)

output. This effect is due to the price elasticity of demand for the air service. At low quantities, a decrease in price leads to a proportionately greater increase in quantity demanded. The result is an increase in total revenue: in this range, the demand is elastic. As the price is decreased from $.54 to $.45, however, there is no change in total revenue, indicating unitary elasticity. At higher quantities, total revenue declines as price is decreased: demand is inelastic. Figure 11.1 shows that *marginal revenue becomes negative just beyond the quantity where total revenue reaches a maximum and at the point of unitary elasticity on the demand or average revenue curve.* One rule for profit-maximization is to produce the quantity at which marginal cost equals marginal revenue; therefore, the monopolist will not produce beyond the quantity at which marginal revenue becomes negative, since marginal cost will rarely, if ever, be negative. When demand is inelastic, producing larger quantities always reduces total revenue. But production of larger quantities will be possible only at the same or higher total costs. Therefore the monopolist never sells at a price in the range where demand is inelastic. This leads to the further conclusion that a *monopolist will be concerned only with the range of output associated with the elastic portion of the demand curve.*

Price and Output Where MC = MR

The precise shapes of the monopolist's cost curves depend on the degree of competition in the markets for productive factors, and on the technology he employs. In the example used here, the cost curves are assumed to be of the same general shape shown in the last chapter. Specific cost data are presented in Table 11.1 and plotted as cost curves in Figure 11.2. The fixed cost of $1,000 per month is the leasing charge for the aircraft. Variable costs are primarily for fuel and maintenance: the latter costs are assumed to increase faster than output at higher quantity levels so that the marginal cost curve will turn upward. The average variable cost curve is not shown because this is required only to determine the firm's short-run shutdown point. Note the other similarities with cost curves examined in the last chapter: marginal cost is equal to average cost at the output

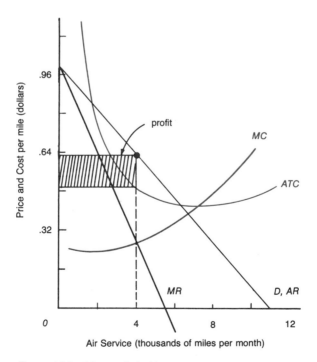

Figure 11.2   Monopolist's Maximum-Profit Output and Price
The monopolist maximizes profit at the output where *MC* equals *MR*, namely 4,000 air-miles per month. The demand curve indicates this quantity can be sold at a price of $.63 per air-mile. Pure profit is the difference between *AR* and *ATC* for 4,000 units.

where average cost is at its minimum level. At lower outputs, marginal cost is less than average cost, and at higher outputs, marginal cost is greater than average cost. Average total cost falls sharply at low output levels, as the fixed costs are averaged over increasing quantities, and then rises as variable costs form a more significant portion of total costs.

Figure 11.2 shows that the monopolist's marginal revenue exceeds his marginal cost on each additional unit up to a quantity of 4,000 miles. At higher levels of output, the additional cost of each air-travel mile is greater than the additional revenue: total profit therefore declines beyond that point. The maximum profit is realized by providing 4,000 miles of air service per month. The demand curve indicates that this quantity can be sold at a price of $.63 per mile. The profit on 4,000 miles is shown in Figure 11.2 as the shaded area between the average revenue and average total cost curves, for an output of 4,000 miles.

Table 11.1 confirms the profit-maximizing quantity indicated by Figure 11.2. The marginal revenue in going from 3,000 to 4,000 miles is $.36 per mile, but marginal cost is only $.26 per mile. If output is increased to 5,000 miles, marginal revenue drops to $.18 while marginal cost rises to $.30. The monopolist should therefore restrict his output to 4,000 miles per month. Note that at this quantity, demand is still elastic: the general conclusion that a monopolist will not produce where demand is inelastic is confirmed in this specific example. The total revenue minus total cost rule for determining maximum profit provides the same result: the final column of Table 11.1 indicates that the maximum profit, of $520 per month, is realized at a quantity of 4,000 miles per month.

Two important observations should be drawn from this analysis of the monopolist's revenue and cost conditions.

First, a monopolist does not necessarily make a profit.

Suppose, in the example used here, that the price of aircraft fuel rises sharply. Marginal costs increase for each output quantity: the marginal cost curve thus shifts upward to MC_1 as shown in Figure 11.3. The average total cost curve also shifts upward. The new marginal cost curve determines a new profit-maximization point at a lower quantity and a higher price. At this new quantity, average total cost exceeds average revenue: the "maximum-profit" level is actually the output at which the monopolist's loss is minimized. This loss is shown as the shaded area in Figure 11.3. *The monopolist will continue to operate in the short run, however, provided that the average variable cost is less than average revenue at this quantity;* otherwise, the monopolist should shut down.

The monopolist can also realize a lower profit or incur a loss even if his marginal costs do not increase. If his fixed cost is increased, perhaps by a new tax on air service operators, the average total cost curve will again shift upward. However, because there is

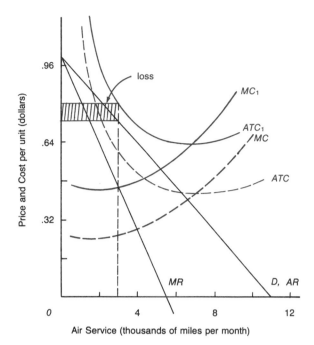

Figure 11.3   Monopolists May Incur Losses
The monopolist's profit illustrated in Figure 11.2 can become a loss if production
costs increase but there is no increase in demand. Increased prices for productive
factors such as labour shift the *MC* curve to MC_1 and the *ATC* curve to ATC_1. The
new profit-maximizing output is the level at which MC_1 equals *MR*. At this level
(about 3,000 air-miles), the selling price indicated by the demand curve is less than
ATC_1 and a loss is incurred.

no change in his marginal costs, the profit-maximizing (or loss-
minimizing) quantity is unchanged. There is no reason therefore for
him to raise his price. He simply absorbs the cost of the new tax by
reducing his profit or increasing his loss. Moreover, this tax cannot
force him to shut down if it was rational for him to operate prior to
the tax because average variable costs are also unchanged.

The second observation is that there is no supply curve for a
monopolist.

A supply curve indicates the quantities which will be offered in
response to various market prices. A supply curve can therefore be
determined for a purely competitive firm because it adjusts its output quantity to the given market price. Although a monopolist has a
marginal cost curve, he does not have a supply curve because his
output depends on both demand and cost for his product. That is,
the monopolist determines profit-maximizing output and then sets
the price at which this quantity can be sold.

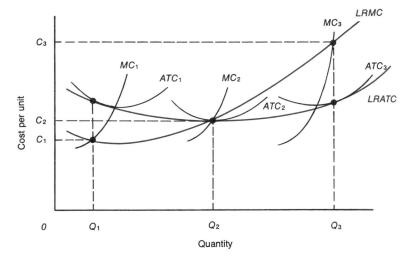

Figure 11.4   Monopolist's Long-Run Cost Curves
The monopolist's long-run average total cost curve, *LRATC*, is obtained by determining the lowest *ATC* for producing each possible level of output. The lowest *ATC*
for OQ_1, for example, is possible only in a plant size represented by ATC_1. The
marginal cost curve, MC_1, associated with ATC_1 is the marginal cost of OQ_1.
Similarly, the marginal cost is found for each output level, these are plotted to
obtain the long-run marginal cost, *LRMC*.

Long-Run Price and Output in Pure Monopoly

The rule that a firm will obtain maximum profit if it produces the
quantity at which marginal cost equals marginal revenue is also
applicable for long-run decisions. In this case, however, it is the
long-run marginal cost that must be considered; as shown in Figure
11.4, this is the marginal cost that is associated with each of the
profit-maximizing output levels for various short-run positions.

The lowest short-run average total cost for producing OQ_1 is
associated with the short-run plant size represented by ATC_1. The
short-run marginal cost for OQ_1 is OC_1; thus the long-run marginal
cost for OQ_1 is also OC_1. Similarly, the long-run marginal cost is
obtained from the other short-run cost conditions, shown as ATC_2
and ATC_3, to produce the long-run marginal cost curve, *LRMC*.

The *LRMC* and *LRATC* curves of Figure 11.4 are reproduced in
Figure 11.5, together with the average revenue and marginal
revenue curves. Assuming that no forces are acting to shift these
revenue curves over time, they are the same revenue curves faced by
the monopolist in the short-run case. The long-run profit-
maximizing quantity, where *LRMC* equals MR_1 is OQ_{LR}; the price is
OP_{LR}. If the monopolist was previously in the short-run position
represented by ATC_1 in Figure 11.4, the long-run price will be lower;

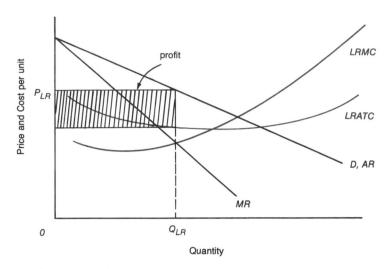

Figure 11.5   Monopolist's Long-Run Equilibrium Output and Price
The monopolist's long-run profit-maximizing output level is the quantity at which
MR equals LRMC, namely OQ_{LR}. The demand curve indicates that this quantity
can be sold at price OP_{LR}. The monopolist's profit is the difference between AR
and LRATC at output OQ_{LR} multiplied by OQ_{LR}.

but his profit will be greater. This can be determined from the fact
that total revenue increases as price falls when demand is elastic,
and LRATC is less than ATC_1 except where LRATC equals ATC_1 at
OQ_1.

Note also that the monopolist's long-run profit-maximizing
quantity is unlikely to be at the level at which LRATC is at a
minimum. More will be said about this observation later in the chapter. Finally, this calculation of the monopolist's long-run equilibrium output and price has assumed that he is able to maintain his
monopoly position, that there is no change in demand, and that
there is no change in the prices of productive factors. Variation from
any of these assumptions would lead to different results.

Determining the Degree of Monopoly Power

The extent to which potential buyers perceive other products as
close substitutes for the monopolist's product determines the extent
of the monopolist's power to decide the price of the product. Judgments about buyers' perceptions of product substitutability do not
provide operation measures of monopoly power, yet some measure
is required if public policies are to be effectively designed for regulating monopolies.

One approach to determining the degree of monopoly power
would be to *compare the monopolist's marginal revenue and his
average revenue.* Since, in pure competition, average revenue or
price is equal to marginal revenue, the wider the gap between these

two, the greater is the degree of monopoly power. The closer the substitutability of other products, the more elastic the demand curve will be, and the closer marginal revenue will be to the price. Thus the difference between marginal revenue and average revenue is a direct measure of the degree of substitutability. The difficulty in determining marginal revenue, however, severely limits the use of this method for estimating monopoly power. The monopolist probably cannot know his demand curve with the accuracy implied in the example used; he is more likely to discover short segments of the curve both by market research and actual trial-and-error. What information he does have will be considered top secret, and thus be unavailable for public policy decisions.

Another approach is to *compare the monopolist's total profit with his normal profit.* The difference between the two can be regarded as a measure of monopoly power. This measure is especially valid if the difference remains substantial for some time, indicating that other firms are not able to enter the industry in the long run. The difficulty with this measure lies in estimating a normal profit; this requires arbitrary judgments about the risk associated with producing and marketing the product and the appropriate values for imputed costs.

A third approach, and one commonly used in view of the difficulties with the other measures, involves the *concentration ratio* for the industry. This is the percentage of the total market sales associated with one firm, or a few of the largest firms, supplying that market. Pure monopoly would be indicated by a concentration ratio of 100 per cent. The next chapter presents a number of concentration ratios for Canadian industries and indicates their value in assessing the market power of the few large firms which dominate some industries.

Price Discrimination

Some monopolists are able to increase their profits by practising *price discrimination: charging different prices to different buyers of the same commodity produced under the same cost conditions.* Price discrimination is quite common even in markets which are not supplied by pure monopolists. Lower prices are charged for children on buses, trains, and planes, at theatres and concerts, and for haircuts, although the cost of such services is seldom different for children and adults. Doctors and lawyers sometimes charge their wealthier patients and clients higher fees, for the same service provided at the same cost, than they charge the less wealthy. These examples of price discrimination, although not cases of absolute monopoly, are examined here because they are possible only when the producer has some control over the price of his product.

Conditions for Price Discrimination

Price discrimination by "price makers" is potentially possible because different buyers are willing to pay different prices for a single unit of a commodity; that is, because individuals have different demand curves for the commodity. But price discrimination can actually occur only if different groups of individuals with different demand curves can be identified and segregated into sub-markets of the total market for the commodity. Thus there are sub-markets consisting of children and of adults in the examples cited above. Not only must the groups having different demand curves be identified separately; it is also essential that the commodity cannot be transferred or resold among individuals in different groups. Otherwise, the group charged the lowest price would resell the commodity to the other groups, until everyone bought at the lowest price and no discrimination would exist. Price discrimination is therefore possible when a supplier can control both the quantity and distribution of the product, when he can distinguish buyers with different demand curves, and when transfer of the product among buyers is impossible, preventable, or more costly than the difference between the prices charged different buyers.

The circumstances meeting these conditions include the following: (a) the product is a service, such as a concert, haircut, or surgical operation, and thus cannot be transferred to anyone else; or (b) one group of buyers is not aware that another group of buyers is paying a different price: an example of this is secret rebates or discounts; or (c) there is a barrier to the transfer of goods from one group of buyers to another: such barriers would include high transportation costs, tariffs, quotas, or embargoes on imports, or explicit restrictions imposed by the seller as a condition of a lower price.

A special case of price discrimination exists when a single buyer may be charged different prices for additional quantities. Electricity and natural gas, for example, are commonly sold according to a rate structure whereby initial quantities have a high price and successive quantities are provided at lower prices. Electricity or natural gas could be transferred to another buyer only by an extension of the power or gas lines, an arrangement forbidden by the suppliers. The differentiated rate structure allows the producer to obtain more of the total revenue represented by the area under an individual's demand curve. The more complex the set of rates, the larger the revenue realized. In other words, if a different price could be charged for each unit consumed, the producer would obtain all the revenue represented by the demand curve, up to the quantity level at which the price no longer exceeded his marginal cost. This is thus another technique for collecting the consumers' surplus described in Chapter 9.

Effects of Price Discrimination

The example of price discrimination among different units sold to the same buyer can be generalized to draw some conclusions about the effects of price discrimination among different buyers in a market. The monopolist who can segregate his market into several groups will increase his output to the point where his marginal cost is equal to the price at that quantity level. The demand curve will become his marginal revenue curve since the price charged for an additional unit will be the marginal revenue for that unit. (Note that in cases of price discrimination the seller does not reduce the price of all units in order to sell an additional unit.) *Thus, equating marginal revenue and marginal cost is, for the perfect price-discriminating monopolist, also equating price and marginal cost.* The consequence of this, as shown in Figure 11.6, is a higher profit and larger output than occurs in the case of a non-discriminating or single-price monopolist.

A single-price monopolist, producing where MC equals MR, would produce OQ_1 at an average total cost of OP_2 and would sell at price OP_3. *His profit is $(OP_3 - OP_2) \times OQ_1$.* A monopolist who can

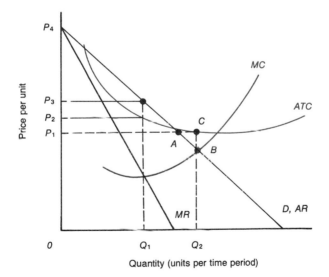

Figure 11.6   Price Discrimination From A Monopolist's Perspective
Price discrimination involves selling the same product at different prices to different buyers. The monopolist who sells at only one price maximizes profit at output OQ_1, which can be sold at price OP_3. His profit is P_2P_3 on quantity OQ_1. Under perfect or complete price discrimination, when each unit is sold at the maximum price a consumer is willing to pay, the demand curve *(D, AR)* becomes the monopolist's marginal revenue curve. Maximum profit is then realized at output OQ_2, the level at which MC intersects the demand curve. Total revenue is the area under the demand curve up to OQ_2, and total cost is $OQ_2 \times OP_1$. Profit for the price-discriminating monopolist is the difference between these two areas, namely P_4P_1A less ACB.

carry price discrimination to its limit by charging a different price for each unit will produce quantity OQ_2, where MC equals AR. His total revenue is the area under the demand curve up to quantity OQ_2, namely OP_4BQ_2; total cost is the average total cost at quantity OQ_2 multiplied by OQ_2, or area OP_1CQ_2. His profit is the difference between these areas, namely triangle P_4P_1A less triangle ACB. From Figure 11.6, it can be clearly seen that the discriminating monopolist has a substantially higher profit and a greater output than a non-discriminating monopolist.

B.   Monopolistic Competition

Monopolistic competition is the case of a market or industry where there are many small firms selling similar but not identical products.

Each small firm supplies only a small share of the total market quantity and hence is not concerned about the reaction of other firms to its price and output decisions. However, because the product of each firm is slightly different from that of other firms, firms' products are not perfect substitutes. Thus, a monopolistically competitive firm's demand curve is not perfectly elastic, with the result that it can adjust both price and output, rather than just output, to maximize its profit. Since there are a large number of firms in the industry, it follows that barriers to entering the industry are negligible. The competitive aspects of this model are thus the existence of many sellers, each with a small market share, and the ease of entry to the industry. The monopolistic aspect is the differentiation of products resulting in a demand curve which is not perfectly elastic, such that individual firms have some effect on market price.

The monopolistic competition model is a reasonably good explanation for a large number of industries, including those producing clothing, shoes, and furniture, as well as numerous retail service industries such as corner drugstores, shoe repair shops, laundries and dry cleaners. Product differentiation in such industries takes many forms: clothing and shoes differ in style, workmanship, and material; small retail establishments vary mainly in their selling conditions such as location, service, and credit policy.

Short-Run Price and Output in Monopolistic Competition

The profit-maximizing rule that applies to monopolists also applies to the firm in monopolistic competition: produce the quantity at which marginal cost equals marginal revenue and set the price for this quantity as indicated by the demand curve facing the firm.

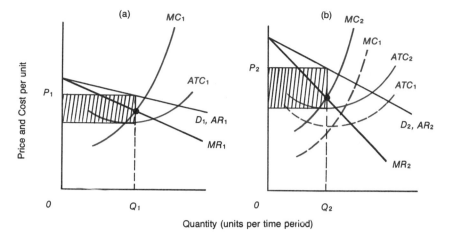

Quantity (units per time period)

Figure 11.7 Advertising Sometimes Increases Profits
A monopolistically competitive firm which does not advertise maximizes its profit, as in Figure 11.7a, at output OQ_1 and price OP_1. By advertising, the firm shifts its demand curve to AR_2 (Figure 11.7b), and its marginal revenue curve to MR_2. Advertising costs shift marginal costs to MC_2 and average total cost to ATC_2. The new profit-maximizing output is reduced to OQ_2, which is sold at a higher price, OP_2. Profit is increased in this case, but a profit reduction could occur when large advertising costs have little effect on the demand curve.

The monopolistically competitive firm faces a highly elastic demand curve because its product is a close but not perfect substitute for the products of its competitors. If the monopolistically competitive firm raises its price slightly it will lose a substantial number of sales, but not all sales, because some buyers will pay slightly more for the closer location of a drugstore or the confidence in a product that has given satisfactory results in the past. Similarly, a price reduction will attract many customers from other producers but some will remain with the firm's competitors.

The cost conditions of firms in monopolistic competition are assumed to be generally the same as those described for firms in other market conditions, except that costs likely include expenditures for advertising and other sales promotion that were unnecessary for the purely competitive firm. However, a monopolist may advertise to raise his demand curve, or improve public relations to prevent government controls. The profit-maximizing output level, OQ_1 and price, OP_1, shown in Figure 11.7a are the short-run equilibrium conditions for the monopolistically competitive firm.

Selling Costs

Maximum profit in the short run can vary, depending on the firm's decisions about *selling costs: the expenditures for sales promotion.* Assume that a firm can shift its demand curve outward and make it less elastic by increasing advertising, paying higher salesmen's commissions, spending more for a more attractive package, and so on. These costs are assumed to vary with the quantity produced, with resulting upward shifts in the marginal cost and average total cost curves as shown in Figure 11.7b. The new marginal cost and marginal revenue curves intersect at output OQ_2, with the new, larger profit shown as the shaded area. The product price also increases, from OP_1 to OP_2.

Many monopolistically competitive firms thus face the further problem of estimating the extent to which their demand curves can be altered in the short run by increasing such selling costs. An advertising program, for example, may not always have the substantial effect on the demand curve illustrated in Figure 11.7b. If the demand curve had remained as it was in Figure 11.7a, despite the additional sales promotion, the new marginal cost curve would have intersected the original marginal revenue curve at a lower output level than OQ_1, the average total cost of that level of output would be higher, the profit would be reduced, but the product price would be higher than OP_1.

Long-Run Price and Output in Monopolistic Competition

In the long run, a monopolistically competitive firm can change its plant size, as can firms in other types of industries, to take account of whatever economies of scale as possible. This possibility will be curtailed, however, by the entry of new firms. The absence of barriers to new firms enables them to enter the industry, attracted by any short-run profits of existing firms. As new firms attract existing customers in the market, the demand curves of existing firms will be shifted to the left. This process will continue until so many firms have entered the industry that a firm's demand curve will be shifted to the point where, at the quantity equating long-run marginal cost and marginal revenue, pure profit has been reduced to zero. This is shown in Figure 11.8. The long-run profit-maximizing output is produced at a plant size (represented by ATC) too small to realize the economies of scale implied by the downward-slope of the $LRATC$ beyond the quantity OQ_1.

C.   Oligopoly

An oligopoly is an industry or market with so few firms that the actions of one firm affect the decisions of other firms in the industry.

"Fewness" does not need to be defined in terms of numbers; the

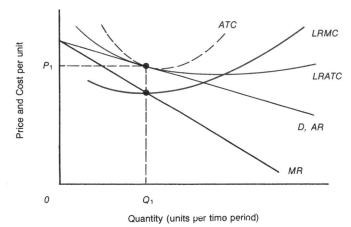

*Figure 11.8 Long-Run Output and Price of A Monopolistically
Competitive Firm*
A monopolistically competitive firm, like firms under other market structures, maximizes profit at the output where *LRMC* equals *MR*, namely OQ_1. The free entry of
new firms reduces pure profit to zero through an adjustment process which decreases the firm's demand and increases its costs until *ATC* is tangent to the
demand curve at OQ_1. However, the firm is not producing at either its short-run
optimum capacity (the minimum level of *ATC*) nor at its long run optimum scale
(the minimum level of *LRATC*).

important fact in an oligopoly is that each firm produces a large
share of the total output of the product concerned. Some oligopolies,
however, may have a number of small firms in addition to the few
large firms dominating the industry. Although the actions of the
small firms are occasionally of some consequence, it is the actions of
the large firms that are significant in oligopolistic behaviour. Because there are only a few major producers, each has some control
over the price of its product. This distinguishes oligopoly from pure
competition. But oligopolists do not have the independence in setting prices that characterize a monopolist; the price and output decisions of one firm affect the decisions of each of the other firms. The
second distinguishing feature of an oligopoly, in addition to the
small number of firms, is thus the *interdependence* of the actions of
firms.

The equilibrium price and output of oligopolistic firms and industries cannot be determined quite as readily as those for pure
competition and monopoly because firms' decisions not only reflect
cost and revenue conditions but also how they *think* other firms in
the industry will react. This unpredictable behaviour has led
economists to suggest that oligopolistic price and output are
*indeterminate: the same set of cost and revenue conditions do not
always lead to the same price and output decision because other
variable factors – primarily competitors' responses – also influence
the decision.*

Price and output are, of course, decided somehow. Several hypotheses have been proposed to describe firms' behaviour in oligopolies but insufficient evidence has been available to validate these. A recent approach has involved applying the *theory of games or strategies* for successive responses to the actions of rivals. However, a lack of data has also limited this approach to the development of an analytical framework.

Conditions for Oligopoly

Conditions fostering the existence of oligopolies are primarily the following: *economies of scale, cost advantages*, and *mergers*.

Economies of large scale make it possible for only one firm to operate profitably in the case of a monopoly; similarly, economies of large scale may prevent more than a few firms from realizing a profit in an oligopoly. Oligopolies often emerge from more competitive conditions in which several firms are operating at a small-scale output level in the short run. Longer-run expansion to realize economies of scale results in fewer firms, each providing a large share of the market quantity, with other firms leaving the industry. This process tends to follow *technological changes* which make economies of large scale possible. Firms which first adapt their production and marketing techniques to the new technology are the ones to remain in the industry; the laggards cannot match the lower prices or improved quality of the other firms and are forced to cease operation. Most of the current oligopolies, such as the automobile, steel, and petroleum industries, once included several other firms which gradually dropped out or were bought by the remaining firms.

Cost advantages enjoyed by existing firms are major barriers to new firms that might wish to enter an oligopoly. A new firm would need to become a large-scale producer immediately in order to realize the low average total cost at which existing firms are operating. But this would require extremely large expenditures for plant, equipment, senior management, advertising, and distribution. Such a venture might be regarded as a high risk by potential creditors or shareholders. In the few cases where new firms do enter an oligopoly, financing is often provided by other large firms which operate in a related oligopoly, and which can realize further economies of scale by sharing management and distribution with the new firm.

Even if a new firm could arrange financing of a large-scale plant, the existing firms would have other advantages which would give them a lower long-run average total cost curve than the new firm would have. Existing firms may control necessary patents or raw materials; have a specialized knowledge of production and marketing in their industry that can be learned only by experience; or have a well-established group of customers or "brand loyalty" that the potential new firm must penetrate.

Mergers are often the outcome of the two other conditions fostering oligopolies, and thus reinforce the oligopolistic nature of an industry. The few firms in an oligopoly, although large, often differ significantly in their output. Two of the smaller firms may merge in order to gain the economies of scale and market power held by the largest firm and thereby be less susceptible to the effects of its actions. Also, each of the firms in the oligopoly may have particular advantages such as outstanding management or established customers and find that they can each improve their cost and profit positions by merging and sharing these advantages.

Short-Run Price and Output in Oligopoly

Different models or explanations of oligopolists' behaviour are based on the nature of their products: these are described as being *differentiated* or *undifferentiated*. The product of each firm in an oligopoly may differ slightly in design or composition, or buyers may simply *believe* that the products are different. The oil companies, for example, put much effort into persuading buyers that their automobile gasolines are significantly different. Other differentiated-product oligopolies include the automobile, tobacco, and soap industries. In other oligopolistic industries, such as those producing primary aluminum, cement, and basic steel, the product is undifferentiated, or essentially the same for all firms.

Oligopolists' Revenues

The interdependence of oligopolists' actions makes it difficult to specify precisely their demand or average revenue curves since the elasticity of demand for the product of a particular firm depends on how other firms react to the firm's price changes. Consider the case of a paint industry dominated by about five major producers. If one firm, currently selling 2,000 gallons per week of its standard white paint at $9.50 per gallon, should lower its price to $8.50 per gallon, its rivals could react in a number of ways. If they do not change their prices, the firm will increase its sales both because the total market sales increase and because it gains sales from its competitors. If other firms also lower their prices, total market sales will increase but each firm will gain a share of this increase roughly proportionate to its previous market share. The firm initiating the price change will increase its sales less than it would if rival firms' prices were unchanged. The demand elasticity is therefore lower in the second case than the first.

The other firms may decide that the price-cutting firm is in financial difficulty and can be squeezed out of the industry if they reduce their prices still further. The price-cutting firm may increase its sales slightly if it has a sufficiently different product or if there is strong brand-loyalty among its buyers; otherwise, its sales will remain unchanged or even decrease. Thus, in estimating its demand curve, the firm must be able to predict how both buyers and other firms will react to its own price changes, and how buyers will react to price differentials between its product and those of other firms.

Is is assumed in the following discussion that an oligopolist will face a normal, downward-sloping demand curve. Although its precise shape or elasticity may not be known, this assumption can still provide important comparisons among alternative oligopolistic situations. In the case of differentiated products the market demand curve is also imprecise, since slightly different products are being treated as if they were the same. The problem is one of determining how different products may be and yet be considered within a single market. Again, a downward-sloping demand curve can be assumed for the industry; the precise position it takes remains in question.

Price and Output in Differentiated-Product Oligopoly

A model of the behaviour of oligopolistic firms whose products are differentiated has been developed to explain why prices tend to remain unchanged despite changing cost conditions. This is the *kinked demand model*. It assumes that if a firm lowers its price other firms will do the same, but if a firm raises its price the others will not follow; and that firms recognize that none will benefit by price-cutting since each would move away from its profit-maximizing output level.

The kinked demand curve facing a firm in this situation is shown as the solid D, AR curve in Figure 11.9. This actually combines segments of two demand curves. Suppose the firm's current price and quantity are OP_1 and OQ_1. If the firm expects that its rivals will match any price change, its demand curve will be the steeper, less elastic one. If all firms raise their prices, this firm will lose some sales, but so will the other firms; if all firms lower their prices, this firm will gain few sales. Alternatively, if the firm expects its rivals to ignore its price changes, its demand curve will be the flatter, more elastic one because a price increase will sharply reduce sales and a price decrease will lead to many more sales.

The firm facing the kinked demand curve, however, expects that its price increase will be ignored by rivals because they can then gain a larger share of the market, while its price decrease will be followed by other firms attempting to preserve their market shares. But all of the firms recognize that there is nothing to be gained if they all reduce their prices. Thus the price remains fixed at OP_1.

One might expect, however, that an increase in costs would cause a firm to raise its price as part of its adjustment to a new profit-maximizing price and output combination. *Within a certain range of cost changes, no such price change occurs.* Figure 11.9

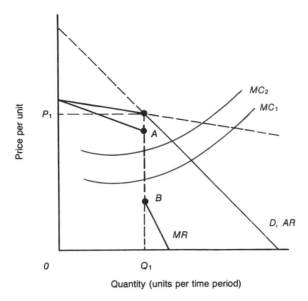

Figure 11.9 Oligopolist's Kinked Demand Curve
An oligopolist is selling OQ_1 units per period at OP_1 per unit. He believes that if he raises his price, the quantity sold will decrease proportionately more (demand is elastic) because rivals will not raise their prices. A price reduction, however, would be matched by rivals. Hence there is a "kink" in his demand curve which produces a discontinuity in the MR curve between A and B. An increase in production costs, shifting marginal costs up to MC_2, has no effect on price and output because MC_2 equals MR at the same output, OQ_1, at which MC_1 equals MR.

illustrates why this is rational behaviour for the firm. While the demand curve has a kink at quantity OQ_1, the marginal revenue curve derived from the segments of the two demand curves has a *discontinuity*, or vertical section, AB, at this output level. If the firm's marginal cost curve is MC_1, marginal cost is equal to marginal revenue at output OQ_1 and the firm is at its maximum-profit position. Suppose an increase in the price of a variable factor such as labour shifts its marginal cost curve upward to MC_2. *The output level at which marginal revenue is equal to the new marginal cost is still OQ_1. The price thus remains at OP_1 despite the cost increase.*

Note that the kinked demand explanation does not account for the initial price, nor can this explanation be expected to apply to all cases of differentiated products. The range within which marginal revenue is constant, and thus the range within which marginal cost changes have no effect on price, depends on the relative elasticities of the two segments of the kinked demand curve.

This model would lead one to expect that:

- prices will remain unchanged in oligopolies even when costs change;

- only substantial shifts in costs will cause prices to change;
- firms will advertise to differentiate their products and thus make the upper segment of the kinked demand curve less elastic, thereby reducing the degree of "kinkiness". This will enhance their opportunity for freedom of action in setting prices.

In the real world, these results are observed: prices of products offered by oligopolistic firms change infrequently, and then in pronounced jumps; and oligopolists generally spend a larger percentage of the selling price of the product for advertising than do firms in other industries.

Price and Output in Undifferentiated-Product Oligopoly

Since oligopolistic firms cannot be certain how their rivals will react, they cannot be certain what their profit-maximizing price and output should be. This is especially true for firms producing essentially the same product as their rivals because buyers' responses to any price difference will be greater than when products are differentiated.

Firms that are uncertain about their rivals' reactions thus have a strong incentive to work together to maximize their joint profits as a means to maximizing their individual profits.

At the same time, as a firm increases its certainty about rivals' reactions by cooperating with them, there will also be an incentive to use this knowledge to operate independently, and thus to improve its profit position still further.

Collusion

Collusion is the joint decision-making of firms, particularly concerning the setting or changing of prices. It rarely occurs in any market other than those characterized by oligopoly, because it is not necessary in monopoly, and too difficult for the monopolistically competitive firm described earlier in this chapter. Collusion can take several specific forms but these can be categorized as *overt or explicit collusion* and *tacit or implicit collusion*.

The most formal type of overt collusion is the *cartel*: an arrangement whereby firms agree to establish a central authority which determines the price and output for the industry, tells firms how much each should produce, and regulates marketing by individual firms. The cartel thus can behave as a pure monopolist. Profit-maximizing output is determined by aggregating the firms' marginal costs to derive the industry's marginal cost curve and finding the quantity at which marginal costs and revenues are equal. The cartel then allocates output quotas among the firms such that each firm is operating at the same marginal cost. The profit of each firm is the difference between the industry price and its own average total cost at the output allocated to it. Individual firms thus have an incentive to reduce their marginal costs relative to that of other firms because this increases both the quota allocated to them and their profit on each unit. While this arrangement would maximize joint profits, cartels are unlikely to obtain the agreement of all firms.

Cartels were common in Europe during the 1920s and 1930s but are now forbidden in most countries by antitrust, anticombine, or unfair trade practice legislation. However, international groups such as OPEC (Organization of Petroleum Exporting Countries) closely resemble cartels and continue to exist because they are subject to no other authority. Less formal but explicit collusion in the form of price schedules which reflect the joint-profit maximization price can also be agreed upon without the formal machinery of a cartel organization. This too is illegal in most countries.[2]

Tacit or implicit collusion is also generally illegal, but this type is more difficult to identify and prove in the courts. A common form of implicit collusion is *price leadership*. One firm, often the largest in the industry, becomes the acknowledged price setter. Whenever it raises its price, other firms do likewise. This pattern serves to reduce uncertainity because the largest firm, knowing that its costs are likely to be lower than in other firms, can expect that other firms will welcome a price increase. Similarly, the smaller firms know that each of the other firms has more to gain by a price increase than by holding price constant once the industry leader has raised its price. They may also fear retaliation if they refuse to cooperate.

In addition to legislation, other factors can prevent or break down collusive activity. These include the *number and size of firms in the industry, the degree of product similarity or differentiation, the rate of technological change, and the temptation to take independent action*. The more firms there are and the more dissimilar they are in size, the weaker will be their sense of interdependence and hence their willingness to act in concert. Agreement is also less easily reached and enforced when seven or eight firms rather than three or four are involved. In an industry where there are a few large firms and a number of small ones, the smaller firms may decide they have more to gain by setting prices below those of the large firms and attempting to increase their scale of operation.

The more differentiated are the products of collusive firms, the more likely are their revenue and cost conditions to be different. But even firms producing the same product may have different cost curves, and thus different profit levels at the agreed price. In either case, some firms may decide they can improve their profits by leaving the agreements. Where products are differentiated by quality, firms may not be able to agree on a price differential commensurate

---

[2] Collusive agreements are forbidden in Canada by the Combines Investigation Act; this and other features of the Act are described in Chapter 12.

with the quality difference. Firms may also believe that they can achieve a greater profit through product differentiation than by cooperation.

In oligopolies where technological change is slow or seems to have been halted, cost conditions are more stable and the possibilities for product differentiation are minimized. Hence there is less incentive for firms to act independently. Conversely, in periods of rapid technological change, each firm may think that by aggressive, individual action, it can dominate the others and reduce the importance of their reactions to its own decisions.

Finally, there is always the temptation to betray an informal price agreement by offering secret price reductions to a few customers in order to take sales from other firms. Alternatively, a firm may simply declare an open price war in the hope of getting and holding customers of the other firms. These secret or open violations of a price agreement are probably the single most significant factor in disrupting collusive activity in an industry. Each firm becomes wary of future agreements with the offender, and often with the other firms as well.

Long-Run Price and Output in Oligopoly

Long-run profit-maximizing price and output decisions are even more difficult for oligopolists than are short-run decisions. In the short run, a firm at least knows its rivals' production capabilities, and hence the range of their possible reactions. In the long run, when plant size and technology can be changed, these factors increase the firm's uncertainty about its competitors' reactions. Otherwise, the same principles would apply that were described for the long-run decisions of monopolistic and competitive firms, namely that each oligopolistic firm should produce the quantity at which its long-run marginal cost is equal to its long-run marginal revenue. Estimation of long-run costs raises the possibility of economies or diseconomies of scale, and estimation of long-run revenues raises the possibility that other firms will enter the industry. Possible barriers to the entry of other firms are the same as those discussed in explaining the existence of oligopolies: the large investment needed to enter the industry and the cost and other advantages enjoyed by the established firms.

Nonprice Competition

Since joint-profit maximization through collusion is illegal and otherwise difficult, and individual profit-maximizing output is subject to uncertainty, oligopolistic firms are likely to engage in *nonprice competition*. This includes the use of advertising and emphasis on product style and quality in order to shift the firm's demand curve to the right, and to make the demand less elastic by increasing product differentiation.

Price decreases, especially the substantial reductions evident in some price wars, often reduce short-run profits and do not result in permanent gains in absolute sales or share of the market since rivals can and usually do follow with similar price decreases. Nonprice competition, however, may enable a firm to make slower but *permanent gains*. Advertising and design changes, of course, increase a firm's costs; hence, nonprice competition may be seen as a kind of cost competition — an attempt to increase marginal revenue as much as possible for a given increase in marginal cost.

Massive advertising has also been shown to form *a barrier to the entry of other firms*. A potential new firm would not only need to incur the same large expenditures to match the advertising budgets of existing firms; it may need to spend even more to alter the attitudes and buying habits of buyers in an established market.

Another advantage to firms of nonprice competition is that *competitors' reactions to nonprice actions can usually be predicted with more certainty*. An advertising campaign tends to provoke a similar campaign, style changes are countered with similar style changes, and promotional games and contests soon compete with other such attractions. Moreover, the cost of an advertising campaign is known in advance; the cost of a price war in terms of increased costs and decreased profits is much more uncertain. Through nonprice competition, a firm hopes that it can do better than its rivals in altering its product or image, and therefore achieve a permanent gain, even if its rivals attempt to do the same.

D. Evaluation of Alternative Market Structures

Four types of market structure have been described: pure competition, pure monopoly, oligopoly (of two types), and monopolistic competition. As a first step toward understanding the significance of alternative market structures, the *conduct or behaviour* of firms and industries under each alternative was examined in terms of output, prices, responses to competitors' decisions, collusive activity, product differentiation, and nonprice competition. Table 11.2 presents a short review of the major features distinguishing different basic market structures.

Performance of Firms

An evaluation of alternative market structures cannot be based only on the conduct of firms. Collusive activity, for example, cannot be judged desirable or otherwise without evaluating its consequences. A further step is therefore required, an evaluation of the performance

Table 11.2

Distinguishing Features of Market Structures

Features	Pure Competition	Imperfect Competition			Pure Monopoly
		Monopolistic Competition	Oligopoly		
			Different Products	Standard Product	
Number of Sellers	many	several	few	few	one
Product Differentiation	none	much (also differing service, location)	little to some	little or none	one product, no close substitutes
Typical Demand Facing Firm	perfectly elastic	quite elastic	moderately elastic, perhaps kinked	same as market, if collusion exists	slightly elastic, as for market
Control over Price	none	little	some	some	much
Competitor Reaction	none	little	much	much	none
Barriers to Entry	none	slight or none	some	some	complete
Examples	some products in agriculture and fishing	some retail stores, clothing, furniture	automobiles, gasoline, cigarettes	aluminum, steel, cement	rare, some public utilities

of firms in terms of their contribution to general economic objectives. It is here that the elaboration of market structure models becomes most useful. No single theory of the firm can include all characteristics of each firm when there is such a diversity of firms in a large economy. Comparing the characteristics and behaviour of any given firm with those of firms in the market structure models, however, often makes it possible to place the firm in a particular category and thus predict how it will perform.

Criteria for evaluating the performance of firms include:

- the efficient use of productive resources;
- innovation in products and techniques to stimulate and adapt technological change; and
- contribution to product variety, providing a broad range of choice corresponding with the range of effective consumer demand for goods and services.

Efficiency

Relative efficiency in the use of productive resources under alternative market structures can be judged, given some strict assumptions, by comparing firms' long-run equilibrium positions. These equilibrium positions are valid, however, only as statements of the *tendencies* of firms, because long-run equilibrium is seldom reached: forces inevitably emerge to change the firm's long-run cost or revenue conditions.

Figure 11.10 is presented in three parts to compare the short and long-run equilibrium positions of firms in pure competition, monopolistic competition, and pure monopoly. Oligopoly is omitted to avoid complicating the diagram further and because the two general cases of oligopoly can be roughly approximated by either pure monopoly or monopolistic competition. To clarify the effects of different revenue conditions, the same cost curves are assumed for each type of firm.

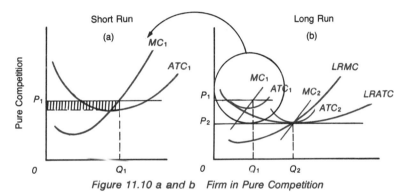

Figure 11.10 a and b   Firm in Pure Competition

A purely competitive firm can realize a pure profit in the short run but not in the long run, at which point it reaches its optimum scale (ATC_2) and capacity, OQ_2. Its price, OP_2, equals $LRMC$.

Pure Competiton. The purely competitive firm may make a pure profit in the short run; it is doing so in Figure 11.10a. Because the firm faces a perfectly elastic demand curve, its marginal revenue is the average revenue for each level of output. Its profit-maximizing output, OQ_1, at which marginal cost equals marginal revenue, therefore is priced at marginal cost, OP_1. However, it is not necessarily producing at the minimum short-run average total cost. The latter would occur only if the demand curve happened to be tangent to the short-run average total cost curve, ATC_1.

In the long run (Figure 11.10b), the firm produces the quantity, OQ_2, at which its long-run marginal cost equals its marginal revenue. Again, its perfectly elastic demand curve is also its marginal revenue curve and long-run output is priced at marginal cost. Because other firms are attracted into the industry by short-run profits, the demand curve facing an original firm is lower than it was in the short-run. The downward shift of the firms' demand curves and their expansion of plant size continue until no pure profit can be made: that is, to the point where long-run average total cost is equal to average revenue or price. Thus in the long run, the purely competitive firm's output is produced at the minimum cost, and output is as large and price as low as possible under pure competition.

Monopolistic Competition. The monopolistically competitive firm may make a short-run pure profit; it is doing so in Figure 11.10c. Because the firm faces a downward-sloping demand curve, its short-run profit-maximizing output, OQ_3, is priced above marginal cost. The difference between marginal cost and price is not large, however, because the typical demand curve facing this firm is quite elastic; the marginal revenue curve thus lies not far below the demand curve. Short-run output would be produced at the minimum average total cost only if the marginal revenue curve happened to intersect the ATC_1 curve at its minimum point.

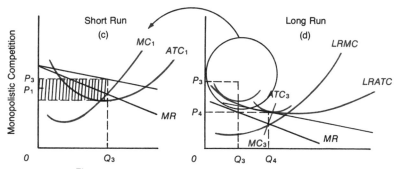

Figure 11.10 c and d   Firm in Monopolistic Competition
A monopolistically competitive firm makes no pure profit in the long run, does not produce at its lowest possible *LRATC*, and its price, OP_4, exceeds its *LRMC*.

In the long run (Figure 11.10d), the firm increases its plant size to produce the quantity, OQ_4, where its long-run marginal cost equals its marginal revenue. The entry of other firms attracted by short-run pure profits shifts downward the long-run demand and marginal revenue curve until no pure profit can be made. However, the downward slope of the demand curve causes this point to be reached to the left of the minimum point of the long-run average total cost curve. *Given the same cost conditions for purely competitive and monopolistically competitive firms, the long-run output of the latter firms will always be less, and the price will be more, than for the former. Furthermore, long-run output, OQ_4 will be priced above marginal cost and produced at more than the long-run average total cost.*

Pure Monopoly. The pure monopoly firm may make a pure profit in the short run; it is doing so in Figure 11.10e. The demand curve it faces is generally less elastic than that for the monopolistically competitive firm; hence, its marginal revenue curve lies further below its average revenue curve at any given quantity, and there is a greater difference between the marginal cost and price of its profit-maximizing output, OQ_5. (Again, short-run output would be produced at the minimum average total cost only if the marginal revenue curve happened to intersect the ATC_1 curve at its minimum point.)

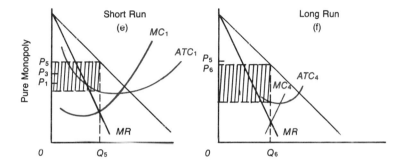

Figure 11.10 e and f A Monopoly

A monopoly firm can realize a long-run profit, and usually produces with excess capacity and at a scale (ATC_4) which does not realize further potential economies of scale. Its long-run price, OP_6, is much higher than its $LRMC$ at OQ_6.

Since new firms cannot enter the industry, the demand curve will not shift in the long run (Figure 11.10f), other things being equal. The firm may, however, need to increase its plant size to produce the output, OQ_6, at which its long-run marginal cost equals marginal revenue. If output *is* increased, pure profit will also increase, otherwise the monopolist would not alter his output. Although the price decreases, there is a greater difference between marginal cost and price. As in the short run, output will be produced at the minimum average total cost only if the marginal revenue happens to intersect the $LRATC$ curve at its minimum point. This is illustrated in Figure 11.11. If the marginal revenue curve is MR_1, marginal revenue equals long-run marginal cost at OQ_1. The lowest short-run marginal cost for OQ_1 is realized with a plant size represented by ATC_1. If marginal revenue is MR_3, output is OQ_3, and is produced at an average total cost shown by ATC_3. Only in rare cases, if marginal revenue is MR_2, is the output OQ_2 produced at the lowest long-run average total cost. However, the price is greater than the average cost, and a pure profit is also realized in the long run.

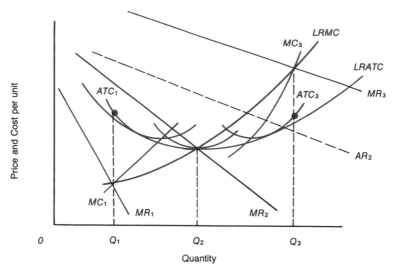

Figure 11.11   A Monopoly May Produce Below, At, or Above,
Its Optimum Scale
Depending on the relationship between a monopoly's marginal revenue and marginal cost curves, a monopoly may produce in the long run below, at, or above its
optimum scale. When marginal revenue is MR_1, the firm produces OQ_1 at less
than optimum capacity and scale. At MR_3, it produces OQ_3 at more than optimum
capacity and with decreasing returns to scale. If the demand curve happens to be
AR_2, the firm produces OQ_2, at which $LRMC$ equals MR_2, at the optimum capacity
and scale which would also be the long-run equilibrium position of a purely competitive firm. However, the monopolist realizes a profit since AR_2 is above $LRATC$
at output OQ_2.

Oligopoly. In the short run, the oligopolist *may* make a pure profit,
will price its output above marginal cost, and only by coincidence
will be operating at its minimum average total cost. In the long run,
if there is freedom to enter the oligopolistic industry, the equilibrium condition resembles that of monopolistic competition to the
extent that the demand curve facing a firm is shifted downward until
it is tangent to the long-run average total cost curve and no pure
profit is realized. Because the ologopolist's demand curve typically
has a greater slope, output is produced at a cost further above the
minimum average total cost than in the case of monopolistic competition.

If, however, there are substantial barriers to entering the industry, there will not be enough new firms to shift the firm's demand
curve downward to the point of tangency with long-run average
total cost. The situation then resembles that of pure monopoly, in
which long-run pure profit is possible and output might only by
chance be produced at minimum average total cost. In either long-
run case, however, oligopolist firms price their output above average
cost.

Comparative Efficiency

The efficiency of firms under alternative market structures may be compared on two grounds: optimum scale of plant and rate of output, and equality of price with marginal cost.

Optimum Scale and Output. Recall from the discussion of costs in Chapter 10 that the *optimum rate of output* is defined as *the quantity at which the short-run average total cost is at a minimum.* The *optimum scale of plant* is the one at which *all economies of scale are realized but diseconomies of large scale have not been incurred.* It is represented by the short-run average total cost curve whose minimum point coincides with the minimum point of the long-run average total cost curve. (See, for example, ATC_2 in Figure 11.10b.) Thus the optimum rate of output using the optimum scale of plant is the quantity at which long-run average total cost is at a minimum. (Note: optimum output should not be confused with the profit-maximizing level of output.)

A brief review of the firms' performance shows that the long-run tendency is for pure competition to lead to both the optimum scale of plant and the optimum rate of output for that scale.

Production under pure competition is therefore at the lowest possible average total cost.

Under monopolistic competition, firms do not quite reach the optimum scale, and produce at less than the optimum rate of output for that plant size. *This is the general criticism of monopolistic competition: that there is necessarily an underutilization of resources because firms operate with excess productive capacity.* Similarly, in an oligopoly to which there is free entry, and in which firms face a less-elastic demand curve than in monopolistic competition, firms tend to have a still smaller than optimum plant size and to produce at still less than the optimum rate of output. *The result is that there usually is even more excess capacity in a free-entry oligopoly than in monopolistic competition.*

Whether firms in pure monopoly and restricted-entry oligopoly will produce at the optimum scale and rate of output is uncertain. As explained above, this would occur simply by chance. The probability therefore is that they will produce in plants either smaller or larger than the optimum; *there will thus probably be some inefficient use of resources in pure monopoly and restricted-entry oligopoly.*

Price and Marginal Cost. Only in pure competition do firms price their output at marginal cost, because these are the only firms facing a perfectly elastic demand curve. (A monopoly which can practise perfect price discrimination prices the *final* unit of output at marginal cost.) The efficiency in pricing at marginal cost may not be so obvious, however, as efficiency in producing at minimum average cost. This second case of efficiency relates to maximizing consumer satisfaction, given the resources available.

Reccall the explanation of consumer surplus in Chapter 9. Consumers are willing to pay more than the price charged for every unit preceding the last unit sold. The lower the price and the greater the quantity, the greater will be consumer surplus associated with any commodity. Now turn to Figure 11.12. Under monopoly, output will be OQ_1, priced at OP_1. Consumer surplus is represented by the area, P_0P_1A. If the industry illustrated in Figure 11.12 is under pure competition, however, the marginal cost curve is the industry's supply curve. Output will be OQ_2 and priced at OP_2. Consumer surplus is much greater than if the industry is a monopoly. Furthermore, output under pure competition is increased to the point where the marginal cost of producing the last unit is just equal to the marginal utility derived from this last unit, as evidenced by the price consumers are willing to pay. Resources are being used as efficiently as possible to provide consumer satisfaction or utility. When this condition is realized in all markets, the maximum possible consumer satisfaction is reached.

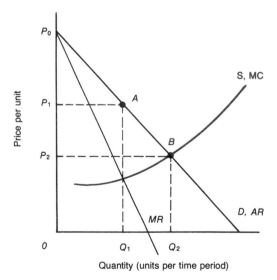

Figure 11.12 Marginal Cost Pricing Maximizes Consumer Surplus
A monopoly facing the cost and revenue conditions show here will produce OQ_1 and sell its output at price OP_1. Consumer surplus is represented by area P_0P_1A. A purely competitive industry with the same cost and revenue conditions will supply OQ_2 which will be sold at price OP_2. Consumer surplus will be increased to P_0P_2B. One advantage of competition for consumers is the increased consumer surplus represented by P_1P_2BA.

Pure Profit. Note that whether pure profit is possible is not an issue in evaluating the performance of firms. In the long run, monopolistically competitive firms, for example, do not realize a pure profit, but they do price output above marginal cost and operate with less than the optimum plant scale. The *persistence* of profits in the long run is of interest, however, as evidence that there is restricted entry to the industry and thus that an oligopolistic or monopolistic situation exists.

How Valid Are the Assumptions? Two of the several assumptions made in comparing the efficiency of resource use under alternative market structures have important implications for this evaluation. One assumption is that the market in question is large enough to accommodate many firms, each of which can attain the optimum plant size in the long run. However, the long-run cost conditions may be such that the optimum output is, for example, 100 units per day produced at a marginal cost and price of $2.00. Market demand may be such that, at this price, only 300 units can be sold per day: only three firms can exist in what would then become an oligopolistic industry. The first three firms to enlarge their plants to this optimum size would survive, with the others leaving the industry.

Changes in technology, often requiring larger fixed costs for more complex equipment, have tended to increase the optimum plant size. In some industries, these changes have occurred faster than the expansion of demand for the industries' products and thus have reduced the number of firms in the industry. If the number of firms were to be increased artificially, by government regulation or court order, the result likely would be lower output and higher prices.

A second major assumption underlying the comparative efficiency of alternative market structures is that these have no differential effect on cost conditions. However, there may be monetary economies or diseconomies to be realized by having fewer firms produce any given level of output. This is not a case of economies of scale within a firm. Rather, it is, for example, the consequence of having one firm instead of ten firms buying raw materials or one firm instead of one hundred firms hiring semi-skilled labour. One large firm usually can influence prices of its inputs more than can a single small firm. This effect is discussed in Chapter 14 in examining the nature of labour markets.

Innovation and Costs

A second general criterion for evaluating the performance of firms is their record for innovation: the use of new raw materials, new sources of existing raw materials, new techniques or processes, and the development of new products, or improved quality in existing products. The latter two types of innovations are relevant to the next section; the first three are considered here because each of them can potentially reduce production costs for existing products.

From the firm's point of view, the incentive to innovate is the possibility of larger profits through cost reductions. A special case of this condition, of course, is the incentive to maintain existing profits or even to survive as new firms enter the industry or market demand falls. All types of firms can realize a profit in the short run and thus all have an incentive to innovate within this period. But the range of potential short-run innovations is limited to changes in the variable inputs: alternative sources of labour or raw materials might be found or a new raw material might be used, provided that these can be substituted within the constraints of the fixed plant and equipment.

In the long run, only the monopolist and restricted-entry oligopolist have an incentive to innovate. Their long-run profits are protected by barriers to entering the industry. Firms under other market structures are unlikely to make long-run innovations because the resulting increased profits would attract even more firms. These would imitate the cost-reducing innovations of the original firms and wipe out profits for any of them. One important exception to this outcome occurs when the innovation can be kept secret for some time or, as is commonly the case, if it requires some time to introduce. A purely or monopolistically competitive firm might decide that the profit to be made in this interim was sufficient to undertake the innovation.

Since there usually are substantial economies of scale in research and development programs, innovation is also more likely to occur in oligopolies where the few firms are large enough to undertake their own research and development programs and to introduce a large-scale technique, such as automated assembly, which represents a cost saving only at high levels of output.

One public policy consequence of the lack of incentive for purely competitive firms to innovate is that governments sponsor, for example, agricultural research and extension programs in an effort to have agricultural commodities produced at lower cost. This policy is sometimes extended to oligopolistic industries, since lower costs, despite increased pure profits, will lead to lower prices and greater output. Similarly, public policy may be directed to the encouragement of oligopolies which have innovation potential on the grounds that output will be expanded and will be sold at lower prices, even though there may be a greater difference between price and marginal cost.

Product Variety

Product variety is also a criterion for evaluating the performance of firms because there is such a great diversity in consumer tastes. A wide choice in products, of varying quality and style, can be produced only at higher cost than if a similar number of identical units were produced. For example, if the only cars made in Canada were standard Fords, Chevrolets, and Dodges, the same number of cars could be supplied each year at lower per-unit costs. But consumers apparently place a high value on variety in automobile models, colours, and options.

Product variety is likely to be greatest in oligopolies. These firms have a large enough plant size to produce great quantities of a standard unit such as a basic automobile chassis or washing machine frame and then add enough superficial features or options to offer several "different" products. Product differentiation also occurs under monopolistic competition but this more often involves variation which has less effect on costs. The threat that other firms will enter an industry and thus reduce profits means that the monopolistic competitor has little scope for introducing a range of styles or colours if these lead to higher per-unit costs. Pure competition, by definition, is restricted to one standard product. No variation will emerge under pure competition unless the market *for each different product* is large enough to support many firms at the optimum plant size; this is obviously quite improbable.

Firms in oligopolies and monopolistic competition will tend to offer different products in an effort to attract sales from their competitors, but the differentiation cannot be so great that it alienates potential customers. North American automobile producers, for example, could have introduced compact cars many years ago but waited instead until the "small car" market was well established and they were forced to compete with imported cars. For one of the domestic producers to have introduced compact cars earlier would indeed have been to offer variety, but it also involved the risk of losing sales to other domestic producers.

Models of Firms' Behaviour: A Critique

The alternative models for behaviour and performance of firms are usually referred to collectively as the theory of the firm. It is clearly useful for predicting the responses of different types of firms to changing revenue and cost conditions, and for designing public policies to create the industrial organization most favourable to the public interest. The theory of the firm has been subjected to much criticism (and has been vigorously defended) for many years. Among the continuing objections, the most important are the following: firms do not necessarily have profit maximization as their primary objective; even if they do attempt to maximize profits, they may not produce at the level where marginal cost equals marginal revenue; and even if they do try to do this, firms may not have enough information about costs and revenues at various outputs to use the theory of the firm.

Profit Maximization. Firms' objectives were considered in the second part of Chapter 10. Although the assumption that profit maximization is the primary objective has had widespread and long support, an alternative hypothesis, that firms seek to maximize sales revenue as a means to maximizing management's prestige and political power, is increasing in popularity. Support for this alternative objective has been cogently presented in J. Kenneth Galbraith's recent book, *Economics and the Public Purpose*. Galbraith argues that separation of ownership and control of the giant corporations has enabled management — Galbraith calls it the "technostructure" — to set its own objectives. These are primarily related to the security of management's position; this in turn requires managers to retain control, earning sufficient and steady profits to satisfy shareholders and isolating the firm from market disturbances by controlling suppliers of raw products and financing expansion with internal funds. Increasing sales and numbers of products provides both direct job satisfaction and prestige. All of these conditions, however, can be incorporated within the traditional theory of the firm. Earning sufficient profit, if not maximum profit, requires an analysis of costs and revenues at different output levels. New products cannot be introduced without regard for their effect on the firm's existing profit position; and at some point, sales maximization encounters diseconomies of large scale. However, Galbraith has effectively portrayed the detailed behaviour of oligopolistic firms striving to protect their position from the entry of new firms, and thus the process by which oligopolies have risen to a dominant position in the modern mixed economies.

Markup Pricing. An attack on the hypothesis of pricing according to the demand curve has provided the alternative hypothesis that firms practise markup pricing: *setting a price which is a specified percentage above the producer's average cost per unit*. This argument suggests that firms calculate the average cost per unit for producing their output and add 5, 10, 20, or 50 per cent to this cost to determine the price. Since the average cost frequently does not include all fixed costs, particularly imputed costs of plant and equipment and a normal profit, the markup is expected to cover these as well as to provide a pure profit. A firm's standard markup percentage often sets a base price which can be modified if the firm thinks demand conditions are changing. If demand and cost conditions are fairly static, the firm can discover the relevant section of its demand curve: a too-high price will result in unsold units and a too-low price will leave the firm unable to fill all orders. A price which just clears its output identifies one point on its demand curve. Since the difference between its total cost and total revenue at this price is the firm's total profit for that level of output, the firm, by altering its output level in either direction, can determine the direction it must move to increase its profit until it has identified a maximum profit output. Earlier it was shown that the output at which total revenue exceeded total cost by the greatest amount is also the output at which marginal cost equals marginal revenue. *Thus, by a trial-and-error process, the firm arrives at the point predicted by the theory of the firm.* It is not important to the theory that the firm determines its output by explicitly equating marginal cost and marginal revenue, but simply that it act *as if* it did this. Given this, the theory remains a valid tool for explaining and predicting firms' behaviour.

Cost and Revenue Information. Another criticism of the theory of the firm is that it assumes that firms have full information about their cost curves and the demand curve they face. One answer is given above: firms may discover the relevant portion of the demand curve by offering various quantities at different prices. The firm may also estimate a larger segment of its demand curve by observing the experience of other firms with similar products, or it may simply ask consumers how much they would buy at various prices as part of its market research program.

Some cost curves are more difficult to estimate. Fixed costs can be determined with reasonable accuracy, except in firms which produce several products using the same plant and senior management. Variable costs present a greater problem due to the difficulty in estimating the marginal productivity associated with successive units of productive factors such as labour. Firms thus tend to assume that marginal productivity and prices of productive factors do not vary with output, at least over the relevant quantity range, and thus implicitly assume constant marginal costs. It was suggested previously that actual experience shows this to be a reasonable or workable assumption in many cases.

Review of the Main Points

1. Pure monopoly is a market in which only one firm produces a commodity for which there are no close substitutes. Monopoly exists because other firms are prevented from entering the industry by barriers such as patents, public utilities, restricted access to raw materials, and economies of scale.

2. A monopolist can set the price at which he can sell whatever quantity he decides to produce. His demand curve is also the market demand curve; since there are no close substitutes it is less elastic than the demand curve facing a firm in any other market structure. There is no supply curve for a monopolist because he does not adjust the quantity produced to a given market price.

3. Monopoly profits are maximized by producing the quantity at which marginal cost equals marginal revenue, but a monopolist does not necessarily make a profit. Marginal revenue, the change

in total revenue for each unit of output, declines with increasing output: the marginal revenue curve is downward-sloping and lies below the average revenue curve.

4. The degree of monopoly power could be estimated by comparing the monopolist's marginal revenue and his price; by comparing his total profit with his normal profit; or, most commonly, by calculating the concentration ratio for the industry.

5. Price discrimination is charging different prices to different buyers of the same commodity produced under the same cost conditions. This is possible when the commodity cannot be transferred or resold because it is a service, or when buyers are not aware that others are paying a different price, or there is a barrier to the transfer of the commodity. A special case of price discrimination is charging a single buyer lower prices for additional quantities. The perfect price discriminator, who could charge a different price for each unit sold, would produce the quantity at which marginal cost is equal to price and would have a higher output and profit than if he charged only one price.

6. Monopolistic competition describes a market or industry in which there are many small firms selling similar but not identical products; the market share of any firm is too small for it to be concerned about reactions of other firms. Products are different enough that the demand curve facing each firm is not perfectly elastic. There is also easy entry to the industry. The firm's profit-maximizing output level occurs where marginal cost equals marginal revenue, but by changing its selling costs the firm may be able to alter its demand curve and hence its maximum-profit output level.

7. In the long run, new firms will enter a monopolistically competitive industry where pure profits have been realized, shifting the demand curves facing existing firms to the left until all firms make only normal profits. The downward slope of the demand curve, however, means that this breakeven point will occur at a lower quantity, higher price, and higher average cost than occurred in pure competition.

8. An oligopoly is an industry or market with so few firms that the actions of one firm affect the decisions of other firms in the industry. Oligopolies develop where there are economies of scale, cost advantages for particular firms, and a tendency for firms to merge.

9. Behaviour of oligopolists may differ depending on whether other firms in their industry produce the same or slightly different products. In the latter case oligopolists are sometimes assumed to face a kinked demand curve: an increase in price will not be matched by other firms but a decrease will be. A firm's price can

therefore remain at the existing price even if there is a change in the marginal cost.

10. Firms in undifferentiated-product oligopolies tend to practise collusion, agreeing to set a common price for their products in order to maximize the total profit for the industry. Collusion is illegal in most countries, but governments can control overt or explicit collusion such as a cartel more easily than tacit or implicit collusion such as price leadership. Collusion is less stable where there are a larger number of firms and firms of varying sizes, where products are less similar, and where technological change occurs more quickly.

11. Oligopolists engage in nonprice competition such as advertising and other forms of sales promotion to avoid the less predictable effects of price wars.

12. The performance of firms under alternative market structures can be evaluated in terms of their efficiency, innovation, and product variety. Purely competitive firms are more efficient than other firms in their use of resources because, in the long run, they produce at the lowest possible average total cost. This occurs in monopoly and restricted-entry oligopoly only if the firms' marginal revenue curves intersect their LRATC curves at the lowest point. Only in pure competition do firms price their output at marginal cost. These advantages of pure competition assume that the market is large enough to accommodate many firms and that firms' cost conditions are the same, regardless of the market structure.

13. Although firms under any market structure may make a pure profit in the short run, and therefore have an incentive to innovate, long-run innovations will occur only under monopoly and restricted-entry oligopoly. Product variety is likely to be greatest in oligopolies.

14. An examination of some basic criticisms of the theory of the firm indicates that these do not invalidate the predications yielded by the theory, even though firms may not follow the same reasoning, in determining their level of output that economists use in explaining why that is the level which firms will tend to choose.

Review and Discussion Questions

1. Draw the typical average revenue and marginal revenue curves for firms and for industries operating under conditions of pure competition, monopoly, and monopolistic competition.

2. Why are there numerous retail automobile dealers but only a few automobile producers?

3. "Firms under imperfect competition are described as price makers; they can therefore set any price they wish for their products." Explain why you agree or disagree.

4. The college-textbook industry appears to be a differentiated-product oligopoly. How do you think the publisher of this book decided how many copies to produce and what price to charge? Do you think the publisher realized the maximum possible profit on this book? If not, explain carefully what advice you would have offered him.

5. List several products you buy from monopolistically competitive firms. What are the specific features of the products or the firms which led you to place these in this category?

6. It has been claimed both that advertising reduces product prices and that it increases product prices. Could each claim be correct? Under what conditions?

Sources and Selected Readings

Backman, Jules. *Advertising and Competition.* New York: New York University Press, 1967.

Bain, Joe S. *Industrial Organization*, 2nd ed. New York: Wiley, 1968.

Chamberlain, E. H. *The Theory of Monopolistic Competition*, 7th ed. Cambridge, Mass.: Harvard University Press, 1956.

Due, John F., and Robert W. Clower. *Intermediate Economic Analysis*, 5th ed. Homewood, Ill.: Irwin, 1966.

Heyne, Paul T. *Private Keepers of the Public Interest.* New York: McGraw-Hill, 1968.

Lancaster, Kelvin. *Introduction to Modern Microeconomics*, 2nd ed. Chicago: Rand McNally, 1974.

Leftwich, Richard H. *The Price System and Resource Allocation*, 5th ed. Hinsdale, Ill.: Dryden Press, 1973.

Machlup, Fritz. *The Economics of Sellers' Competition.* Baltimore: The Johns Hopkins Press, 1952.

Robinson, Joan. *The Economics of Imperfect Competition.* London: Macmillan, 1933.

12 Industrial Organization and Public Policy

A. Industrial Organization in Canada

The performance of firms under different types of market structures, as presented in Chapters 10 and 11, provides an important basis for government regulation of business. Public policy in this area emphasizes the nature of industrial organization, or the conditions influencing the supply side of product markets. Thus the term "market structure" gives way to the term "industrial organization" in the following discussion. Before turning to specific legislation and government programs, however, it is necessary to examine the number, size, and types of firms in the Canadian economy.

Industrial Concentration

One of the measures described earlier for defining monopoly power was the *concentration ratio*. This provides an indication of the number of sellers in an industry relative to the market size. It is usually defined either as the percentage of market sales (or value of factory shipments) of the four largest firms in the industry, or as the number of firms producing 80 per cent of the industry's output. Variations of these measures are also used: number of employees or value of assets may be substituted for sales. Due to the format for reporting data, *establishments* may also be substituted for firms. An establishment is a single plant, perhaps representing only a fraction of a firm's total operation; this approach thus tends to understate the degree of concentration.

Table 12.1 presents evidence on industrial concentration in Canadian manufacturing, using the number of employees as the concentration measure. Concentration in 1961 and 1967 was quite similar to that found for 1948,[1] and there will probably be little change over at least the next decade. Canadian manufacturing is more highly concentrated than American manufacturing, mainly because Canadian markets are much smaller while firms generally are not much smaller than American firms. Moreover, national data understate the degree of concentration in local markets. Table 12.1 shows low concentration in such industries as printing and bakeries. There may, however, be only one such establishment in a small community, implying a high degree of monopoly power in these cases.

---

[1] Gideon Rosenbluth, *Concentration in Canadian Manufacturing Industries.* New York: National Bureau of Economic Research, 1957.

Table 12.1

**Concentration in Selected Manufacturing Industries, Canada, 1967
(number of establishments required to include 80 per cent of
the employees of the industry)**

Industry	Number of Establishments
High Concentration	
Motor vehicles	5
Iron and steel mills	7
Tobacco products	8
Smelting and refining	10
Low Concentration	
Commercial printing	209
Household furniture	284
Women's clothing	303
Sawmills	479
Bakeries	549

Source: Dominion Bureau of Statistics, *Manufacturing Industries of Canada, 1967*.

Size of Firms

Another dimension of industrial organization is the size of firms, which can be measured in terms of sales, employees, or assets. Size is assumed to be important in determining whether firms are likely to be realizing economies of scale, and indirectly suggests areas where industrial concentration may be high. Table 12.2 provides some evidence on the relative size of manufacturing establishments

Table 12.2

Size of Manufacturing Establishments, Canada, 1961 and 1971

Production ($ thousands)	Percentage of the total number of establishments		Percentage of the total value of production	
	1961	1971	1961	1971
0—25	27.7	13.3	0.4	0.1
25—50	14.0	11.9	0.7	0.4
50—100	13.7	13.2	1.4	0.6
100—200	12.8	13.2	2.6	1.2
200—500	13.7	16.8	6.2	3.4
500—1,000	7.2	10.6	7.2	4.8
1,000—5,000	8.6	15.2	26.1	21.5
5,000 and over	2.3	5.8	55.3	68.1
Total	100.0	100.0	100.0	100.0

Source: Statistics Canada, *Manufacturing Industries of Canada, 1971*.

in Canada in 1961 and 1971. Note that establishments producing goods valued at less than $100,000 annually in 1971 represented 38 per cent of the total number of manufacturing establishments but produced only 1.1 per cent of the total value of output. At the other end of the size scale, establishments which individually produced at least $5 million in goods annually, accounted for only 5.8 per cent of all establishments but for 68.1 per cent of the total value of output.

Some of these large firms are included in the list in Table 12.3. Such a list is interesting but has little significance for economic analysis since sales data are not strictly comparable and other firms are omitted for lack of data. (The T. Eaton Co., for example, is estimated to have annual sales exceeding $1 billion, but it does not publish financial figures because it is a private firm.)

Table 12.3

Ten of the Largest Firms in Canada, Measured by Sales, 1974

Company	Sales ($ millions)
Ford Motor Co. of Canada[1]	4,259
Imperial Oil Ltd.	3,713
General Motors of Canada[1]	3,614
Loblaws Cos.[2]	3,060
Bell Canada	2,691
Alcan Aluminum Ltd.	2,338
Chrysler Canada Ltd.[1]	1,929
Massey-Ferguson Ltd.	1,785
International Nickel Co. of Canada	1,685
George Weston Ltd.[3]	1,673

[1]Data for automobile companies not strictly comparable due to different treatment of international sales.
[2]Consolidates U.S. subsidiaries Loblaw Inc. and National Tea Co.
[3]Excludes Loblaws Cos.
Source: Financial Post *Survey of Industrials*.

Type of Firm

The legal form or organization of the individual firm is another aspect of industrial organization. This has been of less importance to economic analysis than industrial concentration or size of firms, largely because one type of organization — the corporation — accounts for a very large proportion of the economy's output. Nonetheless, it is useful to examine the different types of firms to understand why corporations have attained this dominant position, and why the behaviour of some larger corporations has spurred the suggestion that not all firms hold profit maximization as their primary objective.

There are four basic forms of business organization: single proprietorships, partnerships, cooperatives, and corporations. Corporations can be further classified as public or crown corporations, holding companies, corporations holding provincial or national charters, and multinational corporations.

The relative importance of these forms of business in two industry groups, manufacturing and retailing, is illustrated by Table 12.4. Over two-thirds of the establishments in manufacturing were corporations but they accounted for over 97 per cent of the total sales in 1971; just over one-fifth were proprietorships but they produced less than 1 per cent of the total sales. Proprietorships are more significant in retailing, both in percentage of establishments and of sales, but again corporations dominated with the large majority of the sales. In fact, corporations account for the largest share of sales in every broad industry group except in agriculture. In 1966, over 90 per cent of Canada's farms were single proprietorships.

Table 12.4

Type of Organization in Canadian Manufacturing and Retailing

	Retailing		Manufacturing			
	Percentage of Establishments	Percentage of Sales	Percentage of Establishments		Percentage of Sales	
	1961	1961	1961	1971	1961	1971
Proprietorships	72.4	30.9	35.2	22.1	1.7	0.7
Partnerships	8.0	6.1	9.5	5.5	1.0	0.4
Corporations	18.1	58.5	52.9	70.9	96.0	97.4
Cooperatives	0.6	1.0	2.4	1.5	1.3	1.5
Other forms	0.9	3.5	—	—	—	—
Totals	152,256	$16,074 million	33,357	31,908	$23,439 million	$50,276 million

Source: Dominion Bureau of Statistics, *Manufacturing Industries of Canada, 1961 and 1971.*

Single Proprietorships

A single proprietorship is a business or firm wholly owned by one person. The owner almost always manages or operates the business although he may have a number of employees. Proprietorships can be established easily; as easily as going to the city hall to complete a business registration form. Certain types of businesses also require an annual business licence. Apart from farms, proprietorships predominate among retail and service establishments such as confectionery and cigar stores and restaurants, and professional groups such as doctors, dentists, engineers, and consultants of various kinds.

Proprietorships are usually restricted to businesses with low financial requirements because the individual owner must rely on his own assets and whatever he can borrow personally. Moreover, he is often unwilling to undertake large financial ventures because he is subject to *unlimited liability*. This means that creditors can claim his personal assets such as his home, automobile, and furniture, as well as his business assets, should he be unable to meet his financial obligations. One result of unlimited liability has been a greater use of the bankruptcy law whereby an individual can declare his bankruptcy or inability to meet all claims. He can then accumulate personal and business assets again which cannot be claimed by previous creditors.

The major disadvantage of the proprietorship is the difficulty it imposes on obtaining financing to expand a successful business. Profits of proprietorships are taxed as individual income; the owner may find that he is paying as much as 40 per cent of his net profit in taxes and thus cannot depend on savings for business expansion. Borrowing requires collateral which may involve pledging some of his personal assets and perhaps buying additional life insurance. Interest rates paid by small businesses for borrowed funds usually are higher than the rates paid by larger corporations.

Proprietorships come to an end with the owner's death or the sale of the proprietorship's assets to another person or firm.

Partnerships

A partnership is a firm formed by two or more persons who agree to own and operate a single business. The partnership agreement usually specifies what each partner contributes to the firm in terms of funds, management, physical assets, or even prestige; how each will share in the profits or losses; and what each will receive should the business be dissolved. The latter section is important since it has been estimated that only about one-third of partnerships last for more than two years.

Forming a partnership is one method for a single proprietor to obtain financing for a business expansion. It may also provide a means for joining with another single proprietor in a related business, or acquiring some special managerial or technical talent.

Partnerships are subject to the same unlimited liability described for single proprietorships. Each partner should therefore have an equal share in the firm's decisions, although each partner can act independently in the name of the firm, committing other partners to this action, unless restrictions on individual action have been agreed to previously. Partnerships may also include "limited partners" who contribute funds but who do not participate in managing the firm, and who are liable only to the extent of their financial contributions.

A partnership is dissolved by the death or withdrawal of one of the partners. Although it can be reestablished by the agreement of the remaining partners, other partners may use the occasion to leave the partnership, perhaps because they must find the funds to purchase part of the share held by the deceased or withdrawing partner. This uncertainty in a partnership's lifespan can be a serious disadvantage to a successful, growing firm which needs permanence for financing and for holding skilled employees.

Corporations

A corporation is distinguished from a proprietorship or a partnership by two main features: it has *limited liability* and is a *separate legal entity.*

Limited Liability. *Limited liability means that persons who own part of a company are financially liable only for the particular share of the firm's assets they own.* Creditors of an incorporated firm cannot make claims beyond this on the personal and other business assets of individual owners should a firm be unable to meet its obligations. This feature has made it possible for corporations to raise substantial sums by offering small shares to a large number of individuals.

Some firms, however, have used the limited liability feature not to raise funds but to limit the liability of the few owners. These are the private companies whose shares are not offered to the general public. Even if shares are sold privately, the directors can refuse to acknowledge the transfer of ownership. Many family businesses have been limited private corporations in the past, but these are gradually "going public" as the need arises to raise more financing to maintain or expand the business. One of the largest private corporations in Canada, for example, is the T. Eaton Co. Ltd.

Separate Legal Entity. Corporations are created by the granting of a provincial or federal charter which gives them the right to engage in specific business activities as separate legal entities. This means that they have *the same legal rights and responsibilities as an adult human being under civil law regarding property and contracts.* The chief executive officers of a corporation can, however, be prosecuted personally for offenses under the criminal law, even though the actions were taken in the name of the firm. A corporation can be a more permanent form of business than a partnership or a proprietorship, its lifespan being terminated only if it seriously deviates from its stated (albiet broadly worded) purposes or by the decision of its directors. This feature is important in raising funds since owners know that, provided the corporation is soundly managed, they will be able to sell their shares at some future time. Furthermore, specialized or skilled personnel can be more easily attracted because there are reasonable prospects of permanent employment.

Corporation Financing

Corporations obtain financing by issuing shares, selling bonds, or using retained earnings.

Stocks or Shares. A stock certificate is evidence of a share in the ownership of a corporation; the terms stock and share thus are often used interchangeably. Stocks are further classified as common stocks or preferred stocks. *Common stocks* are the basic stocks issued by all corporations. A stockholder receives one vote in the general affairs of the corporation for each common stock held; any individual or group holding 51 per cent of the common stock would therefore be able to control the corporation. In cases where the stock is held by a very large number of persons, control of the corporation can sometimes be gained by holding only 10 to 20 per cent of the stock.

There is no guarantee that a stockholder will obtain the original price of his stock when it is sold or that he will receive any return on this asset, but any profits the corporation may realize and decide to distribute are paid out as dividends in proportion to the number of stocks held.

Preferred stocks also represent ownership in the corporation, but the holder of preferred stock surrenders voting rights in exchange for "preferences": a stated annual rate of return on the face value of the share; the guarantee that this dividend will be paid before dividends are paid on common stocks; and a prior claim against the corporation's assets should it be dissolved. Although the preferred stock carries a stated rate of return (usually 5 to 7 per cent), this payment does not need to be made if there is insufficient profit. Preferred stock therefore sometimes has additional features: a *cumulative* preferred stock, for example, provides for the cumulation of stated dividends until profits are large enough to meet these accumulated obligations.

Corporate Bonds. Corporate bonds differ substantially from stocks in that the amount of the bond must be repaid on or before the stated maturity date; interest payments generally must be made annually unless alternative provisions are made. The bond holder thus is a creditor rather than a part-owner of the corporation and, as such, has a prior claim on the corporation's assets in the event of dissolution.

Internal Financing. The increasing size of corporations, which is usually accompanied by a greater total profit, has made it possible for more corporations to meet their financing needs internally. When expansion or alterations are planned, the directors may decide not to pay dividends and to retain the net profits or earnings for reinvestment in the corporation. *Retained earnings* provide a major financial source for many corporations; and although dividends are less than they would be otherwise, retained earnings increase the value of the common stock. Another internal source is the *depreciation allowance* which is set aside each year to provide for the replacement of plant and equipment. Finally, both retained earnings and depreciation allowances may be used to acquire assets such as government bonds or stocks of other companies; the annual income from these supplements the other two sources.

Ownership and Control of Corporations

The separation of ownership and control of corporations has become a popular theme in the criticism of corporations. Reference has already been made in the previous chapter to Galbraith's description of the managerial "technostructure" which gains control of large corporations to pursue its own objectives. This situation arises when shares are widely held; individual investors each hold perhaps only a few hundred shares of possibly three or four million common shares issued. These small shareholders seldom are familiar with the detailed affairs of the corporation and choose not to spend the time or money to travel to the annual meetings. The managers, many of whom likely are also directors, can therefore easily persuade such shareholders to vote by proxy, assigning these votes to the controlling group.

When management holds control in this way, they may become less concerned with profits as such because they can vote themselves larger salaries, bonuses, and other benefits. Regaining control for other shareholders can be extremely difficult in such circumstances; dramatic "proxy battles" have been fought between incumbent managers and directors and other groups wanting to gain control. An interesting recent development, however, has been the use of annual shareholders' meetings to press policy changes on management. Persons holding perhaps only one or two shares have, through the skillful use of news media, been able to call attention to what is deemed to be the corporation's neglect of specific social and political responsibilities.

Holding Companies

The possibility of maintaining control of a corporation by holding only a small percentage of the stock has stimulated the rise of *holding companies* and *conglomerates*. These are corporations which produce no goods or services but are established explicitly for the purpose of holding stock in other companies. A pyramidal structure of corporations can be built up by holding perhaps 40 per cent of the stock in a company which holds controlling interest in two or three other companies, each of which hold controlling interest in a number of other companies. Thus by investing $1 million in the company at the top of the pyramid, it is possible to control companies whose assets total $100 million or more. Two of the largest holding companies in Canada are Argus Corporation and Power Corporation.

Public Corporations

Crown corporations, or public corporations, enable governments to be directly involved in the provision of goods and services, without subjecting this activity to day-to-day politics. Several crown "corporations" actually are not incorporated; they were created directly by an act of Parliament. Some of them are not far removed from government, since they are *responsible for administrative or supervisory functions comparable to government departments* and draw all of their operating revenue from government budgets. Examples of such corporations at the federal level include the National Research Council, the Atomic Energy Control Board, and the Unemployment Insurance Commission.

Other crown corporations are *responsible for the production or trading of goods and services* and are expected to earn substantial revenues from these activities. Any deficit, however, is provided from government budgets. Examples of these are the Crown Assets Disposal Corporation, the Northern Canada Power Commission, and Atomic Energy of Canada.

A third group of crown corporations are those which are responsible to Parliament or a provincial legislature but which are *expected to cover all costs from operating revenues*. These include, for example, the provincial hydro-electric power commissions, the Canadian National Railways, Polymer Corporation Limited, and Air Canada.

Cooperatives

A cooperative is a unique form of corporation, retaining several of the partnership's features, established by a society of individuals to buy or sell commodities cooperatively, according to a set of principles governing their organization. The cooperative movement originated with a retail store in Rochdale, England, in 1844; the principles governing cooperatives are still commonly referred to as the "Rochdale principles". A similar cooperative store was first established in Canada in 1861. Later, the Antigonish Movement helped Maritimes fishermen start their own cooperatives for selling fish. In the Prairie provinces, grain cooperatives have been an important feature of the social and political as well as economic life of the communities.

There are two basic types of cooperatives: *producer cooperatives* which sell their members' products, and *consumer cooperatives* which buy goods from wholesalers for retailing to their members or which provide financial services such as insurance and loans.

Principles governing most cooperatives include the following:

- Each member has one vote, regardless of the number of shares he holds in the cooperative, to maintain democratic control of the society.

- Each member receives a fixed rate of return on his capital contribution to the society because the society is not intended as a means for increasing one's unearned income.
- Net earnings or profits are returned to the members in proportion to the purchases made or produce delivered by each member, so that members will be encouraged to use the society.

The major advantage of the cooperative is that it can obtain for individuals the benefits of large-scale selling or buying. The growth of some cooperatives has been restricted because, unable to issue shares or bonds as other corporations do, they have found it difficult to raise capital; competition with giant retail chains is increasingly difficult; and management must be able to deal with the democracy of control by the membership:

Nonetheless, cooperatives have a significant role in some sectors of the economy. Approximately one-third of all agricultural products marketed in Canada are sold through producer cooperatives, mainly the grain cooperatives in the prairies. The credit unions and *caisses populaires* in Quebec account for over 10 per cent of all consumer credit.

B.   Public Policy for Industrial Organization

Among other objectives, public policy for industrial organization is concerned with attaining and supporting an industrial structure which will foster the increased efficiency in resource use and the greater total consumer satisfaction that is expected to follow from increased competition. The conditions necessary for an optimal industrial structure, however, are widely considered to be unattainable, if only because the path of technological development appears to be leading the economy further from the basic features of pure competition. Some economists have therefore proposed a modified guide for public policy on industrial organization. This is intended to create what is termed "workable competition" or "effective competition".[2]

Desirable conditions for "workable competition" include a market structure with at least two buyers and two sellers, but preferably more; a mixture of large and small firms; no collusion or coercion among sellers; as much market information as can possibly be made available to buyers and sellers; and no barriers to entry and

---

[2] J. M. Clark, "Toward a Concept of Workable Competition," *American Economic Review*, Vol. XXX, June 1940, pp. 241-56; and J. M. Clark, *Competition as a Dynamic Process*. Washington, D.C.: The Brookings Institution, 1961.

exit. These conditions suggest a blend of oligopoly and monopolistic competition with a leaning toward the latter.

Some existing conditions also contribute to greater competition. These include: the universal competition of producers for the limited incomes of consumers, such that producers of a wide variety of household appliances and furniture are effectively in competition with each other; the high degree of substitutability that exists for many products (aluminum can be substituted for steel or wood in many cases); the rapid pace of invention and innovation, which makes it difficult to maintain monopoly power; and finally, public policy for strengthening competition, which makes firms cautious about assuming control of markets.

Public policy for industrial organization has emerged slowly, uncertain of how to define competition and wavering under strong, persistent arguments that some industries should have only a few sellers. Different policies have been designed to meet different types of problems: policies for monopoly and oligopoly, for the support of existing competition in agriculture, for the protection of consumers by setting standards for products and conduct, and most recently, for Canadian ownership and control of industry.

Public Policy for Monopoly and Oligopoly

Public policy for monopoly and oligopoly has taken three major forms: *anticombines legislation* to prevent reduction of competition; and *public ownership* or *regulatory agencies* to control or set prices for "natural monopolies". These are industries in which the existence of more than one or two firms would waste resources and increase prices.

Maintaining Competition Through Anti-combines Legislation

Anticombines legislation in Canada is consolidated in the Combines Investigation Act. Its purpose is to prevent firms from taking actions which would "unduly lessen competition". Legislation against such restriction of trade was first passed in 1889 and has been modified by new acts or amendments on six subsequent occasions. Despite these revisions, the anti-combines law remains largely ineffective, partly because the Act fails to define what is meant by *unduly* lessening competition. Moreover, the Act exempts the increasingly important service industries such as financial institutions, real estate brokers, and consulting firms. It has also been suggested that the federal government wants to have the minimum legislation necessary to show the public that it is opposed to monopoly, without incurring the disfavour of the business community.

Three general types of activity are forbidden by the Combines Investigation Act: agreements between supplies that would unduly restrict competition; mergers and the formation of monopolies; and a number of restrictive trade practices.

Agreements. The Act forbids suppliers to make agreements which unduly restrict entry into an industry, to fix prices, or to limit production or distribution of goods. Nevertheless, firms are still permitted to make agreements on the exchange of statistics and credit information, definitions of product standards, cooperation in research and development, and restriction of advertising, provided that these do not unduly restrict competition. Since "unduly" is undefined in the Act, the courts have interpreted this to mean that a substantial part of the market (80 to 90 percent) must be affected by the agreement.

This section of the Act also exempts agreements relating to the export of Canadian-produced goods, provided that neither entry into export markets nor domestic market competition is restricted, in recognition that such agreements may make economies of scale possible and hence improve Canadian competition in world markets.

Mergers and Monopolies. The Act also prohibits mergers and the formation of monopolies harmful to the public interest. A *merger* is the acquisition of any control over or interest in the whole or part of a competitor's business, or the control of markets or sources of supply, that has the effect of lessening competition to the detriment of the public interest. A *monopoly* is a situation where one business controls all, or a substantial part, of a particular trade or industry and is likely to operate against the public interest.

Restrictive Trade Practices. A number of restrictive trade practices are made illegal by the Act: price discrimination, loss-leaders ("predatory price cutting"), misleading price advertising, and resale price maintenance. A supplier may not sell at different prices to different buyers who are buying similar quality and quantity; may not sell at lower prices in some localities than in others, or at unreasonably low prices anywhere in order to eliminate a competitor; and may not misrepresent the price of his goods in advertising, especially regarding the "regular" price of the good. Finally, a supplier may not practise resale price maintenance: setting a specific price at which wholesalers or retailers are to sell the good.

Note that Canadian anti-combines legislation makes no reference to *existing* monopolies or industries which are highly concentrated due to earlier mergers. In this regard, the Canadian law is even more limited in its effect than the American antitrust legislation which deals with existing concentration as well as new mergers.

Effectiveness of Anti-combines Legislation

The Combines Investigation Act is administered by the federal Department of Consumer and Corporate Affairs. The Director of the Investigation and Research Branch is responsible for investigating complaints, which may be brought by any six citizens. If the Director finds reasonable evidence of a violation of the Act this is reported to the Restrictive Trade Practices Commission. When the Commission has heard the evidence, including the defendent's statements, the Commission reports to the Minister of Consumer and Corporate Affairs. The Attorney General reviews this report and determines whether legal proceedings should begin. If it appears that there is sufficient evidence of a violation, the case is taken to the Federal Court.

If the court determines that a violation has occurred, a number of penalties are available; imposition of fines or a prison sentence with a maximum of two years; a court order to cease and desist from the illegal practices, or to have the company dissolved in favour of a number of smaller companies; or protective patents, trade marks, or tariffs may be revoked. It is often argued, however, that the adverse publicity of the Commission's report and court hearing are sufficient deterrent to potential violators.

Canada's anti-combines legislation has been largely ineffective, not only for the reasons given previously, but also because the Director has not had sufficient staff to investigate thoroughly what are necessarily complex situations. Moreover, the nature of the violations makes it difficult to establish proof: agreements generally are verbal and that a situation appears to be the outcome of collusion is seldom acceptable evidence. The courts have also refused to consider evidence based on the *economic performance* of firms. One result of this has been that only two merger cases have been taken to court and in each case the defendant was acquitted. Because the Combines Investigation Act is based on criminal law, the courts are concerned with proving that a criminal act has occurred beyond a reasonable doubt.[3] This legal attitude to dealing with what is generally considered an economic problem (apart, perhaps, from such offences as price-fixing) has led to the proposal that a commission concerned with the economic consequences of restrictive practices should replace the courts' responsibility for determining violations:

> ... there would seem to be a valid argument for a less legalistic and a more economic-commission approach to deal with some questions such as mergers. For example, one might want greater justification (unit-cost

---

[3] The Act has been treated as a matter of criminal law because other bases for such federal legislation have been declared *ultra vires*, or unconstitutional, in light of Section 92 of the British North American Act which gives provinces jurisdiction over civil and property rights within a province.

reductions) for a merger in circumstances of high concentration. In some cases, lower costs from a merger might outweigh the anti-competitive potential. The net effect of commission decisions could well be less merger activity in some industries and more in others.[4]

A New Competition Policy?

The extensive and long-standing criticisms of the Combines Investigation Act led the federal government in 1971 to introduce a proposed Competition Act to replace the anti-combines legislation. The proposed Act would have widened the list of prohibited agreements, further reduced the possibility of mergers and price discrimination, established regulations for fee schedules of several service industries, and introduced a Competitive Practices Tribunal, in place of the criminal or civil courts, to render judgments on alleged violations of the Act. However, the proposed Act was so strongly criticized by business, labour, and consumer groups that the government withdrew the draft legislation for further consideration. The government decided to take a two-pronged approach to competition policy: consumer-oriented provisions such as misleading advertising would be separated from provisions dealing with monopolies and mergers. The former were included in a government bill proposed in late 1973 but this was also withdrawn under strong opposition. In late 1975, however, Parliament passed the first half of a bill to amend the Combines Investigation Act; these amendments banned pyramid selling, "bait and switch" selling, re-pricing goods in stock, and misleading advertising. Several service industries were also brought within the provisions of the Act.

The second half of the proposed legislation, relating to monopolies and mergers may be delayed pending a report from the royal commission that was appointed in 1975 to investigate the concentration of corporate power in Canada.

Public Control of Natural Monopolies

In a few industries, a firm's optimum size is so large relative to the market size that only one or two firms can operate efficiently. Such industries are termed *natural monopolies*. Common examples include those providing electricity, natural gas, telephone communication, railroad and local bus transportation. These industries are similar, not only in that economies of scale can often be realized even at quantities larger than the market would buy at low prices, but also in that they are *public utilities*: they provide energy, transportation, or communication used by large numbers of the population. If several firms were in competition in each industry consum-

---

[4] Max D. Stewart, "Industrial Organization," in L. H. Officer and L. B. Smith (eds.) *Canadian Economic Problems and Policies*. Toronto: McGraw-Hill, 1970.

ers might find the service both more expensive and less satisfactory — especially if railway transportation entailed coordinating different timetables; or reaching a telephone subscriber of a different firm required making the connection through a central agency; or competitive ferries at a popular crossing had a record of frequent collisions.

Although the one or two firms in such industries may have the potential to make more efficient use of resources by producing at the lower average costs of large scale, their profit-maximizing quantity may be at a point where average costs are still quite high. In any case, their services will be priced well above marginal cost; this difference will be greater the fewer close substitutes there are for the service provided.

Public policy for natural monopolies therefore involves some means of setting the price, and sometimes the output, for such industries. Two means have been used: *regulatory agencies* which determine prices for specific industries, and *public ownership of the industry*. In either case, the analytical principles for specifying a price are the same.

Figure 12.1 shows the hypothetical revenue and cost conditions for a natural monopoly. The long-run average total cost curve, *LRATC*, is decreasing throughout, reflecting continuing economies of scale. If there were a number of firms in the industry and there were no restriction on entry, or if public policy required breaking up natural monopolies into several small firms, each might be producing approximately quantity OQ_1 for sale at price OP_1. Governments therefore reject this approach and decide to set the price instead. But what should that price be?

The profit-maximizing quantity, and thus the quantity that would be produced in the absence of public regulation, is OQ_2: the quantity at which $MR = LRMC$. This quantity would be sold at price OP_2, which in this particular case is an even higher price than would occur with a large number of inefficient firms.

A public agency might decide that the monopoly should produce where price is equal to marginal cost, since this is the criterion for the optimum allocation of resources. At such a quantity, OQ_4, the monopoly would incur a loss because its average revenue is less than its average total cost. (In the unlikely case that the *LRATC* curve had reached a minimum to the left of OQ_3, marginal cost would be above *LRATC* at OQ_3 and a price equal to marginal cost would enable the monopoly to make some pure profit). Since marginal-cost pricing would usually cause the monopoly firm to go out of business, public policy requires instead that price be set which will give the firm a "fair return". Although this is a difficult concept to define operationally, the fact that the average total cost includes the cost of a normal profit suggests that pricing at average total cost will provide the firm with just enough profit to keep it in business. This would entail producing quantity OQ_3, to be sold at price OP_3.

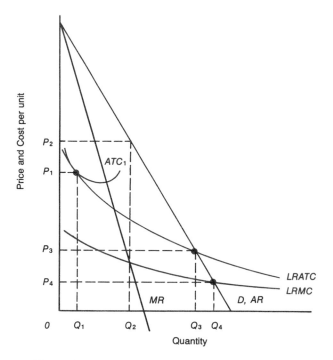

Figure 12.1   Alternative Prices Under Natural Monopoly
A natural monopoly is an industry with extremely large economies of scale: the
LRATC is decreasing throughout the relevant output range. If several firms were
operating in this industry, the output of each, OQ_1, would be sold at a high price,
OP_1, even though no profit is realized. A monopoly firm would produce OQ_2, to be
sold at a still higher price, OP_2. If a regulatory agency were to set the price equal to
marginal cost, OQ_4 would be the quantity that could be sold at OP_4 but the firm
would have a loss equal to the difference between *LRATC* and *AR* at OQ_4. Hence
the agency is likely to set the price at OP_3; at the related output level, OQ_3, the firm
realizes only a normal profit since *AR* equals *LRATC*.

Regulatory Agencies

One approach to implementing public price regulation of
natural monopolies is to appoint a regulatory agency. Boards or
commissions are established by governments for each industry or
utility concerned. These may be appointed by federal, provincial, or
municipal governments in accordance with the scope of the market
served by a particular utility. Any of these agencies, however, faces
the same general problems in setting prices: What is a fair return?
How should the firm's assets be valued in determining a base for
calculations of a fair return? Are the firm's statements of costs
reasonable? Additional problems are also faced by regulatory agencies: Is there a place for more firms in the industry? What are the
relative merits of allowing a utility to discontinue part of its service,

rather than raising the price for all service, to maintain a fair rate of return?

What is a fair return? Setting prices which will enable a firm to realize a fair rate of return on its physical and financial assets has been the traditional principle of public price regulation, but "a fair rate" remains undefined. Economic principles suggest that this should be the opportunity cost of the assets, or the rate that could be earned in another industry, allowing for the higher risk usually found in industries other than public utilities. Regulatory agencies pay some attention to this principle to the extent that they consider the average rate of return for the whole economy. "Fair rates" have thus been defined as about 6 to 9 per cent, with the higher level more common in recent years. When prices reflecting this rate are set, there is, of course, no guarantee that the rate will be realized. Demand and cost conditions may change following the agency's decision. Any actual variation from this rate is therefore taken into account when prices are set in the subsequent period.

What is a fair assets value? The set rate of return is related to the value of the firm's assets to determine what the total revenue should be, and thus what the price should be. Estimating a fair value for these assets raises a controversial issue: should assets be valued at *original cost* or *replacement cost*? The original cost approach gives a more accurate statement of actual costs of land, buildings, and equipment, but does not include enhanced value due to inflation. Depreciation must be deducted but this can be calculated several different ways. Replacement costs, however, require arbitrary estimates which may provoke much dispute in price-setting deliberations. The higher the value of assets, the higher the total dollar return will be for any given rate. Regulated monopolies also lack incentive to restrain their spending for plant and equipment; regulatory agencies must therefore also assure that all such expenditures are necessary.

Are costs reasonable? This approach to price-setting is essentially a matter of adding a fair profit to the firm's costs. A regulatory agency thus is watching for exaggerated cost statements and unnecessary expenditures. Cases of inefficiency or waste are not easily identified and proved; regulated monopolies therefore also lack incentives to control their operating costs.

Other Problems. In examining the cost data of regulated monopolies, boards or commissions will also question whether another firm could enter the industry without seriously reducing the economies of scale realized by existing firms. The possibility of such expansion arises when demand for the service is increasing quickly. For example, boards are required to decide whether a particular air route should be served by one, two, or more airlines, and whether new firms should be added to the television-broadcasting industry.

Secondly, regulated monopolies such as the railways sometimes request permission to discontinue services in an area which is unprofitable, as an alternative to setting higher prices for all services. The regulatory agency faces the difficult task of weighing the social benefits of maintaining the service against the additional cost to be borne by all users of the service.

Regulatory Agencies in Canada

Regulatory agencies are used principally at the federal level; municipalities and provinces have tended to adopt the public ownership approach to natural monopolies. The three major federal agencies are the Canadian Transport Commission, the Canadian Radio-Television Commission, and the National Energy Board.

Canadian Transport Commission. The Canadian Transport Commission was established in 1967 to consolidate several agencies that had regulated different types of transportation. These became Commission committees: the Railway Transport Committee regulates railway services (but no longer the rates), express, telegraph, and telephone communication, and tolls on international bridges and tunnels; the Air Transport Committee licenses and sets rates for commercial air services; the Water Transport Committee licenses and sets rates for commercial shipping on inland waterways, with the important exception of the bulk carriers which constitute much of the Great Lakes shipping; the Motor Vehicle Committee regulates interprovincial commercial trucking and all international motor vehicle transportation; and the Commodity Pipeline Committee licenses interprovincial and international pipelines and sets pipeline rates. The Commission is required by previous legislation to maintain special rates on railway freight transportation for the Maritime provinces under the Maritime Freight Rates Act, and on grain shipping in the west under the Crow's Nest Pass Agreement.

Canadian Radio-Television Commission. All broadcasting in Canada comes under the regulation of the Canadian Radio-Television Commission. This agency regulates the number of firms or stations which can broadcast in each area, their programming, and the proportion of advertising time. It also regulates the cable-television industry by establishing rates and the areas to be served by each firm.

National Energy Board. Responsibility for oil and gas pipelines is shared by the National Energy Board and the Pipeline Committee of the Canadian Transport Commission. They regulate the construction and operation of such pipelines and set the rates or tolls. The National Energy Board also regulates the export and import of electricity.

Public Ownership of Natural Monopolies

In some cases, public ownership of natural monopolies has been favoured not only because of the problems associated with regulatory agencies but also because outright public ownership seemed preferable to the operating subsidies and public capital financing that appeared necessary for some regulated agencies. For example, the federal government amalgamated several railways to form Canadian National Railways, and created Air Canada, which was originally a division of the CNR. Similarly, some provinces have owned hydro-electric power systems since they were established.

Public ownership has two basic advantages. First, since the commission responsible for operating the utility has a direct knowledge of its production costs, it should be able to control them more effectively than can regulatory agencies. This also makes it possible to pursue a "break even" policy, rather than a "fair returns" policy. Second, the commission can take more direct account of the social benefits of its services. This may mean, for example in the case of urban public transit, that the utility should be permitted a deficit to be subsidized from tax revenues. Such a utility thus becomes another municipal service like parks, sewers, and fire protection. A publicly owned utility should be able to take positive action to serve the public interest, whereas a regulatory agency can only prevent a utility from acting contrary to the public interest.

Most urban public transit systems, and water and electricity utilities, are municipally owned. Provincial electricity utilities (which sell power to the municipal systems) are also under public ownership, as are the provincial telephone systems in the Prairie provinces.

Public Support for Restricted Competition

Governments are pressed by consumers and small businesses to legislate against monopolistic practices and decreasing competition. But there is also pressure from other groups to support restricted competition. The latter may take the form of public licensing and chartering to restrict entry, issuing patents for the production of specific items, and even includes governments' own monopolizing of an industry.

Public Monopolies for Non-Economic Reasons. Governments have extended public ownership to some cases which cannot be justified by economies of scale. One common example is the liquor control boards established by the different provinces to be responsible for liquor retailing. The result is a standard price for liquors and wines, by contrast with the experience in several American states of intense price competition and a wider product variety. Provincial governments apparently maintain ownership of liquor retail stores because it is a highly profitable enterprise.

Licensing and Chartering. A major industry to which entry is severely restricted is *commercial banking.* The restriction arises not only because a federal government charter is required to establish a bank in Canada, but also because for a long time no such charters were issued. This enabled existing banks to become so large, including growth due to mergers, that potential entrants were discouraged. The result is a typical oligopoly with almost undifferentiated products or services, where banks rely on nonprice competition — establishing new branches in every new shopping centre, and emphasizing their helpfulness, concern with people, and so on — while deposit and loan rates remain virtually uniform among banks.

Provincial and municipal governments license a number of *occupations* ranging from medicine, dentistry, law, and engineering, through plumbing, electrical, and plastering trades, to undertaking and barbering. Legislation protecting these occupations usually allows the municipality to restrict the number licensed, or allows the occupational association itself to restrict the number of entrants or to raise standards frequently enough to maintain the desired numbers. Some professional associations are also allowed to set their own fee schedules. Licensing of this kind is usually said to be in the public interest to the extent that the public is protected from unsatisfactory service or workmanship. However, prices are higher than if there were unrestricted entry and there is a possibility that the service is worse, especially when an excess demand for such services means the public must accept unsatisfactory work or go without.

Taxis are also licensed by most municipalities. Some cases present the appearance of a natural monopoly because only one or two firms are operating in a city. That this is unnecessary is shown in other cases where several taxi firms are operating, whether in small towns or large cities. The effect of taxi licensing is to create a substantial financial asset for the existing operators: taxi "plates" are said to be worth several thousand dollars in major metropolitan markets. Again, licensing is defended as being "in the public interest", but the public interest probably would be better served simply by setting minimum standards for taxi operation rather than by fixing the number to be licensed.

Patents. Patents constitute legal support for restricted entry without public regulation of the consequences. A patent grants its holder the exclusive right to produce a specific item without direct competition for 17 years. The purpose of the patent law is to encourage the invention of new products and processes. Although this purpose obviously has been served, other undesirable consequences have followed. Firms have been able to extend their protected period by patenting "improvements" on the original item. Some large firms have patented what appears to be every possible aspect of their particular technology. Several years ago, for example, the International Business Machine Corporation acquired patents on all aspects of tabulating machinery, hired most of the known inventors in the field, and harrassed competitors by charging them with patent infringements. Finally, IBM was forced by threat of legal proceedings to make some of its patents available on a royalty basis.

Other governmental support for restricted competition has been discussed previously, including exemption of service industries from anti-combines legislation, and tariffs which protect domestic firms from foreign competition.

Public Support for Existing Competition: Agriculture

Public policies supporting agriculture are directed toward several dimensions of the "farm problem" in Canada.[5] Such policies are intended as much to raise the low average incomes of farmers as they are to encourage competition in the agricultural industry and protect it from the consequences of dealing with other less-competitive industries. These two goals were described by a federal task force on agriculture as "the basic conflict in agricultural policy, a cheap food policy together with a small farm maintenance policy." The following analysis of the farm problem and related public policies could have properly appeared in Chapter 15, along with the examination of income distribution and proverty in Canada; in fact, a full treatment of the puverty problem is not possible without including the agricultural sector.

Major Conditions Facing the Agricultural Industry

The major feature of the agricultural industry is the *large number of producers*. In 1971, there were about 258,000 commercial farms in Canada; such farms have been defined in the census as having at least one acre and annual cash sales of $2,500 or more. These of course include farmers producing diverse products — milk, beef, horticultural products, poultry and eggs, hogs, and so on — but the number nevertheless far exceeds, for example, the number of firms in the retail trade, which is also characterized by many small establishments.

Second, the *price elasticity of demand for farm products in Canadian markets is quite low*, although many individual producers

---

[5] For an excellent presentation of the farm problem in Canada, see D. R. Campbell, "The Farm Problem" in L. H. Officer and L. B. Smith, *Canadian Economic Problems and Policies*. Toronto: McGraw-Hill, 1970, pp. 194-209.

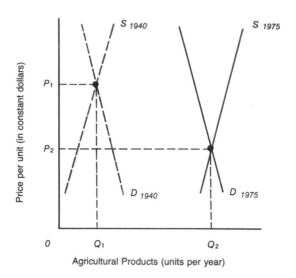

Figure 12.2   Decline in Relative Prices of Agricultural Products
The prices of agricultural products have declined relative to prices of other commodities in the past three decades because improved agricultural productivity has increased supply proportionately more than the increase in demand, and because the demand for agricultural products in general is inelastic.

face the almost perfectly elastic demand curve typical of pure competition. The low market elasticity results in a substantial price reduction, with a decreased total revenue, if output is increased when there is no change in demand. The third major feature is that *supply curves for agricultural products have shifted outward rather quickly* with postwar improvements in agricultural productivity. Because agriculture is such a competitive industry, farmers who do not adopt new techniques, varieties, breeds, or machinery are not able to break even and are forced out of the industry. Those who remain receive lower prices and lower total revenues, as illustrated in Figure 12.2.

The rapid increase in supply has not been matched by a similar increase in demand. The latter is influenced mainly by population and per capita real incomes but Canada's population has grown by only about 2 per cent annually, and much of the increase in per capita incomes allocated to food has been for more food preparation and processing rather than more agricultural products. In high-income countries the income elasticity of demand for food tends to be quite low. The result, as shown in Figure 12.2, is that agricultural prices have fallen *relative* to prices for most other commodities during the postwar period. Occasionally, as in 1951 and 1973-74, farm prices may rise quite rapidly but the gains in real net farm income in these years are more than offset by the long-run decline.

Short-run supply conditions also complicate the problem: *weather and disease can substantially alter output from year to year.* When output is unusually low, prices and total revenue will rise, but frequently this additional income is used to purchase machinery or make repairs that were postponed from previous years. Few farmers are able to save substantial amounts as protection against the bad years. Good weather and larger harvests usually result in lower prices and incomes.

About 20 to 25 per cent of Canada's agricultural products are exported, but they must compete with highly subsidized farm produce in many countries; some foreign governments both subsidize all agricultural production and add a further subsidy for exported agricultural products.

Consequences of Conditions in the Agricultural Industry

There are two major consequences of the conditions described for the agricultural industry: low incomes and unstable incomes.

The low net farm incomes follow mainly from the large number of producers. Since each producer faces a perfectly elastic demand curve (except where output is limited by quotas, as for fluid milk, eggs, and tobacco), he usually produces as much as he can with his fixed assets of land and buildings. With each farmer doing this, the market quantity is usually in the inelastic portion of the market demand curve. This is shown as quantity OQ_2 in Figure 12.3. The industry supply curve is also its marginal cost curve. Hence, if the

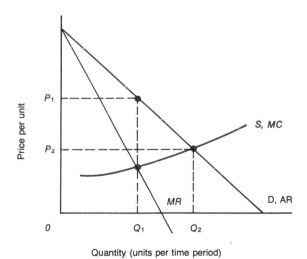

Figure 12.3 *Competition in Agriculture Leads to Lower Farm Incomes*
If a monopoly faced the revenue and cost curves shown here, it would produce OQ_1, to be sold at price OP_1. Competition in the production of most agricultural products results in the production of OQ_2, to be sold at OP_2. Although competition increases consumer surplus, it lowers net farm incomes below what they would be in less competitive conditions unless producers cooperate as monopolistic selling agencies.

industry were a monopoly or an oligopoly, the profit-maximizing output would be determined as OQ_1 (where MC equals MR) and the price would be OP_1. Although marginal cost pricing is desirable for consumers, it results in lower prices and incomes for the more competitive industries such as agriculture.

A further problem arises because producers have tended to plan future production in response to previous prices. The result is instability of farm incomes. Economists have termed this phenomenon the "hog cycle" because it has been prominent in hog production,[6] or the "cobweb theorem" because its diagrammatic explanation resembles a cobweb — as Figure 12.4 may suggest. Suppose the equilibrium price for hogs has been OP_1 with quantity OQ_1 produced. A short-run increase in supply (perhaps due to improved feed) results in a new supply curve, S_1S_1. In the following production period, there is a greater quantity, OQ_2, produced in response to the previous price. The price of hogs then falls to OP_2. Producers

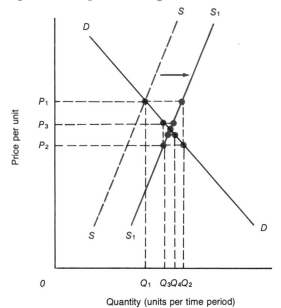

Figure 12.4   The Cobweb Theorem of Income Instability
Farm incomes tend to be unstable to the extent that producers determine the quantity to be supplied in the next period on the basis of current prices. Suppose a market is in equilibrium at OP_1. A shift in supply, to S_1S_1, leads producers to offer OQ_2 with the expectation of price OP_1. But OQ_2 is sold at OP_2. Producers therefore plan to offer only OQ_3; this raises the price to OP_3. Given DD and S_1S_1, this cyclical pattern would lead to a new equilibrium price, but another shift in either demand or supply would start the cyclical process again.

---

[6] For example, the output of hogs in Canada increased in 1967 by 18 per cent over the previous year, remained constant in 1968, declined by 5 per cent in 1969, and then increased again by 18 per cent in 1970.

therefore decide to reduce output to OQ_3, but this increases the price to OP_3. The response to this is quantity OQ_4, and on it goes until the market is in equilibrium again, but at a lower price and larger quantity than before. Meanwhile, of course, either supply or demand, or both, may have shifted, setting off a new cycle of quantity responses to price changes. Since the demand for hogs is assumed to be inelastic, the price increases result in higher incomes; the price decreases produce lower incomes. The outcome is unstable farm incomes.

Public Assistance for Agriculture

Several types of government programs provide public assistance for agriculture. These can be classified as programs to maintain higher, more stable incomes through price supports; to decrease or subsidize production costs; to improve prices through more effective marketing; and to assist in the reallocation of resources within agriculture, or from agriculture to other uses.

Price Support Programs

Often confused with subsidy programs, price support programs consist of a government guarantee that the producer will receive a specific minimum price per unit for his product. If the market price is higher than the guaranteed price, no government payment is made. A subsidy, however, is a payment of a specific amount per unit produced; payment is therefore made regardless of the market price.[7]

The federal government's price support program is conducted under the Agricultural Stabilization Act of 1958. This Act provides for an Agricultural Stabilization Board to set support prices for three produce categories: cattle, hogs, and sheep; butter, cheese, and eggs;[8] corn and soybeans; and oats and barley grown outside the Prairie provinces. The support price must be at least 90 per cent of the previous 5-year weighted average price for each product, but may be higher than this. The Board may recommend to the federal cabinet that support prices be established for a number of other agricultural products, and it may also authorize subsidy payments. Two types of price support may be used: an *offer-to-purchase* produce not sold in the market when the price is set at the guaranteed minimum, and a *deficiency payment* or a payment of the difference between the free-market price and the guaranteed price.

---

[7] The general case of floor prices and subsidies is presented toward the end of Chapter 2.

[8] Price support programs for butter and cheese (and dry skim milk) have been administered by the Canadian Dairy Commission since 1967; and egg production and prices have been the responsibility of the Canadian Egg Marketing Agency since 1972.

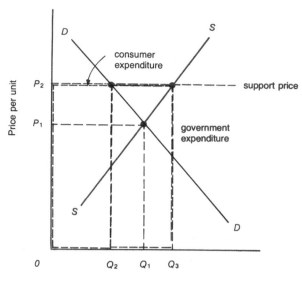

Figure 12.5   Offer-To-Purchase Method
Under the offer-to-purchase method for supporting agricultural prices, the government announces a floor price, OP_2. Producers supply OQ_3 at the floor price, but
consumers buy only OQ_2. The government purchases the balance, $OQ_3 - OQ_2$. If
the equilibrium price and output prior to the floor price were OP_1, and OQ_1, farmers
receive a greater revenue, but consumers pay a higher price and enjoy a lower
quantity and less consumer surplus.

Offer-to-Purchase Method. Under the offer-to-purchase method the
government agrees to buy any unsold produce at the support price.
The effect of this scheme is illustrated by Figure 12.5. Suppose the
equilibrium price of butter, for example, is OP_1 and the quantity sold
is OQ_1. A guaranteed price is now set at OP_2. Producers therefore
decide to increase output to OQ_3, but consumers will buy only OQ_2
units at the higher price. The government therefore buys the unsold
butter, the difference between OQ_2 and OQ_3, at a price of OP_2 per
pound.

What can the government do with the butter it has purchased? It
cannot sell the butter in Canada because consumers have bought all
they will take at the floor price. It may be able to sell some butter in
foreign countries provided that this does not violate antidumping
agreements: that is, international agreements that a product will not
be sold abroad at less than the price received at home. Destroying
produce always provokes public criticism, and donating produce to
low-income countries requires further transportation and administration expenditures. Produce such as butter can be stored for a few
months. If the demand curve should shift rightward and/or the supply curve shift leftward until the equilibrium price was above the
guaranteed price, the government could then add its stored butter to

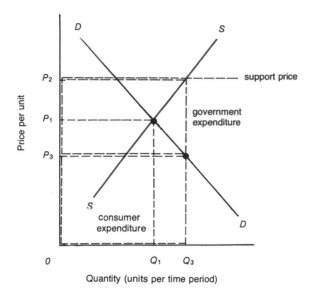

Figure 12.6 Deficiency Payment Method

Under the deficiency payment method of supporting agricultural prices, the government guarantees producers a price of OP_2 per unit. Producers supply OQ_3 units, which are sold in an otherwise free market at OP_3. The government pays producers the difference between OP_2 and OP_3 for OQ_3 units. Consumers pay a lower price than the previous equilibrium price, OP_1, and enjoy a larger quantity, OQ_3, and a larger consumer surplus. Producers' total revenue is OP_2 for OQ_3 units.

the current quantity supplied until the price fell back to the guaranteed price. The probability that this situation will arise within the safe storage period of butter is slight. Moreover, such a support program involves transportation and storage costs in addition to the cost of purchasing the product. Finally, consumers must pay a higher price for a lower quantity of the product. Offer-to-purchase programs therefore are not commonly used. In 1976, offer-to-purchase programs were used only for butter, cheddar cheese, and skim milk powder under the Canadian Dairy Commission's price support program.

Deficiency Payments Method. Under the deficiency payments method for supporting prices, no minimum market price is set. Instead, the government guarantees to pay producers the difference between the national average market price for the product and the support price. Each producer therefore receives the same deficiency payment per unit regardless of the particular market price received for his own produce. The effect of this scheme is shown in Figure 12.6. Assume the same supply and demand curves, equilibrium price and quantity, and guaranteed price, that were used in Figure 12.5. Producers decide to supply quantity OQ_3 at the guaranteed price of OP_2. In this second case, the new market price will be OP_3:

the price at which consumers will buy all of quantity OQ_3. The government payment per unit is the difference between OP_2 and OP_3; this amount is paid for OQ_3 units.

The advantages of the deficiency payments method are that there is no problem of surplus disposal, no additional costs for transportation and storage (although each method has administrative costs), and there is an increased quantity for consumers at a lower price. However, if the demand for the product is inelastic, government payments are higher under a deficiency payments program than under an offer-to-purchase program. Under both programs, using the example illustrated by Figures 12.5 and 12.6, producers receive a total revenue of $OP_2 \times OQ_3$. The portion of this revenue received from consumers is larger under offer-to-purchase due to the inelasticity of demand: total revenue (from consumers) is greater at a higher price. The portion remaining for the government to pay is therefore smaller under the offer-to-purchase method. However, despite the higher government payments required by a deficiency payments program when demand is inelastic, this program is frequently preferred because of its other advantages. Moreover, if demand is elastic, the government payments to producers are lower under the deficiency payments method. Finally, payments can be limited to a specific quantity for each producer, thereby reducing the quantity that will be offered at the support price, and giving proportionately more assistance to the smaller producers.

The deficiency payments method is thus more commonly used by the Agricultural Stabilization Board. This method was in effect in 1975 for hogs, sheep, wool, sugar beets, potatoes, cattle, and Ontario grains.

Production and Transportation Programs

Several agricultural assistance programs are directed to reducing or subsidizing production costs. *Agricultural research* is conducted by the federal and provincial departments of agriculture, with information made available through their publications, demonstration farms, and provincial extension or advisory services. *Loans* are made available to farmers in larger amounts and/or at lower rates than could be obtained normally, under the federal government's Farm Credit Act, Farm Improvement Loans Act, and the Farm Syndicates Credit Act. Some provincial governments also have farm credit legislation. *Tax exemptions* or *rebates* are applicable to some farm items: farmers are eligible for a rebate of the gasoline tax for gasoline used on the farm. No duty is charged on imported farm machinery and most farm supplies.

Subsidies are paid for selected products or specific costs.[9] A

---

[9] See Chapter 2 for an explanation of a subsidy's effect on price and quantity, and the incidence of the benefit.

direct subsidy is paid for milk and cream used in manufacturing butter, cheese and skim milk powder. Subsidies are also paid for the transportation of prairie-grown grains to other provinces, under the Livestock Feed Assistance Act. (Although a subsidy is not paid, prairie-grown grains also benefit from the Crow's Nest Pass Agreement which limits railway freight rates for exported prairie grains to the rates prevailing in 1898). A subsidy is paid to the Canadian Wheat Board to meet the annual cost of storing wheat in excess of 178 billion bushels. The federal government also subsidizes premiums charged under provincial programs for crop insurance.

Marketing Programs

Federal and provincial governments set and administer *grading standards* so that a producer can realize a higher price for high-quality products and so that buyers can have confidence in the uniform quality and size of products.

Marketing boards have been established for almost every agricultural commodity. The Canadian Wheat Board administers a price support program for prairie-grown wheat, oats, and barley by making a guaranteed initial payment to producers. All grain entering into interprovincial or international trade is delivered to and sold by the Wheat Board. Deliveries are based on quotas set by the Board to ration the limited elevator space. All revenue from wheat sales, less operating costs, is distributed to producers such that each producer receives the same price for the same quality delivered to the same terminal.

The federal Farm Products Marketing Agencies Act of 1971 provides for the creation of national marketing agencies for all farm products except those covered by the Canadian Wheat Board and the Canadian Dairy Commission. Under this Act, an egg marketing agency was established to assign quotas to the egg producer's council in each province, based on provincial shares of total egg production between 1967 and 1971. The provincial councils, in turn, assigned quotas to each egg producer.

Provincial marketing boards are established by a vote of the producers of the particular commodity concerned. These boards do not administer price support programs; rather, most boards negotiate with the major buyers, such as food processors, for a minimum price for the commodity. Price differentials for quality differences, and transportation charges may also be negotiated. Some boards have even established processing facilities to compete directly with the major processors. A few provincial boards have also established production or marketing quotas to restrict the total quantity supplied to the market.

The Ontario Tobacco Growers Marketing Board, for example, establishes production "rights", or the right to plant tobacco on a specified number of acres. The effect of this restriction is illustrated

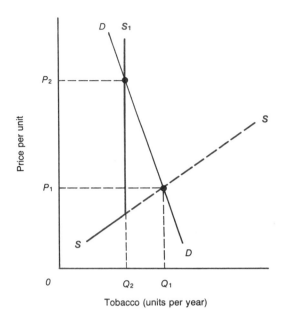

Figure 12.7   Crop Restriction Can Increase Total Revenue
When demand, *DD*, is inelastic, a price increase also increases total revenue. By restricting the quantity of tobacco supplied to OQ_2, tobacco producers can increase the price from its free market level of OP_1 to OP_2, and thus increase the total revenue.

by Figure 12.7. Suppose that in the absence of such restrictions, the equilibrium price is OP_1 and quantity sold is OQ_1. The effect of the restrictive tobacco "rights" is to shift the supply curve leftward and make it perfectly inelastic above its intersection with the former supply curve at quantity OQ_2. The price obtained for quantity OQ_2 is OP_2. Because the demand for tobacco is inelastic (due to the inelastic demand for tobacco products), the total revenue is greater for OQ_2 than for OQ_1. Since tobacco is a more profitable crop than most others, especially when such restrictions are applied, the "rights" increase land values for the owner of an established tobacco farm and cause considerable criticism of this system.

An alternative method of restricting supply is to specify quotas or quantities that each producer is permitted to supply, or for the marketing board itself to withhold part of the total quantity produced. This has the further advantage of controlling the quantity supplied more precisely; when quantity is specified in terms of acres planted, farmers cultivate these acres more intensely to obtain the highest possible yield.

Programs for Resource Reallocation

Programs described in the preceding sections are intended to support farming units which do or could provide a reasonable income for their owners. Some farms however are too small, have land which is too infertile or rugged, or are too far from large markets or transportation facilities, to produce satisfactory incomes even with such assistance programs. The federal government therefore introduced the Agricultural and Rural Development Act (ARDA) in 1961 and the Fund for Rural Economic Development (FRED) in 1966, to assist the reallocation of resources in rural areas. Funds are provided through the small farms development program, for federal-provincial programs for consolidation of farms, shifting land use to other activities such as recreation and tourism, retraining programs for farm owners and labourers, and creating small industries in rural areas.

Effectiveness of Agricultural Assistance Programs

Some of the less expensive programs appear to have been of greatest long-run benefit to Canadian agriculture: research in developing and breeding higher-yielding plants, livestock, and poultry; development of fertilizers, insecticides, and herbicides, and improved production techniques; expansion of information and advisory services, particularly in specialized subjects; and the establishment of marketing boards. Price supports have had some effect in raising farm prices and especially in reducing the instability of farm incomes. There has been rather disappointing progress, however, in dealing with the problem of agricultural surpluses such as wheat, and in coping with the long run causes of rural poverty.

The report of the Federal Task Force on Agriculture, published in 1970, recognized these problems in recommending that farm surpluses be controlled by restricting production and transferring some agricultural lands to other uses; that more emphasis be placed on management training for farmers, supplemented by better market information and forecasts; and that younger farmers in areas or on farms which cannot provide an adequate income by farming alone be provided with retraining and other employment opportunities.

Public Policy for Consumer Protection

In addition to policies directed to different forms of market structure, there are programs or legislation to protect consumers from harmful products and to provide more knowledge of and confidence in consumer products. These are listed briefly to illustrate a number of other ways in which governments regulate business in Canada.

Many of the consumer protection programs are now under the jurisdiction of the federal Department of Consumer and Corporate Affairs, or similar provincial departments. The federal department monitors *advertising messages* to check for illegal or misleading claims: products cannot be described as having certain effects on consumers; other claims that are made must be proven. *Weights* and *volumes* must be specified on packages, and weigh-scales must be checked regularly. *Packages* cannot be misleading: red-and-white-striped packaging for sliced bacon, for example, is forbidden because it can confuse consumers about the proportion of lean meat in the package. *Foods and drugs* are subject to specific legislation to prevent the sale of harmful products and to identify the ingredients of all products. Other products involving consumer safety often, but not yet always, are subject to *safety standards*. It has, for example, taken a number of years to bring children's automobile seats and harnesses under a specified safety standard. Similarly, more safety devices have recently been required for new automobiles.

Furthermore, there are many laws and regulations which have universal application, and which therefore affect the performance of firms. These include, for example, laws concerning environmental protection or waste disposal, housing or buildings standards, land-use zoning, and legislation forbidding discrimination by employers against race, colour, religion, sex, and age.

Foreign Ownership and Control in Canadian Industry

Perhaps the most popular current issue in the Canadian economy concerns foreign ownership and control in Canadian industry. Ownership and control, however, are not synonymous. Ownership of 51 per cent of a corporation's common stock is nominally required to control the firm's affairs, but when shares are held by many people, a smaller percentage may be sufficient. Each of these issues requires separate consideration in examining the foreign ownership and control question. For simplicity, however, this section will use only the term, foreign ownership, unless specific reference to control is necessary.

Table 12.5 summarizes some of the available information on foreign ownership in Canadian industry. Regrettably, no aggregative data are available on actual foreign control although minimum estimates have been developed by including firms in which at least 51 per cent of the common stock is owned by non-residents plus those in which less than 51 per cent is owned by non-residents but for which it is known or believed by the statisticians that control lies abroad.

Similar data for previous years show little change in the percen-

---

[10] See, for example, A. E. Safarian, "Benefits and Costs of Foreign Investment" in L.H. Officer and L.B. Smith (eds.) *Canadian Economic Problems and Policies*. Toronto: McGraw-Hill, 1970, Table 1. The increase in foreign control was most significant in mining and smelting where it rose from 61 to 70 per cent in the 1960-69 period.

Table 12.5

**Ownership and Control of Capital Employed in Selected Industries,
Canada, 1972**

	Total Capital Employed ($ billions)	Canada		United States		Other Foreign	
		Own	Control	Own	Control	Own	Control
				(percentage of total capital)			
Manufacturing	28.4	47	42	44	43	9	15
Petroleum, natural gas	15.0	43	25	46	58	11	17
Mining, smelting	7.8	44	42	46	47	10	11
Railways	6.0	85	98	7	2	8	0
Other utilities	25.9	81	92	16	5	3	3
Above industries plus merchandising, construction	105.0	66	65	27	26	7	9

Source: Statistics Canada, *Canada's International Investment Position*.

tage of foreign ownership but that foreign control has increased slightly in recent years.[10] This trend may be expected to continue, unless the federal and provincial governments decide to implement severe policies to curtail foreign direct investment in Canada. Foreign ownership is increasing because foreign investors, particularly in the United States, are looking more widely for profitable uses of their financial assets and are increasingly buying larger blocks of stock in a few foreign firms instead of bonds and small shareholdings in several firms. Another factor is the growth of *multinational corporations*, or firms which have plants in a number of countries. These are generally firms concerned with product areas where technology is changing rapidly, and where there are thus increasing opportunities for realizing economies of very large scale. Because many countries have retained high tariffs on the products concerned, these large firms are encouraged to establish plants in each country rather than supply world markets from a home base.

The Major Issues

The question of foreign ownership might be included in a chapter on international trade and finance since foreign direct investment obviously has important effects on a country's balance of international payments and its foreign exchange rate. The current issues, however, extend much beyond the matter of international economics, and indeed beyond economic considerations. This is evident in some of the proposals for dealing with foreign-owned firms. The suggestion that such firms be brought under public ownership, for example, has more to do with a general political ideology than with the specific consequences of foreign control. Public ownership may be appropriate, however, if the firm in question is a case of natural monopoly, as described earlier in this chapter.

There appear to be five basic economic issues in the debate on foreign ownership. These concern the relationship of foreign ownership, Canadian economic growth, and the balance of payments; the effect of foreign-owned firms' international trade on Canada's balance of payments; foreign governments' influence on Canadian industry and governments; the behaviour of foreign-owned firms concerning research, development, and employment; and the accelerated depletion of Canada's natural resources. Each of these issues is discussed briefly below but the interested reader is particularly encouraged in this case to pursue the sources bearing on this question which are listed at the end of the chapter.

Economic Growth Versus Balance of Payments Problems. Foreign ownership has generally been defended on the grounds that it would contribute to a substantial increase in the rate of economic growth. However, this argument usually fails to distinguish between an increase in foreign ownership due to the reinvestment of earnings of foreign-owned firms and that due to the importation of capital. The latter case also must distinguish between foreign *direct investment* (ownership of most or all of a firm's physical assets) and *portfolio investment* (holdings of bonds and small blocks of common stocks). Much of the foreign borrowing is done by provincial governments and has no direct bearing on the foreign ownership question; similarly, foreign holdings of small blocks of common shares in Canadian firms is not the nub of the issue. Moreover, much of the increase in the percentage of foreign-owned firms in Canada reflects reinvestment of earnings realized in Canada and borrowing from Canadian financial institutions.

The argument favouring foreign ownership for economic growth reasons thus shifts from the simple importation of capital to the special features of foreign capital. Two claims are made for this; foreign-owned firms are: (1) willing and able to undertake riskier ventures than are Canadian-owned firms because they are part of the large, diverse operation of a foreign parent firm which can afford greater risk; and (2) able to draw on the advanced production, marketing, and financing experience of the parent company. Estimates of the effect of foreign-owned firms on Canadian economic growth vary with the data and assumptions used. For example, one set of estimates concludes that foreign investment (portfolio plus direct) accounted for between 8 and 20 per cent of the increase in per capita real income from 1950 to 1956, depending on the assumptions made

---

[11] R. G. Penner, "The Benefits of Foreign Investment in Canada, 1950-56," *Canadian Journal of Economics and Political Science*, May 1966; and John Helliwell and Julian Broadbent, "How Much Does Foreign Capital Matter?" *BC Studies*, Spring 1972, pp. 38-42.

in the calculations. A more recent calculation suggests that the current level of foreign-owned capital in Canada contributes less than 5 per cent of the current G.N.P.[11]

Earlier criticism was directed against foreign investment rather than foreign ownership since the former necessarily would require that interest payments, and likely some dividend payments, be made abroad for many years hence. If the exchange rate were pegged, this would impose an additional burden on foreign exchange reserves, or if the foreign exchange rate were floating, would increase the price of imports. Foreign ownership, however, has no immediate effect on the balance of payments if earnings are retained in Canada. This does increase the base from which future earnings are paid abroad, however. Earnings transmitted abroad are likely to vary with business conditions; these payments would thus be highest when export earnings were highest.

International Trade of Foreign-Owned Firms. Because they tend to import more and export less than the rest of Canadian industry, foreign-owned firms are said to contribute to a current account deficit and to contractionary pressures on national income. This argument follows from the belief that Canadian subsidiaries are required to import much of their raw material or semi-finished products from foreign parent firms. This, however, is inconsistent with the argument that Canadian subsidiaries are established to get around tariffs preventing foreign firms from exporting directly to Canada. Foreign-owned firms do, in fact, import more than similar Canadian firms but the explanations for this vary; for example, this may be because parent firms export finished products through their subsidiaries rather than deal with independent importers.

That Canadian subsidiaries can be expected to export less than other firms follows from the assumption that Canadian subsidiaries would be restricted to Canadian markets, leaving other markets to the parent firm or subsidiaries in other countries. The evidence does not support this as a general assumption: where foreign-owned firms can be compared with like Canadian firms, the export performance of the two types is similar, "whether one considers all such firms, only the large ones, or only those in manufacturing."[12] This general conclusion is consistent, however, with the existence of specific cases of marketing restrictions and special advantages such as access to the parent firm's marketing system, since the evidence suggests that these features have offsetting effects. Moreover, the export performance of foreign-owned firms can be improved by diminishing the first case and encouraging the second.

Foreign Influence. Current opposition to foreign ownership would appear to be based primarily on the view that Canadian subsidiaries and other foreign-owned firms are or can be a channel of influence

---

[12] A. E. Safarian, *loc. cit.*, p. 117.

on Canadian governments, and the fact that policies of foreign governments are extended to the behaviour of foreign-owned firms in Canada. The latter condition does exist: American-owned firms in Canada are subject to American antitrust legislation and to policies forbidding trade with certain communist countries. Since American antitrust legislation is more effective than Canada's anticombines law, foreign control of this type might be welcomed by most Canadian consumers. There are a few known cases where American-owned firms in Canada were restricted from exporting to communist countries but these represented almost negligible amounts by comparison with Canada's total exports.

Foreign influence through Canadian subsidiaries pressuring the federal government on instruction from the parent firm has not been documented or studied, but there is no reason why the federal government should be particularly susceptible to this kind of pressure. Moreover, such subsidiaries have no bargaining power other than threatening to leave the country, and are more likely to seek government favour rather than express criticism. There have been a few cases of foreign governments pressing the federal government on behalf of foreign-owned firms, but this is a case of normal pleading which can be resisted or not as the federal government chooses.

Research and Employment in Foreign-Owned Firms. The suggestion that there can be foreign political influence through Canadian subsidiaries should be distinguished from the argument that these plants are controlled by the parent firm, frequently contrary to the Canadian public interest. Two specific concerns are the alleged lack of research and development undertaken in the subsidiary and the employment of foreign personnel in senior management, thus curtailing Canada's research and development capacity and reducing job opportunities for highly trained personnel.

Evidence shows that much of the research and development work related to Canadian subsidiaries is done in the parent firm. At the same time the subsidiaries do at least as much research and development work in Canada as similar Canadian firms do. The important question then is why Canadian firms conduct relatively little research and development activity. The association of Canadian subsidiaries with the research and development divisions of the parent firm is one of the major advantages credited to foreign ownership since new technology can be transmitted more quickly through this close international linkage.

Foreign-owned firms do have a higher proportion of foreign personnel in senior management but this can be beneficial in the transmission of management skills to Canadian firms. The loss of employment opportunities for Canadians would be serious only when unemployment in the managerial category is hight. The presence of non-resident directors on the boards of foreign-owned firms in Canada also causes some concern, but it is not clear why they should be expected to act differently from Canadian directors, provided that one assumes the general objective of profit maximization in each case.

Depletion of Canada's Natural Resources. One of the most controversial issues is whether foreign-owned firms should dominate any industry, and particularly the mining industry. The basic question here, however, is whether Canada has an appropriate policy for mining development, including taxation policy, rather than whether foreign firms should be excluded from this field. Nevertheless, an important related problem is that foreign-owned firms extract and export raw materials, such as lumber, pulp, and mineral ores, for processing elsewhere instead of providing the potential employment associated with processing these materials in Canada.

Public Policy on Foreign Ownership and Control

Public policy has evolved more slowly on the question of foreign ownership than on almost any other economic matter. The question became a political issue following the report of the Royal Commission on Canada's Economic Prospects in 1957. Commission chairman Walter Gordon aroused some public support for his criticism of foreign ownership, and particularly for his proposed Canada Development Corporation. Gordon later persuaded the government to establish a Task Force on Foreign Ownership, which produced a report in 1968. This and the Gray Report[13] of 1972 led to the Foreign Investment Review Act of 1973. This provides for a government agency to screen proposed foreign takeovers of Canadian-owned firms as well as new foreign investment in Canada. The basic test for allowing foreign ownership is that it should "bring significant benefit to Canada", particularly in terms of employment, investment, and improved productivity.

The provincial governments have reacted in various ways to the foreign ownership question; some provinces anxiously encourage foreign direct and portfolio investment, while others are more cautious. Ontario, for example, requires that at least 50 per cent of the directors of any provincially incorporated firms be Canadian residents. Such a policy may have popular appeal but economists generally are skeptical about its consequence to the behaviour of firms.

In specific areas, however, public policy has been more restrictive because it is easier to identify the consequences of foreign ownership. Only 25 per cent of the common stock of Canadian chartered banks may be foreign-owned, with no single owner having over 10 per cent.[14] Similar rules apply in broadcasting and publishing of periodicals.

---

[13] Hon. Herb Gray, *Foreign Direct Investment in Canada*. Ottawa: Information Canada, 1972.

[14] The Mercantile Bank is currently an exception, but it must reduce foreign ownership to 25 per cent by 1980.

The slow evolution of public policy on foreign ownership follows not only from governments' attempts to find a compromise between the restrictive proposals of the nationalists and the international orientation of traditional liberals. There appear to be quite different effects of foreign ownership on different groups of people and in different regions of the country. There are also the difficult problems of determining the effects of foreign ownership in particular industries and under a diversity of circumstances. It is the problem of reconciling these various differences which helps explain the difficulty of determining a policy to encourage those effects which are most in the public interest.

Review of the Main Points

1. Canadian manufacturing industries tend to be more highly concentrated than American manufacturing; this leads to an uneven size distribution of firms: about 90 per cent of the total production in manufacturing comes from about 20 per cent of the establishments.

2. There are four basic forms of business organization: single proprietorships, partnerships, corporations, and cooperatives. Proprietorships and partnerships have unlimited liability: creditors may claim the personal assets of the firms' owners should they be unable to meet financial obligations. Corporations have limited liability because they are treated as a separate legal entity.

3. Corporations are financed by issuing stocks or bonds, or by drawing on retained earnings or depreciation allowances. Control of a corporation nominally requires ownership of 51 per cent of the common shares, but in large public corporations, control can be gained with a lower pecentage of the shares. This has led to holding companies or conglomerates which control large accumulations of assets through a pyramidal structure of holdings.

4. Two special cases of corporations are the public or crown corporations established by governments, and the cooperatives established by societies of individuals to buy or sell commodities cooperatively.

5. Public policy concerning monopolies and oligopolies takes the form of anti-combines legislation, and public ownership or regulatory agencies to control natural monopolies: industries in which the existence of more than one or two firms would waste resources and increase prices. The Combines Investigation Act forbids agreements between suppliers that would unduly restrict competition; mergers and the formation of monopolies; and a number of restrictive trade practices. This Act has not been very effective, but new amendments are expected to overcome some of the previous weaknesses.

6. Natural monopolies are common in the transportation, communications, natural gas, and electricity industries because firms have large fixed costs relative to the total output of the market. Such industries are either controlled by regulatory agencies appointed by governments, or are brought under direct control by public ownership. Regulatory agencies usually are required to determine a "fair return" on the firm's assets. The major regulatory agencies in Canada are the Canadian Transport Commission, the Canadian Radio-Television Commission, and the National Energy Board.

7. Public support for restricted competition takes the form of licensing only some persons or firms in some professions, trades, or businesses, and issuing patents which restrict the production of a specific item to one firm.

8. Conversely, there is public support for existing competition in agriculture. This industry has an unusually large number of firms, faces a low price elasticity of demand for its products, has experienced rapid increases in supply, and is subject to sharp changes in product prices due to weather and disease. Consequently, farm incomes tend to be low and unstable. Public assistance takes the form of programs to support and stabilize prices, to decrease or subsidize production costs, to improve prices through more effective marketing, and to assist in reallocating resources.

9. Two types of price supports are used: an offer to purchase produce not sold in the market when the price is set at the guaranteed minimum, and a deficiency payment or a payment of the difference between the free-market price and the guaranteed price. The latter method's advantage is that the government does not need to accumulate stocks of the supported product, although the total deficiency payments are larger than the offer-to-purchase payments would be for a given product, if the demand for that product is inelastic.

10. Other assistance programs include agricultural research and extension services provided by the federal and provincial governments, tax exemptions or rebates on farm supplies, subsidies for production or transportation of some products, and the establishment of marketing boards. Some boards set quotas, which when the demand is inelastic, have the effect of raising the total revenue for the product. Finally, the federal government has been actively encouraging the formation of larger, more efficient farms, and the shifting of land and labour into other industries.

11. Foreign ownership and control of firms in Canada has become a major problem for public policy on industrial organization. There appear to be five basic issues: the relationship of economic growth and the balance of payments to foreign ownership; the

international trade pattern of foreign-owned firms; the influence
of foreign governments on Canadian industry and government;
the research, development, and employment practices of
foreign-owned firms; and the accelerated depletion of Canada's
natural resources. Public policy on foreign ownership includes
the federal government's plan to review proposed foreign
takeovers of Canadian firms and rules concerning the extent of
foreign ownership in some industries, but policy has evolved
slowly because foreign ownership has different effects on different groups of people and in different regions.

Review and Discussion Questions

1. Would you prefer to hold financial assets in the form of corporate
   bonds, as common shares, or as preferred shares? Explain.
   Would your answer be different in a recession than at the peak of
   an economic expansion?

2. Why are corporations relatively more common in manufacturing
   than in retail services?

3. Some economists have proposed that there should be more,
   rather than fewer, mergers in Canada. Why might they argue this
   way? Would you?

4. "All natural monopolies should be purchased by the government
   and be operated by a public commission." Do you agree? Why?

5. It is frequently suggested that urban public transportation
   should be provided at a lower price between 10 a.m. and 3 p.m.
   than at the price charged during rush-hours. How should the
   lower price be determined? What economic arguments could
   you offer in support of this proposal? Against the proposal?

6. One factor in the decline of real income for farmers, relative to
   incomes in many other occupations, has been increased agricultural productivity, resulting in a fairly rapid outward shift of the
   agricultural products supply curve. Does this mean that all efforts to improve agricultural productivity should cease? Why?

Sources and Selected Readings

Bain, Joe S. Industrial Organization, 2nd ed. New York: Wiley, 1968.

Campbell, D. R. "The Farm Problem," in L. H. Officer and L. B. Smith (eds.)
   Canadian Economic Problems and Policies. Toronto: McGraw-Hill,
   1970.

Caves, Richard. American Industry: Structure, Conduct, Performance, 3rd
   ed. Englewood Cliffs, N.J.: Prentice-Hall, 1972.

Economic Council of Canada. Interim Report on Competition Policy. Ottawa: Queen's Printer, 1969.

Galbraith, J. Kenneth. The New Industrial State. Toronto: New American
   Library of Canada, 1967.

Jones, J. C. H. "Mergers and Competition: The Brewing Case" *Canadian Journal of Economics and Political Science*, November 1967, pp. 551-568.

Levitt, Kari. *Silent Surrender*. Toronto: Macmillan, 1970.

Moore, Milton. *How Much Price Competition?* Montreal: McGill-Queen's University Press, 1970.

Paquet, G. (ed.) *The Multinational Firm and the Nation State*. Toronto: Collier-Macmillan, 1972.

Rosenbluth, G. "Concentration and Monopoly in the Canadian Economy" in M. Oliver (ed.) *Social Purpose for Canada*. Toronto: University of Toronto Press, 1961, pp. 198-248.

_____. "The Relation between Foreign Control and Concentration in Canadian Industry" *Canadian Journal of Economics*, February 1970, pp. 14-39.

Safarian, A. E. *Foreign Ownership of Canadian Industry*. Toronto: McGraw-Hill, 1966.

Skeoch, L. A. (ed.) *Restrictive Trade Practices in Canada*. Toronto: McClelland and Stewart, 1966.

Watkins, M. H., et al. *Foreign Ownership and the Structure of Canadian Industry*. Ottawa: Queen's Printer, 1967.

Wilcox, Clair. *Public Policies Toward Business*, 5th ed. Homewood, Ill.: Irwin, 1975.

13

Rent, Interest, and Profit

In Chapters 10 and 11, which were concerned with the prices and output of finished products, the prices of productive factors were taken as given. This chapter turns to a general explanation of the demand for productive factors and then considers the determination of factor prices in the form of rent, interest, and profit. An examination of wage determination in labour markets is reserved for the following chapter.

A. Demand for Productive Factors

Prices of productive factors have an obvious effect on the costs of producing final products, and thus on their prices. Factor prices also allocate or ration factors among industries and firms producing different commodities, and determine the particular combination of resources used to produce each commodity. Of even wider significance is the influence that factor prices have on the total income of the population and the distribution of this income among various groups and individuals. This *functional or factor distribution of income* is determined largely by factor prices because it is individuals who have ultimate ownership or control of the productive factors and who receive the income from the use of them. Each individual's income thus depends on the quantity of each kind of factor services he supplies and the prices of these services.

What are Factors and Factor Services?

Two terms are used in this chapter which are similar, but actually have different meanings: *factors* and *factor services*. A distinction must be made, for example, between one worker and one hour of a worker's labour. A productive factor is something which can make a contribution to the process of producing a good or service. A factor is thus a *stock*, a stock of the potential contributions to production which the factor can provide over a period of time. Factor services are the actual contributions of the factor and are described as a *flow* of the services over a specified period. The prices of factor services are therefore expressed in terms of time periods: the price of labour service, for example, is its hourly wage or annual salary.

The services of many different factors are used in the production of most commodities, but for convenience these different factors are generally classified as *land*, *labour*, and *capital*. This traditional classification, however, no longer represents clear distinctions among different factors. At a time when there were few improvements to land through draining, clearing, or levelling, and few improvements to labour through education and training, these two types of "natural" factors could be differentiated from capital, which was defined simply as a man-made means of production. However, the use of resources to improve the land and the skills of labour, as well as to create new plant and equipment, has blurred this earlier distinction.

A fourth factor is sometimes added to the list; namely, *management* or *entrepreneurship*. This addition emphasizes the particular contribution made by individuals who take the initiative, and the risk, in employing and organizing the other factors in the productive process.

Demand for Factor Services: The Marginal Productivity Theory

There is a basic similarity between the demand for finished products and the demand for factor services. In Chapter 9, consumer demand was explained primarily in terms of the utility or satisfaction obtained from additional units of a given commodity; similarly, producer demand can be explained in terms of the output or revenue obtained from additional units of factor services. This explanation, termed the *marginal productivity theory*, can be illustrated by referring again to the example of the pottery firm used in Chapter 10.

The pottery firm was assumed to use only two productive factors in producing its ceramic coffee mugs, capital and labour. Capital was the fixed factor consisting of five pottery wheels; labour was the variable factor. The firm was assumed to be in a purely competitive industry: it could sell any quantity of its mugs at a constant price of $2 per mug. Since there are many other pottery firms in the industry, this particular firm has no influence on the price of labour services because it employs only a small fraction of the potters in the industry.

Table 13.1 presents some of the production information included in Table 1 of Chapter 10. As an increasing number of man-days are added to the firm's five pottery wheels, the *total product* increases up to the eighth man-day but the *marginal product* decreases after the fourth man-day. Note that the terminology is changed slightly in Table 13.1: what was previously termed marginal product is now termed *marginal physical product* to emphasize that the additional number of units of output are being measured. This distinguishes the additional physical product from the additional revenue associated with additional units of the variable factor. By multiplying the selling price of the product by the marginal physical product, one can calculate the *marginal revenue product*.

The marginal revenue product is the change in total revenue associated with each additional unit of the variable factor.

(Recall that marginal revenue is the change in total revenue associated with each additional unit of output.)

The marginal revenue product and the price of a factor determine a firm's demand for the services of the factor. The profit-maximization rule for determining the output — produce the quantity at which marginal revenue equals marginal cost — can be modified to establish a profit-maximization rule for determining the quantity of factor services to be employed. The purely competitive firm will maximize its profit if it continues to purchase additional units of the factor's service up to the point where the factor's price — the *marginal resource cost* — is equal to its marginal revenue product.

Table 13.1

Marginal Revenue Product of a Purely Competitive Firm

Variable Factor (Man-days of Labour)	Total Product	Marginal Physical Product	Product Selling Price	Marginal Revenue Product
0	0		$2	
1	20	20	2	$ 40
2	76	56	2	112
3	183	107	2	214
4	304	121	2	242
5	410	106	2	212
6	486	76	2	152
7	518	32	2	64
8	520	2	2	4
9	513	−7	2	−14

In the pottery firm example used in Chapter 10, the price per man-day of potters' services was assumed to be $100. (This is evident from the fact that total variable cost increased by $100 for each additional man-day in Table 10.2.) At a price of $100 man-day, Table 13.1 shows that the pottery firm will maximize its profit by employing six potters because the cost per man-day of $100 is less than the marginal revenue product, $152, of the sixth potter. If the firm increased its staff to seven potters, the additional cost would be $100, but the marginal revenue product would be only $64, with a loss of $36 incurred by hiring the seventh potter. Note that this result is the same as that found in Chapter 10 by following the profit-maximization rule for determining the level of output.

By assuming a schedule of alternative prices per man-day of potters' services, the firm's demand curve for this factor can be plotted as in Figure 13.1. As the price (or wage) of potters' services declines, more man-hours are used because the firm can add to its profit as long as the marginal revenue product of the last unit of the factor's service exceeds the price of that unit.

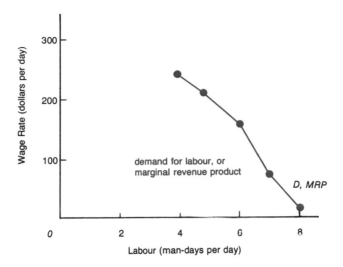

Figure 13.1   Competitive Firm's Demand For Factor Services
Although a competitive firm faces a perfectly elastic demand for its product, its
demand for factor services is downward sloping, due to the diminishing marginal
productivity of variable factors. The firm will purchase the quantity of labour services at which the marginal revenue product, *MRP*, equals the wage rate. Hence
the declining portion of the firm's *MRP* curve is also its demand curve for labour
services.

The marginal revenue product curve is therefore a firm's
demand curve for the services of a particular factor.

Only a portion of the demand curve has been plotted in Figure
13.1; namely, the portion corresponding with diminishing marginal
productivity. As long as marginal productivity is increasing, the
firm will add to its profit (or reduce its loss) by adding more of the
variable factor; this portion of the curve is therefore irrelevant to the
firm's decision. It is only when marginal productivity is diminishing
that the firm must decide how many units of the variable factor it
should employ.

The demand for factor services is said to be a *derived demand*
because such services are useful or desirable only to the extent that
they contribute to the production of final products desired by consumers. Furthermore, other things being equal, a shift in the demand
for a final product will cause a shift in the demand for the factor
services used in producing that product.

One might expect that the market demand curve for a factor's
services would be derived in the same way that a market demand
curve is obtained for final products, by adding horizontally the individual demand curves of all firms. This cannot be done for factor
services, however, because the industry normally faces a
downward-sloping demand for its product; that is, the product price
declines with increasing output, whereas the product price received

by a single firm in a competitive industry remains constant. Consequently, if each firm attempts to expand its output when the price of a factor's services declines, the price of its product falls. The effect of an industry's declining product demand curve is that its labour demand curve is less elastic than the sum of the demand curves of the individual firms.

Elasticity of Demand for Factor Services

The price elasticity of demand for factor services is defined and calculated in the same way as the price elasticity of demand for final products: the percentage change in the price of the factor service. Furthermore, given the degree of competition in the product market, some of the reasons for differing degrees of elasticity are similar to those given for the different elasticities of consumer products. If there are close substitutes for a factor, the demand for that factor's service is likely to be highly elastic. If, for example, a technician is a close substitute for an engineer in a particular process, the demand for an engineer's service is likely to be quite elastic. A small increase in engineers' salaries relative to technicians' salaries will result in a proportionately greater decline in the number of engineers employed (and an increase in technicians employed).

Second, the elasticity of demand for a factor's service will reflect the elasticity of demand for the final product to which it contributes. If the demand for ceramic coffee mugs is quite elastic, a small increase in the price of mugs will result in a substantial decline in the quantity of mugs sold; hence there will be a sharp decline in the number of potters hired to produce the mugs.

Third, the relative significance of the factor in the total production costs of the firm will also influence the elasticity of its demand for the factor. If labour costs represent only a small portion of the total costs, a 10 per cent increase in wages, for example, may have little effect on the quantity of labour employed; but if labour is the firm's major production cost, the same percentage increase in wages may sharply reduce the number of labourers employed.

A fourth factor influencing the demand elasticity of factor services is the rate at which marginal productivity is declining. When the marginal productivity of a factor declines quickly, the demand for that factor is likely to be highly inelastic: even substantial decreases in the factor price result in small increases in the quantity used because the additional units add so little to the total revenue.

Shifts in Demand

The demand curve for a factor's services may shift for any of three general reasons. One of these was suggested above in reference to derived demand. The demand curve for a factor's services is influenced by the demand for the related final product. When the demand for the latter increases, the demand for any factors used in its production is also likely to shift outward. Another major reason for a shift in demand is a change in the productivity of each unit of a factor. This has been especially important in increasing the demand for particular kinds of skilled labour. With improved machinery and plant organization, the productivity of each labourer can be increased, with a resulting increase in marginal revenue product. Labour productivity can also be increased by combining more of the fixed factors — capital and land — with each unit of labour. One worker controlling several automated lathes is more productive than the same worker associated with only one lathe. Labour productivity is also increased by providing additional training for workers. Each of these factors can increase the marginal revenue product of a worker and hence lead a firm to employ more workers at any given wage level.

Finally, as was suggested above in the case of engineers and technicians, a change in the relative prices of other factors can shift the demand curve for a factor. A decrease in the relative wage of technicians will shift inward the demand curve for engineers, to the extent that these are close substitutes. Note, however, that shifts in the demand for factor services usually do not occur within a firm's short-run planning period, unless it is possible to vary the quantity of factors such as labour.

Imperfect Competition in the Product Market

The pottery firm's demand for factor services was derived from a set of assumptions, including the existence of pure competition in the product market. This implied a perfectly elastic demand curve for the firm's product, and hence a constant selling price of $2 per mug. In an imperfectly competitive market, however, the firm would face a downward-sloping demand curve: there would be a lower price per unit for each higher level of output. Moreover, the lower price applies to the total quantity sold. The result, as seen in the discussion of imperfect competition in Chapter 11, is that marginal revenue is less than the average revenue and declines more quickly than the average revenue.

This outcome if found again when the marginal revenue product is calculated for the imperfectly competitive firm. Table 13.2 shows the same production information presented in Table 13.1, but assumes a downward-sloping demand curve: the product's selling price declines with increasing output. Total revenue is obtained by multiplying the price by the total product.

The marginal revenue product in the imperfect competition case must be calculated as the change in total revenue with each additional unit of the variable factor, and *not* by multiplying price and marginal physical product.

Table 13.2

Marginal Revenue Product of an Imperfectly Competitive Firm

Variable Factor (man-days of labour)	Total Product	Marginal Physical Product	Product Selling Price	Total Revenue	Marginal Revenue Product
0	0		$4.00	$ 0	
1	20	20	3.50	70.00	$ 70.00
2	76	56	3.00	228.00	158.00
3	183	107	2.50	457.50	229.50
4	304	121	2.00	608.00	150.50
5	410	106	1.60	656.00	48.00
6	486	76	1.40	680.40	24.40
7	518	32	1.20	621.60	−58.80
8	520	2	1.00	520.00	−101.60
9	513	−7			

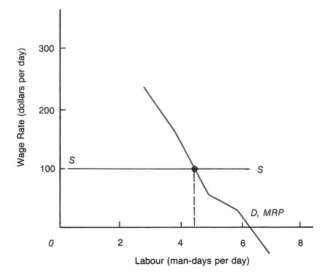

Figure 13.2 Imperfectly Competitive Firm's Labour Demand
An imperfectly competitive firm's demand for labour services (or other productive factors) is less elastic than that of a perfectly competitive firm because it faces a less elastic demand for its product, as well as the diminishing marginal productivity of productive factors. If the labour market is perfectly competitive, the firm faces a perfectly elastic labour supply curve, SS, at a wage rate of $100 per man-day; it will employ just over four man-days per day.

The marginal revenue product schedule is plotted in Figure 13.2 as the firm's demand curve for the factor service. If the price of the factor service remains at $100 per man-day, as assumed previously, the firm's profit-maximizing level of input will be four man-days since the marginal revenue product of the fourth man-day is $150.50, but for the fifth man-day it falls to only $48. This result is in line with the general conclusion reached earlier; namely, that an imperfectly competitive firm will have a lower level of output than a purely competitive firm in the short run, and will underutilize its productive resources, which in this case are the pottery wheels.

MC = MR Versus MRC = MRP

Although there is a close similarity between the calculation of marginal revenue and marginal revenue product, marginal revenue is associated with each additional unit of *output* while marginal revenue product is associated with each additional unit of the factor service or *input*.

Similarly, the profit-maximization rule of equating marginal revenue with marginal cost is used to determine the firm's level of *output*. In order to distinguish this rule from that for determining the profit-maximizing level of *input*, the marginal cost of productive resources is termed the *marginal resource cost*, MRC. The profit-maximizing level of input of factor services is thus defined as the level at which the marginal revenue product equals the marginal resource cost. Each rule, however, leads to the same conclusion since a particular level of output is associated with a specific level of variable factor services.

Demand for More Than One Factor Service

Firms have thus far been assumed to use only one variable factor but of course most productive processes require several variable factors, if only in terms of different types of labour service. How can the firm determine the *profit-maximizing combination of productive resources*? The same rule applies for each input in the combination that was used when only one factor was involved.

The firm should employ each factor up to the point where its marginal revenue product is equal to the marginal resource cost.

Thus the ratio of MRP to MRC for each factor will be equal to 1, and the profit-maximizing rule can be expressed as:

$$\frac{MRP_1}{MRC_1} = \frac{MRP_2}{MRC_2} = \frac{MRP_3}{MRC_3} = 1$$

where the subscripts 1, 2, 3, etc., refer to different factor services. Unless the firm has some influence on the price of factor services such that their prices change with different quantities purchased by the firm, this rule can also be expressed as:

$$\frac{MRP_1}{P_1} = \frac{MRP_2}{P_2} = \frac{MRP_3}{P_3} = 1$$

where P is the price per unit of factor services.

The profit-maximizing rule is used to determine the most desirable combination of factor services at each of various alternative *product* prices. As the product price increases, the marginal revenue product of each unit of factor service also increases, and hence the firm must decide how much more of each factor should be used.

A different rule is required when the relative prices of *factor services* change. In this case, the firm will be seeking the *lowest-cost combination of factor services*. As the relative prices of factor services change, the firm should determine which factor will provide the largest marginal physical product for any given additional expenditure on productive resources. If an additional $100 for semi-skilled labour will yield a higher marginal physical product than $100 for skilled labour, the firm will choose the former alternative. This approach yields the conclusion that

The cost of producing a given level of output is lowest or minimized when the marginal physical product of each factor is the same for any given level of expenditure.

The minimum-cost rule for determining the most desirable combination of resources to produce any given level of output can be expressed as:

$$\frac{MPP_1}{P_1} = \frac{MPP_2}{P_2} = \frac{MPP_3}{P_3}$$

Or if the firm's purchases of factor services influences the prices of these, the rule is expressed as:

$$\frac{MPP_1}{MRC_1} = \frac{MPP_2}{MRC_2} = \frac{MPP_3}{MRC_3}$$

B.   Rent

In everyday language, the term "rent" refers to the price for the use of property, whether this be in the form of land, buildings, furniture, or machinery. The emergence of "rent-all" stores in most Canadian communities has made it possible to rent or hire almost any type of equipment, with the result that the term "rent" is now used to describe payments for the use of a wide variety of items. "Rent" has a narrower usage in economics, although even here the term can have different meanings depending on its context.

Economic Rent and Transfer Earnings

The price for a factor's services is described as having two components: economic rent and transfer earnings. Although this is true for

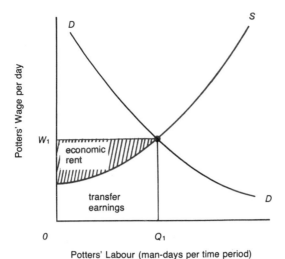

Potters' Labour (man-days per time period)

Figure 13.3 Economic Rent and Transfer Earnings
The labour supply curve facing the industry indicates the wage rate it must pay, for
each unit of labour service employed, to attract labour into the labour force or away
from other industries. But all employees will expect, or demand, the same wage
rate. Hence, each unit of labour service must be paid OW_1, the rate required to
attract the last unit. The difference between OW_1 and the rate indicated by the
supply curve is the economic rent enjoyed by each unit of labour service.

other factors, it will be seen that this distinction is of special importance in the case of land. The meanings of economic rent and transfer earnings can be illustrated by referring to the pottery firms constituting the ceramic mug industry. If the firms wish to employ
additional potters, they must be willing to pay enough so that the
potters will transfer their labour services from other industries.

The minimum payment required to attract resources from other
uses is the transfer earnings of the factor.

The total earnings must be at least this amount, but they may
also be greater. The reason can be illustrated by Figure 13.3. The
industry's demand for potters' services is *DD*; the supply curve for
potters' services is assumed to be upward-sloping since additional
potters can be attracted away from other industries, or into the labour
force, only by offering higher wages. Figure 13.3 indicates that if the
industry wishes to employ OQ_1 potters, it must pay a wage of OW_1.
Only the last potter hired, however, must be paid OW_1 to attract him
into the industry. The other employees will thus be paid more than
their transfer earnings. The difference between the transfer earnings
for each employee and the actual wage OW_1 is a surplus payment the
firms could avoid if they could make separate contracts with each
employee.

Any payment in addition to the transfer earnings is termed
economic rent.

Rent and the Use of Land

The distinction between economic rent and transfer earnings is particularly important in the case of land because the quantity of land is fixed; land cannot be reproduced or destroyed. (There is one exception to this statement: the quantity of land is reduced when an area is flooded, and increased when an area is drained.) The supply curve for land is therefore considered to be perfectly inelastic in both the short run and long run.

The fixed quantity of land is represented by the vertical supply curve in Figure 13.4. In this case, all possible uses of land — agricultural, recreational, residential, and commercial — are treated together. Similarly, the demand for land is represented as a single demand curve. The use of land is defined here so broadly that no other use for land is possible. Hence there are no transfer earnings associated with the price for using land since it does not have to be attracted away from some other use. The full price for the use of land is therefore economic rent.

In this general case, land is considered from the point of view of the entire economy. Some land, however, has several uses while other land may have only one use. The land at the water's edge in many Canadian cities could be used for agricultural, recreational, or residential purposes, as well as for its usual use as the location of warehouses, docks, or offices. This use of the land provides a higher marginal revenue product per acre than if it were used, for example, for agricultural production. Thus, commercial users are willing to pay a higher price per acre for the use of the land. The supply curve

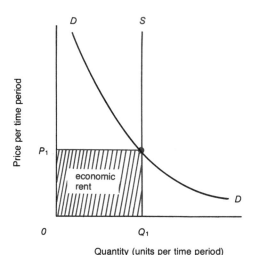

Figure 13.4 Payment For the Use of Land is Economic Rent
Since the quantity of land available is fixed at OQ_1, land has no transfer earnings. That is, land would be made available for productive uses at even an extremely low price. Payment for the use of land is therefore economic rent.

for commercial land in city centres therefore is highly elastic at low prices, as land is bid away from other uses, but quite inelastic at higher prices. The price paid for such land *for commercial purposes* therefore has a transfer earnings component because a certain (low) price must be paid to attract it away from other uses. As the demand curve shifts outward, and the price for using commercial land increases, the economic rent component becomes an increasingly large portion of the price. Alternatively, land such as the Haliburton Highlands of Ontario, the Laurentians of Quebec, or Whistler Mountain in British Columbia, can be used for little but recreation. Even agriculture and forestry is not very profitable in these areas. The price for using this land therefore has virtually no transfer earnings component, but the economic rent increases annually with the increasing demand for recreational space.

The above two cases consider land from the perspective of alternative industries. However, an individual farmer who wants to rent an additional fifty acres would argue that the price he pays for the use of this land represents only transfer earnings since he must pay this price before the landowner will allow him, rather than another farmer, to use the land. From the perspective of the individual producer, this is correct. The size of the economic rent component therefore depends on whether one is interested in determining the surplus value associated with the use of a factor being transferred from another firm or from another industry. From the total economy's perspective, however, the entire price paid for the use of land is economic rent since land exists: it is available for production at any price. This differs from the case of labour services since there is a minimum price which must be offered to attract labour into productive processes.

Recent concern about the private ownership of waterfront land in popular recreational areas provides an example of the economic rent concept applied to public policy. A camping-park operator who rents lakeside land and in turn charges high rates for camping privileges would argue that there is no economic rent or surplus in his prices because he must pay a high annual rent to the landowner. This high rent, however, is due to the fixed quantity of such land available and the increasing demand for its use. It is therefore sometimes suggested that the economic rent component of the return to this land should be taxed away from the landowner since he will make the land available for camping purposes as long as he receives a price which covers the transfer earnings, or the return he would realize from alternative uses such as agricultural production.[1]

Quasi-Rent. The use of buildings is distinguished from the use of land because the quantity of land is fixed in the long run but the

---

[1] This was the essence of a nineteenth-century proposal that there be only one tax, a tax on land. For an explanation of this argument, see Henry George, *Progress and Poverty*.

quantity of buildings is fixed only in the short run. Buildings (or floor space) earn an economic rent due to their inelastic supply in the short run. In the long run, however, some buildings can be demolished or more can be constructed, depending on the expected returns from the use of buildings. The economic rent realized in the short run may thus disappear in the long run; it has thus been termed *quasi-rent* to emphasize its short-term nature.

The concepts of economic rent and quasi-rent are not limited in their application to land and buildings. Rather, these rents occur whenever the quantity of a factor is fixed. One of the best-known cases of quasi-rent (although it is seldom recognized as such) occurs in the high prices paid to famous entertainers and sports stars. The available quantity of top-ranking professional hockey players is limited and cannot be changed in the short run. The transfer earnings component of Bobby Orr's annual salary, for example, might be in the order of $15,000. The balance, amounting to several hundred thousand dollars, is quasi-rent, due to his almost unique ability as a hockey player and the high marginal revenue product realized by any hockey club that can add Mr. Orr to its roster.

C. Interest

Interest is sometimes defined as the price charged or paid for the use of money; it is also defined as the return on capital. The terms "capital" and "money" are sometimes used interchangeably, but an important distinction between these two terms has been made in earlier chapters.

Capital is any man-made means of production, and includes real or tangible items such as plant and equipment, as well as improvements to land such as dams, drainage systems, and paving.

Residential housing is also included because houses are thought of as providing a service over a long period of time, rather than as items which are produced for immediate consumption. Capital, real goods which are used directly in the productive process, must be distinguished from financial assets which represent ownership of, or creditors' claims on, the capital items. A firm's plant and equipment are capital; the stocks and bonds issued by the firm to raise money needed to purchase the plant and equipment are financial assets of the firm's owners and creditors. (A wider concept of capital includes human capital: the improvements to labour due to education, training, and health care.)

A return can be earned both on the use of capital and on the financial assets representing a claim on this capital. However, only if there is a return on capital in terms of real goods and services is it possible for there to be a return on financial assets. A firm which does not use its plant and equipment productively will not be able to pay dividends to its shareholders or interest to its bondholders. A return on financial assets can only be paid out of the returns to real capital items. This is the key relationship between capital and money which is developed in the following sections.

Valuation of Assets

Before turning to the determination of interest rates, it is important to deal with a mistaken impression some people have about what determines the prices of factor services. It is sometimes argued, for example, that land rents are high because the price of land is high. But the argument should be reversed. A particular piece of land may have a high selling price because a high price can be charged for its use.

The value of an asset depends on its yield or net return.

To see why this is so, consider the following example. Suppose someone is considering the purchase of a piece of equipment which can be leased to other users. What is the maximum price he should pay for the equipment? Assume he knows that it can be leased to earn a net income of $1,000 per year, and that the equipment will be obsolete in 10 years. His income from the equipment over the 10-year period will thus be $10,000. If he is to earn a net return on the asset, its price must be less than $10,000, but how much less? This depends on the *opportunity cost* of the money used to purchase the equipment; namely, the best alternative rate of return from another asset. If the highest rate of return one could obtain on any other asset is 8 per cent, then one should not purchase the equipment in question unless at least this rate can be realized.

The maximum price which will reflect this rate of return requires the calculation of the *present value* of the return earned in each of the future years. At an interest rate of 8 per cent, the $1,000 earned at the end of the first year is equal to $925.93 (or $1,000 ÷ 1.08) at the present time. (Conversely, $925.93 loaned now at 8 per cent would increase to $1,000 in one year.) The present value of the $1,000 earned on the equipment in the second year is $1,000 ÷ $(1.08)^2$, and so on for the 10 years the equipment is to be leased. The present value of the sum of the annual income from the equipment can be expressed as:

$$PV = \frac{\$1,000}{(1.08)} + \frac{\$1,000}{(1.08)^2} + \frac{\$1,000}{(1.08)^3} + \ldots + \frac{\$1,000}{(1.08)^{10}}$$

A compound interest table shows that PV is equal to $6,710.

The present value or capitalized value of an asset is therefore equal to the sum of the present values of the annual income earned by the asset, (plus the present value of whatever the asset might be sold for at the end of the period).[2]

This method for calculating the present value of a capital item can also be used to calculate its *internal rate of return*. This is the rate which makes the present value of the future stream of net receipts from a capital item equal to its cost. Suppose the equipment in the example above could be purchased for less than $6,710. The rate required to reduce or discount the annual returns to equality with this lower price would be greater than 8 per cent, and thus greater than the opportunity cost of funds used to purchase the equipment. The internal rate of return would thus be greater than the external rate used for evaluations of the proposed capital item.

The present value calculations provide two approaches for a firm's investment decisions. A firm should purchase a capital item if: (1) its cost is less than the present value of the net returns to the capital item when these are discounted at the best alternative rate of return or the rate on borrowed funds; or (2) the internal rate of return on the capital item is greater than the best alternative rate.

Interest and the Marginal Efficiency of Capital

The marginal productivity theory, introduced earlier in the chapter as a general explanation of the demand for factors of production, has one minor modification when applied to capital. The marginal revenue product derived from a factor's services was expressed as the return per unit of the factor input. In the case of capital, the marginal revenue product is related to the total value of the capital item; this is the same as expressing the marginal revenue product as a rate of return on the total value of the item. But instead of calling this the marginal rate of return on capital, conventional usage has adopted the shorter term, *marginal efficiency of capital (MEC)*.[3]

Whether the marginal efficiency of capital declines as more capital is added to an economy depends on whether the additional capital is used for *capital widening* or *capital deepening*. Capital widening occurs when an economy's labour force is increasing in such a way that the use of capital and labour can be increased in constant proportion. Provided that industries have not reached the

---

[2] The general expression for this formula is $PV = \sum_{1}^{n} \frac{A}{(1 + r)^t}$, where $\sum_{1}^{n}$ represents the sum of n items, and $\frac{A}{(1 + r)^t}$ is the present value of A dollars earned t years hence, when the interest rate is r per cent.

[3] This term was used by J.M. Keynes in *The General Theory of Employment, Interest and Money*, in explaining the significance of the money supply in the determination of an equilibrium level of national income.

point of diminishing returns to scale — and this is unlikely for the economy as a whole — the marginal efficiency of capital will remain constant, or even increase where there are increasing returns to scale.

At an advanced state of economic development, however, increases in the economy's capital stock are likely to result in capital deepening: an increase in the proportion of capital to labour. As the capital deepening process continues, the law of diminishing marginal productivity begins to take effect: the marginal physical product of additional capital (or investment) falls, and thus the marginal efficiency of capital also falls.

Figure 13.5 shows the downward-sloping segment of an economy's *MEC* curve — as the capital stock increases, the *MEC* or rate of return on additional capital declines. The existing capital stock in the economy is valued, in this example, at $300 billion: this is shown as a perfectly inelastic supply curve, *SS*. The intersection of the *MEC* and *SS* curves indicates that the marginal rate of return on capital is 12 per cent.

Suppose that the prevailing rate of interest for business loans is 10 per cent. There will be a strong demand for such loans because firms can earn 12 per cent on each dollar spent for new plant and equipment but pay only 10 per cent for funds borrowed to purchase these capital assets. As firms increase their borrowing and add to their capital, the increased demand for loans will increase the interest rate on loans especially if the money supply is constant. At the

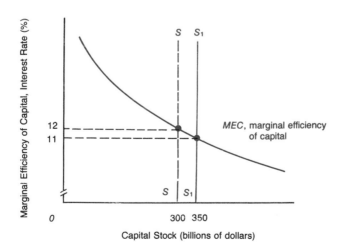

Figure 13.5 Marginal Efficiency of Capital
As an economy's capital stock increases, there is a decline in the rate of return on additional capital, or the marginal efficiency of capital (*MEC*). An increase in the capital stock, from $300 to $350 billion in this example, will occur only if the interest rate is less than 11 per cent, or otherwise investors could not earn a net return on borrowed funds.

same time, the marginal efficiency of capital falls with the increasing capital stock. The result may be that the marginal efficiency of capital is equal to the interest rate at 11 per cent. The equilibrium level of investment, or additions to capital, is reached at $350 billion. No further investment will occur unless the MEC curve shifts upward or the interest rate falls.

The MEC curve will shift upward with improvements in technology. Discoveries of new sources of raw materials and the development of new production techniques and new products usually result in an increased rate of return and additions to the capital stock. The rapid improvements in technology in the past few decades, for example, have resulted in a continuing outward shift of the MEC curve in most industrial countries. There has thus been a substantial increase in their capital stock even though interest rates have not fallen. The tendency toward higher interest rates in recent years, however, may slow this rate of capital accumulation unless there continue to be substantial improvements in technology.

Changes in the interest rate are influenced by many factors, only one of which is the demand for loans to finance new plant and equipment. There is a demand for loans for a number of other purposes: consumers borrow to finance purchases of consumer goods and residential housing, and all levels of government borrow both to finance specific projects such as sewers and roads and to meet general budgetary deficits. The supply of funds available for such borrowers largely depends on the prevailing monetary policy, as explained in Chapter 6.

The Structure of Interest Rates

When interest rates enter into general explanations of economic behaviour, the explanation is often expressed in terms of *the* interest rate in existence at any time. The various interest rates associated with different types of financial assets are referred to collectively as the *structure of interest rates*. This may range from 5 to 9 per cent on bank savings accounts, 12 to 15 per cent on second mortgages, to rates of 18 or 20 per cent on riskier loans.

Variation in interest rates is due to several factors. One is the *time to maturity* of a loan or bond. For example, the federal government's 91-day treasury bills have a much lower interest rate than its 20-year bonds. Interest rates vary for loans or bonds of any given length of maturity due to differences in the *risk* associated with each. A 5-year bond issued by the federal government may have an interest rate of 9 per cent, but a bond of the same maturity issued by a provincial government usually has a slightly higher rate, while municipal and corporation bonds carry a still higher rate, reflecting creditors' judgments about the relative degrees of risk, or the ability of borrowers to repay interest and principal, associated with each type of bond.

The *type of collateral* or security provided by a borrower also influences the interest rate charged. Mortgage rates would be somewhat higher were they not secured by houses. These durable, immovable items obviously offer greater security for a creditor than, for example, the signature of a second person who guarantees to repay a loan should the borrower default.

Interest rates also vary with the *size* of the loan and the *number of installment payments*. A small loan requires as much administration and bookkeeping time as a large loan; similarly, monthly repayments require more time than a single annual payment. Since these administrative costs must be covered by the interest payments, the interest rate on a small loan with monthly payments is substantially higher than on a larger loan of equal risk and maturity that requires only one annual payment.

Finally, interest rates reflect lenders' previous experience with rising prices and expectations about further *inflation*. The higher the expected rate of inflation, the higher the interest rate lenders will require for any given loan, to avoid the possibility of a loss in real income due to higher future prices of goods and services. A general price increase of 5 per cent in one year, for example, would mean that a loan of $100 would buy only $95 worth of goods and services when it was repaid a year later. In this case, a lender would require an interest rate that was 5 percentage points higher than it would be if no inflation were expected.

Although the differences among interest rates on various types of loans and bonds may change slightly, the entire structure or range of rates tends to move up or down simultaneously as the money supply changes. Thus, one can think of a typical or average interest rate when economic theories are expressed in terms of the interest rate. Reference is often made for example to the "prime rate", the rate charged by a chartered bank on large loans extended to its regular and least-risky borrowers, as an indicator of the general level of interest rates.

D.   Profit

What Is Profit?

Profit is another term with one meaning in everyday language and a different, specific meaning in economic analysis. In business, profit is usually defined as the difference between total revenues and the total direct expenditures for materials, labour, and interest. This definition, however, omits important costs such as the opportunity cost of plant, equipment, and land owned by a firm. For a more accurate measure of profit, these costs should be added to direct or explicit expenditures. In this case, profit is the difference between total revenue and the total of explicit and implicit costs.

Profit thus defined represents the return to entrepreneurial activity, after payment has been made or imputed for all other factors of production.

A further distinction is made, as explained in Chapter 10, between *normal profit* and *pure profit*. Normal profit is the minimum profit necessary to retain a firm in a particular industry in the long run. In other words, normal profit is the return to entrepreneurial ability to organize and manage the other factors of production in order to produce a specific commodity. If the return for this activity is insufficient, the entrepreneur will transfer his organizational ability to managing a firm in another industry, just as additional units of a factor's service will be made available only at higher prices.

Any profit greater than the normal profit is termed a pure or economic profit. Note the difference between *economic profit* and *economic rent*. Each is a surplus — an amount greater than that required to attract a factor into a particular use — but economic rent is due only to a fixed or inelastic supply of a factor, whereas economic or pure profit arises because other firms do not enter the industry to reduce the profit realized by each firm.

Risk, Uncertainty, and Profit

Profit is sometimes described as a reward or return to risk-taking. However, this is only one of the reasons for profits. Moreover, a distinction must be made between *calculable and incalculable risks*. Calculable risks are those unfortunate events such as fire and flood which, on the basis of past experience, are certain to happen to some firms, although no one knows which particular firms will be affected in the future. The *probability* that any given firm will experience a fire, flood, death of key personnel, and so on, can be calculated; insurance against loss from such misfortune can be purchased. Since the insurance premiums are another cost of production to the firm, this is not the kind of risks which are implied in an explanation of profits.

Incalculable or uninsurable risks are those which are related to the *uncertainty* of future events. Changes in economic, political, or social conditions cannot be predicted on the probabilistic basis used to predict the occurrence of insurable risks. Social conditions may change consumer preferences, for example, or the willingness of married women to enter the labour force may change, with resulting changes in related product prices and wages. Political conditions can open new export markets or close existing ones, or possibly block the import of raw materials from a particular country. Economic conditions can result in substantial changes in fiscal and monetary policies and tariff policies, or in public policies for assisting research and development. Any of these changes can alter a firm's costs and revenues; thus at any time a firm faces considerable uncertainty about its future profit or loss position. It will of course attempt to predict the changes which will most directly affect its particular operations, but some uncertainty must remain.

Another kind of uncertainty relates not to the economy-wide conditions described above but to the uncertainty associated with particular *innovations*. A new technique, perhaps reflected in more complex equipment, may be expected to reduce production costs. Whether this will actually occur remains uncertain until a firm has made the expenditures to develop and install new equipment. A new product may involve an even greater degree of uncertainty since it may require new machinery and raise special packaging and transportation problems, as well as the uncertainty of consumer acceptance or demand for the product.

Some entrepreneurs will be more willing than others to produce existing commodities or to undertake innovations under higher degrees of uncertainty and therefore, if conditions are favourable, will realize a pure profit. They may of course incur a substantial loss if their predictions or expectations are seriously inaccurate. The lower the degree of uncertainty, the more entrepreneurs or firms there will be in the industry and thus, the lower will be profits in the form of a return to accepting uncertainty or uninsurable risks.

Competition, Monopoly, and Profits

The comparison of firms under different market structures, presented in Chapter 11, emphasize that any of these firms could realize a pure profit in the short run. Whether such profits were made in the long run, however, depended on the degree of freedom that existed for other firms to enter the industry. Thus profits due to innovation could disappear in the long run in the absence of patents or other restrictions to entry.

Another reason for the existence of pure profits, therefore, is the variety of barriers preventing a new firm from entering an industry, and thus permitting existing firms to exercise more control over the price of their product. Monopoly profit is sometimes confused with profit due to innovation because most innovations are protected by patents, a major source of monopoly control. The distinction is important, however, because monopolies or restricted-entry oligopolies are not the sole sources of innovation.

The difference between monopoly profit and profit as a return to risk-taking is significant for public policy purposes. "Monopoly profits" is a cliché often used in a manner that implies all profit attributable to monopolistic conditions is an unnecessary surplus and thus socially undesirable. Under a market system, however, some profit is necessary to encourage innovation which leads to lower costs and improved products. This must be viewed separately from the profit due only to barriers against the entry of other firms. When this approach is taken, it becomes clear that public attitudes toward profits must be reflected in policies to increase competition or to regulate natural monopolies, rather than in simply attacking all profits. One of the advantages often cited for a centrally planned economy, or for public ownership of certain industries, is that under these conditions profit is unnecessary because the state becomes the entrepreneur: profit is not required either to maintain production of given commodities or to serve as an incentive for innovation. In some of the centrally planned economies and in some publicly owned industries, however, it has been necessary to introduce incentive schemes as encouragement for managers to reduce costs and to improve quality.

Review of the Main Points

1. The distribution of income among productive factors depends on the prices of factor services and the quantity of these services supplied. Factors are stocks of potential contributions to production; factor services are the flows of actual contributions of a factor during a specified period. Factors are generally categorized as land, labour, and capital, with the occasional addition of entrepreneurship.

2. The marginal productivity theory is an explanation of the demand for factor services. The marginal revenue product of one unit of factor service is the change in a firm's total revenue associated with the use of an additional unit of the factor's service. A firm will employ additional units only if the price per unit does not exceed its marginal revenue product. The marginal revenue product curve is therefore a firm's demand curve for the services of a particular factor.

3. The demand for a factor's service will have a greater price elasticity (a) the closer the substitutability of other factors, (b) the more elastic the demand for the related product, (c) the larger the cost of the factor in the total production cost, and (d) the more gradual the decline in the factor's marginal productivity.

4. The profit-maximizing quantity of a factor's service to be employed is the quantity at which the marginal resource cost equals the marginal revenue product. The lowest-cost combination of factor services is determined by employing the quantity of each factor's services such that the ratio of the marginal physical product to the marginal resource cost is the same for each factor.

5. The price for a factor's services may have two components: economic rent and transfer earnings. The latter is the minumum price required to attract the factor away from other uses. Economic rent, the difference between transfer and actual earnings, is due to the fixed quantity available of the factor. Quasi-rent is the surplus earnings realized because the quantity available is fixed in the short run, but not in the long run.

6. Capital is any man-made means of production, and includes real or tangible items such as plant, equipment, and residential housing. Financial assets represent ownership of, or creditors' claims on, capital items. The value of an asset depends on its yield or net return. The present value or capitalized value of an asset is equal to the sum of the present values of the annual income earned by the asset, plus the present value of what it might be sold for at the end of the earnings period. The internal rate of return is the rate which makes the present value of the future stream of net receipts from a capital item equal to its cost.

7. A firm should invest in a capital item if the cost of a capital item is less than the present value of the future net returns, or if its internal rate of return is greater than the internal rate on the best alternative project or the interest rate on borrowed funds.

8. The marginal efficiency of capital decreases as an economy's capital stock rises because increasing the proportion of capital to labour (capital deepening) leads to diminishing marginal productivity of capital.

9. The long-run equilibrium level of the capital stock would be reached when the rate of interest equals the marginal efficiency of capital. As long as technological change continues to shift the MEC curve outward, and there is not a long-term rise in interest rates, an economy is not likely to reach the equilibrium level of the capital stock.

10. The structure of interest rates is explained by four main factors differentiating loans or bonds: (1) time to maturity; (2) risk; (3) type of collateral; (4) expected rate of inflation.

11. Profit, the difference between total revenues and the total of explicit and implicit costs, is the return to entrepreneurial activity. Normal profit is the minimum profit required to retain or attract a firm into an industry. Pure profit is the amount by which total profit exceeds normal profit.

12. Profit is realized by firms that are willing to operate under conditions of uncertainty about general economics, political, and social conditions, and about the consequences of its own innovations. Profit can also be realized, even when there is little general uncertainty and no innovation, when new firms are prevented from entering an industry by barriers such as those described for monopolies and restricted-entry oligopolies.

13. Profits are necessary in a market system to induce entrepreneurs to organize other factors of production in productive processes, to produce under conditions of uncertainty, and to undertake innovations.

Review and Discussion Questions

1. "There need not be three categories of productive factors (land, labour, capital) because there is actually only one productive factor: capital." Explain why someone might make this statement. Is it completely true? Why?

2. Explain carefully why the demand curve for a factor's services is downward sloping. Why does the elasticity of demand for labour, over a given price range, vary among firms operating under different product market structures?

3. Suppose that an area of residential land is rezoned for commercial uses. What change, if any, will there be in the economic rent realized on this land? Should any public action be taken concerning changes in economic rent resulting from zoning changes?

4. Why is the interest rate such an important price in the market system?

5. How can one account for the wide range of interest rates that occur at any given time in the economy?

6. "Normal profits, by definition, are enough to keep a firm in a given industry. The government should therefore tax away all profits in excess of normal profits." Do you agree? Why?

Sources and Selected Readings

Barlowe, Raleigh. Land Resource Economics, 2nd ed. Englewood Cliffs, N.J.: Prentice-Hall, 1972.

Boulding, Kenneth E. Economic Analysis, Volume 1: Microeconomics, 4th ed. New York: Harper and Row, 1966.

Due, John F., and Robert W. Clower. Intermediate Economic Analysis, 5th ed. Homewood, Ill.: Irwin, 1966.

Leftwich, Richard H. The Price System and Resource Association, 5th ed. New York: Hinsdale, Ill.: Dryden Press, 1973.

Stonier, Alfred W., and Douglas C. Hague. A Textbook of Economic Theory, 4th ed. New York: Longmans, Green, 1973.

14   Labour Markets, Wages, and Labour Unions

Wages and salaries constitute the largest share of the total income received by all factors of production in Canada. The counterpart of this is that labour costs account for the largest share of total production costs for all goods and services. Consequently, the conditions determining the price of labour services in the Canadian economy warrant careful attention. This chapter first considers the determination of wages under different labour market conditions and then examines the effects of labour unions and the collective bargaining process on wages and employment.

A.   Wage Determination in Labour Markets

Some Definitions

Wages

Payment for labour services takes a variety of forms, and statistical reports of such payments use different terms and definitions, with the result that some clarification of the term "wages" is essential to the following discussion.

Wages, as used in a general analysis of labour markets, include all forms of payment for labour services: not only hourly wages or annual salaries but also commissions, tips, royalties, and bonuses. In addition to these direct payments, indirect compensation in the form of medical insurance premiums and benefits, supplementary unemployment benefits, pensions, and recreational facilities, are also included. Such indirect costs or "fringe benefits" now amount to more than 25 per cent of the direct labour costs in Canada. This all-inclusive concept of wages is thus broader than that implied in the terms, *earnings* or *employment income*, which refer only to the direct payments to labour.

For some purposes, such as an analysis of consumer expenditure patterns, the relevant measure is *take-home pay*; or what remains after deductions such as those for income taxes, social security and unemployment contributions, and union dues; but the emphasis in this chapter is on *gross earnings*: total direct payments prior to payroll deductions. A distinction must also be made between money wages and real wages. *Money wages* are the actual wages paid. An increase in one's money wage of 3 per cent will, however, represent no increase in purchasing power if prices also increase by 3 per cent. Comparisons of money wages paid in different years should thus take account of price changes over the same period; this is done by dividing the current money wage by the Consumer Price Index for the given year. Many studies of wages therefore concentrate on *real wages*, the real income one enjoys in terms of the quantity of goods and services that can be purchased in return for labour services.

Wages are also expressed in terms of the length of time over which the payment is made: $4.50 per hour, $150 per week, $600 per month, or $7,800 per year. Such expressions actually indicate the *wage rate*, the amount paid per unit of time. One variation from this is payment based on the number of units of output produced by a worker, usually referred to as a *piece rate*. In the following discussion, however, labour service is viewed in terms of time periods and thus the wage rate is the appropriate measure of payment. Furthermore, just as the broad structure of interest rates was represented simply as *the* interest rate in the last chapter, the broad structure of wage rates paid to different types of labour and in different areas will be represented for convenience as *the* wage rate.

Labour Service

Another simplification involves a reference to labour service as if all labour services were of the same quality in terms of skills. This is also a convenient means for dealing with a wide range of physical and mental skills and other personal differences which partly account for the range of wage rates. Labour services have become increasingly differentiated in recent years by opportunities for vocational training at all levels of the educational system: the effect of this differentiation is considered further in the section on occupational wage differences.

Labour Markets

A general definition of labour markets would parallel the definition for commodity or product markets: namely, the interaction of buyers and sellers of particular labour services, such that there is a market for each identifiable type of labour service. In an economy which covers as large an area as Canada, there are even more labour markets than distinct types of labour services because individuals are unaware of conditions in distant regions. There are almost as many markets, for example, for unskilled labour as there are municipalities because buyers or sellers of such labour generally find that it does not pay to devote time and expense to searching more widely for lower-wage labour, or higher-wage jobs, at the same skill level, or to incur the related moving costs.

Markets for some other types of labour service, however, especially those associated with higher levels of education, are closely interrelated. On the demand side, an employer may decide that a particular job can be filled equally well by graduates of various technology programs and thus will seek potential employees in the various markets for different types of technologists. On the supply side, a recent graduate in chemical technology may seek employment in the markets for salesmen, research assistants, production supervisors, and so on. Labour markets therefore are more or less distinct or separated depending on the difference in job functions and the mobility of persons offering labour services.

The Supply of Labour

Labour Supply in the Short Run

When the behaviour of firms in product markets is examined, a clear distinction can be made between their decisions in the *short run* and in the *long run*. These terms are also used in describing the supply side of labour markets, but with less precise meanings. For the present purpose, the short run may be defined as the period within which the total population and its level of schooling and training does not vary significantly. That is, the total quantity and quality of potential workers are fixed. In the long run, these factors may change and hence alter the supply of labour.

The supply of labour is a schedule or curve showing the quantity of labour services which will be offered during a specific period over a range of alternative wage rates.

Two major factors determine the short-run supply of labour: the percentage of the population seeking employment or in employment at a given time — the *labour force participation rate* — and the *number of hours per day or week* that these persons are willing to work. The labour force participation rate[1] and the length of the work week are treated separately for empirical studies in labour economics, but for the present purpose they can be treated as one. The decision about whether to enter the labour force can be considered a special case of the decision regarding the number of hours to offer: namely, to offer zero hours or to offer some hours.

The Choice: Labour vs. Leisure. Decisions about the number of hours per week (or weeks per year) to offer as labour services are decisions

[1] The labour force participation rate is defined as the percentage of the population aged 14 years or over who are in the labour force; and recall from Chapter 3 that the labour force consists of persons who are employed and those who are unemployed — as determined by the monthly labour force survey.

about allocating one's time between labour and leisure. In this simple explanation of labour supply, labour is defined as any income-earning activity; leisure is all other activity. This approach assumes that labour services are offered to the market only to earn income which in turn can be used to purchase goods and services; it is further assumed that leisure is also a good, yielding satisfaction or enjoyment. Although this view may seem to ignore the satisfaction that people find in their work, and the dissatisfaction associated with some forms of leisure, such as mowing the lawn, these circumstances are at least partly reflected in labour/leisure decisions. One might also object that individuals are not free to determine how many hours they will work each week because the minimum is set by individual firms and the maximum in many cases is set by legislation. Individuals do, however, have some freedom in choosing whether to work at part-time or full-time jobs, whether to work for a few months or for a full year, whether to take a second job as "moonlighters", and so on.

The labour/leisure choice and the derivation of an individual's labour supply curve can be illustrated using the *indifference curve analysis* that was introduced in Chapter 9 to explain an individual's demand curve. Figure 14.1 presents an individual's indifference curves for different levels of satisfaction derived from various combinations of leisure and other goods (and services) purchased with labour income. Each indifference curve shows that in moving upward along the curve more goods must be purchased to compensate for fewer leisure hours if the same level of satisfaction is to be maintained. A higher-level indifference curve indicates that a greater total satisfaction is realized by combining more goods with a given quantity of leisure.

At a wage rate of $1 per hour, one can enjoy 16 hours of leisure — assuming a minimum of 8 hours for sleeping and eating — but no other goods, or $16 worth of goods and services but no leisure, or any intermediate combination of leisure and other goods. These alternative combinations are indicated by the budget line WW_1. The greatest satisfaction possible at this wage rate is at A, the tangency point of WW_1 and I_1, with 8 hours of leisure being "consumed" and 8 hours of labour offered to acquire $8 worth of goods and services.

A higher wage rate, $2 per hour, will move this person to a higher level of satisfaction shown by point B. Only 5 hours of leisure are consumed because the income from each hour of labour will now buy more goods and services. The move from A to B consists of an *income effect* (A to C) and a *substitution effect* (C to B). The income effect results from the increased wage rate: for any given number of labour hours, the individual receives a higher income due to the higher wage per hour. The substitution effect results from the increased price of leisure: for any given number of leisure hours, the individual "pays" a higher price because more goods and services are forfeited in forgoing an hour of labour at $2 per hour than at $1

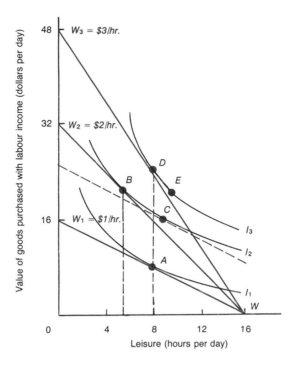

Figure 14.1   The Labour/Leisure Choice
Combinations of leisure and labour income yielding the same level of satisfaction
are shown by the indifference curve, I_1. At a wage rate of $1 per hour, one can
enjoy 16 hours of leisure per day, or goods purchased with 16 hours of labour
income, or various combinations indicated by the budget line, WW_1. (The budget
line assumes 16 hours per day are available for the allocation decision.) Satisfaction is maximized by combination *A*, 8 hours each of leisure and labour. At a wage
of $2 per hour, the optimum combination is *B*, 5 hours of leisure and 11 hours of
labour. The income effect of the wage increase would lead one to "buy" more
leisure, about 9 hours as indicated by *C*, but the substitution or price effect of the
wage increase outweighs the income effect. Since leisure is now more expensive,
one substitutes more goods for leisure, and chooses to offer 11 hours of labour.

per hour. In moving from *C* to *B*, more goods are substituted for
fewer hours of leisure. The substitution effect *outweighs* the income
effect because, on balance, the individual offers more labour time at
the higher wage rate.

When the wage rate rises to $3 per hour, the net result is differ-
ent. Figure 14.1 shows that the most satisfactory combination, represented by *D*, is 8 hours of leisure and 8 hours of labour. Again there
is both an income and substitution effect of the wage increase, (imagine a budget line drawn parallel to WW_2 and tangent to I_3 at *E*), but
this time the income effect outweighs the substitution effect. For a
given number of labour hours, this person can buy so many more
goods that he decides to enjoy more leisure hours than he did at a
wage of $2 per hour.

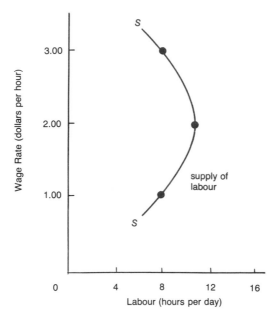

Figure 14.2   Individual's Labour Supply Curve
An individual's labour supply curve can be derived from Figure 14.1. The number
of labour hours offered at alternative wage rates is shown by points *A, B* and *D*.
These are plotted here to produce the supply curve, *SS*. At a wage below $2.00
per hour, the price or substitution effect outweighs the income effect, but the
reverse is true at wage rates above $2.00 per hour.

The quantity of labour offered at each wage rate is plotted in
Figure 14.2. In this particular case, the number of hours worked
increases as the wage rate increases through the lower range of wage
rates, but at higher wage rates the number of hours declines with
further increases in the wage rates. In this example the substitution
effect outweighs the income effect at low wage rates; at higher rates
the income effect outweighs the substitution effect. Which effect
outweighs the other depends on the particular shape of the indifference curves.

The shape of labour supply curves has been the subject of much
controversy among economists.[2] Since actual experiments with different wage rates to determine individuals' offerings of labour services at any given time are not possible, one can only speculate on
the general shape of labour supply curves. Nevertheless, the income

---

[2] For an interesting example of the controversy, see Elliot J. Berg,
  "Backward-Sloping Labor Supply Functions in Dual Economies — The
  Africa Case," *Quarterly Journal of Economics*, Vol. LXXV (August 1961),
  pp. 468-492.

and substitution effects are present in wage changes, and provide useful explanations for the number of hours offered by individuals at different wage rates. There is, for example, some evidence of a backward-bending labour supply curve in the historical data on wages and average length of the work week. Although these data must be interpreted carefully the decline in the average work week from over 60 hours to less than 40 hours during the past century, while real wages have increased substantially, suggests that the income effect has been dominant.

When the supply curves for individuals are aggregated to obtain a supply curve for a market or the economy, the full influence of the income effect is not evident because individuals enter the labour market at different wage rates. That is, the backward-bending portion of one individual's supply curve may be offset by the upward-sloping portion of the supply curve of another individual who enters the labour market at a higher wage rate. It is therefore generally assumed that the economy's short-run labour supply curve is upward-sloping over the relevant range of wage rates, but is highly inelastic.

Labour Supply in the Long Run

An economy's total supply of labour services in the long run is determined primarily by changes in the population due to *international migration* and *birth and death rates*. Where there are no barriers to migration, labour may be expected to respond to changes in the relative real wages of different countries. If the wage rate in Canada, for example, should increase more quickly than in the United States, one would expect that there would be an increasing flow of American immigrants to Canada. A reverse movement of the relative wage rates would result in an increased number of emigrants from Canada to the United States, all other things being equal. The assumption of constancy in other factors influencing migration is clearly not appropriate in light of actual experience with immigration policies and political and social changes in particular countries. Nonetheless, changes in relative wage rates will partly offset or augment the other influences on migration, except where there are complete barriers to migration due to political decrees.

The natural factors of births and deaths, while not directly related to the wage rate, influence the quantity of labour services available in the long run. An increasing birth rate combined with a declining death rate, which was Canada's experience in the 1950s, will increase the total population and thus the potential labour services. The elasticity of the long-run labour supply curve, however, depends on whether the rate of increase in the natural population together with net immigration is proportionately more or less than the rate of increase in real wages.

Wage Determination Under Pure Competition

When product markets were described in terms of alternative structures, emphasis was placed on the number of supplies in different markets because there were assumed to be many buyers in all product markets. In describing the degree of competition in different labour markets, however, both the demand and supply sides must be considered, since the numbers involved on either side can range widely. Until the expansion of the National Hockey League and the founding of the World Hockey Association, for example, there were only two buyers in Canada for the labour services of professional hockey players — the Toronto Maple Leafs and the Montreal Canadiens.[3] A purely competitive labour market therefore requires that there are not only many sellers of a service but also many buyers. The other conditions are also similar to those necessary for a purely competitive product market: workers and employers have full knowledge of market conditions such as job opportunities and wage rates; workers are perfectly mobile; and each worker and employer acts individually in making employment decisions.

Demand for Labour

The demand for labour by an individual firm was examined in Chapter 13. (Refer again especially to Tables 13.1 and 13.2 and Figures 13.1 and 13.2.) Two demand curves were derived, one for a firm in a purely competitive product market and one for a firm in an imperfectly competitive product market. Each of these firms, however, may be buyers in a purely competitive *labour* (or factor) market. For example, the oligopolistic automobile firms enter what are close to purely competitive labour markets when employing typists, night watchmen, or cafeteria workers.

The labour demand curve of the purely competitive firm was seen to be more elastic than that of the imperfectly competitive firm because the former firm faced a perfectly elastic demand, and thus received a constant price for its products. The downward slope of the labour demand curve reflected only the diminishing marginal product of additional units of labour service, whereas the labour demand curve of the imperfectly competitive firm reflected a decreasing product price as well as diminishing labour productivity.

The market demand for labour, as seen in Chapter 13, is less elastic than the summation of the individual firms' demand curves. Moreover, since these usually reflect the demand of firms operating in different product markets it is not possible to make a general statement about the degree of elasticity in the market demand curve.

Shifts in the demand for labour were also explained briefly in Chapter 13. The demand for particular kinds of labour services will

---

[3] Some of the provincial hockey leagues could also be included as buyers if one uses a broader definition of "professional" than is implied here.

shift outward with an *increase in the demand for a commodity* requiring those labour services for its production. The increased commodity demand represents an outward shift of a firm's marginal revenue product curve — its labour demand curve — because a higher price can be obtained for each unit sold.

The labour demand curve will also shift outward if there is an *increase in the marginal physical product of labour*. Because the marginal physical product of labour declines as additional labour is added to a given quantity of other inputs such as capital, an increase in the latter will extend to the point at which diminishing marginal productivity of labour begins, and hence will shift outward labour's MPP curve. A second reason for an increase in marginal physical product is an *improvement in the quality of labour services*, usually resulting from further education or training that makes a given unit of labour more productive.

Single Firm in Purely Competitive Labour Market. The labour supply curve facing a firm in a purely competitive labour market is horizontal or perfectly elastic, as shown in Figure 14.3a, because there are so many buyers of the given type of labour service that a single firm has no control over the wage it pays. If the firm offers a wage below the prevailing rate, OW_1, it will not be able to find any workers because they can obtain the prevailing rate at other firms. Nor will the firm offer a higher rate because it can obtain as many or as few workers as it wants at the prevailing rate.

The firm thus is concerned only with determining the profit-maximizing quantity of labour to be hired at the given wage rate. This quantity will be realized when the marginal revenue product of

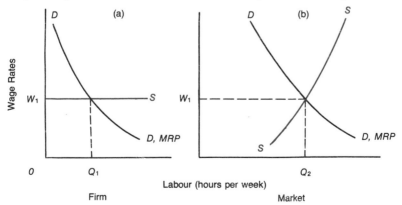

Figure 14.3 Purely Competitive Labour Market
Firms which buy labour services in a purely competitive labour market face a perfectly elastic labour supply curve, such that any quantity can be purchased at the market equilibrium wage rate, OW_1. Given the firm's demand curve, DD, it buys OQ_1 hours of labour per week. The equilibrium wage rate, OW_1, is determined by the intersection of the market demand and supply curves; the equilibrium quantity at this wage rate is OQ_2.

labour is equal to its marginal resource cost. Since the supply curve is perfectly elastic, the marginal resource cost is the same as the average resource cost: the given wage rate. Thus the profit-maximizing quantity is the level at which the marginal revenue product curve, the demand curve, intersects the labour supply curve. For the firm illustrated in Figure 14.3a this is OQ_1 hours per week. In practice, this quantity will be converted into the number of employees to be hired by dividing OQ_1 by the firm's standard work week.

Equilibrium in a Purely Competitive Labour Market

The supply curve for any given labour market is determined by summing individual's supply curves; these in turn are the outcome of the labour/leisure choices made by individuals willing to supply their labour services to the particular market. As noted previously the demand curve is approximated by, but is less elastic than, the aggregate of the firms' demand or marginal revenue product curves. The market equilibrium quantity and wage rate, as shown in Figure 14.3b, is determined at the intersection of the supply and demand curves. If a wage higher than OW_1 exists in the market, the quantity of labour supplied will exceed OQ_2 but employers will want less than OQ_2; the result will be an excess supply of labour, or unemployment. Some labour will be transferred to other labour markets or out of the labour force, while other unemployed workers will be willing to work at a lower wage. Employers thus hire workers only at a lower wage until the rate falls to OW_1 where there is neither an excess supply nor an excess demand. The opposite process would occur if the wage rate were less than OW_1 since employers could actually pay a rate higher than OW_1 for any labour less than OQ_2 without incurring a loss on the marginal unit employed. Thus employers would gradually offer a higher wage rate to attract more workers until OW_1 was reached.

Wage Determination Under Imperfect Competition

Imperfect competition in labour markets may arise because there are either relatively few buyers or relatively few sellers or both. The latter two possibilities are considered in the next section when the economic effects of trade unions are examined. The existence of only one buyer in a given labour market is termed *monopsony*, and the single employer is said to have monopsonistic power. One who has read Chapter 11 could therefore correctly anticipate that the existence of a few buyers in a labour market is termed *oligopsony*, and that they might be expected to act in concert to behave as a monopsonist would.

Monopsony, like monopoly, is rare. The closest case to that of monopsony is the company in a "company town" in mining or logging areas which employs almost everyone in the town's labour force. To the extent that workers are prepared to move to other areas, however, they can participate in a labour market that is larger than the company town. But the cost of moving may be substantial, and employees in remote areas are often unaware of other employment opportunities.

Labour markets may be imperfect for reasons other than the limited number of buyers and sellers. The cost of moving to other areas and the lack of information about other employment opportunities, mentioned above in the case of a company town, are examples of two major limitations on the perfect operation of a labour market : *immobility of labour* and *incomplete knowledge* of labour market conditions.

The effect of these imperfections is to reduce the geographical movement of workers among labour markets in response to changing relative wage rates in these different areas. The supply curve will be further to the right in a low-wage market, and further to the left in a high-wage market, such that the wage difference will be greater when there is immobility and lack of information than if these conditions did not exist. The federal government and some provincial governments therefore have introduced programs to make more information available concerning wage rates and job vacancies in various occupations and areas, to assist workers in moving to other areas, and to retrain workers for occupations where demand is increasing most quickly. Employment counselling programs also provide information to workers who may be unaware that they could seek employment in other occupations with their existing basic skills.

The labour demand curve for a monopsonistic firm is its marginal revenue product curve, as explained previously. It is on the supply side that the monopsonist's condition differs from that of a firm in a purely competitive labour market. Since the labour supply curve facing the monopsonist is the market supply curve, it will be upward sloping. In order to attract increasing numbers of workers away from other labour markets, or into the labour force, successively higher wage rates must be offered. Moreover, the marginal resource cost of an additional worker will exceed the higher wage rate required to attract an additional worker, because persons currently employed by the firm will also have to be paid the same higher wage to retain their services. Thus, for any quantity of labour services hired, the marginal resource cost exceeds the wage rate. The marginal cost of hiring a sixth employee, for example, includes the

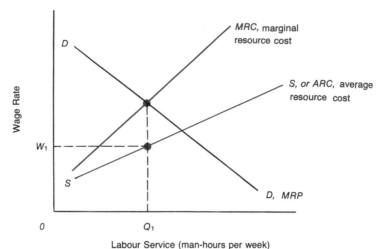

Figure 14.4   Wage Determination in Imperfect Labour Markets
When there are only a few buyers of labour, the buyers face an upward sloping
labour supply curve. A single, or monopsonistic, buyer faces the market supply
curve, *SS*. The supply curve is the firm's average resource cost curve, *ARC*,
because it indicates the wage rate which must be paid to attract a given quantity of
labour. The marginal resource cost, *MRC*, shows the increase in total cost associated with additional units of labour and rises more steeply than the *ARC* curve.
The firm's profit-maximizing quantity of labour, *OQ₁*, is the quantity at which *MRP*
= *MRC*; this quantity can be hired at wage, *OW₁*.

full wage paid to this employee plus the amount required to raise the
wages of the other five employees to the new wage rate. This is
illustrated in Figure 14.4 where the MRC curve is above the supply,
or average resource cost curve, ARC, and rises more steeply. This
situation is similar to that of a firm in an imperfectly competitive
product market: the MR curve was below the AR curve and fell more
steeply because an additional unit could be sold only at a lower
price, but all units were then sold at this lower price.

The profit-maximizing quantity of labour for the firm illustrated
in Figure 14.4 is the quantity at which the marginal resource cost
equals the marginal revenue product, namely OQ_1. The wage rate to
be paid to attract OQ_1 units of labour is OW_1 since the supply curve
indicates that workers will be willing to supply OQ_1 hours per week
at a wage of OW_1. Note that if there had been many buyers in this
labour market (that is, if it had been purely competitive), the equilibrium wage and quantity would both have been greater, because the
equilibrium levels would have been determined by the intersection
of the supply and demand curves.

Figure 14.3 and 14.4 illustrate the cases of perfect competition
and monopsony in the labour market. The effects of labour unions,
acting as monopoly sellers of labour services, are examined in a later
section of this chapter.

The Structure of Wages in Canada

The wage rates determined in the multiplicity of labour markets in Canada constitute the *structure* of wages. The analysis, just presented, of wage determination in competitive and monopsonistic markets has suggested a few reasons for the existence of different wages in different labour markets. These reasons are not sufficient, however, to explain, for example, why some persons are paid $1.50 per hour while others receive $150 per hour.

Such wage differences are assumed to take account of the net advantages of some jobs compared with others. Jobs differ, it is suggested, in five basic ways: pleasantness or disagreeableness of the work, cost of training required, regularity or uncertainty of employment, degree of responsibility and probability of further success. On the basis of such criteria, some jobs would be preferable to others; differences in wages represent the amounts necessary to attract persons into the less desirable jobs. These wage differences that compensate workers for the relative disadvantages of their jobs are usually termed *equalizing differences*.

If all wage differences could be explained as equalizing differences, the commonly observed situation in which higher-wage jobs are associated with some of the best working conditions would not exist. This suggests that a substantial component of wage differences represents a *nonequalizing difference*, that part of the wage difference is compensation for, or is due to something other than, characteristics of particular occupations. The numerous labour market imperfections account for much of such differences: imperfections such as monopsonistic employers, labour unions and professional associations, labour immobility, and inadequate information about labour markets. Differences in labour quality, due to different levels of education or training, also explain a substantial part of wage differentials. The economic rent associated with individuals whose rare skills are much in demand, as explained in Chapter 13, forms a large part of the difference between, for example, the wage paid to a hockey club's outstanding player and that paid to its assistant accountant.

Occupational income data such as those presented in Table 14.1 may provide few surprises. A closer look at more detailed occupational data, however, has revealed important evidence that is not apparent from average incomes reported for broad occupational groups. Occupations vary greatly in the range of wages received by persons within a given occupation, with wider ranges being found in the lowest- and highest-income occupations where there is more irregularity of employment or variation in skills and personal factors than in the salaried occupations at the middle-income levels.

Table 14.1

Earnings by Occupation, Canada, 1973

Occupational Category	Average Earnings of Full-Year Workers*	
	Males	Females
Managerial	$14,731	$8,335
Professional	13,500	7,770
Construction	10,577	**
Sales	10,187	3,942
Processing and Machining	9,463	5,065
Transport	9,382	5,094
Production Fabrication	9,261	4,453
Clerical	8,483	5,584
Service	7,796	3,368
Farming	6,175	2,662

*Workers who reported having worked 50-52 weeks.
**Sample too small for reliable estimate.

Source: Statistics Canada, *Income Distributions by Size in Canada, 1973*.

Education is a major factor in occupational wage differentials. Table 14.2 shows that the higher the average income for an occupation, the higher usually is the percentage of persons in that occupation who have above-average schooling. Formal education not only develops certain occupational skills, it also provides the basis for further training. Several studies have shown that the higher the level of one's formal education, the more likely one is to participate in on-the-job training programs or other forms of continuing education which lead to still higher incomes.

Table 14.2

Selected Occupations, Income and Schooling, Males, Canada, 1971

Occupation	Average Employment Income	Percentage with at least Grade 12 Schooling
All Occupations	$ 6,574	34
Law and Jurisprudence	17,860	97
Architects and Engineers	11,237	86
Teaching	9,014	93
Sales	7,120	43
Fabricating	6,402	23
Construction Trades	6,175	20
Clerical	5,823	47
Farmers	3,699	22

Source: Statistics Canada, *Income of Individuals, 1971 Census of Canada*.

Part of the occupational wage differentials are also explained by the fact that certain occupations have a very high proportion of female workers. There are several implications of such a situation. For example, the annual incomes in such occupations tend to be lower due to what Ostry and Zaidi term "discontinuous work experience", or intermittant participation in the labour force. It is suggested that this "might have prevented female workers from taking up jobs in higher positions or positions of responsibility and thus affected their earnings adversely".[4] Even within narrowly defined occupations, however, male/female wage differentials remain: an Ontario study of more than 2,500 jobs found male wages to be greater by 22 per cent. This difference was almost halved in the case of unionized firms, and was reduced by more than one-third when wages were based on piece rates rather than time rates.[5]

For some predominantly female occupations such as clerical work, there are many qualified persons not currently in the labour force. A slight increase in the wage rate in such occupations may attract a proportionately larger increase in the number of persons willing to enter the occupation at the higher rate. That is, the labour supply curve is highly elastic, resulting in only a small wage increase even though demand may increase substantially.[6] In other occupations, the short-run supply curve is much less elastic; a similar increase in demand results in a much larger wage increase.

Finally, some occupations, such as medicine, dentistry, and law, have a high proportion of self-employed persons. Their reported incomes include some return to capital (a dentist's net income, for example, includes a return to his investment in office equipment and tools) which should be deducted to determine the true payment for labour services. Also, self-employed persons have more freedom in deciding how many hours to work; this tends to be higher than the average number of hours per week for employees.

B. Labour Unions and Collective Bargaining in Canada

Size and Structure of Unions

Approximately one-third of all non-agricultural employees in Canada belong to labour unions. A complete picture of labour or-

---

[4] Sylvia Ostry and Mahmood A. Zaidi, *Labour Economics in Canada*, 2nd ed. Toronto: Macmillan, 1972, p. 289. This source presents a comprehensive examination of occupational, industrial, and geographical wage differentials.

[5] Morley Gunderson, "Male-Female Wage Differentials and the Impact of Equal Pay Legislation," *Review of Economics and Statistics*, November 1975.

[6] Noah M. Meltz, *Changes in the Occupational Composition of the Canadian Labour Force, 1931-1961*. Ottawa: Queen's Printer, 1965.

ganizations should also include members of professional associations, many of which resemble labour unions in some organizational aspects and economic effects. These two types of labour organization traditionally have been treated differently in government policies and legislation; consequently there is less information available on the scope and impact of professional associations than on labour unions.

Union Growth. Union membership in Canada has increased substantially, although not steadily, in terms of numbers and percentage of non-agricultural workers. Public attitudes tended to favour unionism during the two World Wars and the Depression, but employer opposition halted its growth in the 1920s. In the postwar period, unions have expanded steadily but not as quickly as in the 1930s and 1940s because the most easily organized workers had been brought into unions previously, and because occupational growth was greatest in the service sector where union organizing was more difficult. Thus, as Table 14.3 indicates, the percentage of non-agricultural workers belonging to unions declined slightly in the 1960s but increased again in the early 1970s.

Table 14.3

Union Membership in Canada, 1921-1973, Selected Years

Year	Union Membership (thousands)	Total Non-agricultural Paid Workers (thousands)	Union Membership as a percentage of Total Non-agricultural Paid Workers
1921	313	1,956	16.0
1926	275	2,299	12.0
1931	311	2,028	15.3
1936	323	1,994	16.2
1941	462	2,566	18.0
1946	832	2,986	27.9
1951	1,029	3,625	28.4
1956	1,352	4,058	33.3
1961	1,447	4,578	31.6
1966	1,736	5,658	30.7
1971	2,231	6,637	33.6
1973	2,610	7,181	36.3

Source: Canada Department of Labour, *Labour Organizations in Canada, 1973.*

Craft vs. Industrial Unions. Economic analysis of the effects of labour unions requires that a distinction be made between craft unions and industrial unions. *Craft unions* were the first type of labour organization to emerge, and included craftsmen such as shoe makers, carpenters, and printers. These unions consist of members from particular occupations regardless of the firm or industry in which they are employed. They are thus identified as carpenters unions, plasterers unions, electrical workers unions, and so on. *Industrial unions* developed during the 1930s particularly with the rapid growth of the automobile and steel industries. These unions draw their members from specific industries or groups of industries, and thus include workers in many occupations with a wide variety of skills.

Local, National, and International Unions

The organizational structure of labour unions includes local, national, and international unions, as well as federations of unions.

Local Unions. A union member's direct association is with his local union which usually consists of the members in one plant, firm, or local area. Locals range in size from less than ten to over 30,000 members, and may be chapters of a national or international union, or chartered directly by a federation, or independent of other associations.

National and International Unions. National unions, such as the Canadian Union of Public Employees (CUPE), may have many local chapters but these are located only in Canada. An international union often has many locals and a large membership in Canada, but most of the membership and the union headquarters are in the United States. These include some of the largest unions in Canada: United Steel Workers of America (175,000 members) and the International Union of United Automobile, Aerospace and Agriculture Implement Workers of America (107,000 members).

Federations and Congresses. Most unions are in turn affiliated with a federation or congress of unions which acts as a national spokesman for labour unions but has little direct control over individual unions. The Canadian Labour Congress (CLC) includes provincial federations of labour, Canadian branches of international unions, and most national unions. The CLC also has close ties with its American counterpart, the American Federation of Labour and Congress of Industrial Organizations (AFL-CIO). The Confederation of National Trade Unions (CNTU), based mainly in Quebec, comprises about 6 per cent of all union members. Two newer union federations are the Confederation of Canadian Unions (CCU) and the Centrale des syndicats démocratiques (CSD). Other unions, notably the Brotherhood of Locomotive Engineers, are not affiliated with any federation or congress. Table 14.4 shows that more than one-half of all union members are in international unions and that most of these are affiliated with both the AFL-CIO and the CLC.

Table 14.4

Union Membership by Type of Union and Affiliation, 1973

Type of Affiliation	No. of Unions	No. of Locals	Membership	
			Number	Percentage
International Unions	96	4,787	1,443,246	55.3
AFL-CIO/CLC	79	4,445	1,230,735	47.2
CLC only	5	195	139,481	5.3
AFL-CIO only	5	8	619	*
Unaffiliated Unions	7	139	72,411	2.8
National Unions	93	5,177	1,098,763	42.1
CLC	24	2,073	473,720	18.1
CNTU	9	977	163,928	6.3
CSD	8	233	41,000	1.6
CCU	10	43	17,455	0.7
Unaffiliated	42	1,851	402,660	15.4
Directly Chartered Local Unions	133	133	16,056	0.6
CLC	130	130	15,492	0.6
CNTU	3	3	564	*
Independent Local Organizations	158	158	51,571	2.0
Total	480	10,255	2,609,636	100.0

*Less than 0.1 per cent.

Source: Canada Department of Labour, *Labour Organizations in Canada*.

Union Goals, Techniques, and Effects

Union Goals

In earlier chapters, the objectives or goals of consumers and firms were the key to analyzing and predicting the behaviour or decisions of these groups. If one assumed that consumers wish to maximize utility and that firms seek maximum profits, consumption and production decisions followed logically. Behaviour of unions is more difficult to explain and predict because unions appear to have several objectives, some of which can be in conflict with each other. A general assumption is that unions seek to improve the economic welfare of union members by raising wages, including fringe benefits and working conditions. However, this assumption is too simple to take account of a complex combination of union goals. Priorities among these goals vary, of course, among unions, and over a period of time for any particular union.

1. Increased Wage Rate. As suggested above, the most common assumption is that unions attempt to raise the wage rate paid to their members. If a union succeeds in doing so, however, it may reduce the number of workers employed by the firm, unless the demand for labour is shifting outward.

2. Increased Total Income of Union Members. Some unions, recognizing that higher wage rates may result in unemployment, argue that they attempt to increase the aggregate income of all union members. Again, this may be possible but only when the demand for labour is inelastic, if there is no substantial increase in demand.

3. Fringe Benefits and Working Conditions. Particularly when unions have been able to realize recent large increases in wage rates, they may emphasize fringe benefits such as paid holidays, medical and pension benefits, education leave and tuition fees, and so on. Working conditions, including safety devices and equipment, recreational facilities, hours of work, and lighting and ventilation, also tend to receive priority when unions anticipate difficulty in securing large wage gains.

4. Work Rules and Job Security. Unions in industries or occupations where technology is changing quickly often bargain on the pace of work and the number of persons employed for a particular job function. In a few cases, this has led to *featherbedding*, or payment for unnecessary work. Featherbedding is evident, for example, in a union requirement that the railways employ locomotive firemen on diesel locomotives where firemen are not required. This situation arose when the railways switched from steam to diesel engines, and the union successfully opposed the displacement of locomotive firemen who previously had stoked the coal-fired steam engines.

Seniority systems are established to protect the jobs of union members with longest experience in a firm. When lay-offs are required, a seniority system requires that the most recent employees are the first to be laid off.

Grievance procedures also form a part of job security provisions. Arrangements are established whereby any problem or complaint concerning workers can, if necessary, be dealt with at successively higher management levels until a satisfactory solution is reached. If even this fails, the matter is referred to arbitration.

5. Union Security. In addition to seeking improved wages and security for its members, a union is also concerned with its own security. This requires that it preserve its strength by continuing to represent all workers within its potential jurisdiction. One aspect of this is persistent efforts to organize workers in plants or areas which have not been unionized; another aspect is the need to establish a *union shop* — the requirement that a new employee must join the union within a specified period, usually 30 days. This is a compromise between an *open shop* in which union membership is voluntary and a *closed shop* in which employers may hire only persons who have previously joined the union.

6. Political Goals and Activities. Unions also have a number of political goals. Some of these, such as increasing the minimum wage level, are directly associated with labour markets. Other objectives and activities, such as the support some unions have given to the New Democratic Party, are directed to changing more general social conditions.

Union Techniques and Tactics

Unions seek most of these goals in regular negotiations with the management of firms. Other techniques are sometimes used, and in any case, are a potential threat which management must take into account when replying to union demands.

Strikes. An organized strike can be the most effective weapon in gaining a union's objective if the union executive has substantial support among the membership and the financial resources to maintain a strike for what can become a matter of several months. However, if the management knows that members doubt the ability of the executive to secure its demands, or that the members' "strike pay" is meagre, a strike loses much of its potential effectiveness.

Working to Rule and Slowdowns. Instead of a strike, or in cases where organized strikes are forbidden, a union may order its members to "work to rule" or to slow down the pace of their work. Working to rule can cause considerable reduction in the normal work flow because workers generally have found methods to circumvent rules which resulted in delays or because some rules had been ignored. For example, when the postal workers were on a "work to rule" campaign a few years ago, they set aside mail which was not fully addressed, even when its destination was obvious from the address given. Union members may also organize the use of their sick leave so that a large portion of the employees are absent on particular days. Such tactics can be used by the union to show management the degree of its control over the members, indicating that it could, if it wished, conduct an effective strike.

Picketing. Public sympathy for a union's position in a strike is often sought by publicizing the strike through picketing — carrying signs around the property of the struck firm. The general public and members of other unions making deliveries to the plant or employed in the plant are urged not to cross the picket line, thus denying the firm services beyond those supplied by the union members.

Boycotts. A *primary boycott* consists of urging consumers not to buy the products or services of the struck firm. A *secondary boycott* attempts to put pressure on the struck firm by urging employees and customers of other firms not to handle or buy the product of the struck firm. By boycotting a supermarket, for example, unions associated with meat-packing plants might hope to have more effect than through a primary boycott. Because third-party firms can be harmed by this tactic, secondary boycotts are illegal in some provinces.

Collective Bargaining Procedures

The techniques listed above represent the ultimate weapons available to labour unions. The availability of these tactics, however, is more significant than their actual use: about 95 per cent of all labour contracts or agreements signed during the past decade were settled without resort to such means. Instead, the collective bargaining process has been the predominant method used by unions to gain at least some of their demands. (The two-sided nature of collective bargaining is sometimes overlooked: management also uses the process to gain some of *its* demands, especially for improving labour productivity.)

Many steps are involved in arriving at a labour contract through collective bargaining. Briefly, these are the following:

* Where there is not a recognized union to represent the employees of a particular firm, one or more unions may send representatives to organize the employees as a union "local", or the employees may decide to form their own independent union. If there are two or more unions claiming to have the support the majority of workers, or if it is not clear that the majority wish to be represented by a union, the provincial Labour Relations Board conducts an election to determine whether any union, or which one, will be certified to bargain collectively for the relevant group of workers. A majority of all workers eligible to vote is required before certification can be granted.
* When such certification is given, the certified union is legally recognized as the exclusive bargaining agent for the group of employees it represents, and employers are required to bargain with the certified union.
* Shortly before a new collective agreement is to be established, union representatives and management officers meet to review the requests made by both sides. Such items probably include not only wage rates, but also fringe benefits like pensions and health insurance, standard and overtime hours, training programs, work load, seniority rights, grievance procedures, arrangements for technological improvements in the firm, and so on.

- The representatives of the union and management probably will meet many times to discuss these items, perhaps reaching agreement on some and spending much time on two or three areas of substantial disagreement. In almost all cases, the two parties are able to negotiate a new agreement. If this is ratified by a majority of the union members, it is signed by representatives of both sides and becomes the collective agreement which governs wages, fringe benefits, and labour-management relations in the firm for the period, usually one to three years, specified in the agreement. There will also be provisions forbidding a strike or lockout and for arbitrating problems that arise during this period, as well as for earlier negotiations of a new agreement should unusual conditions arise.

- If agreement cannot be reached, the provisions for the next steps vary slightly among the provinces. (Provincial labour legislation governs collective bargaining procedures, with the exception of bargaining in industries under federal jurisdiction: primarily transportation and broadcasting.) Generally, however, a conciliation officer is appointed by the provincial Labour Relations Board to meet with each party in an effort to resolve their differences. About 40 to 60 per cent of collective agreements are reached by the end of this stage.

- When a conciliation officer recognizes that he cannot reconcile the dispute, a conciliation board is appointed to hear presentations from both parties, try to mediate their differences, and in any case, make a formal report and recommendation.

- If a conciliation board's report is not acceptable to both parties, the union members can decide by a vote to strike or to continue bargaining with management representatives. Should the union choose to strike or should the management decide on a lockout (refuse to admit workers to the plant) a *work stoppage* results. Collective bargaining continues, although often intermittently, until either a settlement is reached, or ultimately the union is destroyed or the firm is bankrupt. The latter possibilities occur quite rarely because it is in the interest of both parties to settle at some point rather than incur the high costs of work stoppage.

Although strikes are given considerable publicity in the news media, their importance in terms of man-days lost during work stoppages is slight: in 1974, this amounted to less than 0.5 per cent of the total estimated working time of the Canadian labour force. An issue of increasing importance in the collective bargaining process is the *right to strike in essential services*, and especially in the public service. Strikes by postal workers and air traffic controllers which affect all parts of the country, and by such essential public servants as policemen and firemen, have led many to argue that strikes by public servants should be forbidden. Strikes in the private sector which also affect the public directly — such as in railroads and shipping — or which cause layoffs in other industries due to material shortages, such as sometimes occurs in the automobile industry during a steel strike, have also led to sharp dispute.

The alternative frequently proposed is *compulsory arbitration*, whereby the decisions are made on subject areas of collective agreements by one or three independent persons appointed by each side. This proposal has been just as frequently rejected because it could remove the incentive for each party to strive for a negotiated settlement if each believed it would gain more through an arbitration award, and because compulsory arbitration, for example in Australia, has led to illegal or "wildcat" strikes.

For this reason, some provinces — notably Saskatchewan and Quebec — have removed the compulsory conciliation stage from the collective bargaining process. Too often, this provision was used by either party to lengthen the negotiations in the hope that the other side would eventually yield.

Union Effects on Labour Markets

Unions are sometimes described as monopoly sellers of labour services. This is not strictly correct because unions do not have the ability to sell various quantities of labour services at different prices or wage rates. Rather, some unions can affect the wage rate by altering the labour market in various ways. These include directly restricting the labour supply, changing the labour supply by gaining a higher standard wage rate, increasing the demand for labour, and offsetting monopsonistic power in imperfect labour markets.

Restricting Labour Supply. Most labour unions have supported general measures which would restrict the total supply of labour to the economy in order to gain wage increases as the demand for labour increased over time. Thus, some unions have opposed more liberal immigration provisions, and have encouraged compulsory retirement, earlier retirement, and shorter work weeks. Craft unions have been able to get large firms in important industries like construction to employ only union craftsmen in such essential trades as bricklaying, carpentry, and plastering. The supply of these services is further restricted by requiring long apprenticeship periods, high initiation fees, and sometimes by setting quotas on the annual number of entrants to the trade. The quantity of labour supplied at any wage is therefore less than it would have been under more competitive conditions.

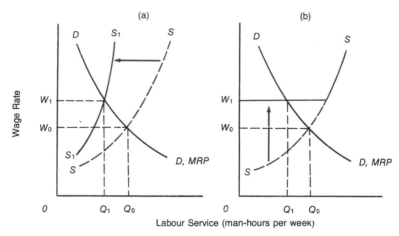

Figure 14.5   Union Effects on Labour Markets
A union which can restrict entrants to an occupation can shift the labour supply
curve, for example, to S_1S_1. Given the demand curve, DD, this will increase the
wage rate to OW_1, but reduce the quantity of labour service purchased to OQ_1. A
union which can impose a higher wage, OW_1, on an industry by collective bargaining effectively shifts the supply curve to W_1S. This reduces the quantity of labour
service purchased to OQ_1.

Effects of supply restriction are illustrated in Figure 14.5a where
the labour supply curve, SS, represents the supply that would be
available in the absence of a union, and S_1S_1 represents the restricted
and more inelastic supply resulting from provisions enforced by a
craft union. The wage rate under the latter condition is higher, at
OW_1 and the quantity of labour employed is lower, at OQ_1, than
would have occurred had supply not been restricted.

Increasing Standard Wage Rates. Industrial unions can try to affect
the total supply of labour to the economy by following the approaches listed above, but they cannot restrict entrants to an industry as craft unions do for certain occupations. Instead, industrial
unions attempt to get all workers in an industry into the union and
then try to obtain a higher standard wage rate. If all workers are
unionized, firms cannot obtain workers at a lower wage, and thus
must pay the agreed rates. This effectively makes the labour supply
curve perfectly elastic or horizontal at the agreed rate, as shown by
the solid W_1S curve in Figure 14.5b. If the union has forced the wage
upward from OW_0, some of the union members will not be rehired.
Thus unions are less likely to press for large wage increases where
there is an elastic demand for labour. Conversely, a wage increase in
cases of highly inelastic labour demand will have proportionately
less effect on employment and will increase the aggregate of wages
paid to those who remain. In such cases, unions may decide that the
increased income more than offsets the unemployment effect.

Increasing the Demand for Labour. Unions which are restrained from pressing for higher wages due to an elastic demand for labour, undertake to shift the labour demand curve outward by assisting employers to improve labour productivity. Since the demand for labour is derived from the demand for products, unions can also try to increase the latter by urging the public, and especially all union members, to buy only union-made goods, by assisting firms in advertising and other promotional activities, and by lobbying the federal government to maintain tariffs against competing imports.

Although these activities have been particularly characteristic of the industrial unions associated with highly elastic labour demand, all unions engage to some extent in these activities because an increase in labour demand, provided that labour supply does not also increase, leads to an increase in both wages and employment.

Offsetting Monopsonistic Power. The three previous cases have dealt with the effects of unions in what are otherwise competitive labour markets. When there are only a few buyers of labour services, and there is a strong union, the condition becomes what is sometimes termed *bilateral monopoly*: the union behaves as if it were a monopoly seller of labour services, and firms which have monopolistic power in the product market tend to be monopsonistic buyers of labour services used mainly in producing those products. Examples of such labour markets include those associated with the automobile, steel, and meatpacking industries.

A bilateral monopoly labour market is illustrated in Figure 14.6. This reproduces the curves for labour supply, SS, marginal resource cost, MRC, and labour demand, MRP, shown in Figure 14.4. The monopsonistic employers will, also as indicated in Figure 14.4, want to hire OQ_1 units of labour at a wage rate of OW_1. If the union could actually act as a single seller of labour, it would want to sell the quantity at which its marginal revenue equals its marginal cost. This requires another curve, $M(MRP)$, which is the marginal revenue the union would realize if it sold various quantities of labour priced according to the demand curve it faces, namely the employers' MRP curve. (Note that the employers' marginal revenue product is *not* the union's marginal revenue; rather, the MRP curve is the union's *average* revenue curve.) The union will thus want to "sell" the quantity at which the $M(MRP)$ curve intersects its supply curve, since the latter is regarded as its marginal cost. The union would therefore demand a wage of OW_2, the wage employers would be willing to pay for OQ_2 units of labour. Neither side, however, has sufficient power to fix its optimum wage level, OW_1 for employers and OW_2 for the union. Although the actual outcome cannot be determined by economic analysis, since the agreed wage depends on the relative bargaining power of each side, the bilateral monopoly model can clarify the wage limits within which bargaining takes place.

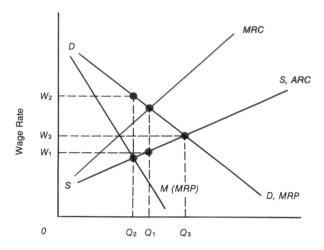

Labour Service (man-hours per week)

Figure 14.6   Bilateral Monopoly in A Labour Market
In a labour market consisting of one buyer, (a monopsonist), and one seller in the
form of a labour union, the wage rate is indeterminate. The monopsonist will want
to buy OQ_1 man-hours per week, at a wage of OW_1. The union's marginal revenue
curve, $M(MRP)$, shows the additional revenue associated with each additional unit
of labour purchased by the monopsonist. Since the union members' supply curve
can be seen as their marginal cost curve, their optimum offering of labour is the
quantity at which their supply curve intersects their $M(MRP)$ curve, or OQ_2. The
employer is willing to pay OW_2 for quantity OQ_2. The actual wage may therefore be
between OW_1 and OW_2; the closer it is to OW_3, the closer is the result to what
would have occurred under perfect competition.

Economists have often expressed some support for the bilateral
monopoly situation — or the presence of countervailing powers —
since the outcome will be similar to that which would be determined
in a competitive labour market. Suppose collective bargaining results in a wage rate of OW_3. This is the rate that would exist at
equilibrium in this market in the absence of employer monopsony
and union monopoly. (The effect of the employers' monopoly power
in the *product* market remains, however, since this is what determines the labour demand curve.) The competitive equilibrium is
further approximated with respect to the quantity of labour offered,
because once the wage rate is set at OW_3, the union will be willing to
supply, and employers will be willing to buy, as much as OQ_3 units
of labour service.

The indeterminacy of the wage rate in bilateral monopoly
models of the labour market has led some economists to develop
bargaining theories of wage determination which include other
economic arguments such as the longer-run costs and benefits to
unions and employers of incurring a strike, and non-economic arguments including the degree of political or public support enjoyed
by each side in a labour dispute.

Union Impact on Wages: Empirical Evidence

On the basis of the analytical models of union effects on labour markets, one must conclude that unions can raise the wage rate above what it would be in their absence. Indeed, this is the commonly held view, that "unions raise wages". Empirical research to test this view has, however, produced rather inconclusive results. A major reason for this is that controlled experiments are not possible: one cannot find situations which are precisely the same in all respects except for the absence or presence of a union. Instead, researchers have focussed on the wage differences between firms or industries which were or were not unionized. But this approach raises questions about the effect of unions on the wages of non-unionized groups. For example, employers may pay higher wages to non-unionized employees so that these employees will be less inclined to form or join a union.

Ostry and Zaidi, after reviewing the research problems and the evidence for union effects on wages suggest that:

> At the present time, techniques of analysis and available statistics are probably too crude to enable the researcher to obtain unequivocal results in relating unionism to the determination of wages or wage structure. For the moment the verdict one way or another can only be the Scottish 'not proven'.[7]

A comprehensive evaluation of the evidence for similar research in the United States has led one economist to state that, "My own best guess of the average effects of all American unions on the wages of their members in recent years would be somewhere between 10 and 15 per cent."[8]

Labour Legislation in Canada

Labour legislation in Canada varies among the provinces because both the provincial governments and the federal government have legislative powers in labour affairs. The provincial legislatures have the major jurisdiction, under Section 92 of the British North America Act which gives the provinces exclusive power to make laws regarding "property and civil rights in the province". Since contracts between employees and employers are questions of civil rights, the terms and conditions of contracts are therefore regarded as coming under provincial jurisdiction. The federal government's powers in that area are limited to legislation concerning industries which are

---

[7] Sylvia Ostry and Mahmood A. Zaidi, op. cit. p. 312.
[8] Albert Rees, The Economics of Trade Unions. Chicago: The University of Chicago Press, 1962, p. 79.

national, international, or interprovincial in nature, such as transportation and communications, banking, and other industries, such as uranium mining, over which the federal government has direct control.

Industrial relations legislation dates back to 1907 when the federal government passed the Industrial Disputes Investigation Act which outlawed strikes in public utilities, mining and railroads until a conciliation board has submitted a report. However, not until the late 1930s was there general acceptance of the principle that an employer had an obligation to recognize and bargain with a union representing the majority of the employees. Legislation embodying this principle was elaborated in the 1940s to include methods for determining questions of union representation and appropriate bargaining units, and requiring negotiation between management and union representatives. Federal legislation enacted during World War II extended federal jurisdiction in labour matters and this set a pattern of legislation which was generally followed by the provinces. Thus there now is an industrial or labour relations act in each province which provides for the establishment of a Labour Relations Board and which specifies the conditions for certification of unions and the procedures to be followed in collective bargaining.

The second major area of labour legislation concerns labour standards and conditions of employment. The Canada Labour Code, the federal government's collection of labour legislation includes, in addition to the Industrial Relations and Disputes Investigation Act, acts that govern minimum wages, hours of work, annual vacations and public holidays, and discrimination in employment. The federal Employees Equal Pay Act requires equal pay for equal work for employees of both sexes. Most of the provinces have acts dealing with the same questions, while some provinces also have legislation on additional matters such as the requirement that employers or employees give notice of termination of employment and the requirement that employers provide maternity leave. All provinces have a Workmen's Compensation Act providing for the payment of compensation to a worker or his dependents in case of accident or industrial disease arising from his employment. Such payments are made from a fund established by a levy on all employers.

Review of the Main Points

1. "Wages" include all forms of payment for labour services, including direct payments and indirect compensation in the form of various benefits and facilities. Distinctions must be made, however, between gross earnings and take-home pay, and between money wages and real wages. Although reference is frequently made to "the" wage rate and "the" labour market, there

are actually many labour markets and therefore many wage rates. Labour markets are interrelated, however, because workers and employers may be in several labour markets at the same time.

2. The short-run labour supply period may be defined as the period within which the total population and its level of schooling and training does not vary significantly. Two major factors therefore determine the short-run labour supply: the labour force participation rate and the number of hours offered per day or per week. These factors reflect workers' decisions about allocating their time between labour and leisure, when leisure is defined as any non-income-earning activity. An individual's short-run supply curve depends on his marginal rates of substitution of labour income for leisure over the range of possible working hours, and the relative size of the income and substitution effects across different wage rates. Although an individual's labour supply curve is thought to be backward-bending, the short-run labour supply curve for the economy is assumed to be upward-sloping, but highly inelastic, over the relevant range of wage rates. The economy's long-run labour supply is influenced primarily by population changes due to international migration and birth and death rates.

3. A firm's demand for labour is determined by the marginal revenue product of workers, and is more elastic the higher the degree of competition in the product market supplied by the firm in question. A firm in a purely competitive labour market faces a perfectly elastic labour supply curve and hence has no influence on the wage it pays; it is thus concerned only with determining the quantity of labour to be hired at the given wage rate. This is the rate at which the quantity of labour supplied to the market is equal to the quantity demanded.

4. The opposite of a purely competitive labour market is a monopsonistic labour market in which there is only one buyer of labour services. The labour supply curve faced by this firm is the upward-sloping market supply curve. The marginal cost of hiring an additional worker exceeds the prevailing wage rate because more must be paid to attract an additional worker. Furthermore, the existing workers must be paid the same wage as the additional worker in order to retain their services. The profit-maximizing quantity of labour for the firm is the quantity at which the marginal resource cost is equal to the marginal revenue product.

5. The structure of wages in Canada reflects many differences in jobs, from working conditions to the cost of training for a particular occupation. Other factors such as monopsonistic employers, labour unions and professional associations, labour immobility, and inadequate information, also have a differential influence on wage rates.

6. Approximately one-third of all non-agricultural employees in Canada belong to labour unions. Craft unions consist of members from particular occupations, while industrial unions draw their members from specific industries or groups of industries, regardless of their occupations. Union organizational structure is based on many local unions which are usually chartered by and affiliated with national or international unions. These, in turn, are affiliated with national or international federations or congresses.

7. Unions have several goals: to increase the wage rate or the total income of union members, to increase fringe benefits and improve working conditions, to maintain work rules and job security, to maintain the security of the union organization, and to promote particular political goals. To achieve these objectives unions may use one or more of various tactics: strikes, working-to-rule campaigns, slowdowns, picketing, boycotts, as well as collective bargaining.

8. The collective bargaining process can involve several steps toward an agreement between union and management representatives. If a union does not exist and two or more unions claim to have the support of the majority of workers, the provincial Labour Relations Board conducts an election and certifies the successful union as bargaining agent for that group of employees. If a union and management representatives cannot agree on a settlement of the issues presented by each side, in most provinces a conciliation officer appointed by the Board attempts to resolve the differences. If this is not possible, a conciliation board attempts mediation and compiles a formal report. If this is unacceptable to either side, the union members can vote to strike or to continue bargaining. If a strike is called, bargaining nevertheless continues until an agreement is reached.

9. Unions can influence the wage rate in several ways: by restricting labour supply, by increasing the basic or standard wage rate in an industry, by increasing the demand for labour, and by offsetting monopsonistic power. This last case is termed bilateral monopoly since a union acts as if it were a monopoly seller of labour services to a monopsonistic buyer.

10. Empirical research on the effect of unions on wages has produced rather inconclusive results, because the data are generally not satisfactory for separating the indirect effect of unions on non-unionized firms and industries. However, the available evidence does suggest that unions have increased the wages of their members by 10 to 15 per cent over what the wages would have been in the absence of a union.

Review and Discussion Questions

1. What impediments are there in the real world to the precise expression of a person's relative preferences for labour income and leisure? Would most people you know in the labour force like to increase or decrease the number of hours they work per week, at the prevailing wage rates? Why?

2. Why have labour unions been formed mainly in the blue-collar occupations?

3. Many unions are opposed to increased mechanization in their industries, yet the existence of strong unions can hasten the rate of mechanization. How can you explain this?

4. Should persons employed in essential services such as police and fire protection have the right to strike? Why?

Sources and Selected Readings

Crispo, John H.G. *International Unionism.* Toronto: McGraw-Hill, 1967.

Federal Task Force on Industrial Relations. *Canadian Industrial Relations.* Ottawa: Queen's Printer, 1969.

Fleisher, Belton M. *Labor Economics: Theory and Evidence.* Englewood Cliffs, N.J.: Prentice-Hall, 1970.

Rees, Albert. *The Economics of Work and Pay.* New York: Harper & Row, 1973.

Jamieson, Stuart. *Industrial Relations in Canada*, 2nd ed. Toronto: Macmillan, 1973.

Kruger, A.M., and N.M. Meltz (eds.) *The Canadian Labour Market.* Toronto: Centre for Industrial Relations, University of Toronto, 1968.

Miller, Richard U., and Fraser Isbester. *Canadian Labour in Transition.* Scarborough, Ont.: Prentice-Hall, 1971.

Ostry, Sylvia, and Mahmood A. Zaidi. *Labour Economics in Canada*, 2nd ed. Toronto: Macmillan, 1972.

Peitchinis, Stephen G. *Canadian Labour Economics.* Toronto: McGraw-Hill, 1970.

15 Personal Income, Poverty, and Regional Disparity

An equitable distribution of rising incomes was one of Canada's basic economic goals listed at the beginning of Chapter 3. Nothing further was said about this goal in describing measurements of Canada's economic performance because, as the Economic Council of Canada has noted, "The goal of an equitable distribution of rising incomes is the most complex of the basic goals and defies any simple, easily grasped quantitative measurement."[1] This goal has therefore been defined by the Council as at least involving the reduction of regional income disparities and the elimination of poverty. These are the two topics considered in this chapter, following an initial examination of current income distribution in Canada.

A. Income Distribution in Canada

Income Distribution Among Productive Factors

In a pure market system, the economy's output of goods and services would be distributed among the population according to the quantity of productive services offered by individuals and the prices of these services. That is, the incomes received would represent purchasing power or claims on the real goods and services available: the more services one could offer or the higher the price of service, the more goods and services one could buy. Distribution as it would be determined by a free market system is modified somewhat in a mixed economy by government regulations and direct intervention. The resulting distribution of income according to the basic types of productive factors — land, labour, and capital — is termed the *functional distribution of income.*

Statistics for the national income and expenditure accounts are not collected and arranged in a way that shows precisely the share of national income going to each type of factor but an estimate of these shares can be obtained from the components of Net National Income. Table 15.1 shows an approximation of the functional distribution of income which treats employee earnings as the return to labour services, and corporate profits, interest, and dividends as the return to capital. Income of unincorporated enterprises (small businesses and farms) represents a combined return to land, labour, and capital used in these businesses.

---

[1] Economic Council of Canada, *Sixth Annual Review: Perspective 1975.* Ottawa: Queen's Printer, 1969, p. 6.

Table 15.1

Functional Distribution of Income, Canada, 1974

	millions of dollars	per cent of total
Employee earnings[1]	77,155	72
Corporate profits[2]	12,533	12
Interest and dividends[3]	7,014	6
Income of unincorporated enterprises[4]	11,079	10
Total (Net National Income at factor cost)	107,781	100

[1] Includes wages, salaries, supplementary labour income, military pay and allowances.
[2] Corporation profits before taxes less dividends paid to non-residents and inventory valuation adjustment.
[3] Interest and miscellaneous investment income, including profits of government enterprises and governments' investment income.
[4] Includes net income of independent professional practitioners.

Source: Statistics Canada, *Canadian Statistical Review.*

The relative share of the national income received by each factor has been fairly stable over a long period of time, with employee earnings representing about 70 to 75 per cent of the total income. If one can assume that about one-half of the income of unincorporated enterprises is a return to labour, the labour share of national income has thus been about 75 to 80 per cent.

Personal Distribution of Income

Sources of Personal Income

The functional distribution of income is based on the components of Net National Income, which also includes income received by corporations and governments but not passed on to individuals. For an accounting of the total income received by individuals, one could turn to the Personal Income account. However, this account includes the current income of private non-commercial organizations, such as charitable organizations and universities, and therefore overstates the incomes actually received by individuals. Instead, personal income statistics are usually taken from a survey of consumers' finances conducted by Statistics Canada. Table 15.2 shows that over 85 per cent of the income of families and individuals is received through employment or self-employment earnings. (Some of the latter, however, may be a return to the plant and equipment used by self-employed professionals such as doctors, engineers, and artists.) Investment income accounts for less than 5 per

cent, while transfer payments represent almost 8 per cent.[2] The latter
include government pension payments, workmen's compensation,
unemployment insurance benefits, family allowances, and so on.

Table 15.2

**Sources of Income of Families and
Unattached Individuals[1], Canada, 1973**

	millions of dollars	per cent of total
Wages and salaries	60,494	79.3
Net self-employment income	4,866	6.4
Investment income	3,365	4.4
Transfer payments	5,923	7.8
Miscellaneous income[2]	1,661	2.1
Total	76,309	100.0

[1] Families are groups of individuals sharing common dwelling units and related by blood, marriage or adoption. Unattached individuals are persons living by themselves or rooming in a household where they are not related to other household members.

[2] Includes retirement pensions, annuities, scholarships, alimony and other items not specified or included in other categories.

Source: Statistics Canada, *Income Distributions by Size in Canada*, 1973.

Size Distribution of Income

Information on the sources of personal income is important in
understanding how persons obtain their incomes in total, but it does
not show how incomes are distributed among the population. The
latter question requires detailed examination in considering the goal
of equitable income distribution. The simplest approach, and thus
the one which receives the most attention, involves the *size distribution of income: the number of individuals and families at each level
of income or in each income group.*

Column 2 of Table 15.3 shows the percentage of families and
individuals whose income levels fall within each of several income
groups, while column 4 shows the percentage of the total income
which is earned by persons within each of the income groups. The
percentages shown in each of these columns are accumulated, starting from the lowest income level, such that columns 5 and 6 show
most clearly the inequality of income distribution. For example,
families and individuals with an income of less than $4,000 in 1973
constituted 20.1 per cent of the population, but they received only
3.9 per cent of the total income. Almost four times as much income
(14.7 per cent) was received by the 4.5 per cent of the population
who were in the income group of $25,000 and over.

---

[2] Statisticians estimate that investment income actually represents about 8
per cent of total income because survey respondents tend to forget about
income such as interest on bank deposits and Canada Savings Bonds.

Table 15.3

**Income Distribution by Size, for Families and
Unattached Individuals, Canada, 1973**

Annual Income	Families and Individuals		Income Received		Percentage of population in this and lower groups (5)	Percentage of Income received by this and lower groups (6)
	Number in Income Group (thousands) (1)	Percent in Income Group (2)	By each Income Group ($ millions) (3)	Percent of Total (4)		
Under $2,000	584	8.2	519	0.7	8.2	0.7
2,000 — 3,999	852	11.9	2,458	3.2	20.1	3.9
4,000 — 5,999	820	11.5	4,062	5.3	31.6	9.2
6,000 — 7,999	744	10.4	5,218	6.8	42.0	16.0
8,000 — 9,999	777	10.9	6,973	9.1	52.9	25.1
10,000 — 11,999	753	10.5	8,238	10.8	63.4	35.9
12,000 — 14,999	941	13.2	12,615	16.6	76.6	52.5
15,000 — 19,999	950	13.4	16,330	21.5	90.0	74.0
20,000 — 24,999	392	5.5	8,645	11.3	95.5	85.3
25,000 and over	322	4.5	11,251	14.7	100.0	100.0
Total	7,135	100.0	76,309	100.0		

Source: Statistics Canada, *Income Distributions by Size in Canada, 1973.*

The degree of inequality in income distribution is illustrated in Figure 15.1, by a *Lorenz curve.* This shows the extent to which the actual distribution of incomes deviates from perfect equality in income distribution. Since the scales used to show the percentage of families and the percentage of total income are equal, perfect equality in income distribution would be represented by a straight line running out from the origin at a 45° angle to each scale. For example, if 20 per cent of the population received 20 per cent of the total income, this would be shown as point A in Figure 15.1; if a further 20 per cent of the population also received a further 20 per cent of the income, this would be shown as point B; and so on.

When the information presented in columns 5 and 6 of Table 15.3 are plotted in Figure 15.1, the result is the bowed-out curve below the equal distribution line. Point C, for example, shows that the 42 per cent of the population who receive annual incomes of less than $8,000 receive only 16 per cent of the total income.

The degree of income inequality is represented by the size of the area between the equal distribution line and the actual income distribution curve: the closer the curve is to the equality line and the smaller the area between the two, the less the income inequality. The Lorenz curves for earlier years have not been plotted in Figure 15.1 because there has been so little change in income distribution during the past two decades that the curves for other years would be almost indistinguishable from the 1973 curve. Table 15.4 shows how little change there was, for example, in the distribution of family

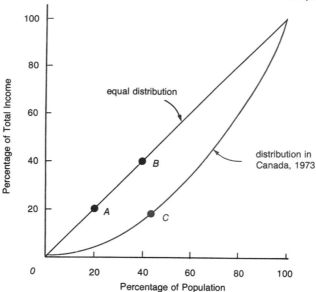

Figure 15.1 Income Distribution in Canada, 1973
A Lorenz curve shows the percentage of the total income received by each percentage of the population. The area between the two curves shows the extent to which the actual distribution varies from equal distribution of incomes.
Source: Table 15.3.

income between 1951 and 1973. Although the share received by the highest-income families declined slightly (from 41.1 to 38.9 per cent), the largest percentage gain during the period was in the next-highest income group rather than in the lower income groups.

Note, however that *equal* income distribution is not necessarily defined as an *equitable* income distribution. Only if the normative judgment is made that social justice requires everyone to have the same income will these two distributions be the same.

Table 15.4

Distribution of Family Income in Canada*

| | Percentage of Total Income Received by Each Fifth | | | |
	1951	1961	1971	1973
Lowest-income fifth of families	6.1	6.6	5.6	6.1
Second fifth	12.9	13.4	12.7	12.9
Third fifth	17.4	18.2	18.0	18.2
Fourth fifth	22.5	23.4	23.7	23.9
Highest-income fifth	41.1	38.4	40.0	38.9
All families	100.0	100.0	100.0	100.0

*Prior to 1965 only non-farm family income was included but the change in survey coverage made negligible difference to the relative distributions.
Source: Statistics Canada, *Income Distributions by Size in Canada*.

Table 15.5

**Transfer Payment Income of Families and
Unattached Individuals, Canada, 1973**

Income Class	Transfer Payments as percentage of Income
Under $2,000	67
$ 2,000 — 3,999	53
4,000 — 5,999	27
6,000 — 7,999	13
8,000 — 9,999	8
10,000 — 11,999	6
12,000 — 14,999	5
15,000 — 24,999	3
25,000 and over	2
All persons	7.8

Source: Statistics Canada, *Income Distributions by Size in Canada*, 1973.

Redistribution of Income

The income distribution illustrated in Figure 15.1 is based on gross, or before-tax incomes. However, these gross incomes do not reflect the distribution determined by the markets for productive factors because transfer payments are included. Without these, the Lorenz curve would be bowed somewhat further out from the equality line. Table 15.5 summarizes the relative importance of transfer payments in the total income of each group. Families and individuals whose total incomes were less than $2,000 in 1973 received 67 per cent of this income as transfer payments. This percentage then drops sharply for successively higher income groups, although even the persons in the highest income bracket received some transfer payments — mainly as family allowances. Transfer payments thus increase the share of the total income going to the low-income groups and reduce some of the inequality that would exist in the absence of such government programs as unemployment insurance and welfare assistance.

Inequality of income distribution is further reduced by the various taxes levied by each level of government. Table 15.6 presents an estimate of the redistribution of income which occurs through the tax and expenditure programs of the combined levels of government. The money income of families shown in the left-hand column is based on estimates of what incomes would be in the absence of government taxes and spending. The effective tax rate shows the percentage of this basic income paid in all forms of taxes — property, sales, income, and so on — to the three levels of government. Note that the tax rate decreases, and then rises slowly above the

$4,000 level. The incidence of public expenditures reflects an attempt to estimate how the benefits of public spending, both as transfer payments and for the provision of real goods and services, are distributed among income groups. The net incidence of taxes and spending shows the substantial redistribution that occurs at the lowest income levels, but above the $3,000 level, the redistribution effect is rather modest. Although these are the results of a study based on 1961 statistics, the general pattern holds true for the 1970s.

Table 15.6

**Incidence of Taxes and Public Expenditures, Canada, 1961
(as a percentage of family money income)**

Family Money Income Class	Effective Tax Rates	Incidence of Public Expenditures	Net Incidence (expenditures minus taxes)
Under $2,000	60.0	162.9	102.8
$ 2,000 — 2,999	32.9	72.8	39.9
3,000 — 3,999	32.2	51.4	19.1
4,000 — 4,999	30.5	42.7	12.3
5,000 — 6,999	32.8	38.7	5.9
7,000 — 9,999	34.2	34.2	0.0
10,000 and over	38.4	29.2	−9.2

Source: W.I. Gillespie, *The Incidence of Taxes and Public Expenditures in Canada.*

Causes of Income Inequality

There are many causes of income inequality. Combinations of these causes can result in very low incomes for some individuals and families, as the discussion of poverty in the next section shows, while other factors can lead to very high incomes. A few factors can by themselves, however, account for substantial income differences: Table 15.7 illustrates two of these, age and education.

Age. Average incomes rise steadily up to about age 45 and then decline almost as quickly to age 70 and over. The increase in incomes is due largely to the experience workers develop in particular jobs or occupations, for which employers are willing to pay a significant premium. By the mid-forties, however, many persons who have been in their jobs for some time have little additional experience to gain, and incomes rise more slowly. This more gradual rise in later years is more than offset, as Table 15.7 shows, by a tendency for some older workers to withdraw from the labour force and the retirement of most persons at ages 65 to 70. The lower income at higher ages is also due partly to the lower average level of education of the older population, but even for persons with a specific level of education the average income declines due to the effect of withdrawal from the labour force.

Education. The effect of education on incomes is now widely recognized. Table 15.7 shows that persons with only some elementary schooling have less than one-third the income received by those with a university degree. Much of the attention that has been given to the effect of education on income, however, has failed to emphasize that other factors are also at work. For example, persons with higher levels of education are more likely to be employed on an annual basis and thus do not face temporary lay-offs or as much unemployment as some other workers experience.

Table 15.7

**Average Annual Incomes by Age and Education,
Canada, 1973**

Age	Average Income	Education	Average Income
Under 20	$1,592	Elementary School	
20 — 24	4,668	None or some	$ 3,858
25 — 34	7,706	Completed	5,469
		Secondary School	
35 — 44	9,139	Some	5,517
45 — 54	8,688	Completed	6,898
55 — 64	7,209	Non-University Post-secondary	
65 — 69	4,315	Some	5,696
70 and over	3,171	Completed	7,542
		University	
		Some	7,494
		Degree	13,342

Source: Statistics Canada, *Income Distributions by Size in Canada*, 1973.

Occupations. In the previous chapter, Table 14.1 showed the average employment earnings in broad occupational categories. Much of the variation among occupations is due to education differences: the average education of labourers is lower than the education of managers. But this accounts for only part of the difference. Other factors such as relative changes in the supply and demand for persons in different occupations can change income differentials fairly quickly: the rapid increase in the number of post-secondary graduates during the 1960s, for example, may narrow the income difference between professional and clerical occupations. More pronounced narrowing of income differentials will likely occur between manual labour and most other occupations. Chapter 14 also outlined other factors, such as degree of responsibility, cost of training, and so on, which explain part of the occupational wage differences.

Weeks Worked. The number of weeks worked per year is a significant factor in explaining earnings differences among occupations. Workers in some occupations, particularly in the managerial and professional categories, are usually employed on an annual basis and are paid for 52 weeks of work. In other occupations, such as farming, logging, and fishing, the work tends to be seasonal and wages are paid for perhaps only 6 or 7 months.

The lower earnings associated with fewer weeks worked, as shown in Table 15.8, would be expected. However, when the average earnings are divided by the number of the weeks worked, one finds that lower *weekly* wages are received by persons who work only part of the year. This accentuates the earnings difference which results from working fewer than 52 weeks. The actual earnings differences shown here, however, are reduced somewhat by the unemployment insurance benefits paid to persons who work less than 52 weeks.

Table 15.8

Earnings by Employment Duration, Males, Canada, 1973

Weeks Worked	Average Earnings from Employment
50 — 52	$10,151
40 — 49	7,547
30 — 39	5,485
20 — 29	3,694
10 — 19	2,086
0 — 9	999

Source: Statistics Canada, *Income Distributions by Size in Canada*, 1973.

Other Causes. Holdings of income-earning assets such as stocks, bonds and real estate are distributed quite unequally, with the result that a large part of the total income from these assets is received by a small percentage of the population. For example, 11 per cent of the income received in 1973 by families and individuals in the $25,000 and over income-group was derived from investments, but investment income accounted for only about 4 per cent of the income of lower-income groups. To state this another way, the 4.5 per cent of the population in the top income-group received 27 per cent of all investment income.

Other causes of income inequality are not so easily identified by objective measurement. Individuals and families experience various kinds of fortune or misfortune which accentuate income inequality: some individuals seem to have had the good luck to be "in the right place at the right time" while others have suffered a series of tragedies including accidents, fires, thefts, and so on. Some of these personal and social causes of inequality are considered more fully in the following discussion of poverty.

B. Poverty

The elimination of poverty has been specified as an essential step toward equitable income distribution. The Economic Council stated this in clear terms: *We believe that serious poverty should be eliminated in Canada, and that this should be designated as a major national goal.*[3]

Can Poverty Be Measured?

Policies and programs to eliminate poverty, and measures of their effectiveness, require an operational definition of poverty. Although there may be general agreement on the need to overcome poverty, there is some disagreement on what constitutes poverty. This is sometimes defined as a condition in which individuals or families do not have the means to meet their basic needs, but any list of basic needs is based on arbitrary judgments. Moreover, the basic needs of families or individuals vary with the specific circumstances of each case.

A second definition of poverty suggests that poverty is a *relative* concept. That is, that the elimination of poverty requires more than just the means to sustain life; it includes the notion of a minimum socially acceptable standard of living. With a general rise in economic and social well-being, it is argued, the minimum acceptable standard also rises. This definition of the poverty level implies that "the poor will always be with us", at least so long as the minimum standard rises faster than anti-poverty programs can assist those below this rising standard.

A third, somewhat similar, view of poverty is based on the size distribution of income described in the last section. As long as the fifth of the population receives such a large share, the bottom fifth are said to be in a state of poverty relative to the rest of the population. In this case an elimination of poverty would require a consensus on a much more difficult question: the most appropriate size distribution of income.

Each of these definitions, however, is concerned only with current income or living standards. Poverty also has a time component, and thus is different from having a low income at any given time. Some persons, notably college students, may have low incomes at one point but have prospects of higher incomes in the near future. This is a substantially different situation from the hopeless cycle of poverty that can perpetuate itself as described in the quotation on the following page.

---

[3] Economic Council of Canada, *Fifth Annual Review: The Challenge of Growth and Change.* Ottawa: Queen's Printer, 1968, p. 105.

The Poverty Cycle

Poverty breeds poverty. A poor individual or family has a high probability of staying poor. Low incomes carry with them high risks of illness;
limitations on mobility; limited access to education, information, and training. Poor parents cannot give their children the opportunities for better
health and education needed to improve their lot. Lack of motivation,
hope, and incentive is a more subtle but no less powerful barrier than lack
of financial means. Thus the cruel legacy of poverty is passed from parents to children.

Source: *Economic Report of the President*. Washington, D.C.: U.S. Government Printing
Office, 1964, pp. 69-70.

The Poverty Line

While recognizing the limitations of income measures of poverty, recent reports on poverty have chosen to define poverty, in the
absence of other operational measures, in terms of the minimum
income believed necessary for meeting basic human needs. Thus the
concept of a *poverty line* has been used to measure and describe the
magnitude of poverty in Canada. In fact, different poverty lines have
been suggested, to take account of different total needs of individuals and of families of various sizes.

Two sets of poverty lines have been used to measure the extent
of poverty: one by Statistics Canada and the Economic Council of
Canada (SC/ECC), and another by the Special Senate Committee on
Poverty. The SC/ECC poverty lines were determined from a study
which showed that, on average, families allocated roughly half of
their incomes to the basic essentials of food, clothing, and shelter. It
was assumed therefore that a family using much more than half its
income on such essentials could be described as at or below the
poverty level. An arbitrary figure of 70 per cent was chosen as the
poverty line; that is, the income level below which families spent 70
per cent of their incomes on essentials. Thus the poverty lines based
on 1969 incomes were established, as shown in Table 15.9, to range
from an annual income of $1,894 for one individual to $5,051 for a
family of five or more persons. However, the Economic Council emphasized the arbitrary nature of the 70 per cent line and offered an
alternate set of poverty lines based on an expenditure of 60 per cent
of family income on the basic essentials. Which set is chosen has
serious implications for estimations of the extent of poverty in
Canada: using 1961 census data, the Council reported 27 per cent of
the nonfarm population were living in poverty if the 70 per cent
level was chosen, but 41 per cent were, if the 60 per cent level was
applied.

The method for establishing the poverty lines reflects the "basic
needs" rather than the "minimum acceptable standard" approach to
defining poverty. If the latter definition were used, the 70 per cent

Table 15.9

Poverty Lines by Family Unit Size, Canada

Family Unit Size	Senate Committee poverty lines	Statistics Canada/Economic Council poverty lines	
	1969	1969	1973*
1	$2,140	$1,894	$2,917
2	3,570	3,157	4,229
3	4,290	3,788	5,397
4	5,000	4,420	6,417
5	5,710	5,051	7,173
6	6,430	5,051	7,875
7	7,140	5,051	8,633
10	9,290	5,051	8,633

*For cities of 100,000 to 500,000 population.

Source: Special Senate Committee on Poverty, *Poverty in Canada*, Table 1, and Statistics Canada, *Income Distributions by Size in Canada*, 1973.

basis for establishing poverty lines would need to be dropped gradually as the percentage of income spent on food, clothing, and shelter by the average Canadian family declined with rising incomes. Holding the 70 per cent basis constant over a period of years would result in a growing gap between the poverty lines and the average family income. Consequently, the poverty lines were revised in 1973 to reflect the income levels of families who spent 62 per cent or more of their annual incomes on food, shelter and clothing. These poverty lines, which were differentiated by size of area of residence in addition to family size, are also shown in Table 15.9.[4]

The Poverty Rate

When the number of families or individuals whose incomes fall below the poverty lines established by the Senate Committee are expressed as a percentage of the total population, the overall poverty rate in Canada in 1969 was found to be 25 per cent: one person in four was in poverty. Table 15.10 presents further evidence on the incidence of poverty, by selected characteristics, using the Statistics Canada definition of poverty lines for 1973. Apart from the high rate for unattached individuals (40 per cent), the poverty rate was highest (16 per cent) among families of two; these include families of two adults or an adult with a dependent child. There was also a high poverty rate in the Atlantic Provinces, where 19 per cent of all families and 45 per cent of unattached individuals are below the poverty line. Rural poverty has been identified as a particular problem; this is verified by the high incidence of poverty found in rural areas. Over 40 per cent of the families headed by a woman — usually

---

[4] Table 15.9 shows the poverty lines for residents of large cities. See the Statistics Canada report cited for poverty lines related to other areas.

widowed or divorced — experience poverty. The low incomes of the
aged are also evident in the high incidence of poverty among those
over 65. Finally, poverty is serious not only among those not in the
labour force but also among the self-employed — mainly the farmers
who were reflected in the high poverty rate of rural areas.

Characteristics and Causes of Poverty

Characteristics of the Poor

Just as it is difficult to define poverty, so it is difficult to describe
the many features that combine to distinguish the poor from the rest
of the population. However, some basic features can be determined
by examining the distribution of poverty within selected sections of
the population. Table 15.10 compares the *distribution* of poverty
with its *incidence*: for example, 19 per cent of families in the Atlantic provinces are below the poverty line, but only 12.5 per cent of all
low-income families are in the Atlantic provinces. More than 60 per
cent of Canada's poor live in Ontario and Quebec.

More than one-half of the low-income families and individuals
live in cities, but almost 30 per cent of the poor families live in rural
areas. Poverty is not strongly identified with any particular age of
family heads, although about one-third of unattached individuals
below the poverty line are 70 or over.

The poor have often been portrayed as lazy or unemployable but
over 50 per cent of the heads of low-income families are in the labour
force, and about 60 per cent of these work a normal work-week for
the whole year. Although 67 per cent of low-income unattached
individuals are not in the labour force, this is a small fraction of the
total poverty group. Moreover, those individuals include many who
neither married nor entered the labour force due to chronic illness or
physical handicaps.

Causes of Poverty

Several of the factors used to describe income distribution and
the incidence of poverty also constitute an explanation of the causes
of poverty. Due to the cyclical, complex process that characterizes
the lives of low-income families, the consequences of poverty are not
easily separated from its causes. However, one can approach the
problem by dealing first with those who are in the labour force but
who derive an inadequate income from their work, and then with
those who have an inadequate income because they are not in the
labour force.

Table 15.10

Incidence and Distribution of Poverty in Canada, 1973
(percentages)

Characteristics	Incidence of Poverty[1]		Distribution of Poverty[2]	
	Families	Individuals	Families	Individuals
Size of family		40.2		
2	16.0		38.4	
3	11.4		17.1	
4	10.3		16.8	
5 or more	14.4		27.7	
Region of residence				
Atlantic Provinces	19.0	44.9	12.5	7.3
Quebec	15.4	40.8	30.8	27.3
Ontario	10.7	37.7	29.8	34.4
Prairie Provinces	16.5	45.5	19.6	18.9
British Columbia	8.9	37.1	7.3	12.0
Place of residence				
Cities	11.9	38.2	57.6	73.2
Small urban areas	16.0	49.8	14.2	13.5
Rural areas	17.3	47.4	28.2	13.2
Sex of family head				
Male	10.8	31.9	73.9	36.1
Female	41.6	47.2	26.1	63.9
Age of family head				
24 and under	16.0	40.6	7.3	22.8
25 — 34	11.7	16.5	20.6	7.3
35 — 44	12.6	18.7	21.4	3.5
45 — 54	9.6	31.4	14.6	7.4
55 — 64	12.3	42.4	13.6	14.5
65 — 69	21.4	51.7	8.4	11.9
70 and over	26.2	66.6	14.2	32.7
Labour force status of head				
Employee	6.8	21.0	35.6	30.3
Self-employed	19.8	37.3	17.7	2.7
Not in the labour force	36.0	69.2	46.6	67.2
Education of family head				
Some or complete elementary	22.0	63.4	54.0	47.8
Some high school	12.9	38.0	28.2	22.3
High school or some	17.2	29.4	16.0	27.3
University degree post-secondary	3.3	12.5	1.9	2.6

[1] Percentage of all families or unattached individuals whose incomes are below the Statistics Canada 1973 poverty lines, shown in Table 15.9.
[2] Percentage distribution of low-income families or individuals within the selected characteristic.
Source: Statistics Canada, *Income Distributions by Size in Canada, 1973.*

The Working Poor. About one-half of all individuals and family heads with low incomes are in the labour force yet are unable to earn an income large enough to lift them above the poverty line. One of the major reasons is *inadequate education and training.* This is frequently the result of growing up in a family that could not provide educational opportunites, or in an area where these were severely limited. Without basic education, a worker lacks the basis for further training, either in technical courses or on the job. Poor *health* may compound the problem: a worker may leave school for health reasons, such as respiratory illness, and may then find that the same problem prevents him from working at certain jobs or for a full-time week and year.

Inadequate training or *geographical immobility* may constrain a worker from changing to another occupation where seasonal effects and economic fluctuations would permit him to work longer periods at a higher hourly or weekly wage rate. *Discrimination* may also bar a worker from a more desirable occupation, especially one where his skills can be utilized more effectively. Such discrimination ranges from racial prejudice through to dislike for a person's appearance or manner; these same factors can sometimes cause as much difficulty in holding an existing job as finding a new one.

Market power of employers, or the absence of union power among employees is a serious problem for low-income workers since they tend to work in non-unionized occupations and industries. Lack of *information* about other employment opportunities may also keep workers in low-wage jobs. They cannot afford the time or money to look for other jobs and many are in remote areas where there is little opportunity for learning about jobs elsewhere.

A large portion of the *rural poverty*, and poverty among the self-employed, is associated with farmers who operate farms of inefficient size, on sub-marginal land (rocky, hilly, or poorly drained terrain), without adequate financing for capital needs, and without training in modern agricultural technology and farm management.

These factors deal mainly with the individual characteristics of the poor, but another serious cause is external to the individual. This is the effect of public *economic and social policies*. Fiscal policies for example, as Chapter 6 showed, require a choice between unemployment and inflation. When the government chooses to fight inflation by pursuing a contractionary policy, unemployment increases. This tends to have its most direct impact on the kinds of workers who constitute the working poor. Because they usually have no special skills, employers are not reluctant to lay them off, knowing that such workers can be found easily when they are required again. They usually have no union protection of their seniority rights; and if they have large families, they cannot easily go elsewhere to look for work. Conversely, an expansionary policy with its attendant inflation reduces the purchasing power of the transfer payments made to both the working and non-working poor, unless such transfer payments are automatically adjusted for changes in the general level of prices.

Other socioeconomic policies, such as the "urban development" process described in the quotation below, have less obvious but longer-term or permanent effects on the poor. The external effects of such public programs usually receive low consideration because the poor lack either the time or the political skill, or both, to defend their position against the policy-makers.

How The Middle Class Creates Poverty

[Note] the middle class orientation of much of our public policy. Consider first our cities, where the majority of the poor live. The central feature of most urban policy has been to accommodate the automobile. This includes massive road building programs into the core, requiring the razing of sites for roads and parking lots. Since the poor are the ones who live adjacent to the core, it is their homes that are removed — typically under the name of urban renewal. Since they can afford only low quality, crowded, and cheap dwellings, they are made worse off by the elimination of the supply of such accommodations, for they must move into newer, higher cost areas that are usually zoned for single family dwelling only.

The same transportation routes permit those with cars to acquire land for housing farther from the city core, and thus subsidize not only their travel cost, but also their housing costs. But with suburbanization based on the automobile, the demand for public transit systems declines, raising the costs of that service to those without cars — again, the poor. In the extreme, public transit is terminated, as in Los Angeles, and the poor become immobilized near the core of the city. When firms also begin to locate at the fringe of the cities because of lower land costs, better transportation, and access to the scarce, more skilled workers who are suburbanites, the poor at the core become pauperized as well as immobilized. Add to this the fact that, as this migration begins to take place from the core to the fringes, the tax base in the inner city declines, forcing decline of the level of much needed social services, and the iron grip of urban poverty grows tighter.

Source: N. H. Lithwick, *Urban Poverty*. Ottawa: Central Mortgage and Housing Corporation, 1971, pp. 54-55.

The Non-working Poor. The low-income family heads and individuals who are not in the labour force have been termed "the welfare poor" by the Senate Committee. They depend on the welfare system because they have no alternative means of support:

> They are the ones left behind by our economic system — the elderly, the sick, the disabled, and women in charge of families which require their presence in the home. . . . A few others . . . are members of the labour force, but work at jobs which do not pay them enough to live on.[5]

The composition of persons receiving social assistance is shown in Table 15.11. Most of this group consist of persons who are permanently disabled or ill (41 per cent) or women who are responsible for their families (26 per cent). The portion who are unemployed (13 per

---

[5] Special Senate Committee on Poverty, *Poverty in Canada*, p. 31.

cent) is unusually high due to the high unemployment rate of 6.6 per cent prevailing at the time these statistics were compiled.

Table 15.11

Persons Receiving Social Assistance, Canada, July 1970 (excluding dependents)

Category	Per cent
Aged (not all over 65 years)	9
Permanently disabled or ill	41
Female heads of families	26
Temporarily disabled	8
Some working poor	3
Unemployed	13
Total	100

Source: Special Senate Committee on Poverty, *Poverty in Canada*.

Anti-Poverty Programs and Proposals

Poverty has been identified as a serious national problem for possibly three kinds of reasons: moral, social, and economic. The existence of such extensive poverty in Canada has been termed a disgrace by the Economic Council, and a national shame by the Senate Committee. Many Canadians realize a moral obligation, on humanitarian grounds, to assist people who are unable to fend for themselves, whether they are in or out of the labour force. The social reasons are somewhat more intangible, involving a concern for social harmony, reducing the hopeless frustration of poverty and its legacy to future generations, and fending off the political strife that would be generated as the poor became more vocal and militant.

The economic burden of poverty, apart from the direct impact on the poor, falls on the rest of the economy in terms of *lost output* and *diverted output*.[6] Lost output is the additional production of goods and services that the economy would have realized had the productive potential of the poor been more effectively developed and utilized. Such additional output would provide the poor with higher incomes and thus directly offset at least a part of the poverty gap. Diverted output refers to the goods and services which could have been produced by the resources required to deal with poverty. Low-income families, for example, usually do not have adequate preventive medical and dental attention and thus may require more

[6] These terms have been suggested by the Economic Council of Canada in its assessment of the costs of poverty as described in its *Sixth Annual Review: Perspective 1975*.

remedial care. To the extent that an ounce of prevention is worth a pound of cure, remedial care demands far more resources, which could have been directed elsewhere, than the resources required for preventive medical care.

Two different approaches are required to deal with the problem of poverty, reflecting the different conditions of the two basic groups constituting the poor: persons who earn low incomes or who are unemployed although they are willing and able to work, and persons who are unable to work for a variety of reasons. The first approach requires improved employment opportunities and conditions; the second requires adequate transfer payments and public services to provide a decent, rising standard of living. In each case, as several reports have argued, the programs must be directed specifically at the problems of the poor if they are to be successful.

Programs to Improve Employment

Underlying any program for improving employment there must be an effective policy of sustained full employment and economic growth, but other specialized programs are necessary if the working poor are to benefit from high levels of aggregate demand. Education and training for example, are often cited as the major means for alleviating poverty. However, Table 15.10 showed that more than 75 per cent of the family heads with less than a complete elementary education were not below the poverty line in 1973, while 6 per cent of those who had completed high school or higher levels of education were below this line. Although more training therefore does not necessarily overcome poverty, training programs are an important component of an anti-poverty program.

The manpower programs described briefly in Chapter 6 are not directly aimed at the poor, but do include some of the poor among their participants. The *Adult Occupational Training Act* provides for basic education or vocational training for persons out of school for at least a year, with maintenance allowances paid if they have been out of school for three years. However, a significant portion of the working poor are excluded from the program by various limitations in its operation. Canada Manpower Centres provide counselling and information on job opportunities but if they are to be effective, people must know about them and seek their services. The Manpower Mobility Program offers grants to assist workers to look for jobs in other areas, and if a job is found, to assist with moving costs.

The *Canada Fair Employment Practices Act* forbids employers to exercise discrimination in their hiring practices for reasons of race, religion, colour, or national origin, but the Act covers only those few industries under federal jurisdiction. Most of the provinces, however, have enacted similar legislation. Similarly, the federal government and most of the provinces have legislation requiring "equal pay for equal work" for female employees.

Assistance for women who are the heads of families is becoming available through provision of day care facilities for children, and a tax amendment allowing the costs of child care to be exempted from income tax.

Programs to Provide Incomes and Services

The major existing programs for providing income to persons not in the labour force are Old Age Security, the Canada Pension Plan, the Family Allowance Act, and the Canada Assistance Plan. Persons who are in the labour force but who are unemployed are assisted mainly by payments from the Unemployment Insurance Commission.

The *Old Age Security Act* provides for a payment of $100 per month (adjusted according to changes in the Consumer Price Index since April, 1973) to all residents over 65 who have been in Canada for at least ten years prior to their application for the payments. A Guaranteed Income Supplement of up to $70.14 per month (also subject to a cost-of-living adjustment) is added to the O.A.S. payment for persons with little or no other income. The G.I.S. payment is reduced by $1 for each $2 of income received from other sources. These rates would provide a single pensioner, as of January, 1975, with $2,451 annually. This is substantially below the Statistics Canada poverty line for a single person, yet in 1969, 28 per cent of all persons receiving Old Age Security payments had no other source of income.

The *Canada Pension Plan*, (or the comparable Quebec Pension Plan), provides an annual pension equal to 25 per cent of the recipients' annual earnings, up to $7,400, averaged over the period during which contributions could have been made. The Plan is financed by employee contributions based on 1.8 per cent of the earnings up to $7,400, with a matching contribution from the employer. Benefits are also paid to the survivors of a deceased contributor and to persons who are unable to work due to mental or physical disability.

Family allowances are not specifically a low-income assistance scheme because they are paid regardless of a family's income. However, the payments do supplement the income of low-income families with children: payments are made at the monthly rate of $20 per child (also subject to price index adjustment since January, 1974). A province may supplement this amount to vary the payment by age of child or number of children. A proposal to modify the family allowance program, by relating the payments inversely to family income, was introduced in Parliament in 1971 but was not enacted.

The *Canada Assistance Plan* (CAP) was introduced in 1966 as the federal government's main program to support its declared war on poverty, and was intended to provide a basis for coordinating the various public welfare programs in each province. Provinces had the option of replacing the shared-cost assistance programs — for the elderly, blind, disabled, and unemployed — with the CAP program to assist all needy persons regardless of the cause of need. All provinces have taken up this option, designing their own programs, for which the federal government pays 50 per cent of the costs.

The benefits provided under the CAP programs vary significantly among the provinces. Some have assigned responsibility for specific assistance programs to municipalities, but share these costs with the municipalities, which are in turn shared with the federal government under the CAP agreements. Municipalities, for example, may provide general welfare payments, child-care services, and homes for the aged.

The provision of medical services to the poor also varies widely among the provinces. Although persons receiving welfare assistance payments receive medical services at no cost in all provinces, most provinces charge premiums for participation in the federal-provincial medical care programs established under the *Medical Care Act*; some provinces cover only part of the doctor's charges; and there are a variety of arrangements regarding the inclusion of drugs, dental care, optical needs, home nursing, and other medical services.

Recognition that housing or shelter costs account for a large share (as much as 50 to 60 per cent) of low-income families' budgets has led the federal government to introduce various programs for low-income housing. In 1973 and 1974, a number of amendments to the *National Housing Act* provided for subsidies to assist with mortgage and rental payments, and grants for housing rehabilitation and neighbourhood improvement. The government's Central Mortgage and Housing Corporation (C.M.H.C.) can make low-interest loans for 90 to 100 per cent of the cost of low-rental housing provided by provinces, municipalities or non-profit groups, and can also contribute a 10 per cent subsidy to certain projects through partial loan forgiveness. The federal government also directly participates by paying 50 to 75 per cent of the deficits on the operation of federal-provincial housing projects.

An important contribution to the incomes of unemployed persons is made through the payments specified by the federal *Unemployment Insurance Act*. This covers almost all employees, with the exception of persons over 70 years or persons receiving payments from the Canada or Quebec Pension Plans, casual employees, and employees who are spouses or dependents of employers or who work for provincial or foreign governments. Payments are equal to two-thirds of the unemployed person's average weekly earnings, up to maximum (in 1975) weekly earnings of $185 per week.

The length of time for which payments are made depends on the length of previous employment. Anyone who was employed for 8 to 20 weeks prior to unemployment receives payments for 8 to 15 weeks, according to the specific length of previous employment. The higher the unemployment rate, however, the longer period payments are extended. Persons who were previously employed for more than 20 weeks may receive payments for up to 18 weeks, with payments again being extended for longer periods according to the current unemployment rate. Still further extensions are based on the extent to which the regional unemployment rate exceeds the national rate.

The current unemployment insurance scheme, introduced in 1971, represents a major change from the scheme which had been in effect since 1941. About 1.2 million workers were added to the employees covered by the scheme, benefits were substantially increased and are now payable for longer periods especially when unemployment rates are high, and contributions from employers and employees have been increased. These contributions cover the basic costs of the benefits, with the federal government paying only the costs of the extension periods due to unemployment rates in excess of 4 per cent.

Minimum wage legislation has often been supported on the grounds that it alleviates poverty by increasing the earnings of low-income workers. However, as the analysis of minimum wages in Chapter 2 indicates, a minimum wage or an increase in the legal minimum wage will probably increase unemployment. The aggregate earnings of persons who remain employed are increased only if the labour demand curve is inelastic. Moreover, some low-wage occupations, such as farm labour, usually are not included in the coverage of the minimum wage legislation.

Proposals for a Guaranteed Annual Income

Welfare assistance systems have long been criticized for their inadequacy, bureaucratic complexity, personal and regional inequity, social stigma, and attitude of charity. An increasingly frequent response to this set of problems is a proposal for a *guaranteed annual income: a guarantee by the federal government that every family or individual would have an income at least equal to some specified amount, often expressed as a fraction of the related poverty line.* Such a guarantee could be realized in alternative ways. One approach would involve reforming the existing welfare system, but this probably would not solve the administrative difficulties, provincial differences in benefits, and the inadequate assistance for the working poor.

The Negative Income Tax

An alternative method for providing a guaranteed annual income is based on the introduction of a negative income tax, a government payment to individuals and families whose other income is below the poverty line but which varies with the amount of this other income.[7] The specific amounts of the payments depend on the various components of the formula used in calculating the government contribution: the poverty line established for each group, the fraction of the poverty line income which is to be guaranteed, and the rate at which the government payment is reduced as other income rises.

The operation of a negative income tax in determining the amount of the government payment is illustrated in Table 15.12. Assume that the government guarantees that no family or individual will have an income of less than 50 per cent of the poverty line income level, and that this latter level is set at $6,000 for a family of four. The guaranteed income is therefore $3,000. Assume also that the government payment (the negative tax) is reduced by $500 for every $1,000 of private income. Thus the effective tax rate on the government guarantee of $3,000 is 50 per cent. Table 15.12 shows, for example, that a family with no other income receives the full amount of the guaranteed income in the form of a negative tax or government payment. A family with $1,000 in private income has its potential government payment of $3,000 reduced by 50 per cent of its other income and thus receives $2,500. Its total income is therefore $3,500. A family which has private income just equal to the poverty line level of $6,000 receives no government payment. Since the potential payment of $3,000 is reduced by 50 per cent of the private income, the potential payment is reduced to zero at $6,000.

Table 15.12

**Negative Income Tax Approach to a
Guaranteed Annual Income
(for a family of four)**

Guaranteed Income Level	Private Income	Negative Tax (Allowance Paid)	Total Income
$3,000	0	3,000	3,000
3,000	1,000	2,500	3,500
3,000	2,000	2,000	4,000
3,000	3,000	1,500	4,500
3,000	4,000	1,000	5,000
3,000	5,000	500	5,500
3,000	6,000	0	6,000

Assumptions: 1. Poverty line for a family of four is $6,000.
　　　　　　 2. Guaranteed income is set at 50 per cent of poverty line income.
　　　　　　 3. Tax on private income up to poverty line level is 50 per cent.

[7] For a specific proposal on the approach, see the Special Senate Committee on Poverty, *Poverty in Canada*, pp. 178-192. The Manitoba government introduced a guaranteed annual income plan in 1975 as a three-year pilot project, with the federal government paying 75 per cent of the cos..

Note that the government thus has three decisions to make in operating a negative income tax method for providing a guaranteed annual income; that is, alternative values can be specified in place of each of the three assumptions made in the calculations for Table 15.12. However, the scheme should be designed so that payments are reduced to zero at the poverty line, and the poverty line should coincide with the income level at which positive tax payments begin. One of the difficulties in introducing a negative income tax scheme, therefore, is to integrate it with the existing income tax structure.

The negative income tax has some significant advantages over the alternative proposals for a guaranteed annual income:

- The scheme is simple to administer: the amount of the government payment is calculated on the basis of income statements submitted to the Department of National Revenue under the existing arrangements for assessing positive income taxes.

- Reduction of the government payment by less than any increase in private income provides a "work incentive". It is argued that if, for example, $3,000 is paid to all families who have other income of up to $3,000, there is no incentive for head of a family earning $4,000 to remain at his job. He would be better off to earn only $2,900 and collect an additional $3,000 from the government. Conversely, if the government payment is reduced by the full amount of other income, a family head earning $3,000 would have no incentive to continue earning even this low amount since he could quit work and receive $3,000 from the government. The fractional reduction of government payments thus provides some financial support while maintaining an incentive to supplement this by other income. Under most of the existing welfare schemes, the welfare payment is reduced by the full amount of any increase in private income, thus largely removing the incentive to seek earned income unless this can be substantially above the welfare payments level.

- There is universal coverage under the negative income tax scheme: all families or individuals with low incomes receive some financial assistance regardless of the reasons for their low incomes. This point also implies, however, that it may be necessary to set different poverty lines for each region of the country if the costs of living vary significantly by region.

C. *Regional Income Disparity*

The goal of an equitable distribution of rising incomes includes two specific objectives: the elimination of poverty, and the narrowing of regional income disparities. The latter reflects the national policy of balanced regional development and the sharing by all regions in the results of Canada's economic growth. It is well known in Canada, however, that there are wide differences in the level of economic well-being among the regions or provinces.

Table 15.13

Regional Income Disparity, Canada, 1973

Region	Average Annual Income		Percent of National Average	
	Families	Unattached Individuals	Families	Unattached Individuals
Atlantic Provinces	$ 9,965	$4,162	78	81
Quebec	12,024	4,967	95	96
Ontario	13,912	5,596	109	109
Prairie Provinces	11,760	4,459	92	87
British Columbia	13,942	5,651	110	110
Canada	12,716	5,149	100	100

Source: Statistics Canada, *Income Distributions by Size in Canada, 1973.*

Regional income disparity or inequality can be illustrated in various ways. Table 15.13 shows the average annual incomes of families and unattached individuals in each major economic region and compares these with the national average. The regional ranking of family income levels — British Columbia, Ontario, Quebec, Prairies, and the Atlantic provinces — is the same as the ranking for unattached individuals, with the average family income in British Columbia about 40 per cent higher than it is in the Atlantic procinces. Income differentials of approximately these proportions have persisted for a fairly long time. Statistics comparable to those shown in Table 15.13 are not available for earlier decades, but the Personal Income statistics of the national accounts offer a similar comparison of income differentials since 1926. These, as presented in Table 15.14, show a continuation of the same general pattern with only minor changes such as Ontario replacing British Columbia as the province with the highest per capita income, and some variation in the rankings of the Prairie provinces. The slight narrowing of the overall inequality of provincial income levels can be seen by comparing the difference between Newfoundland and British Columbia in 1951 (48 vs. 118 per cent of the national average) and between Newfoundland and Ontario in 1971 (65 vs. 117 per cent of the national average). These comparisons are based on total personal incomes including transfer payments. A provincial comparison of earned income per person would show slightly greater differentials since transfer payments reflect one aspect of the government's policies designed to reduce the differentials. Although regional development policies have been directed to parts of all the provinces,

major emphasis — as the income differentials would suggest — has
been placed on the development of the Atlantic provinces.

Table 15.14

**Personal Income Per Person, by Province, Canada
(as a percentage of the national average)**

Province	1926	1941	1951	1961	1971
Newfoundland	—	—	48	58	65
Prince Edward Island	56	47	54	59	64
Nova Scotia	61	78	69	78	77
New Brunswick	65	64	67	68	73
Quebec	85	87	84	90	89
Ontario	114	129	118	118	117
Manitoba	108	93	101	94	94
Saskatchewan	102	59	107	71	82
Alberta	114	80	111	100	100
British Columbia	122	121	119	115	109

Source: Statistics Canada, *National Accounts, Income and Expenditure*, revised data.

Some Causes of Regional Income Disparity

Regional and provincial income disparity has been a basic concern
of public policy in Canada for several decades, but there has been
remarkably little research on the specific sources of the problem and
few efforts at evolving a theory of regional economic development.[8]
However, some factors which appear to explain much of the regional
variation can be identified; these include the relative size and productivity of the labour force in each region, the capital stock and
composition of industrial activity, the availability of natural resources, concentration of population, and proximity to large markets.

Size and Productivity of the Labour Force

Age Composition of the Population. The per capita income of a region
is obviously influenced by the size of its labour force relative to its
total population. Even if there is a high output per worker in a given
region, the income per capita is sharply reduced if the potential

---

[8] For a more elaborate treatment of this topic, see Economic Council of
Canada, *Second Annual Review: Towards Sustained and Balanced
Economic Growth.* Ottawa: Queen's Printer, 1965. This section draws
heavily on that source.

labour force is a small fraction of the total population, since each worker is then supporting a number of dependents. In 1974, for example, the Atlantic provinces had the lowest proportion, about 60 per cent, of its population in the working ages of 14 to 64, while Ontario and British Columbia had the highest proportion, 65 per cent.

Labour Force Participation Rate. This rate is defined as the percentage of the population aged 14 and over who are in the labour force. The provincial labour force participation rates roughly parallel the provincial ranking of incomes per capita; in 1970-74, the participation rate in the Atlantic provinces averaged 50 per cent compared with 60 per cent in Ontario. The lower rate reflects a lower particpation rate among both men and women in the Atlantic provinces.

Unemployment Rate. Since the labour force includes both the employed and the unemployed, a high unemployment rate can compound the effect of a low participation rate on per capital incomes. This has been true for the Atlantic provinces and Quebec where the average unemployment rates during 1970 to 1974 were 9 per cent and 7.8 per cent. Moreover, the combination of a low participation rate and a high unemployment rate suggests that some persons who might have entered the labour force were discouraged from doing so by a general lack of employment opportunities.

The result of these combined factors (age, participation, unemployment) was that in 1974, for example, only 33 per cent of the Atlantic provinces' population was employed, compared with 41 per cent for the whole country, and 43 per cent in Ontario. The Economic Council has estimated that this fact alone accounts for roughly half of the difference between the per capita income of the Atlantic provinces and the national average.

Table 15.15

**Educational Attainment of The Labour Force,
By Region, Canada, 1972**

Schooling Level	Atlantic Provinces	Quebec	Ontario	Prairie Provinces	British Columbia	Canada
	percentage of the labour force					
Elementary some or completed	30	33	21	22	14	24
Secondary some or completed	48	45	58	55	60	54
Post-Secondary some or completed	22	22	21	23	26	22

Source: Statistics Canada, *The Labour Force*, February 1973.

Level of Education Attainment. The preceding factors in this section
are related to the employment rate, but at any given employment rate
there may still be considerable variation in personal income per
capita due to differences in labour productivity, or the value of output per unit of labour service. The regional variation in productivity
or earnings per worker shows the same ranking as the personal incomes per capita, with the Atlantic provinces at about 80 per cent of
the national average. One important reason for the difference in
earned income per worker is the level of education attainment of the
labour force in each region. As Table 15.15 indicates, the labour
force in the Atlantic provinces and Quebec has the highest percentage of persons who have completed not more than elementary
schooling.

Capital Stock and Industrial Composition

Capital Stock. The capital stock of a region can be expected to influence the level of income per worker because the greater the quantity
of physical capital (plant and equipment) associated with a worker,
the greater the value of output per worker tends to be. Estimates of
the physical capital stock by region are not available, but these can
be approximated by comparing the annual rates of real investment
per person in each region over a long period. Such comparisons
show that this rate was about 2.5 times greater in Alberta (the
highest-ranking province) than in Nova Scotia (the lowest-ranking
province), for the period 1951-1964.

Industrial Composition. Since earnings per worker vary substantially
among industries, it is possible that some of the regional variation in
income per worker is due to the particular composition or "mix" of
industries in each region. It is often suggested, that, if more manufacturing firms could be attracted to the Atlantic region, this would
directly increase per capita income in that area. However, when the
average earnings in each region are standardized according to the
industrial composition of the whole country, there is little effect on
the regional variation in earnings. Standardization involves making
the assumption that the industrial composition of a region is the
same as the composition for the country, and then applying the
region's average earnings in each industry to this standard mix of
industries. Since this produces little effect, as shown by Table 15.16,
the regional differences in average earnings must be due to different
earnings levels for any given industry rather than to a region's particular industrial composition. In fact, the slight decrease in earnings in the Atlantic provinces when earnings are standardized for
industrial composition shows that this region has a more favourable
industrial composition than the national average. Attracting mining

or manufacturing firms to the Atlantic region would improve average earnings only if those particular firms paid higher wages than other firms in the same industry. However, the major reason firms locate in low-wage areas is to take advantage of low wages. If the wage level rose significantly, a firm would likely find it more profitable to locate in central Canada where it would be closer to large markets and have lower transportation costs.

Table 15.16

Average Weekly Earnings by Region, Canada, 1969

	Average Weekly Earnings	
	Unstandardized	*Standardized by Industrial Structure for Canada*
Atlantic provinces	$ 97.38	$ 96.79
Quebec	114.24	115.36
Ontario	121.55	120.43
Prairie Provinces	112.64	110.89
British Columbia	129.35	128.71
Canada	117.63	117.63

Source: Sylvia Ostry and Mahmood A. Zaidi, *Labour Economics in Canada*, Table 72.

Other Factors in Regional Income Disparity

Some other factors that appear important in explaining regional income differences affect a region's economy in complex and indirect ways. The discovery of oil in Alberta, for example, and its subsequent impact on the province's economy must account for a large share of the higher per capita income in that province, but the indirect effects of Alberta's petroleum industry are not easily measured. Similarly British Columbia's forests and the wheat lands of the Prairies have conferred natural advantages on these areas which otherwise would probably have much lower per capital incomes.

Another factor, the population concentration in central Canada and in the Vancouver area, represents both a cause and an effect of higher incomes in those areas. The Economic Council has described the process of population concentration and its relation to economic development as follows:

Of major importance is the concentration of population in fairly small geographic areas, in which the most efficient production and distribution is more easily achieved. Moreover, once the process of concentration gets underway, similar powerful forces make it of cumulative importance in growth — production can be scaled still more efficiently to meet enlarging markets; business services and a versatile labour force are close at hand; new technology is more easily developed and exploited; and advanced management skills and enterprise are more readily attracted. It is on this basis that the concept of the "growth centre" as a necessary focus for regional growth has been widely advanced and accepted.[9]

Policies and Programs to Reduce Regional Disparity

The previous section noted that there are substantial differences in the per capita income levels of the different regions of Canada, that these income differences have persisted for a long time, and that the differences are due, in part, to variations in the number of employed persons as a percentage of the population and the productivity of labour. Public policies designed to reduce the regional income disparity in Canada have tried to reduce the influence of these factors, as well as to provide interprovincial income transfers through the federal government. The several different policies can be grouped in three categories: income transfers, general stabilization policies, and specific development policies.

Federal-Provincial Fiscal Transfer Payments

Under the Federal-Provincial Fiscal Arrangements Act, the federal government makes equalization payments to some provinces to compensate them for the lower value of their tax bases in the case of nineteen different taxes or levies imposed by the provinces. The national average revenue yield per capita is calculated for each of the nineteen tax revenue sources; the provincial average revenue yield per capita is then calculated, using each province's tax base (the total value of the category which is taxed) and the national average tax for each item. The difference between the two per capita amounts multiplied by a province's population, represents the equalization payment with respect to the particular revenue source. The calculation is repeated for each of the nineteen taxes — from personal income tax to oil royalties — to determine the total equalization payment to each province. The equalization payments for 1974-75 are shown in Table 15.17. Three provinces, Alberta, British Columbia, and Ontario, do not receive equalization payments because their provincial tax bases are so large relative to the other provinces. Per capita payments to the other provinces follow roughly the reverse ranking of the per capital personal income shown in Table 15.14; that is, the lowest income provinces receive the highest equalization payments per capita.

---

[9] *Ibid.*, p. 127.

Table 15.17

**Equalization Payments[1] Under the Federal-
Provincial Fiscal Arrangements Act, 1974-75**

| | Payment | | | Payment | |
	Total (millions)	Per Capita		Total (millions)	Per Capita
Newfoundland	$182.3	$336	Manitoba	$118.6	$117
Prince Edward Island	41.3	353	Saskatchewan	100.9	111
Nova Scotia	208.5	256	Alberta	—	—
New Brunswick	178.0	269	British	—	—
Quobec	903.2	147	Columbia		
Ontario	—	—			
			Total	1,732.7	

[1]Preliminary estimates
Source: Canadian Tax Foundation, *The National Finances, 1974-75.*

Stabilization Policies

Among the limitations of fiscal and monetary policies described
in Chapter 6 was the differential impact of these general stabilization
policies on the different economic regions of Canada. This is evident, for example, in the relative unemployment rates of the different regions during periods of economic contraction compared with
the relative rates during economic expansion. Figure 15.2 shows

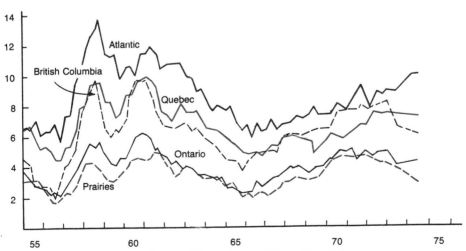

Figure 15.2 Regional Unemployment Rates in Canada
Unemployment rates tend to be highest in the Atlantic provinces and lowest in
Ontario and the Prairie provinces. Although the unemployment rates generally rise
and fall together, the rates tend to show a greater relative decline in expansionary
periods in the low unemployment regions.
Source: Statistics Canada, *Canadian Statistical Review*.

that although regional unemployment rates tend to change in unison with changes in economic conditions, the share of the total unemployment borne by the high unemployment areas such as the Atlantic provinces tends to rise in an expansionary phase. Thus, the low-income regions do not benefit as much as the high-income regions from expansionary policies. Furthermore, policies to restrain inflationary pressures in the high-income regions tend to increase the unemployment rates in the low-income regions, although their share of the total unemployment declines. That is, contractionary policies must be introduced to curtail inflation in the high-income regions before the unemployment rate has dropped to a satisfactory level in the low-income regions. There is thus an inherent conflict in determining national stabilization policies: should the high-income regions be required to accept a higher rate of inflation so that the low-income regions can enjoy a further decline in their unemployment rates, or should inflation be restrained before the unemployment rates have dropped satisfactorily in the low-income areas?

This dilemma raises the question of whether stabilization policies can be designed to have desirable differential effects on each region. Monetary policy is difficult to implement on a regional basis because changes in bank reserves and interest rates tend to have similar, although perhaps delayed, effects across the country. Some slight regional discrimination might be possible in the administration of federal loan programs such as the Central Mortgage and Housing Corporation and the Farm Credit Corporation, but the effect of this would be insignificant relative to the size of the changes required.

Fiscal policy designed to have differential regional effects would require different tax structures in each region and government expenditure programs related to specific regions. Such tax differentials would face political opposition if applied to personal income, but special tax exemptions and deferrals have been used to encourage regional relocation of some corporations. Government expenditure programs generally cannot be directed to specific regions because the goods and services required may not be produced in the regions concerned and because some expenditure programs cannot be varied abruptly to deal with short-term instability. Some specific programs, however, have been introduced to deal directly with regional differences in unemployment rates. The Local Initiatives Program and the Opportunities For Youth program enabled the federal government to make grants in areas with the highest unemployment rates and to approve applications from persons with a high marginal propensity to consume, thus assuring at least a strong beginning for the multiplier effect of these grants. Nevertheless, the basic dilemma of coping with strong inflationary pressures in some regions while unemployment remains high elsewhere remains a serious problem in Canadian stabilization policies.

Regional Development Policies

Throughout Canada's history, the federal government has undertaken a wide variety of programs specifically intended to stimulate the economic growth of the lower-income regions. The net effect of these programs is difficult to determine since estimates of how the regional economies would have performed in the absence of programs must be based on crude assumptions. It would appear, however, that reduction of regional income disparity has been slow and slight.

Tariff Policies. Canada's protective tariff structure was one of the earliest policies designed to encourage regional development but the shift of population westward and the declining relative importance of primary industries has frustrated the original intentions of the National Policy. Rather than participating fully in the growth of manufacturing in Canada, the Atlantic provinces, along with the Prairie provinces and British Columbia, have borne the cost of a tariff structure which has increased the real income of Ontario and Quebec. Thus, the tariff policy, which was to have fostered regional development, has instead increased the need for other development policies.

Transportation Policies. Another early policy for regional development involved the development of a national railroad, and later national highways and airlines systems, to encourage inter-regional travel and shipping of raw materials and finished products. Specific attention was given to the problem of transportation costs for producers in the Maritimes in the form of the Maritime Freight Rates Act which provided for federal subsidies to reduce freight rates by 30 per cent for rail shipments moving from eastern Canada to the central and western areas. Prairie grain producers were also assisted by the Crow's Nest Pass Agreement, which provided for lower freight rates on grain shipped to the west coast, and by the construction of the St. Lawrence Seaway.

Manpower and Education Policies. The federal government's manpower policies are discussed in Chapter 6 and the cost-sharing arrangement for post-secondary education is described in Chapter 8. Although these policies are applicable to all regions, the potential effect of the program is greatest in the low-income regions where education levels are lowest and labour mobility is essential for overcoming structural unemployment.

Incentives Policies. A program to encourage the development of population and economic growth centres in depressed areas was established in 1962 under an Area Development Agency; in 1969, this agency was replaced by the Department of Regional Economic

Expansion to administer a new Regional Development Incentives Act. This provides for federal grants, special depreciation allowances, and loans, to encourage the location of firms in designated areas.

Rural Adjustment Policies. A number of programs have been introduced to assist resource allocation within rural areas, or from rural to urban areas. The Prairie Farm Rehabilitation Act (PFRA) provided for assistance in land conservation, dam construction, and irrigation systems. A more recent program, under the Agricultural and Rural Development Act, involves developing new uses for marginal farmlands and new employment opportunities for persons who are unable to realize an adequate income from farming operations. A somewhat similar program, the Fund for Rural Economic Development (FRED), was designed to assist specific large areas of concentration of rural poverty through federal-provincial agreements on intensive development projects in New Brunswick, Manitoba, Quebec, and Prince Edward Island.

Review of the Main Points

1. Equitable income distribution is not easily defined, but it is considered to include at least the elimination of poverty and the reduction of regional income disparities.

2. Income distribution can be examined in different ways: one is functional distribution, or the distribution among productive factors according to the price and quantity of each general type of factor. The relative share of national income received by each factor category has been fairly stable, with labour receiving about 75 to 80 per cent, and the remainder going to capital and land.

3. The size distribution of income, or the number of individuals and families at each level of income, shows that, for example, families and individuals with an income of less than $4,000 in 1973 constituted 20 per cent of the population but received only 4 per cent of the total income. A Lorenz curve shows the deviation of the actual distribution of incomes from perfect equality in income distribution. The degree of inequality in employment and investment income is reduced by government taxation and expenditures.

4. The causes of income inequality are complex, but some of the basic factors include age, education, occupation, and number of weeks worked per year.

5. Poverty is difficult to define. It has been defined as having an income below a certain absolute level, or below a level which rises as the population's average income rises, or as the lowest-income groups having a very small share of the total income.

Similarly, poverty is difficult to measure. The concept of a poverty line is based on the income level below which families need to spend womewhat more than half (for example, 70 per cent) of their incomes on the basic essentials of food, clothing, and shelter.

6. The poverty rate is the percentage of the total group, in different categories, whose incomes fall below the poverty-line income. The proverty rate is highest: among individuals and families of two; in the Atlantic provinces; in rural areas; among families headed by a female; among persons over age 65; and among persons with no secondary school education. However, the distribution of the poor shows that over 60 per cent live in Ontario or Quebec, are roughly equally distributed across the age groups, and that about 50 per cent are in the labour force.

7. The working poor are not able to earn more for many reasons: inadequate education or training, poor health, geographical immobility, discrimination, market power of employers, lack of employment information, inadequate financing and management training for farm operations, and the adverse effects of several economic and social policies. The non-working poor include persons who are permanently disabled or ill and women who remain at home to care for dependents.

8. Poverty is considered a serious national problem for moral, social, and economic reasons. The latter include the cost of lost output and diverted output associated with poverty. Lost output includes the goods and services that could be produced if the productive potential of the poor is more effectively developed and utilized. Diverted output includes the goods and services which could be produced by the resources required to deal with poverty.

9. Anti-poverty programs include those to improve employment and to provide incomes and services directly to the poor. The former include manpower programs providing occupational training, counselling and placement, and mobility assistance; anti-discrimination and equal pay legislation; and day-care facilities. Programs to provide incomes and services include transfer payments under the Old Age Security and Guaranteed Income Supplement, Canada Pension, and federal-provincial welfare assistance programs; medical care programs, and low-income housing.

10. Since welfare assistance programs have not satisfactorily dealt with the low-income problem, a guaranteed annual income has been proposed. This could be provided in various ways; a common proposal involves a negative income tax whereby the federal government would guarantee persons a minimum income

but the government payment would be reduced with increasing levels of income received from other sources.

11. The average personal or family income differs significantly across the major economic regions of Canada, such that the average family income in British Columbia is 40 per cent higher than it is in the Atlantic provinces. The reasons for regional income disparities include the age composition of the population, the labour force participation rate, the unemployment rate, the level of educational attainment, the capital stock per capita, and the industrial composition. Other important factors cannot be expressed so precisely; these include the indirect effects of important natural resources such as forests and petroleum, and the complex effects of population concentration on economic growth.

12. Public policies to reduce regional income disparities have included income transfers, general stabilization policies, and specific development policies. The Federal-Provincial Fiscal Arrangements Act provides for federal equalization payments to some provinces to compensate them for the lower value of their tax bases. It is difficult to design stabilization policies which do not adversely affect one region while benefiting another region because inflationary pressures tend to develop in the higher-income regions while the unemployment rate is still high in the lower-income regions. Regional development policies have included protective tariffs (which benefited only central Canada), and programs for transportation, manpower and education, industrial incentives, and rural adjustment.

Review and Discussion Questions

1. What is the difference between the functional and personal distributions of income? How are these two concepts related?

2. Do you think the existing distribution of income is equitable? Why? If not, use a Lorenz curve to describe the distribution you believe is equitable. Outline the programs you would advocate to achieve this result. If you think the existing distribution is equitable, what steps must be taken to maintain this distribution?

3. Think of two persons whose incomes you know are quite different. List as many reasons as you can for the difference in their incomes.

4. Develop a definition of poverty without including the general concept of a poverty line as described in this chapter. What difficulties do you encounter in devising such a definition?

5. Can the war against poverty ever be won? Explain. Outline what you believe to be the most effective anti-poverty programs, in

light of the data provided in Table 15.10 on the incidence and distribution of poverty.

6. Some people are in favour of modifying the existing welfare system and increasing the amounts paid, others favour a reduction in welfare payments, while still others favour a negative income tax. Decide which position you favour and outline the arguments supporting your position and opposing the other positions.

7. Average earnings in Ontario are among the highest in Canada, yet Canada's manufacturing industry is also concentrated in Ontario. Why do not more manufacturing firms locate in the lower-wage provinces?

Sources and Selected Readings

Adams, Ian, et al. *The Real Poverty Report.* Edmonton: M.G. Hurtig, 1971.

Brewis, T.N. *Regional Economic Policies in Canada.* Toronto: Macmillan, 1969.

Economic Council of Canada. *Second Annual Review: Towards Sustained and Balanced Economic Growth.* Ottawa: Queen's Printer, 1965.

————. *Fifth Annual Review: The Challenge of Growth and Change.* Ottawa: Queen's Printer, 1968.

Green, Christopher. *Negative Taxes and the Poverty Problem.* Washington, D.C.: Brookings Institution, 1967.

Harrington, Michael. *The Other America: Poverty in the United States.* Baltimore: Penguin Books, 1963.

Lithwick, N.H. *Urban Poverty.* Ottawa: Information Canada, 1971.

Podoluk, Jenny R. *Incomes of Canadians.* Ottawa: Queen's Printer, 1968.

Special Senate Committee on Poverty. *Poverty in Canada.* Ottawa: Information Canada, 1971.

Index